Monumenta Archaeologica
Volume 21

The Cotsen Institute of Archaeology
University of California, Los Angeles

Roman slag heap at Mitsero *Mavrovounos* (SIA 4; *bottom left*) and Modern period mine at Mitsero *Kokkinoyia* (SIA 11), from the southeast

The Sydney Cyprus Survey Project

SOCIAL APPROACHES TO REGIONAL ARCHAEOLOGICAL SURVEY

Michael Given and A. Bernard Knapp

with contributions by

Dina Coleman, Lita Diacopoulos, Timothy E. Gregory, Vasiliki Kassianidou,

Nathan Meyer, R. Scott Moore, Jay Noller, Helen Saunders, Kylie Seretis,

Joanna S. Smith, Neil Urwin, Sven Van Lokeren, Lisa Wells, and Caroline Whitehill

and

Peter Grave, Priscilla Keswani, Sturt Manning, Elinor Ribeiro,

Robert Schon, and Haddon Wright

Monumenta Archaeologica 21
The Cotsen Institute of Archaeology
University of California, Los Angeles
2003

Library of Congress Cataloging-in-Publication Data

    Given, Michael.
    The Sydney Cyprus survey project : social approaches to regional
    archaeological survey / by Michael Given and A. Bernard Knapp with
    contributions by Dina Coleman ... [et al.].
        p. cm. — (Monumenta archaeologica ; v. 21)
    Includes bibliographical references.
     ISBN 1-931745-04-8
     1. Cyprus—Antiquities. 2. Cyprus—Civilization 3. Cyprus—History.
    I. Knapp, Arthur Bernard. II. Coleman, Dina. III. Title. IV. Monumenta
    archaeologica (University of California, Los Angeles. Institute of
    Archaeology) ; v. 21.
     DS54.3.G56 2003
     939'.37—dc21
                2003000831

Undertaken with the assistance of the Institute for Aegean Prehistory.

Contents

CONTENTS

List of Illustrations

List of Tables

Preface

Understanding the social organization of space is a central facet of understanding archaeological data—anywhere, anytime. Whether excavating a pueblo complex in the southwestern United States, sampling an obsidian quarry in West New Britain, or intensively surveying a 65 km^2 swatch of the igneous-sedimentary zone in the foothills of Cyprus's Troodos Mountains, we should be able to establish and improve methodologies that inform us about the ways people lived (and earned a living), interacted, worshiped, and died; how they structured and modified the landscapes in which they dwelt, hunted, fished, or farmed; and how they organized their social relations around the regional resources that sustained them. In other words, we need to understand better how people use their landscapes—from mines and quarries to farms and shrines to urban centers and all the space in between—and to consider how material culture correlates with this use of space to amplify the diversity of social organization we see among humans.

The starting point in any such archaeological endeavor must be a regional approach to the landscape. Regional survey projects in the Mediterranean usually incorporate historical and contextual focuses, which provide a fuller, more inclusive vision of past landscapes than does a purely ecological approach. Landscapes comprise not just environmental zones, ecological diversity, and settlements; they also represent the focus of human activity, the medium and context within which archaeological evidence is produced, distributed, abandoned, preserved, or destroyed. Landscapes thus frame and shape the way people act, even as people continuously alter the face of their landscapes. (The term *landscape* is defined and discussed at greater length in chapter 7.5.)

One of the main themes that characterizes Mediterranean regional survey archaeology, and one of the more important aspects of landscape archaeology anywhere, is the study of the rural landscape and the way it is affected by urban dynamics. The developing interest in the nature of rural habitation and resource exploitation is both innovative and provocative and has helped to situate small, well-dated rural sites in their regional cultural contexts. Regional surveys have also given impetus to urban archaeology in the Mediterranean. Survey work monitors variations in the density of artifacts across the landscape, and this variation at times can be related to the extant documentary information on urban centers.

There is much to be said for incorporating into survey archaeology an approach that attempts to treat the landscape at the individual, local, regional, and Mediterranean-wide scale. Siting and developing settlements within these past landscapes was conditioned by individual social relations and ecologies at the local scale; by more inclusive social, economic, and ideological structures operating at the regional scale; and by the changing fortunes of a wider Mediterranean economy. In the past, archaeologists perhaps made too much of the distinction between the timeless, wholesome, and "past" countryside and the superficial, degenerate, and "present" urban center. This attitude disguises how closely towns were integrated with the arable lands surrounding them and how changing social relations in the countryside can generate much of the economic base upon which urban centers rely. In fact, there was not only interaction but also complementarity between these different sectors of the landscape, and survey evidence helps us to consider the associated long-term patterns of stasis, change, accumulation, and cultural transmission.

Regional survey data also make it possible to assess major historical trends (for example, the emergence and development of large estates, changing demographic patterns, expansion or contraction in mining and agriculture) from an entirely different perspective. Even so, and despite the wealth of historical documentation available on mining, deforestation, overgrazing, manuring, and intensive agricultural practices, we still understand very little about the complex relationship between land use, resource exploitation, and landscape change in the Mediterranean basin. For example, we consider spatial variation in the landscape as an inevitable result of population growth or surplus production, when it could just as easily result from changing agricultural strategies dictated by nucleated or dispersed settlement. Moreover, it is most likely that the low-density artifact distributions that appear so frequently in the landscape were at least in part an accidental by-product of manuring. In other words, artifacts were spread throughout arable fields in the landscape chiefly because they were incorporated in farmyard manure. Finally, despite all the regional survey work that has been done over the past forty years in the Mediterranean, it is still very difficult to establish an overall landscape history of the region: There are too many different approaches, attitudes, and methodologies.

These are some of the more general concerns, ideals, and methods that have motivated the Sydney Cyprus Survey Project (SCSP). Readers will have to judge for themselves whether we have successfully considered, implemented, or resolved any of them. Because we sought to gain better insight into the variability and social impact of agricultural systems, resource exploitation, human mobility, and other human actions within the landscape, SCSP utilized a range of specialist expertise—both analytical and social—beyond that of regional survey and Cypriot archaeology: geology, archaeometallurgy, geomorphology, geobotany, satellite imagery, historical archaeology, and ethnography—all facilitated by an interlinked database and Geographic Information System (GIS). In so doing, we sought to meet one of the greatest challenges faced by Mediterranean regional surveys, namely to combine ecological approaches to past landscapes as developed by natural scientists with the concerns of social archaeologists, in particular the interface between human action and the environment.

When I first began to consider the notion of conducting an intensive regional archaeological survey, I was asked if Cypriot data were robust enough to engage an archaeology of landscapes. I felt then and I feel now that such a question is entirely irrelevant: More important is the fact that we have completed this exercise, developed a viable if always changing methodology in striving for some measure of understanding, and confronted a range of questions and issues. It is hoped that others who work on Cyprus, or in landscape archaeology anywhere, may assess, and perhaps benefit from, our work and move on from here.

– A. Bernard Knapp

Acknowledgments

In concept, this project began in 1982, while I was on a brief holiday visit to Cyprus with my future family (this volume is dedicated in part to one of my stepdaughters who was with me at the time). On the good advice of CAARI (Cyprus American Archaeological Research Institute, Nicosia), scholars and residents such as Stuart Swiny, Steve Held, and Anita Walker, and with the encouragement of the then director of the Department of Antiquities of Cyprus, Dr. Vassos Karageorghis, we set out to explore the foothills of the Troodos, in the region that supported the modern mining sites near the villages of Agrokipia, Mitsero, and Kambia. One of my main research interests at the time was the archaeology, anthropology, and social history of mining, and my aim was to conduct a survey in a region or regions that had never been surveyed before, at least not from an archaeological perspective. As we drove on the back roads in and around the villages of Mitsero and Politiko, I had little idea that it would take a further ten years to implement these ideas and that I would return with a team of Australians to live in a house owned by the Hellenic Mining Company and located just outside the village of Mitsero.

In practice, the Sydney Cyprus Survey Project (SCSP) began while I was an Australian Research Fellow in Mediterranean Archaeology at Macquarie University, Sydney, an appointment funded by the Australian Research Council. I am most grateful for the generous support of the Council, whose Large Research Grant for the years 1995 to 1997 made SCSP a reality. I am also grateful for the collegiality and kindness of everyone in the Ancient History Documentary Research Centre at Macquarie University, in particular Emeritus Professor Edwin Judge; they ensured that my research was carried out uninterrupted by the daily fracas of an academic department.

Since 1996, SCSP has been based in the Department of Archaeology, University of Glasgow, Scotland. Dr. Michael Given, who joined the project as a team leader in 1995 and became Field Director in 1996, was appointed British Academy Institutional Research Fellow in Glasgow's Archaeology Department in 1998/99. This factor has helped to ensure SCSP's prompt publication; both he and I are grateful to the British Academy (now the Arts and Humanities Research Board) and to Glasgow's Department of Archaeology for financial, institutional, logistical, and collegial support. I personally am most grateful to Michael, without whom this final product would have been infinitely longer in the making. In addition, we would both like to acknowledge especially the commitment, dedication, and intellectual input to all aspects of SCSP by Nathan Meyer, whose personal circumstances precluded fuller involvement in the making of this final monograph.

The five seasons of fieldwork and one study season carried out by SCSP have been funded by the Australian Research Council, the Institute for Aegean Prehistory, the National Geographic Society, the British Academy, Macquarie University, the University of Glasgow (Robertson Bequest), the Carnegie Trust for the Universities of Scotland, and the American Schools of Oriental Research. The project is sponsored by the University of Glasgow and the American Schools of Oriental Research; its permit to survey was provided and renewed by successive Directors of the Department of Antiquities, Cyprus (Drs. Demos Christou and Sophocles Hadjisavvas), to whom we are most grateful. We were very fortunate to have both scholarly and logistical support from the Cyprus Geological Survey, especially from its former Director Dr. George Constantinou and from Dr. Andreas Panayiotou (now the Minister of Agriculture). We also gratefully acknowledge the assistance over the years of the Hellenic Mining Company (in particular Mr. Constantine Xydas and Dr. George Maliotis); the Cyprus Forestry Department's Remote Sensing Centre (especially Andreas Panayi and Nikos Shamarias), and the Cyprus American Archaeological Research Institute (especially former directors Stuart Swiny and Nancy Serwint, and Secretary Vathoulla Moustoukki, who makes everything possible). The early days on the project in Cyprus succeeded largely because of the support and knowledge of Dr. Steve O. Held, and the enthusiasm of Dr. Pitsa Kenti: I owe them both a debt I can never repay. We appreciate the contributions made to our prehistoric pottery analysis by Diane Bolger and Jennifer Webb and thank Iain Banks for carrying out a geomagnetic survey of Politiko *Phournia*. We also wish to thank the wonderful people of Mitsero—especially Andriani Kosta Loïzou, Andreas Papanastasiou, Konstantinos Ttaouxis, and Loïzos Xinaris and even the denizens of the "communist cafe"—and the rest of our survey area for their hospitality and forbearance. To all the many other individuals and institutions too numerous to mention, SCSP extends its warmest thanks.

In addition to the publication team who made this book possible, and in particular Helen Saunders (myriad illustrative and graphic contributions), we are indebted to several other scholars who worked with us on various aspects of SCSP over the years, from consultants and database manager to team leader: Ian Johnson (University of Sydney); Priscilla Keswani (Independent Scholar); Thomas Hillard (Macquarie University); Sturt Manning (University of Reading); Paul Sant Cassia (University of Durham); James D. Muhly (American School of Classical Studies, Athens); Alice Kingsnorth (American River College, Sacramento, CA.); Murray McClellan; David Rupp (Brock University, Ontario); Stuart Jeffrey (University of Glasgow); Eberhard Zangger (Independent Scholar). Thanks also to team leaders Susan Bain (Edinburgh), Julia Burnet (Sydney), Bradley Creevey (Newcastle, NSW), and Haddon Wright (Sydney); and to all the fieldwalkers, illustrators, and photographers from five seasons' work. A special thanks goes to Carole McCartney (Paphos) who stepped in at the last minute and identified some exceptionally clear examples of Pre-Pottery Neolithic chipped stone at two places of special interest (POSIs); this information has been incorporated into the final text. Finally, but by no means least, I wish to thank the marvelous chefs who made the incredibly hard work of each day dissipate in a cornucopia of Mediterranean and Asian haute cuisine: Andriani Kosta Loïzou, Julia Burnet, Trish Pemberton, Thelma Lowe, Tracy Ireland, Lori Dibble, and Annie Evans: SCSP just would never have been the same without you.

– A. Bernard Knapp

SCSP Team Members

1992
Steve O. Held
Ian Johnson
Priscilla Keswani
A. Bernard Knapp
Eberhard Zangger
Pitsa Kenti

1993
Julia Burnet
Bradley Creevey
Steve O. Held
Ian Johnson
Priscilla Keswani
A. Bernard Knapp
Lynn Meskell
Haddon Wright
Louise Zarmati

1995
Julia Burnet
Rod Clough
Bradley Creevey
Lita Diacopoulos
Emmanuel Gabet
Michael Given
Timothy E. Gregory
Steve O. Held
Ros James
Ian Johnson
Vasiliki Kassianidou
Pitsa Kenti

Priscilla Keswani
Alice Kingsnorth
A. Bernard Knapp
Murray McClellan
Megan Mebberson
Annette Moore
Christopher Papalas
Trish Pemberton
Paul Sant Cassia
Kylie Seretis
Lisa Wells
Haddon Wright

1996
ZoAnna Carrol
Dina Coleman
Matthew Daskivich
Michael Given
Ann Goldberg
Peter Grave
Timothy E. Gregory
Fiona Herring
Brett Hill
Heath Hughes
Vasiliki Kassianidou
Priscilla Keswani
A. Bernard Knapp
Pamela Kottaras
Thelma Lowe
Anne Mackay
Nathan Meyer

Samantha Moody
R. Scott Moore
Jay Noller
Janie Ravenhurst
Paul Sant Cassia
Kylie Seretis
Joanna S. Smith
Sharne Thomas
Karen Ulrich
Neil Urwin
Anthoulla Vassiliades
Haddon Wright

1997
Susan Bain
Dina Coleman
Bradley Creevey
Lita Diacopoulos
Lori Dibble
Caitlin Evans
Jo Finkel
Robyn Gerth
Michael Given
Timothy E. Gregory
Thomas Hillard
Tracy Ireland
Stuart Jeffrey
Vasiliki Kassianidou
A. Bernard Knapp
Michelle McLean
Nathan Meyer

R. Scott Moore
Shona Nicol
Jay Noller
Libby Percival
Lara-Ann Proctor
Robert Schon
Kylie Seretis
Ingrid Shearer
Jacqueline Smith
Joanna S. Smith
Robert Suttie
Natalie Swords
Karen Ulrich
Neil Urwin
Sven Van Lokeren
Lisa Wells
Lyn Wilson
Caroline Whitehill

1998
Dina Coleman
Annie Evans
Ian Evans
Michael Given
Timothy E. Gregory
Jean Humbert
Vasiliki Kassianidou
A. Bernard Knapp
Sturt Manning
Nathan Meyer
R. Scott Moore

Jay Noller
Chris Parks
David Pettegrew
Elinor Ribeiro
Dorella Romanou
Kylie Seretis
Joanna S. Smith
Krista Ubbels
Sven Van Lokeren
Anthoulla Vassiliades
Caroline Whitehill

1999
Dina Coleman
Denise de Joseph
Lita Diacopoulos
Michael Given
Timothy E. Gregory
Vasiliki Kassianidou
A. Bernard Knapp
Nathan Meyer
R. Scott Moore
Jay Noller
Helen Saunders
Kylie Seretis
Joanna S. Smith
Luke Sollars
Neil Urwin
Sven Van Lokeren
Lisa Wells
Caroline Whitehill

STRANGERS IN THE LANDSCAPE

Michael Given and Kylie Seretis

To 'our' farmer, wherever in time and space he may be…

In the grey mist of an early morning a farmer was standing in front of his house, yawning and scratching himself and looking out through the olive trees. Distant goat bells clanked dully through the mist as a herdsman set off on his daily wandering circuit. The farmer squinted up at the still weak sun, and looked round his small property. The house was small, but firmly built; it had foundations of stones from the ravine, walls of mud brick, and a new roof of tiles from the village. A separate shelter at the back held the potter's wheel that his wife used, and in the yard in front the farmer kept his hoes and plough and storage jars for the olive oil.

He looked again across his olive grove and suddenly stiffened. In a distant field four figures appeared through the mist, all of them wearing strange hats and brightly coloured clothes. They were walking in line a couple of donkey lengths apart, continually stooping to the ground and picking things up. It was his field, and he knew there was nothing to collect; the wheat had just been reaped, and the olives would not be ready for three months.

The figures reached the edge of the field and gathered under an olive tree, the farmer watching them intently. They all had coloured bags which contained many things which seemed important to them, though quite clearly none of it was food. They spent a lot of time under the tree. The farmer shrugged, and began to search across his courtyard, picking up the few limestone slabs that were left loose on the surface and throwing them into the next field. He had paved the courtyard the day before, after bringing in the slabs from the white hill down the valley; the stones from the ravine were useless for this work.

Under the olive tree the four had finished and were packing up their bags again. The sun had dissipated the mist, and the shadows cast by each individual blade of stubble were growing shorter.

'That was a really good unit,' said Lita, as she stuffed her clipboard into her pack. '147 sherds. It's going to be a good day, I can tell.'

'Team Central strikes again,' answered Bradley. 'Told you so.' He frowned at the scanned aerial photograph on his clipboard, and looked up again through the olives. 'OK, there's Unit 1360, all ready and waiting for us. Let's hit it.'

The four of them shouldered their bags and lined up along the edge of the next field. As they began to move across it, the farmer came down to the edge and stood there leaning on his staff and watching them carefully.

'There's some tile here,' said Michael, stooping to pick up a chunky corner of coarse terracotta.

'Anyone else found some slag?' asked Bradley from the far end of the line.

'No,' answered Kylie, looking about her just in case.

'Bradley always finds the slag,' said Lita, looking about her as well.

'It's his magnetic personality,' commented Michael, who hadn't found any either.

Bradley gave a mock bow, and frowned at his clipboard again. 'We stop at that olive tree,' he said.

'Which olive tree?' asked Michael. 'The whole place is packed with olive trees.'

'The one with all the shade under it for writing up.'

They continued across the field, clicking their clickers every time they saw a sherd, counting tiles and slag and *pithos* and lithics and handles in their head, and continually stooping to pick up likely-looking sherds. The farmer shook his head in bewilderment, and walked back to his courtyard to start loading the donkey. He was taking a double load to the market in the village today: two sacks of wheat, and a pile of jugs that his wife had pulled out of the kiln yesterday. She'd suddenly started going in for those fancy handles made out of two sausages of clay, and she'd been making him go miles with the donkey to get the sort of clay she wanted. A bit of a waste of time, in his opinion; after all, a water jug was a water jug. But they did sell; there was a market for jugs. Probably because everyone dropped them all the time. He heaved the sacks of wheat up into the panniers, and carefully balanced the jugs on top and between them. He'd be walking beside the donkey today, not riding it.

The archaeologists collected under the olive tree, pulling off their bags with relief.

'What d'you think of these, Michael?' asked Bradley, handing across three small slabs of limestone.

Michael turned them over in his hands, examining them sceptically. 'Stones,' he said briefly, and gave them to Kylie.

'Yes, I'm pretty sure they're natural,' she agreed.

'Spoilsports,' grumbled Bradley. 'I think they're floor slabs, or paving stones. And anyway, how did they get here? This is all pillow lava, and these are limestone.'

He thought for a moment. 'OK, we won't collect them. Lita, could you make a comment that there are several pieces of limestone slab in the southeast corner of the field.'

'OK,' answered Lita, pulling out her clipboard and writing on the Unit Sheet. 'Is this still lower pillow lava?'

'Yes,' answered Bradley, briefly looking around him. 'And fluviatile terrace.'

Lita nodded, and repeated what she was writing under her breath: 'Surface – plough; landuse – orchard; terraces – nil.'

'Sherds?' she asked.

'75' said Bradley.

'62,' said Kylie.

There was a pause.

'Michael?'

Michael looked up with a start. 'What? Oh yes, sherds. Hang on.' He looked round him. 'Anyone seen my clicker? Ah, here it is. 61.'

'And I had 73,' said Lita, frowning as she did the arithmetic. 'That makes – 267. That's pretty good, isn't it?'

'We're onto something, if you ask me,' agreed Bradley.

'There's tile as well, isn't there?' said Michael. 'Do you think there's enough around for this to be a settlement?'

'Ah, it depends how you define a settlement,' put in Kylie. 'Is it just density of sherds?'

'Tile as well.'

'But is that enough?'

They looked out from the shade of the olive tree at the ploughed field sitting innocently in the bright sunshine.

'Maybe we're on the edge of a settlement,' said Bradley at last.

'Halo?' suggested Michael. There was no answer.

After a few minutes Bradley pulled himself to his feet and squinted out from the shade of the olive tree.

'You lot stay here for a minute. I'll just go and check out the next unit.'

He walked across the corner of the farmer's courtyard and looked around him, glancing down at his clipboard. The farmer, still loading his donkey, paused briefly, holding the jug he was about to tie onto the donkey.

'Lita!' called Bradley suddenly. The farmer jumped, and dropped the jug which hit a paving stone at his feet and shattered into a dozen chunky sherds. He snatched up the broken handle and hurled it furiously at Bradley, who was staring at his clipboard again, totally oblivious. The handle missed him and went sailing out into the field beyond.

'Yes?' answered Lita from under the tree.

'Can you mark down Unit 1361 as "Not surveyed – no visibility".'

'OK.'

Bradley turned round and examined the small field beyond the farmer's house.

'And this one is 1362, which we'll do.'

He waited, but there was no action from under the tree.

'Come on, gang. Let's do it!'

'Slave-driver,' commented Michael pleasantly. He yawned, and one by one they came blinking out from the shade of the olive tree. The farmer tapped his donkey on the flank with his staff, and stared disgustedly at the four archaeologists as he urged the donkey on towards the village.

Twenty minutes later, the archaeologists had finished their next unit. Kylie stooped under the branches of an olive tree at the far side of the field.

'Where are you putting the sherds?' she asked.

Bradley cleared a space in the earth.

'Here you go.'

In turn they dumped the sherds each had collected from the unit. Bradley began picking through them.

'Lot of handles from this field, aren't there? Must have been doing a lot of pouring.'

'That's a nice one,' said Lita, pointing at a handle made of slightly finer fabric, with a division going down the length of it. 'Is that Late Roman?'

'Don't know. What d'you think, Michael?'

'Let's see,' said Michael, stretching across and taking it from him. 'Well, it's made of two cylinders of clay pressed together. And the fabric's unusual. But I haven't a clue about its date. Priscilla will know.'

'I'm going to go and check out the next units,' said Bradley. 'We'll do another quick one and then have second breakfast.'

The sun was fierce and high when the farmer returned from the village. A little before his house, a battered Vauxhall Viva was parked neatly in the stubble beside the path. He looked at it, mystified and a bit suspicious, and looked carefully round his fields. And sure enough, there they were, four figures in a line across the field, clicking something with one hand and stooping down to pick things up with the other. He stopped the donkey and watched them for a few minutes. What was it they were picking up? As far as he could see, it was just garbage. Well, why not? At least they weren't taking his figs. But why didn't they come and talk to him? If it was garbage they wanted, he could tell them where there was heaps of the stuff; behind his house, for example.

The archaeologists slumped gratefully into the shade of another olive tree, and began sorting the finds and filling in the sheets.

'It's really hot today,' said Lita.

Bradley looked at his watch. 'That's it for the day, team. We'll wrap up this one and go home. And there'd better be some beer in the fridge.'

'Where d'you think all this slag is coming from?' asked Michael.

'Search me, mate. We had, what was it, about a thousand in the last unit.'

'And a total of 74 in this unit,' put in Lita, looking at her Unit Sheet.

'Who knows?' said Bradley, shrugging. 'Come on, let's go.'

They walked down the track to where the farmer was standing opposite the car.

'Oh look,' whispered Lita. 'There's a farmer, and look, he's got a donkey as well. Shall we go and talk to him?'

'Where is he?' asked Kylie.

'Not sure we've got time,' said Bradley, checking his watch.

'We need to enter all this data,' agreed Michael. 'And it's not fair on Trish if we're late for lunch.'

The car lurched out of the field and onto the track, and the farmer raised a hand in acknowledgement. The archaeologists drove past without seeing him, and he shook his head with a sad smile as the car headed off down the track.

The Villa Bernard was full of the usual pre-lunch activity. Conversations about slag heap sections and beautiful lithics and the heat and the lack of cold beers were floating round the courtyard, as the teams came in from the field and swapped accounts of the morning's doings. Trish was in the kitchen frying halloumi; Priscilla was sitting at the table counting and dating the bags of sherds; Lita was tapping at one of the computers, entering the data from the morning; Kylie and Michael were out the back washing sherds; Bradley was telling Haddon about slag found in fields, and Haddon was telling Bradley about slag found in slag heaps.

'Oh look,' exclaimed Kylie. 'Here's that nice handle we found.' She brushed it carefully, and rinsed it in the muddy water.

'How do you think it got there?' asked Michael, looking up from the uninspiring coarse ware rim he was washing.

'You know,' she said, turning it in her hands, 'there's a person behind every sherd.'

'And a deposition process. It's probably been ploughed half way round the field.'

'But it still got there somehow. Somewhere there's a story about the man or woman who broke this jug and left the handle there.'

'I supposed,' mused Michael. 'But how do we find that story? All we can talk about is drift from sites, or background scatter from agricultural use, or an isolated sherd from casual crossing of the landscape. Where do you get your story from?'

'I tell you what. That farmer that Lita saw. I'm sure he could talk about how a sherd gets where it does. He must have some stories.'

'What farmer is this?' asked Haddon, who had been listening from the side.

'Just a farmer that Lita saw today,' answered Kylie. 'He probably knows all sorts of things about what we're looking for.'

'Maybe he's a ghost from the past,' suggested Haddon with a mischievous glint in his eyes.

'There's your story,' said Michael suddenly, looking across the bowl of muddy water at Kylie.

'Yes,' she answered, looking thoughtfully at the handle. 'There's the story.'

The goat bell rang for lunch, and soon the conversation had changed to fried halloumi and beer and the importance of tabasco sauce.

A tray of sherds rested where the salad bowl had been, and Priscilla was staring glumly at an undateable sherd.

'That's one of ours,' said Kylie, coming past and looking over her shoulder. 'None of us knew what it was.'

'I've got news for you,' answered Priscilla. 'Neither do I.' She turned it over in her hands and compared it with the rest of the tray. 'Yes. This is Period UNK.'

'Unk?'

'Unknown.' She picked up her pen and wrote quickly across the Finds Sheet, explaining to Kylie as she wrote. 'Batch 3. Quantity: 1. Material: P; that's Pottery. Fabric: CL; that's Coarse Light. Form HN, for handle. No decoration. Period: UNK; that's –'

'Unknown,' chimed in Kylie.

'That's right. And Comments: one plain ware split handle. And that's that. Exciting stuff, isn't it?'

Kylie smiled non-committally and went off to see if her computer was free. Michael was digitizing the day's units, poring over the Field Sheet as he moved the cross-hair along the unit boundaries. At the end of the unit he pressed '1' and looked at the screen in satisfaction as the new unit blinked and filled itself in.

Kylie looked over his shoulder. 'So where's the farmer then?'

Michael moved the mouse so the cursor rested in the corner of Unit 1379.

'That's where Lita saw him.' He moved it up to the top of the screen. 'And that's probably where he lives; right in a field with bad visibility that we couldn't survey.'

'I wonder what sort of house he has,' said Kylie.

'Well, there were a few bits of tile in the next unit. And there were those three limestone blocks that Bradley found. So…'

'Tiled with a paved courtyard. Sounds very nice.'

Michael nodded vaguely, pressed 'D', and began digitizing the next unit.

In a small house in an olive grove, a farmer and his family were hungrily eating their bread and yoghurt. The farmer talked about his trip to the village, and his success in selling the wheat and jugs for a decent price. He wiped out his bowl with a scrap of bread, and leant back against the wall of the house.

'There were four strangers here today,' he announced.

'From the village?' asked his wife.

The farmer jerked his head in denial.

'From another village? From another country?'

The farmer looked round at his wife and children.

'From another world,' he declared solemnly.

His younger daughter stared up at him, her eyes wide and round. 'Tell us the story, Daddy! Please tell us the story!'

The farmer smiled, and began to speak.

Michael sat at his improvised desk beside the kitchen sink, watching the print-head tacking backwards and forwards. There was a tap at the door, and he turned to see Bernard's tall figure standing in the doorway behind him.

'I just wanted to remind you,' said Bernard, 'that I'll need your report on the Medieval to Modern Periods by the end of the week.'

"I'm working on it. I've just been doing that area between Malounda and Klirou we did today."

The printer screeched out the last line, and the paper fed out of the top and fell on the floor.

"Here you are," said Michael triumphantly, picking it up. "Hot off the press."

He handed it over, and Bernard began to read.

Once upon a time there lived in this house a brave hero, who travelled round the country helping good people against dragons and devils and other monsters. Now, one day he was working in his fields when he saw four beings from another world who appeared before him out of the mist. They all wore outlandish clothes of unimaginable colours, and each had exotic headgear of different aspect. They walked in a chain across his fields, and they could neither see anyone nor hear anyone; for they were beings from another world. Now, when he saw these strange beings, our brave hero went out to accost them. But they neither saw him nor heard him. So he set himself to understanding who they were and what they were doing. But he could not ask them as he could with his own kind, so he must watch them and see what they did. And he saw that they bore little grey stones in their hand which made a clicking sound as they walked; and he saw that they stopped every three paces to gather another stone from the field. They crossed the field, and they huddled together like sheep under a tree before crossing the next field. And it seemed to our hero that they were taking stock of the land and making count, so as to pluck it from the hands of its rightful owner for their own use and enjoyment. And then one of them, their leader, who was tall and brave almost like our hero himself, came out against our brave hero. He bore strange weapons and uttered outlandish cries. The fight was fierce, but the leader of the strange beings was vanquished by a mighty throw from our brave hero's arm. He took his minions with him and vanished into the mist whence he came. And thus was our brave hero's house preserved, and our country protected for ever and eternity.

All transects walked during the 1995 season produced considerable quantities of material from the Medieval (1191–1571), Ottoman (or Early Modern; 1571–1878), and Modern (1878–present) periods. This material derived both from settlement sites and from background scatters deposited as a result of agricultural use. Three areas of particular interest were surveyed on a wider scale than was done in the transects: the olive groves east of the church of *Panayia Odhiyitria* at Aredhiou; the area round the church of *Panayia Khrysopandanassa* at Malounda; and the fields between Malounda and Klirou. This last area is particularly remarkable for its extensive scatter of Ottoman material, though there are also considerable quantities of Late Roman and Medieval, and a lesser amount of Classical to Early Roman. The correlation between this material and the agricultural land is very clear. The area is a flat fluvial terrace with good soil and a major water course, the river Akaki, immediately to the west. It has clearly been cultivated for centuries; some olive trees are several hundred years old. A scatter of pottery covers some 10 units in varying concentrations, though unfortunately there was a similar number of units which could not be surveyed because of poor visibility due to high stubble and standing crops. Much of the scatter of material appears to be background associated with intensive agricultural use over a long period of time. In Units 1359-1361 the sherd counts were high enough to suggest the presence of a settlement in the area, especially when combined with a certain amount of tile. These units may represent a halo of material which has drifted from a nearby settlement due to agricultural processes.

A jagged rock stood silhouetted against the stars, and the lights of Mitsero shone out into the moonless night from far below. Dark shapes moved around the rock, talking and laughing and passing up the brandy sour. Above loomed the massive outline of the summit of Mount Kriadhis.

A little distance from the rock Haddon stood smoking and looking up at the summit. He turned suddenly to Michael, the lights of Mitsero sparkling in his glasses.

'I wonder where that farmer of yours is now,' he said softly.

'The farmer? Well, I think he's up on that hill now, watching us and wondering what we're up to.'

'Oh, do you think so?' broke in Lita from behind. 'I'm sure he is. He's with us all the time.'

'Yes, that's right,' agreed Kylie. 'He's up on that hill, or down in his olive grove, standing in the doorway of his house with the firelight at his back, wondering when we're going to go up and talk to him.'

The fresh night breeze blew softly on their faces as they looked up at Mount Kriadhis and down over Mitsero and their darkened survey area.

'Well,' said someone at last, 'Time to go, I suppose. We've got work to do tomorrow.'

They gathered the empty bottles and plastic cups, and set off back to the Villa and to bed.

In the cool of the early morning four archaeologists were walking across a field, counting slag and tiles and picking up sherds from the long shadow of the stubble. Distant goat bells rang out from across the ravine, and every shout of the herdsman could be heard through the clear, still air. The archaeologists finished their unit, and sat by an olive grove to fill in their sheets. In the distance a solitary figure stood watching them, leaning on his staff.

'Lita,' said Bradley suddenly. 'Isn't that your farmer again?'

'Oh, I think it is,' she answered, craning her neck to see. 'Can we go and talk to him? I think it'd be really good.'

'I don't see why not,' answered Bradley. 'We've done all our figures for this unit.'

'I'd be interested to see what he says about sherds drifting from settlements into the fields,' agreed Michael. 'What do you think, Kylie?'

'Oh, let's,' she answered. 'After all, he might have a story to tell us.'

The four archaeologists waved, and began walking across to where the farmer was standing. He waited, leaning on his staff, and smiled as he watched them approach.

Team central recording a survey unit
east of Aredhiou, June 1995.

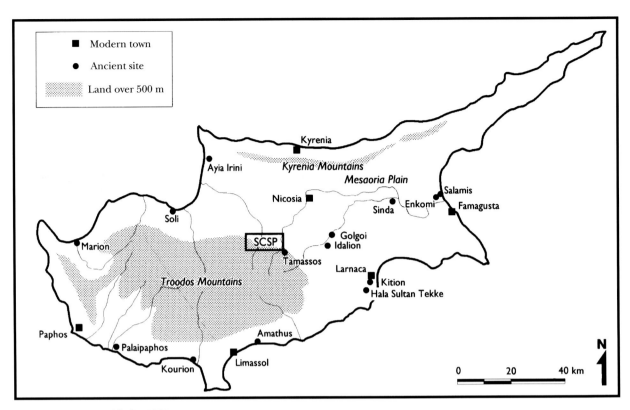

Figure 1.1 Cyprus, with the SCSP survey area

Figure 1.2 View from Kriadhis looking north, 1995

1

THE SYDNEY CYPRUS SURVEY PROJECT

1.1 Introduction and Overview

A. Bernard Knapp

The Sydney Cyprus Survey Project (SCSP) devoted five seasons of fieldwork (1992–1997) to an intensive ar-chaeological survey in the north-central foothills of the Troodos Mountains on the eastern Mediterranean island of Cyprus. We conducted this regional archaeological project in a 65 km^2 area in and around the modern villages of Politiko and Mitsero (figures 1.1, 1.2). This pedi-montane region has always been reputed for its natural resources, not least the copper-sulfide ore deposits of Cyprus's Lower Pillow Lavas, which in this region lie adjacent to the fertile agricultural plain. (For a detailed description of the SCSP area, see chapter 7.1 "Human and Physical Landscape Dynamics.") One of our primary goals is to understand through archaeo-logical data and to exemplify through archaeological practice the relationship between the production and distribution of agricultural and metallurgical resources, on the one hand, and the changing configurations of a complex society and the individuals within it, on the other. Accordingly, the proximity of igneous foothills and sedimentary plain was of strategic importance in selecting this area for regional survey work. In part, then, SCSP was designed to locate archaeological "sites" and to determine the patterning of settlement through time, in relation to both metallurgical and agricultural resources.

Fotiadis (1997:106–107) recently observed that processual archaeologists designed survey projects to in-vestigate eco-environmental issues by sampling at a regional scale. He maintains, quite rightly in our opinion, that regional projects instead should begin with the essential question, what is a region?, and with an attempt to understand the geohistorical unity there may have been in the area. Practical considerations will also dictate and delimit the configuration and extent of the region selected, and most archaeological survey projects will, for differing reasons, consciously choose more than one morphostratigraphic unit or environmental zone. Unlike many processual archaeological surveys, SCSP selected a region (actually a portion, or "sample," of a larger region to limit the scope of the work) based not only on its spatial and geomorphological attributes but also on what we perceived to be its likely cultural coherence within the northern Troodos region and its historical continuity in terms of mining zones and agricultural communities. We develop this perspective in more detail in chapter 2.1, "The Goals of a Regional Survey."

SCSP is the first coordinated attempt anywhere in the Troodos to identify and locate industrial sites and agricultural villages; to reconsider and redefine the existence of a proposed site hierarchy (mining/resource sites, agricultural villages, urban centers); and to reconstruct early industrial and agricultural landscapes (Manning and Conwell 1992; Rupp 1986). The term *industrial sites* refers to installations such as smelting or roasting sites, slag heaps, spoil heaps, mines (adits, galleries, open-cast), or anything else (fluxes, ores, gossans) related to the extraction and production of copper from Cyprus's sulfide ore bodies (Knapp and Seretis 1996:11–12; Knapp 1999a). The term *agricultural villages* refers to sites whose main role in a settlement system is to provide subsistence support, primarily for themselves but at times for other components of a settlement hierarchy, for example, for the miners who work nearby, or for "rural sanctuaries" (Knapp 1999b:232–236). Examples in the SCSP area are Aredhiou *Vouppes* (SCY010; Knapp et al. 1994:336–338) and Politiko *Phorades* 2 (SCY101; Given et al. 1999:32–34).

However, we want to emphasize that SCSP is interested not only in sites but also in human-land relations throughout the landscape, in fact, in the total landscape (chapter 7.5). The study of social landscapes makes it possible to consider how people interact with a landscape in terms of their own individual experience (Ashmore and Knapp 1999). Our framework for interpretation is the belief that the study of people cannot be separated from the study of their environment and, conversely, that the environment will alter as humans alter their society. People tend to modify their surroundings profoundly and have the capacity to move more sediment in any given year than all known geological processes combined. SCSP is dealing with the human transformation of a landscape over a period of seven thousand years; in evaluating this specific landscape we seek to integrate such diverse fields and techniques as archaeology, ethnohistory, geomorphology, ecology, geographic information system (GIS), and satellite imagery into landscape reconstructions, as well as into social and economic reconstructions of a distinctive region. We consider not only how humans transform the landscape they inhabit but also how natural history and natural resources affect sociocultural development and change.

We begin (chapter 1) by presenting our perspective on social archaeology and indicating how that perspective engages the study of agricultural and industrial landscapes. Then we recount some participant experiences in the field, following which we present a background of previous research in the study area. In chapter 2, we consider the differing goals and concerns of contemporary regional survey to situate and highlight our own theoretical outlook and methodological procedures. There are several areas where we believe SCSP has made notable, if not unique, contributions to regional survey practice in the Mediterranean—integrating geomorphology, GIS, and aerial photography; combining geobotanical survey and satellite imagery; incorporating historical archaeology and ethnohistory into archaeological field survey; engaging archaeometallurgy in the study of prehistoric and historic mining; and assessing the use of lithics in a historical landscapes—and we discuss these in some detail.

In chapter 3, we present our methodology in full, from sampling, mapping, and testing through fieldwalking and analytical procedures for all classes of material. We also explain the reasoning behind our use of terms such as *place of special interest* (POSI) and *special interest area* (SIA). The methodology, laboratory, and dating procedures involved in each specialist enterprise that SCSP has sought to integrate are discussed in full: GIS, pottery and lithic studies, geomorphology, archaeometallurgy, ethnohistory, and historical archaeology. In other words, we treat a diversity of issues relating to the SCSP survey universe and our techniques for sampling, analyzing, and interpreting that domain. The discussion of these core methods—and the new perspectives from chapter 2—should be of interest to anyone interested in regional studies, in any discipline, anywhere in the world.

Chapter 4 represents the empirical heart of this study: For each relevant SIA and POSI, we present the physical landscape (geomorphology, vegetation, natural resources), the historical context (including discussion of relevant documentary evidence), the field methodology (including sampling, gridding, and collecting), analytical maps and assemblages, GIS thematic maps (with artifact density by period), and an integrated but concise summary of the overall landscape. We give summaries of the artifacts from each SIA in tabular format, while in chapter 5 we present a catalog of our most representative artifacts, including brief descriptions, photographs and drawings, comparanda, and references for all categories of material culture considered—pottery, chipped stone, special finds (for example, picrolite, glass, metal), and for archaeometallurgical materials (particularly analytical results).

In chapter 6, specialists in each of five chronological eras—Neolithic to Bronze Age, Geometric to Classical, Hellenistic to Roman, Byzantine, Medieval to Modern—present a diachronic landscape history. In so doing, they engage thematic issues related to communications, material culture patterns, modes of production, types of settlement, and land-use patterns as indicators of politico-economic organization. In each case, we attempt to reconstruct the SCSP landscape during a particular time frame, but within the wider perspective of a diachronic Cypriot landscape.

In chapter 7, the concluding discussion, we broaden the perspective to assess inhabited Cypriot landscapes from the diverse viewpoints that our data both allow and demand: natural and anthropogenic landscapes, industrial and agricultural landscapes, and ideational landscapes. Our aim is to present an integrated discussion of social landscapes—from archaeological, historical, geomorphological, geobotanical, and archaeometallurgical perspectives—within the SCSP survey universe. This chapter represents our attempt to provide a holistic overview of a regional survey project, integrating material culture within an interpretative context shaped and framed by contemporary social archaeology.

1.2 The Social Archaeology of Industrial and Agricultural Landscapes

A. Bernard Knapp

To the extent that nature presents itself to humans as so much raw material to fashion, space is no longer a container, field, or ground that holds, engulfs, or supports other things but is itself a contingent product, a sediment of human practice, a construction in the material and not merely semantic sense of that word—in short, an artifact. (Biersack 1999:9)

In writing about landscapes, archaeologists often tend to overlook the human experience of place. The social archaeology of a region must focus on human settlements, from the individuals and households that comprise them to the cultural landscape that contextualizes them. People use places and features in the landscape—fields, hills, caves, forests and streams—to produce food and resources, express formal design, make social statements, live their lives, and bury their dead. Such places are imbued with deep personal, ideological, and economic significance. These are some of the social aspects of the landscape that SCSP seeks to explore and understand.

Even where landscapes are regarded chiefly as mythic space, people participate actively in that space (for example, Denevan 1992; Taçon 1999). Despite our predilection to see landscapes as natural, it is impossible to deny that they are also social and cultural. Some regard the landscape as a mediation between the natural and the social, one aspect of Bourdieu's *habitus,* the routine social practices through which and within which people experience their world (Knapp and Ashmore 1999:20–21). By the very act of dwelling in the landscape, people not only identify with it; they actively order and transform it. The environment becomes manifest as landscape only when people experience space as a complex of places. Kealhofer (1999:61) conceives of this as a dialectic and compares it to the "structuration" of Giddens (1979) wherein people create places that define space; in turn their identities become defined by place. To understand how social identity and landscape articulate, we have to understand the active role of landscapes, that is, how place is formed, maintained, and continuously reconfigured (Kealhofer 1999:62).

As archaeologists, we explore the meaning and memory, the remnants and legacies of individual landscapes. This is the study of social meaning in past landscapes. Where once the landscape was seen simply as a backdrop against which human activities were carried out, we believe that landscapes exist only when they become contextualized, perceived, and experienced by people. In other words, we would not separate the study of any society from the study of its environment: The two develop and change in tandem. SCSP is concerned with understanding social dynamics in a landscape that has been used continuously over the past seven thousand years; in so doing, we consider not only the human transformation of the landscape but also the effect that natural history and the exploitation of natural resources may have on social developments and social change in that same space.

SCSP's methodology and philosophy and offshoots (for example, the excavations at Politiko *Phorades,* most recently Knapp et al. 1999, 2001) represent our attempt to engage field survey within a social archaeology. The long-term, sociohistorical perspective of this project forms an important research focus of its several principal collaborators. The interactive study by diverse specialists using innovative technologies to reconstruct past landscapes has

Figure 1.3 Team East at SCY209 in 1997

enabled SCSP to make a different kind of contribution to the archaeological history of Cyprus. Moreover, we continue to emphasize the outstanding cultural significance of key industrial and agricultural landscapes so that they may be recognized as worthy of preservation and protection. Only through interdisciplinary survey, excavation, exploration, and social analysis can one gain a better awareness of the early agricultural and industrial landscapes that typify the island of Cyprus.

1.3 Archaeological Survey: Views from the Field

Michael Given

Fieldwalking teams kept notebooks, in which they gave general descriptions of work in progress and commented on team discussions, problems, and state of mind. A brief selection of quotations from these notebooks gives some flavor of doing fieldwork in the northern foothills of Cyprus's Troodos Mountains. More importantly, it puts the people—at least the fieldwalkers—back into their landscape (figure 1.3). The interpretations, analytical maps, and conclusions of this volume are based on actions taken and decisions made by individuals working in the survey area, and it is important to understand the context. This section comes with appreciative thanks to the fieldwalkers (identities obscured by random initials) and the authors of the field notebooks.

The early days were spent experimenting with methodology and discussing terminology:

There are clear fields ("plots") but in between we are having difficulty defining the area to be surveyed. What has happened to our "quadrat" method? Could we call this "transect strip" instead of quadrat? We need to stick to an agreed-upon method.

As in all such enterprises, the discussion could occasionally become quite intense:

Tension in the field—too many generals and the cavalry keep advancing. Much evidence of a former forest cover. Almost enjoyed the bickering—light hearted—though A was flustered or frustrated by B. C's constant control was almost as difficult—in retrospect, quite funny.

With time and much hard work, everyone gained experience, and the system began to come together:

Did a lot of the map reading today from scans and aerial photos, which was fun and a huge learning experience. We fairly much stuck to the transect and covered our 50 m band. Sorted and cataloged finds late tonight and had to fix up various mistakes. This sort of work needs a lot of cross checking.

On occasion, particularly in the rough terrain in the southeast of the survey area, fieldwalking could become quite adventurous:

Climbed up a steep crumbly limestone slope and back down till we reached a sheer drop comprised of crumbly limestone. From there it ran into a lovely smooth limestone watercourse. We all nearly died going down a cliff, and we are now kissing the prickly ground at the bottom. One reinforced terrace, one core, two lithics—is it really worth it? Sang theme from Indiana Jones, applied sunscreen, and moved on.

A variety of difficulties and problems had to be faced and resolved, or at least written about so that they could be borne in mind during data interpretation. One such was the problem of early morning light:

Unit 5042. 6.50–7.10 a.m. The unit consisted of a freshly plowed field. The sun was very low in the sky and cast confusing shadows...the lines of the plow became vast dark gullies.

Or there were animals:

The setting up of the line was somewhat delayed when a flock of goats invaded our area and mistaking the flags for some tasty flower munched through 500E/ 510N–500E/550N, and no doubt redistributed some pottery en route.

Or problematic maps and scansheets:

> Bit of trouble....We have started in a new area, SCY215—and the scansheet grid is all wrong. Rather than being 10 by 10 cm, the grid is 6.4 by 7.2 cm—what kind of navigation tool is that to give to people? Fortunately, being pretty good at what we do, we're making our own.

Or 'illness':

> Getting over our hangovers not too badly, but we're all dead tired. So bad that we couldn't even face the pub today—I'm sure we'll manage to make up for it tomorrow.

Worst of all, perhaps, were visits from the director, field director, and various specialists:

> We had a visit from the bigwigs halfway through walking the unit. One helpfully (cough, cough) commented that we missed picking up a handle fragment on one side of the field...and X commented that it was *only* 35°C, that it was a very pleasant temperature, and that he couldn't understand what we were complaining about.

The heat regularly reached the high 30s. Particularly by the end of the morning, it could often affect concentration:

> Unit 3655. Start 11:00. End 11:45. Huge unit. Cut crop. Smack dab in centre of valley. 'Drain' trench on SE side...and raw (rah!) material for lithics. Great beach lots of groovy music ,great men, needs gridding as a POSI. We all volunteer to come back. Yay! Also a temple. Ate monkey brains and snakes. The saga continues tomorrow.

Meanwhile, back at the house in Mitsero (generally known as the "Villa"), the artifact specialists and database managers worked away. Conditions may have been cooler, but they were not necessarily easier. As well as the basic reading of the artifacts, there were tedious and frustrating problems in the data that had to be laboriously corrected:

> Trying to deal with problems from SCY101. Two units do not have pottery, and at least one has too much. 1599 has five bags, which equals 50, but 20 in database. We find one bag with 20. Completed re-reading of pottery from SCY101 the best we could.

A frequent problem with working at the Villa was that there were various distractions and chores:

> Wednesday. Most of day spent with septic tank, washing machine, Seychelles, and pulling pottery for illustration. The last is a time-consuming process. Trip to Tamassos in pm. No pottery reading. Rain in evening. A real thunderstorm.

But for field teams and lab specialists alike, there was always the satisfaction of getting the job done in the end. Sometimes there was even the chance for a quick one after work...

> Stopped off in Klirou for our post-survey drinks and crisps. Got back a bit late and everyone had been worried about us. Isn't that nice?

1.4 Background and Previous Research
Michael Given

Until SCSP began work in 1992, the area between the western edge of Politiko village and the village of Mitsero was effectively archaeological terra incognita. The Department of Antiquities, Cyprus, had carried out several small-scale rescue excavations, mainly of Roman tombs near the villages of Politiko, Klirou, and Mitsero. Guidebook writers such as Rupert Gunnis (1936) and topographers such as Jack Goodwin (1984) noted tombs and other chance finds, and many villagers have a good knowledge of the antiquities discovered in the immediate area of their village. Dr. George Constantinou, former director of the Cyprus Geological Survey, noted slag heaps and other antiquities associated with mining in the course of his research in the area (Constantinou 1972) and has been very generous in sharing his knowledge with SCSP. The few other brief discussions of sites or finds in the area are mentioned in this report where relevant.

Two separate projects, on the boundary and just beyond the survey area, have been the most notable forerunners of SCSP: various excavations at Tamassos and the Akhera Survey. The ancient city-kingdom of Tamassos flourished from the Cypro-Geometric III to the Byzantine period, and much of the eastern part of our survey area lies within its territory. In 1885, 1889, and 1894, three sanctuaries, a glass workshop, and a large number of tombs, some of them very opulent, were excavated by Max Ohnefalsch-Richter (1893:6–11; Buchholz and Untiedt 1996:19–21). These included twenty-nine tombs immediately north of the later monastery of Ayios Mnason, which do fall into SCSP's SIA 6 (see chapter 4.6; Buchholz 1974:574–577).

Excavations at the locality Chomazoudhia, on the northern edge of Politiko and just outside the SCSP survey area, were carried out from 1970 to 1981 by the Deutsche Tamassos-Expedition from the Deutschen Archäologischen Institut in Berlin, led by Hans-Günter Buchholz (1973, 1974, 1978, 1985a, 1985b, 1994; Buchholz and Untiedt 1996). These excavations uncovered a major sanctuary and accompanying buildings dating from the Cypro-Archaic I to Late Roman periods, short stretches of the Archaic and Classical city wall, and portions of the Cypro-Archaic aristocratic tombs left untouched by Ohnefalsch-Richter. The Deutsche Tamassos-Expedition also examined the cemeteries in the immediate vicinity and undertook other investigations into rural sanctuaries and the timber and copper resources of the region, although no intensive survey was carried out (Buchholz and Untiedt 1996:21–22). Recent spectacular mortuary finds from Tamassos include carved sphinxes and lions (Christou 1996; Solomidou-Ieronymidou 2001).

One survey project preceded SCSP in this general region: the Akhera Survey from the State University of New York at Albany, directed by Paul Wallace. The Akhera Survey held one season of fieldwork in 1979, in an area stretching from Mitsero north to Meniko, with its southernmost 9 km² overlapping the northwest corner of the SCSP survey area (Wallace 1982). Most of the work focused on the Akhera area 2.5 km to the north of SCSP, but the slag heaps at Mitsero *Mavrovounos* (our SIA 4), Mitsero *Kouloupakhis* (SIA 3), and Agrokipia *Kriadhis* (SIA 1) were also investigated, with pottery being collected and the slag analyzed (Koucky 1982). The analysis of this pottery was entrusted to Charles Adelman, and although SCSP was given charge of the actual pottery, we were unable to arrange any satisfactory schedule of work and publication with Dr. Adelman.

2

CONTRIBUTIONS TO REGIONAL SURVEY ARCHAEOLOGY

2.1 The Goals of a Regional Survey

Nathan Meyer and A. Bernard Knapp

> Two things are new: the joining together of archaeological and historical data and the adherence to a single, spatiotemporal frame at the scale of the region. Connecting archaeological with historical populations in a common geographical frame leads to a long-term demography, a simple and obvious idea, yet empirically based curves such as these are rare if not absent from the world literature. (Kowalewski 1997:303)

To investigate archaeologically the long-term relationships between social structures and human agents, the ideal scale of analysis is at the regional rather than the site level (Barker 1995b:3). Regional studies, including regional survey projects, have only recently become an accepted archaeological endeavor; the need to defend survey methodologies was still felt throughout the 1970s (for example, Schiffer et al. 1978; Ammerman 1981:63). Archaeologists, for example, debated the use of statistical analysis and the importance of sampling design and called into question the validity of the "site" as the basic unit of analysis. Even today there remains some unease with the actual nature and especially the means of recording and interpreting survey data. Some recent works call for redefining the scale of analysis to the microregion (Gaffney and Tingle 1988) or to the community (Kolb and Snead 1997; Canuto and Yaeger 2000), although both approaches assume intensive survey strategies and neither seem aware that Trigger (1967, 1968), in his early work on settlement pattern analysis, had already formulated three general levels for study: buildings, communities, and regions. Thus, it is fair to say that archaeologists have yet to resolve some fundamental methodological issues in regional survey practice. Have methodological goals and concerns, coupled with our increasing ability to produce microscopically detailed knowledge about the physical and material facets of the landscape, outstripped our ability to integrate survey results, data analysis, and interpretation (Alcock et al. 1994)? How can we breach the gap between ever-more refined regional survey methodology, on the one hand, and on the other the burgeoning literature on the archaeologies of landscape (Ashmore and Knapp 1999)?

Ideally, regional survey projects conduct basic research into the locational, social and environmental aspects of the landscape. Although collecting and processing environmental data have always constituted a major element in interdisciplinary survey projects (for example, Cherry et al. 1991; Barker 1995a, 1995b; Philips 1989; Larsson, Callmer and Stjerngnist 1992), integrating environmental data into social or cultural frameworks has proved more difficult (McGlade 1995; Knapp and Ashmore 1999:5–8). Interpreting mineral, floral and faunal, hydrological, or pedological data requires a range of specialist expertise and, while lending an atmosphere of interdisciplinary collaboration, also has the effect of increasing the impact of hard science on archaeological data generation, interpretation, and publication.

An eco-environmental approach to understanding past human societies has long been integral to both anthropology (Biersack 1999) and archaeology (Trigger 1989:247–250), and carries within it a regional element. The neoevolutionary models of Leslie White and Julian Steward already posited a materialist basis to the forms that human culture would take, and the environment was one of these bases (Trigger 1989:290–291). Steward (1937), for example, implicitly adopted a regional approach by emphasizing the necessity of studying human interaction with the environment—the subsistence economy, population size, and settlement patterns. In turn, this affected the development of large-scale interdisciplinary projects, especially those studying the origins of agriculture (for example, Braidwood and Howe 1960). Any attempt to study the patterning of socioecological dynamics required a frame of analysis beyond the single site. The environment, particularly as a restraining or enabling parameter, was emphasized in the context of systems theory, economic anthropology, and the new ecology.

The *Annales* school likewise influenced archaeological attempts to integrate the study of the environment with human history (Cherry et al. 1991; Bintliff 1991; Knapp 1992). Within Braudel's (1980) *longue durée* and *conjoncture* (respectively, long-term and medium-term history), geological, spatial, and environmental structures are seen to exert a strong influence upon stability, development, and change in human society. One major critique of a specifically Braudellian (as opposed to an *Annaliste*) approach to studying the past is the lack of emphasis on the individual agent and on human motivation, major concerns in social archaeology today. Nonetheless, an *Annales*' model of the past certainly has the scope to deal with the individual in history or prehistory and, in addition, offers an important way to integrate environmental data into an interpretative framework.

The critique of environmental determinism, or ecofunctionalism, stemmed in part from the realization that settlement patterns were affected by diverse interrelated factors, not just adaptation or reaction

to the environment (Trigger 1989:310; Wylie 1993:24). The inclusion of social theory into archaeology (for example, Hodder 1982; Renfrew 1984; Shanks and Tilley 1987) has added a more nuanced understanding of the ways in which the landscape affects and is affected by human action. Whereas eco-environmental approaches generally focused on economic factors and privileged "rational and common sense approaches to subsistence and exploitation of the environment" (McGlade 1995:113), more recent approaches, such as landscape archaeology (Knapp 1997:11–13; Ashmore and Knapp 1999), utilize textual analysis with an emphasis on perception, experience, and the symbolic aspects of the landscape (Tilley 1994) or examine the dialectical relationship between socioeconomic formations and the environment (Ruiz et al. 1992). The new approaches also adopt a theoretical framework that insists on the irreducibility of the human-environment relationship, a relationship characterized by human ecodynamics (the environment as a co-evolving phenomenon inseparable from human society, McGlade 1995) rather than by self-regulating, equilibrium-seeking systems.

Eco-environmental approaches and settlement-pattern analysis are closely related in regional studies, but both have been criticized as being overly reductionist or based on deterministic principles that rely upon uniformitarian assumptions. Perhaps too often the critique of reductionist models and assumptions has been framed as an either/or proposition: Either you use reductionist models and underdescribe the reality of the past (or perpetuate ideologies about an unknowable past), or you subscribe to ramified, situated descriptions of past cultures (or the inability to know the past because of its ramified and situated nature). In fact, reductionist models are the first, necessary step toward a nuanced description of the past. Such models require a data set to which they can be applied, and regional survey is a critical component of creating those data sets.

The environment's role in shaping human society has long been bound up with site-location analysis and hence with settlement patterning across the landscape. Settlement archaeology was defined as the study of both synchronic and diachronic social relationships using settlement-pattern data (Trigger 1967:151). While the connection between settlement archaeology and cultural ecology is clear, the idea behind the Viru Valley Project (Peru) was that settlement patterns could be used to understand not only socio-ecological relations but also other social dimensions (Willey 1953:1; Ammerman 1981; Trigger 1989:282). By accumulating data on the regional scale, Willey was able to recognize long-term demographic continuities in the Viru Valley and to consider social change as the result of internal rather than external impetus (Trigger 1989:284). Moreover, in settlement archaeology, each site was seen in relation to all others in the settlement pattern or settlement hierarchy, not simply valued for itself or seen as representative of a culture. In turn, the settlement pattern could be analyzed as a hierarchy of sites, along with the various factors that influenced the different scales. Thus, the recording and understanding of site variability in the regional archaeological record was also an implicit goal of settlement archaeology.

The techniques and practices of settlement archaeology, including regional approaches to field surveys, were critical in the evolution and development of what today is termed the *archaeology* or *archaeologies of landscape* (Knapp 1997:4–7; Knapp and Ashmore 1999). Although such developments may appear prima facie to be theoretical in nature, in fact they are based heavily on strict chronological control of material collected in field surveys (Ammerman 1981; Feinman 1994). Temporal change is often lumped into a single spatial dimension, with breaking points recognized only when there are major shifts in the settlement pattern (Dewar 1991, 1994; Kintigh 1994). In this situation, archaeologists need to move from the static remnant to the past dynamic of settlement patterns. To establish temporal control of a data set in regional survey, large quantities of material must be collected. Appropriate collection strategies should include not just diagnostic finds but items such as lithic debitage or badly worn body sherds belonging to coarse-ware pottery because such materials will yield chronological information if one studies lithic reduction sequences or if the pottery fabrics are distinguishable through thin-section or microscopic analyses. Whether or not a survey project collects large quantities of material, it is also important to assess carefully the degree to which what is collected is representative of what was left behind in the field.

Politico-economic analysis of settlement patterns has been emphasized in a series of publications (for example, Flannery 1976; Sanders et al. 1979; Renfrew and Shennan 1982; Knapp 1997) discussing how economic resources—for example, control of prestige or scarce goods versus control of social storage surplus—influenced the rise of elites and by extension elite centers within a regional setting. Such emphases on resource control, social ranking and stratification, and the development of complex societies necessitate an analytical frame of mind that goes beyond adaptation to economic circumstances or environmental parameters. Other studies have considered the role of ideational categories in settlement patterning (for example, Kus 1982, 1987; Ashmore and Knapp 1999). Regional analysis offers an important key to understanding the emergence and growth of complex social systems.

Another major influence on the contemporary experience of landscape and space is sometimes termed *cognitive geography* (Tuan 1977; Downs and Stea 1977; Gould and White 1986; Portugali 1992) or *ideational landscapes* (Knapp and Ashmore 1999:12–13). The evaluation of cognitive maps makes it clear that the Cartesian space scrutinized so carefully and "scientifically" by archaeologists or anthropologists often bears strikingly little resemblance to the mental maps of nonwestern or prehistoric societies and individuals (for example, Kus 1982). Ideational landscapes are meant to elicit an insider's perspective that may provide moral messages, recount mythic histories, or record genealogies. This term is thus meant to be more comprehensive than *sacred* and embraces other kinds of meanings embodied in landscapes. Bender et al. (1997:150) suggest that peoples' ideas about their world, as well as their social identities, would have mediated every part of a prehistoric landscape. The ideational landscape approximates in meaning Johnston's (1998) "inherent" notion of landscape, that is, one not separately perceived but embedded within ways of living and being.

SAMPLING STRATEGIES AND REGIONAL ARCHAEOLOGICAL SURVEY

As part of his new design for archaeology, Binford (1964) maintained that research projects needed to be regional in scope if they wished to isolate and study cultural change and evolution. To understand the nature and formal characteristics of a "site," as well as its spatial "structuring," one had to know how that site varied from other sites within the greater study universe. Because cultures are adaptive primarily to ecological factors, he argued, archaeologists must be able to articulate the relationship between past cultural activity and local ecology. Moreover, the best way to investigate that relationship—from the scale of the artifact to the entire study universe—is to adopt a regional perspective. Binford's design was fully in accord with the focus on new ecology in anthropology at that time (Kottak 1999:23–25).

Given that archaeologists seek representative and reliable data and given that time and resources are usually limited, sampling is usually regarded as the most viable methodological approach. Binford turned aside claims that such sampling rendered the archaeologist a mere technician by pointing to a running analysis of data, with each successive methodological step informing the next. In other words, a successful application of sampling methods required not just a research objective but the capacity to refine that objective as demanded by the reality of ongoing fieldwork and research. From his early statements on the mission of archaeological research, Binford set regional researchers the task of understanding human relationships with the environment and the nature of settlement patterns within a regional context—two areas of major concern we have already noted. In what follows we focus first on sampling techniques and afterwards look at issues beyond sampling.

PROBABILITY SAMPLING

Ammerman (1981:78) believed that Binford had sold sampling as an uncomplicated panacea for improving data collection and the quality of archaeological inferences. More recently, he linked the original troubles within quantitative archaeology (and sampling in particular) to the unsophisticated adoption of statistical methods from other disciplines (Ammerman 1992: 233). However archaeologists may react to these opinions, statistical analysis is here to stay, and we often reap benefits from its use, from radiocarbon dating to physical anthropology (for example, Aldenderfer 1987; Shennan 1997).

Although today most regional survey projects introduce some level of sampling into their research design, there are several problems in doing so. Many of these problems arise because we lack prior knowledge of the number of entities and their location or makeup and often we are dealing with areal coverage rather than point coverage. Nance (1983:291) points out that we are trying to learn about previously unknown entities (using what he terms *a discovery model*), yet the most commonly used sampling methods are derived from disciplines unconcerned with discovery, making their application to archaeological contexts, at best, problematic. To apply sampling in a discovery situation, archaeologists not only require sampling techniques specific to archaeological contexts, but also an understanding of the level of effort needed to find the cultural remains they seek.

In regional survey, sampling some fraction of the overall population and measuring certain parameters are usually handled arbitrarily by defining areal units and investigating formal variation within these units. Termed *element sampling*, the statistical techniques used in analysis are not relevant to investigating the formal variation in materials of interest found within the areally defined elements. The latter is actually cluster sampling (Ammerman 1981; Nance 1983:298): What is being studied is not the areal unit itself but rather the elements recovered within that unit (that is, often we are not just counting the number of occurrences per unit but also studying the variability of those occurrences). All regional surveys involve multistage cluster sampling unless the entire areal expanse of the survey universe is inspected, or the intensity of inspection does not introduce a second level of subsampling by virtue of gaps in the survey team's ability to investigate the region. If particular loci of cultural materials undergo highly intensive investigation after discovery, a further level of subsampling is introduced. Each of these subsamples involves potential sources of sampling error and at the same time necessitates different statistical procedures.

One of the main difficulties with sampling an unknown population is that we are ignorant of the degree of spatial aggregation. Deviations from the mean are likely to be accentuated in conditions of spatial aggregation, meaning that greater numbers of observations must be made to arrive at an acceptable confidence level. One potential solution to this dilemma is to stratify the survey universe along lines calculated to diminish intrastratum variability (Nance 1983:308, Plog et al. 1978:402–403). Here stratification means separating the survey universe according to self-evident categories; clearly this is most effective where a great deal is already known about the survey population (rarely the case in archaeology). Schiffer et al. (1978:4) suggest that the sample size needed to cope with aggregation can rise dramatically with the degree of aggregation, quickly reaching a point at which the cost of probabilistic survey is prohibitive, thus making purposive (biased) survey techniques more desirable and realistic.

Archaeologists also need to understand that the higher the degree of variability, the larger the sample must be to approximate the variability to acceptable tolerances, with similar implications for aggregated elements. For extremely rare entities, however, the sample size may have to go close to 100% coverage to recover the entity. A further source of sampling bias in regional survey involves the issue of edge effects (Nance 1983:310, Plog et al. 1978:396–400; McManamon 1982:201), where the number of occurrences encountered is actually greater than that predicted, given the sample fraction. This results from the fact that some material which lies outside the actual survey fraction (transect, quadrat, and so on) nonetheless has an edge within that fraction. Edge effects are accentuated by certain unit shapes and, in general, are more pronounced with long, thin units.

Finally, Schiffer and colleagues (1978:3) have pointed out that to select the appropriate techniques for estimating target parameters, one must know the abundance and location of sample elements (again, rarely the case in archaeology). Yet such knowledge is not an either/or proposition, which is one reason why multistage approaches to sampling are advisable, where knowledge from each stage would lead, ideally, to ever more appropriate techniques and more accurate estimates.

As indicated earlier, resource constraints frequently necessitate the use of sampling in regional surveys. Although statistical analysis may help us understand the correct approach to sampling, observations from regional surveys:

> ...have severely challenged the belief that patterns from one area are necessarily representative of an entire region. As a result, it is now generally agreed that much larger samples than had hitherto been thought necessary are required before they are representative of a whole and that the study of changes over long periods requires something approaching total samples. (Trigger (1989:311)

Beyond the technical difficulties of correct statistical procedures, there is a serious question as to whether or not sampling, on the one hand, and predictive models, on the other, are effective tools for regional survey issues or the questions we seek to

answer in that enterprise. Ammerman (1981:79; also Cherry et al. 1978:31) notes that sampling concerns and the needs of spatial analysis often pull in opposite directions. This leads us to the prominent debate over the use of total versus sample coverage in regional archaeological surveys.

SAMPLING VERSUS FULL COVERAGE

Fish and Kowalewski (1990) claim that the data archaeologists require to understand complex intraregional relations cannot be obtained through sampling. They contend, further, that full coverage survey makes it possible to pose and answer anthropological questions that depend upon a completely representative sample of variability. Such questions or research need to include the study of spatial patterning; the recognition of boundaries between cultural groups or large, diffuse sites; and the reusability of regional survey data.

Plog (1990) observes that the two methodologies might be mutually beneficial. Cowgill (1990), however, maintains that spatial sampling borders on the useless and possibly is misleading for an understanding of spatial patterning. However, the issue of intensity cannot be resolved simply by adopting a strategy of full coverage survey. Rather, intensity must be related to research goals—in particular the recovery of rare types, one of the claimed benefits of full coverage survey. In fact, the full range of issues and problems encountered in sampling procedures must also be considered in full coverage survey. The conclusion to be drawn, then, is that while full coverage may lead to clearer spatial analysis of site distributions and to fuller understanding of the flow of information and materials within a region, there remain several variables that may adversely affect survey observations and results.

Before moving on, we can summarize the problems with sampling as follows:

1) Quantitative techniques have often been poorly understood and applied in archaeology, in part because of the naive application of statistical methods drawn from outside the discipline.

2) There are serious questions concerning the use of sampling as an effective tool for answering some critical questions that arise in regional survey studies.

3) The use of sampling techniques in regional survey projects requires critical reappraisal.

THE RECOVERABILITY OF MATERIALS

Moving beyond the intricacies of sampling design or the benefits of full coverage versus sampling strategies, here we focus on the broader environment within which survey work takes place and the overwhelming effect this may have on the usefulness of survey data. Schiffer et al. (1978) concisely summarize the problems:

- *Obtrusiveness*—this is the probability that elements of special interest to the archaeologist will be discovered by a particular technique. For example, given the technique of small bore soil sampling, it is more likely that large, common, and dense sites will be obtrusive than will small, rare, and low-density sites.

- *Visibility*—this refers to the variability in the observer's ability to detect an element of interest introduced by environmental factors such as inflated soils, dense ground cover, precipitation, weather conditions, the quality of light, the attention of the fieldwalker, and so on.

- *Accessibility*—this indicates the effort it will take to reach any particular location in the survey universe. Among the factors that contribute to accessibility are terrain, weather extremes, impenetrable vegetation, the lack of decent access roads, and land title restrictions.

Our understanding of all three factors remains decidedly imprecise and our methods for handling them ad hoc. Moreover, even though there have been attempts to record how survey results may be affected by these factors (for example, Nance 1983:314–316), there is as yet no systematic body of experimentation oriented toward resolving these issues.

In an interesting exception, Wandsnider and Camilli (1992) sought to understand how certain characteristics (color, size, shape) of surface deposits might affect survey results. Their question is: given a certain level of intensity, how accurate (free from bias or distortion) are survey results (the "document") given certain characteristics in the surface deposits of material culture (the "record")? Their

seeding experiments led to the conclusion (Wandsnider and Camilli 1992:182–183) that our impression of a landscape with hot spots (or sites) is heavily reinforced by traditional survey methodology; that the population of isolated occurrences is 8 to 17 times larger than those recovered; and that concern for the quality of survey results created through normal fieldwalking techniques is not misplaced, because these results do not reflect accurate representations of the material record, particularly in low-density areas.

Accordingly, Wandsnider and Camilli (1992:182–188) suggest that field survey projects should decrease the spacing between fieldwalkers and slow the pace of survey and that they should carry out systematic seeding programs to evaluate the accuracy of the materials collected. Nonetheless, even this type of experimentation is unlikely to produce a body of baseline data that can be used by any survey in any context. This is perhaps best indicated by Ammerman's (1985) work in Italy, which highlighted the limitations that time places on survey results, whether in clearly unstable land surfaces, such as dunes, or on less obviously transient surfaces, such as worked fields. Ammerman's repeated visits to agricultural fields and the differing results from these visits provide an important lesson here (Ammerman 1985, 1995; Terrenato and Ammerman 1996). Nonetheless, as Davis and Sutton (1995) argued in response to Ammerman, the issues surrounding visibility are manifold and there are several alternatives—for example, an intensive survey methodology, a longer term perspective on the cultivation history of an area, consideration of currently-used agricultural methods—to resurveying when the aim is to evaluate the effects of changing land-use strategies on the surface density of artifacts.

This prolonged debate helps to underscore a fundamentally important point in survey methodology: Survey data can never be complete without recording and understanding the gross surface characteristics and variability that fall under the rubric of visibility. If there is as yet no single corrective to this problem, it is still clear that more effort must be directed specifically toward resampling and seeding experiments as part of intensive survey methodology.

There is another set of methodological decisions that must be made before or during the course of survey work, which also affects our capacity to understand survey results. This is the definition of the actual survey universe (chapter 3.1).

2.2 SCSP Contributions to Regional Survey Archaeology

Nathan Meyer and A. Bernard Knapp

Regional survey projects in the Mediterranean have given impetus to both urban and rural archaeology, particularly in their capacity to monitor variations in artifact density across the landscape. Such variation is then related to information on populations and habitation contained in documentary or ethnohistoric evidence or derived from excavations (Cherry 1983:388–389; Bintliff and Snodgrass 1988). Intensive regional surveys have also been able to distinguish between changing patterns (for example, nucleated, dispersed) of settlement in towns, villages and the surrounding countryside (Lloyd 1991:233–235; Alcock 1994:175–180). Local social factors or political agendas, such as landowning elites, can strongly influence rural residence patterns (for example, Cherry et al. 1991:469–470; Lloyd 1991:233–234; Jameson et al. 1994:323). A holistic perspective on landscape and settlement will benefit from the use of an intensive survey strategy, in which off-site artifact scatters—even if in aggregate—paint a broad picture of the material culture that characterizes a region. Within Mediterranean landscapes, settlement patterning and settlement types often seem to have been conditioned by the distribution of natural resources or by access to local or regional trade systems (Wagstaff and Cherry 1982:246–248). In no case is that better exemplified than on the island of Cyprus.

Although Cyprus produced and traded copper throughout the Mediterranean world from about 2500 BC, its primary ore-production area had never been examined from a regional archaeological perspective until the inception of SCSP in 1992. During five field seasons (1992 to 1997), SCSP sought to trace settlement patterns and to understand long-term history (from the Neolithic to the present) in a key mineralogical resource zone, the foothills of the northern Troodos Mountains. We have tried to build creatively on the achievements of past and present survey work elsewhere in the Mediterranean, to employ the optimum technology available in a problem-oriented framework, and to present a long-term material and ethnohistoric perspective on Cyprus's

social, economic, and cultural history. Our systematic, intensive survey methodology was developed and practiced within an interdisciplinary context informed by archaeological and ethnohistoric theory and experience. By working continuously with a geomorphological team and a geobotanist in the field, we greatly improved our understanding of site-preservation factors and human modification of the landscapes, past and present.

Our survey data, GIS, and database analytics, as well as documentary and ethnographic research, have provided new insights into factors associated with cultural development and economic change on Cyprus and into the social and historical trajectories of mining and agricultural communities. SCSP fieldwork demonstrates that the north central Troodos region has as much, if not more, potential than any other on the island for revealing both industrial (mining, smelting) sites and the agricultural villages that supported them. In addition, SCSP data and resources already have provided new insights into social change at the local level and into Cyprus's role in overseas trade. The results of SCSP research, furthermore, will enhance the study of Cyprus's agricultural and industrial landscapes and help preserve the cultural heritage of historically known mining communities. We also believe it will add a useful new chapter to survey methodology on Cyprus and in the Mediterranean.

One long-range goal of SCSP has been to identify industrial sites or farming villages situated near copper resources and associated with the mining, production, and trade of copper. Because the primary production sites and agricultural villages that provided the resources and subsistence goods on which coastal emporia relied were virtually unknown six years ago, SCSP has already filled a large gap in the archaeological record. In this publication, we also assess the impact of broader eastern Mediterranean phenomena on the local northern Troodos area, for example how regional or imperial economic systems affect local polities and the people within them. Questions related to the scope, extent, and cultural or politico-economic significance of an early agro-industrial society, as well as attitudes to the mining landscape, have always formed important theoretical foci of SCSP. Our work on industrial landscapes, economic and social history, and the integration of geohistorical, anthropological, and geomorphological approaches into field archaeology have helped us to maintain an integrated, social archaeology, as well as a viable, human-science methodology.

By focusing on specific human activities in the landscape, using the analytical units of special interest area (SIA) and place of special interest (POSI) as described in chapter 3, we have observed and examined several distinct patterns in the relationships among human activity, the environment, and past or current industrial and agricultural landscapes. From the alluvial plains in the eastern part of the SCSP area come large quantities of sherds, which fluctuate gradually throughout the landscape without forming specific high-density areas. This phenomenon may be due in part to plowing, in part to manuring, but we also have to consider how the landscape was being used to produce such a pattern. Did the alluvial plains in the Late Roman and Medieval periods, for example, have a much broader and sparser spread of human activity than they do now? If so, why is the spread of pottery so much wider than the expected halo around each settlement, which is no doubt owing to the well-attested dumping and manuring in the fields nearest the village (Christodoulou 1959:41)?

For the more readily identifiable artifact density peaks, there are clear patterns relating site location and function. Mining and smelting sites can be expected in the igneous zones, with agricultural support villages nearby but in the sedimentary zone or on alluvial plains. In areas of limited arable land, Archaic to Roman settlements tend to be built on small knolls overlooking whatever agricultural land there is. From the Roman period onward, settlements on the major alluvial plains tend to drift slowly across the landscape through time; from the Medieval period successive churches may mark the changing focus of the settlement.

In general, for the later historical periods, cultural material is spread across the entire survey universe. The exception is Byzantine material, thus far identified in very few survey units. Medieval to Ottoman material is found throughout the SCSP area and in high concentrations around the modern villages of Malounda and Aredhiou, with a clear peak in the sixteenth century AD (cf. Toumazou et al. 1998:19). Bronze Age material, on the other hand, was restricted to the easternmost sectors of the survey area. Because of the topographical orientation of the river valleys within and beyond the survey area, this con-

centration of Bronze Age material appears to coincide with similar finds from sites to the north and then northwest of our area (for example, Akhera, Meniko, Akaki, Dhenia).

Mining activities were carried out in the SCSP area from the Bronze Age at least to the end of the Roman Empire; analytical work (radiocarbon dating, slags) has allowed us to establish firm chronological and technological parameters. The Bronze Age smelting site of Politiko *Phorades* 1 reveals archaeometallurgical and technological developments unprecedented on an island that has been producing copper at least for the past four thousand years. We have examined the technology of mining, and the productive processes overall, in the context of the mining community (Knapp 1999a). All mining activity and its material remains in the survey area and beyond represent specialized production and trade, as well as economic growth, and vindicate the call for an archaeology of mining (Knapp, Pigott, and Herbert 1998). With the research activities and fieldwork of SCSP, we now feel we can also make a call for the social archaeology of agriculture.

2.3 Pottery Strategy and Chronotypes
Nathan Meyer

Regional archaeological survey faces a challenge. Survey archaeology needs to move on from simply supplying period components to a survey unit to the type of analysis that can inform us of the size of the period component and of the functional classes of materials found in that unit. Counting, collecting, and analyzing pottery forms the backbone of regional survey recording in the Mediterranean. Within the SCSP study universe, pottery has no equal in any other artifact or ecofact class; in terms of abundance, chronological ubiquity, and potential for refining analysis, pottery—and the burden on pottery studies—cannot be underestimated. At the same time, however, regional survey in north-central Cyprus has had to deal with quantities of pottery, and pottery data, about which literally nothing was known previously. How can we make the progress we want in regional survey archaeology unless we find good tools for dealing with unknown pottery?

Briefly described, the goal of pottery studies within SCSP's broader practice was to assist in the identification and sizing of the chronological components of the unit; the understanding of the possible functions within a unit (for example, habitation, seasonal use, agriculture, industrial activity); and the study of trade and other interactions within and beyond the study area.

To meet these goals, a regional survey project in a pottery-rich area such as Cyprus must define and systematize the types of observations made on pottery and carry them out in a standardized manner. At any stage of investigation, comparability of observations must be maintained among team members in the field and pottery specialists in the lab. If comparability is not maintained, then the results of a particular stage of fieldwork cannot be applied usefully in further stages of research. Likewise, observations must be contextualized within the practice of the observer. For the purpose of creating a language within SCSP that could be used to discuss these central concerns, we developed four categories for the study of pottery: quantitative, analytic, reflexive and experimental. Each of these categories is treated in detail in chapter 3.7. Here we introduce a core SCSP concept that enabled our study of pottery: the chronotype.

The concept of the chronotype (a SCSP neologism) contributes to the discourse on pottery studies and to the development of information systems designed to support the study of pottery. A chronotype is not simply a synonym for *ware;* rather it is both a categorization of artifacts and a form of archaeological informatics. Thus, we would define a chronotype as follows:

- A chronotype is—with varying degrees of refinement—identifiable on the basis of form, fabric, and surface treatment (diagnostic is the commonly used term).

- A chronotype has a specific temporal range.

- A chronotype has a specific but broadly defined function associated with it.

Chronotypes also relate to each other in a significant fashion: Like nested bowls, they are arranged in series of hierarchies arranged around the common themes. At the top of a chronotype hierarchy are the most weakly typed chronotypes (for example, COUNK: coarse ware, unknown). *Weakly typed* means that the form, surface treatment, date, function, and even (to some extent) fabric of such a chronotype

are described only vaguely. At the other end of a hierarchy would be a very strongly typed example: Here the form, fabric, surface treatment, date, and function are all well and narrowly defined. For example, our chronotype system has both Fine ware-Roman and Fine ware-African Red Slip. The former is used only when a pottery specialist knows by virtue of fabric analysis and surface treatment that (s)he is looking at a piece of fine ware pottery, one from a broad span of time but one that is definitely Roman; as such it is not very well placed in time. African Red Slip, however, is much more specifically dated, though it too is a Roman Fine ware.

The reality of imperfect knowledge, both in the absolute sense (within archaeology generally) and in the narrower sense (knowledge on a specific archaeological project), makes it imperative that pottery analyses facilitate the coherent organization of pottery that is only vaguely identifiable. In this way, by allowing for weakly typed chronotypes, we still encourage systemization.

By leveraging the chronotype concept for our pottery studies, we have accomplished the following: In most cases, we created data with a robust and consistent naming scheme for pottery that carried a date and a functional category, which is vital for further analysis. Secondly, we processed large amounts of materials quickly, knowing that with a chronotype attached to a batch of pottery, we would be able to review these batches against each other and the chronotype description for inconsistencies. Finally, we created a dynamic process whereby the chronotype was always open to revision: we did this by including in the analytical process (and supporting data tables) the ability to augment or overwrite the descriptions of chronotypes. In so doing, we established a further data set that, upon review and analysis, could actually provide a mechanism for reviewing the validity of a chronotype and changing or extending its description, or even adding new subtypes.

Such a development is essential in dealing with pottery for which our knowledge is highly imperfect. For example, the ability to capture pottery as COUNK—coarse ware, unknown, and to assign fabric, form, and surface treatment descriptions means that we can begin to break down these unknowns into finer groupings, as our descriptive database grows and as we unravel archaeological contexts which can provide temporal refinements. The goal is to promote pottery from weakly typed chronotypes such as COUNK to one more strongly typed.

As fully evolved by the end of our project, a chronotype had the following structure:

1) *Chronotype:* the name;
2) *Surface Treatment:* how the pottery vessel's surface is finished;
3) *Form:* a standardized description of the shape of the pottery vessel;
4) *Fabric:* a standardized description of the fabric of the pottery vessel;
5) *Function:* a standardized term for the our understanding of the pottery vessel's function;
6) *Period:* assignment of a SCSP period.

For our future projects, the chronotype definition will drop period and expand to contain the following:

7) *Chronotype-Above:* the name of thechronotype, if any, of which another example is a subtype;
8) *Specific-Date-Begin:* an integer for the beginning date, expressed as negative for BC dates;
9) *Specific-Date-End:* An integer for the ending date, expressed as negative for BC dates;
10) *Citation:* published studies of the chronotype;
11) *Node Number:* within the project database and following the hierarchy established by *Chronotype-Above,* the nodes number from 10 forward (10 being the lowest). Numbers 0 through 9 are reserved for tying regional survey data sets to each other.

With these refinements, we expect the information systems aspect of the chronotype to expand considerably. As developed within SCSP (detailed further in chapter 3.7 "Pottery Collection, Pottery Analysis, and GIS Mapping," and exemplified in chapter 4) the information-systems aspect of the chronotype allowed us to assess coherently period and function within our units of study (for a list of chronotypes, see appendix C).

We want to move away from organizing our information system by periods and move toward organizing it by calendar dates. By using a chronotype classification with real, assigned dates we solve the vexing problem of having to relate (within the same information system) different artifact classes and their often different period schemas. Moreover, by adding explicit data representations

(*Specific-Date-Begin, Specific-Date-End, Chronotype-Above,* and *Node Number*) of the implicit hierarchical associations of chronotypes (in time and in type), we will enhance our ability to study chronotypes in relationship to each other by extracting data from the database in a precise fashion. *Node Number* and *Chronotype-Above* tie chronotypes together in a hierarchy. Real dates tie chronotypes together across hierarchies. With these tools in place, the archaeological information system can provide a very robust inquiry.

Finally, it is important to emphasize that the chronotype system grew up out of uncertainty. Pottery analysis on Cyprus is not always as advanced, particularly in the later periods (Medieval to Modern) as it is in other regions of the Mediterranean. The ability to systematize uncertainty was critical for the success of SCSP. The chronotypes we developed represent the first step toward building a base of pottery comparanda that should prove highly useful to archaeologists working in Cyprus and the eastern Mediterranean. We hope to have the time and financial support to develop macroscopic and petrographic data for each of our chronotypes and to make this information available as a research tool. The flexibility of the chronotype system as designed, together with our continued development of archaeological information systems, should allow for further refinement of this tool as we continue our work in Cyprus.

2.4 Geomorphology and Archaeological Survey
Lisa Wells

If one primary goal of regional archaeological survey is to understand patterning in social and economic relationships as reflected in settlement patterns, then regional survey must be placed in a framework that allows for the interpretation of the environmental and geomorphological contexts of sites or artifacts of interest. Without an appreciation of landscape evolution, the likelihood of misinterpreting archaeological survey data is considerable. Understanding the geomorphology of the landscape provides a context for determining the stability and relative age of landscape surfaces, which in turn makes it possible to carry out spatial analyses of the artifacts on these surfaces. Unless this fundamental geological information is included in surface survey, a secure interpretation of the human landscape is impossible, because:

1) knowing the geological context of an artifact provides a framework for determining whether that artifact is in situ or has been reworked by geologic or taphonomic processes;

2) establishing the age of surfaces relative to the times of land use allows us to interpret the archaeological relevance of sterile surfaces (whether depositional, erosional, or never occupied);

3) reconstructing the physical landscape at the time of occupation or use allows for an understanding of the environmental context of sites and features;

4) our experience suggests that once the morphostratigraphy and chronostratigraphy of the physical landscape have been established, the success rate in finding artifacts, especially from the oldest occupations, increases dramatically.

Three distinct kinds of geomorphological data are needed for reconstructing ancient landscapes: stability, chronology, and palaeoenvironment. Without such information it is impossible to distinguish which changes in artifact distribution result from natural as opposed to anthropogenic factors. The geomorphologist commonly begins by determining the processes that formed a surface and the relative age of that surface. Such work results in a standard classification of the landscape.

Unfortunately, these primary geological data are frequently unintelligible to archaeologists (Wells 2001), and the data must be manipulated into a form that presents the landscape in terms that will be useful. For SCSP, we found landscape stability to be one of the most important tools in interpreting artifact distribution. Bedrock stratigraphy (placement within the ophiolite and marine sedimentary complex) was also important for interpreting land use patterns, for example industrial or mining landscapes versus primarily agricultural landscapes.

Determining the relative stability of a geomorphological surface allowed us to decide whether artifacts were in situ or had been reworked by geological processes. At the level of a POSI or SIA we were able to remove reworked artifacts from the database prior to reconstructing human settlement and activity patterns. These data were also useful in understanding the sterile areas encountered during transect survey. Sterile regions that have undergone substantial sedimentation or erosion are products of geological processes. In depositional areas, sterility was tested by subsurface investigations. Relatively stable, low-gradient surfaces that lacked artifacts were interpreted as representing regions that had never seen significant levels of human activity. Where regions had been stripped of all surface sediment, however, it was impossible to resolve whether people had ever settled there. Regions with extremely high artifact density that lacked surface architectural remains, but at the same time were located on nondepositional (yet stable) surfaces, constituted something of a conundrum. On the Quaternary terraces of the Akaki River, for example, alluvial sediments are too thin to accommodate site burial, while erosion has been insufficient to remove preferentially the substantive fine-grained sediment and concentrate the artifacts in a lag deposit on the surface. Thus we must return to archaeological interpretations of these anomalous artifact concentrations.

The determination of the relative age of a geomorphological surface allows us to project which parts of the landscape were extant during a particular period of occupation. If we are attempting to understand the spatial relationships between archaeological loci we must also attempt to reconstruct the land surface during the period of interest. In the SCSP area, changes in the position of the river channels, drainage divides, and large net erosion have dramatically altered the appearance of the landscape during the Holocene. The combination of archaeological survey data with a morphostratigraphic analysis of the landscape is a powerful tool for reconstructing those parts of the landscape that existed in the past. If we combine this temporal view of the landscape with a palaeoenvironmental interpretation, we can begin to reconstruct the environmental context of archaeological sites, and, as a result, we can determine which aspects of a settlement pattern were driven by the distribution of natural resources. It is the combination of these data that allows us to determine, for example, that the smelting site of Politiko *Phorades* 1 (SCY100) was built on the banks of a broad braided stream channel some 4 m above the modern entrenched channel. The richness of our interpretations of ancient landscapes is clearly enhanced by this interdisciplinary technique.

It is easiest to incorporate the collection of geomorphological data into the sampling strategy when the geomorphological study is begun prior to establishing the survey methodology. The most useful information for survey design is an analysis of surface stability and relative age, as it allows for a stratification of the landscape based on the highest likelihood of artifact discovery. Some level of random sampling is clearly necessary to avoid prejudicing the survey. Once the impacts of geomorphological processes on artifact distribution have been resolved, the survey can focus on those areas of the landscape that were extant during the periods of interest and that have been relatively stable subsequent to those periods of interest. As the archaeological component of SCSP had begun before geomorphological work began in earnest, there are some modest limitations in the compatibility of archaeological and geomorphologic survey data. The problem is most significant for data collected in the early years of the survey project (1992 to 1993). From 1995 onward, however, SCSP's geomorphologists and archaeologists worked together to modify and develop the interdisciplinary methodology presented here.

Archaeological settlement patterns reflect how humans have used the landscape through time and reveal a combination of environmental, economic, cultural, and aesthetic choices. By integrating an understanding of the physical evolution of the landscape into settlement pattern analysis, we are able to understand better which of these choices were predicated by the distribution of natural (hydrologic, biologic, geologic) resources and changes in the distribution of these resources through time. Only when we account fully for the impact of physical changes do the social and cultural patterns become clear.

2.5 Geobotanical Survey

Neil Urwin

Where the factors that influence plant growth and distribution are anthropogenic in origin, or are associated with exploitable resources such as groundwater or minerals, the response in the vegetation—if it can be read—is generally termed a *botanical indicator*. Botanical indicators may be seen at the individual species level or at the vegetation community level. The aim of SCSP's geobotanical component was to investigate botanical indicators on archaeological POSIs in the survey area.

The concept of individual botanical indicator species has long been known and used in agricultural activities and prospecting. The science of geobotany, which incorporates and systematizes this information, was developed in Russia in the eighteenth century and was used primarily for geological and mineralogical surveys. Brooks and Johannes (1990) discuss the seminal work of the Russian Karpinsky and his followers and describe a number of major principles which they established. Two of these principles are directly relevant to the development of SCSP's geobotanical analysis: (1) reliance should be placed on an examination of the whole vegetation community and not just on one or two characteristic plants within it; (2) a favorable climate will tend to nullify the effects of toxic elements in the substrate. Geobotany tends to be a more powerful tool in semiarid areas or in Mediterranean type climates. In these conditions the elemental content of the soil moisture gradually increases to insupportable levels for some species.

During the second half of the twentieth century, archaeologists amplified geologists' work on botanical indicators, once parallels were recognized between survey for geological features and the investigation of buried or surface archaeological features (Constantinou 1982; Brooks and Johannes 1990). The science of geobotany has benefited in recent years from commercially available satellite imagery, and the information technology associated with it, and from sophisticated computerized techniques for statistical treatment of raw data, which can evaluate subtle variations in the compositions of plant communities.

The SCSP survey area fulfills the need for a semiarid climate to maximize the geobotanical indicators of human indicators. It is sparsely settled but extensively farmed, especially along the wide flats of the Akaki River and the foothills of the Pillow Lavas. In the south and east of the area, pine forest predominates on basaltic soils. The pine species, *Pinus brutia var. cretica*, is susceptible to gross levels of phytotoxicity in soils, but it appears to be extremely tolerant of lower elemental concentrations in the soils associated with slag heaps or mining spoil. Moreover, it forms a single species canopy community and therefore offers little opportunity to investigate species or community changes.

In the rolling country where the Pillow Lavas intersect with sedimentary strata, there are large areas of dry shrublands on poor, shallow soils. These vegetation communities range in a continuum from batha (a sparse low, dry heath, very poor in species numbers) to garrigue (a tall shrubland). The major garrigue/batha dominants are *Thymus capitatus* (thyme) and *Sarcopoterium spinosum* (thorny burnet). In general terms, *Sarcopoterium* is more suited to alkaline soils, and *Thymus* is more suited to the soils of basaltic origin. These preferences, by no means exclusive, are expressed by the relative proportions of each in the garrigue/batha communities. *Thymus* appears to avoid soils with strong metalliferous qualities (especially copper); it was not observed to grow on slag heaps where soil cover was extremely shallow. *Sarcopoterium* appears to be far less affected by metalliferous soils and will grow on slag heaps whatever the soil level.

The development of geobotanical hypotheses for the SCSP study area is based upon previous work by a number of researchers examining the ways in which past settlement activities and their enduring remnants as archaeological features affect the edaphic environment and therefore the present-day conditions for vegetation growth and distribution. The essential characteristics of these effects have been discussed in the literature (for example, Horler et al. 1981; Brooks 1983; Bell et al. 1985; Hodcroft and Moore 1988; Brooks and Johannes 1990). The major categories of effect, collated in Hodcroft and Moore (1988) and developed further by Brooks and Johannes (1990), led them to posit three categories of response to buried archaeological features:

- *Geobotanical effects*—comprising unusual plant populations or subdued growth;

- *Spatial/spectral vegetation stress effects*—including dwarfism/gigantism and discoloration;

- *Temporal vegetation stress effects*—where various growth effects (premature flowering, retarded growth, delayed senescence, and premature senescence) are manifest in different seasons of the year.

In the sparse, perennial vegetation of Cyprus's low rainfall areas, where plants are stressed for the majority of the growing season, only geobotanical ef-

fects at their most spectacular (the emergence of unusual plant populations over archaeological sites) are relevant and measurable. Following an initial examination of these effects in the context of the SCSP environment, we propose a further subdivision of geobotanical effects that result from: changes in soil chemistry, comprising phytotoxic effects, nutrient enrichment effects, and pH (soil acidity) changes; changes in soil structure and drainage, comprising physical effects related to compaction, soil aeration, and soil moisture; geomorphological processes independent of the archaeological features, comprising the processes of erosion, deposition, floods, and catastrophic land movement that can physically relocate materials or affect overburden conditions; and traditional agricultural, horticultural, or other cultural practices—examples of these effects are enduring seed stores in the soil (*Allium* and camomile at Roman sites) and long-lived horticultural plantations (olives, chestnuts).

The effects of buried, weathering slag and other metallurgical remnants of the copper-smelting process on soil chemistry are complex and dependent upon the scale of the enterprise, the materials used, the type of smelting process and the local climate. Brooks and Johannes's (1990) review of a number of case studies of vegetation on smelting sites indicates that the emphasis lies at the indicator species level and is on the ubiquity of certain celebrated species (usually herbs) as regional indicators. Discussion of community is largely limited to descriptions of the phytosociological alliances (after Braun-Blanquet 1932) within which the species fall, rather than about changes within the makeup of these alliances as a response to site effects. Unsurprisingly, none of the species cited in these studies occurs on Cyprus, but many of the mechanisms by which the effects of soil chemistry and soil physics result in characteristic vegetation have resonance in the present study.

Germany's Harz region has a long history of copper smelting and has provided researchers with an opportunity to chart the progress of vegetation succession over slag deposits over a span of seven to eight hundred years (Schubert 1953/1954a, 1953/1954b). A decrease in phytotoxicity effects as the deposits aged was noted; in addition, the physical/topographic weathering of slag heaps and the patterns of accumulation of topsoil interacted with the leaching of heavy metal salts—a combination of soil chemistry and localized geomorphological effects—to delimit vegetation growth. In Zaire's fourteenth-century Kabambian copper-smelting sites, indicator species were absent when remains were buried beneath a thick, nonmetalliferous surface layer (Malaisse and Brooks 1982). Smelting in Northern Italy's Bronze Age caused phytotoxicity—a toxicity that remains after three thousand years—which has left an absence of vegetation (Preuschen 1964).

Soil data from smelting sites and associated slag deposits in the SCSP area have returned analyses with significantly high iron, copper, and sulfur content. Phosphorus, potassium, and magnesium are more variable but are also in generally elevated levels in these soils. Iron and copper (and to a lesser degree, magnesium) are readily taken up in soil carbonates and organic matter (forming organo-metallic compounds). Copper and magnesium have strong phytotoxic characteristics for many plant species at higher concentrations. At lower concentrations in the soil (or when bound up in slag and released very slowly over time) they can, along with iron, provide soil chemistry environments unsuitable for some plant species that would otherwise be common on that soil type when uncontaminated.

We propose that such a mechanism would cause a change in the species array and the relative abundance of community dominants on a site. The autecologies of the batha/garigue dominants, *Thymus* and *Sarcopoterium*, differ in their respective responses to elevated levels of metals in soil. While no bioassays have been performed to confirm this for the SCSP study area, it is assumed that the variable distributions of these and other key species over smelting or slag sites are, in part, a response to soil chemistry and thus a form of geobotanical indicator. Detectable effects of physical changes in the soil environment and landscape as a result of archaeological features were expected to be less obvious. Conditions of soil moisture and aeration are extremely variable over the study area. Changes in these factors as a result of past human activities, in this type of vegetation, are more likely to result in changes in vegetation density over the landscape than in detectable species change.

The remaining two geobotanical effects listed above, cultural practices and geomorphological processes, are of less importance to the present study. The effects of past cultural practices, which retain seeds in the soil to the present day, are direct botanical indicators in themselves, although at the species level only. The effects of geomorphological processes are mainly detected as an increase or decrease in the effects of an archaeological site on soil chemistry and soil physics.

Following an initial ecological reconnaissance, two hypotheses were developed for testing in the SCSP study area. Reconnaissance confirmed that the vegetation and land cover characteristics of the areas of interest were dominated by a low batha/garrigue vegetation, where changes in the relative abundance of major elements readily detected by observation might be measured in the field and confirmed by statistical analysis.

The first hypothesis relates to SCSP's objective of examining the potential for developing predictive models or methods for site detection and site-landscape integration from, inter alia, environmental factors:

1) that the naturally occurring vegetation of the study area, by adaptation to a range of physical and chemical environmental conditions, can indicate the existence and location of sites of past human activities of archaeological interest.

The second hypothesis follows from the first and is designed to test the potential to develop a remotely sensed predictive tool:

2) that the geobotanical indicators that characterize sites of past human activity of archaeological interest can be detected reliably by remote sensing and, if so, can be used as a geographic prediction tool at the regional level.

To test these hypotheses and to develop geobotany and satellite imagery as a predictive tool for archaeological survey, geobotanical investigation was carried out at nine naturally vegetated POSIs. This involved the collection of botanical data from a series of sample units both on and off each POSI, the multivariate analysis of this data, and the interpretation of the relevant satellite images. The results of this work suggest that archaeological sites, particularly copper smelting sites, can be indicated by the natural vegetation occurring on them as a result of chemical and possibly physical effects in the soil environment. Thus, in environmental conditions such as those prevailing in the SCSP survey area, geobotanical survey and satellite imagery can be used effectively as a predictive tool in discovering and investigating human activity across the landscape.

2.6 Archaeological Survey and Archaeometallurgy

Sven Van Lokeren and Vasiliki Kassianidou

Over the past three decades, archaeometallurgy has come a long way as an interdisciplinary field of research (Knapp, Pigott, and Herbert 1998; Shennan 1995). These developments have been accompanied by methodological diversification but constrained by inherent limitations in the analytical techniques applied to materials research. Until the early 1980s, metallurgical studies focused on the technical examination of metal artifacts and on presenting site plans of metallurgical installations. Up to that time, then, the discipline was engaged primarily in technological studies and used an art historical approach accompanied by scientific analyses within a linear chronological framework. This entire intellectual approach rested on assumptions of technological progress and cultural diffusion (Tylecote 1976).

By the 1980s and early 1990s, researchers began to pay more attention to newly excavated remains, especially the byproducts of metal processing, such as matte and slag, and to refractory materials such as tuyères, furnace lining, and crucibles (for example, Bachmann 1982a:2–7; see also chapter 3.6). Fieldwork became regional in scope, while the main analytical focus came to revolve around the properties of installations and the performance of materials. This is well exemplified in the combination of historical studies, experimental reconstruction, laboratory analysis and contextual evaluation of mining and furnace remains at such sites as Timna in Israel (Rothenberg 1990a, 1990b) or Mount Gabriel in Ireland (O'Brien 1994). Thus, archaeometallurgy belatedly adopted an eco-environmental approach still prevalent in pottery and lithic studies (Arnold 1993; Rosen 1997).

In the analytical realm, this still forms a key objective of SCSP's archaeometallurgy program (see chapter 5.4). SCSP's attempt to model archaeometallurgical systems, however, is based only partially on such technical data. Along with many other regional survey projects in the Mediterranean, we are interested in contextualizing analytical data on a larger scale. More distinctively, SCSP seeks to examine the social significance and symbolic values of technical production systems as well as the manipulation of

technology in politico-religious contexts (for example, Herbert 1984; Hosler 1994).

The reluctance to embrace social theory in a strongly analytical field seems to have diminished. Various social approaches to an industrial past now seek to integrate the study of the socioeconomic, spatial, and ideological dimensions of past industrial communities with the history of technology and the reconstruction of practical production techniques (Knapp, Pigott, and Herbert 1998). The emphasis lies on mining communities as social constructs, based on a shared interest and occupation rather than on a fixed location. Throughout mining history, settlements and structures were always notoriously temporary or transitory. As an interdisciplinary regional survey project, SCSP is ideally suited to the study of such diachronic archaeometallurgical phenomena (see chapter 2.1 and Knapp 1999a; more generally, see Braudel 1980).

Many archaeometallurgical survey projects today are influenced by an intellectual framework focusing on the technological diversity and linear diachronic evolution encountered in the "pure" sciences (for example, Raber 1987; Rothenberg and Blanco-Freijeiro 1981). SCSP, however, has attempted to study the relationship between a (reconstructed) production process and its social or economic role. In attempting to investigate and integrate economic, technological, and social factors, SCSP seeks to further both methodological and theoretical developments in archaeometallurgy. The interaction between landscape and society needs to be reassessed from a holistic perspective, one in which miners and smelters create the archaeometallurgical landscape, which in turn modifies their social and economic conditions. This dialectic and the spatial setting that contextualizes it (Knapp 1997:72) must be the ultimate aim of any social archaeometallurgy.

Technology and society can be reintegrated usefully into archaeometallurgical research by applying the *chaînes opératoires* model (Leroi-Gourhan 1943; Lemmonier 1993; Pfaffenberger 1992; 1998). This model serves to unify an archaeometallurgical sampling design, the analytical procedures, and the material reconstructions and in turn links these factors to the socioeconomic organization and spatial distribution of metal production. Such an approach demands only that we conceptualize an archaeometallurgical landscape as made up of production units represented by their diagnostic debris. SCSP's problem-oriented research design aims to balance prevailing views on sociotechnical systems and mining communities by integrating social archaeology and archaeometallurgy.

To recognize this spatial distribution of technologically distinct components, SCSP has applied archaeological methods of systematic recording to all archaeometallurgical sites. From the outset, finds such as slag, furnace fragments, and other archaeometallurgical waste products were included in the list of archaeological artifacts recorded by field teams throughout the survey area. These teams were trained prior to fieldwalking in recognizing several types of archaeometallurgical remains to increase qualitatively and quantitatively the data recovered (Merkel et al. 1994). No other archaeological, or indeed archaeometallurgical, survey project undertaken on Cyprus has ever approached the issue of recording ancient mining or metallurgical sites and archaeometallurgical materials in the same manner. As a result, the dispersal patterns of waste products (slag in particular), as well as the diachronic development of technologies and associated production sites, can be analyzed in detail by our GIS. Archaeometallurgical products have finally joined the established range of archaeological remains (pottery and lithics) traditionally studied in such a manner. As a result, we have been able to map and assess archaeometallurgical and contemporary mining practices—as well as postdepositional disturbances—across the entire landscape, not just within mines and slag heaps already known to be industrial sites.

SCSP owes a large debt to previous research that included valuable information on site locations and ore types. The first to record ancient mines and slag heaps were mining engineers and geologists (Bruce 1949; Lavender 1962). Prospectors used the (ancient) slag heaps to locate copper ore deposits and at the same time considered through analyses the possibility of extracting copper from the slags. According to Bear (1963:191), the earliest chemical analyses of Cypriot slags were published by Gaudry in 1862. Because the copper content was quite low, this idea was not followed through. Slag heaps, however, were quarried systematically during the earlier part of the twentieth century, when slag was used as road metal and in cement manufacture (Bear 1963:190).

The fact that slag heaps were economic deposits in themselves, not just indicators of ore deposits, meant that their location was often mentioned in geological publications (for example, Bear 1963: Fig. 3) and in the archives of the mining companies. From the archives of the Hellenic Mining Company, for example, Stos-Gale et al. (1998) list eighty-five slag heaps with information on location and relative size. Mining engineers also recorded ancient mining debris when it was encountered (see chapter 4.11), but these ancient mines have now been destroyed; Bruce (1937, 1949) remains the most informative source on ancient galleries and adits.

The interest of the geologists and mining engineers lay in the economic exploitation of the slag heaps, not in their archaeological and historical significance. Thus, slags were defined as Roman or Phoenician on the basis of color (reddish-brown slags were argued to be Phoenician while dark brown to black slags were Roman), because it was assumed that the mines had been exploited chiefly during these periods (Bruce 1937:642). This color-based division was soon recognized to be false, not least because black slag was also found at the Late Bronze Age site of Apliki (Muhly et al. 1980:86).

Only in the 1970s did scholars begin to take a more active interest in the archaeometallurgy of Cyprus. Most attention fell on the analysis and interpretation of the archaeometallurgical finds coming from excavated urban sites and on the organization of copper production and trade during the Late Bronze Age (for example, Bachmann 1982b; Tylecote 1982; Knapp 1986a; Muhly 1982, 1989; Gale 1991). Some papers, however, presented analyses of slag samples collected from slag heaps (for example Tylecote 1971, 1977; Zwicker et al. 1972). These publications usually focused on the analytical results and the information such analyses offer on smelting technology; in general they offered no information on the date of the heaps, nor did they try to integrate them with the archaeological sites in the immediate vicinity. Zwicker (1986) was the only scholar to use radiocarbon dating and to publish the results. Koucky and Steinberg took samples from many of the main slag heaps, including those in the SCSP area, and tried to create a system for classifying the different slag types (Koucky and Steinberg 1974, 1982a, 1989). They did not, however, collect samples following the strata clearly visible in the sections. Furthermore, a number of the conclusions they drew from their field work and the analytical results can be contested, based on results from SCSP as well as other projects (see chapter 5.4).

Metallurgical sites were recorded more systematically during the course of two archaeological surveys undertaken in the Paphos district. The Canadian Palaepaphos Survey Project (CPSP) noted some slag heaps and other sites with metallurgical activity, took slag samples for analysis, and presented some preliminary conclusions (Fox et al. 1987). Raber's survey of mining and metallurgical sites in the Polis region of western Cyprus investigated the organization of the mining and smelting industry, as well as issues of technology (Raber 1984, 1987). Raber (1987:301), however, found it difficult to date the slag heaps because most of the associated pottery was made up of coarse wares. Recently Walter Fasnacht and his team, who have been excavating the Archaic to Hellenistic period smelting workshop of Ayia Varvara *Almyras*, have also initiated a survey of the area around the site (Fasnacht et al. 1997; Fasnacht 1999:180–181).

Although much work has already been done, SCSP has attempted to address previously neglected issues by using an array of new procedures. Although all these projects noted the location of slag heaps, none recorded them in any great detail. Some tried to date them, usually with recourse to pottery found on their surface; this practice resulted in problems as the pottery was often found to be undiagnostic, or else unrelated to the time period when the slag was deposited. Published papers rarely give information on the provenance of analyzed samples within a slag heap, even though a sample taken from the surface could be hundreds of years younger than one taken from the lower layers. All these factors present serious problems for looking at diachronic archaeometallurgical landscapes. Because slag heaps like Mitsero *Kokkinoyia* and *Sykamies* have been formed over several centuries (most likely with time gaps in production), they become stratified and should be approached as an archaeological section (Bachmann 1982a:6). Although such an approach has been adopted in other mining areas (for example, Rothenberg and Blanco Freijeiro 1981:104), SCSP was the first to apply it in Cyprus. Making use of stratigraphic sampling in this way has helped us to integrate production sites into a wider landscape approach. The methods used in recording these sites are described in some detail in chapter 3.6.

2.7 Historical Archaeology, Oral History, and Field Survey

Lita Diacopoulos, Michael Given, and Kylie Seretis

No longer do regional survey projects stop at the end of the Roman period. In Greece, for example, an influential school of settlement history is examining changes in settlement patterns from the Medi-

eval period to the twentieth century (Bintliff 1997b, 1997c; Sutton 1994). The wealth of information in Ottoman administrative records about the political organization and economy of the countryside increasingly has been exploited and integrated with archaeological survey data (Davis 1991; Kiel 1997). The pottery of the post-Roman period is being studied not just for the artistic value of particular pieces but for the social and historical analyses demanded by assemblages systematically collected on intensive survey projects (Vroom 1998). Contemporary societies among which archaeologists work—especially the villages where they stay—are no longer seen as mere comparisons to throw light on whatever periods of antiquity happen to be the focus of interest: It is now generally agreed that recent periods have as much intrinsic archaeological interest as any other (for example, Lee 2001).

In Cyprus, beyond some historical, art historical, and numismatic studies, there has been comparatively little work on the archaeology of the post-Roman periods. Medieval sugar mills at Kouklia (von Wartburg 1983) and Kolossi have been excavated, as has a fifteenth-century industrial structure at Malloura (Toumazou et al. 1998:176–177). Structures such as threshing floors (Whittaker 1999) and a nineteenth-century water mill (Morris 1984) have been examined and described. Artifact studies are minimal compared to earlier periods, although there are some important exceptions: chert blades from threshing sledges (Kardulias and Yerkes 1996); pottery and its distribution in the southwest of the island (Gregory 1987, 1993); "traditional" pottery (Ionas 1998); and Ottoman tobacco pipes (Baram 1995a). Medieval and Ottoman sites are mentioned in the reports of extensive surveys (Baird 1985:346–347), and were examined rather more systematically by the Canadian Palaepaphos Survey Project (Rupp 1986:38–39). Documentary sources for Medieval villages have also been examined in detail (Grivaud 1998). Otherwise, however, few attempts have been made to investigate the landscapes of post-Roman Cyprus on a systematic, intensive, and interdisciplinary basis (Given 2000:209).

SCSP's contribution to the archaeology of the Medieval, Ottoman, and Modern periods is threefold: (1) the systematic collection of artifacts across the survey area and the analysis of their distribution using geomorphological studies and GIS; (2) an examination of standing buildings and other features in the landscape, such as houses, cemeteries, field shelters, and water mills; (3) a series of interviews in the village of Mitsero to investigate the ethnohistory.

An intensive survey methodology allows the analysis not just of sites, or hot spots within the landscape, but of a wide range of human activities taking place outside the principal towns and settlements. Indications of these activities are particularly clear in the transects crossing the survey area. The halo of material around the main Medieval to Modern villages, resulting from manuring and dumping in the closest fields, is visible in the alluvial plains of the SCSP region. Pottery distribution patterns support in general terms the principle of nucleated settlement during these periods, but there are various exceptions and subtleties. The long-term perspective to which regional survey lends itself so well shows interesting continuities and discontinuities: For example, Medieval and Ottoman material on major settlements and in good agricultural areas is nearly always found together, and there is a close correlation between Late Roman and Medieval settlements.

The second aspect of SCSP's approach to the post-Roman periods is the investigation of specific monuments, features, and other relevant POSIs. One major focus was the village of Mitsero itself (SIA 5), particularly its traditional houses and cemetery, where the material evidence is related to oral information and documentation. The landscape around villages such as Mitsero is equally important. Descriptions of taking grain to the water mill to be ground, for example, could be compared with our studies of the six mills of the survey area. Studies of the thresh-ing floors (*alonia*) at Mitsero were important for understanding the agricultural landscapes of the Ottoman and Modern periods and for investigating the lithic technologies of the area.

The third approach consists of gathering oral information from villagers, mainly from Mitsero, and from employees of the Hellenic Mining Company. The purpose here was to supplement our knowledge and understanding, obtained from other sources, of the social and economic issues contributing to the present character of Mitsero, its inhabitants, and its immediate environs. In particular, we aimed to incorporate local experience to provide a specifically human dimension to the archaeology of the more recent past. This was particularly valuable for the investigation of the history of mining in the area. As with all other kinds of evidence, the oral information had to be sampled and evaluated in terms of its accuracy and relevance to our research questions and compared to other oral accounts, material remains, and documentary evidence.

In spite of their long archaeological neglect in Cyprus and elsewhere, the Medieval, Ottoman, and Modern periods are rich in material, in their levels of social and economic complexity, and in issues of significant archaeological interest. This applies particularly to the SCSP area, which saw a high level of population and a wide variety of different social structures during these centuries. By integrating a range of disciplines and field methods, SCSP hopes to demonstrate the appropriateness of a socially focused, intensive regional survey to the study of the recent past.

3

METHODOLOGY AND ANALYTICAL PROCEDURES

3.1 The Survey Universe

Nathan Meyer and A. Bernard Knapp

Defining the survey universe is perhaps the most basic decision in regional survey methodology. (Plog et al. 1978:384) To select such a study region, one must consider the nature of the boundaries chosen and whether the area chosen should be stratified into smaller analytical units. Ideally, archaeologists should conduct regional surveys within an area that was culturally bounded in the past, what Fotiadis (1997:106) terms a geohistorical unit. As logical as it may seem, determining the parameters of a cultural unit is problematic for several reasons: by definition, regional surveys involve diachronic research, usually covering millennia of human history and the concomitant shifting of cultural boundaries; even where the problem orientation of a survey is focused on a particular stage in the past, the areal extent of the targeted cultural expression is seldom clear; and permits to conduct survey work are handled by modern administrative units, not past cultural groupings.

An intermediate position between a culturally bounded survey universe and one randomly selected might be one defined by natural boundaries, such as rivers or mountains (Plog et al. 1978:385). Because natural boundaries sometimes correspond to cultural borders, this apparently tidy notion is appealing. However, two further problems emerge: First, which natural phenomena might best delimit a culturally bounded unit, or survey universe? Even if natural features such as mountain chains or rivers are regarded as appropriate choices, this is not the case with modern vegetation patterns (Nance 1983) or hydrology regimes. The second problem is the very concept of the boundary, which suggests a lack of extra-community interaction, or at the very least, interaction across a boundary. This concept gains much of its appeal from an uncritical internalization of modern political and administrative units. Finally, to reemphasize a point made earlier, regional survey implicitly recognizes the relevance of the natural environment to cultural forms.

Where a specific area is characterized by high variability in site or artifact density, it may be useful to divide the survey universe into a stratified sample. This exemplifies a more general principle: Specific survey methods and the level of intensity should be set according to the nature of the area being surveyed in terms of site size and density estimates, where known, and in terms of the natural conditions. Given a finite pool of resources to be allocated across a project, there may be sound reasons to stratify the survey universe according to common-sense principles and then to sample within those stratifications to test the assumptions. For example, if one-quarter of a survey region is situated at a slope considered inhospitable to habitation and/or too expensive in terms of time commitment, it may make sense first to delimit that area and sample it at a lower level of intensity.

Such stratification and variation of survey effort across a given region may introduce other analytical problems. For example, how comparable are results from areas where survey effort or strategy has varied? In addition, one must be aware of a direct correlation between reduced survey intensity and the reduced probability of locating uncommon materials, single component "sites," and other rarely occurring items.

The concept of a survey universe holds strong sway in the design of regional survey projects and may be regarded as a methodological backdrop against which field research is carried out. Given a finite amount of resources and a defined expanse as the survey universe, the entire area can be covered at a certain level of intensity or else a sample of the whole may be carried out at a greater intensity. Proponents of sampling cite the larger number (relative to areal expanse) of sought-after occurrences recovered through sampling and the greater variability of types, with smaller and less prominent occurrences more properly reflected in the data set (Plog et al. 1978). We reiterate here only that such a restriction of resources reinforces our quantitative approach to the archaeological record by offering the potential for broad knowledge through statistical sampling.

SCSP SURVEY UNIVERSE

SCSP's survey universe is a naturally defined area, the interface between the igneous (metal-bearing) ore bodies and the sedimentary (arable) soils. This contact zone is transverse to the drainage network and includes drainage basins that have a wide variety of discharge and arable land surface. The SCSP region also has proved to be important for investigating the articulation between agricultural and mining sites in an early industrial landscape. Because of the great variability in terrain and archaeological material across the survey universe, we decided early (1995) that we had to stratify our survey universe according to purposive principles and then to sample within those strata to test our assumptions.

Our initial stages of survey work were designed to provide a systematic coverage of the survey universe and at the same time to generate information that could be applied constructively to the succeeding stages of research. The goal was to develop a broad understanding of the cultural remains and recoverability potential across the survey region before any stratification was undertaken. Accordingly, we adopted a multistage research design and tried to make it as flexible as possible. During the early stages we chose to sacrifice areal extent in favor of intensity. As we moved on to the succeeding stages of the fieldwork and research, we had explicit reasons for adopting a different strategy, but the overall goal remained to examine as much of the survey universe as possible at a level of intensity appropriate to the particular recovery goals of that stage of research.

SCSP has built an extensive database of quantitative cultural, environmental and social information about the survey universe. The natural resource wealth of the survey area has been mapped and catalogued, while initial patterning in the relationship between human activity and the landscape has been observed and discussed. Finally, our field and laboratory methodologies have been developed, refined and tested.

3.2 Definitions and Dating

A. Bernard Knapp and Nathan Meyer

DEFINITIONS

Landscape components are sometimes categorized in terms that are either excessively reductionist for example—spaces, networks, nodes—or inadequate for the kind of survey endeavors undertaken by most archaeologists today. Landscape historians tend to see the landscape as comprised primarily of elements such as land, boundaries, monuments, and settlements (Muir 1999:50–60). Within archaeology, similar terminological issues affect regional studies of the landscape.

For instance, the debate over the meaning of the term *site*, indeed the very concept of site, has a direct bearing on regional research programs and strategies. Attempts to operationalize the concept of a site in archaeological field survey may lead to quite arbitrary categorizations: The Southwest Anthropological Research Group (SARG), for example, defined a site as an analytical unit having a minimum of five artifacts per m² (Plog and Hill 1971:8). Because some regional survey projects fail altogether to define sites, should we conclude that they carry around a mental template of a site they are then prepared to identify in the field (Fotiadis 1992:133)? Most archaeological sites, unlike those studied by landscape historians (Muir 1999:75–84), are difficult to define in the field specifically because their limits are not immediately apparent (Dunnel and Dancy 1983). Within the SCSP survey area, this is particularly apparent in the alluvial terraces. Even where surveys seek only to define distributional densities in the field, in their final analyses they often attempt to examine clusters as possible indicators of a site (Fotiadis 1992). Plog et al.'s (1978:389) notion of site in survey archaeology is based upon an ability to interpret relationships among the constituent elements of a site. Archaeologists often have an implicit notion that site equals community, and community in turn equals society (Fotiadis 1992). Thus a site is a society that may be interpreted through analysis of the relationships among its constituent parts. And yet, in our view, a site is a locale that can be interpreted not only with respect to its constituent parts, but also within the regional context of other sites.

Early proponents of siteless survey (for example, Thomas 1975) pointed out that nonsedentary populations leave minimal material evidence in the landscape. We would add that, at times, even sedentary peoples carry out activities in the landscape that leave few material indicators. Ebert (1992:7–15) has claimed that site-based methods of investigating the past inhibit progress in archaeological survey strategy; yet in seeking to validate surface archaeology he makes an untenable attack on the concept of the site. While we would agree that it is important to problematize the notion and definition of sites, the lack of chronological control does not necessarily mean that material cannot be dated. Nor does the boundedness of concentrated cultural material mean that spatial analytics cannot extend beyond its limits.

Archaeological survey methodology, including sampling theory, is often misunderstood because of a failure to be explicit about the nature of the units discovered. To define the makeup and stratification of SCSP's survey universe, we begin by discussing the terminology associated with the analytical unit of discovery.

SCSP sought to examine the total landscape and its use, exploitation, development, and change in the face of long-term human activity. In such an approach, a site is more of an interpretative construct than something that can be strictly observed and defined; in this we follow closely Cherry et al. (1991:45–47). Defining a site also requires a detailed knowledge of localized patterns of artifact distribution and landscape use across the full range of spatial and chronological scales, as well as an awareness of taphonomic and geomorphological processes. In other words, there is a great deal of variation in what exists during different periods, under differing conditions of visibility, and within different parts of the survey area. Another significant issue in defining sites as artifact clusters or even on the basis of habitational elements is that a site's boundaries are often indeterminable. Thus, it is not so much a question of where the site is as where it isn't. If a site is an artificial construct (Cherry et al. 1991:34, note 2), then site distribution is meaningless without adequate information on overall artifact-density distributions, meaningful criteria to construct sites from these density-distributions, and the capacity to assess environmental data. Another relevant point in considering the SCSP region is that we have large, very broad areas of high artifact density as well as other evidence indicating human exploitation of almost the entire stable landscape; only areas stripped of all surface soils (usually by erosion) appear to be devoid of artifacts. Such factors actually confound the concept of site, which might be defined more readily and clearly in regions with less dense land use.

Our decision to begin with a systematic sample and to employ the methodology of a siteless survey reflected a commitment to gain as much information as possible about the area of our investigations before making any attempt to characterize it and, ultimately, to stratify it. In this mode, our analytical unit was the survey unit itself. Wherever we found agricultural plots clearly defined in the field and on aerial photographs, they formed our basic recording unit. Such units are characterized by roughly uniform land use, topography, vegetation cover, often even slope and aspect; they are distinguished from other units by a change in any of these factors, or by a field boundary, fence, hedge, road, stream, and so on. Where agricultural fields, vineyards, orchards, and similar aspects of the landscape were not clearly defined, we used transect recording and defined units according to topographic, geological, or even artificial boundaries (for example, roads). We also attempted to limit these arbitrary units to 100 m or less in length (Knapp et al. 1992:323–326; Knapp and Johnson 1994). The data from any analytical unit consist of raw numbers of artifacts and quantifiable observations on geomorphological factors, ecofacts, and other spatial components (for example, slope, aspect, and the like). Yet we assumed from the outset that our higher level research goals, which impel us to understand the social aspects of any human community as expressed by material in the landscape, would require us eventually to shift our analytical unit from landscape features to something that is itself a construct of our research process.

We accept, therefore, that there is a certain tension between the type of siteless survey conducted in field plots and transects, on the one hand, and on the other the attempt to discuss sites, settlements, and settlement hierarchies in more theoretical terms bearing on the research goals and questions in which this project is interested. Methodologically, our field strategy evolved to incorporate the concept of POSIs (places of special interest) and SIAs (special interest areas). POSIs are limited in horizontal expanse and in their diversity of material: for example, lithic scatters or dense pottery concentrations, a water mill, a sheepfold, or the remains of a smelting furnace. SIAs, on the other hand, are more complex, broader in horizontal area and usually multifunctional, containing material from different time periods, and occasionally made up of several different POSIs. As an example of an SIA, we would cite Politiko *Kokkinorotsos*, the upper part of a river valley some 600 m across that includes a broad range of evidence for mining, smelting, and habitation activities from the Late Bronze Age to the Classical period (see chapter 4.7; Given et al. 1999:34–36). In dealing with SIAs, a variety of techniques are involved—from casual walkovers, to sample transects, to "block" survey (see chapter 3.3), to gridded collections, and measured plans and sections. In effect, POSIs and SIAs represent a further stratification of our survey universe.

To address our research goals, it was essential to develop definitions that would facilitate the analysis of settlement patterns through time. Given the diverse types and dating of material recovered by SCSP teams over five field seasons, we feel that we are better able to assess exactly what constitutes specific uses of the landscape: for example, lithic production areas, smelting sites, mines, slag heaps, rural sanctuaries or churches, farmsteads, and agricultural settlements. With the aim of creating usable categories and key concepts to investigate and articulate our research goals, we work with the following explicit definitions.

Sites. SCSP regards the entire landscape as a more-or-less continuous distribution of cultural material generated by people in social space, in some cases redistributed secondarily by further human activity or natural processes. Within this sociocultural landscape, where there are interpretable material expressions (peaks of artifact density), we believe we are dealing with a site as constructed by the archaeologist. While an isolated artifact, particularly a rare or unusual one, may elicit interest and concern, interpretation beyond formal analysis will prove difficult. Hence sites are likely to be density peaks of either single or multiple artifact classes that provide an opportunity to discuss functional interrelationships between data elements. Thus, we are working with site definitions that encompass a rather broad spectrum, from agricultural features, to rare representations of specific periods, to lithic processing locales, to metallurgical installations. Additionally, we have included in our working definition of a site evidence of dense but undifferentiated pottery scatters that we currently regard as the result of agricultural field maintenance.

Settlements. SCSP defines a settlement as any site having material culture remains in close association with architectural features spread over a hectare or more or including several distinct structures. Wherever a dense scatter of sherds is accompanied by an equally dense spread of roofing tiles and building rubble that could indicate contemporary architectural remains, we tentatively regard such a combination of features as a settlement. This supposition, however, would have to be demonstrated by further field reconnaissance and more intensive sampling. Prehistoric sites without architecture present more specific problems (for example, Bintliff et al. 1999): Lithic scatters may be sites, but never settlements. In this rather closely delimited definition, a group of farmsteads would comprise a settlement, but a single farmstead or sheepfold would not. Slag heaps, lithic scatters, and industrial installations, in other words, may be regarded as sites, but not as settlements. Where we have a slag heap with the re- mains of a habitational structure, as at Mitsero *Kouloupakhis* (see chapter 4.3), we also have a site but not a settlement (even if other remains immedi- ately surrounding the slag heap may suggest otherwise).

Our ultimate goal is not to create static defini- tions of sites or settlements: These must be viewed as provisional definitions through which we engage in a dialogue about the complexity of material ex- pression in the landscape. In classifying these sites and settlements as they change through time, with reference to their internal organization as well as their spatial and functional relationship to other sites and settlements within the survey area, our goal is to make meaningful statements about the emer- gence and development of social landscapes and human communities in the northern Troodos foot- hills of Cyprus.

DATING

Members of the SCSP team with specialist knowledge (of pottery, metals, lithics, and so on) studied, re- corded, and dated material collected in the field, unit by unit. Such study is based largely on compari- son with known objects and materials (comparanda), usually from excavated sites, survey work, and other field projects carried out elsewhere on Cyprus. In addition, the SCSP has a study collection of chronotypes and other objects that are especially characteristic of material found in the survey area. A chronotype (see chapter 2.3) is a specific pottery ware or type (for example, Base Ring, African Red Slip, Sgrafitto ware) which represents the essence of pottery styles that have a clear chronological signifi- cance (see also chapter 3.7). The identification of specific chronotypes represents a particularly useful step in the process of studying and recording ob- jects, since these are specific types of pottery or other material that are both readily identifiable and char- acteristic of one particular period. Chronotypes, therefore, can be used with some certainty to sug- gest the presence of a chronological component for an individual unit.

Information about objects was recorded on forms that focus on identification, characterization, and chronology of individual pieces and groups of pieces and identification of chronological periods that may be associated with individual units. The

former process is designed primarily to record the identification of single objects from units, as far as that can be determined on the basis of available in- formation; this provides the basic data from which we draw conclusions about chronology, function, and so on. The latter process takes into consideration the totality of the objects analyzed from a unit to indicate which chronological periods are repre- sented in the material from the individual units. This means that individual items of various types may be given greater weight, or that the number of items from a particular period may be considered, in de- termining chronological components with a unit or in assigning that unit to a chronological period. At times, SCSP staff members responsible for analyzing material brought in from the field conferred with members of a survey team to ask whether individual objects were common or rare in the unit or whether they could provide other useful information to help in understanding the scope of material found in the individual units (chapter 3.7).

The geomorphological team sought to provide at least partial reconstructions of the physical land- scape during the various occupational periods, to place POSIs, sites, or settlements within the context of the natural environment at the time of their oc- cupation. Such reconstructions required good chronological control for the Holocene deposits, both archaeological and geological. Determining the age of archaeological deposits fell to the pot- tery, metal, and lithic specialists. The geochronology was more challenging: Descriptions of soil chrono-sequences and catenas (soil profiles across a change in topography, which show the ef- fect of elevation and relief on soil development) provided a geochronological sequencing and rough age estimates as well as information about amounts of surface erosion across the landscape. Rock-weath- ering features and lichens were described and measured to develop relative chronologies for rock surfaces, including those in structures such as ter- race walls. Radiocarbon analysis of detrital charcoal and soil carbon provided numerical age estimates for fluvial and check dam sediments at a number of locations across the SCSP study area. These nu- merical age estimates then were used with the relative methods to delimit more precisely the tim- ing of erosional and depositional events. Furthermore, cultural artifacts were used as fossils to constrain the age of sedimentary sequences. As

Table 3.1 Chronological periods

Abbreviation	Period	Dates
EP	Early Prehistoric	9000–2500 BC
PeB	Prehistoric Bronze Age	2500–1700 BC
PoB	Protohistoric Bronze Age	1700–1000 BC
PH	Prehistoric (EP–Geometric)	9000–750 BC
Geo	Geometric	1050–750 BC
Ar	Archaic	750–475 BC
GA	Geometric to Archaic	1050–475 BC
Cl	Classical	475–312 BC
GAC	Geometric to Classical	1050–312 BC
AC	Archaic to Classical	750–312 BC
He	Hellenistic	312–100 BC
ClHe	Classical to Hellenistic	475–100 BC
ER	Early Roman	100 BC–AD 300
HER	Hellenistic to Early Roman	312 BC–AD 300
LR	Late Roman	AD 300–750
REL	Early–Late Roman	100 BC–AD 750
Byz	Byzantine	AD 750–1191
Med	Medieval	AD 1191–1571
Ott	Ottoman	AD 1571–1878
Mod	Modern	AD 1878–2000
MM	Medieval to Modern	AD 1191–2000
HA	Historical Antiquity (Ar–LR)	750 BC–AD 750
Hi	Historical (Ar–Mod)	750 BC–AD 2000
PC	Post Classical (He–Mod)	312 BC–AD 2000
Unk	Unknown	9000 BC–AD 2000

with any fossil material, such artifacts provide maximum age estimates on the sediments they have been incorporated into or buried by, and minimum age estimates for materials they overlie.

With respect to archaeometallurgy, it is clear from detailed examination of the ancient slag heaps in the SCSP area that production once was carried out on a considerable scale, spread over hundreds of years. In the slag heap at Mitsero *Kouloupakhis* 1 (SIA 3), for example, structural remains uncovered in the sections during modern quarrying operations suggested a date for occupation and helped us to reconstruct the production process (even though ^{14}C analyses of charcoal embedded in that slag heap subsequently revealed that the slag heap was later than the structure). We also noted considerable variation in the internal structure and characteristics of the slags themselves, which may indicate changes in production processes through time. In general, however, the archaeometallurgical team relied primarily on pottery and tile fragments collected from sections of slag heaps and spoil heaps to date smelting activities and to refine interpretations of the contemporary copper industry. Where sites had no pottery, or where stratified pottery consisted of

coarse wares that did not permit a specific chronology, whenever possible we collected charcoal samples for radiocarbon dating; these at least suggest a time span during which mining and smelting activities took place. Charcoal entrapped in the slags and on working floors has been sampled extensively for radiocarbon dating (the results are discussed in chapter 5.4); such samples provide cross-checks on pottery dates and help us to understand the history of Cypriot metallurgy. Unless pottery, tools, or remnant tool marks are found in mining adits or galleries, it is difficult to determine the chronology of their construction; occasionally their size, shape, and location within geological deposits may provide an indicator. In some cases, the method of construction and the treatment of the wood in these adits or galleries provide chronological information but only radiocarbon or dendrochronological dating can establish secure age determinations.

SCSP assigns material collected by the field teams to a range of period designations (table 3.1). As some material is more precisely datable than others, some of these are broad expanses of time that include two or more specific periods. This is closely integrated with our chronotype system (see chapter 2.3).

3.3 Mapping and Fieldwalking Procedures
Michael Given and Nathan Meyer

SCSP used a systematic intensive survey strategy, well-developed and widely used in other areas of the Mediterranean (and in world archaeology generally) but previously adopted only to a limited extent on Cyprus. We achieved the following:

- walked 1,550 survey units at approximately 5-m spacing between fieldwalkers, covering 6.54 km², or 9.94% of the survey area;
- detected the background artifact scatter across the survey area and estimated its density and correlation with the topographic and environmental characteristics of the landscape;
- identified and investigated 11 SIAs and 142 POSIs within the landscape;
- counted in the field 87,600 sherds of pottery, pithos and terra-cotta, and 8,111 tile fragments;
- collected and analyzed 29,235 diagnostic, unique, or indeterminate sherds of pottery, tile, and

terra-cotta and 2,846 lithics; all were entered into the project's database and exported to the GIS;

- refined our intensive survey methodology and GIS analysis, which should improve the quality and increase the quantity of various types of data from all periods of the Cypriot past.

Our basic field strategies have been to walk 50-m–wide transects north-south across the entire survey area at 500-m intervals, to obtain a broad systematic sample of the survey area, in particular an overview of archaeological material and exposure conditions that typify the region's diverse topography, geology, and land use; to utilize spatial information entered daily into the GIS to determine which topographic, geological, and land-use factors may have conditioned the occurrence of exposed cultural materials; to conduct block survey of SIAs that showed extensive evidence of early industrial, agricultural, or settlement activities; to investigate POSIs, designated by obtrusive remains or densities of artifacts.

MAPS AND AERIAL PHOTOGRAPHS
Nathan Meyer and Caroline Whitehill

One of the chief problems SCSP had to overcome was the lack of the standard Cypriot 1:5000 topographic maps in the survey area. In a refinement of earlier attempts to address this problem, we made use of enlarged aerial photographs to create a base map of the entire survey region (Knapp and Johnson 1994). Using the GIS program MapInfo, these photographs were scanned and registered to the UTM grid, with grid lines of 100-m spacing superimposed on the base map. Mapping sheets were generated from the base map for use in the field. Each A4-size mapping sheet (or field sheet), aligned in a north-south direction and produced at a scale of 1:2500, showed a 500 x 200 m portion of the aerial photographs, with the Universal Transverse Mercator (UTM) grid overlaid on it.

This process was fairly efficient for transect work, but ultimately did not offer the degree of horizontal accuracy required for more detailed investigations. For example, on a 1:50,000 map, a pencil point dot is roughly the equivalent of a circle of 10 m in diameter. Add to that camera distortion and plane tilt, and the inaccuracy can rise to 100+ m.

This problem was overcome through the generous assistance of the Cypriot Geological Survey and the Cypriot Lands and Survey Department, from whom we acquired a set of 1993/1994 aerial photographs and corresponding camera fiducials. These images, as compared to those from the 1960s, more closely resembled the built and natural environment in which we were working. From Lands and Survey, we were given geographical positioning system (GPS) readings for survey points in our study area. The GPS points we were given were purposely degraded in accuracy by ± 2 m in three dimensions. These points are on the Cyprus Geodetic Reference System of 1993 (CGRS'93), a coordinate system that is itself tied to the European Terrestrial Reference Frame (ETRF); the exact relationship between CGRS'93 and ETRF, however, is not available.

With accurate survey points from 1993, our task was then to gather further GPS readings for our 1993/1994 aerials. We did this in two phases: first tying together all the survey points of the Department of Lands and Survey with accurate readings, and second, from these points taking at least four and often upward of a dozen GPS readings for each aerial photograph. The Trimble 4600LS Survey Grade GPS that we used consists of two receivers, one of which acts as a mobile base station and the other as a rover. Accuracy for static survey (rover stationary) is subcentimeter within 10 km.

The 1993/1994 aerial photographs were then rectified using the Erdas Imagine 3.1.0 geometric correction, rectification, and export utilities. Geometric correction of each photograph was required to remove image distortion caused by lens distortion, plane tilt, and parallax. Focal length, lens distortion, and fiducial coordinates used for geometric correction were obtained from the Cypriot Department of Lands and Survey. Once camera components were corrected, a minimum of four GPS ground control points (< 5 cm precision) were used to georeference accurately the image pixels. Photo rectification/warping was achieved through a maximum of ten iterations of bilinear correlation and least squares analysis. Once rectified, the images were cropped to remove the photo headers and fiducial marks using the Erdas raster resampling tool. The images were then exported and restored from an Erdas pyramid format (.IMG) to TIFF format for use in MapInfo. The TIFF images were then registered as image tables in MapInfo using rectified geo-coordinates measured in Erdas Imagine. Once registered as a MapInfo table, the rectified images were easily integrated into the SCSP MapInfo database.

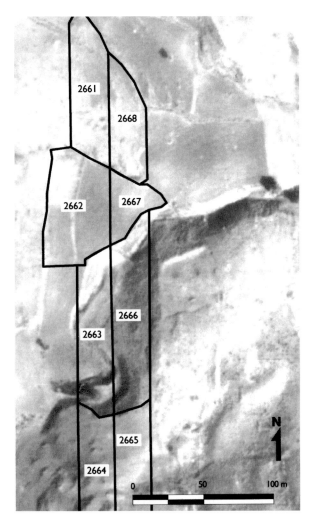

Figure 3.1 Part of transect 513.5, showing standard transect units and two "souvlaki" units. *Based upon the aerials of the Department of Lands and Surveys with the sanction of the Government of Cyprus. State copyright reserved.*

The creation of these photo-maps began as a solution to a problem (the lack of sufficient detailed topographic maps), but ended up as an innovation that we believe improves on standard field techniques. The photo-maps were extremely useful in the field. Not only were they used for recording archaeological units, but they were also used by other specialists for detailing field observations. Having photo-maps with overlain 100-m grids allowed us to address specific grid sections. Finally, when the photo-maps serve as a base layer for the survey units (chapter 4), they provide for documentation of the survey area that is easy to read and rich in information.

In our daily fieldwalking, surveyed units were outlined and numbered sequentially on the field sheets, while the data associated with each unit in the field were recorded on a separate form. Survey unit outlines were digitized from the field sheets using MapInfo. Data collected in the field for each survey unit—spatial, geobotanical, artifactual—were entered into the project's database and were exported regularly to MapInfo. The resulting table could then be opened and combined with the digitized outlines, while the outcome was saved as a new table for analysis.

TRANSECT SURVEY

In five seasons, SCSP participants walked some 92 km of survey transects, which, for the most part, were 50-m wide and composed of units no more than 100-m long and surveyed at 5-m spacing between fieldwalkers. Our aims in walking these transects were to: build up a large body of artifactual and ecofactual data representing our entire survey area, for subsequent GIS analysis; investigate a representative sample of different geological and topographic zones within the survey area; and discover SIAs and POSIs for further investigation.

The basic element that made up survey transects (as well as block surveys; see below) was the survey unit. In uncultivated ground, units were 25-m wide, corresponding to five fieldwalkers walking 5 m apart. Units were defined at their beginning and end by natural divisions such as a break in slope, a significant change in vegetation, or a gully line. If there were no such division, the unit would be ended after 100 m, even if there were no artifacts. The outline of the unit was drawn on the field sheet, and later digitized. Transects were always two units wide, giving a total width of 50 m in uncultivated ground.

In cultivated fields we used a slightly different system of defining units, known as the "souvlaki method," so called because these survey units generally projected beyond the normal 25-m–wide strip (figure 3.1), just as lamb chunks project out from a spit. A plowed field is clearly one discrete unit: Artifacts will be moved around within it by the plow, but not regularly from one field to the next, and in most cases a field's geomorphology, vegetation, and physical characteristics are homogeneous. In cases where a field extended beyond the normal 25-m-wide unit, the extra portion was included in the survey unit, with some team members walking an extra strip to maintain the 5-m spacing. This was done only when 50% or more of the entire survey unit lay within the

Table 3.2 Survey unit form, with codes for database entry. Each field sheet comprised forms for three separate units and the list of codes.

Status

SU	Surveyed
PR	Prohibited Area
GR	Garden/Walled Area
SC	Standing Crops
ST	Stubble
DI	Disturbed Area
BI	Built Area
NS	Not Surveyed

Method

FT	Fixed Width Transect
SO	Souvlaki

Topography

BH	Bedrock Hilltop
CH	Cliff Base/Face-Hillside
CS	Cliff Base/Face-Stream
CP	Clifftop/Plateau Edge
CD	Closed Depression
FP	Floodplain
GU	Gully
HB	Hillside-Bedrock
HS	Hillside-Soil/Plant Cover
HC	Human Constructed
IB	Isolated Bedrock Hilltop
IM	Isolated Mesa Hilltop
MP	Mesa/Plateau
PI	Piedmont
RB	Ridge-Bedrock
RS	Ridge-Soil/Plant Cover
C	River Channel/Bed
RT	River Terrace
SAB	Saddle-Bedrock
SAS	Saddle-Soil/Plant Cover
SB	Spur-Bedrock
SP	Spur-Soil/Plant Cover

Geomorphology

AV	Alluvium
AVB	Alluvium Basalt
AVC	Alluvium Chalk
AVL	Alluvium Limestone
BA	Basalt
CH	Chalk
FA	Fanglomerate
LI	Limestone

Sediment cover

<10	Less than 10 cm
10-30	10 to 30 cm
>30	Greater than 30cm
BR	Bedrock
UK	Unknown

Surface character

AGC	Angular Gravel/Clay-Silt
AGL	Angular Gravel/Loam
AGS	Angular Gravel/Sand
AWG	Angular Washed Gravel
CL	Clay/Silt
LO	Loam
RGC	Round Gravel/Clay-Silt
RGL	Round Gravel/Loam
RGS	Round Gravel/Sand
RWG	Round Washed Gravel
SA	Sand
VA	Variable

Erosional patterns

SS	Stable Surface
FR	Few Rills
MR	Many Rills
MG	Many Gullies
FG	Few Gullies
MGFR	Many Gullies, Few Rills
MGMR	Many Gullies, Many Rills
FGFR	Few Gullies, Few Rills
FGMR	Few Gullies, Many Rills

Soil color

Use Munsell soil color chart
VA	Variable; only for Gossan/Slag

Modern land use

BA	Batha (sparse vegetation)
BI	Built/Industrial
CO	Cultivation (other)
FA	Fallow
FO	Forest (Pine)
GA	Garrigue (Low Scrub)
GP	Grass/Pasture
MA	Maquis (Tall Scrub)
OR	Orchard/Grove
VI	Vineyard

Slope

FL = <1   SL = 1-5   MO = 6-10
ST = 11-20   VS = >20

Aspect

FL=Flat   N   NE   E   SE   S   SW   W   NW

Unit: _____

Easting: _____

Northing: _____

Status: _____

Method: _____

Ground Visibility (%): _____

Background Confusion: 0   +   ++

Topography: _____

Geomorphology: _____

Sediment Cover: _____

Surface Character: _____

Erosion Pattern: _____

Soil Color: _____

Modern Land Use: _____

Slope: _____

Aspect: _____

Terraces   Nil / Trad. / Cut / Unclear

N/A / In Use / Abandoned

	Counted	Collected	Bags
Sherds:	_____	_____	(w/tile)
Pithos:	_____	_____	(w/tile)
Tile:	_____	_____	_____
Glass:	_____	_____	_____
Slag:	_____	_____	_____

Estimated?   Slag: Yes   Ore/Flux: Yes

Ore/Flux:	_____	_____	_____
Metal:	_____	_____	_____
Ground stone:		_____	_____
Lithics:	_____	_____	_____
Other:	_____	_____	_____

Comment:

POSI?   Yes   No

original survey transect. In cases where the transect crossed the edge of a very large field (that is, one in which the survey unit was less than 50% of the field), the survey units were confined to 25 m (see also Knapp et al. 1992).

Within each survey unit, we recorded a range of locational, environmental, and archaeological information. This included basic data such as the unit number, location, status (for example, surveyed, standing crop), and method (transect, souvlaki). The percentage of the ground visible beneath the vegetation was decided after discussion among the team, as was background confusion, the extent to which red or gray stones, for example, made it more difficult to identify sherds. Topographical, geomorphological and environmental data collected consisted of topography, geomorphology, sediment cover, surface character, erosion pattern, soil color, modern land use, slope, aspect, and terraces (table 3.2). The choices were listed as a series of codes on the unit sheet, and were further explained in a detailed field manual.

In each unit, the teams collected a representative sample of cultural materials: pottery, chipped stone, ground stone, metals, slag, ores and fluxes, glass, and tiles. All other, mainly nondiagnostic, material was simply counted and left in the unit. Slag, ore, and flux were estimated when they were too numerous to count.

The pottery collection strategy as it evolved by our third season (1996) was designed to correlate quantitatively what was counted versus what was collected. Each of the five fieldwalkers collected one sherd of each discernible category of ceramics they found in their 5-m strip. Thus a common ware or form would have multiple examples in the collected sample, but we did not have to collect excessive quantities of pottery from the field. In each collection, accordingly, there might be as many as five sherds that were essentially identical (same fabric, same type or subtype of vessel, same portion of the vessel: for example, 5 rim fragments of African Red Slip, form 106). Similarly, if it had very little sgraffito, the collection might contain only two sgraffito body sherds and one base. These figures could then be related to the total count of sherds from the unit, and used to project how much Roman or Medieval pottery (for example) the unit contained (see chapter 3.7).

All these data were recorded on unit forms using a series of codes (table 3.2). As well as the forms,

one team member kept a field book with a running commentary on the units, the finds, any problems in procedure or interpretation, and general comments on the team's health and state of mind (see chapter 1.3).

PLACES OF SPECIAL INTEREST

The purpose of reinvestigating places of special interest (POSIs)—both density peaks and the appearance of rare components—was to develop further our definitions and understanding of sites and settlements, so that we could approach our higher level research questions with the appropriate units of analysis. Depending on the nature of the POSI, we pursued different strategies. Predominantly, however, what we did was to attempt to collect more, better, and different data concerning both artifacts and ecofacts. These data are both qualitative and quantitative.

Each POSI was given an identification number prefixed with SCY and a name according to the Cypriot convention of Village *Locality* (for example, SCY114—Mitsero *Lambadhiotissa*). Where there were several POSIs in the same locality, they were numbered sequentially (for example, SCY116—Politiko *Kokkinorotsos* 1; SCY117—Politiko *Kokkinorotsos* 2). After the discovery of a new POSI during transect survey, the teams ended their most recent survey unit and conducted a brief investigation of the character and boundaries of the POSI. At this stage a POSI reporting form was filled in and a quick sketch map made. Once this was accomplished, the team would continue with the transect, beginning on the far side of the POSI. The information on the reporting form was used later to decide whether and how the POSI should be reinvestigated.

POSIs within the SCSP survey area vary enormously, ranging from scatters of pottery on plowed fields and isolated clusters of chipped stone to rubble piles and standing monuments. Because of this variety, we devised a series of strategies for recording and analyzing them that were appropriate for each case but easily comparable between cases. Discernible ruins and standing buildings were mapped, using a theodolite and EDM for the more complex examples (for example, SCY023; chapter 4.4), and virtually all POSIs required a location map of some sort. More complex were the cases where artifact scatters gave the only indication of past human activity within the landscape. Depending on the extent and density of those scatters, three different methods were used to record them: iron cross, fixed grid, and gridded circles.

Iron cross. Where a pottery scatter was distinct and discrete (not very common in the SCSP landscape), it was important to establish its limits as well as its date. This was conveniently and efficiently achieved by means of an iron cross (for example, SCY209; plate XLV; cf. Cherry et al. 1991:29–30). The survey team laid out two lines across the POSI, crossing each other at right angles, and collected pottery and other artifacts from a series of circles along the lines. These circles were generally 2-m in diameter and 10 m apart, unless there was good reason to increase or decrease the resolution. Each circle was termed a subunit, and given a cardinal coordinate in relation to the center of the cross (E1, N2, and so forth). A team member collected a representative sample of pottery from each circle, according to the normal survey unit procedure, with occasional full collections as a means of testing the collection method. Further collections were made in the four quadrants between the lines, again making a representative sample.

Fixed grid. Some artifact scatters were small and dense, with a considerable amount of variation within a restricted area. This particularly applied to lithics scatters on relatively undisturbed ground (for example, SCY019; plate XLIII; chapter 4.13). To record and analyze these cases required broader coverage and finer resolution, as supplied by a fixed grid covering the entire POSI. The squares (again, termed subunits) varied from 1 to 5 m, depending on the intensity and resolution required, and the team collected a representative or full sample as appropriate. Ideally the geomorphologists worked alongside the survey team, and used the grid to reference their surface stability map of the POSI. Once the grid was laid out not every square needed to be collected: in some cases (for example, SCY010; chapter 4.12) the team collected every other square on a checkerboard pattern. Conversely, the team often realized that they needed to extend the grid beyond what they had originally planned. This was easily done, thanks to a numbering system for the subunits which used cardinal coordinates (N5E2, S2E1; see, for example, SCY200; chapter 4.17).

Gridded circles. Many artifact scatters fell somewhere between the last two types in terms of extent and density. They required a greater sample than an iron cross, but were too large to attempt a fixed grid. In these cases a series of circles laid out on a grid provided a very useful compromise (see, for example, SCY132; chapter 4.2; plate VI). The usual standard consisted of circles 2 m in diameter and 10 m apart center-to-center, with the opportunity of making further representative collections from the squares between them. As always, the size and spacing of the circles could be varied depending on the resolution required, as long as the sampling methods within them remained the same.

These three methods—iron cross, fixed grid, and gridded circles—could also be used in combination, when appropriate. At SCY010, for example, the team laid out a fixed grid on the area with the densest artifacts and the most stable surface, and used an iron cross in the adjacent plowed field, while the previous season's transect provided context at a wider level (chapter 4.12).

SPECIAL INTEREST AREAS

There were various reasons for designating an area as a Special Interest Area (SIA):

- when there were highly obtrusive elements of interest (for example, an ore body with ancient slag heaps and a modern mine);
- when several POSIs situated close to each other appeared to be associated or related and the whole area required more general investigation;
- when transect survey revealed a very wide spread of pottery that was not concentrated in one specific location.

As SIAs typically extended at least 500 m in each direction, a single 50-m-wide transect was clearly not a sufficiently large sample to answer questions about variations in material culture. In such situations, the transect was broadened so that the survey units covered as much of the area as was needed; this we termed *block survey*. Usually the units were contiguous, conforming to field boundaries where these existed.

Apart from the greater number and extent of the survey units, the methodology used in block survey was identical to that of the transects in terms of fieldwalking, collection strategy, and recording information, so that the data from transects and block survey are compatible. In most cases transects ran into the block-surveyed area from north and south, thus giving helpful context on both sides of an SIA. Because the different SIAs varied greatly in character, several techniques were used to investigate them. These techniques were also used in combination:

- *General walkover.* This helped to define the edge of a major pottery scatter, discover new POSIs, and improve the understanding of the resources and topography of the area. In most cases a topographic map was made, using the aerial photos and existing GIS layers as a base.

- *Investigation of individual POSIs.* Most SIAs include within them several POSIs; SIA 7, for example, contains 21. When examined individually and then related to each other, they contribute to an understanding of the entire landscape.

- *Block survey.* This approach was most useful for defining the spread of cultural material. Much of the pottery found on arable land consisted of a broad spread of varying densities, rather than small, defined density spikes. This meant that block survey was often more appropriate than defining several distinct POSIs.

- *Sample transect.* If it was not possible to block survey an entire SIA, a transect could be used, running across it or across a feature of particular interest. This was done, for example, in SIA 7 (plate XXIX).

3.4 Geomorphology Procedures
Lisa Wells

The primary geomorphological task for SCSP was to reconstruct how geological processes affected the distribution of artifacts across the landscape. To this end, geomorphological field mapping and aerial photographic interpretation of the SCSP survey area were compiled as a separate layer in the GIS. These data were subsequently analyzed using statistical methods within the GIS as well as nonnumeric interdisciplinary investigations. These last consisted of visits to SIAs and POSIs by archaeologists, geomorphologists, and other specialists, who discussed together the observed relationships between landforms and artifacts.

MAPPING PROTOCOL

In contrast to the archaeological maps, the geomorphical maps provide continuous coverage of the entire survey area. The area was first mapped at a small scale (roughly 1:16,000) after which higher resolution, larger scale maps (up to 1:500) were inset within the smaller scale maps. The higher resolution maps are focused around POSIs, SIAs, and places of particular geological interest. Apart from some of the more remote and highly eroded regions, most areas were checked in the field. The upper Mitsero Basin (south of UTM 3,876,850) was the only area to receive greater geological than archaeological attention (Whitehill 1999; see chapter 4.8).

Aerial photographic interpretation was the first level of inspection for all subsequent geomorphological studies. By interpreting the aerial photographs, we created a GIS layer where each polygon represented a region of internally consistent geomorphological characteristics. An example of a GIS data file for each mapped unit is given in table 3.3. Each polygon therefore has a consistent slope and aspect and is usually bounded by a distinct change in slope or aspect. These polygons thus represent regions formed predominantly by a single geomorphological process (for example, fluvial deposition or hillslope erosion) within a discrete period of time. As a result, the mapping units can be considered morphostratigraphic units. According to Frye and Willman (1962:112), "A morphostratigraphic unit is defined as comprising a body of rock that is identified primarily on the basis of the surface form it displays; it may or may not be distinctive lithologically from contiguous units; it may or may not transgress time throughout its extent."

Table 3.3 Example of a GIS data file for a geomorphological layer

Surface type	Stability	Erosion	Soil	Agricultural terraces	Area*
Qaf	Erode	Bound	Mat	Oldter	
Hfg	Incise	Gully	Absent	Modche	
Qct	Erode	Bound	Mat	Oldter	
Qcg	Stable	Gully	Mat	Absent	
Hhf	Dep	Absent	Imat	Absent	
Bp	Strip	Gully	Absent	modter	

* Area calculated by MapInfo polygons

Because units are grouped stratigraphically based on their surface characteristics (vertical position, weathering and soil development, depositional morphology), relative ages can be assigned to each unit (Wells 2001) and correlations can be made between drainage basins. The rigor of the age estimation increases as more information is gathered. For example, an age estimation based solely on aerial photographic interpretation of surface characteristics is less rigorous than one based on field examination of soils and surface characteristics, which is in turn less rigorous than one based on the radiocarbon analysis of included charcoal or an age constraint based upon archaeological materials. Individual stratigraphic units may transgress time (that is, they may have different ages at different locations within the deposit), and the time represented by a unit is not constant. The Holocene geomorphological units probably formed over periods from a hundred to a few thousand years, while the Pleistocene units may represent up to ten thousand or twenty thousand years, or even more for the oldest units.

Within the database, morphostratigraphic units are indicated by standard geological symbols (table 3.4). The first letter of the symbol signifies the relative age of the deposits. Undifferentiated Quaternary deposits are given the designation Q; where it was possible to determine that sediments or landforms are of Holocene age, the abbreviation H was used (for example, Ha is Holocene alluvium; Pa is Pleistocene alluvium). If further relative age differentiation was possible, the second letter (o = older; m = middle; y = younger) indicates the position of the unit within the stratigraphy. These stratigraphic subdivisions can be considered consistent relative ages within drainage basins. Between drainage basins any correlation based simply on the stratigraphy must be considered tenuous. The lithology of the deposits is given by the final one or two letters of the geological abbreviation. The first of these indicates origin or depositional environment (for example, Qa for alluvial, Qe for eolian, and so on) while the final letter is a description of the lithology (Qag for alluvial gravel; Qal for active or abandoned floodplains).

In addition to the standard morphostratigraphic subdivisions of the landscape, additional observations and classifications were made of each mapped subunit (table 3.5). These include a stability

Table 3.4 Geological symbols for morphostratigraphic units

A	Surface soil horizon with high organic matter or other indication of soil formation
Ap	Plowed surface horizon
Bt	Soil horizon into which clay has accumulated
C	Altered parent material (the sediment on which the soil formed)
Cox	Soil horizon of oxidized parent material
R	Rock

Alluvial units (Qa or Ha)

Qa	General areas of alluvium
Qal	Alluvial deposits of floodplains and terraces (Relative age modifers are common in this category: Qoal is older than Qmal is older than Qyal; Qoyal is older than Qmyal is older than Qyyal.
Qaf	Alluvial fan
Qap	Pediment alluvium
Qac	Alluvium with a large colluvial component; on hillslopes or along low order ephemeral streams
Pat	Pleistocene alluvial terrace
Hat	Holocene alluvial terrace

River channels and gullies (Qf or Hf)

Qfg	First- to second-order gully cut into bedrock
Qfr	River channel incised to bedrock
Qff	Active floodplain and point bars (below 100 yr flood stage)
Qfc	Palaeo-channels

Colluvium (Qc or Hc)

Qc	General areas of colluvium
Qcg	Gravelly colluvium
Qcf	Fine grained colluvium
Qca	Transitional alluvial/colluvial units
Qcc	Active talus cones
Qct	Triangular talus facets (separated from source on upstream end)
Qcl	Landslides or slumps

Modern anthropogenic (Mh) or pre-modern anthropogenic (Qh or Hh)

Mhm	Modern mine tailings
Hhm	Ancient mine tailings
Mhq	Modern quarries
Hhq	Ancient quarries
Hhf	Sediments trapped behind anthropogenic structures and terraces
Hht	Anthropogenic terraces

Bedrock (B)

Bo	Undifferentiated ophiolites
Bp	Pillow basalt
Bd	Sheeted dike
Bb	Basal group
Bu	Undifferentiated sedimentary rock
Bl	Limestone

measure (plate I), erosional landforms, soil stratigraphy, and the presence or absence of agricultural terraces and check dams (a hillslope terrace contours across an hillslope trapping colluvium, while a check dam crosses a river, rill, or gully and traps alluvial sediment). A field entitled

Table 3.5 Geomorphological observations and classifications

Stability

stable	A horizon intact across surface
unstab	A horizon removed from over 30% of surface
eroded	A horizon removed from entire surface and sub-A horizons exposed extensively
strip	All surface soil and sediment stripped from surface
incise	Actively incising channels and gullies
dep	Surface being buried by active deposition
cons	Anthropogenic construction
both	Marked variability in erosion characteristics across surface

Erosion landforms

rill	Surface bisected by active rills
gully	Surface bisected by active gullies
bound	Surface bounded by active gullies
none	Surface has no rills or gullies
fill	Gullies are filled behind checkdams

Soil stratigraphy

soil	Soils on surface are intact
thin	Soil on surface has been partially stripped and thinned
k	Carbonate soil horizon exposed at surface
strip	Soil has been stripped from surface
none	Soil has not formed substantially on surface

Agricultural terraces and check dams

Yes	Stone hillslope terraces or check dams present on surface
None	Stone hillslope terraces or check dams absent

Note: Space left blank if not observed on aerial photograph and no field check. Presence of check dams was often noted in the "surfmod" field.

"surfmod" was used to provide room to catalogue other observations of each polygon, for example, the name of a town on the unit.

GEOMORPHOLOGICAL MAPPING OF SIAS

We conducted a high-resolution geomorphological investigation at every SIA (except SIAs 1 and 11, where the landscape had been obliterated by modern open-cast mining). These studies included the production of a map at an appropriate scale for comparison with the archaeological data and detailed descriptions of the subsurface stratigraphy and soils wherever exposures were available. These maps are generally represented as a separate layer in the GIS as the data collected were not always compatible with the small-scale geomorphological map described above. Thus, the classifications of the data collected follow the general guidelines presented here, but may vary slightly as required by the stratigraphy encountered at each particular location.

Subsurface investigations focused on describing the soils and sediments within a particular sequence.

The sediments were classified on the basis of grain size distributions, sedimentary structures, lithological facies, and degrees of weathering. Lithostratigraphy was then used to interpret the environment of deposition at a given point in time. Standard soil descriptions were made of morphostratigraphic units of interest as well as soil catenas (cross-slope sequences) to show the topographical control on soil development. Soil development could then be used as an indicator of the relative age of a depositional unit, as well as an indicator of human impact on the surface.

Where they were available in surface exposures, we collected detrital charcoal and artifacts to provide geochronological control on the stratigraphy. Both types of fossils provided maximum ages for the sediments in which they were included. Charcoal samples were submitted for radiocarbon analysis by conventional or AMS procedures. Bulk soil was also collected for radiocarbon analysis, a procedure that is generally considered to yield a Mean Residence Time (MRT) age estimate (Trumbore 2000). Because young charcoal continues to be incorporated into the soil after the landform has stabilized, these MRT ages must be younger than the age of the original landform on which the soil developed.

ESTIMATION OF EROSION

In a limited number of landscapes within the SCSP area, we carried out high-resolution geomorphological studies to estimate the rates and quantities of erosion within the landscape. These studies can be grouped into two broad categories: landscape deflation studies and serendipitous sediment trap studies. Where possible, both types of analysis were completed in an individual drainage basin or landscape region. The areas of focused erosion studies were the Kouphos Basin (in part, SIA 7), Mitsero Basin (SIA 8), Lambadhiotissa Basin (see SCY114), and the southern hillslopes of Kriadhis, just north of Mitsero village.

The landscape deflation studies consisted of high-resolution morphometric mapping of each area. These are essentially topographic maps (with contour intervals of 10 to 50 cm) constructed either with a GPS or theodolite. Many of these maps have not been tied to an absolute elevational base. The morphostratigraphic surfaces (for example, an alluvial terrace) were then identified on the topographical grid, and synthetic surfaces were drawn to reconstruct the former landscape at the position of the terrace. The volume of rock and sediment that must have been removed to create the present landscape was calculated by comparing the synthetic landscape with the modern landscape and, as it were, subtracting the difference. If an age estimation for the reconstructed landscape is available, then a rate of erosion can be calculated if one assumes that erosion has been constant subsequent to the incision of the surface (for a detailed description of the method see Gerth 1998).

Human-constructed check dams are found commonly within eroding basins. The sediment trapped behind the check dams stems from the upstream parts of the basin and can be used to estimate the volume of sediment coming downstream. Stratigraphic study of the check dams and their associated sediments shows that individual dams were constructed by up to ten different wall-building events. Each wall was built on top of and usually slightly behind the preceding wall. As each individual wall is associated with a package of sediment capped by an agricultural soil, there was some significant time lapse between each wall-building event. Changes in the lithology of the sediments indicate changes in erosion processes upstream. Detrital charcoal and soil organic matter are common in these sequences, and so numeric age control is relatively straightforward. Changes in the rate of erosion upstream can be calculated by comparing the sedimentation rates of each package of sediment.

3.5 Geobotanical Procedures and Satellite Imagery Interpretation

Neil Urwin

SCSP's geobotanical investigations aimed to test the hypotheses that vegetation patterns can indicate past human activities and that certain patterns revealed on satellite images can be used as a predictive tool to discover such locations of human activity (see chapter 2.4). To achieve this we carried out an extensive survey of the vegetation over archaeological sites during two field seasons (June 1996 and August through September 1998). Data were analyzed statistically and, where significant results were obtained, were used as "ground truthing" or field reference ar-

eas for a series of focused satellite imagery interpretations and classifications.

To produce viable results, geobotanical examination had to focus on naturally vegetated areas, in other words an area unmanaged by humans, even if it includes weed species and agricultural escapes as well as native, indigenous, or endemic types. The number of POSIs occurring in such naturally vegetated areas was small. This was not unexpected as the revegetation of an archaeological site implies a degree of abandonment unusual in this extensively exploited landscape. However, this factor limited to nine POSIs the number of cases in which we could consider these hypotheses.

The design of the vegetation survey for these areas had to respond to the requirements for testing both hypotheses, namely statistical analysis of sampled data to investigate whether geobotanical indicators existed and the application of remote sensing (in this case, satellite imagery) to these indicators. The sampling strategy, therefore, needed to determine the size of the sampling unit and what botanical data to collect.

SAMPLING UNIT (SU)

The choice of the SU size underpins all subsequent analyses and therefore warrants special consideration. The unit size for the geobotanical data collection was selected on the basis of a number of technical and practical criteria. Optimum SU size for multiple variables is chosen through field trials whereby increasing unit size is plotted against information collected in each. The optimum unit size comes at the point where an increase in SU size yields no, or minimal, increase in data.

This exercise showed that due to the limited number of plant species growing in the harsh environment of the study area, the unit size that sampled over 90% of the species present is quite small, around 5 x 5 m (25 m²). However, the sparseness and uneven spatial distribution of species meant that a larger SU size, on the order of 10 x 10 m, was needed before the spatial abundance (as measured by percentage cover) was accurately sampled.

Several other considerations contributed to the selection of 10 x 10 m as the standard SU size. This SU size was found to be sufficiently small to pick up vegetational features associated with small archaeological features (spoil heaps, smelting sites) without compromising sampling on the larger ones (slag and sherd scatters).

SU size was also influenced by the requirement to investigate remote sensing applications. The imagery chosen for this aspect of the survey was SPOT Panchromatic imagery, which provides the maximum spatial resolution (smallest pixel size) of readily available imagery, namely 10 x 10 m. A ground SU size of comparable proportions would be needed to take advantage of this spatial resolution.

In the field, "belt" transects were laid across individual POSIs consisting of an adjoining series of 10 x 10 m quadrats. In this way the transects could be used to sample both the vegetation on the POSI and the vegetation adjoining it. A control was thus established so that by comparing adjoining quadrats along the transect, or adjacent quadrats where transects were not possible, it would be possible to detect any change in the vegetation because of conditions within the POSI.

COLLECTION OF VEGETATION DATA

The type of data collected needed to be suitable for statistical analysis to test the first hypothesis (to investigate whether geobotanical indicators exist) and for the application of satellite imagery to test the second hypothesis (to investigate site prediction using remote sensing of the indicators).

Data commonly collected in geobotanical surveys fall into three broad categories (Brooks and Johannes 1990). These are species presence/absence; species density/spacing; and species cover. Species presence/absence is self explanatory and includes no spatial measures. Species density/spacing (Braun-Blanquet 1932), on the other hand, records spatial data, but is assessed on a qualitative scale of five classes, with no quantitative spatial measures. Species cover (Grieg-Smith 1964) is usually expressed as a percentage and is based on the assumption that the above-ground parts of a plant, called the canopy, are projected on the ground. The concepts of layering (tree layer over shrub/understory layer over herb/ground cover layer) and overlapping within layers means that the total cover of all species within an SU will often exceed 100%.

Since the geobotanical relationships to be examined were expected to be at the community level rather than the individual level, and since the satellite imagery data were based on the reflection from the sum total of land cover entities within a pixel, we concluded that a spatial data set for the vegetation was essential. Of the two spatial data set types, species density/spacing was rejected because the assessment was considered to be too coarse to pick up the subtle changes in vegetation that might be encountered over sites and that statistical analysis is capable of detecting. To investigate vegetation change at the small scale imposed by the sampling strategy, the most detailed, spatially related data set was required; this is provided by species cover.

Accordingly, all identifiable plant species present within an SU in each of three layers were recorded for their projective foliage cover. The layers sampled were the tree layer, the understory (shrub) layer, and the ground cover layer. Species were identified and taxa reported by primary reference to the standard botanical reference for the area (Meikle 1977). The percentage cover of bare soil and bare rock was also sampled within each unit. (The statistical analysis chosen ensured that SUs would not be correlated on the basis of having similarly large proportions of bare ground, especially if the relative abundance of their respective species arrays were different.)

Field techniques were developed using a measured and taped 10 x 10 m quadrat, initially gridded into 2 x 2 m squares. Percentage cover of species within each grid square was estimated by eye and added together to give the measure for the whole quadrat.

STATISTICAL ANALYSIS

To determine whether the vegetation on POSIs was significantly different from the vegetation adjoining or surrounding them required a particular kind of statistical analysis. This analysis needed to illuminate the degree of similarity and dissimilarity among and between a set of SUs based upon multiple variables represented by their species cover data. Additionally, the analysis needed to do this without subjecting the data to distorting manipulations that might have masked or changed the original, spatial nature of the data set, and so reduce its validity as a selector of reference areas for any subsequent satellite imagery interpretations. The multivariate analysis considered to be the most suitable, given the foregoing conditions, was the hierarchical cluster analysis.

This analytical technique is modified from the original work on cluster analysis as a simple distance matrix comparison between variables by Lance and Williams (1968) and has been further examined by Everitt (1974) and Hartigan (1975). The hierarchical analysis has intuitive appeal because it is based on the underlying principle that at each stage of clustering the variance within clusters is minimized with respect to the variance between clusters (Ludwig and Reynolds 1988). In this way it encompasses the duality of "homogeneity within clusters and heterogeneity between clusters" (Brooks and Johannes 1990). This duality provides a safeguard against false correlations (for instance, a correlation between SUs based on similar large percentage cover scores for a single variable, such as bare soil).

The usual way of summarizing the results of a hierarchical cluster analysis is a dendrogram. Ludwig and Reynolds (1985) describe the process of delimiting homogeneous groups of SUs from the information provided by clustering (cutting the stems of the dendrogram) as a subjective one. The point separating the information into a set of discrete clusters is, in most cases, readily apparent, but it should also be chosen with some knowledge of the data set and the potential for clustering it contains.

To maximize the likelihood that any changes in the vegetation community revealed by the cluster analysis were the result of environmental features associated with the site of archaeological interest, only those SUs within the same geomorphological area were compared. Thus, any differences identified would be less likely attributable to changes in geology or soils and would more likely reflect real changes in the vegetation.

Initially, all species within each SU were used as variables in the cluster analysis. This included species with a cover of less than 2%. Percentage cover scores below this level frequently represented a single occurrence of a species (especially in the shrub stratum) in a 100 m² quadrat. A second phase of clustering was then undertaken using as variables only those species whose cover scores 2% or more within an SU. This procedure was based upon the assumption that those species with a spatial abundance of < 2% in a quadrat were occasional or opportunistic occurrences and did not characterize the vegetation community as a whole. However, it was recognized that these individual occurrences often represented valid geobotanical indicators themselves. The two phases of clustering therefore made it possible to identify sites where the whole species array best indicated the site and those where changes in the relative abundance of community dominants indicated the site. The distinction between species-level and community-level indicators was important, since only those sites that showed differentiation at the community level have a chance of being remotely detected.

In some cases, where a cluster contained a discrete grouping of SUs of on-site vegetation but was "contaminated" by a small number of off-site control units, a further examination of within-cluster relationships between sample units was required. An ordination analysis (after Goodall 1954) was chosen for this. Although the results of an ordination analysis often suggest discrete groupings, it is not primarily a method of grouping, but rather of arranging samples in relation to a multidimensional series or continuum (that is, real-world vegetation patterns). Its use in this analysis is based upon the work of Jensen (1979), who showed that a seemingly natural and useful community grouping may follow secondarily from the results of an ordination analysis applied to subsets of larger data sets already split by grouping/clustering.

The most readily applicable ordination strategy is Principal Components Analysis (PCA) because it extracts the maximum amount of variance from an already grouped data set. In PCA, the scores from a resemblance matrix of all variables are extracted in descending order of magnitude, such that the corresponding PCA components represent successively greater to lesser amounts of variation in the matrix. Hence the first few PCA components (usually two, so that the results can be depicted as a two-dimensional scatter plot) will represent the largest percentage of the total variation. PCA can also operate successfully on a small data set provided it is free of outliers, although in general at least five cases (SUs) for each observed variable is considered a minimum.

Multivariate clustering of the botanical data sampled for eight sites of archaeological interest with natural vegetation indicated a significantly different on-site vegetation for a number of them when compared with control (off-site) vegetation samples. Sites that showed significantly different vegetation at the community level were investigated further for their predictive value via remote sensing (satellite imagery). Those that showed differentiation only at the species level, although exhibiting positive geobotanical correlation, were considered unsuitable for remote sensing investigation, since the differences most likely would be undetectable at the ground resolution of the satellite imagery.

SATELLITE IMAGERY INTERPRETATION

Development of the Satellite Imagery Application. The most commonly used form of remote sensing in archaeology has been aerial photography, employed successfully since World War I for detection of varied features and landscape patterns. The development of aerial photographic media has progressed through black-and-white photography, color photography, black-and-white infrared photography, color infrared photography, multispectral photography, radar scanning, and microwave imagery. Gummerman and Lyons (1971:131), writing at a time when the use of satellite imagery for land survey was in its infancy, summarized the main applications of each medium and noted the decrease in spatial resolution through the progression. Although these authors and others (see, for example, Stringer and Cook 1974; Lyon 1975) point out that there has been a concurrent and extremely valuable increase in spectral resolution in the later media, this has not been directly compensatory. Instead, the later forms of imagery, including satellite imagery, which lack the spatial resolution of photography, have mainly been promoted for their ability to provide a synoptic overview which is "as necessary in archaeology as the spotting and identification of individual cultural features" (Gummerman and Lyons 1971:131).

The synoptic overview application underlay much of the satellite imagery use in archaeology over the next two decades. Well-known and influential examples of such applications occur in the work of Stringer and Cook (1974), Pope and Dahlin (1989), Madry (1987), and Cox (1992). All used satellite imagery for its ability to provide a regional or subregional perspective on the patterns of landscape and distribution of sites. The advantage of satellite imagery for this kind of work is threefold (Ireland and Urwin 1993):

- It provides a regional perspective available only through aerial photography with large and cumbersome mosaics.
- It provides a cost-effective coverage of large areas.

- It corrects or minimizes many of the common and frustrating deficiencies in photography, such as cloud cover, distortion, shadow, and lack of georeferencing.

Each of the surveys cited, however, and many others not referenced here also used the special applications related to spectral resolution offered by these products in their analyses. Stringer and Cook (1974) and Cox (1992) used the infrared wavelengths of multispectral satellite imagery to map large-scale landform features in Alaskan archaeological village sites and Cumbrian peat lands, respectively. Madry (1987) used satellite imagery to help investigate the physical environment and its relationship to cultural features such as ancient road networks, political boundaries, and archaeological sites in the Burgundian landscape. Pope and Dahlin (1989) used satellite imagery in the investigation of large-scale spatial patterns associated with Mayan agriculture and settlement, following on, controversially, from work with radar imaging systems by Adams et al. (1981). The progression has been toward increasingly specialized applications of the multispectral satellite data, while still retaining the synoptic overview application of the imagery.

The present study operates at the lower end of the technology scale of remote sensing use, usually relegated to overview applications, and examines the characteristics of spatial resolution limitations and the potential to use them as part of the experimental design of a landscape survey. The imagery pixel, which is the limit of spatial resolution, is treated in the present study as a form of data-sampling unit, paralleling the use of SUs in the multivariate cluster analysis of the vegetation quadrats.

Imagery data comes in the form of averaged light signatures from everything reflecting light within a pixel, for each pixel comprising an image. Rather than mourning the loss of feature detail within the 100 m^2 of the pixel, the experimental design has made use of the fact that the pixel light signature is an accumulation of all light emissions from within the pixel. The design is based upon the assertion that the resultant light signature of a pixel is influenced by all the light-reflecting features within it and that these influences must at some stage be sufficient to produce an average light signature for that pixel which is different from that of an adjoining pixel lacking those features. Therefore, a classification of the image by a strategy that selects for the appropriate similarities and differences among and between the pixels will be, at least partly, classifying on the effect of the sum of those internal features, that is, at the subpixel scale.

This assertion is less far-reaching and therefore less exacting when it is recognized that the present study is not looking at small archaeological features but rather at the percentage cover patterns of the dominant species that make up the vegetation community on and around those features. Nevertheless, focusing at such a small scale brings with it a range of methodological considerations to ensure that sites are located with very high accuracy on the image and that the classification strategies using data derived from such a tight focus on the image will produce valid results.

Imagery classification. The first consideration in selecting the imagery type for the investigation was spatial resolution. Beyond this study's requirements related to the selection of vegetation quadrat size, it was also critical that the maximum level of spatial resolution in commercially available satellite imagery be used, which necessitated the use of panchromatic SPOT imagery with a 10 m ground resolution.

Use of panchromatic imagery limited the satellite data to wavelengths in the visible spectrum. Given the types of areas under investigation, this posed no significant problem. The subject variable was surface vegetation, not subsurface conditions that might require the additional use of infrared wavelengths. The nature of the vegetation also obviated the need for data from light wavelengths outside the visible spectrum. The vegetation is a perennial, woody shrubland in a semiarid environment that shows community changes through changes in relative abundance of species dominants rather than through chlorosis, senescence, or dwarfism/gigantism, which would only be revealed with the use of multispectral imagery data (further discussion in Ireland and Urwin 1993).

Two 1990 SPOT panchromatic images (courtesy, the Cyprus Department of Forestry, Ministry of Agriculture) were used to provide full coverage of the study area, along with a July 1986 archive panchromatic SPOT scene with full coverage. Where possible, the later image was used in order to minimize the likelihood of land cover changes between the date of image capture and the field sampling. Data en-

hancement and classification of the SPOT digital data were undertaken using the image processing software Idrisi for Windows version 1.01.004, which allowed processing both in the lab and in the field.

Initially, the raw images were resampled onto a UTM grid. Clusters of SUs (or vegetation quadrats), sorted by the clustering analysis into discrete groups, were accurately located on the images using recent aerial photography, which had previously been digitized and resampled to the same UTM grid by MapInfo or, where available, by direct UTM coordinates from field GPS readings. Only those clusters that showed statistically significant results in relation to the archaeological sites and that reflected vegetation community makeup (that is, from data sets of species variables with > 2% areal coverage) were admitted.

Clusters were delineated as polygons on the image using Idrisi's on-screen digitizing facility. The completed polygons representing the clusters on the image are called training areas. In effect, these are reference areas that train the computer to recognize this combination of pixels anywhere else on the image. The training areas were converted by Idrisi into *subject area signatures*. This is a measure of the cumulative light signatures of all pixels within the training-area polygons expressed as maxima, minima, and mean wavelength frequencies. Training areas for deriving signatures of other areas on the image, for which values are needed to provide the background to the classification (such as village areas, water bodies, quarries, grain/grass fields), were also added. These were interpreted easily on the image and required little field validation.

Once assembled, the subject area signatures can be used to classify the satellite image into a thematic map; this is a geographic extrapolation of each of the subject area signatures over the rest of the image, identifying and classifying areas with the same signature as the reference areas. The area signature for a cluster of vegetation SUs known to be growing over a POSI is compared with the light signatures of all areas on the image to show if and where matches occur. Similarly, the signatures for background areas, such as forest or quarries, are also matched with any other like areas on the image. In this way, the iterative series of classifications results in a new map of the image based upon the nominated themes of the subject area signatures (plate II).

Like all image processing software, Idrisi incorporates a number of classification strategies based upon matching all light signatures. The one used for classification of the SCSP vegetation data is the MINDIST (minimum distance) strategy. Unlike the alternatives, it does not rely on measures of covariance between adjoining pixels and, therefore, does not require a statistically significant number of sample areas for its training signatures. Instead it compares the mean light signatures of adjacent pixels (with +/- standard deviation) and, therefore, does not require a large number of pixels for each reference signature. This feature was essential for the SCSP exercise, where light signatures for the vegetation over areas of archaeological interest often comprised only three or four pixels.

The use of satellite imagery classification to form a thematic map is an iterative process requiring intensive operator input. The components of the image are refined until the best classification is achieved. To safeguard against operator-induced bias in the classification of the areas of interest, the "best picture" is defined as the one in which all the other major components (which are background values and largely independent of the area of interest) are mapped correctly. The complete classification of an image means that all pixels of that image have been assigned to a signature group on the basis of the classification strategy.

In this case, the MINDIST strategy assigns pixels to a signature group if it is within a standard deviation of the mean of that signature. Thus, when all pixels have been assigned to signature classes and the background signatures have been mapped correctly and checked by aerial photography and field inspections, the signatures of vegetation over archaeological sites (including the original training area and the extrapolation to other predicted sites) are assumed to have been assigned consistently.

Since the SUs within the clusters were only those from within a homogeneous geomorphological area, it follows that the highest confidence areas of the results of the satellite imagery classification (in this case, a thematic map) are those areas within the same geomorphological boundary. Any findings on the predictive value of the process are therefore confined to the geomorphological area within which the classification is located. If it proves that vegetation change can be detected and that change detection has a role in site prediction, then it will be for these small subscenes rather than for the survey universe as a whole.

3.6 Archaeometallurgical Procedures
Vasiliki Kassianidou

RECORDING OF ARCHAEOMETALLURGICAL SITES

The survey area includes a number of archaeometallurgical POSIs ranging in date from prehistory to the twentieth century AD. These POSIs can be divided into three major groups representing the three major steps in the process of extracting metal from its ores: mines; areas where SCSP teams found evidence of ore processing in the stages before smelting, such as beneficiation and roasting; and smelting sites that, apart from the small primary smelting workshop at Politiko *Phorades* 1 (SCY100), are, in fact, major slag heaps representing large-scale production over a considerable period of time.

Often, the three groups are all represented within the same SIA, as in the case of SIA 7 (Politiko *Kokkinorotsos*); in other cases, only one part of the process is represented, namely smelting, as is the case with the two larger slag heaps at Mitsero *Sykamies* (SCY024) and Mitsero *Kouloupakhis* (SCY021).

The recording and scientific analysis of archaeometallurgical finds and POSIs has played an important part in SCSP. A number of archaeologists specializing in ancient metallurgy (Rod Clough, Vasiliki Kassianidou, Sven Van Lokeren, and Haddon Wright) have participated in the fieldwork, both as field team leaders and as a team specifically involved in recording remains associated with ancient mining and extractive metallurgy. At the beginning of each season, fieldwalkers were introduced to basic archaeometallurgical terms, and were shown examples of common archaeometallurgical finds, such as different types of ores and fluxes, slags, and refractories. This proved particularly important in the case of some refractories, namely tuyère fragments, which are often rather small in size and could easily be overlooked or misinterpreted as pottery. To impress upon fieldwalkers the importance of these finds, they were given handouts explaining the various processes involved in the extraction of the metal, the raw materials and tools involved, and the waste products left behind.

The method used to record POSIs was developed on the basis of suggestions made in several specialized publications (Bachmann 1982a; Craddock 1989; Kassianidou 2001), as well as on the experience of other large-scale archaeometallurgical projects already published (for example, Timna [Rothenberg 1990a, 1990b]; Huelva Province [Rothenberg and Blanco Freijeiro 1981]; Thasos [Wagner and Weisgerber 1988]). Special attention was paid to all these POSIs, which were recorded in detail. General plans and section drawings of each POSI were made in situ. Because these archaeometallurgical POSIs formed an integral part of the survey area, the field teams conducted intensive block survey in the units around them, while various specialists analyzed and studied the material that came from them. SCSP's holistic approach enabled us to place each area where some type of metallurgical activity took place in its appropriate chronological, cultural, and environmental context. As a result, we are in a better position to formulate models regarding the organization of the copper industry in the landscape through time (see chapter 2.6).

Mines. Almost all we know about ancient mines in the SCSP area comes from the little that has survived extensive open cast mining during the twentieth century AD. Along the walls of these mines, we have detected the remains of galleries, adits, and shafts (vertical or near-vertical passages linking the surface with an ore body), which in the case of Mitsero *Kokkinoyia* (SIA 11) are sometimes lined with wooden supports. The position of all such supports has been recorded in maps and section drawings; in the case of wood-supported galleries, we have made detailed drawings showing their construction.

Adits—horizontal or gently sloping passages driven from the surface to an ore body—have also been recorded in areas where deposits were found to be uneconomical for modern, large-scale, open-cast exploitation. The problem with such adits, whether isolated or clustered (as is the case with those found in the open-cast mines), is that they are extremely difficult to date. As was the case in antiquity, modern mining initially was based on systems of adits, shafts, and galleries (a level or mined-out area within the mine); it was only in the 1960s that mining by open-cast methods began in Cyprus. Furthermore, mining companies often sank exploratory adits in areas where there was a possibility of finding economically productive ore deposits. Unless pottery (as is the case with one of the adits in Mitsero *Kokkinoyia*), tools, or remains of tool marks are found in the galleries or on their walls, we cannot be sure that any of these constructions are ancient. Nonetheless, their

size, shape, and location within the geological deposits may offer some indication. The wood-supported galleries of the Kokkinoyia mine are perhaps the best candidates for ancient mining remains: Their method of construction and the treatment of the wood is similar to those of the ancient galleries discovered when twentieth-century mining first began (Bruce 1937:648). Indeed, some of the wood from Kokkinoyia has already been analyzed by radiocarbon and found to date to three different periods: ninth to seventh centuries BC; sixth to third centuries BC; and third to fifth centuries AD (Panayiotou 1989a:85).

Spoil heaps and roasting remains (*Vasiliki Kassianidou with Peter Grave*). At SCY022 (in SIA 1, Agrokipia *Kriadhis*) and SCY116 (in SIA 7, Politiko *Kokkinorotsos*), we recorded spoil heaps of material derived from mining, beneficiation, and the roasting processes. In both cases, modern workings had sectioned these remnants and exposed them. With permission from the Cypriot Department of Antiquities, these sections were cleaned back, photographed, and recorded in detailed drawings. The components of each layer were described in as much detail as possible and, subsequently, some samples were collected from each one, both representative (most common material in the section) and random (fragments picked from the section without any prior screening). No pottery was recovered in either of these sections, but in both we recovered small amounts of charcoal, which enabled us to date these remains by radiocarbon analyses.

In both POSIs some strata consisted of very finely crushed material, and sediment column samples were taken for micromorphological analysis. As preservation of the structure and orientation of the sediment column is essential for this type of analysis, the column first had to be partially consolidated in situ. An open-topped container was used as a resin reservoir against the section, the edges of the container were pressed into the section, pegged into position, then sealed with a putty mixture. A polyester two-part resin was mixed and slowly poured into the container to promote resin infiltration of the now-isolated section of the column. The reservoir was eventually filled to the top and the resin left overnight to penetrate further and harden (work coordinated by Dr. Peter Grave).

The following day, the partially consolidated and hardened column was labeled (with the top indicated) and removed from the section. It was placed into a resin-resistant, foil-lined ditch dug to the same dimensions but deeper, to allow additional resin to encase the sample fully. The block was again left overnight to harden and a second label applied to the surface. The resin-encased blocks were then shipped to the University of New England (Armidale, New South Wales, Australia) for further preparation. This involved a more continuous resin consolidation, using vacuum impregnation of a three-part polymer. The resulting consolidated blocks could then be sectioned readily and polished without damaging the sediment structures. Both thick and thin sections were prepared for structural and mineralogical analysis.

The large-scale features of the section were examined and recorded with a Wild macroscope equipped with a rotating stage, transmitted polarizing light source and trinocular photographic head. A petrological microscope was used to study microscopic and mineralogical features of the sediment, and a Joel Scanning Electron Microscope (SEM) equipped with an Energy Dispersive Spectrometer (EDS) provided secondary electron imaging and an elemental profile of the section. Analysis at each level was done to ensure that the same sequence of sediments was being examined at each analytic scale (analytical results are presented in the POSI reports).

Slag heaps. The vast slag heaps could not possibly be sectioned with simple archaeological tools, such as picks (small or large) and trowels. Quarrying for road metal, however, has produced large bulldozer cuts that often left sections visible in the slag heap so that the stratigraphy could be recorded. Over four field seasons, we described and recorded in detail three major slag heaps: Mitsero *Kouloupakhis* (SCY021), Mitsero *Sykamies* (SCY024) and Mitsero *Kokkinoyia* (SCY219). Sections were cleaned back, drawn, and photographed, while samples of slag, charcoal, and pottery were collected from each of the strata. The charcoal and pottery enabled us to date the smelting activities and to suggest the time it took for such slag heaps to form. We have also undertaken scientific analysis of slag samples from all slag heaps. The analysis of samples from different layers of the same heap enabled us to consider possible technological and organizational changes, while examination of different slag heaps allowed us to compare the ore and flux deposits these workshops used.

In the case of Politiko *Phorades* 1 (SCY100), we also had to take into consideration the singular na-

ture of the material and the ongoing erosion of the site by the modern stream. We therefore decided to collect all refractories and diagnostic samples of slag (on the basis of shape, size, type, and adhesions/inclusions) that had eroded out of the section and were lying on the bank of the modern creek. The section was cleaned back and recorded using the same method as the other archaeometallurgical sections, but with an important geomorphological contribution because we needed to understand the changing activities of the stream.

ANALYSIS OF ARCHAEOMETALLURGICAL FINDS

In the survey units themselves, the teams collected diagnostic metal objects, slag, ores, and fluxes, and counted all nondiagnostic material. This information was recorded on field sheets, entered into the survey unit database, and exported to the GIS for spatial analysis. The finds brought back to the fieldhouse were examined and described wherever relevant, and this information was entered into the archaeometallurgy database. This gave us important information on the distribution of archaeometallurgical activity throughout the entire survey area, as well as in the specific SIAs and POSIs. Going through samples collected by the field teams, for example, we found in two units fragments of plano-concave slag cakes characteristic of the smelting workshop at Politiko *Phorades* 1 (SCY100); before the discovery of Phorades such slag cakes would have presented a real enigma.

SCIENTIFIC ANALYSIS OF THE FINDS
Vasiliki Kassianidou with Sven Van Lokeren

Throughout the span of the project, we collected hundreds of samples of slag, furnaces, furnace wall material, tuyères, ores, and fluxes. These materials now form a substantial reference collection of archaeometallurgical finds from ancient Cyprus. Clearly, we could not analyze them all, so we selected material from POSIs where metallurgical activity was intense: the three slag heaps (SCY021, SCY024, SCY219), the two spoil heaps/roasting sites (SCY022, SCY116), and two other POSIs with significant amounts of slag (SCY011, SCY204). The study of finds from Politiko *Phorades* 1 (SCY100) will be published separately although, for comparison, ten samples from Phorades were also analyzed as part of this project.

Scientific analysis of slags from all POSIs except Mitsero *Kokkinoyia* (SCY219) was undertaken at the National Centre for Scientific Research (*Demokritos*) in Athens, at the University of Glasgow, and at the Institute of Archaeology, University College, London. The samples, mainly slags and furnace conglomerate, were described and then sectioned with a diamond saw. The slice was set in epoxy resin and polished according to standard metallographic methods. Polished sections were subsequently studied under a reflected light microscope as well as a SEM equipped with an EDS.

The copper slags were analyzed for major, minor, and trace elements by combining the analytical results of three different X-ray fluorescence (XRF) techniques. These analyses were carried out in collaboration with A.G. Karydas, S. Galanopoulos, and T. Paradellis, all from the Laboratory for Material Analysis Institute of Nuclear Physics, NCSR *Demokritos*. The specific nature of the slags, namely the high iron content, determined an experimental methodology quite different from the one that is usually adopted in XRF spectrometry. Quantitative analysis of copper slags using either XRF spectrometry with a conventional X-ray source (X-ray tube, radioisotopes) or SEM and PIXE is considerably reduced in accuracy because of the intense background that is recorded below the iron characteristic X-rays. In this experimental approach, three different X-ray sources were used to produce almost monoenergetic incident X-ray radiations, each of which excited selectively a certain group of elements. This procedure resulted in an improved accuracy of the concentrations obtained (better signal/background ratio, minimization of secondary interelement corrections), and in lower minimum limits of detection for some elements of interest (sulfur, selenium).

The XRF techniques employed for the analysis of the copper slags are the following :

- *Proton-induced XRF.* The principle of this technique is that a low-energy proton beam is used at first to produce the characteristic X-rays from a primary target. This X-ray radiation induces fluorescent X-rays from the sample under analysis (Karydas and Paradellis 1993; 1998). For the analysis of copper slags, a chromium-pure metal was chosen as a primary target, and a proton beam of energy 1.5 MeV

was used. The advantage of the technique is that the chromium characteristic X-rays excite selectively only the elements Al, Si, S, Cl, K, Ca, and Ti. The absence in the recorded X-ray spectra of the iron characteristic X-rays offers a significantly better signal/background ratio in the energy region where the above elements are detected.

- *Secondary-target-tube-excited XRF.* A secondary target transforms the composite X-ray spectrum emitted from an X-ray tube to an almost monoenergetic X-ray radiation. Since selenium is an element of great importance in the analysis of copper slags, the experimental conditions were optimized for its determination. Thus, an yttrium oxide (Y_2O_3) pellet was employed as the secondary target of a Mo anode X-ray tube, and an xyz geometry was employed to minimize the spectral background (Zarkadas et al. 1998). Using this technique, we determined the concentrations of the elements V, Cr, Mn, Fe, Ni, Cu, Zn, Ga, Ge, As, Br, and Pb.

- *Radioisotope-induced XRF.* For the quantitative analysis of elements with atomic numbers in the range $38 < Z < 68$, an annular radioactive source (Am-241) was used. This source, after proper filtration, emits a monoenergetic radiation of energy 59.6 keV. This mode of analysis was included in our experimental procedure, as in some cases the Barium oxide concentration was found to be varied in the 0.1–1% w/w range.

The analysis of all recorded X-ray spectra was performed by AXIL. For each detected element, a calibration constant was determined experimentally by measuring the fluorescence signal either from a compound or a pure form of this element. This procedure results in calibration constants with an uncertainty of about 4%.

After analyzing all the recorded spectra, the determined peak areas were converted to elemental concentrations using a simple iteration scheme. For every analyzed sample, the corresponding data from the three X-ray sources were considered together in this scheme. The necessary interelement secondary corrections are much less important when adopting this procedure, thus improving the accuracy of the results. The uncertainty of the measured concentrations is estimated to be about 5 to 7%.

Apart from bulk chemical analysis, phase and microanalysis of the samples were also carried out. Polished sections were prepared following standard metallographic procedures and these were studied under reflected light of a Leica metallographic microscope. Some of the samples were also studied under a SEM (Leo Microscopy Stereoscan S360, University of Glasgow), equipped with an integrated energy dispersive X-ray microanalyzer (Linch Analytical AN 10855). The microanalyzer enabled the determination of the chemical composition of the various mineral phases, as well as that of the metallic inclusions within these samples. In an effort to confirm the identification of the crystal phases, some of the samples were also analyzed by X-ray diffraction (XRD).

Scientific analysis of the Mitsero *Kokkinoyia* (SCY219) slags was undertaken at the Wolfson Laboratories, Institute of Archaeology, University College London. The slag samples, nine in total, were first morphologically and macroscopically investigated and described (Bachmann 1982a; Koucky and Steinberg 1982a). They were then prepared according to standard metallographic methods with subsamples being mounted in epoxy resin, followed by grinding and polishing (Scott 1991:61–69). Optical polarizing microscopy was supplemented by XRD mineral-phase identification. Finally, we undertook semiquantitative SEM-EDX analysis of the main mineral phases, metal-rich and matte inclusions, and any remaining ore or gangue encountered. This procedure was followed to allow comparative studies with other published and dated Iron Age material such as slags and metal finds from Ayia Varvara *Almyras* and the Sha survey (Fasnacht et al. 1992, 1996, 1997).

The results of all analyses are presented in chapter 5.4 and are discussed further under the relevant POSIs in chapter 4. All analytical work at Glasgow was supported by a grant from the National Geographic Society (NGS 5506-95).

3.7 Pottery Collection, Pottery Analysis, and GIS Mapping

Nathan Meyer and Timothy E. Gregory

As outlined in chapter 2.4, the study of pottery was a critical component of SCSP. Our goal was to develop a measurement of pottery (Pottery Index) that would indicate the strength of a specific period within a unit. Additionally, we wanted to be able to assign functional meaning to our pottery. Although very generalized at the level of the individual observation (see table 3.7 for functional categories), our intention was that the functional data would provide us with the opportunity to look at how these generalized categories might combine to create knowledge about a specific unit or across the survey universe. We aimed to do this by incorporating the pottery data into GIS maps that could convey more and different information than prose. Pottery study, then, was the key analytical aspect of our study of survey units in the broadest sense. Elsewhere in this monograph, we have discussed the critical mitigating evidence of geomorphology as it affects understanding our artifact observations (chapter 3.4). Geomorphological data, however, were only one of several observational or analytical factors affecting our pottery data.

QUANTITATIVE OBSERVATIONS

Quantitative field observations for SCSP were taken within standardized methods for recording the appearance of specific artifacts and ecofacts, including those that might affect artifact observations. Ecofacts of particular concern in this context were the percentage of the ground obscured by heavy vegetation, background confusion caused by other materials, and the effects of ambient light, as well as the analysis of the local geomorphology. Briefly, as fully evolved, the SCSP field strategy for developing solid quantitative pottery data was composed of four observations taken in the field: (1) the absolute count of pottery, (2) an estimation of percentage of ground obscured by vegetation, (3) an estimation of the severity of background confusion, and (4) an ordered sequence of observations meant to estimate the depth and state of erosion of sediments.

The degree to which these observations were consistent across field seasons, geographical areas, teams, and specific collection units is the measure of the comparability of the data. For this reason, the final quantitative analysis of SCSP pottery data had to follow these guidelines:

- 1993 data had internal inconsistencies and differences to the 1995 to 1997 data, including intensity measures, ecofact measures, and collection techniques. These factors make those data very difficult to use in a comparative fashion. The Period Confidence data (see further below, under *Analytical Strategies*) can be mapped to form a minimal expression for some (but not necessarily all potential) periods for any given unit. Therefore, across a specific period these data can be compared to data collected subsequently. As we finished the 1993 season, we were acutely aware that the mass of unknown pottery we were seeing in the units needed to be dealt with.

- Pottery data from the 1995 season were collected and read in a manner evolving toward our chronotype system. Thus, it is of variable structure and consistency. Materials perceived as diagnostic or potentially diagnostic for all periods were collected, giving us a relatively accurate understanding of the periods represented in the unit and confidence of that period designation. Our ability to project from what was collected to what was counted, however, is not as robust and structured as it is for 1996 to 1997. Therefore, for a given period, we can compare confidence data to other seasons but raw quantitative data must be used cautiously.

- In 1996 and 1997, the chronotype collection system was in place (and became more robust with time). Likewise, the chronotype pottery-reading system was in place with similar positive implications. For these seasons, therefore, we are able to project from quantities collected to quantities counted in a structured and replicable manner. These data can be compared with confidence within the 1996 to 1997 seasons and with care for the 1995 season. Period confidence data are comparable across these two seasons and can be used side-by-side with the 1993 data (for a specific period across all units) and with those from 1995 (for looking at all periods within a unit as well as a period across units) as well.

ANALYTICAL STRATEGIES

The analytical portion of SCSP's pottery studies was multifaceted and began in the field itself. We developed a pottery collection strategy with the following goals: (1) to attempt a complete visual inspection of

the surface and take a complete count of observed pottery; (2) to collect as few pieces of pottery as possible, for reasons of ethics and practicality—we did not feel entitled to strip the surface of artifacts, nor did we have the resources to process such a vast quantity of materials; (3) to collect pottery in a manner that achieved a completely representative sample of the observed material, thereby creating a structured relationship between materials observed and counted.

There is a clear tension between the items 2 and 3 in this list. In the 1993 and 1995 seasons, the collection strategy followed the practice common in survey projects in the eastern Mediterranean: Diagnostic pottery and lithics were collected from each survey unit and brought back to the project laboratory for analysis. This procedure has obvious methodological problems, chief among which is a failure to consider the relationship between the numbers of artifacts noted and counted in the field (overall density) and the examples collected and brought back to the laboratory. In addition, there are problems with the typical designation of diagnostic pottery as rims, handles, and so on, since many nondiagnostic sherds (for example, body sherds) can in fact provide important chronological and/or functional information. Finally, many projects necessarily grapple with the uneven knowledge of artifacts among members of the survey teams, resulting in a less than satisfactory sampling of the pottery within the areas examined.

While it was clear that we could not afford to collect all the materials we saw, we also believed that any collection method that focused on diagnostics (as commonly interpreted) would in no way bring back data truly representative of what was observed on the ground. All the same, we could not expect field teams to follow some complicated practice for collecting a standardized percentage of observed categories. As a compromise, we chose the following method. As field team members made their counts of pottery, (s)he collected one piece of each type that appeared different from all the others they had observed. In practice this meant that the team member picked up the first piece of pottery (s)he observed and each piece thereafter which seemed different. The axes of difference were the following: fabric (color, texture, inclusions), surface treatment (slips, glazes, decorative elements), vessel body part (rim, neck, neck/shoulder, handle, body, foot) and

Table 3.6 List of pottery fabrics

Code	Description
CD	Coarse Dark
CL	Coarse Light
CR	Coarse Red
FW	Fine Ware
PI	Pithos
T	Tile
TD	Thin Dark
TL	Thin Light
TR	Thin Red

Table 3.7 List of pottery functions

Code	Function	Usages
AR	Architectural	Domestic and public architecture
CU	Coarse Utility	Domestic cooking, domestic dining, light industry
FW	Fine Ware	Domestic dining, ritual dining, burials, offerings
HU	Heavy Utility	Domestic storage, light industry, heavy industry, transport
LU	Light Utility	Domestic dining, kitchen, light industry, burials, offerings
PI	Pithos	Nonportable storage, light industry, heavy industry
PO	Personal Object	Adornment, personal interaction
SYM	Symbolic	Domestic and public ritual, burial art, offerings, informational messaging
UNK	Unknown	Unknown
UT	Utility	General utility

thickness (roughly estimated). In theory, then, the collection of materials from a unit could include up to five pieces that were, for all practical purposes, identical. Crews were given training on reading pottery in this fashion. We believe that this system, in combination with our laboratory processes, was effective at gauging the kinds and amounts of pottery in the unit.

During analysis in the laboratory, we made extensive use of the chronotype system in the reading of the pottery and design of our database (for full discussion, see chapter 2.4; for list of chronotypes see appendix C). Pottery collected in the field was divided into batches. A batch is a group of pottery for which all the observations made under the chronotype system would be the same, for example, all AMCL (amphora, Classical) body sherds from a single unit would be described as one batch. This saved recording and keying time, without losing any information. Where possible, a batch was assigned a strongly typed chronotype during processing, for example ESB2 (Eastern Sigillata B II). Other batches, of necessity, were assigned a weakly typed chronotype,

such as COUNK (coarse ware, unknown). Pottery batches were weighed as a control for counts. Standardized observations were taken for form, fabric (table 3.6) and surface treatment. These readings were not strictly necessary for very strongly typed chronotypes but will prove invaluable to future work on the analysis of the weakly typed chronotypes.

Each chronotype was assigned to one (and only one) function (table 3.7). Clearly, we could not tell precisely what use each object had; this designation is intended as a device which divides the material into several mutually exclusive categories, based on the characteristics of the chronotype, what is known—or can be surmised—about its use and, often, its fabric.

Period confidence measure. Our initial attempt at assessing period components for each unit was the Period Confidence Measure. As specialists worked through the batches, they assigned a confidence rating for each of the period designations used by SCSP (see table 3.1). The period confidence measure is a combination of quantitative and subjective assessments. Thus, a unit with one or two objects probably assigned to a particular period might be given a certainty of 1, while a certainty of 3 would result if those objects were clearly derived from that period. Likewise, three or four confidently identified objects from a particular period would result in a certainty index of 5. There always is some degree of uncertainty that is difficult to quantify, and the experience of the individuals assigning the chronological components is an important asset. This, then, is the strength of our period confidence measure: it combines solid quantitative data with a judicious measure of subjective assessment. We relied upon period confidence measures to guide our revisit and POSI survey tactics, and to prompt further discussion and analysis of the pottery in these units.

Adjusting for field conditions. To make a meaningful comparison of the counts of pottery in one unit with another, we had to correct for both the size of the unit and the conditions within the unit that affected our ability to observe pottery on the surface. The correction for area is dealt with below (see *Factoring in Unit Area*). The correction for conditions within the unit—visibility and background confusion—is represented in the following schematic equation:

$$acp = cp + vc + bgc$$

where acp is adjusted count of pottery in a unit, cp is count of pottery in a unit, vc is correction for visibility, and bgc is correction for background confusion.

Precisely how visibility and background confusion should be factored here was a matter of debate. Though SCSP has certainly not solved this problem for all situations, our experimental data enabled us to solve it for our context. The specifics of this reasoning are given below (under *Experimental*).

Weighting appearance of specific chronotypes. Gross or factored counts of total pottery are valuable for assigning further stages of research. Ultimately, however, we want to discuss material occurrences in terms of specific periods. To get totals for a period, we had to add up the totals for specific batches of pottery from within the unit by chronotype. To arrive at these numbers, we had to build a relationship between the pottery collected and analyzed in the chronotype system, on the one hand, and on the other the counts of pottery seen but not collected in the units. A representation of this equation is:

$$pqc = acp * (cc/pc)$$

where pqc is projected quantity of chronotype, acp is adjusted count of pottery in a unit (from equation given above), cc is count of sherds in chronotype batch, and pc is count of pottery collected in a unit. The actual equation used was somewhat more complex. Our goal was to project what share of the pottery counted (of which we knew nothing other than the count) was taken by a specific chronotype represented in pottery collected. There was a consensus, however, on the part of those doing the pottery analysis, that the data were skewed. This skew, we reasoned, was the result of two specific factors: First, given our field collection technique, a strongly typed chronotype had an absolute limit to the number that would be collected, no matter how many were seen. The stronger the typing, the lower that number would be. Secondly, consider a situation where in a certain unit there are 100 sherds actually on the ground, divided into chronotype A and chronotype B, and that the ratio between them is 1:4 (20:80). If 50 of these sherds are discovered in nearly the same ratio (~10:40), and thus far 49 have been discovered, the probability that the fiftieth sherd will be of chronotype B is higher than that it will be of chronotype A. The actual probability would

be complex to calculate, and would have to take into consideration the relative obtrusiveness of the sherds, the degree of clustering, and so forth. Still, we felt this was notable enough to warrant consideration, particularly when taken with the first factor.

Our goal was not to increase the overall amount of pottery counted, but instead to affect that number as little as possible while rearranging how individual chronotype batches were weighted within that total. After doing various exploratory analyses of the data, we settled on a weighting of the counted chronotypes as follows:

$$wc = cc + ((cc - acc)/10)$$

where wc is weighted count of sherds in a chronotype batch, cc is count of sherds in a chronotype batch, and acc is average count of sherds per chronotype batch. This gave us less than a 1% error over nearly four thousand batches of pottery. Using wc in the above equation for projected chronotype count, we get the following amended equation:

$$pqc = acp * (wc/pc)$$

where pqc is projected quantity of chronotype, acp is adjusted count of pottery in a unit (from equation given above), wc is weighted count of sherds in a chronotype batch, and pc is count of pottery collected in a unit.

Factoring in unit area. At this point we had established a corrected total count of pottery for the unit and developed figures for the total number of sherds per period. All that remained was to factor both of these by the actual area of the unit in order to create comparability across units of different sizes. This, in fact, was done for all artifact classes. For pottery, it was accomplished simply by dividing the individual counts by the area of the unit and then scaling it so that it became a number that could effectively be mapped (that is, showed differences readable by the human eye). For an individual chronotype within a unit the equation we used was:

$$apqc = (pqc/a) * s$$

where apqc is projected chronotype count in a unit adjusted for area, pqc is projected chronotype count in a unit, a is area (derived from MapInfo polygons), and s is scaling number (10,000 was used).

Developing the pottery index. Once this was accomplished it was only a matter of adding up all sherds with chronotypes of the same period, at which point we obtained the expected number of sherds for a period based upon:

- how many sherds were counted in total for a unit (cp);
- how many sherds were collected for that unit (pc);
- a correction of that count based on visibility and background confusion (acp);
- how many sherds of a specific chronotype were collected (wc);
- the projected total of that chronotype (pqc) in the unit as a percentage of the adjusted total pottery: pqc = acp * (wc/pc);
- a factoring of that projected count for a chronotype so that it was equivalent across units of different sizes (apqc); and
- the sum of the apqc for a specific period.

This summing up for a specific period gives us the pottery index for that period in that unit. When mapped in the GIS, it allowed us at a glance to assess the relative presence of periods within a unit as well as across units. It could likewise be used with total counts of pottery to assess relative pottery presence across units. To summarize, the pottery index was (1) corrected for unit size, visibility, and background confusion; (2) based on a weighted projection of what percentage of the total observed pottery would be claimed by the collected chronotype batches.

REFLEXIVE DATA

Ultimately, the numbers we generated had to be situated within our own practice. Regional surveys have long attempted to generate information on their practice by capturing fuzzy data on the human and natural conditions within which quantitative observations are made. Examples of reflexive data would be whether the fieldwalker was feeling ill, whether it was blistering hot or cool and rainy, or whether the team was in a funk after four fruitless days in the hot sun. Before now, such data have not been leveraged into any systematic tool kit for factoring against observations. In this regard, SCSP made no methodological progress. Such progress will have to be predicated on extensive experimental collections targeted at a specific fuzzy data element (for example, running crews against seeded lots in a variety of temperatures). It is questionable whether the amount of cost and energy expended on these experiments could be afforded by any one project. If it is to be done, it will be done only over a number of years, across a number of projects. For SCSP then, such reflexive data remain at best anecdotal and useable only to question a specifically anomalous finding. For example, if a unit was expected to have a high density of pottery but turned out to have very little, it would be worth checking the team log books to see if excessive heat or tiredness might have affected data collection (see chapter 1.3 for examples).

Another class of reflexive data consists of the resurvey of units that have previously been visited. SCSP engaged in a variety of such efforts. Some of these were simple repeat visits where we used our standard field methodology. Others were total collections, geared toward providing some insight into the collection procedures we had established. Yet others were revisits during which we conducted intensive survey using gridded circles or other delineated subunits where team members scoured the ground on hands and knees. Unfortunately, we have had neither the time nor the resources to investigate fully the nature of our findings—a project that we will take on in subsequent fieldwork and publications.

EXPERIMENTAL DATA
Nathan Meyer and Robert Schon

A critical, and unfortunately underrepresented, class of reflexive data is experimental. We treat it separately because we regard its importance as vital. Survey data are often difficult to comprehend because we have no meaningful way to ascertain how effectively we are collecting those data. Experimental work, particularly seeding experiments, is important in this regard. SCSP's program of experimental archaeology was designed to help the project gain tighter control over data collected by fieldwalkers, by assessing the sherd discovery performance of our field teams. SCSP was sensitive to the fact that the data generated by survey archaeologists reflect not what we know as the archaeological record (what's out there), but rather the archaeological document (what we actually found) (Wandsnider

Table 3.8 Summary of experimental seeding fields

Field	Area (m²)	Visibility	Confusion	Sherds	Description
1	1250	70%	+	100	Stubble. Glare in early morning sun. Rocky soil matrix. Sherds in 2 clusters, plus sparse isolates.
2	3200	55%	++	50	Broad, sparse scatter. Some sherds in rock piles and field margins.
3	625	25%	+	20	Prickly garrigue, reducing visibility and access.
4	2500	85%	+	108	Orchard with ploughed, sorted soil. Sherds clustered in center of field.
5	625	90%	0	20	Orchard on plowed terrace.

and Camilli 1992). The latter is a subset, a sample, of the former. SCSP experiments were designed to test the congruence of these two phenomena. We posed the question: What is the difference between what we found and what was actually out there in the first place? Because these types of experiments are relatively rare in the literature, we give an in-depth accounting of our findings.

The experiments. Three hundred sherds were selected from our pottery discard pile, and each one numbered, weighed, and its longest dimension measured. The last two figures provide a relative index of each sherd's size and, by extension, relative obtrusiveness. Prior to seeding, the clean sherds were placed in a mud-bath and made dirty again in order to simulate field conditions. We selected five evidently sterile fields for the experiments, classifying each one according to its plant cover and soil matrix (table 3.8). The numbered potsherds were strewn over the fields and their locations noted to the nearest 10 cm.

Four teams of five fieldwalkers spaced 5 m apart walked the fields as if they were regular survey units, filling out paperwork, calling out findspots, and filling in field sheets at the end. Team members flagged each sherd they saw, instead of collecting it. This enabled us to repeat the experiments for each team without having to perform the arduous and difficult task of replanting sherds. After the fields were walked, the serial number of each flagged sherd was noted.

Results. While the numbers for each team varied, the overall pattern of recovery for each field was similar (figure 3.2). When visibility was limited by wheat stubble, performance was better in the field with the greater density of materials. Field 4 was a surprise, as conditions were such that greater recovery rates were expected. Fields 3 and 5 were identical in total surface area and artifact density. Visibility was drastically better in field 5. As the chart demonstrates, visibility was a factor, as recovery rates were almost always improved in field 5; however, it is not, as we had assumed, the primary factor.

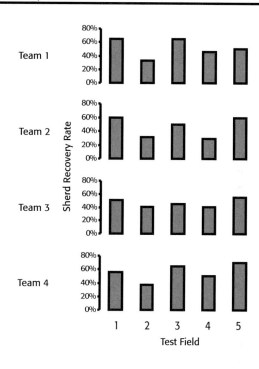

Figure 3.2 Seeding experiments: sherd recovery rates

When comparing the different field teams, in no instance was the difference between the best and worst performance greater than 20%. However, this may be a significant enough amount to warrant consideration. The bars in the chart also show that no single team was "the best." Team 1, for instance was the top performer in fields 1 and 3, but came in last in field 5 and second to last in field 2. Experience levels were roughly consistent among the teams with the exception of team 4, which consisted of senior staff members, all of whom had extensive survey experience. Their recovery totals for all exercises combined do exceed those of the others but, as fields 1 and 2 demonstrate, experience is not always an advantage.

Leveraging the experiments. In hindsight, it is clear that we needed to control more variables in these experiments. The experiments as performed have too much variation in the density, clustering and volume of sherds. Additionally, times of day and intensity as a measure of time spent in the fields should have been better controlled. These observations, and the fact that we needed more seeding experiments overall, are the lessons learned. Still, the work accomplished is a significant component of our thinking and rare in the literature. A main goal for SCSP was to advance survey methodology, and these experiments are a step in that direction.

The experiments were taken not just for the sake of experimenting: SCSP extracted value from these experiments and exploited what we learned, particularly for factoring our pottery index. For this process, we chose to focus on visibility and background confusion, as these were the observations taken in the field that held the greatest promise for quantification. We were surprised that visibility did not seem to have as big an impact on recovery rates as we had expected. In contrast, background confusion seemed to show a larger impact. The challenge, then, was to find an equation that would, starting from the known number of sherds in the field, give us a good estimation of what would be recovered. Unlike normal field procedures, we took numerous readings of visibility and background confusion. Thus, whereas our field data contained only one reading for visibility and one reading for background confusion (arrived at by consensus of the team members), our experimental data were made up of eleven readings each. We took advantage of this and used the average readings. The subsequent method was essentially that of data exploration.

We began by resolving a limitation in the manner in which observations on background confusion were made. Whereas visibility was recorded as a percentage of surface visible, background confusion was taken as either 0, +, or ++. These latter were not of use for quantitative analysis and, moreover, no diagnostic tools were provided to team members to help them measure background confusion (unlike for visibility, where team members had such tools). The first step in attempting to get an equation for factoring background confusion was to assign values to the 0, +, and ++ recordings. Initially this was set at 0, 1 and 2, with 0 signifying that 20% of the artifacts were obscured and 2 that 60% were obscured.

The experimental data seemed to indicate that background confusion had much more impact on observations than visibility and so we chose to hold the background confusion constant. To project what

number of a known population of sherds would be lost in the background confusion we used this equation:

$$\text{bans} = \text{ans} - (\text{ans} * (\text{bg}/100))$$

where bans is actual number of sherds, factored for background confusion, ans is actual number of sherds on the ground, and bg is background confusion. For example, where background confusion was recorded as 40% (+ in our recording system) of a known population of 50 sherds we would expect background confusion to cause us to miss 20 of these sherds:

$$50 - (50 * (40/100) = 30$$

On the other hand, the experimental data for visibility seemed to indicate that it was not as large a factor in recovery rates. We experimented with ways to reduce the overall impact of visibility on the pottery index and settled for this equation:

$$\text{vans} = \text{ans} - (\text{ans} * (((100\text{-}v)/4)/100))$$

where vans is actual number of sherds, factored for visibility, ans is actual number of sherds on the ground, and v is background confusion. This equation illustrates that we chose to flatten the effect of visibility of sherd observation by a factor of 4. For example, where visibility was rated at 60% (that is, 40% of the surface obscured), of a known population of fifty sherds we would expect visibility to cause us to miss five of these sherds:

$$50 - (50 * (((100\text{-}60)/4)/100)) = 45$$

Taken together, these two equations combine to give us an equation that allows us to predict how many sherds of a known population will be observed under recorded conditions of visibility and background confusion:

$$\text{ons} = \text{ans} - [(\text{ans} * (\text{bg}/100)) + (\text{ans} * (((100\text{-}v)/4)/100))]$$

where ons is the observed number of sherds. For example, where the actual number of sherds on the ground was fifty, the visibility reading 60% (that is, 40% of the surface obscured), and the background confusion rating 40% (that is, 60% of the sherds not lost in the background confusion), we would predict that our teams would observe 25 sherds:

$$50 - [(50 * (40/100)) + (50 * (((100\text{-}60)/4)/100))] = 25$$

Table 3.9 Percent errors with average visibility and 20 to 60% background confusion

Field number	Flattened visibility	Background confusion (% not obscured)	Total sherds (actual)	Total sherds (predicted)	Percent error	Counted sherds (actual)	Counted sherds (predicted)	Percent error
1	92.50	62.00	100	99	1	58	55	3
2	88.75	46.00	50	41	18	18	17	2
3	81.25	64.00	20	20	0	11	9	10
4	95.75	50.00	108	88	19	43	49	6
5	97.25	72.00	20	17	15	12	13	5
(Average)					(10.6)			(5.2)

Table 3.10 Percent errors with average visibility and 12 to 72% background confusion

Field number	Flattened visibility	Background confusion (% not obscured)	Total sherds (actual)	Total sherds (predicted)	Percent error	Counted sherds (actual)	Counted sherds (predicted)	Percent error
1	92.50	61.00	100	100	0	58	54	4
2	88.75	37.00	50	51	2	18	13	10
3	81.25	64.00	20	20	0	11	9	10
4	95.75	43.00	108	102	6	43	41	2
5	97.25	76.00	20	16	20	12	14	10
(Average)					(5.6)			(7.6)

Previously we stated that the equation for working up from the observed number of sherds to the actual number of sherds on the ground would look like this:

$$acp = cp + vc + bgc$$

where acp is adjusted count of pottery in a unit, cp is count of pottery in a unit, vc is correction for visibility, and bgc is correction for background confusion. We can now drive into vc and bgc as follows:

$$vc = (cp * (100/(100-((100-v)/4)))) - cp$$

and

$$bgc = (cp * (100/(100-bg))) - cp$$

This gives us the completed equation as follows:

$$acp = cp + [(cp * (100/(100-((100-v)/4)))) - cp] + [(cp * (100/(100-bg))) - cp]$$

Using these two equations gave us encouraging results (table 3.9). We felt that some percentage error based on calculations using visibility and background confusion was to be expected given that there were other factors at play. However, we did not believe that across all of our units, the average error should be as high as 11%. We also wanted percentage error values that were closer together no matter which way

the equation was run (from known population to observed numbers or from observed numbers to predicted population).

It was our conviction that we were treating visibility correctly, barring some minor refinements. We decided that perhaps our range for background confusion was off. Remembering that we recorded background confusion in the field as 0, +, ++ and had previously assigned these a range of values from 20 to 60% (that is, 80 to 40% of the sherds would not be lost in background confusion). By exploring these values we found that broadening the range and starting it at a lesser value gave us the results we wanted. The new scale ran from 12 to 72 and produced average errors that were closer together (table 3.10).

Finally we decided to try another permutation that would acknowledge that some of the readings taken for background confusion and visibility should be considered erratics. Although this was possible for visibility, it was not practicable for background confusion given the limited range of possible readings (0, +, ++). For visibility, we used only those values that fell within ten points of the median. This final revision gave us percent errors that were closely aligned and, we felt, within a reasonable tolerance (see table 3.11).

Summary of seeding experiments. In retrospect, it is clear that we should have done more and better experiments. With such data, survey projects will be better able to draw conclusions about material ex-

Table 3.11. Percent errors with visibility less erratics and 12 to 72% background confusion

Field number	Flattened visibility	Background confusion (% not obscured)	Total sherds (actual)	Total sherds (predicted)	Percent error	Counted sherds (actual)	Counted sherds predicted)	Percent error
1	92.81	61.00	100	99	1	58	54	4
2	90.21	37.00	50	51	2	18	14	8
3	82.50	64.00	20	19	5	11	10	5
4	96.81	43.00	108	101	6	43	43	0
5	97.63	76.00	20	16	20	12	15	15
(Average)					(6.8)			(6.4)

pressions across their survey units. As it was, we were able to use our findings from the experiments to devise an equation that allowed us to correct for visibility and background confusion. The result (when combined with corrections for areal extent) was our pottery index. The role of the experimental data in this process was basic. Any attempt to factor survey observations without experimental data would be impossible and erroneous.

Were our experimental data adequate, both quantitatively and qualitatively, to justify using them to correct for visibility and background confusion? On the one hand, some may argue it was not: Five fields and four teams do not create an excess of data. On the other hand, if we had not corrected for visibility and background confusion at all, it would have been tantamount to failing to correct for the unit area. SCSP's approach to unit survey was intensive and, as such, one has to consider the totality of the unit: The failure to factor in area, visibility, and background confusion would have greatly skewed our pottery index and rendered the data much less useful. Ultimately we have learned valuable lessons that we are taking into our next survey projects. Each member of the team should record critical values, such as visibility and background confusion. Over the course of an entire project, these average values for the unit are certain to be more accurate than if only one reading is taken. Teams should have diagnostic kits for taking such critical readings. We supplied this for visibility but not for background confusion. In the future, we would propose having field members use a catalogue of photographs of the survey region. From this they can select an image for visibility that most suits the current unit (time of day, quality of light, nature of vegetation). A separate image can be selected for background confusion by matching a visual inspection of the surface to catalogue images. These diagnostic image catalogues are

certain to provide quick, comparative, and relatively accurate readings (given a good selection of images). Extensive and well-controlled experiments should be carried out against the actual landscapes represented in the catalogue of images. Survey methods must evolve to incorporate exploration of experimental data.

CONCLUSION

SCSP made what we believe to be significant strides in advancing survey methods in Cyprus. The chronotype cataloguing and information system worked seamlessly with our pottery analyses and GIS mapping to present a new level of integrated information. We developed a quantitative database of pottery—counted, collected, and analyzed—that is yet to be fully scrutinized. The results of our resurvey work will require additional study before publication. The beginning we made on experimental work has given us vital insight for future work.

Ultimately, a social archaeology at the regional scale, or a landscape archaeology that seeks to come to terms with the average person's experience, has to deal with many facets of knowledge. In terms of pottery analysis, the easy part is the study of the well-known types. The truly difficult part involves coming to terms with the mass of imperfectly known pottery; one member of our team affectionately called them "the nasty wares." We did not achieve all our goals in this regard, but we are well placed to make more advances; our chronotype catalogue continues to grow and we plan to publish it in the future along with macroscopic and petrologic data.

Our pottery index, although imperfect, has brought a great deal more rigor to the mapping of pottery data then was the case before we began work. As a document of that work, the GIS maps speak volumes about the level and types of materials we encountered. Integrating this knowledge with future surveys will surely provide insight into topics with which we continue to wrestle, most notably the social meaning of the large, relatively thin spreads of pottery we encountered.

3.8 Chipped Stone Procedures

Dina Coleman

Methods for recording chipped stone data were equivalent to those used for other archaeological materials during field survey. In the field, these involved recording the quantity and location of all cultural materials in transect survey units, identifying notable scatters of chipped stone as POSIs, and in both cases counting all pieces and collecting a representative study sample. This was combined with a systematic recording of raw materials and potential sources. In the laboratory, all collected pieces were measured, described, and analyzed, and a representative selection was drawn and photographed for publication.

At the beginning of each season, fieldwalkers examined the SCSP study collection and learned the characteristic attributes of Cypriot chipped stone material, for example bulbs of percussion, platforms, concentric rings, cores, and shatter debris. They were also shown the common geological materials used for local chipped-stone production. This improved the survey teams' ability to identify cultural artifacts in the field, and to be consistent in selecting a representative sample from survey units. During the fieldwalking of transect survey units, all items of chipped stone were counted, and a representative sample was collected. This allowed us to build up a picture of off-site distribution across the entire landscape of the survey universe.

Areas with unusually high numbers of artifacts were defined as POSIs, particularly if they were on unplowed and relatively stable surfaces. Survey teams returned to these POSIs for full investigation. An initial stage whereby artifacts were located and marked by pin flags allowed a visual impression of their distribution. This distribution was then recorded by means of a grid with an appropriate size of collection square, usually 2 or 3 m. Artifacts from all squares were counted, and a representative selection was collected for full analysis in the laboratory. At the same time the project geomorphologists carried out a surface stability map to assess the degree to which the

artifacts might have moved since deposition. An important aspect of the methodology was interdisciplinary discussion on site among the survey team, the lithics specialist, and the geomorphologist.

The collected material was analyzed to determine the types of stone implements used in the survey area, as well as their possible function, date, and manufacturing technology. Each stone collected in the field and brought back to the laboratory was accessioned. This process involved measuring the length, width, and thickness of the stones in centimeters, weighing them in grams, classifying their geological material, and identifying the "type" of chipped stone. Type categories included cores, flakes, shatter, scrapers, blades, borers, choppers, *dhoukani* points, and utilized flakes. Within these type categories were a series of subcategories used to describe specific production characteristics, utilization evidence, and effects of postdepositional weathering, such as lichen growth and patination. Definitions for chipped stone terms followed those of Crabtree (1972) and Tixier (1974).

The sampling of chipped stones resulted in a study collection of more than 2300 pieces, which were representative of most stages of reduction sequences. The quantitative data resulting from the examination of this collection were entered into a database that could be exported to the project's GIS. This allowed an analysis of the spatial distribution of chipped stone assemblages, as well as an investigation of the relationships between chipped stones and associated artifacts. These relationships provided insights into cultural and, in some cases, temporal contexts.

The identification of the geological materials used for chipped stone manufacture was an important part of our examination of the local chipped-stone industry. These materials primarily consisted of chalcedony, fine-grained cherts, jasper, basalt, and some limestone, all of which are local materials. This information too was recorded in the database and exported to the GIS for spatial analysis. Local investigation was conducted around each POSI with significant collections of chipped stone, and it became clear that geological materials were regularly acquired from nearby outcrops and stream beds. Interpretation of geological maps, along with investigation in the field, also determined that higher quality materials, particularly fine-grained cherts, were often exported to areas several kilometers from their geological sources.

Although chronological sequences for Cypriot chipped stone assemblages remain in a developmental stage, we were able to estimate chronologies for assemblages from several sites. This estimate was based primarily upon the dates of associated artifacts, such as diagnostic ceramics and metallurgical finds. Further methods used to assist in establishing approximate chronologies for the chipped stones involved (1) comparisons between SCSP materials and dated Cypriot chipped stones from excavated sites; (2) geomorphological events and landscape alterations; (3) the identification of SCSP single-period sites datable by associated artifacts; (4) evidence of patination, weathering scars, and lichen growth on chipped stones; (5) recognizable and comparative patterning among SCSP chipped stone assemblages; and (6) ethnographic information (specifically for *dhoukani* implements). These methods did not serve to provide conclusive information in each case, but they aided in narrowing down potential chronological sequences for SCSP's chipped-stone assemblages.

3.9 Historical Archaeology and Oral Information

Lita Diacopoulos and Kylie Seretis

Within the SCSP area lie the modern villages of Mitsero, Malounda, Ayia Varvara, Agrokipia, Aredhiou, and Klirou. Given our limited resources and time constraints, we chose one village for detailed study. Mitsero has been home to SCSP participants since 1993, and during that time project members fostered good relationships with many of the local villagers, who from the outset showed a genuine interest and a willingness to share their knowledge of the recent past. These factors, alongside Mitsero's close association with both mining and agriculture, made the village an obvious choice for our interviews and at the same time contributes to SCSP's long-term goal of investigating industrial landscapes.

Beginning in 1997, historical, oral, and archaeological information was systematically collected concerning Mitsero village, the surrounding mines, and associated features. This included survey of the modern remains of the Kokkinoyia mine (SIA 11), the Agrokipia mines (SIA 1), the Kokkinopezoula mine and associated administrative complex (Mitsero *Yeropalloura*—SCY363), the Ayia Marina washing plant, the Kriadhis washing plant, and the associated workers' houses.

For Mitsero itself, chronological and other information was collected on houses, amenities (for example, lighting and water supply), the roads, shops, coffee houses, cemetery, and the church, and agricultural activities such as threshing, including the use of threshing floors and threshing sledges.

COLLECTING ORAL INFORMATION

A significant part of the 1997 field season involved gathering oral information from the villagers, mainly from Mitsero, as well as from employees of the Hellenic Mining Company. The purpose of collecting this information was to supplement our knowledge and understanding of various social and economic factors contributing to the present character of Mitsero, its inhabitants, and its immediate environs, which we had previously obtained from other sources. In particular, our research aims to incorporate the local experience in providing a specifically human dimension to the study of the archaeology of the more recent past in this part of Cyprus. As with all other kinds of documentary evidence, the oral information had to be sampled and evaluated in terms of its accuracy and relevance to our research questions. For this reason, our oral sources included a wide cross section of the local community, including both farmers and retired mine workers as well as shop owners, all of whom had lived in Mitsero for a significant part of, if not all of, their lives. This information contributed to our understanding of different aspects of local life, which we could also cross-reference for reliability with other oral accounts and/or material and documentary evidence.

Five people were interviewed formally, but informal conversations and inquiries with a number of other people were also recorded in field notes. Most informants were middle-aged or older and male, with the exception of one female. All interviews were conducted in Greek and in a relatively casual and relaxed fashion, usually over a cup of Cypriot coffee. The purpose of the interview was explained and permission was sought prior to the taking of notes and photographs of individuals. All of those approached expressed interest and were eager to participate. Keeping conversation restricted to the subject of our inquiry proved to be our only problem. Conversation often became sidetracked to other interesting but unrelated topics. In particular, most informants were very keen to recount to us local folklore, especially that relating to specific toponyms, churches, local saints, and landform features. Each individual's version of the same story had certain different details and we recorded all of them.

Alongside the interviews and the oral information, we also had the opportunity to observe and record some of the "traditional" activities still practiced by a number of older people in Mitsero, for example, the making of *trahana* (cracked wheat and yogurt, boiled and dried for making soup) and yogurt. This also involved visiting the local automated mill at Kato Moni where raw wheat was processed into flour and *konari*, a coarser ground wheat used in making *trahana*, while preboiled wheat was made into *pourgouri*, or cracked wheat.

RECORDING MATERIAL EVIDENCE

A significant part of this study involved the recording of the physical layout of the village. A 1923 plan of the village was used as the basis for mapping features that included the roads, houses, church, cemetery, and threshing floors. Along with filling out a recording form for each feature, a photographic inventory was made as part of the recording process. This map shows only the older pre-1923 section of the village, so a considerable effort was made to record the new additions. A clear distinction can be made between the older layout of the village and more recent developments, with obvious differences in building construction, house layouts, land allocation, and street widths. While developments in the new section were noted generally, we concentrated on studying the older section.

Given the overwhelming effort it would require to study an entire village, we chose three areas on which to focus our research: studying settlement through houses, church, and cemetery; studying mines and mining through the associated buildings as well as the industrial sites; and studying agriculture through the associated equipment, tools, and threshing floors (*alonia*).

General sketch maps were made to locate our work in each of these areas. All houses in the central area of the village were recorded. One house was selected for detailed recording and study on the basis of the carved decoration visible on the doorway main internal arches. Rubbings were made, along with measurements of the individual designs, and photographs were taken. A video recording was made of the house, the doorway, and the arch, while oral information was gathered on this house. We also made a brief video of the village, recording such

areas as the coffee houses, supermarket, church, cemetery, and some of the streets and houses.

The village street names (first introduced in 1996) were recorded. Along with the street signs have come individual letter boxes. We investigated the village cemetery and recorded the location, names, ages, and dates of death for all graves in the cemetery. General sketch plans were made for each of the mines, showing the location of the industrial buildings, machinery, and equipment in relation to the spoil heaps. In addition to the use of recording forms, we also undertook a detailed photographic inventory. The *alonia* were mapped as far as they could be identified physically. Nine were located and mapped in detail; an aerial photograph of the village from 1948 shows at least twenty-seven *alonia* in the village.

DOCUMENTARY RESEARCH

A preliminary investigation of the documentary records was undertaken by Kylie Seretis prior to the 1997 field season. In 1998, a range of information related to the Mitsero mines—for example, the costs of drilling, building construction, the amounts and types of minerals produced by each mine, and so on—was collected from the Annual Report of the Department of Mines and from information provided by the Geological Survey Department and the Hellenic Mining company. Census records show general population figures for the village from the 1890s.

Specific company records relating to the day-to-day operations and running of the mines proved harder to find. During the process of recording the material remains at the office and administrative buildings at Mitsero *Yeropalloura* (1 km west of Mitsero village on the road to the Kokkinoyia mine), we came upon a number of records in one of the abandoned buildings. These records (in Greek) contain information relating to workers' wages, clothing purchased, and safety, as well as a wealth of maps of several mining regions in Cyprus.

The Hellenic Mining Company lent us a composition of aerial photographs from 1948, taken by a private British company. The existence of these maps was previously unknown and, when compared to the 1973 and 1993 series previously purchased by SCSP from the Department of Lands and Survey, they provide invaluable direct evidence for all the changes that have taken place in the village landscape between 1948 and the 1970s.

4

SURVEY RESULTS

Ⅰn this chapter, we present a comprehensive selection of the SIAs and POSIs recorded by SCSP over five field seasons. We retain on disk and local servers at Glasgow University data on all POSIs and SIAs examined but present the following because of their material, spatial, methodological, analytical, or interpretative significance. For most of these SIAs and POSIs, we publish a full spate of relevant information:

- location (by UTM grid, cadastral map, and aerial photographs),
- physical landscape,
- historical context,
- field methodology,
- block survey or intensive collection strategy,
- materials and dating, and
- landscape-based conclusion

SPECIAL INTEREST AREAS (SIAs)

4.1 SIA I: Agrokipia *Kriadhis*

Compiled by Vasiliki Kassianidou Team leaders: Susan Bain, Bradley Creevey, Michael Given
Archaeometallurgy: Vasiliki Kassianidou, Haddon Wright, Sven Van Lokeren Micromorphology: Peter Grave
GIS analysis: Nathan Meyer Pottery: Timothy E. Gregory, Joanna S. Smith

Grid reference: 513300/3878100
Cadastral map: XXIX/54
Aerial photograph: 1993, run 177, no. 46
Survey units: 1301–10, 2013, 2100–2106, 2611–18, 5058
POSIs: SCY022: Agrokipia *Kriadhis* 1 (spoil heaps, roasting debris); SCY103: Agrokipia *Autinina* (lithics, pottery); SCY203: Agrokipia *Kriadhis* 2 (north and west side of mine); SCY204: Agrokipia *Kriadhis* 3 (archaeometallurgy, pottery); SCY220: Agrokipia *Kriadhis* 4 (slag scatters); SCY221: Agrokipia *Kriadhis* 5 (mining timbers); SCY222: Agrokipia *Kriadhis* 6 (slag scatters)

Agrokipia *Kriadhis* (SIA 1) comprises the modern mine of Agrokipia and surrounding fields. Ancient metallurgical features and finds abound in this area. Open-cast mining has destroyed most ancient mining installations, reversed much of the stratigraphy, and created enormous spoil heaps that cover nearly all the fields surrounding the modern mine (figure 4.1). In spite of this, some remnants of ancient mining and smelting activity have survived and were recorded systematically in the 1995 and 1997 seasons. Based on the pottery and ^{14}C dates, the activities around the Agrokipia mine date from the Geometric to Classical periods; thus our work here sheds light on metal production during one of the most important, cosmopolitan periods of Cyprus's past.

PHYSICAL LANDSCAPE

The Agrokipia mine is located on the southeastern slopes of Kriadhis, between the modern villages of Agrokipia and Mitsero. According to Bear (1963:70), the upper pillow lavas here occupy a narrow zone of about 460 m between the sediments and the lower pillow lavas. The inclined shaft of the modern mine passed through 135 m of various sedimentary formations (shales, chalks, cherts, marls, and sands). Within these geological formations there were three important cupriferous deposits, all of which were extensively mined in the past (Panayiotou 1989a:85). One of the ore bodies lying between 150 and 180 m below ground level was never covered by a gossan capping (Bear 1963:42). Lacking this surface indicator, the deposit was never exploited in antiquity but was detected in the twentieth century because of an anomaly obtained by gravity measurements (Bear 1963:71). The deposit, which consisted of both low- and high-grade cupreous ore, was mined from 1958 to 1964, when a drop in the world price for pyrites made its exploitation economically unfeasible (Bear 1963:71; Panayiotou 1989b:35).

The other two lens-shaped deposits, in contrast, lay fairly close to the surface within the upper pillow lavas and were covered by a prominent gossan (Bear 1963:71). The deposits were separated from each other by 30 m of pillow lava. The larger of the two consisted of low-grade noncupreous pyrites, while the smaller had cupriferous pyrites containing about 1% copper and small amounts of sphalerite (Bear 1963:71; Panayiotou 1989a:35). The ores were exploited by open-cast methods between 1952 and 1971 when this mine too was abandoned (Panayiotou 1989b:35). According to Rickard (1930:299), however, when the mines were first opened there were patches of up to four hundred tons of covellite ore contain-

Figure 4.1 SIA 1: Agrokipia-Kriadhis mine from the northeast. SCY022, top left

ing 12% copper. Such deposits would have been exploited and almost completely exhausted by ancient miners and metalworkers.

Apart from the copper ore deposits there was also an auriferous deposit 15 to 20 cm thick, located at the base of the oxidized zone of the gossan (about 6 m below the original surface and above the secondary enrichment zone). The gold came in the form of a soft crumbly material with the peculiar property of passing into liquid slime when pressed between the fingers (Bear 1963:184). Free sulfuric acid contained in this material (Constantinou 1992:352) made it highly corrosive and would burn the hands of the miners, who thus named it "devil's mud" (Bear 1963:185). Agrokipia's devil's mud contained 200 to 1000 g of gold per ton and was mined extensively between 1939 and 1940 (Bear 1963:189). Although devil's mud was of great significance to the modern mining industry of Cyprus, it was not exploited in antiquity (Kassianidou and Michaelides 1996).

HISTORICAL CONTEXT

One of the earliest references to ancient metallurgical remains in this area is found in Sakellariou (1890).

In the chapter on Tamassos he referred to the mines of this ancient kingdom, stating that they were located in the village of Agrokipia where most of the houses were built out of slag (Sakellariou 1890:201). Davies (1928–1930:75) noted that Agrokipia had two slag heaps, which he believed to be of Hellenic date because of the type of slag as well as the find of a seventh-century terra-cotta in their midst. The best description of Agrokipia's ancient mines comes from Rickard and is worth quoting in full:

> At Agrokipia (meaning "field-garden") two miles from Mitsero (meaning "very little") the village is built upon a black slag dump, and old workings have been found underneath the church. Two caved galleries can be seen on the outskirts of the village. Westward near the apparent gossan outcrop, there are remnants of red slag, of a coarse ropey kind, imputed to the Phoenicians, and near by are some shallow old workings. Half a mile further from the village a drill was at work, under the direction of Mr. Manlis [this is C. P. Manglis, a Cypriot engineer working for Cyprus Mines Corporation who is also mentioned by Bruce (1937:639)]. He informed me that he had found an iron pick, weighing 2.1 pounds in an ancient drift. At this place were numerous ancient galleries going as much as 200 feet underneath the surface. The entrance of the incline at 35 degrees, with steps, could be seen on the hillside. The slag and gossan looked alike, both being reddened by oxidation but the presence of bits of charcoal in the slag and its vesicular structure served to differentiate. Virtually none of these remains have survived modern mining activities. (1930:299)

According to Koucky (1982:243), wooden bowls and wooden hammer handles from the mines of Agrokipia were kept in the office of the Hellenic Mining Company. Koucky also states that their team found numerous Cypro-Geometric sherds along the exposed south wall of the open-cast mine and the possible foundations of a small Cypro-Geometric settlement in the southwest corner of the pit. Koucky and Steinberg collected and analyzed samples from Agrokipia as part of their project on Cypriot slags (Koucky and Steinberg 1982a:128). In their classification (Koucky and Steinberg 1982a: 119), the Agrokipia slags are of type P, which is blocky and highly oxidized and is what used to be called Phoenician-type slag.

The mines of Agrokipia *Kriadhis*, like those of Mitsero, are believed to have belonged to the an-

OPPOSITE: **Figure 4.2 SCY022-1a: section:**
1, Mixed, disturbed modern fill; **2,** Erosional material from pillow lava; **3,** Charcoal, ash, marl, crushed gossan; **4,** Gossan, iron-stained marl, and charcoal; **5,** Gossan, slag (small pieces), chalk/limestone-fine material; **6,** Crushed slag, charcoal, coarse material, gossan; **7,** Iron oxide; **8,** Iron oxide with more chalk/limestone; **9,** Iron oxide; **10,** Fine pieces of gossan, slag, charcoal; **11,** Fine-medium sized material, charcoal, slag (small pieces), small amount of gossan, ochre; **12,** Iron oxide; **13,** Large chunks of furnace material, roasting conglomerate, charcoal, gossan; **14,** Limestone/chalk, small amount of iron oxide; **15,** Iron oxide; **16,** Limestone/chalk, small amount of iron oxide; **17,** Crushed fine material, small pieces crushed slag, chalk; **18,** Marl base with chalk, limestone, and some iron oxide; **19,** Medium-large chunks of slag, gossan, and charcoal; **20,** Crushed chalk, small amount of iron oxide; **21,** Gossan, small amount of roasted ore (?), charcoal, fine reddish material; **22,** Crushed slag, some gossan, limestone, chalk; **23,** Very fine gossan, crushed chalk (small pieces); **24,** Crushed slag, roasted gossan, charcoal, iron oxide, small amounts of limestone/chalk; **25,** Same as **22** with some roasted ore/gossan; **26,** Left, Large chunks of furnace conglomerate, roasted gossan, charcoal, limestone, chalk, slag, Right, Finer material with tapped slag; **27,** Charcoal, crushed gossan, chalk, limestone, medium tap slag; **28,** Large chunks of furnace conglomerates, slag, crushed ore/gossan (roasted); **29,** Gossan, roasted gossan, chalk, limestone, and tapped slag (medium); **30,** Crushed gossan, chalk/marl, fine yellow material; **31,** Roasted gossan in yellowish material; **32,** Charcoal, crushed roasted gossan, iron oxide, pillow lava; **33,** Crushed pillow lava; **34,** Roasted ore, pillow lava, small pieces of charcoal; **35,** Charcoal, chalk and limestone, crushed pillow lava; **36,** Red ochre, crushed with some charcoal; **37,** Crushed limonite with silica; **38,** Fine layers of red clay, some sparse charcoal; **39,** Crushed limonite with silica; **40,** Crushed ore, pillow lava, iron oxide; a little charcoal; **41,** Packed marl, clay, with some iron oxide coloring; **42,** Charcoal; **43,** Clay, marl, pillow lava with large chunks, some small charcoal pieces

cient kingdom of Tamassos (Sakellariou 1890:214), which lay approximately 8 km to the southeast. Based on pottery collected in POSIs located at the mine and in the surrounding fields, as well as the ^{14}C dates, most mining and smelting activity dates from the Geometric through Classical periods. Because so little is known about copper production during the Geometric period, it is important to be able to demonstrate that mines were exploited at this time (this is also supported by radiocarbon dating of samples from SCY116). The Archaic period is much better known and generally recognized as one of the main periods of Cypriot copper production on the island, and no doubt the island flourished

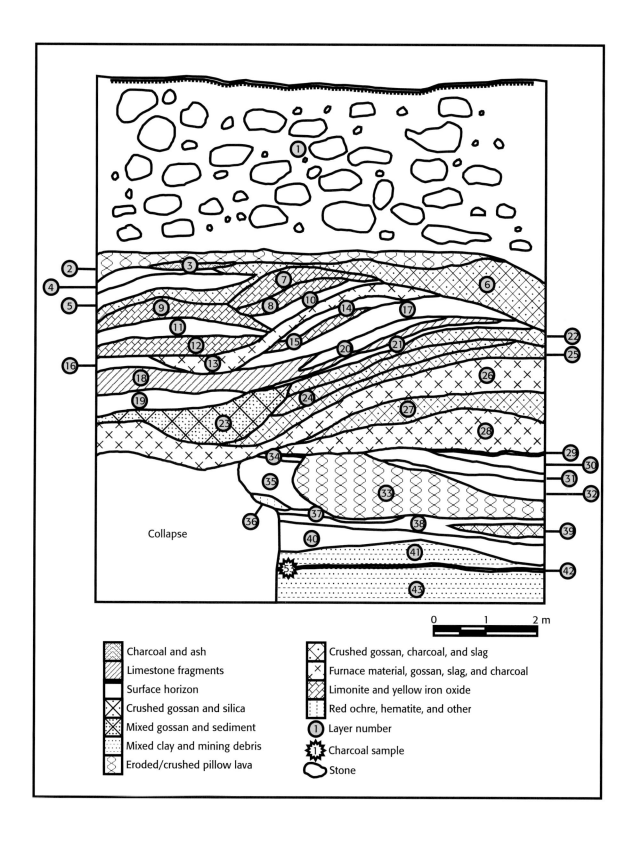

Collapse

0   1   2 m

Charcoal and ash

Limestone fragments

Surface horizon

Crushed gossan and silica

Mixed gossan and sediment

Mixed clay and mining debris

Eroded/crushed pillow lava

Crushed gossan, charcoal, and slag

Furnace material, gossan, slag, and charcoal

Limonite and yellow iron oxide

Red ochre, hematite, and other

① Layer number

✦ Charcoal sample

◯ Stone

at that time at least in part because of the booming copper industry (Gjerstad 1948:459). The mines also seem to have been exploited during the Roman period, as there are two slag heaps in the vicinity of Agrokipia village: One is under the old village church dedicated to Panayia Khrysopandanassa (SCY131). Both heaps are disturbed but appear to have Late Roman pottery associated with them (Koucky 1982:243).

FIELD METHODOLOGY

The open-cast mine of Agrokipia *Kriadhis* lies just west of transect 513.5, and some survey units here (1301–10) were investigated in 1995. The systematic survey of the area (units 2611–18) was carried out mainly in 1996. In 1997, unit 2612 was resurveyed and assigned a new number, 5058. A large part of the transect could not be surveyed because it lies under the enormous spoil heaps of the modern open-cast mine; this factor will affect any interpretation of the survey data (plate III).

The actual open-cast mine and the surviving ancient metallurgical debris were investigated systematically during the 1995 season by Vasiliki Kassianidou and Haddon Wright, and a preliminary report on the work followed (Kassianidou and Wright 1996). The sections were drawn, photographed, and described in detail in field notebooks. Once recording was complete, representative samples were taken from all layers. These samples consisted mainly of mining debris (such as gossan), furnace conglomerate, slag, and related material. Soil samples from the different layers were also collected, as they may include (and thus help to identify) ground ore. On the same basis during the 1997 season, Sven Van Lokeren and Bradley Creevey recorded further sections and features, such as mining timbers and slag scatters, and collected any extant pottery. Charcoal was collected wherever present, and some of the samples were submitted for ^{14}C dating. The results are presented and discussed below.

SCY022: AGROKIPIA *Kriadhis* 1

This POSI is located on one of the artificial terraces in the eastern part of the open-cast mine. Here, ancient piles of mining and roasting debris were dissected by bulldozers and are now visible as verti-

cal sections along 35 m of the north-south face of the open-cast mine. Three sections (subunits SCY022-1a, 1b, and 1c) were cleaned back to expose the stratigraphy and allow proper recording and sample collection. In what follows, the reader should bear in mind the extent to which the entire landscape has been modified and realize that the entire ore deposit and surrounding host rock have been removed by bulldozers. We can see only what has survived and are looking at it from a completely artificial perspective.

SCY022-1a: MINING AND ORE BENEFICIATION WASTE HEAP

This 7 x 6 m section contains forty-three distinct, stratified layers of material (figures 4.2, 4.3). Although the top layer consists of modern mining debris, which derives from the terrace lying directly above, we are confident that the other layers have maintained their original stratigraphy. We base this statement on the presence of a natural outcrop of pillow lava to the north of the layers, which was unaffected by modern mining and seems to have acted as a protective barrier for the stratified deposits. The bulldozers apparently cut through two ancient spoil heaps that partly overlap. The lower layers cover the full extent of the section. Because of the partial collapse of the section and the overgrowth, we were unable to reach the base of the deposit and therefore do not know its full extent. The spoil heaps consist of a sequence of layers comprised mainly of crushed gossan, which sometimes alternates with layers of crushed calcareous material (limestone, chalky marl) and layers of roasted ore and gossan intermixed with ash and charcoal (for example, layers 3, 6, 14, 24, 29). Significant quantities of furnace or roasting conglomerate were found in layers 13, 26, and 28. Smelting (tap) slag was observed in several layers but appeared to consist of scattered pieces rather than any consolidated deposit. Layer 38, at least, appears to represent an abandonment, since it consisted of hard-packed, eroded material devoid of ore, flux, or any other metallurgical remains.

Samples of some layers with finely crushed material were also collected at this time by Peter Grave for micromorphological and elemental analysis (plate IV). The results of the analyses suggest that, overall, the present sediments have been heavily

Figure 4.3 SCY022-1a: layers of ancient spoil from ore treatment. The vertical tape measure is 9.5 m.

altered. With their abundant ash and charcoal content, initial pH levels should have been very basic and highly corrosive, rather than the moderate pH of 4 to 4.5. The micromorphological analysis provides supporting evidence for alteration with the identification of abundant small ($< 60\ \mu$) crypto-crystalline pore spaces and evidence of partial dissolution of many of the quartz grains present. Postdepositional formation of gypsum crystals contrasts with the elemental analysis of the sediment matrix (EDAX scanning of the prepared thin sections), where an average of only 3 to 5% sulfur was present. At least part of the elemental deficit may be due to the initial corrosive conditions that promoted dissolution and mobilization of some sediment components before the pH became equilibrated. Where present, slag consisted of an extensive mullite crystalline phase (commensurate with formation at high temperatures). Elemental analysis of the sediment matrix, however, did not detect copper. If, as we have assumed, these sediments were deposited as a byproduct of beneficiation and smelting (as indicated by the presence of slag), the process was either very efficient or the copper ore was very low grade. The charcoal remains were identified as *Pinus* species by

Naomi Miller (MASCA, University of Pennsylvania Museum of Anthropology and Archaeology).

A mining gallery of unknown date is located approximately 10 m west of the foot of the section. The gallery is too narrow and unstable to permit safe entry and therefore was not investigated further.

SCY022-1b: MINING AND ORE BENEFICIATION WASTE HEAP

Approximately 25 m to the south of the two heaps and along the same north-south face of the open cast was another area with nineteen stratified layers; this too was cleaned and recorded (figure 4.4). Like the top layer in SCY022-1a, the same layer in SCY022-1b was made up of material disturbed or redeposited during modern mining activities; however, an outcrop of pillow lava bordering the area to the south served to assure integrity of the stratigraphy. Pieces of furnace or roasting conglomerate were observed in layers 5 and 6. The majority of the deposits here consisted of much finer material, mainly bright red iron oxide powder, which may indicate that ore was ground to a powder in this area. Furthermore, unlike any of the layers in SCY022-1a, layers 9 and 9a

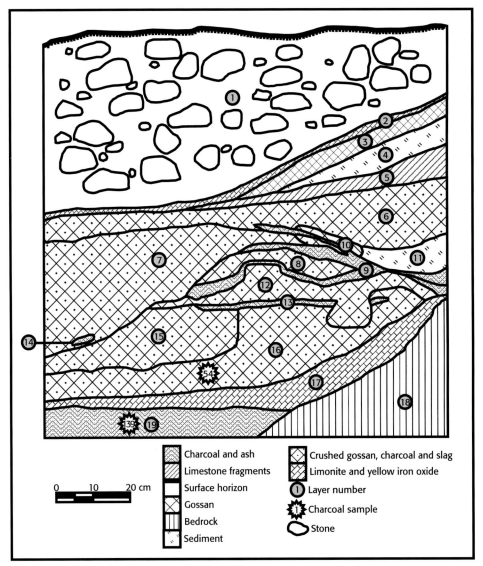

Figure 4.4 SCY022-1b: section: **1**, Mixed, disturbed modern fill; **2**, Limonite, marl; **3**, Crushed gossan; **4**, Sediment fill; **5**, Limonite, marl, chalk, limestone, furnace material, gossan; **6**, Crushed gossan, charcoal, furnace material, slag; **7**, Crushed roasted gossan, charcoal, copper ore, slag; **8**, Crushed roasted gossan, charcoal, copper ore, slag; **9**, Ash, charcoal, roasted gossan, possibly ore; **10**, Crushed roasted gossan, charcoal, copper ore, slag; **11**, Sediment fill, crushed roasted gossan, charcoal; **12**, Crushed roasted gossan, charcoal, slag; **13**, Charcoal, ash; **14**, Charcoal, ash; **15**, Roasted gossan, charcoal, slag; **16**, Crushed roasted gossan material, slag, ?ore; **17**, Marl, limonite; **18**, pillow lava; **19**, Charcoal, ash

consisted almost entirely of very fine, ashy material.

In layer 6 we found the only piece of fired clay in the entire POSI. This is probably refractory material, perhaps a piece of lining from a roasting furnace or some other metallurgical installation. Slag was encountered with slightly greater frequency than in area SCY022-1a, but the quantities are still too limited to warrant the identification of Area 1b as a smelting zone. A single sherd found near this section, like most others found around the mine, dates to the Archaic period. It is a Greek import, the

handle of a skyphos or kylix. Its relation to the actual deposits is unknown and, given the degree of disturbance, we cannot make too much of its chronological significance.

SCY022-1c: MINING AND ORE BENEFICIATION WASTE HEAP

Over the two years that elapsed since the first SCSP fieldwork in the mine (1995), erosion had exposed in the area between the two sections pieces of furnace conglomerate similar to the ones found in SCY022-1a. We therefore decided to investigate this area (1997), and a section measuring approximately 4 x 2 m was cleaned back and drawn (figure 4.5).

Judging from the inclination of the layers, this seems to be another heap of mining waste and roasting debris. Since the lower, relatively horizontal layers 37 to 43 consist of gossan, bedrock outcrops, and the actual bedrock, we may assume that they represent the original surface on which the heap was formed. The presence of charcoal in layer 39 may be the earliest indicator of some activity on this surface. As in the case of SCY022-1a, there are a number of layers (or lenses) that consist almost entirely of furnace conglomerate (layers 4, 13), others that consist of crushed gossan frequently mixed with charcoal (layers 9, 14, 27), and others that contain ash (6, 8, 14).

SCY022: DISCUSSION

The location of SCY022, the nature of the stratified material, and the form of the deposits all indicate that we are dealing with a spoil heap consisting of waste that derives from mining, mineral dressing, and roasting. Mineral dressing is the essential preparative step to the smelting process, in which the metalliferous minerals are concentrated by removal of most gangue material.

Beneficiation of ores has two main advantages: It reduces the amount of slag produced during smelting and limits the amount of fuel needed to smelt the charge. Ore beneficiation consists hand cobbing and selecting the fragments of ore that are richer in metal, crushing the rock using stone or iron hammers (depending on the time period) on mortar stones, grinding the crushed mineral to produce a powder, and, finally, washing the powder to remove the lighter gangue material. These steps are usually undertaken in close proximity to the mine, to avoid the unnecessary carting of large amounts of ore—which contain but a small percentage of metal—to the smelters. According to Forbes, "The ancients generally picked or enriched the ores before transport and hence such operations were mostly conducted at the pit-head and not in metallurgical centers" (1966:223). According to Craddock (1989:187), debris produced during beneficiation of the ore results in numerous small heaps of rock fragments of fairly uniform pea size. Mining debris, on the other hand, consists of variable-sized rocks.

The nature of the material in SCY022-1a and SCY022-1c—namely, crushed ore, fine powder, charcoal, and the like—is consistent with waste material produced in ore beneficiation. Most strata consisted of crushed gossan and iron oxides, probably the waste material produced once the copper-rich nodules of ore had been selected and taken away. If this interpretation is correct, the absence of mortars and grinders should be noted although it could be entirely coincidental and result from the fact that we are only observing a section through the slag heaps.

The other common material from these deposits is furnace conglomerate, which consists of pieces of ore, charcoal, slag, and related materials fused by fire. We believe that this material has resulted from the roasting of the ore, an essential part of smelting sulfide ores. Roasting may also be considered as a step in beneficiation, one which most likely took place near the mines. The fragment of fired clay found in layer 6 of SCY022-1b (sample A60) may come from the lining of a roasting furnace. Roasting furnaces as depicted by Agricola (1950:350) were open π-shaped structures facing the direction of the wind. Just such a roasting furnace, dating to the Hellenistic period, has been found at Ayia Varvara *Almyras* in Cyprus (Fasnacht 1989:63). However, a built installation is not necessary; a loosely piled heap mixed with wood could suffice (Craddock 1989:190).

It is not clear whether the mining gallery exposed adjacent to SCY022-1a is contemporary and therefore related to the spoil heaps. According to Bruce (1937:647; 1949:214), deposits very similar to SCY022 have been found throughout the island and were originally interpreted as gossan outcrops. It is only due to the presence of charcoal and other artifacts that they were eventually identified as being anthropogenic (Rickard 1930:299); they have since been referred to by geologists as "false gossans" (Koucky and Steinberg 1982b:149). One of the best examples of a false gossan was located at the Mavrovouni mine, which exploited the largest ore deposit on the island and produced a wealth of ancient mining remains (this mine now lies in Turkish-occupied territory). When investigated, the artificial Mavrovouni gossan was found to consist of "the thoroughly oxidized remains of a Roman or Phoenician stock pile of pyrite ore" (Bruce 1949:214). It is interesting that this ancient spoil heap was also associated with ancient galleries which, according to Bruce (1937:647), ran beneath the heap in geological

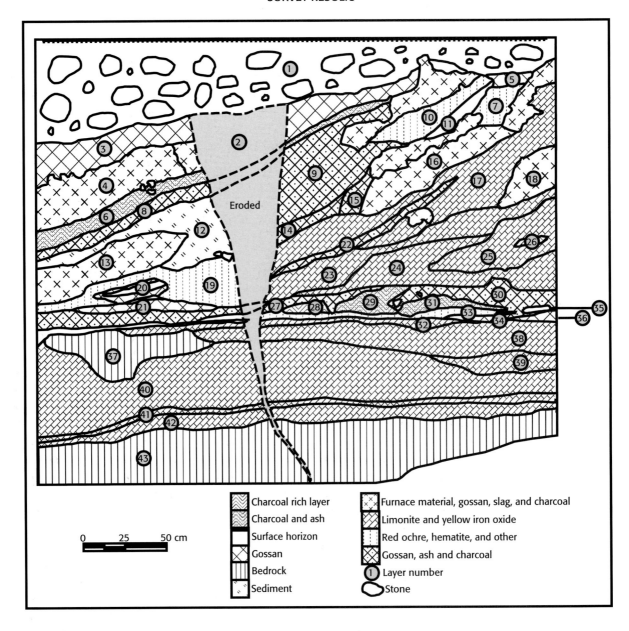

Figure 4.5 SCY022-1c: section: **1**, Mixed, disturbed modern fill; **2**, Gully/erosion; **3**, Crushed/roasted gossan (dark red/brown); **4**, Furnace conglomerate, gossan, charcoal; **5**, Limestone, iron-oxide (pink-orange-white); **6**, Ash layer, gossan (gray-yellow); **7**, Gossan (red-brown); **8**, Ash, crushed gossan (orange); **9**, Ash, charcoal, crushed gossan (orange-brown); **10**, Gossan (dark red); **11**, Gossan (light brown); **12**, Sediment fill (gray); **13**, Furnace conglomerate, charcoal, slag (red/orange/brown/black); **14**, Ash, charcoal, limonite (gray-yellow); **15**, Same as **14**; **16**, Charcoal, gossan, roasting debris (dark orange, red); **17**, Limonite (yellow); **18**, Same as **13**; **19**, Gossan, iron oxide/hematite (dark red); **20**, Gossan (orange); **21**, Gossan (orange); **22**, Ash, limonite (yellow, black); **23**, Same as **22** (dark yellow); **24**, Gossan (yellow); **25**, Gossan (yellow); **26**, Gossan (yellow); **27**, Crushed gossan, small charcoal pieces (brown); **28**, Charcoal layer (dark brown-black); **29**, Ash, charcoal (brown); **30**, Crushed/roasted gossan, charcoal; **31**, Ash, charcoal (brown); **32**, Limonite (dark yellow); **33**, Crushed gossan (violet); **34**, Crushed gossan (red); **35**, Crushed gossan (violet); **36**, Crushed gossan (violet); **37**, Bedrock outcrops (grayish-gray); **38**, Gossan, limonite (dark red-cream yellow); **39**, Gossan (dark orange-yellow); **40**, Limonite (bright yellow); **41**, Limonite (bright yellow); **42**, Limonite (bright yellow); **43**, Bedrock

strata that did not seem to contain ores of commercial value. This observation, as well as the nature of the material, led Bruce to conclude that the Mavrovouni remains represented a roasting heap and that the galleries running beneath it were constructed to facilitate air circulation.

Koucky and Steinberg, on the contrary, have interpreted such deposits as "large leach piles" used in the hydrometallurgical extraction of copper from the ores (1982b:167). The existence of ancient hydrometallurgy is very controversial and has been rejected by several scholars (Muhly 1986:52; Salkield 1982). Considering the amount of slag present on Cyprus, it seems most unlikely that the extraction process involved anything other than the roasting and smelting of sulfide ores.

SCSP's work at Agrokipia *Kriadhis* represents the first systematic investigation of an ore-roasting deposit. As stated above, the nature of the Kriadhis deposits indicates that these remains derive from ore beneficiation which, apart from crushing and sorting, included roasting. The material preserved on the piles are those parts of the ore poor in copper, which were therefore dumped with the rest of the gangue. The analysis of this material enables us to draw some important conclusions regarding this rather elusive aspect of the complex processes involved in ancient copper production.

Only three sherds were collected in the vicinity of these sections. One is an imported Greek Black Glaze kylix or skyphos handle, dated to either the sixth or the fifth century BC. Although the dating of this sherd corresponds well with the pottery collected in other nearby POSIs and archaeometallurgical units (units 2102–2105, 2013), we have to bear in mind the extent of disturbance to this area before considering the relevance of this find to the actual mining activities. The same considerations hold true for the other two sherds from SCY022, one of which dates to the Late Roman period and the other to the Medieval to Modern periods.

A notable amount of Archaic to Classical pottery was collected in (archaeometallurgical) units 2100–06 and 2013 (cat. 2102.12.1, 2105.5.1, and 2105.8.1), all of which lie on terraces of the modern mine between SCY022 and SCY204 (table 4.1). Thirty-three sherds date to the Archaic and Classical period, with a high proportion of decorated, table, and imported wares (mainly imported Attic Black Glaze vessels associated with drinking, for example, torus

Table 4.1 SCY022: analyzed pottery (including units 2013, 2100-06)

Chronotype	Period	Qty
Cooking ware-Ar	Ar	1
Double Rolled Strap Handle	Ar	1
Wide Shallow Bowl-Ar [2105.5.1]	Ar	1
Amphora-AC	AC	1
Amphora, Greek [2105.8.1]	AC	1
Amphora, Torpedo	AC	1
Greek Red Slip	Cl	1
White Painted-Cl	Cl	1
Black Glaze-AC	AC	9
Black-on-Red-AC	AC	1
Pithos-AC	AC	1
Plain ware-AC	AC	9
Unknown-AC	AC	1
White Painted-AC	AC	4
Wide Shallow Bowl-AC	AC	1
Basin-LR	LR	1
Cypriot W4	MM	2
Plain White-HA	HA	1
Red Slip-HA	HA	1
Coarse ware-Unk	Unk	1
Unknown-Unk	Unk	1
TOTAL		41

Note. Figures in brackets refer to cataloged items (see chapter 5.1).

foot no. 2105.2.1); there are also several storage vessels, notably an imported Greek amphora (cat. 2105.8.1). This pattern suggests some connection with elite activities rather than mining and ore processing. The question thus arises whether these finds actually date the mining activities.

To resolve such issues, charcoal samples were collected from all the SCY022 subunits and four of them were submitted for radiocarbon dating (appendix B). The calibrated dates indicate that the spoil heaps date to the late Geometric, not to the Archaic to Classical period. We know very little about mining and metallurgical activities during Geometric times, and here we have good evidence that the mines were active and copper was produced, if not exported, at this time. The fact that there is so much Archaic and Classical material (especially of the sixth and fifth centuries BC) in and around the modern mine may indicate a continuation if not an intensification in extracting copper from this ore deposit.

SCY203: AGROKIPIA *KRIADHIS* 2: SLAG SCATTERS NORTH AND WEST OF THE MINE

Fieldwalking during 1997 discovered concentrations of both pottery and tap slag on the north and west

Table 4.2 SCY203: archaeometallurgical subunits

Subunit	Description
SCY203-1	Broken tap slag in modern dump; 6m diameter holes (ventilation shafts?)
SCY203-2	Tap slag scatter approximately 6 x 4 m. Modern shaft
SCY203-3	Open-cast gallery 25 x 0.8 m. Possibly ancient
SCY203-4	Dense layer of crushed tap slag, approximately 15 x 8 m. Road metalling?
SCY203-5	Ends of mining galleries in west face of pit: 0.6 x 0.6 m; 0.6 x 1.5 m. Rough and irregular: probably ancient
SCY203-6	Filled-in gallery approximately 3 m deep and 1.5 m wide; pre-twentieth century

Table 4.3 SCY204: analyzed pottery

Chronotype	Period	Qty
Amphora-Ar	Ar	2
Cooking ware-Ar	Ar	6
Plain ware-Ar [SCY204.4.12.1]	Ar	3
White Painted-Ar [SCY204.3.5.1]	Ar	5
Amphora-Cl	Cl	4
Bichrome-Cl	Cl	1
Black-on-Red-Cl	Cl	1
Lamp-Cl	Cl	1
Plain ware-Cl [SCY204.3.3.1.1]	Cl	5
Plain White-Cl	Cl	8
Red Slip-Cl	Cl	2
White Painted-Cl	Cl	1
Wide Shallow Bowl-Cl	Cl	1
Amphora-AC	AC	11
Amphora, Torpedo	AC	2
Bichrome-AC	AC	1
Black Glaze-AC [S-0029]	AC	1
Black-on-Red-AC	AC	1
Cooking ware-AC	AC	12
Double Rolled Strap Handle-AC	AC	1
Plain ware-AC	AC	18
Rolled Lug Handle	AC	1
White Painted-AC	AC	6
Red Slip-HA	HA	1
Tile-PC	PC	1
Unknown	Unk	2
TOTAL		98

Note. Figures in brackets refer to cataloged items (see chapter 5.1).

sides of the mine, about 100 m from the edge of the pit. One of these consisted of a concrete base with slag inclusions, surrounded by modern debris and a sparse spread of surface slag. A larger and denser concentration of smaller fragments of slag was situated 50 m to the east of this first scatter. Here the slag was associated with a floor of obscure date and purpose, which consisted of pocked limestone cobbles forming a 7 x 5 grid of squares, each measuring roughly 2.4 x 2.2 m. The slag looked as if it had been deliberately put in channels between the cobble bases. The other concentrations in SCY203

were divided into six subunits along the western and northern edges of the mine (table 4.2).

SCY204: AGROKIPIA *KRIADHIS* 3: SLAG SCATTER

SCY204 (units 2102–2106) consisted of a considerable deposit of slag, charcoal, and pottery, some still in situ but most heavily disturbed by modern mining and eroding out of the sides of the bulldozed terraces. This deposit is situated approximately 80 m north-northwest of SCY022. Its most important feature was a layer of crushed tap slag lying on one of the few definitive bedrock areas in the mine, with Archaic and Classical pottery eroding onto and over the slag from ancient dumps and work floors to the southeast of it. The well-preserved state of the pottery suggests it has only very recently eroded out of the relevant strata. The area was mapped, drawn, and divided into four subunits for collecting pottery and slag samples (figure 4.6). Bulk chemical analysis of three slag samples from SCY204 revealed that they contain a low amount of copper (below 0.7%) and significant amounts of manganese (see chapter 5.4).

The stratified layers near the top of the bulldozed terrace (subunit 1) contained pottery (table 4.3) and some possible tomb remains overlying earlier layers of crushed gossan. These gossan layers, situated beneath a top layer of compacted, crushed tap slag about 30-cm thick, contained limestone cobbles with Archaic to Classical pottery in situ (for example, cat. S-0029). Subunit 2 contained eroded material, mainly slag and pottery, while subunit 3 was comprised of several slag scatters with Archaic to Classical pottery (for example, cat. SCY204.3.3.1.1, SCY204.3.5.1), as well as part of an Archaic "Astarte" type figurine (cat. SCY204.1.1; see chapter 5.3). Subunit 4 corresponds to a distinct but also eroded area with imported limestone cobbles and Archaic pottery (for example, cat. SCY204.4.12.1). When this subunit was originally discovered in 1995, it contained archaeometallurgical material such as tuyères and furnace lining; in subsequent years, however, it has become badly eroded.

The material in SCY204 represents a complex set of features whose interpretation is complicated by the partially preserved stratigraphy in a very eroded and highly disturbed context. A stable platform with an in situ floor level of slag was situated on top of one of the few indisputable bedrock areas in the modern mine. The Archaic to Classical material appears both

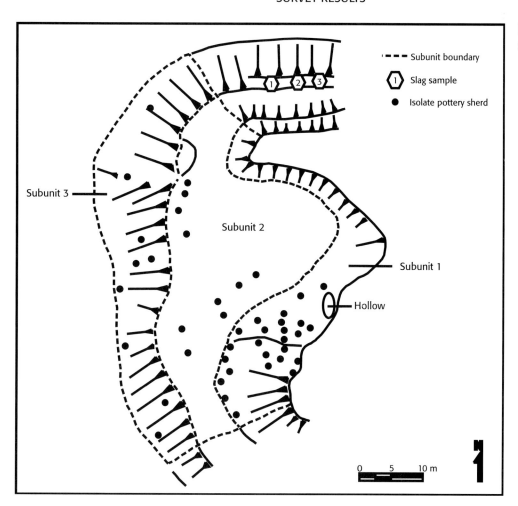

Figure 4.6 SCY204: sketch plan

above and below the slag on eroded slopes and in subunit 3, which is largely intermixed with slag. This area nevertheless offers the opportunity to establish a tentative stratigraphy for the northeastern side of the mine. The pottery (of Archaic to Classical date) eroding from the gully is so well preserved that it probably derives from a concentrated pocket, perhaps a corner of a structure or a tomb, in or just above the layers of crushed ore, gossan, and slag in subunit 1. We might thus envision a layer of work floors (and/or dumps) dating from the Archaic to Classical periods and lying above the slag layer in this part of the modern mine. These work floors would have been contemporary with the roasting and ore crushing floors to the south in SCY022 and possibly with the undated mining remains along the opposite side of the mine. Can this mean that the slags—and subsequently the smelting activities—date to an earlier period, contemporary with the spoil heaps? Such a situation would correspond with the smelting workshop of the Geometric period. However, because the slags are manganiferous and contain such low

amounts of copper, they may date to a much later period (the Roman, to which all other manganiferous slags from the SCSP area belong—see chapter 5.4). Their association with Archaic to Classical material is easily explained as the result of the severe disturbances caused by modern mining activities.

SCY220: AGROKIPIA *KRIADHIS* 4: SLAG SCATTERS NORTH OF MINE

On the north side of the mine lie a series of eroded slag scatters, on either side of a modern track. None of them contained any pottery, and all were heavily disturbed by the modern exploitation at Agrokipia *Kriadhis*. The two main concentrations were SCY220-1a, a hard-packed horizontal layer about 50 cm long and 2 to 3 cm thick, and SCY220-1d, a small packed layer of crushed tap slag about 100-cm long and 30-cm thick, situated on a small ridge. Small scatters of weathered tap slag were also intermixed with crushed gossan in subunits 2 to 4 in the northern area of the modern mine, on top of the modern spoil heaps. subunit 3 was merely a small cavity overgrown with thyme, about 60 cm deep and 50 cm wide.

SCY221: AGROKIPIA *KRIADHIS* 5: MINING TIMBERS

Three rows of mining timbers, the remains of galleries, were cut by bulldozers at a point about 70 m east of the lake at the bottom of the mining pit, on one of the lower platforms of the mine. Subunit 1 contained a small layer of compacted slag, clay matrix, silica, and pyrite, along with some pottery, in front of a row of three small props in a line 60-cm long. Subunits 2 and 3 consisted of two rows of timber supports in heavily eroded gullies and on the ridges in between those gullies. No pottery was found there. Some pieces seem to be broken planks, which would have been used between the supports as lagging to prevent rubble from falling in the gallery, or as a ceiling to prevent collapse (cf. SIA 11: chapter 4.11).

When the soil was cleaned back from some of the supports in subunits 1 and 3, they appeared to rest either on bedrock or on a hard soil layer. The soil in the interior of what must have been an original gallery was unfortunately almost completely eroded out. Later erosion gullies or channels actually followed the axis of each gallery, which strengthens our belief that we are dealing with in situ mining remains, although possibly of recent mining activity. The pottery from SCY221 consisted of one piece of Archaic/Classical Black Glaze, one sherd of Late Roman cooking ware, and one coarse ware sherd of unknown date. Given the highly eroded nature of the area, these could have originated higher up the side of the mine. Two of the mining props had plastic sheeting attached, but a few pieces of timber were extensively replaced by secondary minerals, often a sign of older workings (Bruce 1937).

SCY222: AGROKIPIA *KRIADHIS* 6: SLAG SCATTERS (EAST SIDE)

Subunits 1 to 4 of SCY222 were made up of out-of-context slag scatters often mixed with modern waste or mining debris; these units were located on the artificial plateaus of the modern spoil heaps on the northeastern and eastern side of the mine. Compared to SCY203, these are much smaller and more likely to be secondary dumps.

Subunit SCY222-1 (513330/3877950) was a modern dump of concrete mixed with pieces of crushed tap-slag on both sides of a modern dirt track. Subunit SCY222-2 (513330/3877980), situated about 20 to 30 m to the northeast, was yet another very superficial scatter of weathered, crushed tap slag about 7 m across. It was intermixed with modern waste material and surrounded by small spoil heaps on top of the artificial plateau formed by the modern spoil heaps. The third slag scatter, subunit SCY222-3 (513340/3878010) was about 1.5 m long, 0.6 m wide, and 1.0 m thick, and consisted of a layer of heavily weathered slag, mixed with furnace conglomerate. The scatter was located on the edge of the uppermost plateau of the modern spoil heaps, about 30 m to the northeast of the second subunit. Subunit SCY222-4 (513280/3878080), at the northeastern edge of the modern spoil heaps and about 50 m northeast of SCY220-1, was a roughly circular and superficial scatter of crushed tap slag, measuring about 1.5 m across. No pottery was associated with any of these finds.

BLOCK SURVEY

Most areas in the direct vicinity of the mine lie beneath the enormous modern spoil heaps and therefore could not be surveyed at all. Several slag scatters and other remains of mining and archaeometallurgical activity were recorded individually. Most of the twenty-three units that SCSP managed to survey revealed a sparse spread of sherds and almost no tiles.

The survey units closest to the mine (2611–12, 1615–18 see plate III) contained pottery dated primarily to the Archaic and Classical periods (table 4.4). Of those that could be identified well enough to suggest their function, three categories—table, storage, and kitchen wares—were present. Of these, very few were decorated wares (White Painted and Red Slip) and only two were imports (both Greek Black Glazed ware). In comparison with other POSIs in SIA 1, there was a notable decline in the number of pieces that might be associated with trade or with elite ceremonial (votive or drinking) activities. A single pithos sherd (cat. 2612.21A) suggests that storage continued to be a feature of this material. The presence of some Medieval and Modern sherds in these units perhaps results from proximity to a modern road. As one moves away from the mine, the number of Archaic sherds trails off and is replaced by a small amount of Late Roman pottery.

Fourteen sherds provide minimal evidence for activity in the Hellenistic to Roman periods, and even the Medieval to Modern material is surprisingly scarce, given the proximity to the village of Agrokipia. The nine Medieval sherds provide the most precise dates, including one from a thirteenth- to fourteenth-century Lemba ware bowl. The Ottoman pottery is even less distinctive, with four glazed sherds roughly datable to the seventeenth to eighteenth centuries, while the modern pottery is very recent, dating to the last fifty years

CONCLUSION

Clearly Agrokipia *Kriadhis* was exploited extensively during the Geometric, Archaic, and Classical periods, a time when copper production on Cyprus may have reached a peak level of activity. Because the closest major Archaic to Classical site is Tamassos, it is usually assumed that the kingdom of Tamassos controlled the mines as well as the production of copper.

Modern operations initially revealed and later destroyed ancient mining galleries that seem to have exploited rich covellite deposits. What remain today are parts of the spoil heaps (for example, SCY022) from the mining operations, and the scattered remains of a slag heap (SCY204). Although significant amounts of Archaic and Classical pottery have been found in the terraces of the modern mine, the amount of disturbance everywhere makes it likely that these sherds are out of context. Nonetheless, radiocarbon dating has provided arguably secure dates for mining operations at Kriadhis, which seem to have started already during the Geometric period.

The most interesting part of SIA 1, however, is the way operations were distributed around the mine. Recall once again that this landscape has been altered extensively and in a way can be seen as reversed: A large open-cast mine lies where once a hill would have stood and large spoil heaps cover what would have been the fields surrounding the hill. We must also bear in mind that although there is currently a single open-cast mine, only part of the removed ore body was in fact cupriferous, the rest being low-grade pyrite and therefore of no use or importance to the ancients. Taking all this into consideration, we can begin to look at the distribution of the operations related to the extraction of the ore, the beneficiation (including roasting) and the smelting. The first two seem to have taken place at the southeastern end of

Table 4.4 SIA 1: analyzed pottery from block survey

Chronotype	Period	Qty
Amphora-Ar	Ar	1
Black Glaze-Ar [2611.1.1]	Ar	1
Cooking ware-Ar	Ar	3
Double Rolled Strap Handle-Ar	Ar	1
Green ware	Ar	2
Plain ware-Ar	Ar	3
Soft Red-Orange	Ar	3
Wide Shallow Bowl-Ar	Ar	1
Amphora-Cl	Cl	1
Greek Red Slip	Cl	1
Plain ware-Cl	Cl	1
Plain White-Cl	Cl	11
White Painted-Cl	Cl	1
Amphora-AC	AC	4
Amphora, Torpedo	AC	1
Black Glaze-AC	AC	9
Black-on-Red-AC	AC	1
Cooking ware-AC	AC	10
Pithos-AC	AC	2
Plain ware-AC	AC	31
Plain White-AC	AC	6
Unknown-AC	AC	1
White Painted-AC	AC	7
Wide Shallow Bowl-AC	AC	1
TOTAL Archaic to Classical		103
Black Glaze-He	He	2
Cypriot Sigillata	ER	1
Red Slip-ER	ER	2
Amphora-LR	LR	1
Amphora, LR1	LR	2
Coarse ware-LR	LR	2
Coarse ware, Wheel-Ridged	LR	1
Cypriot Red Slip	LR	1
Cypriot Red Slip 1	LR	1
Phocaean ware (LR C)	LR	1
TOTAL Hellenistic to Late Roman		14
Cypriot Glazed	Med	2
Cypriot Glazed VII	Med	1
Cypriot Glazed VIIIB	Med	4
Cypriot Glazed XI	Med	1
Lemba ware	Med	1
Cypriot Glazed, Brown/Green [1307.1.1]	Ott	2
Ottoman Glazed	Ott	2
Brick	Mod	3
Contemporary Imported Asian	Mod	1
Contemporary Yogurt ware	Mod	1
Fine ware-Mod	Mod	1
Tile-Mod	Mod	1
Brown Glazed ware	MM	1
Coarse ware-MM	MM	1
Cypriot W1	MM	55
Cypriot W4	MM	1
Glazed ware	MM	6
TOTAL Medieval to Modern		84
Plain White-HA	HA	5
Red Slip-HA	HA	2
Pithos-PC	PC	4
Tile-PC	PC	2
Coarse ware-Unk	Unk	82
Cooking ware-Unk	Unk	13
Unknown-Unk	Unk	1
TOTAL		311

Note. Figures in brackets refer to cataloged items (see chapter 5.1).

the mine, where we have recorded the presence of spoil heaps. Smelting likely took place near the northeastern part of the mine and is spatially removed from the initial stages of ore preparation. This situation may result from the availability of ore and fuel. The spoil heaps are in the direct vicinity of the cupriferous ore deposit.

The trees growing in this area would have been used in both the mines and in the roasting furnaces. By setting up smelting operations at a distance, one could exploit the trees growing on another part of the hill. Moreover, the most noxious fumes—a by-product of the metallurgical process—are produced during the roasting of the ore. By setting the roasting operations at a distance, the people operating the smelting furnaces could have avoided these fumes. Unlike smelting furnaces, roasting furnaces do not need to be tended and, once the ore has started to burn, it can be left for days.

The predominantly Archaic to Classical pottery collected in the POSIs within the mine and in the units immediately surrounding it may indicate a contemporary settlement or installation associated with the mine. The high number of Greek imports, both fine table (drinking) wares and amphorae (East Greek), is striking. Excepting the pithoi, all the material from SIA 1, including the Astarte figurine, may well derive from tombs. However, it is equally possible that they came from elite residences with limited storage facilities in this area. Considering the overall pattern of the Archaic and Classical pottery in Cyprus, this material does not differ in form but it may differ in function. Very little is known about residential areas, whether common or elite. If this material is residential, it adds significantly to the broader picture of Cypriot Iron Age material culture within the SCSP area. If it is residential and elite in nature, the Astarte figurine might well be taken to reflect close relations between copper production and elite ideology, as was the case in the Bronze Age (Knapp 1986b; 1996b). This material and its contrast to that in SIA 7 provide, one way or another, a new perspective on patterns of residence and social status in connection with mining areas during the Iron Age. Several questions arise concerning the relationship between such an elite settlement or cemetery and the mine itself.

If Agrokipia *Kriadhis* was indeed an elite settlement contemporary with the mining and smelting activities, we must consider why it was located so close

to the mine and the smelting workshops. Did those who controlled production situate themselves as close as possible to the workshops manufacturing this precious commodity? Or, if this was a cemetery contemporary with the mining and smelting activities, what does that tell us about the status of the miners and metalsmiths of the Iron Age in Cyprus? Does the Astarte figurine demonstrate relations between copper production and elite ideology? It is also possible that the final stages of production—refining of black copper and casting into ingots—would have taken place at Tamassos, where metal producing workshops have been found among the temple complex (Buchholz 1978:165–66).The presence of slag heaps associated with Late Roman pottery at some distance from the mine (within the modern village of Agrokipia) recalls the situations noted at Mitsero *Sykamies* (SCY024) and particularly at Mitsero *Kouloupakhis* (SIA 3). In all these cases, slag heaps of the Late Roman period arose at some distance from the mine.

4.2 SIA 2: Klirou *Manastirka*

Compiled by Kylie Seretis Team leaders: Robert Schon, Haddon Wright Archaeometallurgy: Vasiliki Kassianidou Geomorphology: Jay Noller Pottery: Timothy E. Gregory, R. Scott Moore, Joanna S. Smith

Grid reference:	517300/3873500
Cadastral map:	XXXVIII/16
Aerial photograph:	1993, run 174, no. 198
Survey units:	3000–49, 4052–81
POSIs:	SCY132: Klirou *Manastirka* (church, pottery, tile, slag); SCY201: Klirou *Lithinon* (Roman tombs); SCY211: Klirou *Mazovounos* (pottery on knoll)

The church of Panayia tou Lakhni sits at the top of a small ridge in the center of a cultivated valley (plate V, figure 4.7), with a stream immediately to its east and the steep-sided wooded mountain of Vournia 500 m to the west. The modern village and major Roman settlement of Klirou are situated 2 km to the northwest. The church was substantially rebuilt in 1993 and the top of the knoll bulldozed, but there are rubble piles to the west and a dense scatter of pottery and tile fragments all around. The pottery continues across the surrounding fields, indicating extensive, long-term human activity in the area. Between the

Figure 4.7 SIA 2 from the southeast, with the church of Panayia tou Lakhni toward the left

church and the stream, a dense concentration of slag fragments adds to the striking material presence in this area. To the northwest is Klirou *Lithinon* (SCY201), the steep-sided eastern slope of Vournia, where there was a major Roman cemetery.

PHYSICAL LANDSCAPE

SIA 2 is located within a flat-floored alluvial valley eroded out of pillow basalts and basal group rocks of the Troodos ophiolite. The principal drainage, the Argaki tis Myrenas, is ephemeral, and has its head just 1 km south of SIA 2. To the north, the valley opens out onto the broad alluvial plain of the Akaki River and its tributaries, of which the Myrenas is one of the largest. The upper Myrenas valley is drained by three streams: the Myrenas, the westernmost and largest; a central stream impounded by check dams in its upper reach; and an eastern stream. All stream courses are entrenched down to the basalt bedrock below Pleistocene alluvial fill. A medial bedrock ridge separates the central and eastern streams. The church of Panayia tou Lakhni (SCY132) is located at the northern end of this ridge.

The western slope of the upper Myrenas is underlain by steep alluvial fans more than 5 m thick. The ridge at their head is underlain by a large intrusion in the Basal Group, which is unusual for the survey area. The composition and character of this intrusion allows it to yield cobbles to boulder deposits and finer material to colluvium and fan deposits. These deposits have weathered on the slope to a clayey B horizon that varies from reddish brown to red. They continue downslope to the broad alluvial plain to the north. The eastern slope of the upper Myrenas valley is underlain by sheeted dikes of the Basal Group. The orientation of these dikes gives the landscape the northern trend of its ridgelines and water courses. Erosion of the vertical intrusions gives this west-facing slope of the valley its markedly steep character.

Soils in the area fall into one of four categories and are distributed according to the underlying geology (for abbreviated terms, see table 3.4):

1) Red, stony A/Bt/Cox soil profiles, rich in iron oxide and clay, developed on the western slope

and the main valley floor) (Pleistocene alluvial terrace [Pat]);

2) Dark brown, clayey A/Bt/Cox/R soil profiles, lightly calcic, along and east of the central Manastirka ridge (Pat);

3) Grayish brown loamy A/C/R profiles of the stream bottoms (Holocene alluvial terrace [Hat]);

4) Brownish gray to gray Ap/R soil profiles in agricultural terraces and check dam fills, mainly in the eastern half of the area.

The loss, or rather erosion, of soil from the Cypriot landscape is one of its intriguing and most obvious features. The Manastirka valley is no exception, as much of the area surrounding SIA 2 results from erosion. The quality of the soil reflects in part its erosional history. The thick red soil of Pat underlies a more stable and persistent surface, whereas soil is thin to absent on the gullied basalt slopes to the east. This difference reflects a number of cumulative factors related to the internal character of the deposits and the soils that have developed within them. Check dams trap sediment in the upper reaches of the central stream, whereas the eastern stream is largely unprotected and deeply incised. The smoothing of the landscape in the central valley is due to agricultural displacement of soil. Recent development of terraces in the valley has concentrated on the steep western and eastern slopes, benching deep into bedrock without apparent efforts to conserve the native soil. Those terraces being developed in 1996 to 1998 typically saw their soils being buried at the bottom of fill prisms.

HISTORICAL CONTEXT

Gunnis and other brief twentieth-century accounts describe the church simply as a shedlike building between the village of Klirou and the Macheras mountains and mention the "monastic ruins" that surrounded it (Gunnis 1936:275; cf. Jeffery 1918:303; *MKE* 7:151). The locality name of Manastirka implies the presence of a monastery. The church has recently undergone extensive reconstruction, finished in 1993, and there are several modern icons inside. Late in 1999 a small "spring" was constructed about 150 m to the east of the church. This is a small stone structure about 2 m in height and 1.5 m in width, holding a number of modern printed icons and several lamps and oil burners. The water is piped into the back of the structure, which may be tied to local folklore relating that the holy water from this Panayia is miraculous and can cure skin problems and children's diseases (Paraskevopoulou 1982:144).

FIELD METHODOLOGY

After preliminary reconnaissance of the area, the church and the immediate part of the ridge on which it stands were designated SCY132: Klirou *Manastirka*. It soon became clear that the entire area was significant. The scatter of pottery in the surrounding fields was widespread and in some places extremely dense; local people visiting the church told us about tombs and an ancient settlement in the area, and the published accounts refer to a monastery that preceded the church. Accordingly the entire valley was declared a Special Interest Area (SIA 2) and was block surveyed in 1996 and 1997.

The aims were to investigate the relationship between the different archaeological, geomorphological, historical, and ethnohistoric components of the area and to search for any spatial variations among the material. We conducted block survey in the fields surrounding the church, produced a detailed geomorphological map, analyzed the archaeometallurgical remains on the eastern slope of the ridge below the church, and examined the actual POSI—the knoll with the church and the slag concentration (SCY132)—using an iron cross and gridded circles.

SCY132: KLIROU *MANASTIRKA*: GRIDDED CIRCLES

The first investigation of Klirou *Manastirka* took place in 1996 but could only be preliminary because the slopes of the ridge on which the church stands were thick with wild oats and grass, severely limiting visibility. An iron cross of nine circles was laid out on the southeast slope in an area planted with young olives, where the visibility was marginally better. This was supplemented by a much larger series of gridded circles and grabs in the fields to the south, carried out in 1997 (see plate VI). There is a clear concentration of material close to the church, with tile reaching twenty pieces per m² and pottery twenty-five per m². Most of the datable pottery in this area is Medieval to Modern (table 4.5), decreasing from 9.6 sherds per m² to 1.6 at the bottom of the slope, farthest from the church. This is in contrast to the slag, which gradually increases in density moving away from the church, reaching fifty-six pieces per m² at the southeastern end of the line.

The work to the south of the church in 1997 consisted of sixty-nine circles, which were 2 m in diameter and set out 10 or 20 m apart, with grabs in between. Only in the northernmost circle nearest the church did the figures approach in quantity those laid out southeast of the church. Elsewhere total densities of pottery and tile were much lower, typically ranging from two to five pieces per m². Twenty circles had no pottery at all. For specific periods, there was a low concentration of Geometric to Classical pottery in the southeast, with between 0.3 and 1.0 sherds per m²; this seemed too localized to be general background from manuring, dumping, or erosion. Hellenistic to Roman pottery was even lower but more widespread, and its typical array of 0.3 to 0.6 sherds per m² is more likely to derive from manuring or possibly erosion from upslope. Medieval to Modern material, although substantially less than that adjacent to the church, was broadly and evenly spread; typical figures ranged from 0.5 to 1.0 sherds per m².

GEOMETRIC TO CLASSICAL

Thirty-nine of the sherds collected were identified as Geometric, Archaic, and/or Classical. Most are undiagnostic coarse ware, or other undecorated wares. A small amount of Cypriot Red Slip, Greek imported fine wares, and a knobbed base amphora fragment are most diagnostic of the Archaic to Classical periods. The nature of the material collected is not suggestive of a specific activity in the area, but its very localized spread might suggest a tomb or other concentrated deposit.

HELLENISTIC TO ROMAN

Of the 771 sherds collected from SCY132, none were identifiably Hellenistic, and only three were Early Roman, all fine wares. One of these was a locally produced Cypriot Sigillata body sherd dating to the first century AD; the other two were imported first century AD Eastern Sigillata A produced in Syria. Of the forty-three Late Roman sherds (5.6%), nine were fine wares, and twenty were amphora sherds. Most fine wares were locally produced Cypriot Red Slip (CRS): two unidentifiable; one CRS form 8 (sixth century AD?); and four CRS form 9 (580–700 AD). There was also one piece of African Red Slip,

Table 4.5 SCY132: analyzed pottery

Chronotype	Period	Qty
Red Slip-Ar	Ar	5
Black Glaze-Cl	Cl	2
Fine ware-Cl	Cl	2
Green ware-GAC	GAC	4
Amphora, Knobbed Base	AC	1
Coarse ware-AC	AC	13
Plain ware-AC	AC	2
Plain White-AC	AC	10
TOTAL Geometric to Classical		39
Cypriot Sigillata	ER	1
Eastern Sigillata A	ER	2
African Red Slip	LR	1
Amphora-LR	LR	10
Amphora, LR 1	LR	7
Basin-LR	LR	2
Basin, Piecrust Rim	LR	1
Coarse ware-LR	LR	3
Coarse ware, LR Wheel-Ridged	LR	5
Cooking ware-LR	LR	3
Cooking ware, Dhiorios Pot	LR	1
Cypriot Red Slip	LR	6
Cypriot Red Slip 9	LR	1
Flat-Grooved-LR	LR	2
Phocaean ware 10	LR	1
Amphora-Byz	Byz	1
TOTAL Hellenistic to Byzantine		47
Cypriot Glazed	Med	2
Cypriot Glazed IV	Med	1
Cypriot Glazed VIIIB	Med	1
Cypriot Glazed IX	Med	2
Cypriot Glazed IX Late	Ott	2
Cypriot Glazed XI	Med	1
Cypriot Glazed, Brown and Green	Ott	2
Cypriot W3	Ott	5
Cypriot W6	Ott	12
Cypriot W7	Mod	55
Lapithos ware, Green	Mod	1
Pithos-Mod	Mod	1
Tile-Mod	Mod	4
Water Pipe-Mod	Mod	1
Coarse ware-MM	MM	50
Cypriot W1	MM	8
Cypriot W4	MM	188
Glazed ware	MM	1
Pithos-MM	MM	7
Tile-MM	MM	14
TOTAL Medieval to Modern		358
Plain White-HA	HA	14
Amphora-Hi	Hi	3
Pithos-PC	PC	20
Tile-PC	PC	50
Tile, Corinthian Pan	PC	2
Tile, Flat Pan	PC	3
Coarse ware-Unk	Unk	210
Cooking ware-Unk	Unk	23
Unknown-Unk	Unk	2
TOTAL		771

and a Phocaean ware form 10 (570–625 AD) from Syria, perhaps showing continuity with the early Roman Eastern Sigillata A sherds from Syria. The amphora sherds show a similar pattern. The majority were locally produced, but two were definitely not produced on the island: one was probably from Africa, and the other from the eastern Aegean.

The Late Roman collection of sherds includes transport, cooking, fine and coarse wares. With the exception of the Late Roman frying pan, all the standard Late Roman chronotypes—including a Dhiorios cooking pot, Late Roman basins, and a piecrust rim—were present. SCY132 clearly indicates a thriving area that had commercial ties with all parts of the Late Antique world. While the majority of sherds grouped toward the AD 400 to 700 time period, it seems clear that there was continuity throughout the Roman era.

MEDIEVAL TO MODERN

Of the 771 sherds from SCY132, 349 (45%) were from the Medieval to Modern periods. Of these, 268 could not be identified any more closely than Medieval/Modern, a problem encountered across SIA 2 as a whole. Interestingly, proportions of periods and chronotypes were very similar within SCY132 as in SIA 2, which vindicates in general our use of the two collection strategies in tandem. In terms of pottery function, most concentrations of material were too small and inadequately dated to indicate the presence of the reported monastery.

SCY201: KLIROU *LITHINON*: REPORTED ROMAN CEMETERY

What may have been an ancient cemetery lies on the steep eastern slope of Vournia, 700 m northwest of the church of Panayia tou Lakhni. It was first brought to our attention by villagers from Klirou, who reported that gold and glass bottles had been found in tombs there. This might indicate a cemetery of Roman date. A brief investigation showed that the slope was heavily eroded and had been bulldozed for roads and agricultural terraces. Only one probable tomb entrance was discovered, a rectangular pit (1.1 x 1.7 m) with a depth of approximately 0.4 to 0.7 m and containing no pottery.

SCY211: KLIROU *MAZOVOUNOS*: ARCHAIC TO CLASSICAL SANCTUARY

On a stony, unplowed hilltop marking the southern extent of our work at SIA 2, we discovered a dense, highly localized scatter of fine pottery. First surveyed as unit 4052, the very distinctive character of the finds led us to redefine it as a POSI (SCY211). Elsewhere in SIA 2, Archaic to Classical material tends to be very worn, and forms a minute percentage of the total assemblage. Of the twenty-eight sherds found at SCY211, however, twenty-five (89%) are of Archaic to Classical date. These sherds were noticeably larger and sharper than in the rest of the SIA, suggesting that they have been recently exposed, and perhaps represent a specific use area rather than being an indicator of generalized activity across the landscape.

The pattern of vessel types is consistent with that from the rest of SIA 2, but the percentage of indeterminate vessels (12%) is remarkably low. Almost the entire assemblage can be identified with specific types of vessels, and several can be assigned specific dates. Vessel shapes include skyphos (cat. 4052.9.1), medium-deep bowl (cat. 4052.15.1,2,3) and wide, shallow bowl, as well as other small bowls and a juglet. In addition, there are four fragments of storage vessels, including pithoi (for example, cat. 4052.6.1), and seven in a fabric appropriate for cooking. The dates are primarily Cypro-Archaic II, but a few pieces appear to be Cypro-Classical I. These dates provide a very specific period of use for SCY211, from the sixth to early fifth centuries BC.

Two terra-cottas were discovered in SCY211. Catalog 4052.2.1 (chapter 5.3) is a terra-cotta horse figurine SRO fabric, which, judging from a small protrusion from the figure's right leg, appears to have formed part of a chariot group. Catalog 4052.3 is not identifiable as a specific type but may be part of a figurine. Its two holes do not fully pierce the object. The presence of pithos fragments argues against these items being tomb material. There is no tile from the unit, and almost none on the slopes below (in contrast to the area round SCY132). The figurines, the unusually large number of small bowls and plates, and the rather friable, possibly nonfunctional nature of some of the pottery suggest that this small hilltop may have been used as a local cult area.

METALLURGY

The low central ridge on which the church stands and the higher eastern ridgeline appear to have been mined for both copper ore and construction stone. Premodern prospection pits dot this hillslope, and are located in mineralized zones of basalt between dikes. Copper oxides are frequently evident in the basalts, and red and green jasper are common. Hand-excavated trenches are present over much of the central ridge and some adits were found. On the eastern slope were large rubble piles, tens of cubic meters each: These were perhaps mining spoils, most of which are now buried beneath modern agricultural terraces. Alternatively, the piles of boulder-sized basalt blocks might represent quarried construction stone for use in houses, check dams, or terrace walls.

Slag (but no ore) appears in a single pile 100 m east of the church and is scattered as cobble-sized field stones in nearby agricultural fields. Its distribution seems to follow field boundaries rather than geomorphological zones. A terrace wall on the northwest flank of SCY211 was made up predominately of large slag cakes.

BLOCK SURVEY

Although sherds from all periods are distributed throughout SIA 2, there are several obvious concentrations, three of which coincide with increased numbers of tile fragments (plate VII). The concentration with the greatest number of tiles surrounds the church (SCY132); another lies in the orchards 400 m to the north; and a third is situated in the fields to the southwest. SCY211 shows up as a single, isolated area of high density, with no tiles.

GEOMETRIC TO CLASSICAL

The distribution map of Geometric to Classical pottery shows a general, rather sparse spread of material across the entire SIA (plate VIII). There are three apparent peaks: SCY132, which has a substantial Archaic component (the remainder could be Archaic or Classical); SCY211, which has similar material but is much more restricted in size; and two units to the west (3128, 3129), where the clearly datable pottery is weighted toward the Classical period.

Table Wares. Several table wares are represented

across SIA 2 and are particularly striking in the large number of definable bowls (cat. 3020.11.1), cups, and plates (table 4.6). They comprise not just plain wares (light fabrics) but also some storage vessels (for example, cat. 3000.14B.1), kitchen wares, and the SRO fabric. The last can be very friable (for example, a carinated body fragment, cat. 3049.4B.1, possibly of Cypro-Archaic II date) and seems impractical for daily use or for serving food or drink. Many other items in SIA 2 are made of this material, including large storage vessels and the terra-cottas from SCY211.

Light Utility Wares. There are several sherds of what we term kitchen ware, including one identifiable as part of a jug (3043.15.1); these may also have served more general purposes, in addition to cooking. There may also be a link between kitchen ware and SRO, with the two fabrics mingling in some vessels (for example, 4052.7.1 and 4052.8.1). SIA 2 is full of red clay, which may have been used for the producing the majority of Archaic to Classical material in this area.

Special Purpose Vessels. Pottery vessels with more specific uses include a basin (3049.6) and a possible scoop handle (3043.12) of plain white fabric. Basins may have many functions, including industrial activities; they also appear as offering bowls in tombs and sanctuaries. Scoops appear to be part of sanctuary paraphernalia (Buchholz 1994).

Loomweight. This item (cat. SCY132.1.1.1, chapter 5.3) is disc shaped, probably Classical or Hellenistic in date (Chavane 1975:84–85), and bears the impression of a finger ring on one part of the curved edge. The decoration on the ring appears to represent either a vessel, or a figure standing on a baseline and holding an unknown object. As a single piece the loomweight does not tell us much but the labeling of weights may be an identification mark made by the weaver or, alternatively, may be a way of marking weights so that the weaver knows where in a fabric to insert a special weave (Smith 1999). Loomweights appear in domestic areas and sanctuaries and, on Cyprus, are rarely found in tombs (Smith 2002).

Industry. Although no specific clay source or kiln has been found in SIA 2, it is likely that pottery manufacture occurred somewhere in the area. The SRO and cooking ware fabrics appear to be local products. Pottery was also being produced in SIA 6 but in a different way that led to a high-fired product that was reduce-fired to produce a buff surface (see

Table 4.6 SIA 2: analyzed pottery from block survey

Chronotype	Period	Qty	Chronotype	Period	Qty
Amphora-Ar [3000.14B.1]	Ar	1	Coarse ware-Med	Med	1
Cooking ware-Ar	Ar	9	Cypriot Glazed	Med	6
Medium Deep Bowl-Ar [4052.15.1,2,3]	Ar	2	Cypriot Glazed VII	Med	1
Pithos-Ar [4052.6.1]	Ar	4	Cypriot Glazed VIIIB	Med	2
Plain ware-Ar [3020.11.1]	Ar	4	Cypriot Glazed VIIIBL	Ott	1
Soft Red-Orange-Ar [4052.9.1]	Ar	24	Cypriot Glazed IX	Med	1
Terra-cotta Figurine-Ar	Ar	1	Cypriot Glazed IXL	Ott	1
Wide Shallow Bowl-Ar	Ar	2	Cypriot Glazed XI	Med	1
Black Glaze-Cl	Cl	6	Cypriot Glazed, Brown and Green	Ott	3
Plain ware-Cl	Cl	3	Cypriot W3	Ott	5
Plain White-Cl	Cl	35	Cypriot W5	Ott	1
Soft Red-Orange-Cl	Cl	2	Cypriot W6	Ott	5
Green ware-GAC	GAC	1	Ottoman Glazed	Ott	3
Basin-AC	AC	1	Purple Painted ware	Ott	1
Coarse ware-AC	AC	1	Brick	Mod	1
Cooking ware-AC	AC	4	Coarse ware-Mod	Mod	19
Pithos-AC	AC	1	Cypriot W7	Mod	11
Plain ware-AC	AC	19	Fine ware-Mod	Mod	6
Plain White-AC	AC	5	Lapithos ware, Green	Mod	1
Terra-cotta Figurine-AC	AC	1	Lapithos ware, Yellow	Mod	1
Wide Shallow Bowl-AC	AC	1	Brown Glazed	MM	9
			Coarse ware-MM	MM	22
TOTAL Geometric to Classical		127	Cypriot W1	MM	151
			Cypriot W4	MM	58
Black Glaze-He [4052.25.1]	He	1	Glazed ware	MM	12
Coarse ware-He	He	1	Pithos-MM	MM	15
Red Slip-He	He	1	Tile-MM	MM	3
Çandarli ware	ER	1			
Coarse ware-ER	ER	1	TOTAL Medieval to Modern		341
Cooking ware-ER	ER	2			
Cooking ware, ER Cooking Pot	ER	5	Plain White-HA	HA	14
Cooking ware, Square Rim Pot	ER	2	Pithos-PC	PC	37
Cypriot Sigillata [4069.3.1]	ER	4	Tile-PC	PC	39
African Red Slip	LR	9	Tile, Corinthian	PC	5
Amphora-LR	LR	1	Tile, Corinthian Pan	PC	8
Amphora, LR 1	LR	11	Coarse ware-Unk	Unk	448
Basin-LR	LR	3	Cooking ware-Unk	Unk	21
Coarse ware-LR	LR	9	Fine ware-Unk	Unk	1
Coarse ware, LR Wheel-Ridged	LR	19	Table ware-Unk	Unk	2
Cooking ware-LR	LR	3			
Cypriot Red Slip	LR	11	TOTAL		1160
Cypriot Red Slip 3	LR	1			
Cypriot Red Slip 9	LR	3			
Flat-Grooved-LR	LR	3			
Frying Pan-LR	LR	6			
Phocaean ware (LR C)	LR	4			
Phocaean ware 10	LR	1			
Pithos-LR	LR	4			
Red Slip-LR	LR	1			
Tile-LR	LR	7			
Fine ware-REL	REL	1			
Red Slip-REL	REL	2			
TOTAL Hellenistic to Late Roman		117			

Note. Figures in brackets refer to cataloged items (see chapter 5.1).

chapter 4.6). Both areas used an iron-rich clay, but in SIA 2 the pottery was mostly low-fired, while that in SIA 6 was high-fired, often over-fired and partly vitrified. The absence of wasters and other kiln products in SIA 2 makes it impossible to determine any locus of production. SRO was found throughout the SCSP area but in much smaller quantities. It may be

that this fabric originated within SIA 2 but was used more widely throughout the survey area.

The character of the pottery from SCY211 suggests that it was a small sanctuary. The remainder of the pottery, including that from SCY132, is indicative of small-scale storage and possibly household level activities. At least some of the Archaic to Classical pottery found in units beyond SCY211 probably stems from erosion and/or from movement as a result of agricultural activities.

HELLENISTIC TO ROMAN

In contrast to the Geometric to Classical periods, the Hellenistic to Roman material in SIA 2 is much sparser (plate VIII), and is preponderantly Late Roman in date. The thin spread of material overall may indicate manuring or general land use.

As in the rest of the survey area, very little Hellenistic material (0.3%) was discovered. Of the three Hellenistic sherds found—a coarse black slipped body sherd, a red slipped body sherd, and a black/brown slipped rim—two came from SCY211. All three were most likely locally produced between 150 and 50 BC.

The seventeen Early Roman sherds represent only 1.5% of the total numbers from SIA 2. Most were discovered in the northern section of the SIA, with a clear grouping of both fine ware and cooking ware in units 3011, 3012, 3014, and 3015. Of the 1160 sherds found in SIA 2, 98 (7.5%) were Late Roman, representing a range of cooking, storage, and fine wares. The thirty fine-ware sherds include items locally manufactured on Cyprus (Cypriot Red Slip, Late Roman Red Slip) as well as fourteen imports (African Red Slip, Phocaean ware). This division of material may indicate some affluence, assuming that imported wares were more expensive than local wares. The dates of the fine wares are consistently weighted toward the end of the Late Roman period, fifth to seventh centuries AD. The number of storage/transport sherds is fairly high (30 sherds, or 35%); these were predominately Late Roman 1 amphorae, manufactured at Amathus, Kourion, and Nea Paphos during this period and perhaps used to transport and store olive oil.

MEDIEVAL TO MODERN

The Medieval to Modern pottery can be dated more specifically than that from other periods; here it is dominated by modern material (plate IX). There is only a light scatter of Medieval material, which is most unusual in the SCSP region, particularly for an area that has a church and a moderate scatter of Late Roman pottery. The Ottoman material is clearly concentrated around the church, and coincides closely with the distribution of tiles (plate VII). This pattern is similar to that from unit 3000 (immediately east of the church), where the 27 sherds recovered date from the Medieval, Ottoman, and Modern periods. SCY132 shows similar concentrations in the area of the church.

These distributions must be regarded as tentative because of the high proportion of unknown and Medieval/Modern pottery: Of 1160 sherds from SIA 2, 472 (41%) are unknown and 270 (23%) are Medieval/Modern (without being more specifically determinable). Looking at the more precisely datable sherds (table 4.6), the twelve Medieval pieces represent a very modest level of activity, with the earliest dating to the fourteenth to fifteenth centuries and the most abundant to the sixteenth century. There was no obvious spatial patterning of these pieces. The twenty Ottoman pieces can be dated only generally within the seventeenth to nineteenth centuries AD. The Modern pottery is relatively nondescript, with 31 of 39 sherds being plain or coarse wares. Of the 270 less-diagnostic Medieval to Modern sherds, 209 (77%) belong to the relatively ubiquitous brown fabrics we term W1 and W4.

CONCLUSION

The valley now dominated by the church of Panayia tou Lakhni has seen a wide variety of activities from the Archaic through Modern periods. Often these activities are difficult to tie down spatially, in part because the knoll where the church stands was bulldozed during renovation in the early 1990s. The slopes of this knoll show a slight concentration of Archaic and Classical material, while the likely functions of the material found in this part of the valley—cooking, pottery-making, and weaving—are suggestive of the activities that took place during these periods. Another smaller knoll to the south of the church, with its terra-cotta figurines and dedicatory bowls made in local kilns, may have been a small Archaic to Classical rural shrine. Small cult places are found throughout the Cypriot landscape (see chapter 7.5; Knapp 1996a; Loulloupis 1989; Wright 1992). Limited-scale copper smelting probably took place during this period, perhaps in association with work at Klirou *Koutis* (SCY205) 500 m to the northeast.

There seems to have been a substantial level of activity in this area during the Late Roman period but with only a slight focus on the slopes around the church. Presumably a settlement in the area produced the light scatter of storage vessels and fine wares, both local and imported. This material may have come from the Roman town at Klirou, 2 km to the northwest, but judging from our understanding of the Roman landscape elsewhere in the SCSP area, the material more likely came from smaller local estates or farms. The soil loss and erosion seen in the drainages and the surrounding hillslopes clearly derives from a long history of intensive agriculture in the area.

Medieval to Modern material shows a substantial spread throughout the valley, with a distinct concentration immediately south and east of the church, increasing in density toward the church itself. This concentration might have been associated with the monastery that reportedly existed in the ruins around the church, long since bulldozed and destroyed. The nature of the material, particularly the large number of tiles, does not contradict this suggestion, although most of it is difficult to date precisely. The broader spread of material from this period is clearly associated with agricultural activities, as are the check dams and the general smoothing of contours in the lower parts of the valley. Today, after its long history of settlement, agriculture, and industry, the valley is a rich agricultural area with a well-frequented church and easy access from the neighboring village of Klirou.

4.3 SIA 3: Mitsero *Kouloupakhis*

Compiled by Vasiliki Kassianidou
Team leaders: Bradley Creevey, Robert Schon
Archaeometallurgy: Rod Clough, Vasiliki Kassianidou,
Haddon Wright Geobotany: Neil Urwin
Geomorphology: Lisa Wells GIS analysis: Nathan Meyer,
Vasiliki Kassianidou Pottery: Timothy E. Gregory,
R. Scott Moore, Joanna S. Smith

Grid reference:	511600/3878400
Cadastral map:	XXIX/53
Aerial photograph:	1993, run 177, no. 43
Survey units:	1004–10, 1253–67, 2000–15, 4000–38
POSIs:	SCY021: Mitsero *Kouloupakhis* 1 (slag heap); SCY342: Mitsero *Kouloupakhis* 2 (spoil heap, pottery)

The slag heap at Mitsero *Kouloupakhis*, one of the largest in the survey area and indeed in the whole of the Troodos mountains, is what defines this area as an SIA. It is located on relatively flat land near the base of the

large hill at Kriadhis, approximately 1 km northeast of Mitsero village. The heap is now dissected by a modern road and has been quarried extensively over the last fifty years (plate X).

The Kouloupakhis slag heaps are particularly interesting because they are not situated in the direct vicinity of any mine: They lie approximately 1.5 km from the Kokkinoyia mine and 2 km from the Agrokipia mines. Apart from ascertaining the date and form of the metallurgical activities represented in the waste dump, one of our main aims at SIA 3 was to investigate the archaeological material from the surrounding units and to determine whether any settlements, cemeteries, or workshops could be associated with the slag heaps.

PHYSICAL LANDSCAPE

Mitsero *Kouloupakhis* is located in a transitional zone between colluvial sediments draping the southern slope of Kriadhis and the alluvial deposits of the Likythia River (plate X). This river bounds the western edge of SIA 3 while the confluence of five Likythia tributaries is located just to the southwest. A number of small gullies cut through and bound the extent of this area.

The steep step in the rivers that defines the southern perimeter of the village of Mitsero is located at the interface between the altered and highly eroded upper pillow lavas and the less altered, less erodable lower pillow lavas. As a result, the colluvial gravel that drapes the southern slopes of Kriadhis is comprised exclusively of limestone fragments which have buried an eroded bedrock surface. Where active gullying has removed the protective cover of accumulated gravel sediments, referred to as the talus drape, erosion into the altered upper pillow basalts is extremely rapid (estimated by Gerth 1998). With such rapid deflation rates, it is not surprising to find low artifact densities in the survey units within the active gullies or the units in the southeast sector of the SIA. Archaeological data from these areas, therefore, must be interpreted with this reality in mind: The surveyed units in this POSI drape across landforms of a variety of ages and geologic origins.

The oldest parts of the landscape are Pleistocene talus facets (Qct), which are the remains of limestone colluvium deposited over eroded bedrock or Pleistocene river gravels that are preserved on spur ridges between the active gullies. The deposits are commonly triangular to diamond shaped in map view, hence the term *facet*. The colluvium is at most 2-m thick, often much thinner, and it seems that this deposit once formed a continuous blanket around the southern slope of the mountain. Soils formed on the surface suggest that this colluvium is late Pleistocene in age, perhaps associated with deposition during the Last Glacial Maximum. At the bottom edge of these talus facets, and set somewhat below them indicating a younger age, are early Holocene alluvial deposits (Hoal). These sediments make up the distinct bench at the base of Kriadhis and surrounding much of Mitsero. Below this surface there is a thin cover of alluvial debris (3 m maximum thickness) overlying a somewhat planar eroded bedrock surface referred to as a strath. The strath and the associated overlying sediment resulted from a distinct period of valley widening within the Mitsero Basin, during which the streams had a more braided character and when the climate perhaps was moister so that stream discharges were higher than today. Upstream in the Kryon Neron branch of the Likythia, charcoal from soils on the surface of this stratigraphic unit produced a radiocarbon age of circa 10,000 years calendar years BP (GX1-25438, see appendix B; Whitehill 1999); this provides a minimum age for the stabilization of the alluvial surface in the Mitsero Basin and the subsequent incision of the streams below this surface.

After the abandonment of the Holocene alluvial surface resulting from the shift to river incision, gullies began to erode back into the slopes of Kriadhis. The early/mid-Holocene talus cone in the middle of the SIA has largely been stripped of its overlying sediment and there are numerous bedrock outcrops on the surface of this talus cone (Hct). A small intermediate Holocene alluvial terrace (Hmal) is located under the south side of the village. This surface lies stratigraphically between an older and a younger Holocene alluvial surface and we therefore assign it a mid-Holocene age. This middle Holocene alluvial surface appears to be contemporary or slightly younger than the early/mid-Holocene talus cones that drape off the hillsides. Evidence for the subsequent period of river incision is found in the terrace riser (Hr) that separates the older from the younger Holocene alluvium. The relief of this step between the two surfaces records the minimum amount of river in-

cision that occurred during this time. The surfaces are modified by extensive agricultural terracing, the youngest of which appears to have been bulldozed into the steep slope of the riser. Inset below the Holocene colluvium and the mid-Holocene terrace riser is the surface of the youngest alluvial deposit of the Likythia (Hyal) basin. This surface, which forms a low terrace adjacent to the modern stream, may flood during extreme storm events.

Most material from SIA 3 is distributed on early Holocene and Late Pleistocene geomorphologic surfaces (plate XI). The primary locus of human activity appears to drape over the Holocene talus cone at the mouth of the gully (the gully that traces up from unit 4015) and onto the adjacent older Holocene alluvial terraces. These two geological units, Hct and Hoal, are relatively stable surfaces and maagriculture, are otherwise in their original context.

The only survey unit (1000) on the middle Holocene alluvial terrace is, in fact, an interfluve terrace between the streams at the Likythia confluence. No artifacts were found there and it is likely that surface erosion by the rivers as well as recent human land-use may have removed human-made materials from this location.

GEOBOTANY

The large Kouloupakhis slag heap supports a sparse shrub stratum with a dense herb and grass layer. The community dominants are *Sarcopoterium spinosum* (spiny burnet), *Ononis spinosa,* and *Hyparrhenia* sp. The site is surrounded by waste, disturbed ground, or cropping areas. To rule out the possibility that the vegetation on this slag heap was merely typical of waste and/or disturbed ground in that area, it was compared with the vegetation of a nearby spoil heap adjoining a modern adit and with other batha areas. The sampling unit for the Kouloupakhis slag heap was positioned to sample as far as possible the vegetation on that part of the slag heap with the most weathered (least quarried) surface below topsoil. The multivariate clustering analysis identified the sampling unit (quadrat W16Q1) over the slag heap as a stand-alone outlier at both the species level and the community level (figure 4.8).

The analysis suggested that the individual species growing on the slag heap at low densities (*Papaver rhoes, Palinuris spina-christi, Centaura creticum,*

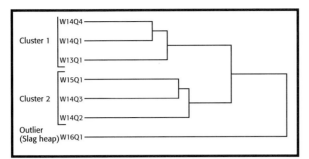

Figure 4.8 SIA 3: geobotanical dendrogram showing identical analytical results of (1) all species and (2) >2%

and *Achnatherum calanagrostis*) acted as specific indicators, since they were largely absent in the vegetation of the other sampling units. Additionally, the analysis showed that the relative abundance of the community *dominants (Sarcopoterium spinosum, Ononis spinosa,* and *Hyperrhenia* sp.) and their density over the area (90% vegetative cover) was indicative of the POSI.

The outlier sampling unit (quadrat W16Q1) was used as a training area in the satellite imagery classification to establish a subject area signature for the slag heap. All other signatures established related to background land cover values (grain, quarry, trees, water, batha, garrigue, waste ground). The thematic map shows several areas with the same vegetation signature as that on the slag heap, distributed throughout the piedmont geomorphological unit of north Mitsero (plate XII). In particular, the classification showed several small areas with vegetation/cover characteristics that are the same as that of the Kouloupakhis slag heap within a large triangular area surrounding it. Two of these areas, SCY021E-1 and SCY021E-2 (plate X), which adjoin units 1266 and 1267, exhibit large surface slag pieces. SCY021E-1 was identified in the thematic map with a much smaller area than recent ground surveys have found. This factor suggests that much of the current vegetation on SCY021E-1 is uncharacteristic of slag, probably due to recent (post-1955) disturbance. This finding points toward extensive past smelting activity in the area resulting in a relatively wide distribution of small buried slag heaps. Alternatively, these indicators may be flagging the present remnants of one or two huge slag complexes of the past.

HISTORICAL BACKGROUND

There are references to the Mitsero slag heaps in earlier publications on the mines of Cyprus (for example, Rickard 1930:287, 299; Bruce 1937:660), as well as in the state archives (SA1/1301/1910: Red 1). There, the presence of some ancient walls in the area of Mitsero village was recorded in 1910 but permission to excavate them was not granted. The slag heap has also been visited, recorded and sampled by several previous scholars (for example, Tylecote 1977:318; Zwicker 1986:97; Panayiotou 1989a:86). Koucky (1982:243) published a short description of the slag heap in an appendix to the preliminary report of the Akhera Survey, and together with Steinberg illustrated a general section of the Mitsero slag heap which shows the architectural remains (Koucky and Steinberg 1982a:123). Furthermore, slag samples from Kouloupakhis, as indeed from all the other slag heaps in the survey area, were included in their study of ancient slags from Cyprus (Koucky and Steinberg 1974; Koucky and Steinberg 1982a). Zwicker (1986:97) published a radiocarbon date of a charcoal sample collected from "a Mitsero slag heap" (others are located at Sykamies and Kokkinoyia). This date—from charcoal sample H 6155–5854, Cy538—was 470±150 AD, which is comparable to the dates of samples SCSP collected systematically from the Kouloupakhis slag heap.

We know very little about the administration of the copper industry in Cyprus during the Late Roman period, and in the past it has often been argued that copper smelting had ceased by the fourth century AD (Davies 1928–30:84; Bruce 1937:640; Bear 1963:2; Raber 1984:144). The systematic recording and study of this POSI, therefore, has enabled us to dismiss once and for all this notion and to gain some insight into the scale and local organization of an "industrial" copper smelting workshop of the Late Roman period.

FIELD METHODOLOGY

The units which form the eastern edge of SIA 3 (units 1002–14) were initially investigated in 1995 as part of transect 511.5. Because this transect lies to the east of the POSI, we decided to conduct a block survey in the units which surround it to the north and the northwest (units 1253–67). In the same year, an archaeometallurgical team led by Rod Clough systematically recorded SCY021, described below. In 1997 another team block surveyed the units south and west of SCY021 (units 4000–4038).

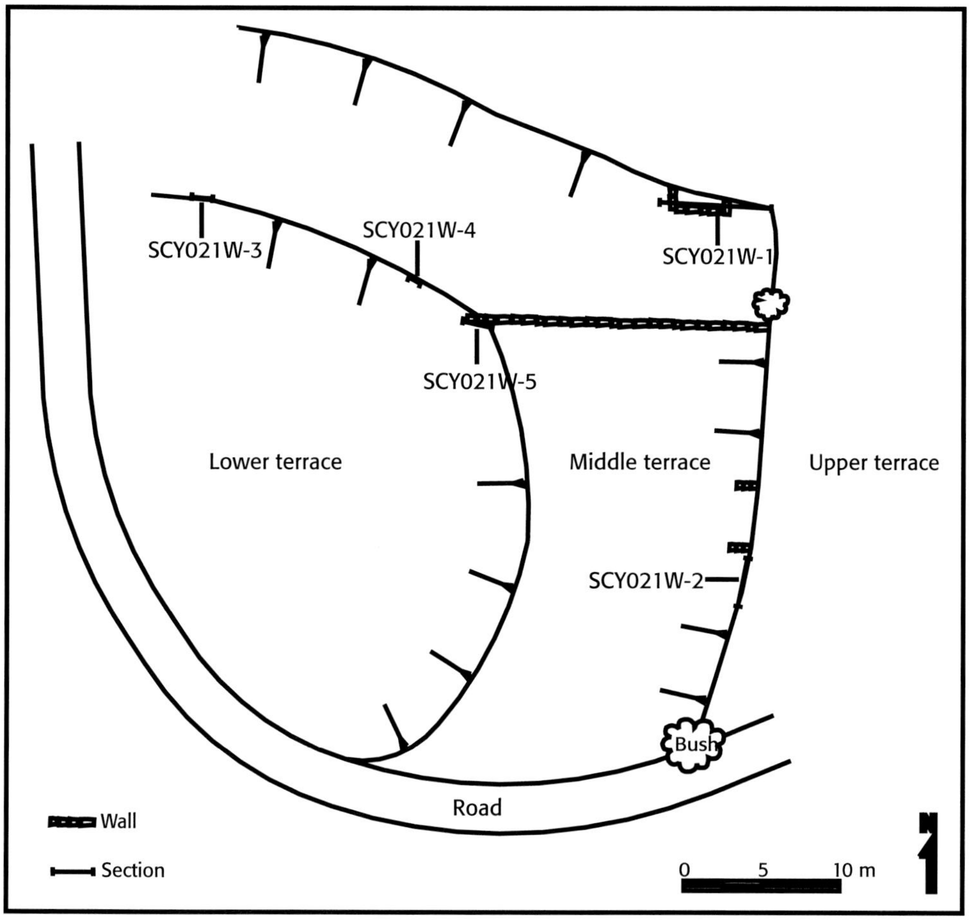

Figure 4.9
SCY021: plan

SCY021: MITSERO *KOULOUPAKHIS* 1: SLAG HEAPS

Like all other slag heaps on the island, Kouloupakhis has suffered from modern exploitation: A substantial part of it has been quarried for use as road metal. Its full extent can only be approximated from 1948 aerial photographs (Hellenic Mining Company) and from earlier publications. According to Rickard (1930:299), the slag heap was drilled and found to be 24 m (80 ft) deep, which led to an estimate of 600,000 tons of slag.

Modern quarrying has divided the slag heap into three components and created artificial terraces within each of these (figure 4.9). The largest component, which we defined as SCY021W, has an estimated diameter of 60 m and a height of 5 m. To the east lies the second largest component (SCY021E), with an estimated diameter of 35 m and a height of 5 m at the exposed face. Most of the southern section of the original slag heap has been quarried away or removed during the construction of the road; only a small part survives within units 4006 and 4007.

The sections created by the quarrying enabled us to inspect and record the stratigraphy of the heap. Permission was obtained from the Cypriot Department of Antiquities to clean back the sections, and systematically to record and collect samples from each one (for a preliminary report on this work, see Clough in Knapp and Given 1996:308–16).

SCY021W-1: BUILDING SECTION WITHIN SLAG HEAP (UNITS 2000–2002)

SCY021W-1 is the most widely exposed section of the slag heap, in which substantial architectural remains were incorporated (figures 4.10, 4.11). The section clearly shows distinct layers consisting either entirely or partly of slag, furnace material, slagged stones and refractory ceramics, layers rich in ash and charcoal, as well as layers of limestone fragments and mixed material which may have come from collapsed walls and the like.

A point of major cultural interest is that substantial architectural remains were found beneath all this industrial waste. In SCY021W-1, the removal of large

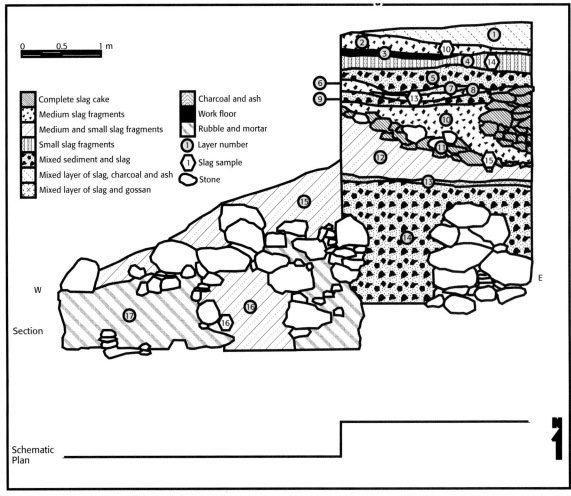

Figure 4.10 SCY021W-1: section: **1**, Sediment, slag, charcoal, ash, some pottery; **2**, Medium slag fragments; **3**, Thin layer of small slag fragments, ash, mortar; **4**, Small slag fragments; **5**, Small slag fragments, ash, mortar; **6**, Small slag fragments; **7**, Slag, gossan, pottery; **8**, Medium fragments of tap slag; **9**, Mixed sediment and slag; **10**, Large fragments of coarse cakes of tap slag; **11**, Tap slag cakes, limestone building material; **12**, Medium and small slag fragments; **13**, Fine ash layer, furnace wall material; **14**, Furnace material, furnace and tap slag of various sizes; **15**, Medium and small fragments of tap slag; **16**, Medium and small fragments of furnace slag; **17**, Mortar, stone

Figure 4.11 SCY021W-1: slag heap and structure; 25-cm scale in center of photograph

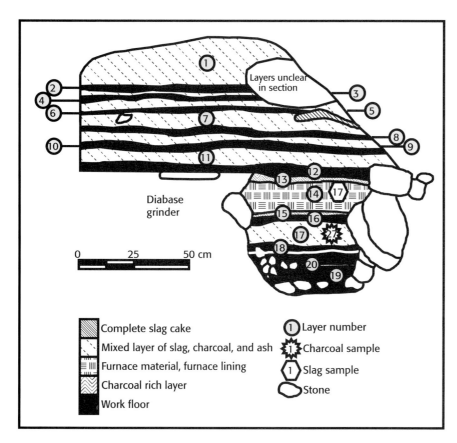

Figure 4.12 SCY021W-2: section: **1**, Slag/charcoal in matrix of charcoal, ash, ore, slag dust; **2**, Plastered work floor (WF 1); **3**, Slag/charcoal in matrix of charcoal, ash, ore, slag dust; **4**, Plastered work floor (WF 2); **5**, Slag/charcoal in matrix of charcoal, ash, ore, slag dust; **6**, Plastered work floor (WF 3); **7**, Slag/charcoal in matrix of charcoal, ash, ore, slag dust; **8**, Plastered work floor (WF 4); **9**, Same matrix as **1**; 15-20 cm slag pieces; charcoal; **10**, Plastered work floor (WF 5); **11**, Same matrix as **1**; pottery, stone furnace material; **12**, Plastered work floor (WF 6); **13**, Charcoal rich layer; **14**, Orange red furnace fragments, coarse pottery, fused and slagged stones, large charcoal fragments; **15**, Charcoal rich layer; **16**, Plastered work floor (WF 7); **17**, Small fragments of slag, plaster, charcoal; **18**, Plastered work floor (WF 8); **19**, Plastered work floor (WF 9); **20**, Charcoal rich lens; **21**, Diabase grinder

Complete slag cake
Mixed layer of slag, charcoal, and ash
Furnace material, furnace lining
Charcoal rich layer
Work floor

Layer number
Charcoal sample
Slag sample
Stone

Figure 4.13 SCY021W-2: workshop floors

quantities of slag has exposed the corner and part of the face of a rectangular structure built of limestone blocks and lined with a mixture of stone and mortar. What appears to be an opening may have been created by the partial collapse of the wall. The exposed walls are almost 2-m high and 50-cm wide, but their full height is unknown because the present ground level is artificial. Most of the slag that fills the cavity does not have a ropy surface typical of the tap slag from the rest of the heap; instead it has a rough, somewhat friable surface in which small pieces of charcoal were incorporated.

More walls, some of which were at least 15 011111m long, protruded from other exposed sections of the slag heap (figure 4.11). Moreover, according to Konstantinos Ttaouxis, who worked for the Hellenic Mining Company on the construction of the road that dissected this slag heap, there was a substantial wall (circa 1.5 to 2 m across) running from the slag heap under what is now the road. Unfortunately, the remaining evidence is so fragmentary that it is difficult to understand the relationship among all these architectural remains and consequently to ascertain the shape of the building of which they were part. Nonetheless, because most of the exposed walls have an east-west orientation, we assume that they form part of the same, rather substantial, building complex. We also assume that the construction and use of the buildings predates the creation of the slag heap, although some of the walls seem to be associated with some of the archaeometallurgical features. The date of the buildings can only be approximated on the basis of the pottery finds and on one ^{14}C date from charcoal found upon one of the plaster floors in SCY021W-5.

The discovery of building remains within a slag heap is not unprecedented, either on Cyprus or elsewhere in the Mediterranean. Impressive architectural features have been found in the slag heaps of Rio Tinto, also dating to the Roman period, and at the site of Corta Lago in southwest Spain (Rothenberg and Blanco Freijeiro 1981:101–102). On Cyprus itself, remains of walls have also been documented in the slag heaps at Skouriotissa and Petra (Kalavasos).

SCY021W-2: WORKSHOP FLOORS (UNIT 2002)

SCY021W-2 is located at the eastern extension of the exposed slag heap (figure 4.9). The subunit consists of a series of nine plastered floors, presumably the working surfaces of metallurgical activities, interspersed with accumulated debris of varying composition which lies between two limestone walls set obliquely to the section (for a detailed description of the layers, see figure 4.12). Once again, the lower levels were never reached as they lay below the present ground level of the quarried terrace.

Between the floors (layers 2, 4, 6, 8, 12, 16, 18, and 19) were compacted layers (1, 3, 5, and 7) which consisted of charcoal, ash, ore and finely crushed slag (figure 4.13). This material is characteristic of foundry workshops, where large waste materials are removed to the dump while the finer material, usually fine black dust, accumulates on the floor. Floor 6 (layer 12) was exposed horizontally and on it was found a smooth, diabase grinding stone. Fragments of small mortar stones with cavities 10 cm in diameter were also found in the direct proximity of this section. A much thicker layer (14) consisted largely of furnace wall fragments made of coarse, organically tempered clay, slagged stones, and large pieces of charcoal. Samples of slag and charcoal were collected from all layers in this section for analysis (chapter 5.4).

SCY021W-3: LOWER TERRACE, WEST SECTION (UNIT 2003)

This section of the lower terrace provided clear evidence of constructional phases and the abandonment of buildings prior to the advent of copper smelting at the site (figure 4.14). Beneath the layers of slag were at least five layers of sediment, two of which could be floors. Each of these layers has cultural material, in particular material related to building construction: chips of limestone, mortar and tile mixed with some pottery. The fact that we found no slag or other metallurgical debris in any of these earlier levels may indicate that they predated smelting activities.

SCY021W-4 AND SCY021W-5: FACE OF LOWER TERRACE (UNIT 2003)

Subunits SCY021W-4 and SCY021W-5 are located in the middle of the lower terrace. SCY021W-4 is a circular bowl-shaped structure 60 cm in diameter, possibly with stone-lined walls (figure 4.15). There was clear evidence of burning, with layers of ash and charcoal, and a roof tile in the fill. The presence of ash and

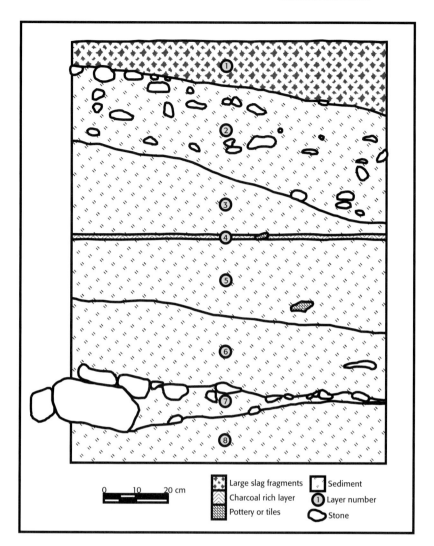

Figure 4.14 SCY021W-3: section:
1, Large slag fragments; **2**, Limestone chips, stones, pottery, in sediment; **3**, Plaster and mortar mix; **4**, Charcoal rich layer; **5**, Harder earth; **6**, Plaster and chalk layer; **7**, Remains of a wall; **8**, Building debris, plaster, limestone

Figure 4.15 SCY021W-4: section: **1**, Slag; **2**, Limestone and pottery fragments; **3**, Red sediment with pottery, furnace material; **4**, Charcoal rich lens; **5**, Lighter more compact layer; **6**, Limestone and plaster layer with thin dark layer on top

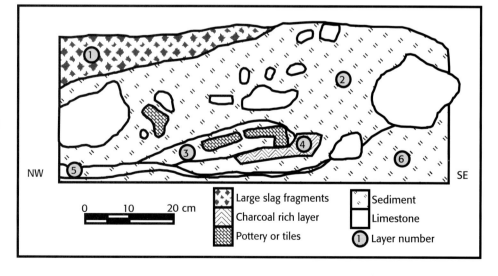

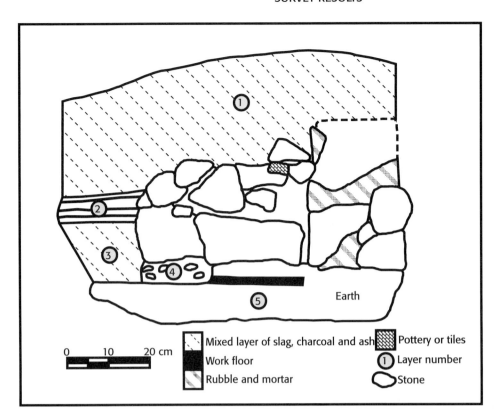

Figure 4.16 SCY021W-5: section: **1**, Slag, charcoal and ash; **2**, Compact plaster layer; **3**, Fine ash material; small slag fragments, cupriferous material; **4**, Foundation layer; **5**, Plaster floor

Earth

Pattern	Legend	Pattern	Legend
	Mixed layer of slag, charcoal and ash		Pottery or tiles
	Work floor	①	Layer number
	Rubble and mortar		Stone

0   10   20 cm

Figure 4.17 SCY021W-5: building remains

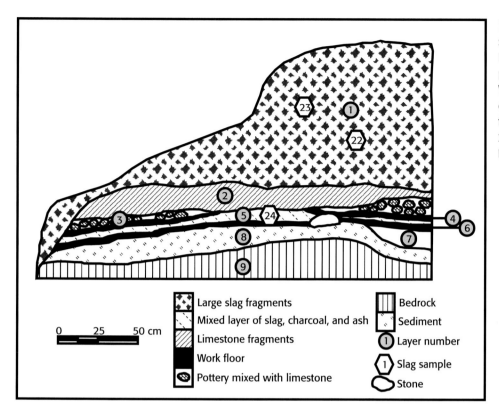

Figure 4.18 SCY021E-1: section: 1, Slag; 2, Limestone mixed with pottery; 3, Pottery; 4, Work floor 1; 5, Slag, charcoal, ash; 6, Work floor 2; 7, Floor section 2; 8, Sediment; 9, Bedrock

Legend:

- Large slag fragments
- Mixed layer of slag, charcoal, and ash
- Limestone fragments
- Work floor
- Pottery mixed with limestone

0   25   50 cm

- Bedrock
- Sediment
- (1) Layer number
- (1) Slag sample
- Stone

the absence of evidence for vitrification and slagging render this feature an unlikely candidate for a metallurgical installation. It seems more likely that it was an oven or kiln. Charcoal samples were collected from the lower levels of the fill.

SCY021W-5 consists of wall remains 3 m to the east, constructed on a foundation layer of limestone chips and soil (figures 4.16, 4.17). The wall was built of limestone blocks set in thick layers of fine white plaster. Associated with this wall were remnants of hardpacked plaster floors, one of which lay over a deposit of fine slag, cupriferous material, and charcoal. In an effort to date the use of the building, we collected and dated a sample of the charcoal lying on the plaster floor. The calibrated ^{14}C age range for this sample is AD 74 to 241 (1 sigma with 68% certainty) and Cal BC 15–Cal AD 339 (2 sigma with 95% certainty, see appendix B). The date can serve as a terminus ante quem for the construction of these buildings.

SCY021E-1: (UNITS 2004, 2006)

A second, somewhat smaller, section of the original slag heap (SCY021E) is located approximately 50 m east of SCY021W. At the bottom of the exposed section was a series of working floors but no architectural

remains (figure 4.18). These floors are not dissimilar to the workshop floors of SCY021W-2, and consist of a dark brown/black dust rich in charcoal, ore, and slag fragments. As in the previous section, among the slag remains we found fragments of pottery indicating the date of the smelting activity.

SCY021: ARCHAEOMETALLURGICAL FINDS

The most striking archaeometallurgical finds from SCY021 were the complete slag cakes, weighing between 40 and 55 kg. A typical slag cake from SCY021E-1 is about 42 cm long, 62 cm wide and 17 cm thick; the standard weight is about 55 kg (chapter 5.4). These slag cakes have a fan-like shape with the typical flows on the surface and a convex base, indicating that they were tapped into a pit. Some of the slag fragments have multiple layers that may result from continuous or serial tapping.

Bulk chemical analysis of 10 slag samples from this POSI has detected quite low levels of copper (below 1% in all but two samples), which is expected for slags of this period. The majority of the analyzed samples are manganiferous, with three examples containing over 39% manganese oxide. Thus it is clear that, by this time, the benefits of manganese as a

Table 4.7 SCY021: analyzed pottery (including units 2000–2007, 2015)

Chronotype	Period	Qty
Cooking ware-Ar	Ar	10
Red Slip-Ar	Ar	2
Soft Red-Orange-Ar	Ar	5
Plain ware-Cl [SCY021.2.7.1]	Cl	1
Plain White-Cl	Cl	1
Coarse ware-GAC	GAC	2
Pithos-AC	AC	1
Plain ware-AC	AC	5
White Painted-AC	AC	2
Coarse ware-He	He	1
Fine ware-He	He	2
Cooking ware-ER	ER	2
Red Slip-ER	ER	1
Amphora-LR	LR	3
Amphora, LR 1	LR	5
Coarse ware-LR	LR	14
Coarse ware, LR Wheel-Ridged	LR	6
Cooking ware-LR	LR	1
Cypriot Red Slip	LR	5
Cypriot Red Slip 9	LR	1
Pithos-LR	LR	1
Red Slip-LR	LR	1
Lamp-REL	REL	1
Red Slip-REL	REL	4
Cypriot W4	MM	2
Cypriot W5	Ott	2
Plain White-HA	HA	1
Pithos-PC	PC	3
Tile-PC	PC	3
Tile, Cover	PC	1
Coarse ware-Unk	Unk	40
Cooking ware-Unk	Unk	3
TOTAL		132

Note: Figures in brackets refer to cataloged items (see chapter 5.1).

fluxing agent were well known and the locally available manganese-rich umbers had been added to the charge of the smelting furnaces (see chapter 5.4).

In his description of Kouloupakhis, Koucky (1982:243) describes the layers according to the type of slag they contained. What is striking about the slag heaps, however, is not that the layers are composed of different types of slag (probably indicative of different conditions in the furnace and not necessarily a significantly different technology), but rather that the size of the slag pieces differs in each layer. For example, in SCY021W-1 (figure 4.10) there are concentrations of complete slag cakes (layers 10 and 11), as well as layers of small crushed fragments of slag (layers 4 and 6). Clearly this phenomenon is not coincidental or natural. In other words, these layers cannot possibly have formed haphazardly when the large pieces of slag were

dumped on the pile. Rather, it seems to indicate that a specific method was followed for disposing of the waste produced in the smelting workshops.

The large quantities of crushed slag require explanation. Because the chemical and microscopic analyses carried out on these slag samples revealed very little copper, we can dismiss the possibility that metallic copper was mechanically removed by crushing the slag. Even if this were the reason behind the crushing of the slag, what workshop activity could explain its sorting into different sizes?

Among the finds from this POSI are a number of stone mortars and grinding stones (chapter 5.4), some of which are broken and thus may have been thrown as waste on the slag heap. Other mortars or grinding stones, however, seem to be in situ (for example, one found in SCY021W-2). Bruce (1937:660) also mentions that stone tools made from hard rock were found in the slag piles of Mitsero, while Tylecote (1977:319) comments that at Kouloupakhis he saw an odd shaped mortar stone containing a channel.

The size of the slag cakes is related to the size of the smelting furnaces, which must have been quite large. Remains of these smelting furnaces were found among the slag pieces. In Kouloupakhis we found slagged rocks (igneous rocks, such as diabase and gabbro, able to withstand high temperatures) and slagged pottery tiles, as well as fragments of slagged refractory clay—the last either a clay lining over a stone structure or part of a furnace wall entirely made from refractory clay. Unfortunately, none of these is preserved well enough to enable us establish the shape or to calculate the diameter of the furnace. Only excavation could resolve some of the manifold questions raised by the archaeometallurgical remains of Kouloupakhis.

SCY021: POTTERY

One hundred thirty-two sherds were collected from the surface of the slag heaps, the surface of the terraces, and within the stratified layers (table 4.7). Of 52 diagnostic pieces, 37 date to the Late Roman period. Most of the unknown pieces were found on the surface rather than in the stratified deposits, although two Classical sherds (for example, cat. SCY021.2.7.1) found in the subunits with architectural remains may suggest an early date for their construction.

Most of the Late Roman sherds are from coarse-ware vessels, amphorae, and pithoi. The fragment of a lamp handle and four sherds of table ware are the only exceptions. This assemblage accords well with the nature of this POSI, essentially the waste dump of an industrial site. Coarse ware may be related to the preparation of food, pithoi to the storage of food and drink, and amphorae to the storage or serving of beverages.

The pottery found in the stratified layers of the slag heap provides some indication for the date of the smelting activities. Unfortunately, the fine wares (mainly Cypriot Red Slip) could date anytime between 400 and 700 AD. There are, however, some diagnostic pieces among the coarse ware. For example, some Late Roman amphora 1 handles date from the early fifth to mid-seventh centuries AD, and three wheel-ridged sherds date from the fourth to sixth centuries AD. According to the pottery, the smelting activities can date only to the Late Roman period.

SCY021: DATING

In an effort to substantiate and refine the dates provided by the pottery assemblage, samples of charcoal were selected from several points in this POSI for radiocarbon dating (appendix B). The earliest date stems from a sample collected on the floor of the building remains in SCY021W-5. The calibrated date of Cal AD 74 to 241 (1 sigma) falls within the Early Roman period. As suggested above, it provides a terminus ante quem for the construction of the buildings. It may also be related with the beginning of smelting activities in this area. The three other samples derive from the stratified slag deposits and are therefore associated with the period during which the smelting workshops were active. The calibrated dates fall within the Late Roman period and correspond well with the relative dating of the strata based on the pottery. The two samples collected from the workshop floors of SCY021W-2 are dated to Cal AD 263 to 431 (1 sigma), while the third sample—from the higher layers of SCY021W-1 and associated with furnace wall fragments—dates to Cal AD 435 to 599 (1 sigma). This final sample is perhaps the most significant of the four, as it provides solid evidence for the continuation of smelting activities on the island after the fifth century AD.

SCY342: MITSERO *KOULOUPAKHIS* 2: ADIT AND SPOIL HEAP

Approximately 100 m northeast of SCY021 is an adit associated with a small spoil heap. This adit is approximately 125 m long and leads to a circular chamber approximately 20 m in diameter and 2 to 3 m in height. Its date cannot be ascertained since there were no finds from the interior; it could be a modern exploration adit. The spoil heap consists essentially of material removed during construction of the adit; it contained no pottery. The pottery collected from the area around the adit and spoil heap all dates to the Archaic and/or Classical periods.

BLOCK SURVEY

In the fifty-two units of SIA 3 where we conducted block survey, a total of 858 sherds were collected, not counting 132 sherds from SCY021. In general, sherd densities were low and tile densities even lower in comparison with other SIAs. High concentrations of artifacts were observed in the units just north of the POSI. Although these areas have been disturbed by modern agricultural activities, they are stable surfaces with the finds in their original context. The exception is unit 4041 which had a relatively dense spread of pottery, dated mainly to the Archaic and Classical periods, but with some Hellenistic (for example, cat. 4041.4.1) and possibly late Geometric material (for example, cat. 4041.14.1). This is an actively eroding surface and, therefore, the context of the material lying on the surface is uncertain.

The units in the direct vicinity of the slag heap (1259, 1263–64) produced most of the tiles as well as the pottery, which is almost exclusively of Late Roman date (plate XIII). To the north, in units 1253 to 1256, the majority of the sherds date to the Hellenistic period, with some examples mainly from the Archaic and Archaic to Classical periods (for example, cat. 1254.1.1), and with a few occurrences of Early to Late Roman pottery.

Of the fourteen Hellenistic sherds, most were coarse wares with but few fine wares, such as Black Glazed (table 4.8). Only a few sherds of the Early Roman period were identified; the diagnostic ones date to the first century AD. Although the number of Hellenistic sherds is limited, it is significant when compared to other areas in the SCSP region; this suggests some Hellenistic activity that diminished during the Early Roman period before it became the location of an industrial-scale smelting operation in the Late Roman period. Perhaps, then, it is not

Table 4.8 SIA 3: analyzed pottery from block survey

Chronotype	Period	Qty
Chalcolithic Red-Burnished	EP	1
Coarse ware-PoB	PoB	1
Plain ware-PoB	PoB	4
TOTAL Prehistoric		**6**
Amphora-Ar	Ar	4
Bichrome-Ar	Ar	1
Cooking ware-Ar	Ar	3
Black-on-Red-Ar	Ar	1
Green ware-Ar	Ar	1
Pithos-Ar	Ar	1
Plain ware-Ar	Ar	9
Red Slip-Ar [1257.12.1]	Ar	5
Soft Red-Orange-Ar [1257.13.1]	Ar	5
White Painted-Ar	Ar	2
Wide Shallow Bowl-Ar	Ar	2
Terra-cotta Figurine-GA [1010.1.1]	GA	1
Amphora-Cl	Cl	4
Black Glaze-Cl	Cl	3
Plain ware-Cl	Cl	4
Plain White-Cl	Cl	10
Green ware-GAC	GAC	4
Plain ware-GAC	GAC	4
White Painted-GAC	GAC	1
Amphora-AC	AC	21
Amphora, Pithoid	AC	7
Black Glaze-AC	AC	5
Coarse ware-AC	AC	3
Cooking ware-AC	AC	14
Fine ware-AC	AC	1
Pithos-AC	AC	1
Plain ware-AC	AC	19
Plain White-AC	AC	6
White Painted-AC	AC	5
TOTAL Geometric to Classical		**147**
Black Glaze-He	He	4
Coarse ware-He	He	9
Fine ware-He	He	1
Coarse ware-ER	ER	4
Cooking ware-ER	ER	1
Cypriot Sigillata	ER	2
African Red Slip	LR	3
Amphora-LR	LR	21
Amphora, LR 1	LR	12
Basin-LR	LR	5
Coarse ware-LR	LR	13
Coarse ware, LR Wheel-Ridged	LR	18
Cooking ware, Dhiorios Pot	LR	3
Cypriot Red Slip	LR	6
Cypriot Red Slip 1 [1009.1.1]	LR	1
Cypriot Red Slip 9	LR	2
Frying Pan	LR	3
Pithos-LR	LR	2
Tile-LR	LR	1
Red Slip-REL	REL	1
TOTAL Hellenistic to Late Roman		**112**

Chronotype	Period	Qty
Byzantine Glazed, Local	Med	1
Coarse ware-Med	Med	1
Cypriot Glazed	Med	2
Cypriot Glazed IVA	Med	1
Cypriot Glazed IVC	Med	2
Cypriot Glazed VII	Med	1
Cypriot Glazed VIII	Med	2
Cypriot Glazed IX	Med	4
Cypriot Glazed XI	Med	1
Cypriot W1 Early	Med	2
Glazed ware, Italian	Med	1
Imported Sgrafitto ware	Med	1
Lemba ware	Med	1
Cypriot Glazed IX Late	Ott	5
Cypriot Glazed, Brown and Green	Ott	4
Cypriot W3	Ott	3
Cypriot W5	Ott	13
Cypriot W6	Ott	1
Ottoman Glazed	Ott	4
Purple Painted ware	Ott	4
Tile-Ott	Ott	1
Turkish Pipe [1007.2.1]	Ott	2
Brick	Mod	8
Coarse ware-Mod	Mod	1
Contemporary Eastern Mediterranean	Mod	17
Contemporary Imported Asian	Mod	8
Contemporary Imported European	Mod	1
Contemporary Local wares	Mod	4
Contemporary Yogurt ware	Mod	5
Cypriot W7	Mod	47
Fine ware-Mod	Mod	8
Lapithos ware [4023.24.1]	Mod	1
Lapithos ware, Green	Mod	1
Lapithos ware, Yellow [4023.25.1]	Mod	9
Pithos-Mod	Mod	1
Tile-Mod	Mod	4
Brown Glaze	MM	7
Cypriot W1 [1005.1.1]	MM	20
Cypriot W4	MM	99
Glazed ware	MM	17
Pithos-MM	MM	2
Tile-MM	MM	9
TOTAL Medieval to Modern		**326**
Plain White-HA	HA	24
Pithos-PC	PC	2
Tile-PC	PC	12
Tile, Corinthian	PC	2
Tile, Corinthian Pan	PC	1
Tile, Laconian	PC	4
Coarse ware-Unk	Unk	208
Cooking ware-Unk	Unk	7
Fine ware-Unk	Unk	2
Table ware-Unk	Unk	2
Unknown	Unk	3
TOTAL		**858**

Note: Figures in brackets refer to cataloged items (see chapter 5.1 for pottery, chapter 5.3 for figurines and Turkish pipe).

unreasonable to suggest that the buildings under the slag heaps of SCY021 could date to the Hellenistic period, taking into consideration that the radiocarbon dates indicate a terminus ante quem in the Early Roman period.

Ninety sherds (10.5%) date to the Late Roman period. Fourteen were fine wares, nine of which were Cypriot Red Slip (CRS) forms; one was a locally produced red slip, and three were imported African Red Slip (ARS), dated AD 300 to 700. Of the locally produced CRS, one dates to the fourth to fifth centuries AD, two to the sixth century AD, and seven to the years between AD 300 to 700. Twenty-five sherds were locally produced Late Roman 1 amphorae (LR1), at least one being a late version dated around AD 700. Such amphorae were manufactured at Amathus, Kourion and Nea Paphos during this period, and most likely carried or stored olive oil. There is at least one Aegean amphora sherd which, along with the ARS sherds, shows external trade or contact. The Late Roman sherds demonstrate the standard grouping in the period between AD 400 to 700.

This Late Roman assemblage reveals a good cross section of the standard Late Roman wares discovered in the survey area, with LR1 amphorae, CRS, Dhiorios cooking pots, frying pans, and basins. It is indicative of a prosperous area dependent on local products, with little access to foreign pottery. The presence of Dhiorios cooking pots, fairly scarce in the SCSP area, would seem to indicate a degree of affluence, as people were clearly buying cooking wares from outside the area, rather than the poorer quality, locally produced wares. The high number of LR1 sherds seems to indicate that goods such as olive oil were being shipped in or out of the area.

A number of tombs have been discovered in this area, some excavated by the Cypriot Department of Antiquities. Villagers from Mitsero have also reported the presence of tombs in the immediate vicinity. The possibility exists, therefore, that the pottery of Classical and Hellenistic periods may be related to a cemetery rather than a settlement.

Three pieces from the Medieval period probably date to the thirteenth to fourteenth centuries AD (Cypriot Glazed IVA and IVC), all from unit 4000 in the southwest corner of the SIA. The other seventeen Medieval pieces were spread throughout the area without any notable concentration (plate XIV). Ottoman material was slightly more numerous with thirty-seven pieces, including five sherds of Cypriot Glazed IX Late from the earlier part of the period and two Turkish pipes. Much more substantial were the 105 pieces from the Modern period, with concentrations in the northwestern and southwestern parts of the SIA, close to the modern village houses.

The units from the southwestern part of SIA 3 (1002–1007) also contain mainly Modern material, while units 1008 to 1010 have some Iron Age (for example, cat. 1010.1.1) and Roman material. Geomorphological indicators, however, suggest that these units lie on the youngest alluvial surfaces in SIA 3, less than eight hundred years old. The artifacts collected from these surfaces thus were most likely redeposited, the result either of river erosion or of the anthropogenic movement of materials for manuring.

CONCLUSION

Most of SIA 3 is situated on well watered, arable land currently cultivated for cereals and fruit trees. Based on the survey data, the first clear evidence of human occupation in this area dates from the Archaic to Classical periods. The remains of these early periods, however, are overshadowed by the impressive remnants of an industrial-scale copper-smelting workshop dating to the Late Roman period.

Although there are three significant cupriferous ore bodies within a radius of 2 km from the slag heaps at Kouloupakhis, there are none in its direct vicinity. One of the main issues that must be addressed, therefore, is why this specific location was chosen for the establishment of such a workshop. To function smoothly, a smelting workshop requires ores, fuel, and fluxes. The fuel used is charcoal, and although at present Kriadhis hill is nearly denuded, in the past it would have supported good charcoal sources such as *Quercus alnifolia*. Chemical analyses of the slags from Kouloupakhis detected a significant amount of manganese (chapter 5.4), which suggests that umbers were used as fluxes in the smelting furnaces of the Late Roman period. On Kriadhis there are several umber outcrops, so fluxes would have been readily available as well. The Likythia River and its tributaries would have provided the necessary water for ore beneficiation, clay preparation, and drinking, as well as refractory clay and igneous rocks for the construction of the furnaces.

Whereas Kouloupakhis is not in direct proximity to the mines of Mitsero or Agrokipia, it is nonetheless an appropriate location for establishing a smelting workshop, as it is within easy reach of four of the five essential raw materials. Another reason for its choice may have been the availability of fuel; it is entirely possible that the forests around the mines had been depleted by earlier workshops. Based on the pottery collected in the slag heaps of Kokkinoyia (SCY219) and Agrokipia *Kriadhis* (SCY204), the peak of smelting activities must be dated to the Archaic and Classical periods. The extra advantages of readily available water and manganese fluxes which, according to chemical analysis, were used only in the Roman period and not earlier, made Kouloupakhis an ideal place for smelting copper ores.

The slag heap is clearly the result of large-scale production, which must have employed a significant number of workers. We should therefore consider where all these people might have lived and where they would have been buried. The distribution of Late Roman pottery within SIA 3 shows a concentration just north of the slag heap. Because it is unlikely that a settlement would have been located so close to copper workshops with their by-products of poisonous sulfur dioxide fumes, we might suggest that these artifacts indicate the location of some kind of mining camp for the workers (Kassianidou 2000), or administrative buildings for the people in charge of the operation.

4.4 SIA 4: Mitsero *Mavrovounos*

Compiled by Michael Given
Team leaders: Julia Burnet, Michael Given, Robert Schon
Archaeometallurgy: Vasiliki Kassianidou, Sven Van Lokeren
Geomorphology: Lisa Wells GIS analysis: Nathan Meyer,
Michael Given Lithics: Dina Coleman Pottery: Timothy E. Gregory, R. Scott Moore, Joanna S. Smith

Grid reference:	509500/3877600
Cadastral maps:	XXIX/52, XXIX/53
Aerial photograph:	1993, run 177, no. 41
Survey units:	Survey: 2500–2508, 2512–14, 2539–75, 4042–50
	Archaeometallurgy: 2009–11, 2050–53
POSIs:	SCY023: Mitsero *Mavrovounos* (Medieval settlement); SCY024E: Mitsero *Sykamies* East (Eastern slag heap [figure 4.19]); SCY024W: Mitsero *Sykamies* West (Western slag heap)

Mavrovounos or "black hill" lies in a stretch of river valley dominated by the twin slag heaps that give the locality its name (plate XV). The western heap is more than 50 m across and some 20 m high; the eastern one is 70 m at its widest point and about 10 m high. Archaeometallurgical examination of several sections through these slag heaps has revealed valuable evidence on ancient smelting procedures and industrial organization, with clear examples of waste management. Detailed mapping of the rubble piles and block survey in the surrounding fields allowed us to investigate one of SCSP's best-preserved historical settlements and to study how it exploited local resources. Immediately adjacent to the west are the rubble piles of a Medieval settlement, named Maurochio in Venetian sources and abandoned in the seventeenth century AD. The fields and olive groves in the vicinity have considerable quantities of pottery, ranging in date from the Iron Age to the Ottoman period. These diverse material traces of metallurgy, agriculture, and habitation from several different periods were clearly part of a broader network of human activity across the entire landscape of the Mitsero region (for a general view of this area, see the frontispiece).

PHYSICAL LANDSCAPE

Mitsero *Mavrovounos* is situated about 440 m asl on a small hill at the downstream end of a low spur running along the upper Mavrovouniotis River Valley. The river itself runs past the settlement and slag heaps eastward into the Mitsero basin, while steep-sided Mount Lambadhousa rises another 180 m in elevation immediately to the north (see figure 4.19). The modern village of Mitsero is easily accessible 2 km down the river valley to the east, while to the west runs a road that crosses over into the next deep valley, that of the Peristerona River. The upper pillow basalts of the area have abundant dikes and have been altered and mineralized. Jasper veins associated with this dike complex provide a good local source for lithic materials.

The Mavrovounos landscape is incised into the upper pillow basalts and the downslope fringe of Pleistocene talus slopes of the southwestern slope of Mount Lambadhousa. Where the paleosol has been preserved, these talus slopes are underlain by a 1 to 2 m thick paleosol, moderately developed in

Figure 4.19 SCY024E: eastern slag heap from the southeast

coarse pebble to cobble colluvium. Gullies have eroded into the talus and their downslope ends coalesce into narrow flat-floored gullies with thin (< 0.3 m) deposits of colluvium and alluvium. These deposits are inset several meters below the remnant surfaces of the talus. As the gullies further coalesce into a third order drainage, the valley floor widens and there are 1 to 1.5 m of alluvial deposits in the lowest channel bottoms. Soils on the valley slopes, including the area around Mavrovounos, are underlain by thin (generally < 0.25 m), stony and organic-poor soils on basalt bedrock.

The modern soil in this part of the Mavrovouniotis River valley is not very fertile and has largely been stripped from the surrounding hillsides. Only on the small hillock just south of the site does it appear that older soil is preserved. On the hills immediately surrounding Mavrovounos there is only 10 to 20 cm of poorly developed A horizon directly overlying unweathered bedrock, while on the southern hillock there is 40+ cm of A and B horizon overlying intensely weathered bedrock. This difference in soil thickness suggests that the landscape directly surrounding Mavrovounos has undergone intense late Holocene erosion, accounting in large part for the absence of artifacts beyond the small hill where Mavrovounos is located.

The surrounding landscape has abundant modern and ancient agricultural terraces. Because of the igneous dikes that crop out at the surface, rectilin-

ear patterns are formed on the landscape by the intersection of dikes and terraces. Large erosional bowls at the headwaters of first- and second-order streams further attest to the active erosion of this landscape. These upper ends of the drainages have only minor or failed check dams within them. Lower down, nearly all the third to fourth order streams, and a few first and second order streams, are filled with recent sediment trapped behind check dams. Agriculture would have been limited to small areas behind check dams and upslope of hillslope terraces for at least the last five hundred to a thousand years.

The combination of extensive late Holocene hillslope erosion and recent sedimentation behind check dams results in a landscape surrounding SIA 4 with very few artifacts remaining in situ. Artifacts from any earlier occupation of the region may be trapped at the base of the check dam sequences or may have been washed out of the Likithia drainage basin entirely. The Mavrovounos settlement and slag heaps are located in a somewhat more stable position at the downstream end of a Pleistocene talus slope. While the surface soils have been stripped, the underlying carbonate soil horizons are discontinuously exposed across this surface. Additionally, the slag heaps and structures themselves, as well as the thick botanical cover, increase the stability of the region directly adjacent to the knoll.

We found no evidence for natural springs in the surrounding landscape, and the nature of the chan-

Figure 4.20
SIA 4:
geobotanical
dendrogram of
species at > 2%

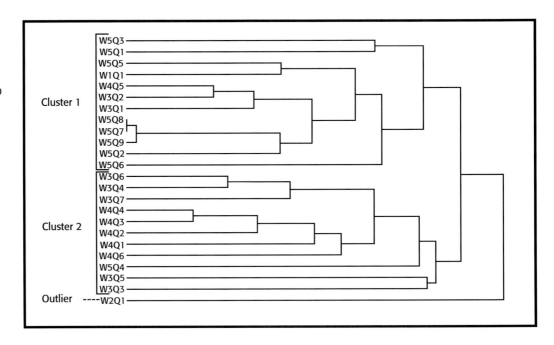

nel fill indicates that these channels have flowed only during wet season storms for at least the past few hundred years, if not for most of the later Holocene. A surviving well at the north end of the western section of the settlement (SCY023b; see plate XV) was 30 m deep, with 20 m of water recorded in early September 1997. This comparatively shallow water table, observed here and in the mine at Kokkinoyia, as well as an abundance of modern wells across the surrounding landscape, suggest that agriculture has depended on ground or rain water at least since the Medieval occupation. No evidence was found for higher channels or higher flow regimes associated with the slag heaps at this SIA, but given the extensive erosion here it is not inconceivable that such evidence has entirely eroded away.

GEOBOTANY

The vegetation community associated with the slag heap was dominated by *Sarcopoterium spinosum* and grasses (especially *Hordeum* spp.), and had a site density of 50% areal coverage. On the edges of the slag heap, the vegetation became more dense and the species richness increased, with the addition of *Rhamnus oleoides* and *Avena fatua* as codominants.

Because of the complexity of the area, a large number of quadrats was sampled for vegetation. Six quadrats were sampled over the Sykamies slag heap (SCY024), seven over the settlement (SCY023), and 11 control quadrats sampled parallel environments

to both. By limiting the species variables to those with > 2% cover in the sample units, two large clusters of 11 and 12 sample units were sorted. While sample units for the medieval ruins (transect W3 quadrats) were present equally in both clusters, those from the Sykamies slag heap (transect W4 quadrats) were all within one cluster (cluster 2) (figure 4.20).

The failure of sample units over the medieval village ruins to sort into definable groups was expected, because the ruins were largely above ground and the differences among the sample units were not based upon vegetation but rather on the amount of standing stone structures in each. The sample units indicative of the slag heap were more strongly correlated. An ordination of the sample units within cluster 2 by PCA confirmed the correlation of the sample units over the slag heap, and indicated internal groupings within cluster 2 (figure 4.21).

The sorting of transect W4 quadrats and the subsequent ordination by PCA enabled three training areas for vegetation communities over slag to be used in the classification of the satellite imagery. These were: cluster 2a: eastern edge of Sykamies (W4Q1, W4Q2); cluster 2b: western edge (W4Q6) and cluster 2c: center (W4Q3, W4Q4)

Background training areas for quarries/mines, olive groves, and control areas of batha were established on the image. Even though the sample units over the medieval village ruins were not differentiated statistically, they were added as background training areas to help characterize this large area on the image.

The MINDIST classification strategy provided a thematic map (plate XVI) that delineated a clear pattern of land cover types identifying the Sykamies slag heap. The subscene extrapolation within the Piedmont geomorphological unit correctly identified the known, smaller slag heap in the immediate area (SCY024W) and predicted another site (SCY208), which a preliminary field inspection showed to have a light slag scatter, pottery sherds, and possible mine workings.

HISTORICAL BACKGROUND

There are no references to the Mavrovounos area in ancient sources. However, because it lay only 12 km from Tamassos, it is likely that the mines formed part of the well-known copper resources of that city (Strabo 14.6.5; Stephen of Byzantium, s.v. Tamassos). The next closest Archaic to Roman city is Soloi, 28 km to the northwest. Rickard (1930:300) mentions a large slag heap at the foot of the Koroni escarpment overgrown by pines, while Jeffery (1918:302–303) reports traces of an ancient settlement connected with the mines on the sides of Corona Hill. In his discussion of the Kokkinoyia mine, Bear (1963:100) comments on the size of the slag heap and how this provides evidence of extensive ancient mining activities. The slag heaps were surveyed in 1979 by a team from the State University of New York at Albany, who reported "early Byzantine sherds" and "mixed high silica and high manganese type slags" (Koucky, in Wallace 1982:243). The samples collected from Sykamies (described as "Kokkinoyia, south of mine near main road") were analyzed by Koucky and Steinberg who, on the basis of associated pottery, dated them to the Late Roman to Early Byzantine period (Koucky and Steinberg 1982a:128).

The Medieval settlement (SCY023) is rather better known from documentary sources. A set of produce and population statistics from the late fifteenth century, soon after Cyprus was taken over by the Venetians, records that "Casal Mavrovunos" belonged to the Grand Commandery of the Knights of St. John, along with other villages of the area such as Kato Moni, Akhera, Mitsero, and Agrokipia (de Mas Latrie 1852–1861 III:502–503). The settlement also appears on a series of European maps, beginning with that of Ortelius in 1573 (Stylianou and

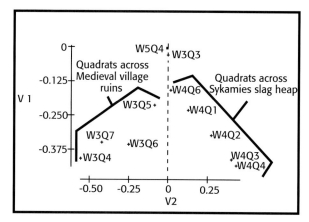

Figure 4.21 SIA 4: PCA scatterplot of cluster 2

Stylianou 1980:257) and continuing into the eighteenth century (Stylianou and Stylianou 1980:291, 304, 314, 322, 337, 372, 397). A slag heap is marked on Kitchener's map of 1885 and immediately to the west of it is the locality name Mavrovouno. The ruined settlement and its church of Ayios Yeoryios are well known in the modern village, where there is a strong tradition about its abandonment because of a plague. Its presence is noted in various topographical writers (Kliridhis 1961:168; Goodwin 1984:1088; *MKE* 10:85).

FIELD METHODOLOGY

We used various field methodologies in investigating Mavrovounos, as appropriate to different research questions and cultural features. The rubble piles of the settlement and the site of the Ayios Yeoryios church were shown to us in 1995 by Andriani Kosta Loïzou of Mitsero village. Initial fieldwalking of the area came as part of transect 509.5, which gave us excellent context to the north and south, and showed an abrupt fall-off in material. The whole area was then examined by block survey using relatively small units to give reasonable resolution.

The archaeometallurgical investigation of the slag heaps consisted of examining and drawing the sections made by bulldozers collecting slag for road metal in the 1950s and of sampling some stratified sherds from these sections. A short preliminary report was published in 1996 (Kassianidou and Wright, in Knapp and Given 1996:321–23). We divided the two separate sections of the settlement (SCY023a, SCY023b) into small subunits following the rubble piles or natural features, and artifacts were recorded on that basis. The field between these two sections

Figure 4.22
SCY024: sketch
plan

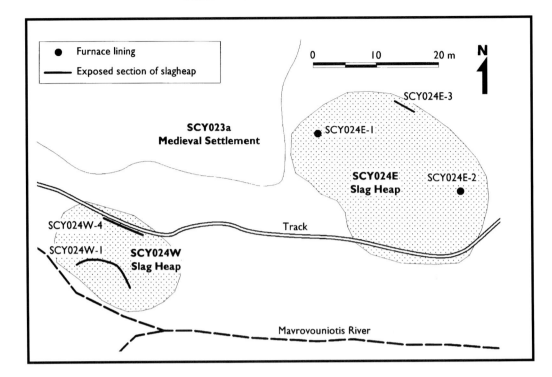

(SCY023c), which was rich in pottery, was surveyed by means of gridded circles 2 m in diameter and 10 m apart, to examine the distribution of material immediately adjacent to the settlement. The main area of the settlement (SCY023a) was mapped using a theodolite and an EDM.

SCY024: MITSERO *SYKAMIES*: THE SLAG HEAPS

The slag heaps, the largest in the survey area, lie 500 m southwest of Kokkinoyia mine, where impressive remnants of the ancient mines still survive today (SIA 11; see chapter 4.11); it is reasonable to assume that this is where the smelters obtained ore for their furnaces. The modern open-cast mine of Kokkinopezoula with its impressive gossan lies approximately 1 km to the southeast, but according to George Constantinou (conversation with author 1 July 1996) that area had not been exploited in antiquity because the copper content of the cupreous pyrites was probably too low to be extracted with the means and technology available.

As is the case at Mitsero *Kouloupakhis*, the slag heaps have been quarried with bulldozers and dissected by modern dirt roads, which created vertical sections enabling us to record the stratigraphy at specific points (figure 4.22). Other features such as such as furnace remains on the surface of the slag heaps,

as well as two possible adits in its direct proximity, have also been recorded.

SCY024W-1: WESTERN SLAG HEAP (AREA 1, UNIT 2050)

The southwest heap has the shape of an elongated, truncated cone, its peak lying just south of the modern road that cuts through its northern edge. The top flat surface of the heap is 30.5 m from north to south and 42.0 m from east to west, while the southern base of the cone is 52.0 m long. The height is estimated to be 20 m. On the southern part of the heap there is an artificial section almost 4 m high, which reveals clearly the stratigraphy of this anthropogenic mountain of metallurgical waste (figures 4.23, 4.24). At the lower part of the section there is a substantial amount of loose material which obscures the lower layers of the slag heap.

The westernmost heap consists almost entirely of tapped slag, although there are some fragments of furnace lining (mainly slagged stones but also clay; see chapter 5.4), as well as some pottery. The slag is mostly black in color, with some examples having a bluish-black surface characteristic of manganese-rich slags. As in the case with SCY021W (Mitsero *Kouloupakhis*) it is interesting that the layers of the slag heap are composed of similar sized fragments

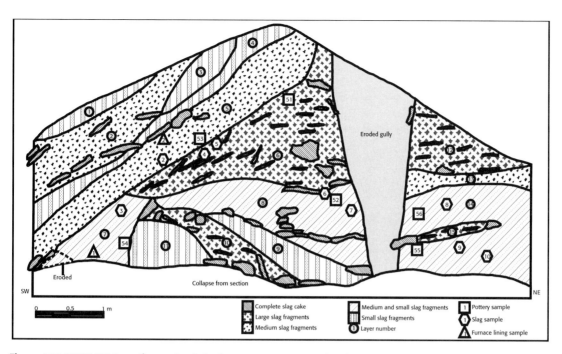

Figure 4.23 SCY024W-1: section: **1**, Small slag fragments; **2**, Compacted medium tap slag fragments; **3**, Small slag fragments; **4**, Small slag fragments; **5**, Compacted medium tap slag fragments; **6**, Large fragments of tap slag cakes; **7**, Tap slag fragments, various sizes; **8**, Small-medium tap slag fragments; **9**, Small slag fragments; **10**, Large tap slag cake fragment; **11**, Small slag fragments; **12**, Large fragments of tap slag cakes; **13**, Compacted medium tap slag fragments; **14**, Small to medium tap slag fragments; **15**, Large fragments of tap slag cakes. Note: layers 8 and 14—as may layers 6 and 12—may be the same layer. An erosion gully between them makes it difficult to ascertain.

Figure 4.24 SCY024W-1: slag heap from west

Table 4.9 SCY024: analyzed pottery (including units 2009–11, 2050–2053)

Chronotype	Period	Qty
Amphora-AC	AC	2
Plain ware-AC	AC	3
Plain White-AC	AC	5
Fine ware-Cl	Cl	1
Amphora-LR	LR	7
Basin-LR	LR	4
Coarse ware-LR	LR	6
Coarse ware, LR Wheel-Ridged	LR	5
Cooking ware-LR	LR	1
Cooking ware, Dhiorios Pot	LR	4
Red Slip-LR	LR	1
Spirally Grooved	LR	1
White Painted-HA	HA	1
Cypriot W6	Ott	1
Tile-Ott	Ott	1
Amphora-Historical	Hi	1
Pithos-PC	PC	1
Tile-PC	PC	1
Tile, Corinthian Pan	PC	1
Tile, Flat Pan	PC	1
Coarse ware-Unk	Unk	34
Cooking ware-Unk	Unk	1
Unknown	Unk	1
TOTAL		84

of slag. For example, there are layers that consist of small or finely crushed pieces (for example, layers 1, 3, 4, 8, 9, 11 in figure 4.23) and layers that consist of medium sized fragments (for example, layers 2, 5, 13). Among these there are large, almost complete slag cakes, again very similar to the ones from Kouloupakhis.

Keeping in mind that this is an artificial section at a random point of the heap we can still make some general remarks on the stratigraphy. Unlike the situation at Kouloupakhis (see figure 4.10), some layers (1 through 5) are not horizontal but slanted, which indicates that the waste material was dumped over an already formed mass of slag. Roughly horizontal layers (for example, 8 and 14) may indicate an effort to create a working platform where new furnaces were built and smelting continued in the same general area.

Slag samples were collected from the various strata (figure 4.23), and ten of them were analyzed by XRF. All the samples contained very low levels of copper (below 1% in all but one sample), which is expected for slags of this period. As in the case of the slags from SIA 3, the majority of these samples were manganiferous, with one example containing 41.5%

manganese oxide (see chapter 5.4). The flux used was also umber, a mineral that consists of mainly of iron oxides but also contains significant concentrations of manganese oxide.

Six samples of pottery were also collected from the stratified layers but, unfortunately, only one of these could be securely identified (Late Roman); the others were of unknown date (table 4.9). Various other pieces of pottery were collected either from the surface or from the collapsed material of the cleaned section. Again, apart from a couple of Archaic sherds and some coarse ware of unknown date, the majority of the pottery is Late Roman. This fits well with the general picture of the slag heap: its size, the size of the slag cakes, the type of furnace lining, and so on, are very similar to those of Kouloupakhis, which was also Late Roman in date.

SCY024W-2: POSSIBLE MINING ADIT

A small adit was recorded 30 m northwest of the north edge of the settlement (SCY023) and approximately 350 m northwest of SCY024W-1. It is 5 m long and cuts through the gossan and into the pillow lavas at an angle of 45 degrees. It has a maximum width of 195 cm at the entrance (which decreases further inside) and a maximum height of 79 cm. It is unclear what its function is, and impossible to know whether it is an ancient or modern exploration adit.

SCY024W-4: NORTHERN SECTION OF WESTERN SLAG HEAP (AREA 2, UNIT 2051)

This subunit is located approximately 8 m northeast of SCY024W-1, and forms part of the north vertical face of the slag heap created along with the modern dirt road. It is 1 m high and its stratigraphy is rather unclear. The slag once again was predominantly broken tap slag, but there were also some fragments of furnace slag as well as pieces of furnace lining. One open body sherd of white painted pottery was collected from this section, but its date is uncertain.

SCY024E-1: FURNACE MATERIAL, NW CORNER (AREA 3, UNIT 2052)

The approximate dimensions of the top surface of the eastern slag heap are 70.5 m north-south and 53.5 m east-west. SCY024E-1 is located on the surface of the eastern slag heap approximately 20 m west-

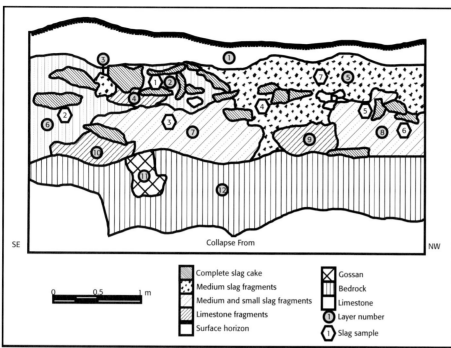

Figure 4.25
SCY024E-3: section:
1, Surface horizon;
2, Small slag fragments; **3**,
Medium slag fragments;
4, Limestone rocks;
5, Medium slag fragments;
6, Small slag fragments; **7**,
Medium-small slag fragments;
8, Medium-small slag
fragments;
9, Limestone rocks;
10, Limestone rocks;
11, Gossan; **12**, Bedrock

SE   Collapse From   NW

Complete slag cake   Gossan
Medium slag fragments   Bedrock
Medium and small slag fragments   Limestone
Limestone fragments   Layer number
Surface horizon   Slag sample

0   0.5   1 m

northwest of SCY024E-2. It consists of a large concentration of furnace lining fragments and slagged stones, exposed by recent bulldozing, and seems to be in situ. This material probably represents the remains of a badly preserved smelting furnace, but it is impossible to ascertain its size or form. Charcoal was also found in association with this installation and was sampled for ^{14}C dating (appendix B). The date (Cal AD 418–538, at 1 sigma) falls well within the Late Roman period. This date is very similar to that of one of the charcoal samples from SCY021, which was also related to furnace remains, and confirms that smelting activities continued during this period. No pottery was associated with this feature.

Apart from surface sampling, further testing of the deposit for stratigraphy and context was impossible, as we decided not to destroy the material present. The discovery of a smelting furnace on top of the slag heap need not be surprising, as it is a common phenomenon elsewhere. Working space for the construction of new furnaces was created wherever necessary, especially on a slag heap. This often resulted in the disturbance of the stratigraphy and even sometimes in the reversal of the chronological sequence (Bachmann 1982a:6).

SCY024E-2: ROASTING REMAINS, E SECTION (AREA 4, UNIT 2053)

This subunit lies on the surface of the slag heap on the eastern side (figure 4.22). It consists of a con-

centration of roasted ore, charcoal, and slagged stones, and like the previous subunits has been disturbed by modern bulldozing. These remains may or may not be in situ. The mixture of roasted ore, earth and charcoal (conglomerate) found here is similar in appearance to that found at in Layer 3 of SCY022-1a (see figure 4.2). Baked earth and furnace lining were also observed, along with one large slagged stone (see chapter 5.4). Once again, no pottery was observed.

SCY024E-3: SECTION ON NORTH OF EASTERN SLAG HEAP (AREA 3, UNIT 2052)

This section apparently indicates the northern limit of the eastern slag heap, and its stratigraphy was revealed by a square cut on the site of the hill (figure 4.25). The 1-m thick slag deposit lies on top of the pillow lava bedrock and is covered by a thick layer of topsoil (layer 1—about 20 to 30 cm).

There are a number of large, complete slag cakes, but the majority of the slag is broken into medium or small pieces. As observed both in the Sykamies West slag heap (SCY024W-1) and at Kouloupakhis (SCY021W-1), the slag fragments seem to be sorted by size, forming separate layers or lenses as shown in figure 4.25. Five samples of slag were analyzed (see chapter 5.4). Their chemical composition is similar to that of

Figure 4.26 SCY023a: main (eastern) part of the settlement

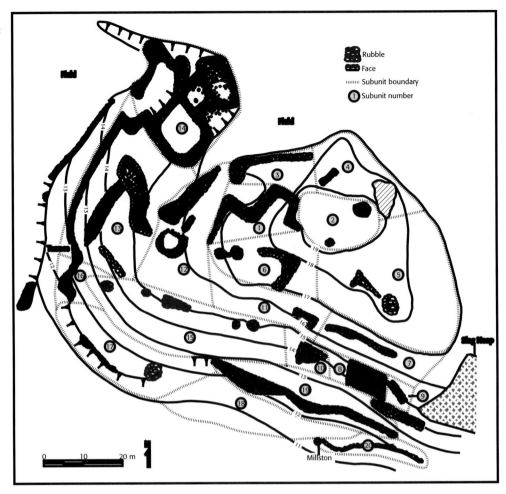

the samples from SCY024W-1. The majority are manganiferous and they all contain low levels of copper. The slags from SCY024E-3, however, contain higher amounts of zinc, which may indicate the exploitation of a different deposit or a different vein within the same ore deposit.

Apart from some small lenses consisting of limestone rocks, there were no other finds from this section. The only piece of pottery found in this subunit was an Archaic sherd collected from the surface of the plowed field in front of the slag heap, and so not necessarily associated with it.

SCY023: MITSERO *MAVROVOUNOS*: THE MEDIEVAL SETTLEMENT

The western end of the east slag heap (SCY024E) runs directly onto a small hill or knoll, whose slopes and summit are covered with piles and lines of rubble, thickly overgrown with hawthorn, terebinth, thorny burnet, and wild grasses. This rubble marks the settlement of Mavrovounos or, in the Italian version used on the sixteenth- and seventeenth-century maps, Maurochio. The principal part of the settlement lies on the western and southern slopes of the knoll (SCY023a). One hundred meters to the northwest a low ridge runs down toward the river, with more rubble piles, a well, and a series of artificially leveled platforms (SCY023b). Between these two parts of the settlement lies a field that mostly derives from accumulated sediments because of a large check dam on its southern edge, across a small first order gully (SCY023c).

The most characteristic feature of the settlement's position is its location on a knoll immediately above the river in the upper part of a valley. Thus it was close to the water supply, by means of wells going down to the water table, and it did not occupy prime arable land. This compares well with Politiko *Phorades* 2 (SCY101), Klirou *Manastirka* (SIA

2) and, to some extent, Mitsero village. Such a situation may also provide more of a breeze, for comfort and for winnowing grain on the threshing floors. The choice of a site immediately adjacent to the ancient slag heaps also seems relevant, particularly because that choice is reflected in the settlement's name.

Many of the rubble piles, though large, are fairly amorphous, and give only a general idea of the layout of the settlement (figure 4.26). Only in two examples (subunits 8 and 14) are the outlines of entire structures clear. The dating of this settlement rests largely on the pottery found within it. Because the area was so overgrown, most pottery was found on the rubble piles and tended to consist of large pieces, as the smaller pieces fall through. This may account for the high proportion of large pithos fragments and large jasper cores. The field between the two parts of the settlement (SCY023c) is of particular importance because of the amount of diagnostic material recovered there.

SCY023a: THE STRUCTURES

Subunit 8. In the southeast corner of the settlement (figure 4.26) is the clear outline of a building that measures 10 x 5 m. The long axis follows the contour and, as the slope here is relatively steep, the northern part at the rear must have been dug into the bank, and the front, southern wall built up to make a platform. There was a considerable amount of pottery in and next to this structure, including some sixteen sherds of Medieval to Modern coarse ware and another two that were certainly Medieval; three sherds of galeftiri, of which one was Medieval and the other two Medieval to Modern. Two glazed fine ware pieces can be dated more precisely to the sixteenth century. The galeftiri (spouted pan) is a common form across the settlement, particularly as only the spouts and rims are easily identifiable, and was probably used for milking, like its modern equivalents.

Subunit 14. There is a particularly clear complex in the northwest corner of the settlement, consisting of a courtyard on the south and two rooms to the north, one leading off the other. Allowing for the space taken up by the rubble collapse, the courtyard measures some 10 x 12 m. There may be an additional structure on the west. The extent of the collapse means that passages and doorways are not detectable. This organization of space, with successive rooms abutting on their long sides and leading off a courtyard, is a familiar type in the surviving late Ottoman and early colonial village houses of Cyprus (Christodoulou 1959: 67; Ionas 1988: 51–52). Of the ten pieces of pottery found within this structure, the one datable glazed piece is a seventeenth-century Cypriot Glazed IX Late body sherd. Four pieces of pithos cannot be dated any more specifically than Medieval to Modern, and the same applies to three coarse ware sherds. It is very probable that the storage facilities provided by the many pithos fragments found in the settlement date to the period when it was inhabited.

Subunit 19. Along the southern edge of the settlement runs a long line of rubble spilling down the front of an artificial terrace. The quantity of rubble seems far too great for it to be a collapsed agricultural terrace wall. It may have been a retaining wall for a house platform or perhaps a street along the front of the structures in subunits 10 and 8. Another possibility is that it marked the southern limit of the settlement, whether as a retaining wall or a larger defensive wall. If this is the case, it would be a continuation of the wall running down the western limit of the settlement (along the western edges of subunits 14, 13, 16), and turning eastwards through subunit 17. After the abandonment of the settlement this long platform seems to have been cleared, presumably for agricultural purposes. There is sufficient lichen on the rubble to make it clear that it does not result from recent field clearance, so it presumably dates to a time not long after the abandonment of the settlement, perhaps the eighteenth or nineteenth century. The pottery found in subunit 19 includes one glazed piece from the sixteenth century, three Medieval/Modern pithos fragments, two Medieval to Modern tile fragments, and a sherd of Medieval to Modern coarse ware, as well as six coarse ware and tile fragments of unknown period.

Subunit 20. Judging by its construction and the smaller volume of rubble, the wall in subunit 20 seems to be a more recent agricultural terrace. The subunit nonetheless is important for the pottery found within it. As usual, much of the coarse ware can only be dated to the Medieval to Modern periods, although one of these is part of the rim and handle of a galeftiri. Apart from one Medieval glazed piece, this subunit has a more substantial Ottoman component, with three plain glazed sherds, two of them brown. There is also a large olive millstone

Table 4.10 SCY023: analyzed pottery

Chronotype	Period	Qty
Amphora-AC	AC	1
Double Rolled Strap Handle-AC	AC	1
Plain ware-AC	AC	1
Amphora-LR	LR	3
Amphora, LR 1	LR	2
Coarse ware, LR Wheel-Ridged	LR	6
Cypriot Red Slip	LR	1
Cypriot Red Slip 10	LR	2
Phocaean ware 10	LR	1
Red Slip-LR	LR	1
TOTAL Archaic to Late Roman		19
Cypriot W1 Early	Med	5
Cypriot Glazed	Med	3
Cypriot Glazed IIIB	Med	1
Cypriot Glazed IVC	Med	1
Cypriot Glazed V	Med	2
Cypriot Glazed VIII	Med	2
Cypriot Glazed VIIIB	Med	6
Cypriot Glazed IX	Med	5
Cypriot Glazed XI	Med	3
Glazed ware, Italian	Med	1
Cypriot Glazed VIIIB Late	Ott	1
Cypriot Glazed IX Late	Ott	5
Cypriot Glazed, Brown and Green	Ott	7
Cypriot W3	Ott	3
Cypriot W5	Ott	2
Cypriot W6	Ott	13
Ottoman Glazed	Ott	1
Contemporary East Mediterranean	Mod	4
Contemporary Imported Asian	Mod	1
Cypriot W7	Mod	20
Brown Glaze	MM	8
Cypriot W1	MM	9
Cypriot W4	MM	212
Glazed ware	MM	2
TOTAL Medieval to Modern		317
Tile-MM	MM	7
Plain White-HA	HA	10
Pithos-PC	PC	1
Tile-PC	PC	9
Tile, Cover	PC	1
Tile, Flat Pan	PC	2
Coarse ware-Unk	Unk	60
Cooking ware-Unk	Unk	2
Unknown	Unk	9
TOTAL		437

(mortarium) with a diameter of 105 cm and a thickness of 75 cm; on each face are roughly square sockets. The shape and dimensions are very similar to those of millstones found on Hellenistic to Late Roman sites in Cyprus (Hadjisavvas 1992:17–19).

SCY023c: GRIDDED CIRCLES

Although pottery was collected from each subunit within the settlement (SCY023a), numbers there never exceeded 0.8 sherds per m^2 because of the poor visibility. The slightly denser units clearly coincided with the main structures (subunits 8, 9, 12, 17, 20), but this is probably due to their larger areas of rubble where pottery could be seen more easily.

For this reason, we surveyed intensively the large field lying immediately west of the main part of the settlement by means of gridded circles (plate XVII). Counts of slag fragments were very high, with up to 21.3 pieces per m^2 in the eastern corner. There was clearly more slag in the northern and eastern corners, and less downslope to the south. This suggests that the slag derives from the eastern slag heap and from reuse as building material in the settlement and nearby field walls, though sedimentation behind the check dam at the south of the field will have covered up a certain amount of premodern material. The pottery shows a similar pattern, though not so marked, perhaps because potsherds are lighter than slag fragments and are more easily displaced downhill by the plow. Geometric to Roman material is scarce; Medieval to Modern, by contrast, is relatively dense, with up to 2.55 pieces per m^2. This is too high to be manuring or dumping, and it clearly derives from the settlement immediately adjacent and upslope to the northeast.

SCY023: DATING

Because of the precision with which we can date the Cypriot Glazed (CG) series of Medieval and Ottoman pottery, examining that material in particular from Mavrovounos is the best means we have of dating the period of occupation of the settlement. Because of the poor visibility in the settlement itself, we had to include material from the gridded circles in SCY023c (table 4.10) and from the block survey. Some of the block survey pottery may not represent settlement, of course, and this count is only the barest indicator of intensive activity within the landscape.

Of the eighty-five glazed sherds from SIA 4 datable to within one or two centuries, there are fifteen from the thirteenth to fifteenth centuries, fifty-four from the sixteenth century alone, and sixteen from the seventeenth to eighteenth centuries. The peak of the settlement was clearly the sixteenth century, as is common elsewhere in the survey area. This also fits in with the local tradition of the village being abandoned a few hundred years ago because of the plague; one informed source in the village even declares that it happened in 1700, a date that matches in general terms the lichen on the rubble heaps.

BLOCK SURVEY

The density map for sherds of all periods (plate XVIII) shows a very marked rise in material approaching SIA 4 along the transect from the north and south, which is clearly in keeping with a major smelting site and settlement. The lack of material in the surrounding landscape, however, needs to be seen in the context of the major erosion that has taken place across it (see above). On an older surface we would have expected at least a halo of material round the SIA reflecting agriculture, movement and other activities in the landscape.

The same map shows the very localized distribution of tile, clearly focused just round the church of Ayios Yeoryios (SCY328). The forty-six tile fragments from unit 2564, a small unit immediately below the church, were of the thick rectangular type with a flange at one end, typically measuring about 20 x 30 cm. These are characteristic of churches from at least the Medieval period onward. Other than these church tiles, there are very few tile fragments from the SIA: there were only three from the circles and grab samples in SCY023c and six from the settlement itself. The houses of Mavrovounos clearly had flat roofs made of branches, reeds and earth, just as those of Mitsero did until the 1930s.

Archaic to Classical. The distribution of the Archaic and Classical material is clearly weighted toward the north end of the SIA (plate XIX). Units 4051 and 2547 have significant amounts, as does unit 2508 further to the north, and in general the map has a "patchy" quality, with three small but distinct density spikes. These are set against a general low background level, normally associated with no more than agriculture or general casual activity in the landscape. It may be that these spikes represent tombs or clusters of tombs. There is almost nothing from the two settlement areas and the gridded circles and grab samples between them. Small amounts were found in the surface collection of the Sykamies East slag heap (SCY024E) and from the collapse in front of the south section of the Sykamies West slag heap (SCY024W-1). The section in the eastern slag heap (SCY024E-3) had one stratified piece.

Most of the Archaic to Classical material consists of plain ware vessels (for example, cat. 2514.1.1) and storage jars, which could be either tomb or settlement materials (table 4.11). There is not much kitchen ware, a certain number of decorated vessels, many storage vessels, many closed jugs or jars, and no pithoi. Few of these sherds are diagnostic, but there is enough in these various units to verify an Archaic and Classical component. The pieces are somewhat worn and, while this wear was not extensive, they are certainly not as sharp as sherds from funerary or archaeometallurgical contexts. The Archaic to Classical component of SIA 4 might well represent a cemetery, but the possibility of a settlement cannot be ruled out.

Hellenistic to Late Roman. The material from these periods is slight. Only one unit (2572) reaches a pottery index of 900; all others are substantially less (plate XIX). That said, there is a very even spread of material across the SIA, at a level which in alluvial plains seems to correspond to agriculture and manuring. This does not extend into areas to the north and south, probably because of the extensive erosion in these areas. As so often happens in the survey area, the dominant period is the Late Roman.

Byzantine to Modern. In common with much of the survey area, even those with substantial Late Roman and Medieval components, there was no identified Byzantine material from Mitsero *Mavrovounos*. Medieval material is widespread, although the densities are not especially high and the pottery index never exceeds 4000 (plate XX). This is more or less equivalent to figures at the similar settlement of Klirou *Ayios Mamas* (SIA 9). The material is clustered in the western part of the SIA, immediately north and west of the settlement. There is also a very clear concentration of material in the southwest, on the far side of the river from the settlement. This is due in part to the church of Ayios Yeoryios, but it may also represent a further extension of the settlement, undetected by other means.

Levels of Ottoman pottery were low (only 2% of pottery collected from SIA 4), and Modern is even lower (1%). It is, however, hard to take this as proof of the seventeenth-century abandonment of Mavrovounos, since another 55% of the pottery could have dated anywhere in the Medieval, Ottoman or

Table 4.11 SIA 4: analyzed pottery from block survey

Chronotype	Period	Qty	Chronotype	Period	Qty
Amphora-Ar	Ar	1	Coarse ware-Med	Med	1
Bichrome-Ar	Ar	1	Cypriot Glazed	Med	23
Green ware	Ar	1	Cypriot Glazed IV	Med	1
Plain ware-Ar	Ar	2	Cypriot Glazed IVC [2501.5.1]	Med	1
Red Slip-Ar	Ar	4	Cypriot Glazed V	Med	2
Soft Red-Orange-Ar	Ar	2	Cypriot Glazed VII	Med	5
Bichrome-Cl	Cl	1	Cypriot Glazed VIII	Med	1
Plain ware-Cl [2514.1.1]	Cl	1	Cypriot Glazed VIIIA	Med	1
Plain White-Cl	Cl	7	Cypriot Glazed VIIIB	Med	24
Amphora-AC	AC	7	Cypriot Glazed IX	Med	20
Amphora, Torpedo	AC	3	Cypriot Glazed XI	Med	6
Plain ware-AC	AC	29	Cypriot W1 Early	Med	2
Plain White-AC	AC	6	Maiolica ware	Med	1
White Painted-AC	AC	1	Zeuxippos ware	Med	1
			Cypriot Glazed VIIIB Late	Ott	3
TOTAL Archaic to Classical		66	Cypriot Glazed IX Late	Ott	11
			Cypriot Glazed, Brown and Green	Ott	6
Black Glaze-He	He	1	Cypriot W3	Ott	3
Red Slip-He	He	1	Cypriot W5	Ott	1
Çandarli ware	ER	1	Ottoman Glazed	Ott	4
Coarse ware-ER	ER	2	Coarse ware-Mod	Mod	4
Cypriot Sigillata	ER	1	Contemporary Eastern Mediterranean	Mod	1
African Red Slip	LR	1	Cypriot W7	Mod	4
Amphora-LR	LR	2	Fine ware-Mod	Mod	1
Amphora, LR 1	LR	5	Lapithos ware, Yellow	Mod	1
Basin-LR	LR	1	Pithos-Mod	Mod	1
Coarse ware-LR	LR	2	Tile-Mod	Mod	1
Coarse ware, LR Wheel-Ridged	LR	8	Brown Glaze	MM	4
Cooking ware, Dhiorios Pot	LR	1	Coarse ware-MM	MM	39
Cypriot Red Slip	LR	2	Cypriot W1	MM	526
Cypriot Red Slip 9	LR	1	Cypriot W4	MM	58
Frying Pan	LR	1	Glazed ware-MM	MM	70
Phocaean ware (LR C)	LR	2	Pithos-MM	MM	86
Pithos-LR	LR	1			
Spirally Grooved	LR	2	TOTAL Medieval to Modern		913
Amphora-REL	REL	1			
Red Slip-REL	REL	2	Plain White-HA	HA	5
			Amphora-Hi	Hi	2
TOTAL Hellenistic to Late Roman		38	Pithos-PC	PC	32
			Tile-PC	PC	24
			Tile, Laconian	PC	1
			Coarse ware-Unk	Unk	328
			Cooking ware-Unk	Unk	3
			Fine ware-Unk	Unk	1
			Unknown	Unk	2
			TOTAL		1415

Note: Figures in brackets refer to cataloged items (see chapter 5.1).

Modern periods. This is a much higher proportion of Medieval to Modern pottery than that from SCY023 (17%). The Medieval pottery is widely spread in time, ranging from the thirteenth to sixteenth centuries, but with a clear preponderance in the sixteenth century. Proportions of Ottoman and Modern period

pottery from the block survey were very slightly lower than in SCY023.

Lithics. The main raw material in the area is red jasper, which is plentiful, particularly just north of this SIA. There were four chunky red jasper cores in the main part of the settlement (SCY023a), and another three came from the intensive collection in the gridded circles (SCY023c). There is also some chalcedony in the area, and often the jasper has veins of chalcedony. The pieces of crypto-crystalline silicate are clearly intrusive to this area. There are many varieties of red jasper scrapers, which follow no particular pattern; people were using what came to hand. Because several blade cores were found, we can presume there was some sort of blade technology, even though there are no actual complete blades.

One characteristic type of tool found across SIA 4 consists of a large, heavy, red jasper chopper. Two utilised flakes of brown jasper and one of chalcedony were found in SCY023c. Unit 2501 contained an important assemblage of lithics that stands out from the rest of the area. Two threshing sledge blades were recovered from the block survey, in two almost contiguous units on the western edge of the western part of the settlement (4046 and 2543). Since this area is slightly raised above the rest of the settlement, it would be appropriate for threshing floors.

CONCLUSION

The slag heap of Mitsero *Sykamies* is clearly associated with the mine of Kokkinoyia. As argued elsewhere for Kouloupakhis, its location at a small distance from the mine may in fact be due to the availability of fuel and water. The Mavrovouniotis stream runs a few meters from the edge of the western slag heap, and it is possible that this provided the workshops with clay, igneous rocks and the necessary water. Smelting activities at Sykamies clearly date to the Late Roman period, which makes them later than such activities at the Kokkinoyia slag heap (SCY219). This may indicate that the fuel around the mine had already been exhausted either in the smelting furnaces or even in the mines themselves, as a number of the galleries at Kokkinoyia are lined with wooden supports.

The shape and spread of the slag heaps of Mitsero *Sykamies* fit well with the formation process described by Tylecote (1977:324; see chapter 5.4). There are flattened layers that may have been used as working surfaces, and there are inclined layers over them indicating the abandonment of the specific spot and the move to another. That the surface was used as a working space is clearly indicated by the badly preserved remains of a smelting furnace found in SCY024E-1.

The Medieval settlement of Mavrovounos was built immediately adjacent to the slag heaps, and certainly named after it. Its relationship with the surrounding landscape was very different, being primarily based on agriculture. The quantities of pithos fragments found suggest a major storage function, presumably of oil, wine, or grain. A notable feature of the landscape around Mavrovounos is the small number of aged olive trees, particularly when compared to Ayios Mamas and Malounda. The olive millstone, judging from published parallels, is more likely to be ancient than medieval. Given the lack of arable land and the erosional nature of the surrounding landscape during most of the Holocene, it is unlikely that Mavrovounos relied heavily on cereal agriculture. The only other main economic options are vines and herding.

Nearby Medieval villages, most notably Akhera (*MKE* 3:100), paid tax to the Grand Commandery in wine, and there are still many vineyards in the immediate area of Mavrovounos. As for herding, there are three possible goat folds in the hills to the north and south of the village, two of them within view of it: Mitsero *Kalorka* (SCY115), which is certainly Medieval; Mitsero *Moutti tou Trimithou* (SCY324), which may be a goat fold and unfortunately produced no dateable pottery; and Mitsero *Klouvaes* (SCY325), which is late Ottoman or early Modern. When combined with the numerous galeftiri fragments from the settlement, this suggests that pastoralism succeeded the industrial economy of Late Roman Mavrovounos.

4.5 SIA 5: Mitsero Village

Kylie Seretis and Lita Diacopoulos

Grid reference: 511400/3878000
Cadastral map: XXIX/53
Aerial photograph: 1993, run 177, no. 43
POSIs: SCY202: Mitsero *Kato Alonia* (threshing floors); SCY300: Mitsero *Rhodanos* (gold mining structures); SCY301: Mitsero *Kokkinopezoula* (mine); SCY320: Mitsero *Ayia Varvara* (foremen's settlement); SCY321: Mitsero *Kolasis* (mineworkers' housing); SCY358: Mitsero (village cemetery); SCY359: Mitsero (House of Symbols); SCY363: Mitsero *Yeropalloura* (mine office complex)

In 1997 and 1998, we systematically collected historical, oral, and archaeological information on Mitsero

Figure 4.27 Mitsero village with Kokkinopezoula mine in the background

village, the surrounding mines, and associated features (figure 4.27). An investigation of this changing landscape from the late nineteenth century to the present day forms a critical part of understanding how both agricultural and mining practices have an impact upon, and form the character of, modern Cypriot villages and their inhabitants. Such an investigation also provides a unique opportunity to attempt to understand local people and their relationship to place through their own descriptions of the past in comparison to the physical remains. It also provides the researcher a rare opportunity to glimpse lifestyles that are rapidly changing beyond recognition.

The village of Mitsero is located 25 km southwest of Nicosia. It is bounded immediately to the north by the hill Kriadhis and to the northwest by Lambadhousa hill (plate XXI). The mines of Kokkinoyia and Kokkinopezoula are located, respectively, to the northwest and southwest. The mine of Agrokipia Kriadhis lies 2 km east (immediately north of Ayia Varvara and west of Agrokipia).

HISTORICAL BACKGROUND

From archaeological sources, we know of a settlement on the site of Mitsero dating back to the Archaic period and surviving through to the Late Roman period (see chapter 4.3). The village of Mitsero first appears in the historical record in a late fifteenth-century Venetian document on population statistics, which includes "Casal Micero" in the property of the Grand Commandery (de Mas Latrie 1852–61, III:502). It also appears on a 1578 map as Micero (Stylianou and Stylianou 1980:273), in another sixteenth-century document as Mitseron (Kyrris 1987:130), and in 1705 as Mytsero (Hidiroglou 1971–1972:334). Between 1573 and 1768 nine different maps name it as Micco, although several of these are likely to be uncritical copies of their predecessors (Stylianou and Stylianou 1980: 257, 291, 304, 305, 314, 322, 337, 372, 397). Goodwin (1984) suggests the name derives from the *matsikoridon* or *mitsikoridon*, the Greek Cypriot word for a type of daffodil, which metaphorically can mean little flower or little girl. According to Mr. Loïzos Xinaris from Mitsero, one of our most helpful and knowledgeable informants, the name derives from *mitson ieron* or small church, because of the size of the current church's predecessor.

According to a strong local tradition, reported by various topographical writers (Kliridhis 1961:167–68; Goodwin 1984:1088), Mitsero is only about three hundred years old. It had three Medieval predecessors: *Mavrovounos* (SIA 4), *Lambadhiotissa* (SCY114), and an unlocated settlement at Koroni somewhere on Lambadhousa. This last may be a confusion with Mavrovounos (cf. Jeffery 1918:302–303). According

Figure 4.28 Church of Arkhangelos Mikhail

to a dramatic local narrative, these settlements were struck with plague three hundred years ago and, because the wells and cisterns were infected with the disease, the surviving inhabitants moved east to make a new start and founded Mitsero. According to Loïzos Xinaris, there were only six founding families: Hatzitheophani, Pasouli, Hatzikyprianos, Hrysi, Kokkonia, and one other. The documentary sources suggest that Mitsero dates to the fifteenth century or before, but our archaeological dating of the abandonment of Mavrovounos to the seventeenth century (chapter 4.4) fits well with this local tradition, and there may well have been a secondary occupation or founding of Mitsero in the seventeenth century.

Until the late 1920s, Mitsero was predominantly an agricultural village. Like many villages of the late nineteenth and early twentieth centuries on Cyprus, there is little or no textual information relating to Mitsero and its development. This situation only changes with the interest of the Hellenic Mining Company (HMC) and its mining operations within the general area, to which the historical development of Mitsero is closely tied from the later 1920s. Until 1935, interaction with Nicosia was minimal, not least because it required a two-day round trip. There were no roads, only footpaths. The first dirt road was constructed in 1935 to service the gold processing plant built in Mitsero and other mining activity in the area.

Government census data from the British Colo-nial period and afterward (1881–1973) shows a steady and substantial increase in population. The population of Mitsero increased from 145 in 1881 to 265 in 1911, 498 in 1946, and 705 in 1973. This increase was tied to the development and industrialization taking place on the island, particularly the development of the mining industry.

FIELD METHODOLOGY

We sought to obtain historical and oral information and we conducted a survey of the physical remains in and around Mitsero. The survey was carried out over a period of three weeks in August and September 1997. Because of the sheer volume of information available and the difficulties of sorting through it all in the time available, a detailed strategy was developed to address specific research questions related to social and technological change within the village over the past century. We also considered how such change is related to the identity of the village and the villagers (see chapter 2.7).

VILLAGE BUILDINGS

The village church, dedicated to Arkhangelos Mikhail, dates to the 1860s and is located in what was the center of the village, surrounded by a sand-

Figure 4.29 General view of the House of Symbols showing images on external arch

Figure 4.30 Mitsero village cemetery

stone and plastered wall (figure 4.28). The building has been painted white and the wooden doors blue, while the windows have metal grates and the roof is tiled. The belfry, a later addition to the church, is decorated with a relief of two lions facing each other. Several icons are located inside the church.

The original village school is located immediately to the south of the church and is visible on the 1923 village plan. The former school building is now used by the Christian Society of the Women of Mitsero and for Sunday school. The building itself has been restored, first in 1975 and again in 1995. It appears to have the original arches and sandstone window and door surrounds, although restoration has made it difficult to see what was original and what is new.

The first coffee house in Mitsero (plate XXI for locations of coffee houses) was opened in 1940 (it is now the "right-wing" coffee house). Another coffee house opened up opposite the church (currently the youth club). Kostas Loïzos opened the DIKO (center-right wing) coffee house in 1956. In 1965 the "left-wing" coffee house opened opposite the first one, which immediately turned the old coffee house into a right-wing establishment. Although the political inclinations of the inhabitants of modern Cypriot villages is beyond the scope of this study, it may be noted that such a distribution of coffee houses—and their almost exclusively male clientele—would not be unusual anywhere in the Republic of Cyprus.

An abandoned house constructed of stone and mudbrick located near the church in the old section of the village was of particular interest because of its elaborately carved stone entrance and central arch. We called this The House of Symbols (SCY359) and recorded the house, its courtyard, and the sculptures (figure 4.29). The large carved stone entrance has a total of 20 relief panels, depicting motifs such as flowers, birds, animals, and a horse with chariot and rider. The entry leads into a large room with a decorated internal arch, with another 23 relief sculptures including religious images such as the Archangel Michael, other angels, stars of David, and St. George killing the Dragon.

Stone carving and decoration is common in nineteenth-century houses and is particularly characteristic of houses in the Karpass peninsula (Papadimitriou 1992) (although it can be found island-wide). Located in the old village center near the old school, the olive press, and the church, this house appears to be one of the oldest remaining in the village. It may be dated either to the end of the

nineteenth century or, more likely, to the first decade of the twentieth century.

Mitsero cemetery (figure 4.30; SCY358) is located just northwest of the village. It comprises two clearly distinct sections: an older one containing graves from 1941 to1987, and a newer one with graves dating from 1987 onward. The old section is located in the northern part of the complex, and is surrounded by a stone wall that also separates it from the new section to the south. An ossuary with a tiled roof, wooden double doors, and a window facing east into the cemetery is located in the northeastern corner near the entrance. The graves face east and are arranged in irregular rows, and grave enclosures vary from marble to concrete and metal. The larger and newer cemetery to the south is surrounded by concrete, white-painted walls, higher than the stone walls of the old section, with a large metal gate, wide enough for vehicle access in the eastern wall.

AGRICULTURE

Prior to the opening of the mines in 1930, Mitsero was an agricultural village. Oral accounts stress that the villagers were self-sufficient (figure 4.31). Produce was grown and consumed within the village, while exchanges of goods took place between individual villagers. Ionas (1998:148) notes a similar situation for pottery producers, who tended to trade their products for farm produce or other goods. Generally produce was not sold outside the village. There were no shops in the village until 1947, and the three most important goods—soap, sugar, and petrol— were purchased from Klirou, an important market center for tradespeople such as bootmakers and blacksmiths. Other tradespeople—saddlemakers, dhoukani flint knappers, and merchants of various textile items—traveled about and visited the villages.

Each family in the village had its own threshing floor (aloni) (see also Whittaker 1999). Villagers who lived in the southern half of the village had their threshing floors in Pano Alonia, while those who lived in the northern part had their threshing floors in Kato Alonia (SCY202; figure 4.32). The continued growth and development of the village, in particular the advent of modern housing has resulted in the destruction of almost all the threshing floors at Pano Alonia. Grain would be piled up in the northern part of the threshing floor and every evening, when the northern wind picked up, the winnowing would take place. A 1948 aerial photograph of Mitsero village shows clearly the numerous alonia both in Kato and Pano Alonia.

Figure 4.31 Mr. Loïzos Xinaris in his home, with agricultural implements

There was no mill in Mitsero itself. The grain would be taken to Malounda where a couple of watermills did the work (for example, SCY308); otherwise the grain was taken to Pitsilia or Peristerona. Almost every family in the village had its own donkey and/or ox used for the plows, as well as for threshing and transport. They also kept sheep, goats, and possibly pigs.

The area of Kato Alonia is overgrown today. Close inspection, however, reveals the large stones that formed the threshing floors. Two alonia are cut by a road that leads down to the Hellenic Mining Company house "Seychelles" (see below) and to the village slaughter house. Generally the alonia are circular or nearly so, and range from 8 to 15 m across. They are paved with large river stones, slabs of limestone, and in some cases large slag cakes, probably from the nearby slag heap at Kouloupakhis (SCY021). In the eastern corner of this area lies a disused threshing machine, common all over the island.

Another major component of the agricultural economy in Mitsero was olive cultivation. Although no longer in existence, the village olive press is marked on the 1923 map and was mentioned by the villagers. Its location was pointed out to us and corresponded well to the location on the map. Today this area is generally unused and overgrown with weeds; some of the more recent village houses are located immediately around it. The olive press was hand-operated rather than mechanized. It was a wooden structure, later replaced by a metal structure, manually operated by two large stone wheels. The olives were harvested between October and December; during the summer months this press was used to press grapes for making wine.

THE HELLENIC MINING COMPANY AND THE MITSERO MINES

In 1926 the Anonyme Hellenic Company of Chemical Products and Manures applied for a mining lease over an area near the village of Mitsero (PWD MBAR 1926: 2). At this time, the company already held six prospecting permits near the villages of Mitsero, Agrokipia, and Eliophotes in the Nicosia district, and was carrying out systematic prospecting by underground work and drilling operations. Most of these prospects were in areas where there was evidence of ancient workings and slag heaps. New galleries were sunk and existing ancient galleries were opened and drilled deeper.

In the 1930s, this company held four prospecting permits in the Nicosia district, two in the Limassol district and two in the Paphos district. In 1933, they were granted a new mining lease for the Troodos Asbestos Mines, formerly granted to the Troodos Chrome and Asbestos Company Ltd. (*ARIM* 1933:11). By 1936, the abandoned mines of Mitsero and Agrokipia were discovered to have appreciable value in gold and silver. The company began to strip overburden from the Agrokipia deposit in preparation for open-cast mining. A 50-ton cyanide plant was erected near Mitsero. The plant was intended for the treatment of ore from the Agrokipia deposit and other gold bearing deposits within the Mitsero and Sha-Kambia lease areas (*ARIM* 1937:4). By 1940 the final remaining gold deposits had been mined and treated at the plant, which was then dismantled and transported for use elsewhere.

In the late 1940s, the company contracted an aerial survey over its mining and prospecting concessions. In 1950 geophysical prospecting was undertaken in the Mitsero-Agrokipia lease area. However, it was not until 1952 that a new ore body was located at Mitsero *Kokkinopezoula* and an iron pyrite deposit of some significance was discovered. Under-

Figure 4.32 SCY202: threshing floors at Mitsero *Kato Alonia*

ground exploration using adits then commenced at the Kokkinopezoula ore deposit (*ARIM* 1952:4; 1953:4), and further prospecting was undertaken in the Kokkinoyia area. This prospecting resulted in the discovery and mining of pyrites in an old open-cast mine at Agrokipia that had previously been worked for gold.

In 1954, the Hellenic Mining Company (HMC) placed orders for the necessary equipment to transfer the company's main operations from the Kalavasos *Vasiliko* district to the Mitsero *Agrokipia* area. Extensive prospecting had shown sufficient reserves of iron pyrites to warrant the installation of a modern treatment plant, and a modern crushing and flotation plant on the Mitsero *Agrokipia* lease. By 1955, plans were drawn up for a new loading station on Morphou Bay, near Karavostasi village (*ARIM* 1955:4–5). Toward the end of 1957 a bill entitled "The Hellenic MC Ltd (road and jetty)" was published for information and passed. This law made provision for the company to construct and maintain a new access road to the Mitsero treatment plant and to construct and maintain a stockpile, loading station, and pier in the vicinity of Karavostasi for their products (*ARIM* 1957:1–3).

MINING SETTLEMENTS AND MINERS' FACILITIES

Between 1954 and 1965, the HMC rented one of the old mudbrick houses in the village and turned it into a general store for the employees of the company. Employees could purchase groceries at a subsidized price and, at the beginning, bread was supplied free of charge. In the 1950s, the HMC built a large, two story building known as Seychelles to house its single male workers. Seychelles is located just beyond and to the north of the village, northeast of the threshing floors. Originally designed for the miners with bedrooms upstairs and down, and a large kitchen and dining room downstairs, this building has also been home to foreign geological teams (and to SCSP in 1993). In 1995 the building housed Ukrainian miners brought to the island to work for the HMC; since that time the building once again lies deserted.

Another larger structure for housing miners was planned at Mitsero *Kolasis* (SCY321). Located on the outskirts of both Ayia Varvara and Mitsero, this structure was only partially completed. Although the HMC began work on it in the 1960s, it never functioned as intended, and the front section of the block was only completed in the mid-1970s to house Greek Cypriot refugees from the 1974 Turkish invasion.

The HMC also set up a small foremen's settlement at Ayia Varvara (SCY320), halfway between Mitsero and Agrokipia, in order to house the company's managers and their families. Ayia Varvara consists of a single street of houses, on either side of the road. The buildings are prefabricated and all have wooden framed fences. The settlement has a church of the same name (Goodwin 1984: 308). The houses are still owned by the HMC and its workers still live there. Various members of SCSP teams lived in two houses in Ayia Varvara in 1995 and 1996.

Located nearly 1 km to the west and half way up toward Kokkinoyia mine (SIA 11) are the remains of the Kokkinopezoula office complex with five buildings and various pieces of equipment (SCY363: Mitsero *Yeropalloura*). Still visible are notices and signs to inform workers about safety issues. Within some of the buildings several other documents still survive: There are numerous maps of geophysical surveys of all HMC properties, as well as documents relating to the employees and to company purchases. The office complex was also home to a number of Greek Cypriot refugee families from the north after the 1974 Turkish invasion. Evidence of this is clearly visible in some of the rooms where, among other discarded items, a baby's cot lies disintegrating. Just below this complex is the building used by the HMC as a hospital; it is constructed of bricks and plaster, with wooden shutters and a brick and plaster garage. The verandah is constructed on stone with concrete steps leading to it. The building now houses geological and soil samples.

MINES AND MINING STRUCTURES

The three large-scale mines in the immediate area of Mitsero are Mitsero *Kokkinoyia* (SIA 11; see chapter 4.11), Agrokipia *Kriadhis* (SIA 1; see chapter 4.1), and Mitsero *Kokkinopezoula* (SCY301). The Kokkinopezoula mine is located 1 km west of Mitsero village. Operations here began in 1952 and initial work was done by the underground method; by 1956, however, open-cast mining was under way. Operations ceased in the late 1960s.

Several indicators suggest that numerous structures were located on the site of Kokkinopezoula. For example, there are fragments of asbestos roofing and metal frames all around the area; there are

remains of a number of concrete, and concrete and stone structures; and there are several concrete bases with fixtures for the connection of equipment. An interesting feature of these remains is the method of construction. The stone and mudbrick walls, built using local traditional techniques, bear witness to Mitsero's isolation from "global" technological advances in the mid-twentieth century. As with the mine at Agrokipia *Kriadhis*, a considerable amount of the material remains has been destroyed by the nature and process of open-cast mining.

Mitsero *Rhodanos* (SCY300) consists of the remains of a 1930s gold processing plant. The main structure is a large concrete base, with metal fixtures that originally would have been attached to a large superstructure. On either side of this main block are two stone structures (walls?) whose original function is unknown. There are two large stone water containers on the hill slope, respectively above and below the concrete slab. A great deal of slag scattered around this area could derive either from an ancient slag heap disturbed by the present concrete structure or more likely from recent attempts to rework the slag.

MITSERO: MINING SETTLEMENT OR AGRICULTURAL VILLAGE?

The old center of the village (figure 4.33) is evident from the church, the old school, and the oldest houses in the village (for example, SCY359). The 1923 map also shows the olive press in this central area. This central focus continued well into the 1960s or early 1970s with the opening of numerous coffee houses. For the older members of the community, it remains the central square of the village.

In contrast, the newer section of the village, mostly inhabited by children of the people who reside in the old section, has no center or village square. The focus has changed from a village with a central orientation to one where everything is dispersed: the school, the new supermarkets, and the service station are all located along the stretch of main road that cuts through the village. This may reflect in part new and different attitudes to space and distance, influenced by new road systems and changes in transport. For example, most new houses have garages and most people work in Nicosia.

From oral interviews with individuals we obtained crucial information—otherwise unobtainable—on the mining and agricultural character of Mitsero. In many

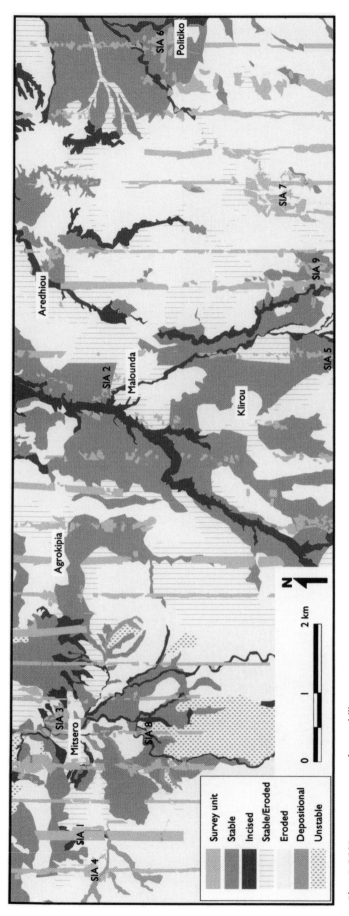

Plate I SCSP survey area: surface stability

Survey unit
Stable
Incised
Stable/Eroded
Eroded
Depositional
Unstable

SIA 1
SIA 4
SIA 3
Mitsero
SIA 8
Agrokipia
SIA 2
Malounda
Klirou
Aredhiou
SIA 9
SIA 5
SIA 7
SIA 6
Politiko

N

0   1   2 km

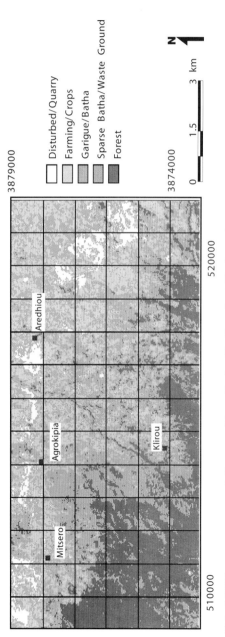

Plate II SCSP survey area: vegetation map (thematic classification of satellite image)

Disturbed/Quarry
Farming/Crops
Garigue/Batha
Sparse Batha/Waste Ground
Forest

3879000
3874000
510000
520000

Mitsero
Agrokipia
Aredhiou
Klirou

N

0   1.5   3 km

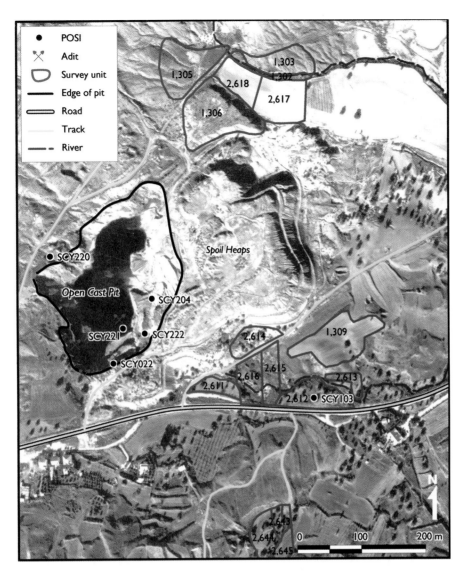

Plate III SIA 1: topographical map. *Based upon the aerials of the Department of Lands and Surveys with the sanction of the Government of Cyprus. State copyright reserved.*

Legend:
- POSI
- Adit
- Survey unit
- Edge of pit
- Road
- Track
- River

1,305 1,303 1,302 2,618 2,617 1,306

SCY220

Spoil Heaps

Open Cast Pit

SCY204

SCY221 SCY222

SCY022

2,614 1,309

2,615

2,616 2,613

2,611 2,612 SCY103

2,643
2,644
2,645

0   100   200 m

N

Plate IV SCY022-1a: thin sections from micromorphological analysis

0   2.5   5 cm

For information on how to read the GIS maps, please see Appendix D.

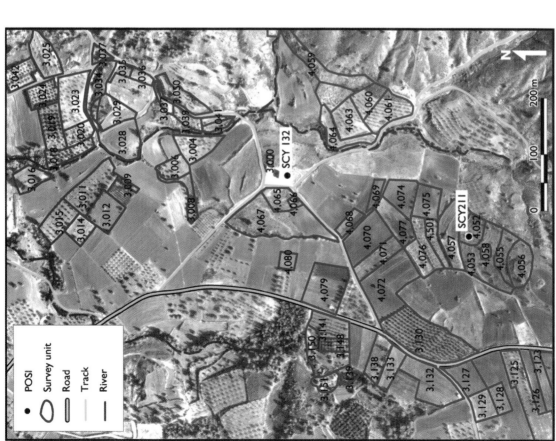

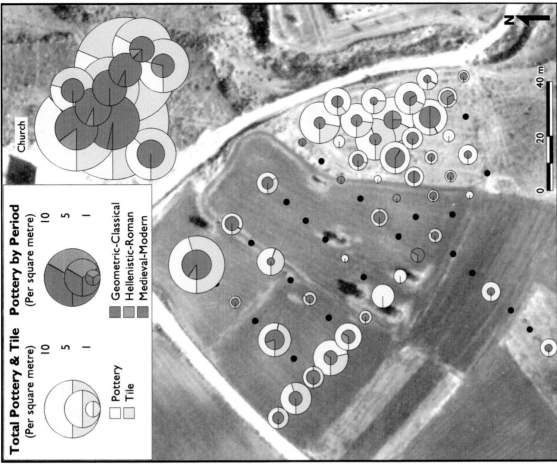

Plate VI SCY132: iron cross and gridded circles. *Based upon the aerials of the Department of Lands and Surveys with the sanction of the Government of Cyprus. State copyright reserved.*

Plate V SIA 2: topographical map. *Based upon the aerials of the Department of Lands and Surveys with the sanction of the Government of Cyprus. State copyright reserved.*

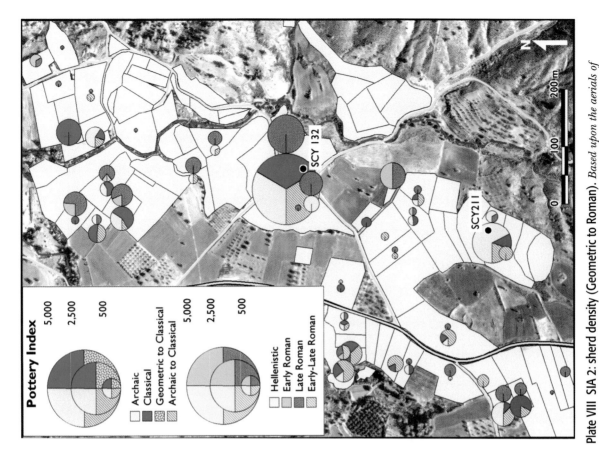

Plate VIII SIA 2: sherd density (Geometric to Roman). *Based upon the aerials of the Department of Lands and Surveys with the sanction of the Government of Cyprus. State copyright reserved.*

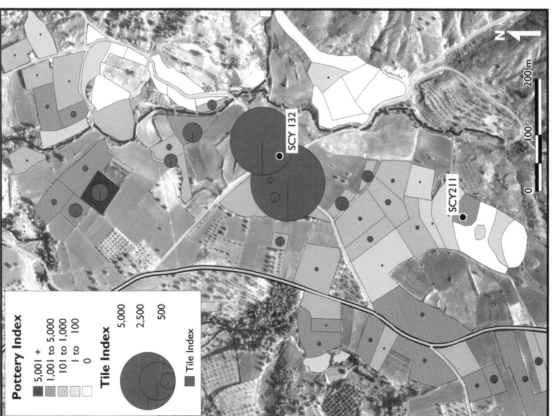

Plate VII SIA 2: sherd and tile density (all periods). *Based upon the aerials of the Department of Lands and Surveys with the sanction of the Government of Cyprus. State copyright reserved.*

For information on how to read the GIS maps, please see Appendix D.

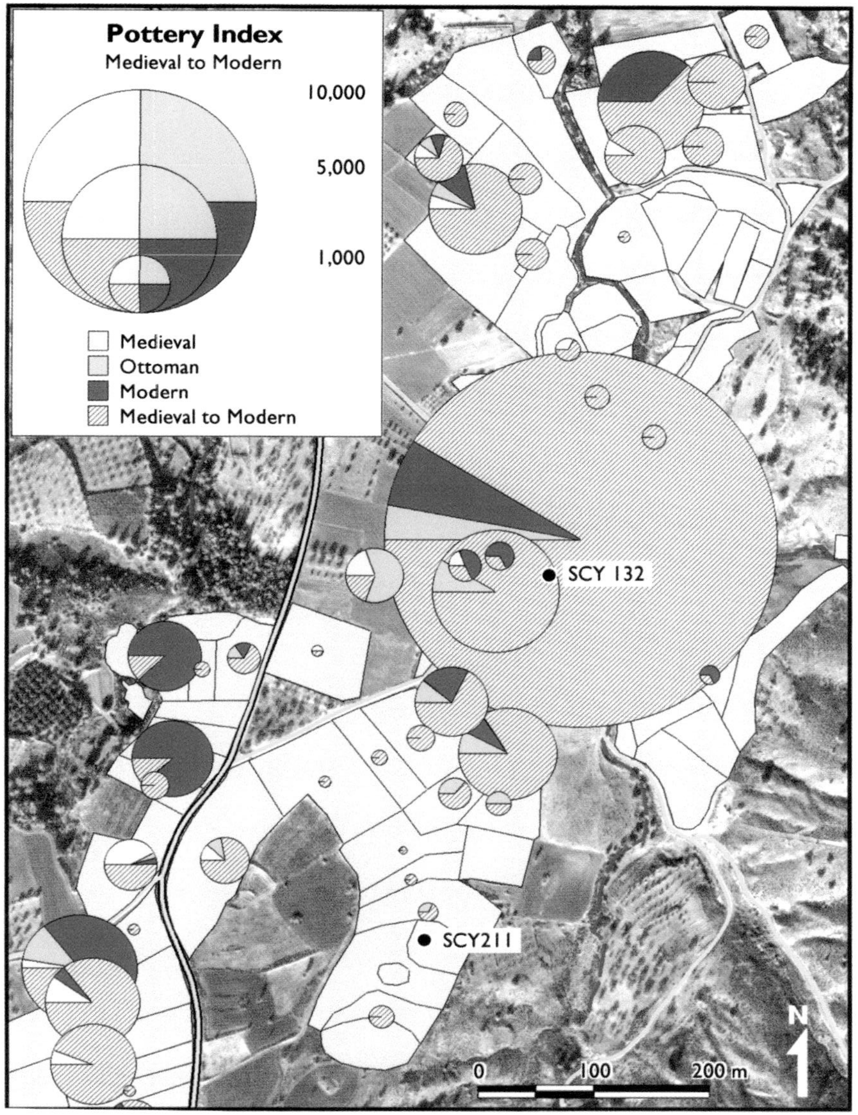

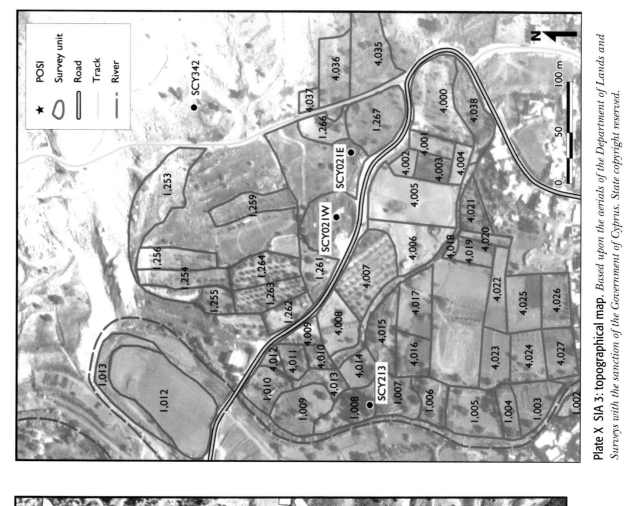

Plate IX SIA 2: sherd density (Medieval to Modern). *Based upon the aerials of the Department of Lands and Surveys with the sanction of the Government of Cyprus. State copyright reserved.*

Plate X SIA 3: topographical map. *Based upon the aerials of the Department of Lands and Surveys with the sanction of the Government of Cyprus. State copyright reserved.*

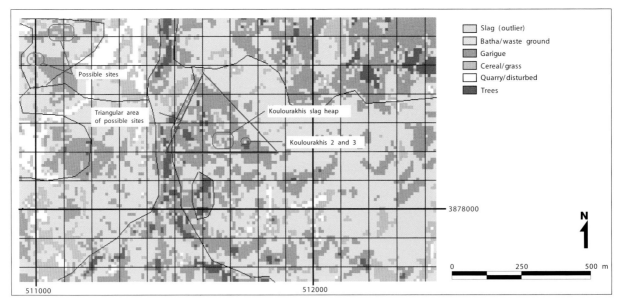

Legend (Plate XII):
- Slag (outlier)
- Batha/waste ground
- Garigue
- Cereal/grass
- Quarry/disturbed
- Trees

Possible sites

Triangular area
of possible sites

Koulourakhis slag heap

Koulourakhis 2 and 3

3878000

511000   512000

N

0   250   500 m

Plate XII   SIA 3: geobotanical map (thematic classification of satellite images)

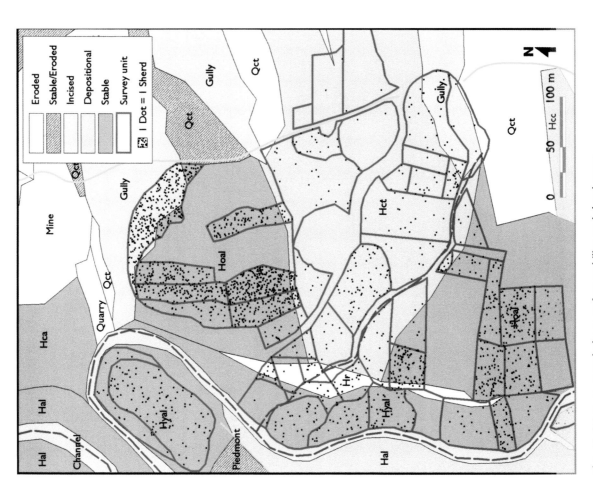

Legend (Plate XI):
- Eroded
- Stable/Eroded
- Incised
- Depositional
- Stable
- Survey unit
- I Dot = I Sherd

Gully

Qct

Qct

Qct

Gully

Hcc

N

0   50   100 m

Hct

Qct

Mine

Hoal

Hoal

Hr

Quarry   Qct

Hca

Hyal

Hyal

Hal

Channel

Piedmont

Hal

Plate XI   SIA 3: geomorphology, surface stability, and sherd count

For information on how to read the GIS maps, please see Appendix D.

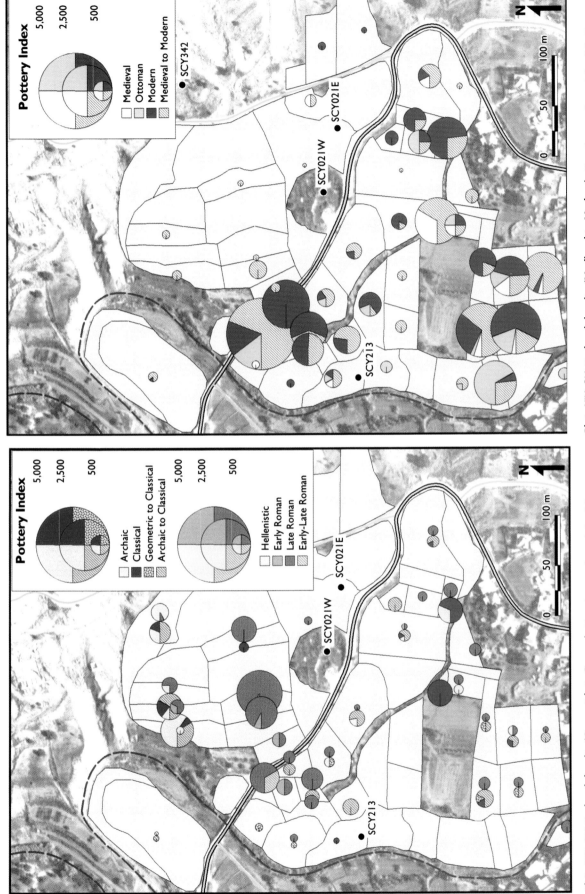

Plate XIII SIA 3: sherd density (Geometric to Roman). *Based upon the aerials of the Department of Lands and Surveys with the sanction of the Government of Cyprus. State copyright reserved.*

Plate XIV SIA 3: sherd density (Medieval to Modern). *Based upon the aerials of the Department of Lands and Surveys with the sanction of the Government of Cyprus. State copyright reserved.*

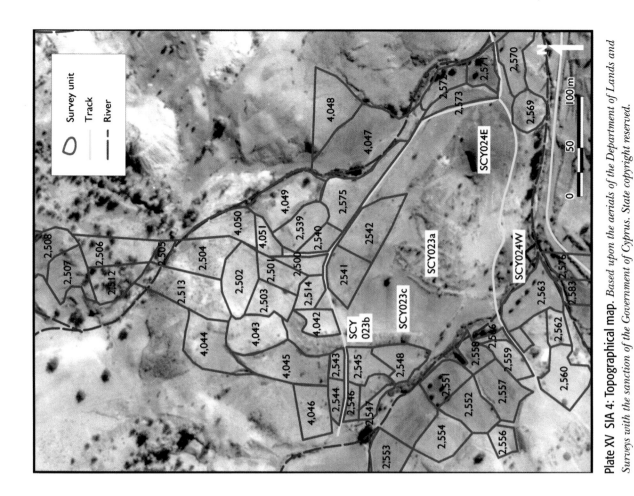

Plate XV SIA 4: Topographical map. *Based upon the aerials of the Department of Lands and Surveys with the sanction of the Government of Cyprus. State copyright reserved.*

Legend:
- Survey unit
- Track
- River

Survey units labeled: 2,508, 2,507, 2,506, 2,512, 2,505, 2,504, 2,513, 4,050, 4,051, 4,049, 2,539, 2,540, 2,575, 4,048, 4,047, 2,502, 2,501, 2,500, 2,514, 2,541, 2,542, 2,573, 2,571, 2,570, 2,569, SCY024E, SCY023a, SCY024W, 2,503, 4,043, 4,042, 2,543, SCY 023b, SCY023c, 2,563, 2,576, 2,583, 4,044, 4,045, 2,545, 2,548, 2,559, 2,562, 2,560, 4,046, 2,544, 2,546, 2,547, 2,551, 2,552, 2,557, 2,558, 2,566, 2,553, 2,554, 2,556

Scale: 0, 50, 100 m

Plate XVI SIA 4: Geobotanical thematic map

Legend:
- Batha Control 1
- Batha Control 2
- Cluster 2a
- Cluster 2c
- Cluster 2b
- SUs on Medieval Site
- SUs on Medieval Site
- Disturbed /Spoil
- Olive Grove 1
- Olive Grove 2
- Garigue Control 1
- Garigue Control 2
- Batha Control 3

Labels: Potential site, Slag heap, Sykamies slag heap Clusters 2b and 2c

Coordinates: 3878000, 510000

Scale: 0, 150, 300 m

For information on how to read the GIS maps, please see Appendix D.

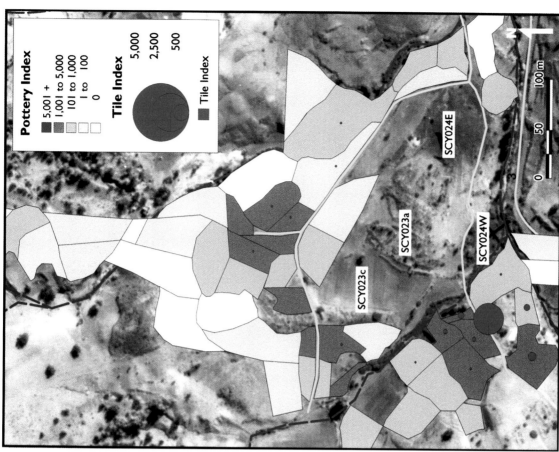

Plate XVIII SIA 4: sherd and tile density (all periods). *Based upon the aerials of the Department of Lands and Surveys with the sanction of the Government of Cyprus. State copyright reserved.*

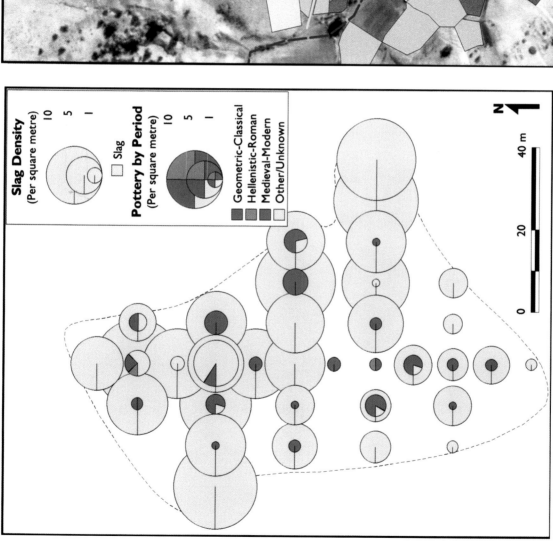

Plate XVII SCY023c: slag and pottery density (all periods)

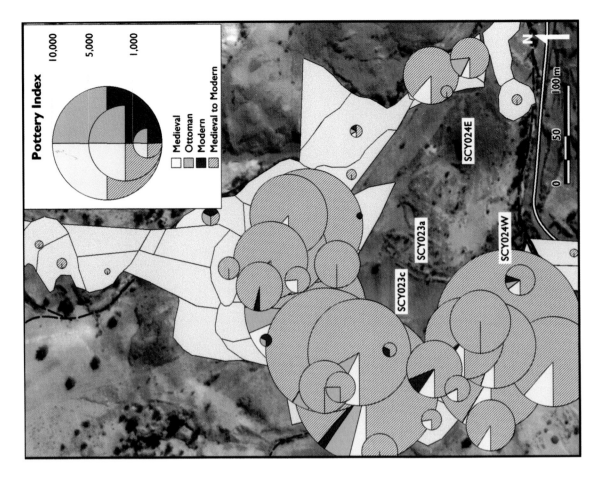

Plate XX SIA 4: sherd density (Medieval to Modern). *Based upon the aerials of the Department of Lands and Surveys with the sanction of the Government of Cyprus. State copyright reserved.*

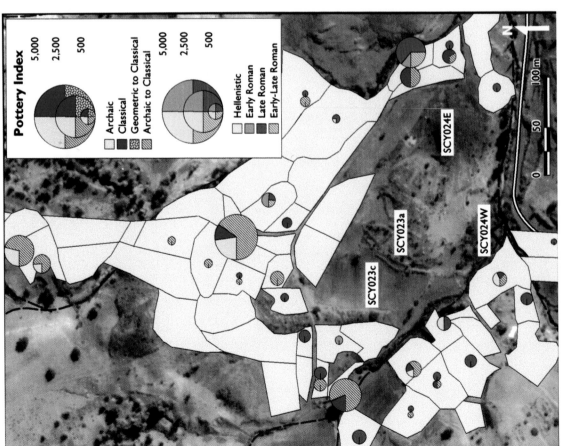

Plate XIX SIA 4: sherd density (Geometric to Roman). *Based upon the aerials of the Department of Lands and Surveys with the sanction of the Government of Cyprus. State copyright reserved.*

For information on how to read the GIS maps, please see Appendix D.

Plate XXI SIA 5: topographical map of Mitsero and surrounds. *Based upon the aerials of the Department of Lands and Surveys with the sanction of the Government of Cyprus. State copyright reserved.*

Plate XXII SIA 6: topographical map. *Based upon the aerials of the Department of Lands and Surveys with the sanction of the Government of Cyprus. State copyright reserved.*

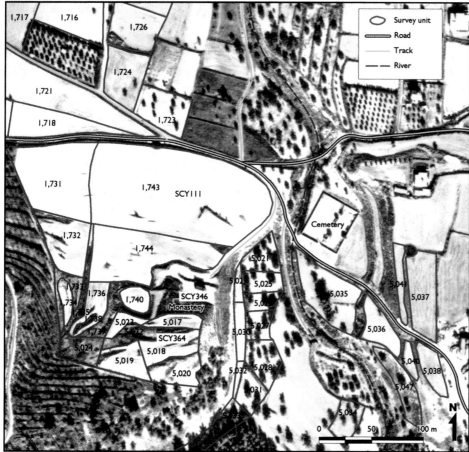

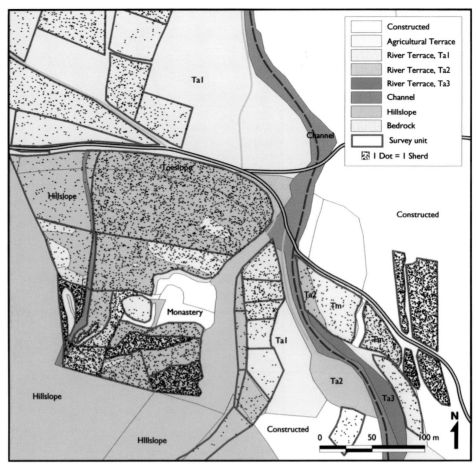

Plate XXIII SIA 6: Geomorphology and sherd count

Legend:
- Constructed
- Agricultural Terrace
- River Terrace, Ta1
- River Terrace, Ta2
- River Terrace, Ta3
- Channel
- Hillslope
- Bedrock
- Survey unit
- 1 Dot = 1 Sherd

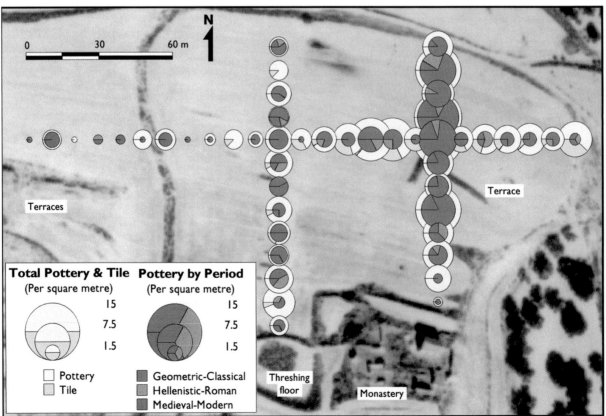

Plate XXIV SCY111: iron cross. *Based upon the aerials of the Department of Lands and Surveys with the sanction of the Government of Cyprus. State copyright reserved.*

Total Pottery & Tile
(Per square metre)
15
7.5
1.5

Pottery by Period
(Per square metre)
15
7.5
1.5

- Pottery
- Tile

- Geometric-Classical
- Hellenistic-Roman
- Medieval-Modern

For information on how to read the GIS maps, please see Appendix D.

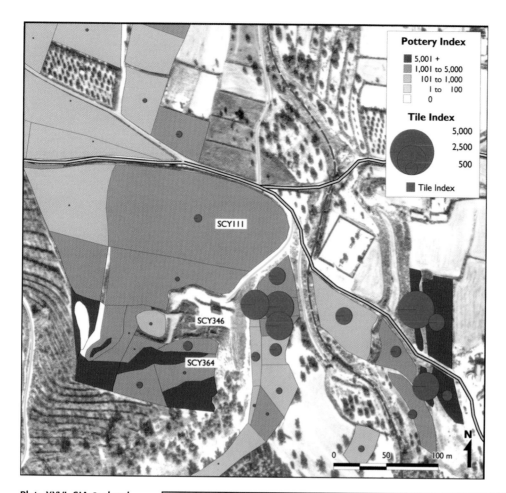

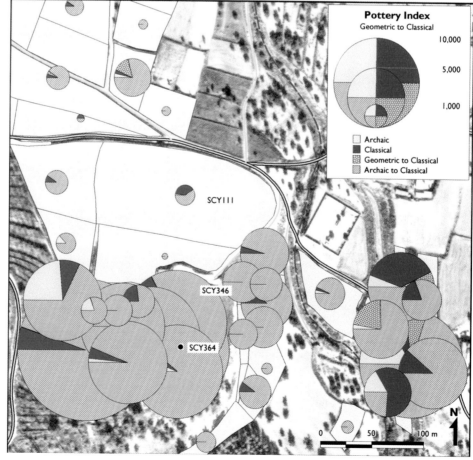

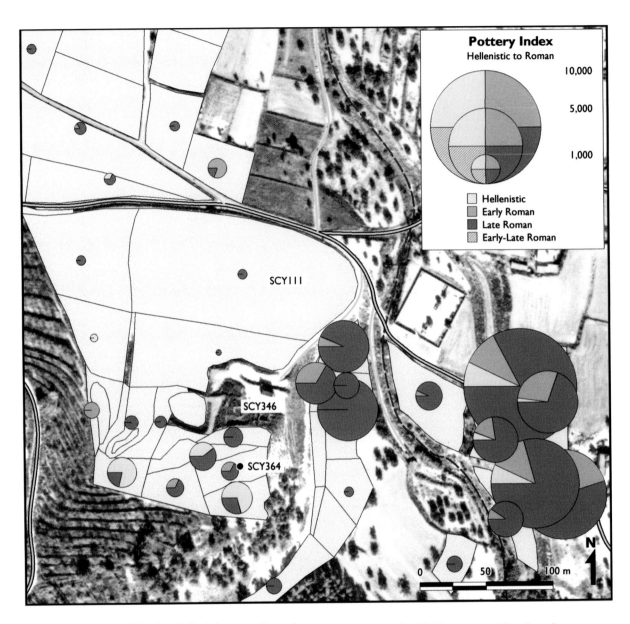

Plate XXVII SIA 6: sherd density (Hellenistic to Late Roman). *Based upon the aerials of the Department of Lands and Surveys with the sanction of the Government of Cyprus. State copyright reserved.*

For information on how to read the GIS maps, please see Appendix D.

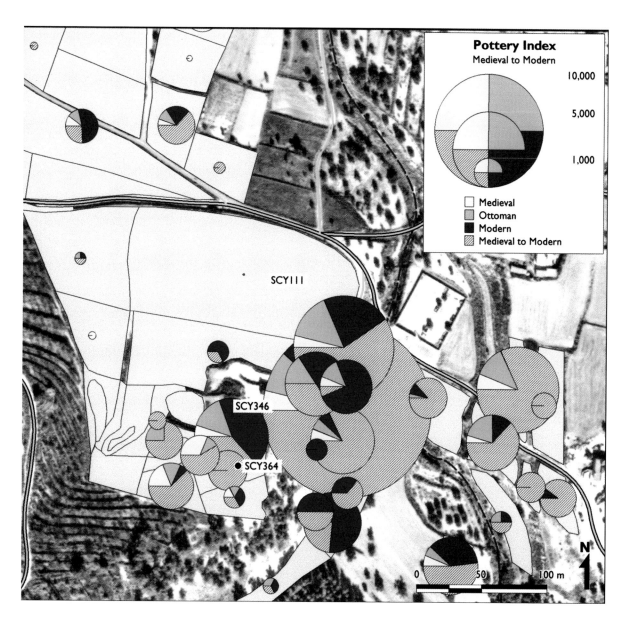

Plate XXVIII SIA 6: sherd density (Medieval to Modern). *Based upon the aerials of the Department of Lands and Surveys with the sanction of the Government of Cyprus. State copyright reserved.*

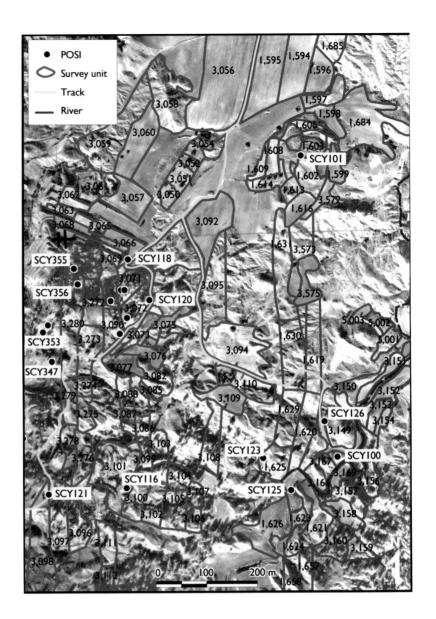

Plate XXIX SIA 7: topographical map.

Based upon the aerials of the Department of Lands and Surveys with the sanction of the Government of Cyprus. State copyright reserved.

Legend:
- POSI
- Survey unit
- Track
- River

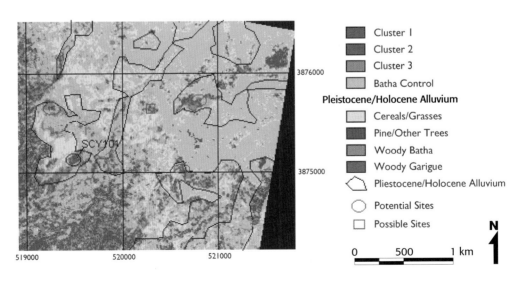

Legend:
- Cluster 1
- Cluster 2
- Cluster 3
- Batha Control

Pleistocene/Holocene Alluvium
- Cereals/Grasses
- Pine/Other Trees
- Woody Batha
- Woody Garigue
- Pliestocene/Holocene Alluvium
- Potential Sites
- Possible Sites

3876000
3875000

519000   520000   521000

0   500   1 km

N

Plate XXX SCY101 and area: annotated thematic satellite image with potential sites

For information on how to read the GIS maps, please see Appendix D.

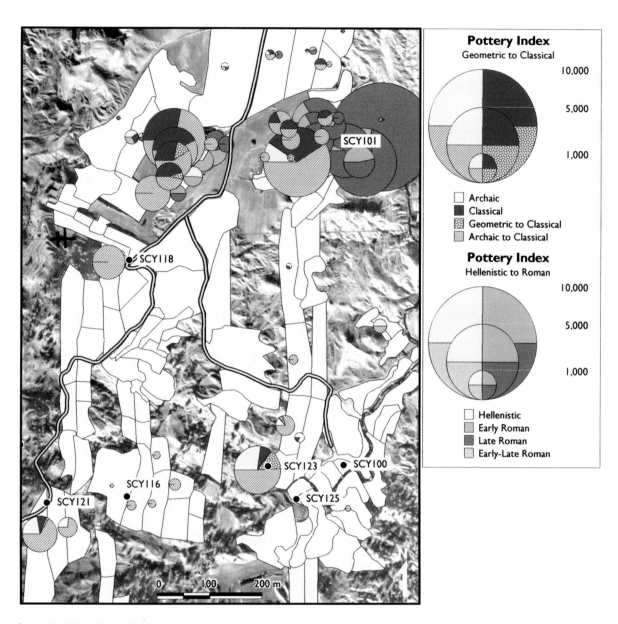

Plate XXXI SIA 7: sherd density (Geometric to Roman). *Based upon the aerials of the Department of Lands and Surveys with the sanction of the Government of Cyprus. State copyright reserved.*

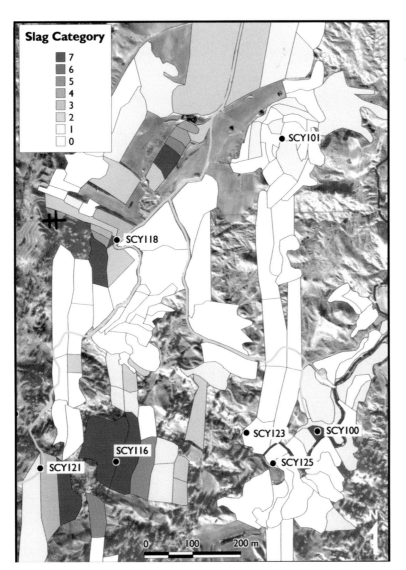

Slag Category

- 7
- 6
- 5
- 4
- 3
- 2
- 1
- 0

SCY101

SCY118

SCY123   SCY100

SCY116

SCY121   SCY125

N

0   100   200 m

Plate XXXII SIA 7: slag density. Survey units are categorized by numbers of slag fragments (7 = slag heap). *Based upon the aerials of the Department of Lands and Surveys with the sanction of the Government of Cyprus. State copyright reserved.*

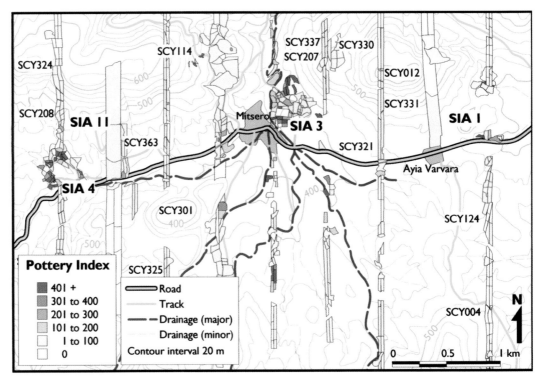

Plate XXXIII SIA 8: Mitsero Basin with SIAs, POSIs and sherd density

SCY324   SCY114   SCY337 SCY330
                                 SCY207   SCY012
SCY208   SCY331
        SIA 11   Mitsero   SIA 1
                SCY363   SIA 3
                                        SCY321
        SIA 4   Ayia Varvara
                        SCY301   SCY124

SCY325

Pottery Index

- 401 +
- 301 to 400
- 201 to 300
- 101 to 200
- 1 to 100
- 0

— Road
— Track
– – Drainage (major)
– Drainage (minor)
Contour interval 20 m

SCY004

N

0   0.5   1 km

For information on how to read the GIS maps, please see Appendix D.

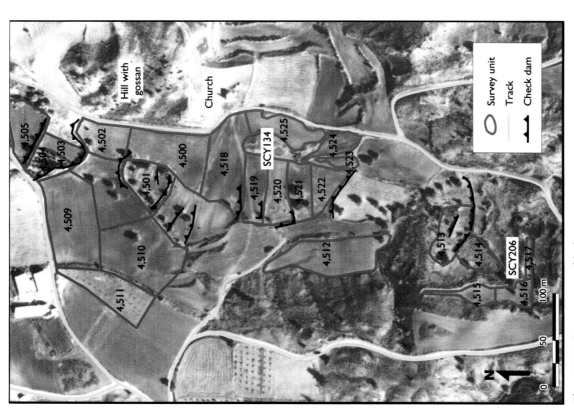

Plate XXXV SIA 9: sherd and tile density (all periods). *Based upon the aerials of the Department of Lands and Surveys with the sanction of the Government of Cyprus. State copyright reserved.*

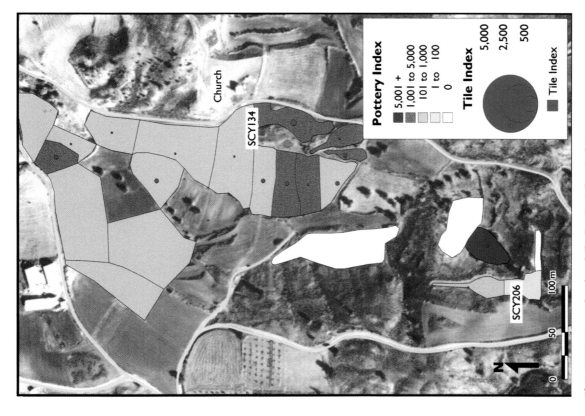

Plate XXXIV SIA 9: topographical map. *Based upon the aerials of the Department of Lands and Surveys with the sanction of the Government of Cyprus. State copyright reserved.*

Plate XXXVII SIA 10: topographical map. *Based upon the aerials of the Department of Lands and Surveys with the sanction of the Government of Cyprus. State copyright reserved.*

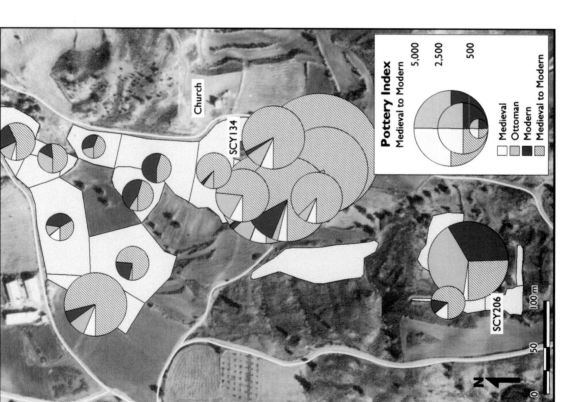

Plate XXXVI SIA 9: sherd density (Medieval to Modern). *Based upon the aerials of the Department of Lands and Surveys with the sanction of the Government of Cyprus. State copyright reserved.*

For information on how to read the GIS maps, please see Appendix D.

Plate XXXIX SIA 10: sherd and tile density (all periods). *Based upon the aerials of the Department of Lands and Surveys with the sanction of the Government of Cyprus. State copyright reserved.*

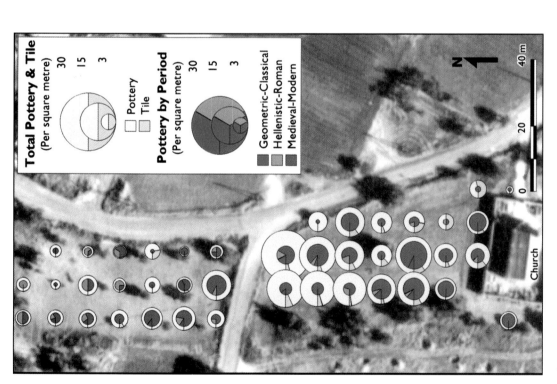

Plate XXXVIII SCY112: gridded circles. *Based upon the aerials of the Department of Lands and Surveys with the sanction of the Government of Cyprus. State copyright reserved.*

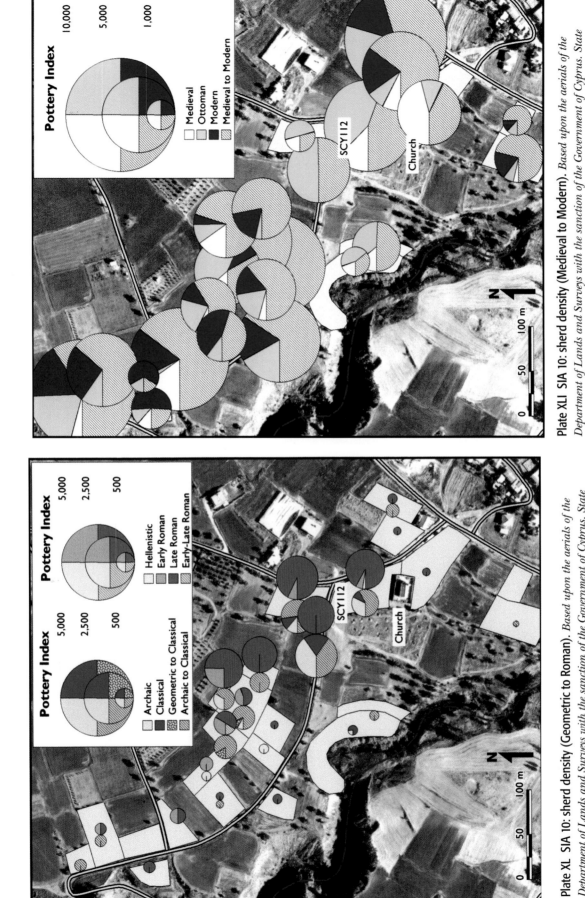

Plate XLI SIA 10: sherd density (Medieval to Modern). *Based upon the aerials of the Department of Lands and Surveys with the sanction of the Government of Cyprus. State copyright reserved.*

Plate XL SIA 10: sherd density (Geometric to Roman). *Based upon the aerials of the Department of Lands and Surveys with the sanction of the Government of Cyprus. State copyright reserved.*

For information on how to read the GIS maps, please see Appendix D.

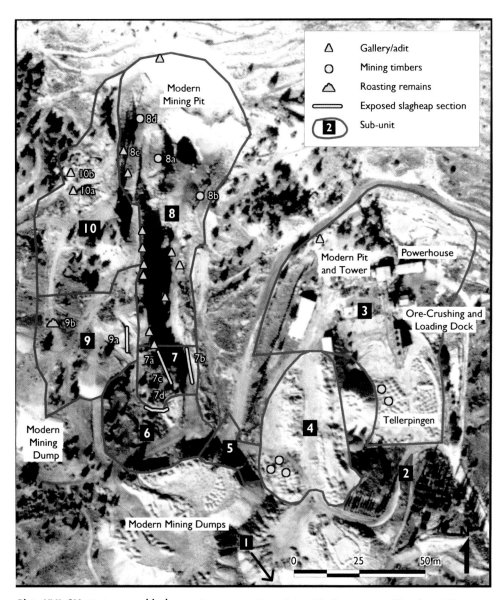

Plate XLII SIA 11: topographical map. *Based upon the aerials of the Department of Lands and Surveys with the sanction of the Government of Cyprus. State copyright reserved.*

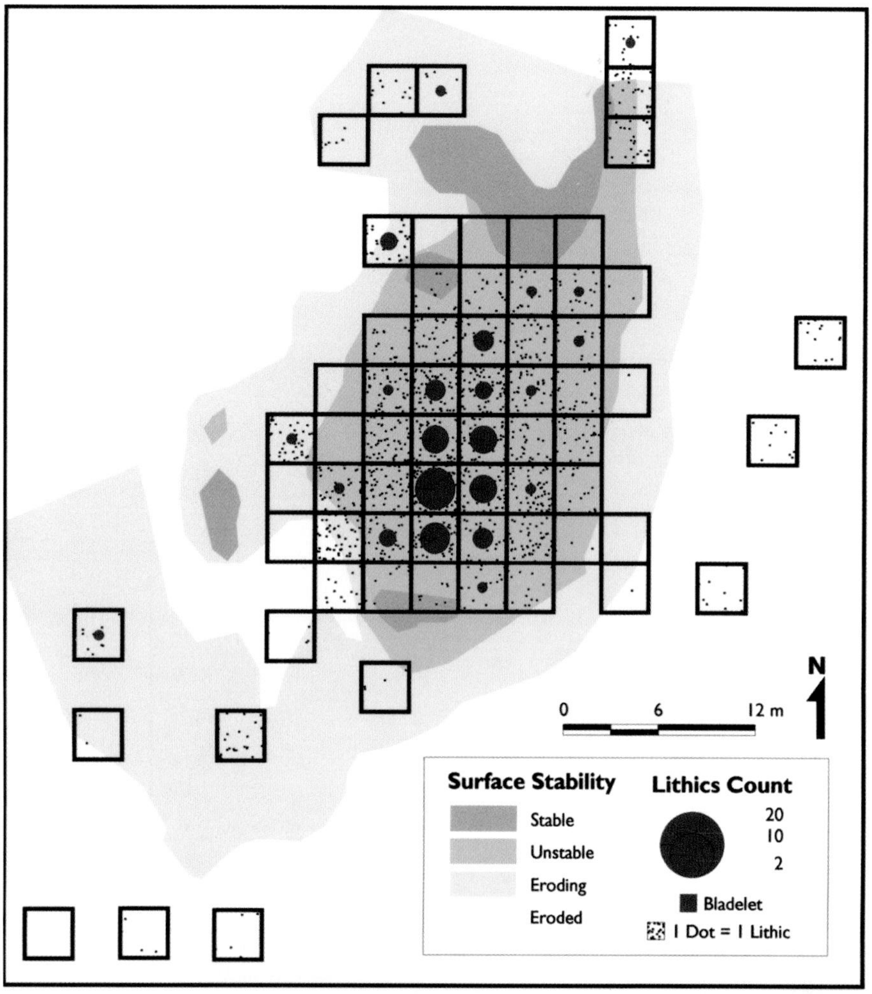

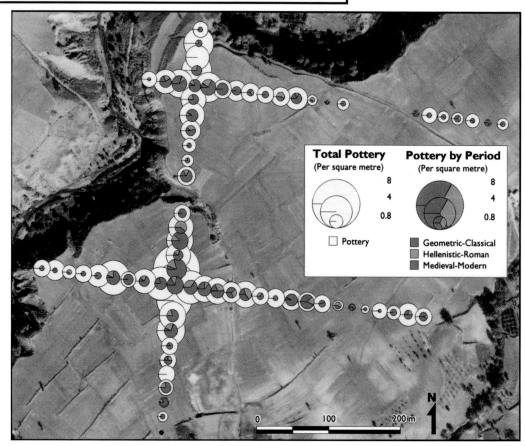

Plate XLIII SCY019: surface stability, lithics count, and bladelet count

Surface Stability

- Stable
- Unstable
- Eroding
- Eroded

Lithics Count

- 20
- 10
- 2
- Bladelet
- 1 Dot = 1 Lithic

0   6   12 m

N

Plate XLIV SCY110: total pottery; pottery by period. *Based upon the aerials of the Department of Lands and Surveys with the sanction of the Government of Cyprus. State copyright reserved.*

Total Pottery
(Per square metre)

- 8
- 4
- 0.8
- Pottery

Pottery by Period
(Per square metre)

- 8
- 4
- 0.8
- Geometric-Classical
- Hellenistic-Roman
- Medieval-Modern

0   100   200 m

N

For information on how to read the GIS maps, please see Appendix D.

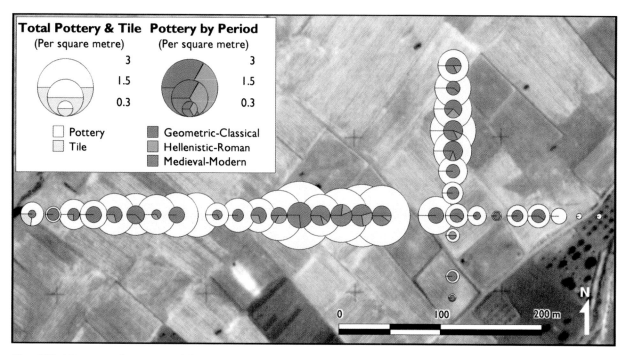

Plate XLV SCY209: total pottery and tile; pottery by period. *Based upon the aerials of the Department of Lands and Surveys with the sanction of the Government of Cyprus. State copyright reserved.*

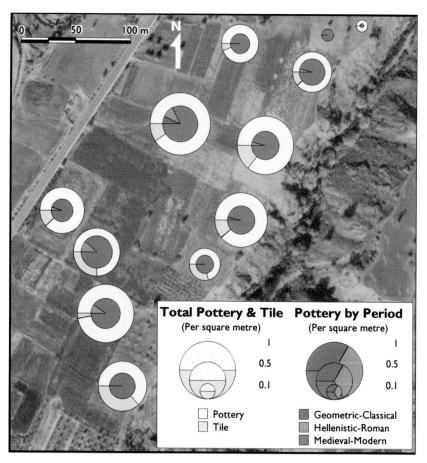

Plate XLVI SCY215: total pottery and tile; pottery by period. *Based upon the aerials of the Department of Lands and Surveys with the sanction of the Government of Cyprus. State copyright reserved.*

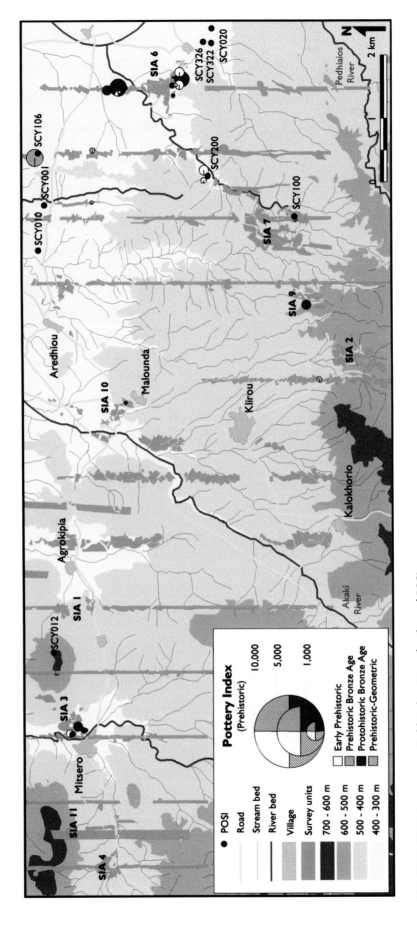

Plate XLVII SCSP Survey area: Prehistoric pottery density and POSIs

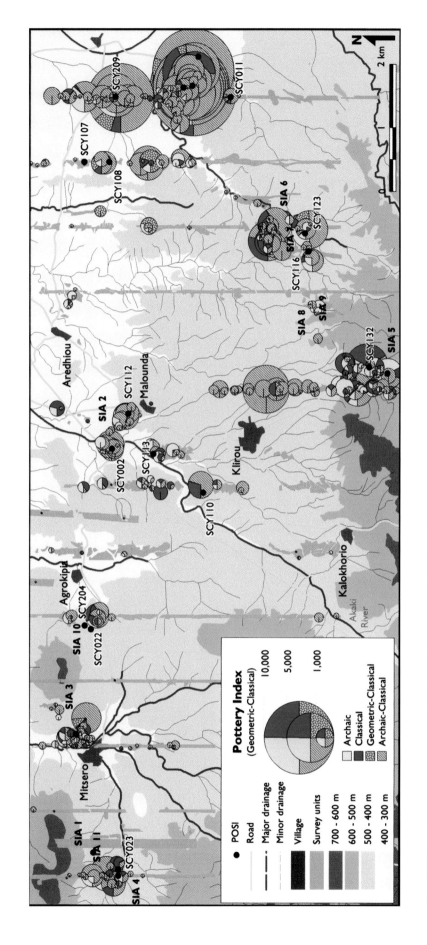

Plate XLVIII SCSP Survey area: Geometric to Classical pottery density and POSIs

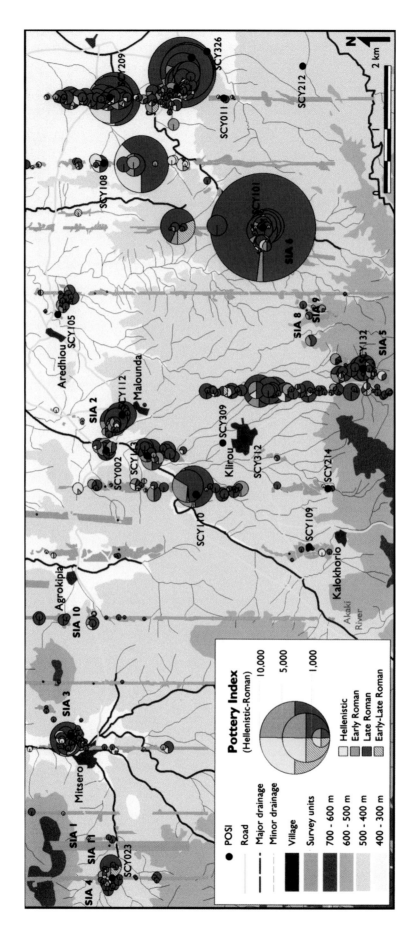

Pottery Index
(Hellenistic-Roman)

10,000
5,000
1,000

Hellenistic
Early Roman
Late Roman
Early-Late Roman

● POSI
Road
Major drainage
Minor drainage
Village
Survey units
700 - 600 m
600 - 500 m
500 - 400 m
400 - 300 m

N

2 km

SCY209
SCY326
SCY011
SCY212
SCY108
SCY101
SIA 6
SCY105
Aredhiou
SIA 8
SIA 9
SIA 2
SCY112
Malounda
SCY132
SIA 5
SCY002
SCY143
SCY309
Klirou
SCY312
SCY170
SCY214
SCY109
Agrokipia
SIA 10
Kalokhorio
Akaki River
SIA 3
Mitsero
SIA 1
SIA 7
SCY023
SIA 4

Plate XLIX SCSP survey area: Hellenistic to Roman pottery density and POSIs

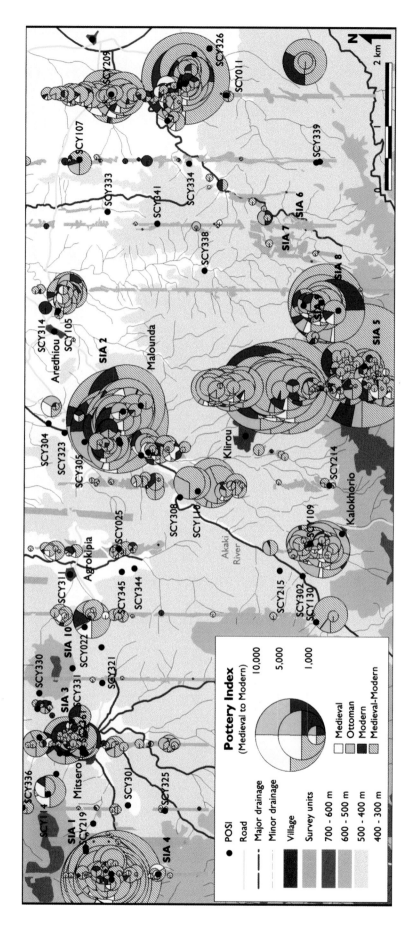

Plate L SCSP survey area: Medieval to Modern pottery density and POSIs

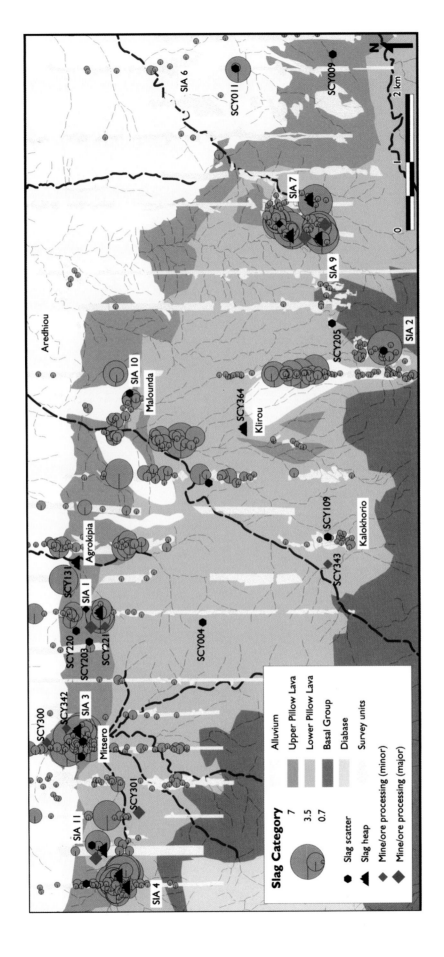

Plate LI SCSP survey area: geology, slag distribution, and archaeometallurgical POSIs (slag category 1 = light scatter; 7 = slag heap)

Slag Category

7
3.5
0.7

● Slag scatter
▲ Slag heap
◆ Mine/ore processing (minor)
◆ Mine/ore processing (major)

Alluvium
Upper Pillow Lava
Lower Pillow Lava
Basal Group
Diabase
Survey units

SIA 6
SCY011
SCY009
N
2 km
0
SIA 7
SIA 9
SCY205
SIA 2
Aredhiou
SIA 10
Malounda
SCY364
Klirou
SCY109
Kalokhorio
SCY343
Agrokipia
SCY131
SIA 1
SCY220
SCY203
SCY221
SCY004
SCY300
SCY342
SIA 3
Mitsero
SCY301
SIA 11
SIA 4

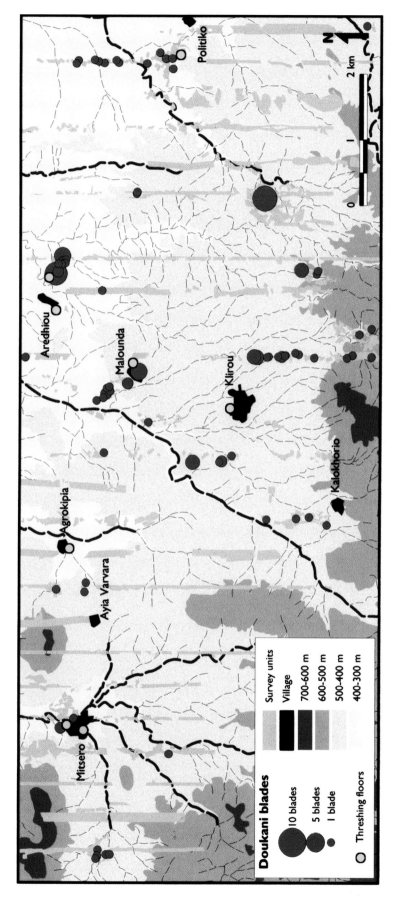

Plate LII SCSP survey area: distribution of threshing sledge (doukani) blades and threshing floors

Doukani blades

10 blades
5 blades
1 blade

Threshing floors

Survey units

Village
700–600 m
600–500 m
500–400 m
400–300 m

N

2 km

0

Politiko

Aredhiou

Malounda

Klirou

Agrokipia

Ayia Varvara

Kalokhorio

Mitsero

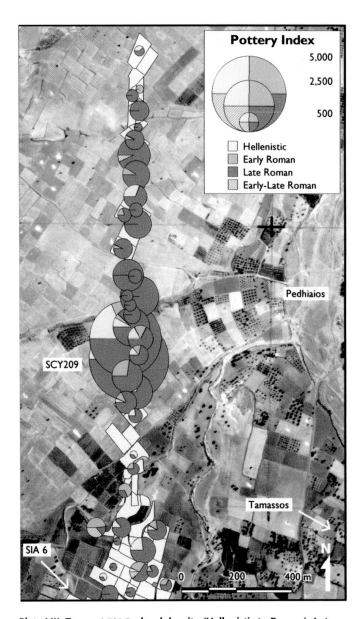

Plate LIII Transect 521.5: sherd density (Hellenistic to Roman). Late Roman manuring patterns and farmstead/estate in the Tamassos Plain. *Based upon the aerials of the Department of Lands and Surveys with the sanction of the Government of Cyprus. State copyright reserved.*

For information on how to read the GIS maps, please see Appendix D.

Figure 4.33
View from new school across to the old section of the village

respects the impact of mining and agriculture on the lives of the villagers is best exemplified in their own stories. In recounting their own links with the land through agriculture, for example, they still identify themselves and their "history" with a village lifestyle and the practice of agriculture rather than mining. This perhaps reflects the importance, in terms of social memory, of the greater depth of time devoted to a traditional way of life. When questioned directly on issues relating to the mines, the villagers would always answer. However, during regular conversations, either prior to or after the interviews or when we saw people in the street, they preferred to tell us of myths and folk tales. Unless specifically questioned, the villagers seldom raised the subject of mining.

Agriculture has been practiced for generations and is part of the oral and historical tradition of the village and its inhabitants. Modern mining, on the other hand, is recent and has taken place only over the last generation; thus, it is less a part of the villagers' sense of identity. Yet the impact, physically and economically, of mining in undeniable. Perhaps, in the hearts of the generation that remembers a time before the mines, it is tied to the perceived loss of tradition, echoed by many older Cypriots (not just in Mitsero but across the island): *That's the problem with the new generation, no sense of their history.*

Mining occurred in two major phases in the twentieth century in the Mitsero area. The first phase involved the extraction and processing of gold and silver in the 1920s and 1930s. The second phase saw the mining of copper pyrites from the 1950s onward. It was the extent and scale of the second phase of operations that played a key role in the changing nature of the village. The small-scale operation that occurred in the 1930s involved a number of local villagers (men) who were, however, still able to maintain their agricultural pursuits. With the increased scale of operations in the 1950s this was no longer possible. At the same time, the more recent period witnessed the introduction of new technologies such as steam threshing machines, electric water mills and the tractor. Fields either were abandoned or people were hired to tend the fields (suggesting, incidentally, a disposable income much higher than previously known or available). In the 1980s and 1990s the fields were usually kept by the older members of the family, while the younger generation worked and often lived in Nicosia. A few fields were used for cash crops.

With regard to general amenities, the village owes much to the mining company. The first road connecting the village to Nicosia was a dirt road constructed by the HMC in the 1930s; in the 1960s the tarred road was constructed. Electricity was first supplied to the village in the 1960s, with all homes supplied by the 1970s. The first water fountain was connected in 1946 and a photograph of this is visible in the Colonial annual report for *1948 (Annual Report* 1948:28). This fountain is no longer visible but is still in place under a monument to the missing in the village square. Other water fountains in the village bear the emblem of the Republic of Cyprus and were installed in 1960.

In the oral tradition of the village, the mine at Kokkinopezoula is associated with illness. It is not that the mining company had a bad history or a high accident rate. Rather, the villagers make that association because of the deaths of several former miners who had worked in the underground mines at Kokkinopezoula and ended up with silicosis. The Hellenic Mining Company had a good safety record, in particular for the mines around Mitsero. However there are sobering and poignant reminders of the dangers associated with working in the mines and the issues relating to health and safety. A stretcher lies abandoned 10 m from the Kokkinoyia mine shaft, for example, and still visible on the walls of the Kokkinopezoula office block are numerous posters dictating mine safety.

The changing relationships between agriculture and mining during the last one hundred years of occupation in Mitsero are best expressed as a series of three phases:

1) *Pre-Mining Phase (up to and including the 1920s).* During this period the primary income (mainly subsistence) for the villagers derived from agricultural pursuits. There were no main roads, and access to other villages and to Nicosia was by means of unpaved tracks. Physical evidence for ancient metallurgy existed in the form of large slag heaps but there was no contemporary mining.

2) *Mining Phase (1930–1970s).* During this period a number of the villagers worked for the mines; the men worked in the mines and in communications, while the women worked in the company canteens and shops. Agriculture still played a role in village life but as a secondary pursuit in terms of income. Food produced locally was

supplemented by the village store. Miners were bused from all over the island to work in these mines. A critical development in the 1950s was the construction of a modern road from Nicosia to Mitsero, reducing an all-day trip to a matter of one hour. As with any large-scale industrial process, open-cast mining led to permanent changes in the landscape.

3) *1980s to Present.* The large mines of Kokkinoyia, Kokkinopezoula, and Kriadhis are now quiet; the large machinery lies unused and rusting away, or is gone, sold by the HMC for scrap, or "stolen." The large spoil heaps remain, a constant and familiar legacy in the landscape as to what lies below the surface (see also Knapp 1999b). The only mining that takes place around there now is the sand extracted from an area just northwest of Mitsero village, where the hillsides are continually blasted away by dynamite.

As with many villages in the Mediterranean area, Mitsero can be seen as a place that has elements of both traditional and modern culture. Older women and men (in their 60s and 70s) still do things in the traditional way, from making yogurt to tending fields. They live in mudbrick houses that have not radically altered in shape, form, or even contents to that of their parents and grandparents. For the younger generation, the facade is that of the modern. They drive new cars and live in new houses; yet, elements of the past are retained. Some move into the houses of their parents when they pass on, modernizing but maintaining traditional elements.

The physical impact of mining on the village and the villagers of Mitsero is evident in a number of ways, most obviously in the form of the large spoil heaps characteristic of open-cast mining. Less obvious, but just as important, is the impact of the mines visible in the new main road from Nicosia to Mitsero (which now bypasses the village), the shops, the coffee houses and other public amenities that came in the wake of the HMC's operations. Today very few people in the village work for the mines. Yet the impact of mining, and the change from an economy based on agriculture to one reliant on external employment, usually in the urban environment of Nicosia or elsewhere, has been of great significance.

4.6 SIA 6: Politiko *Ayios Mnason*

Compiled by Michael Given

Team leaders: Susan Bain, Haddon Wright
Geomorphology: Caroline Whitehill GIS analysis: Nathan
Meyer, Michael Given Pottery: Timothy E. Gregory, R. Scott
Moore, Joanna S. Smith Terra-cottas: Joanna S. Smith

Grid reference: 521500/3876500
Cadastral maps: XXX/57, XXX/58
Aerial photograph: 1993, run 176, no. 54
Survey units: 1698–1747, 5017–47
POSIs: SCY111: Politiko *Ayios Mnason*
                     1 (gridded circles); SCY346:
                     Politiko *Ayios Mnason* 2
                     (monastery); SCY365: Politiko
                     Ayios Mnason 3 (sanctuary)

The church and ruined monastery of Ayios Mnason are situated at the top of a steep bluff immediately above the Katouris River (plate XXII, figure 4.34). On the far side of the river lies the edge of the Medieval to Modern village of Politiko and the site of its Archaic to Late Roman predecessor Tamassos. A more gentle slope runs northwards from Ayios Mnason and into the fertile alluvial plains below. This slope has been known for over a century as one of the principal cemeteries of ancient Tamassos, an identification made clear not just by the artifacts on the surface but also by surviving Roman chamber tombs.

Intensive survey in the whole area of Ayios Mnason was directed at a range of issues over several different periods. Could surface survey detect the boundary of ancient Tamassos on its west side and how it changed over time? Could we distinguish between material derived from the settlement, the cemetery, and the Archaic to Classical sanctuary lying immediately south of the monastery, discovered in 1977? How many of the apparent patterns in the surface distribution of artifacts were actually due to the complex geomorphological processes taking place on the hillslope? What did the architectural and artifactual remains of the monastery, along with any relevant historical documentation, tell us about monasticism and land use in the Ottoman period? To answer these questions, Politiko *Ayios Mnason* (SIA 6) was investigated using a variety of appropriate survey methodologies in 1995 and 1997.

PHYSICAL LANDSCAPE

The monastery of Ayios Mnason is located on a chalk hillslope just north of the contact zone between the Miocene sediments and the upper pillow lavas. Below the monastery are some ten agricultural terraces, a few of which have been maintained, though others are discontinuous or buried (plate XXIII). There is a small channel running down the western side of the slope below the monastery, with several check dams preserved at its head. Most of the terraces created by this channel have been plowed out. Even though the entire slope has been modified with agricultural terraces, a subtle remnant ridge and swale topography is still observable in the western part of the fields.

Soil cover on the hillslope consists of thin colluvium (about 10 to 90 cm, the most representative thickness being 10 to 20 cm). This colluvium is thinnest downhill from the agricultural terrace walls. In these areas there is actually an Ap-R soil sequence: Essentially the only soil that exists has been plowed and lies directly on the bedrock (for geomorphological terms, see table 3.4). The soil cover is thickest where it is trapped behind the terrace walls. Judging by the erosion at the base of these terrace walls, particularly the large L-shaped one 75 m north of the church, at least 30 cm of soil have been lost since they were built, because of plowing, erosion, or deliberate redistribution. The amount of buildup behind the same wall, which comes to almost 1 m, implies not just gradual sedimentation from this erosion process but also an actual importation of soil or manure. At the foot of the slope there is a substantial buildup of soil, partly because of a long continuous terrace wall, parts of which still run alongside the road.

This movement of soil is clearly relevant to patterns of sherd distribution: Higher densities at the foot of the hillslope than on the slope itself may well be the result of these erosional processes. It is also clear that different soil-management and land-use practices have been carried out here. Currently it is all under cereals, but the terrace walls and the concentration of sediment behind them imply crops such as olive trees, which require specific areas of deep sediment rather than a broad spread of shallow sediment, as cereals require.

Above the monastery, to its south, the slope alternates between artificial plowed terraces (Tm) and

Figure 4.34
SIA 6: view from the
northeast

plowed hillslope sediments (Hp). All these have been plowed to bedrock and some are separated by narrow strips of exposed rock. The bedrock here is comprised of coarse reef deposits of the Koronia formation, with underlying Lapithos chalks. The surviving tombs have been dug through the cap of Koronia reef limestone into the softer chalks underneath.

The steep bluff to the east of the monastery has clearly lost substantial portions of soil in the recent past. The local goatherd recalls the eastern wall of the monastery being bulldozed down the bluff when the church was renovated in the 1970s or 1980s; the south wall of the monastery now ends abruptly at the top of the slope. This disturbance clearly has been exacerbated by erosion. The fields at the base of this bluff, in the river terrace along the Katouris river (Ta1), have considerable amounts of colluvial debris plowed onto the agricultural surface (Ap), which was derived from the bluff.

HISTORICAL BACKGROUND

For much of the last three millennia Politiko *Ayios Mnason* was dominated by the nearby ancient city-kingdom of Tamassos and its Medieval to Modern successor, the village of Politiko. By the seventh century BC Tamassos was one of about ten autonomous city-kingdoms in Cyprus, notable now for a series of seventh- and sixth-century BC elite-built tombs and a large sanctuary to the Cypriot goddess at Chomazoudhia, some 700 m east of the monastery (Buchholz and Untiedt 1996, with references). As well as controlling the local copper mines, almost

certainly including those at Politiko *Kokkinorotsos* (SIA 7), Tamassos benefited from the broad alluvial plain that stretches to the north and west of the monastery of Ayios Mnason.

Closer to the city were the cemeteries, ranging in date from the Cypro-Archaic to the Late Roman periods and extending along the western and northern edges of the city. Max Ohnefalsch-Richter excavated in the 1890s twenty-nine tombs at Ayios Mnason in six days (Buchholz 1974:574–577). Other excavations in the same area produced pottery, terracotta sarcophagus fragments, and grave goods from the Roman period (Buchholz 1974:570–574). In 1973, a Cypro-Archaic tomb was reported (Karageorghis 1973:612); in 1978 an infant's sarcophagus (Buchholz 1978:200) was found. Both were from the Ayios Mnason area.

Ayios Mnason himself, according to Orthodox church tradition, was a companion of Ayios Iraklidhios and was baptized by St. Paul at Tamassos on his visit to the island in AD 45. He became the second bishop of Tamassos and was buried beside Iraklidhios (Cobham 1908:224–226). His traditional resting place, then, is in the Monastery of Ayios Iraklidhios, on the southeastern edge of Politiko, rather than in his own monastery on the western edge. The monastery of Ayios Mnason never achieved the same wealth and prestige as that of Ayios Iraklidhios, as is clear from Ottoman period travelers and administrative documents. Today the area is used solely for agricultural and pastoral purposes, apart from the monastery church, rebuilt for use during the saint's festival on October 19.

FIELD METHODOLOGY

The first work that SCSP carried out in the area of Ayios Mnason was as part of transect 521.5 in 1995; because of the quantity of material, this was expanded into a full block survey (units 1698–1747). In 1997 block survey was extended to cover a wider area and to fill in some gaps left by the earlier team because of standing crops and stubble (units 5017–5047). In the same season the fields below the monastery were examined at a much finer resolution by means of gridded circles; this area was designated SCY111. The ruins of the monastery (SCY346) were mapped with a theodolite and EDM at a scale of 1:100, and a geomorphological map and examination of the entire SIA were carried out.

SCY111: POLITIKO *AYIOS MNASON* 1: GRIDDED CIRCLES

Because of the clear variations in material within the large survey units north of the monastery (1743–1744), we decided to resurvey this area with lines of circles (plate XXIV). Two parallel lines of 2-m diameter circles every 10 m were laid out running north to south, bisected by another line running east to west. A total collection strategy was adopted for the eastern of the two north-south lines, and a standard representative collection procedure was used for the remaining two.

The total pottery and tile figures (table 4.12) show substantial densities, with up to 12 sherds per m² (plate XXIV). There is a clear peak toward the east, and a falloff going west away from Tamassos and Politiko. When broken down into periods, there is a broad and relatively even scatter of Geometric to Classical pottery, averaging 0.75 sherds per m². This contrasts with the 0.2 sherds per m² that seems characteristic of agricultural background scatters from this period, for example 800 m to the north at Episkopio *Kallinikos* (SCY209; see chapter 4.18). Geomorphological mapping showed a considerable degree of erosion down the slope, so much of this material may derive from the denser areas near the top.

The Hellenistic to Roman material is much lower in density, averaging 0.25 sherds per m², and has a similarly even distribution, apart from a slight falloff toward the west. These levels are more in keeping with an agricultural background scatter, and block

Table 4.12 SCY111: analyzed pottery

Chronotype	Period	Qty
Amphora-Ar	Ar	1
Plain White-Cl	Cl	1
Coarse ware-GAC	GAC	8
Green ware-GAC	GAC	4
Rolled Lug Handle-GAC	GAC	1
Amphora-AC	AC	12
Amphora, Pithoid	AC	5
Amphora, Torpedo	AC	2
Cooking ware-AC	AC	2
Pithos-AC	AC	3
Plain ware-AC	AC	43
Plain White-AC	AC	7
Rolled Lug Handle-AC	AC	5
Terra-cotta Sculpture-AC	AC	10
Tile-AC	AC	3
White Painted-AC	AC	4
Amphora-LR	LR	20
Amphora, LR 1	LR	3
Basin-LR	LR	1
Coarse ware-LR	LR	4
Cooking ware-LR	LR	1
Cypriot Red Slip 2	LR	1
Frying Pan	LR	1
Pithos-LR	LR	3
Spirally Grooved	LR	1
Lemba ware	Med	1
Cypriot Glazed, Brown and Green	Ott	2
Cypriot W3	Ott	1
Cypriot W6	Ott	8
Brick	Mod	1
Cypriot W7	Mod	37
Cypriot W4	MM	101
Pithos-MM	MM	2
Plain White-HA	HA	1
Pithos-PC	PC	9
Tile-PC	PC	45
Tile, Corinthian Pan	PC	10
Tile, Flat Pan	PC	6
Coarse ware-Unk	Unk	111
Cooking ware-Unk	Unk	5
Table ware-Unk	Unk	2
Unknown-Unk	Unk	4
TOTAL		492

survey showed there was very little at the top of the slope that might produce eroded material further down (see plates XXV to XXVIII).

The higher levels of datable pottery in the easternmost of the two north-south lines result from the total collection strategy used in those circles. As most of it is Medieval to Modern in date, it follows that much of the pottery being left in the field at this POSI dates to these periods. Correlations between total pottery counts and Medieval to Modern

Table 4.13 SIA 6: terra-cotta sculpture and figurine fragments.

Description	Survey Units
SCULPTURES	
Ear	SCY111.500E600N
Eye with eyebrow	5017
Fingers	5024
Hand, right, life-size [5022.1.1]	5022
Hand, doweled, life-size [5037.1.1]	5037
Feet, moldmade	5017
Foot, smaller than life-sized	5020
Body with necklace	SCY346.west
Stamped clothing [5019.19.1]	5019
Drapery	5017
Two decorated body or clothing fragments	5036
Unidentifiable painted fragment	5022
Other fragments of terra-cotta sculpture	(73 pieces)
FIGURINES	
Female figurine fragments, moldmade [5027.17.1]	5017 (x 2)
Standing figurines, handmade [5040.1.1]	1721, 1724, 1726, 5036, 5040
Horse figurine, handmade	1741

Note: Figures in brackets refer to cataloged items (see chapter 5.3).

pottery counts at other POSIs suggest the same phenomenon (for example, SCY110; see chapter 4.15). The Medieval to Modern pottery from these totally collected circles averages 3.2 sherds per m², with an apparent fall-off going up the slope. This is too large a figure to attribute to manuring, though it may be owing to unusually heavy dumping from Politiko village. More likely, it should be linked to the monastery, with the material nearest it removed by erosion. A further possibility is that the pottery bears some association to the curious L-shaped terrace wall crossed by the line of circles.

SCY365: POLITIKO *AYIOS MNASON 3*: ARCHAIC TO CLASSICAL SANCTUARY

Although several Archaic to Classical sanctuaries are known in the area of Tamassos (Buchholz and Untiedt 1996:25–32; 45–52), none was known in the area of Ayios Mnason. Fragments of seven terra-cotta figurines found by SCSP could have come either from tombs or from a sanctuary (Karageorghis 1987:22; 1995; 1998). These figurines represent handmade human (cat. 5040.1.1) and animal (cat. 1741.8A.1) figures as well as mold-made female figures (cat. 5017.37.1 and 5027.17.1). More explicit, however, if harder to identify in the field, were 96

fragments of large-scale terra-cotta sculpture, which derived from both small statuettes (for example, cat. 5017.39.1) and near life-size statues (for example, cat. 5022.1.1 and 5037.1.1). Such pieces are found most often in sanctuaries during the Iron Age (Karageorghis 1993); some of the best-known examples come from Ayia Irini (Gjerstad et al. 1935:642–824) and Pera Frangissa, 4 km southeast of Ayios Mnason (Buchholz 1991).

Though spread over much of the area of SIA 6, these terra-cotta sculpture fragments show a clear pattern of distribution, and are thus discussed together. The heaviest concentration lies immediately above and to the south of the monastery, with a peak in unit 5018 (21 pieces); the two units immediately north of it have 8 pieces each. Clearly a certain amount is trickling down the hill, the result of hillslope erosion. More still have fallen down the heavily eroding bluff on the eastern side of the monastery, which explains the twelve pieces lying in the fields at the base of the bluff. Less easy to explain are two units (1741, 5045) on the western edge of the SIA, which have seven pieces each. These could not have been transported from above the monastery by erosion. Similarly there are four pieces of terra-cotta sculpture and 1 figurine fragment on the eastern side of the Katouris River. These apart, it is clear that the sanctuary was immediately south of the monastery.

As well as the fragments of large terra-cotta sculpture and statuette fragments (table 4.13), a small juglet was found in the main concentration, possibly a miniature or nonpractical but symbolic juglet (cat. 5019.20.1). Miniature vessels are often found in sanctuaries both in the Bronze and the Iron Ages (Dothan and Ben-Tor 1983:53–110; Buitron-Oliver 1996:67–68), but seldom, if at all, in tombs. Another miniature was found on the east slope.

Terra-cotta figurines and sculpture alone are not indicative of a sanctuary. Terra-cotta figurines in particular were regularly placed in tombs. Some of the figurines from Ayios Mnason may have come from some of the known tombs in the area. Only in Polis during the Classical period were terra-cotta statuettes and statues, of seated or reclining figures, placed in tombs (Flourentzos 1994:164; Raptou 1996:225). Standing figures, however, both life-size and over-life-size, and statuettes, particularly those with elaborate jewelry (for example, from SCY346.west), are most typical of sanctuaries during the Archaic and Classical periods (Karageorghis 1993). The elaborate jewelry suggests that the statues may have represented females (Karageorghis 1993:94). Given the rarity of terra-cotta tomb sculpture on Cyprus during this period, and the jeweled and elaborately clothed figures (for example, cat. 5019.19.1), it is most likely that the Ayios Mnason material stems from a sanctuary rather than tombs. The discovery of several feet from standing statues supports their definition as standing figures.

It is possible that Ayios Mnason was the production site for terra-cotta statuary in addition to or instead of its use. Given the roof tiles of Classical type (Salles 1983:110–12), it is likely that a building of some importance stood here, which would suggest that the statues were deployed symbolically, not just manufactured. As discussed further below, Ayios Mnason was definitely a locus of ceramic production during this period, possibly including terra-cottas. The association of this sanctuary with production has parallels among many other Cypriot Iron Age sanctuaries with associated workshops (chapter 6.2; Smith 1997:90–91).

SCY346: POLITIKO *AYIOS MNASON* 2: THE MONASTERY

The ruins of the monastery were mapped at a scale of 1:100 with a theodolite and EDM; the few artifacts visible in the thick undergrowth were collected in two subunits corresponding to the two main wings of the structure. The monastery essentially consisted of a courtyard with the church in the middle, double rows of rooms along the west and south sides, and a simple wall on the north and along the top of the bluff on the east (figures 4.35, 4.36). Some twenty years ago the church was restored, and in the process the courtyard was bulldozed, the edges of the west and south wings removed, and the wall on the north and east sides destroyed. This last wall had separate entrances for the monks going into the monastery proper and for the general public who were restricted to the church.

Built into the north side of the church is a volute stele with a crescent and disc motif in its calyx, which probably once marked a fifth-century BC grave in the vicinity. Near the southwest corner of the courtyard is a single-chambered Roman tomb with three arcosolia (rock-cut sarcophagi surmounted by arches). This may have been a rival candidate for the final resting place of the saint, or it may have been reused as a water cistern for the monastery.

The west and south wings, rather than being single rows of rooms along a portico, were two rooms deep, often with no apparent doorway leading into the inner room. The size of the rooms also varied considerably. There may have been a portico along the front of the south wing, but most traces of it were cut by the bulldozer clearing a platform around the church. One marble column, presumably from Roman Tamassos, lies at the east end of the south wing, and may have been brought in for a portico. As the floor level is about 1 m higher up than that of the church, originally there would have been steps leading up from the courtyard but now destroyed by the bulldozer. The walls in the south wing are built of cut limestone blocks, carefully mortared and packed with smaller stones and a few tile fragments. Most of the walls of the west wing are of a simpler masonry with no mortar or packers; some of these have collapsed into vague lines of rubble (figure 4.35).

The western wall of the monastery is of considerable interest. At the south end, it is built of large rough chunks of the local limestone with no packers, very different from the standard Ottoman period masonry of the other walls of the monastery, which are built of basalt river cobbles and small limestone packers. Immediately north of this is a stretch where the wall has been cut from the bedrock formed by the same limestone. This cutting is as much as 50 cm deep, so that the westernmost room is lower than the top of the bedrock ridge to its west. Further north the line is continued in more standard masonry but with a thickness of 75 cm instead of the usual 50 to 55 cm of the other monastery walls. It seems likely that much of this wall, which continues to the north end of the west wing, predates the current monastery building and was reused.

Artifacts collected from the monastery structures were few, mostly because of the overgrown state of the ruins. Of 19 sherds collected from the west and south wings, four were Medieval to Modern pithos fragments, five were tiles (all of unknown date, apart from one Ottoman piece), and four were coarse wares of unknown date. An Ottoman glazed piece and a Modern Lapithos ware rim are such divergent types that they need not be associated with the monastery, while the three pre-Medieval pieces are typical of the rest of SIA 6.

From Archbishopric records and a plaque inside the church, we know that the church and monastery were rebuilt in the 1770s and in 1836 (Jeffery

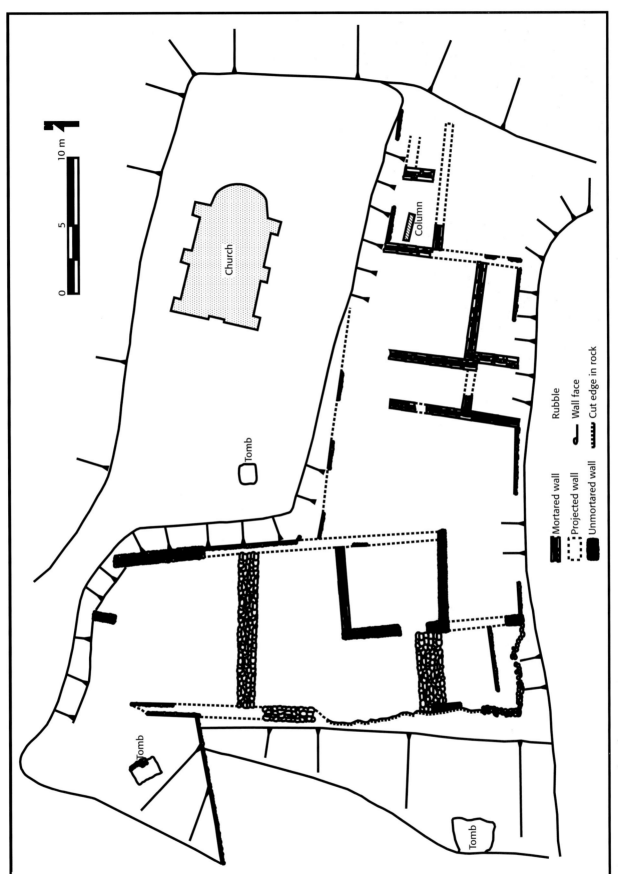

Figure 4.35 SCY346: plan of monastery

Figure 4.36
SCY346:
monastery and
church from the
northeast

1918:211; Gunnis 1936:397–399; Tsiknopoullou 1967:81). The mapped remains are presumably from 1836, though it is not known how complete this rebuilding was. The best description of the monastery in the Ottoman period was made by the Ukrainian monk and traveler Basil Barsky in 1735. The few monks made their living "partly through agriculture, by the sweat of their brow, and partly through collecting alms each year in the surrounding Christian villages" (Barsky 1996:78–79). Just over forty years later, the Archbishopric Property Codex of 1777 gives a very different picture of the monastery's economy. As well as 148 household items and 33 items of church equipment and books, it had a flock of 240 sheep and goats, 50 *skales* of vines (1 *skala* = 625 m²), 132 skales of olives, and extensive fields and orchards in the territories of the neighboring villages. In 1825 it boasted a total of six monks (Tsiknopoullou 1967:81).

A community of six or so monks with few or no dependents can engage in intensive agricultural production on a scale larger than individual families; this was generally the case with the monasteries of the Ottoman period in Cyprus. Immediately to the west of the monastery is an important piece of evidence for this production, in the form of an unusually large threshing floor (unit 1740). This is a roughly elliptical field, carefully leveled by means of a high terrace wall on the north and deeply cut into

the hillside on the south. Unlike the neighboring fields, it is full of stones, with limestone slabs and imported basalt river stones, typically between 15 and 20 cm across. Block survey produced four threshing sledge blades from the general area below it, as well as a jasper core on the floor itself. Measuring about 30 m east to west and 25 m north to south, this aloni is considerably larger than the usual family threshing floors in the villages (typically no more than 15 m in diameter) and is more suited to the large-scale production of grain that went on in the monasteries and estates of the period (Given 2000:227; Whittaker 1999).

BLOCK SURVEY

Eighty-one units were surveyed in SIA 6, including the part of transect 521.5 that runs in from the north. Of these, the forty in the southern half of the SIA are of greatest interest for answering questions about the limits of Tamassos/Politiko, its cemeteries and sanctuaries. The map showing sherd densities for all periods together (plate XXV) shows that four of these units are among the eleven densest units in the entire survey area. The intensity of human activity that this represents is clearly connected to the presence of a major city spanning the Iron Age to Late Roman periods. The densest areas are the hillslope running down from Tamassos on the eastern side, and the area of the monastery, cemetery, and sanctuary. The falloff moving west and north away from Tamassos is very clear.

The distribution of tiles, mostly undatable, is very different (plate XXV). There are very large quantities (tile index of 3000) on the slope running down from Tamassos on the eastern edge of the SIA and on the low river terrace west of the river and at the base of the bluff. Moving to the top of the bluff and into the monastery area, there is an abrupt change. There are a few units with modest amounts (tile index of about 300 to 400) but nothing remotely approaching the quantities that lie to the east. The large amounts on the low river terrace are clearly not a result of erosion down the bluff, as there is so little at the top. They could not have been naturally transported from the eastern side of the Katouris River, so they must be more or less in situ. This tile distribution coincides best with the Late Roman pottery (see below) and is probably related to a broad westward expansion of Late Roman Tamassos.

Only twelve prehistoric sherds were found in SIA 6, in spite of its proximity to the Bronze Age settlements and cemeteries of Politiko *Lambertis*, Politiko *Troulia* (SCY322), and Politiko *Ayios Iraklidhios* (table 4.14). As is often the case, a large proportion of pottery, particularly the coarse wares, was undiagnostic, or could be attributed only to very broad periods.

GEOMETRIC TO CLASSICAL

The map showing pottery densities for the Geometric to Classical periods (plate XXVI) is clearly dominated by Archaic to Classical material. Taking this period as a whole, there are two major concentrations: the slope running down from Tamassos on the east and the area south of the monastery. The first is presumably a result of close proximity to Tamassos; the second is due to a combination of the sanctuary and the looted cemetery. In both cases the figures are very high indeed. Three units have pottery indices higher than 10,000, which represents a remarkable amount of material. Interestingly, the low river terrace west of the Katouris has comparatively little. Given that at least some of this pottery is likely to have fallen down the bluff from the very dense units above, there may have been but little activity here in the Geometric to Classical periods.

No pottery from SIA 6 can be dated definitively to the Cypro-Geometric period (table 4.14). Several Cypro-Archaic and Cypro-Classical pieces are clearly diagnostic of specific periods. These pieces range in date from the Cypro-Archaic I, but mainly Cypro-Archaic II, period (cat. 1733.10.1, 1741.13.1, 1742.1B.1) through the Cypro-Classical I and II periods (for example, cat. 1741.24B.1, 1746.2.1, cat. 1733.2.1) with most pieces dating between Cypro-Archaic II and Cypro-Classical II. The survey material suggests that Ayios Mnason was an important locus of activity during the Archaic and Classical periods, particularly from the sixth to fourth centuries BC and perhaps earlier, in the seventh to eighth centuries BC; this activity certainly continued into the Hellenistic period.

A particularly interesting group of pottery from SIA 6, mostly from the area of the sanctuary just south of the monastery, consists of a series of wasters and other vitrified and misfired pieces. These include wasters, a warped piece, a piece that is almost vitrified, and what may be vitrified exterior kiln material. A related group, but more widely scattered across the SIA, consists of sherds that had been cut or sliced before firing. One is very clearly a vessel (cat. 5019.44A.1) cut at the junction of the neck and shoulder, smudged with a finger; it is now green and clearly a waster, though it retains the original form of a vessel. A second piece from this same unit is of an identical vessel type but has not been cut. It is also green and may be another failed attempt at a vessel. Many of these cut pieces are flattened, although originally they may have been wheelmade. None is decorated or visibly part of recognizable statue parts, and the sliced flat edge is left unworked. These cut pieces are green, hard fired, and somewhat vitrified, suggesting that they were overfired. They were probably made from the same iron rich clay as the remaining pottery, which was high-fired and reduced to produce a light, sometimes buff color (Hocking 1999). The thirteen cut and flattened pieces may have been failed vessels cut up and used to support successfully manufactured vessels and perhaps terra-cottas in kilns.

The large number of storage vessels is a very striking feature of SIA 6 in the Archaic and Classical periods. Pithoi (cat. 1741.1.1) and other transport (for example, cat. 1733.3.1, 1733.2.1, and 1742.1B.1) and storage vessels (for example, cat. 1740.1.2 and 1741.13.1) were found across all areas of SIA 6. Although the units in the far north of the SIA do not follow the pattern of the other areas in terms of pottery production and cult items, they do have a similar pattern of storage vessels. This applies to the Greek amphorae as well as to storage vessels in general. Similarly, decorated and undecorated cups (for example, cat. 1746.2.1), bowls (for example, cat. 1733.10.1), jugs and jars (for example, cat. 1741.24B.1) appear to be spread evenly across the SIA. Like the storage vessels, they seem to represent an overall pattern to which the more unusual production and cult material is added. One jug (cat. 1742.4.1) bears a mark that, if viewed from the side, may be the Cypriot Syllabic sign *a*, added after firing. Pot marks are found on contemporary vessels from sanctuaries such as that at Kourion (Masson 1996:179–180, nos. 2, 35).

HELLENISTIC TO ROMAN

The distribution map (plate XXVII) indicates a much higher level of activity in the Late Roman period, although there was clearly some activity in the eastern and western areas at all periods. The most striking concentration is once again on the slope of the hill below Tamassos, east of the Katouris River, though this never quite attains the same levels as during the Geometric to Classical periods (plate XXVI). There is a middling amount of activity on the low river terraces west of the Katouris; given how little there is on top of the bluff to the west, not all of this can have fallen down from above. When taken with the distribution of tiles (plate XXV), it may be that the Late Roman city extended beyond its walls. The low densities of material south of the monastery, where there is a known Roman necropolis, is striking, particularly in comparison to the vast amounts from the Iron Age to Classical periods. With pottery indices never more than 1000, this seems to represent a general background scatter due to looted and disturbed tombs.

The thirty-three sherds (1%) dated to the Hellenistic period may be small statistically but they constitute one of the largest collection of Hellenistic sherds in the SCSP area (table 4.14). With several late Classical pieces, there is more evidence of continuity from the Classical into the Hellenistic and Early Roman periods here than anywhere else. This certainly fits with the known dates of the nearby sanctuary of Chomazoudhia (Buchholz and Untiedt 1996:32–33). Of twenty-five fine wares, twenty-three were Hellenistic black glaze, one was early red slip, and one was a Hellenistic fish plate dating to the

second century BC. This concentration of fine wares, including the fish plate, shows a high degree of affluence in the area, which must be indicative of the propinquity of Tamassos. The high number of fine wares and low numbers of utility wares provide further indicators of Hellenistic/Early Roman tombs.

The seventy-two sherds (2.3%) dating to the Early Roman period echo the Hellenistic material in the high numbers of quality pieces. Of sixteen fine ware sherds, nine were locally produced (Cypriot Red Slip and other red slips), and seven were imports (Eastern Sigillata A, B, and B2). These eastern sigillatas are from Syria and date from the first century BC to the first century AD. One major contrast with the Hellenistic period is that there are considerably more cooking ware sherds (fifty), which might be expected in a densely inhabited area. There are also several standard early Roman cooking pot rims, common throughout the SCSP area. It is tempting to see the imported wares associated with the cemetery and the local fine wares and cooking wares indicating a settlement, probably the edge of Tamassos.

There were 272 sherds (8.6%) dating to the Late Roman period, which is the characteristic proportion of Late Roman to other material across the survey area. This represents a fairly complete collection, and among the unusual items in the assemblage are: an Aegean Red Amphora sherd, a Late Roman pithos, two early African Red Slip forms 45 and 50, twelve other pieces of African Red Slip, and one piece of Egyptian Red Slip A (cat. 5044.10.1). These all reflect the effects of nearby Tamassos, if not the edge of the city itself east of the Katouris. With the exception of the pithos, these pieces show that items were being imported and making their way inland. Toward the end of the Late Roman period, SIA 6 does not show the same grouping as the others, being more evenly distributed throughout time. Once again this is probably the result of its proximity to Tamassos.

MEDIEVAL TO MODERN

The post-Roman periods (plate XXVIII) show a very different pattern. The intense activity on the hillslope east of the Katouris River has almost entirely gone. Clearly the focus of settlement had receded sharply, either because of a contraction in the settlement or a shift in its position. Certainly the church of Ayios Theodhoros in the oldest part of the village of Politiko, restored in 1888 after what was already a long life (Jeffery 1918:211; *MKE* 11:372), is a good 500 m southeast of Ayios Mnason, and even with its recent expansion the village has reached only the top of this slope. The break with antiquity is clear.

A concentration of material on the low river terrace west of the Katouris is never very high (maximum pottery index of 4000); it may derive partly from material pushed down the bluff from the monastery when it was bulldozed during the restoration of the church. Further west, there is only a general background count (pottery index of less than 1000), which is probably due to manuring and dumping in the fields closest to the village. It seems surprising that there is so little material immediately to the north and west of the monastery. Counts from the monastery itself are also relatively low, although that is at least partially due to thick vegetation within the ruins.

Of 3122 sherds collected from SIA 6, 675 or 22% were Medieval to Modern, an unusually low proportion in comparison with most other SIAs (table 4.14). Of the 71 specifically Medieval sherds, thirty-five were otherwise undiagnostic glazed pieces. The well-dated glazed wares were spread unusually across the thirteenth to sixteenth centuries; the nine sherds from the thirteenth to fourteenth centuries comprise strong representation from a period that is elsewhere attested primarily by few sherds. The sixteenth century material is also significantly represented, though this is a more common phenomenon.

The Ottoman period has a significant total of eighty-one sherds, all of which are reasonably well dated. Some forty-four of these come from the seventeenth and eighteenth centuries, the commonest being the twenty-nine sherds of Cypriot Glazed with Brown Slip and Green Paint. The rest are dated to any time from the seventeenth to nineteenth centuries. With the village of Politiko and two monasteries in the immediate vicinity, this area was clearly still flourishing during a period more commonly associated with depopulation and abandonment.

CONCLUSION

The principal significance of SIA 6 lies in the indications it gives of human activity on the margins of a large settlement. Tamassos was not the only Archaic to Classical city-kingdom to have one or more sanc-

Table 4.14 SIA 6: analyzed pottery from block survey

Chronotype	Period	Qty
Coarse ware, Chalcolithic	EP	1
Red-on-White	EP	2
Pithoid Tub	PoB	1
Pithos-PoB	PoB	7
Plain White, Handmade	PoB	1
TOTAL Prehistoric		12
Amphora-Ar	Ar	7
Amphora, pithoid [1742.1B.1]	Ar	1
Bichrome-Ar	Ar	1
Black-on-Red-Ar	Ar	2
Cooking ware-Ar	Ar	6
Green ware-Ar	Ar	3
Pithos-Ar	Ar	7
Plain ware-Ar	Ar	8
Red Slip-Ar	Ar	5
Soft Red-Orange-Ar	Ar	17
Wide Shallow Bowl-Ar	Ar	1
Amphora-Cl	Cl	6
Amphora, Knobbed [1733.2.1]	Cl	1
Black Glaze-Cl	Cl	6
Cooking ware-Cl	Cl	6
Fine ware-Cl	Cl	1
Plain ware-Cl [1741.24B.1, 1746.2.1]	Cl	27
Plain White-Cl	Cl	43
Stroke Polished	Cl	4
Tile-Cl	Cl	3
White Painted-Cl	Cl	3
Wide Shallow Bowl-Cl	Cl	2
Coarse ware-GAC	GAC	8
Green ware-GAC	GAC	15
Pithos-GAC	GAC	1
Plain ware-GAC	GAC	1
Amphora-AC	AC	153
Amphora, Knobbed Base	AC	2
Amphora, Pithoid	AC	50
Amphora, Torpedo	AC	52
Basin-AC	AC	5
Bichrome-AC	AC	2
Black Glaze-AC	AC	5
Black-on-Red-AC	AC	3
Coarse ware-AC	AC	3
Cooking ware-AC	AC	100
Double Rolled Strap Handle-AC	AC	2
Fine ware-AC	AC	1
Green ware-AC	AC	26
Lamp-AC	AC	1
Pithos-AC	AC	43
Plain ware-AC	AC	353
Plain White-AC	AC	50
Red Slip-AC [1742.4.1]	AC	3
Rolled Lug Handle-AC	AC	22
Unknown-AC	AC	1
White Painted-AC	AC	39
Wide Shallow Bowl-AC	AC	2
TOTAL Geometric to Classical		1103

continued

Table 4.14, *continued*

Chronotype	Period	Qty	Chronotype	Period	Qty
Amphora-He	He	3	Cypriot Glazed VI	Med	1
Black Glaze-He	He	24	Cypriot Glazed VII	Med	1
Black Slip-He	He	1	Cypriot Glazed VIIIB	Med	6
Coarse ware-He [5041.11.1]	He	4	Cypriot Glazed IX	Med	10
Fine ware-He	He	1	Cypriot Glazed XI	Med	3
Fish Plate-He	He	1	Glazed ware, Italian	Med	1
Plain ware-He	He	1	Imported Sgrafitto [1709.27.1, 5026.8.1]	Med	4
Red Slip-He	He	1	Lemba ware	Med	1
Amphora-ER	ER	1	Coarse ware-Ott	Ott	1
Çandarli ware	ER	7	Cypriot Glazed VIIIBL	Ott	1
Casserole, Angular Offset	ER	1	Cypriot Glazed IXL	Ott	9
Casserole, Cypriot Flanged	ER	3	Cypriot Glazed, Brown and Green	Ott	29
Coarse ware-ER	ER	2	Cypriot W3	Ott	15
Cooking ware-ER	ER	34	Cypriot W5	Ott	4
Cooking ware, ER Cooking Pot	ER	3	Cypriot W6	Ott	16
Cooking ware, Offset Rim [1708.14.1]	ER	2	Ottoman Glazed	Ot	6
Cooking ware, Square Rim Pot	ER	8	Purple Painted ware	Ott	2
Eastern Sigillata A	ER	1	Tile-Ott	Ott	1
Eastern Sigillata B	ER	3	Turkish Pipe	Ott	1
Eastern Sigillata B II	ER	3	Brick	Mod	6
African Red Slip	LR	13	Coarse ware-Mod	Mod	8
African Red Slip 45 [1745.1.1]	LR	1	Contemporary Eastern Mediterranean	Mod	29
African Red Slip 50	LR	1	Contemporary Imported Asian	Mod	14
Amphora-LR	LR	30	Contemporary Imported European	Mod	4
Amphora, Aegean Red	LR	3	Contemporary local wares	Mod	3
Amphora, LR 1 [5041.32.1]	LR	57	Contemporary Yogurt ware	Mod	2
Basin-LR	LR	15	Cypriot W7	Mod	58
Basin, Piecrust Rim	LR	16	Fine ware-Mod	Mod	1
Coarse ware-LR	LR	21	Lapithos ware	Mod	1
Coarse ware, LR Wheel-Ridged	LR	23	Lapithos ware, Green	Mod	3
Cooking ware-LR	LR	21	Lapithos ware, Yellow	Mod	8
Cypriot Red Slip	LR	10	Pithos-Mod	Mod	8
Cypriot Red Slip 1	LR	3	Tile-Mod	Mod	11
Cypriot Red Slip 2	LR	2	Brown Glazed ware	MM	8
Cypriot Red Slip 9 [1743.28.1]	LR	9	Coarse ware-MM	MM	2
Cypriot Red Slip 10	LR	3	Cypriot W1	MM	5
Egyptian Red Slip A [5044.10.1]	LR	1	Cypriot W4	MM	309
Frying Pan	LR	6	Glazed ware	MM	23
Flat-Grooved	LR	17	Pithos-MM	MM	6
Phocaean ware (LR C)	LR	1	Tile-MM	MM	14
Phocaean ware 3 [5037.4.1]	LR	3			
Phocaean ware 10 [5039.13.1]	LR	3	TOTAL Medieval to Modern		679
Pithos-LR	LR	4			
Red Slip, Roman	LR	2	Plain White-HA	HA	32
Spirally Grooved	LR	4	Red Slip-HA	HA	3
Tile-LR	LR	3	Amphora-Hi	Hi	8
Coarse ware-REL	REL	2	Pithos-PC	PC	58
Red Slip-REL	REL	3	Tile-PC	PC	77
			Tile, Corinthian	PC	2
TOTAL Hellenistic to Late Roman		381	Tile, Corinthian Pan	PC	30
			Tile, Flat Pan	PC	13
Coarse ware-Med	Med	1	Tile, Laconian	PC	1
Cypriot Glazed	Med	35	Coarse ware-Unk	Unk	569
Cypriot Glazed IIIB	Med	1	Cooking ware-Unk	Unk	44
Cypriot Glazed IV	Med	2	Fine ware-Unk	Unk	5
Cypriot Glazed IVB	Med	1	Table ware-Unk	Unk	2
Cypriot Glazed IVC	Med	2	Unknown-Unk	Unk	8
Cypriot Glazed V	Med	2			
			TOTAL		3015

Note: Figures in brackets refer to cataloged items (see chapter 5.1).

tuaries immediately beyond the confines of the city: Idalion is the most notable example, but Golgoi and Kition have similar patterns. Every city and settlement from the Archaic through the Late Roman periods had extensive cemeteries around them, particularly along the approach roads. By comparing the known Roman cemetery around Ayios Mnason with the characteristic functions, condition, and density of the artifacts on the surface, we can now recognize the signature" of a cemetery on the outskirts of a city. This was very different from the Medieval period, when graves were placed in the churchyard at the heart of the settlement. Because of manuring and dumping practices in the *sokhorafa*, the fields closest to the village, there is again a halo of material around a Medieval to Modern settlement, clearly visible at Ayios Mnason (chapter 7.4).

The landscape of Ayios Mnason obviously has been more than a supplier of practical necessities such as crops, building blocks, and communications routes. With its Archaic to Classical sanctuary, a long-lived necropolis, and a monastery, right down to the recent rebuilding of the church and SCSP's own appropriation of the Saint's name, Ayios Mnason represents a succession of sacred landscapes. Often one was adopted into another, as with the Roman tomb at the heart of the Christian monastery, or the Classical grave stele built into its church. The location of the monastery and its ancient western wall might even retain a memory of the earlier sanctuary. The changes also reflect the radical differences between cultures and their landscapes: the Medieval and Ottoman dead, unlike their Roman predecessors, abandoned Ayios Mnason to rest within their community around the village church.

4.7 SIA 7: Politiko *Kokkinorotsos*

Compiled by A. Bernard Knapp
Team leaders: Susan Bain, Dina Coleman, Haddon Wright
Archaeometallurgy: Vasiliki Kassianidou, Sven Van Lokeren,
Haddon Wright Geobotany: Neil Urwin Geomorphology: Jay
Noller GIS analysis: Nathan Meyer, A. Bernard Knapp
Lithics: Dina Coleman Micromorphology: Peter Grave
Pottery: Sturt Manning, R. Scott Moore, Elinor Ribeiro,
Joanna S. Smith

Grid reference: 519500/3875100
Cadastral maps: XXXVIII/8, XXXIX/1
Aerial photograph: 1993, run 175, no. 235

Survey units: 1594–1629, 3050–3120, 3148–72, 3272–80, 3571–79, 5048–52
POSIs: SCY100: Politiko *Phorades* 1 (ProBA stratified slag deposit); SCY101: Politiko *Phorades* 2 (Roman estate); SCY116: Politiko *Kokkinorotsos* 1 (ore roasting, beneficiation); SCY121: Politiko *Kokkinorotsos* 6 (slag heap); SCY123: Politiko *Phorades* 3 (Archaic to Classical pottery); SCY125: Politiko *Kannouris* (check dam or retaining wall); SCY126: Politiko *Phorades* 4 (lithic scatter) (For POSIs on gossan ridge, see table 4.18.)

In the pillow lavas some 3 km southwest of Politiko, an extended gossan ridge runs south above a branch of the Kouphos River. Ancient slag and other archaeometallurgical debris are scattered across the surrounding fields and hillsides, and exposed in road sections and stream beds. Such features and materials all bear witness to the long-term, widespread production of copper in this area. In addition, the upper Kouphos River Valley is crucial for investigating the relationship between mining, agriculture, and human settlement. Accordingly we designated this area SIA 7 and called it Politiko *Kokkinorotsos* ("red rock") after the locality name of the gossan (plate XXIX). The general region around Kokkinorotsos, with its substantial slag heaps as well as numerous adits and other mining remains, was first shown to us in 1995 by Dr. George Constantinou (former director, Cyprus Geological Survey) who had recorded it during his own doctoral research (Constantinou 1972).

SIA 7 offers a unique panoply of data that makes possible an integrated understanding and interpretation of the relationship between human activity and the natural environment. As examples, we can point to (1) the symbiotic exploitations of two major natural resources, metal-bearing ores and arable land; (2) a range of site types which vary as much as the landscape itself; (3) the perspective gained from abundant geomorphological and geobotanical data which facilitate a unique assessment of the human impact on the landscape; and (4) sufficient artifactual and spatial data to consider environmental constraints on human activity.

PHYSICAL LANDSCAPE

The landscape of SIA 7 is underlain and controlled by its bedrock geology. During the Cretaceous era, active volcanoes and springs of metal-rich boiling water were surrounded by a restful seascape of lava pillows. These metal-rich mounds are high points of land that have been exploited over more recent millennia for their copper ores. The exhumation of this primeval submarine landscape reflects the dominant modern geological process of erosion, which has reduced the area to a series of "badlands," that is, bedrock exposed by the near total loss of soil. This inexorable denudation of the Troodos foothills has been accelerated regionally and interrupted locally by the entry of successive generations of humans into this landscape.

SIA 7 lies within the drainage basin of the Kouphos "creek," a tributary to the major river, the Pedhiaios. The headwaters of this basin lie upstream from SIA 7, along the major north-south geographical drainage divide. The Kouphos is an ephemeral stream, discharging surface waters only during and immediately following winter rains or summer thunderstorms. The winter, frontal systems exact a measured change to much of the watershed, whereas the thunderstorms are much more energetic and result in quick, profound changes to the affected parts of the watershed.

Mineralization in the lower pillow lavas southeast of Klirou village is widespread, with scattered slag heaps indicative of frequent mining activity in antiquity (Bear 1960:104–105; 1963:83). Geochemical prospecting has shown, for example, that the gossan at Kokkinorotsos contains over 1000 ppm of copper, a major anomaly and one of obvious commercial significance. Indeed, the number of modern exploratory shafts and adits confirms the contemporary mineralogical richness of SIA 7.

The POSIs of SIA 7 are found on a number of representative elements of the precultural features of the Kouphos landscape. SCY116–SCY121 are on a ridge capped by ore-bearing rocks (the gossan). Like the Kouphos and its tributaries, this ridgeline parallels the dominant northeast trend of the bedrock features. SCY100, SCY123, SCY125, and SCY126 are on earlier courses of the Kouphos stream. SCY125 is a small check dam constructed of large stones preserved on a ridge approximately 100 m upstream

(southwest) from Politiko *Phorades* (SCY100). SCY101 is situated atop a rounded knoll that is part of a prominent, erosion resistant, east-west trending flow unit within the pillow lava formation. All of these POSIs owe their presence in the modern landscape to one or more factors favoring their preservation over their erosion and loss.

Surrounding the POSIs of SIA 7 are badlands, largely stripped of soil and of any extensive context for the surface archaeological record. Some scholars view the Kouphos badlands as the result of ancient deforestation. Although this interpretation follows on from a basic understanding of soil conservation, we have yet to fix firmly the date or dates of this presumed triggering mechanism (loss of vegetative cover) and to link that mechanism with its responses (soil erosion and increased stream sediment). Nonetheless, in our investigations we have found some direct and highly circumstantial evidence of human entry into and use of this watershed. First, and in the form of direct evidence, we may cite the character of stream deposits in association with the smelting workshop at SCY100. Excavations have shown that the workshop was located on the banks of the Kouphos. The channel dimensions and floodplain sediments were very much as they are today, with one important distinction—the stream was aggrading—that is, the Kouphos was raising the elevation of its bed through deposition of sediment, a very small advance in what had been a millennium or more of accelerated erosional retreat. The amount of sediment coming down the Kouphos, some of which is visible behind the check dam at SCY125, must have been substantial. The end of this aggradation phase at SCY100 could have been triggered by construction of the dam, effectively reducing the power and sediment load of the Kouphos below the dam at SCY125.

Because the channel morphology was similar to that of today, we can rule out a significantly wetter climate. In fact, initial study of soils from this landscape point to a similar climate over the past five thousand years. Given that streams reflect a balance between load (the amount of sediment carried) and power (amount of flow, slope, channel morphology), we suggest that sediment yield from hillslopes increased around the time that the Phorades workshop flourished (beginning of the Late Bronze Age). Increasing sediment yield coupled with changing climate means either a delayed landscape response to an earlier change in climate, or a change in vegetative cover. This latter change could be affected by deforestation, overgrazing, and/or substitution of a new vegetative cover (for example, agriculture). Circumstantially, one could then support a scenario in which the workshop and landscape change was linked. Clearing the land of forest cover, in however limited a fashion, would have provided fuel for the smelting operation at SCY100. This in turn would have precipitated the release of sediment which would ultimately have buried the workshop materials and sealed them until exhumed by its parent, the Kouphos, during the twentieth century AD. Unfortunately, many parts of the Kouphos basin have lost their record of human occupation and use through the obliterating effects of gully erosion.

Were it not for the construction of check dams in gullies of the Kouphos basin, this entire area would today be of limited use. The broad agricultural plains of the lower watershed owe their existence to check dams constructed in prehistoric times, perhaps as early as the Late Bronze Age at SCY125, and to the numerous check dams built during the Late Roman period (near SCY101). Of further interest is the fact that many of the stones used in constructing these dams are either exotic to this landscape or else come from the nearby ore bodies along the gossan ridge. That these stones come from different areas might also suggest a connection between mining enterprise and local agricultural activity. Modern barley fields clearly owe their existence to the foresight of Roman, Byzantine, and certainly Ottoman farmers who constructed and maintained these long-standing structural conservators of soil.

GEOBOTANY

Where the pillow lavas and sedimentary strata meet, there are large areas of dry shrub lands on shallow soils: These shrubs range from batha (an extremely sparse and depauperate species) to garrigue (a tall and thicker shrub). The major garrigue/batha dominants are *Thymus capitatus* (thyme) and *Sarcopoterium spinosum* (spiny burnet). *Thymus* is rare on soils with strong metalliferous qualities (like copper sulfides) and in this area did not grow on slag heaps where soil cover is extremely shallow. *Sarcopoterium*, on the contrary, is much less affected by metalliferous soils and will grow on slag heaps even in the shallowest of soils. These varieties are very common in SIA 7, along with low grasses, *Pinus brutia* and, rarely, hawthorn.

Of the nine concentrations of archaeological material within the SCSP study area that underwent geobotanical investigation, three (SCY100, SCY101, SCY121) were in SIA 7. More specific geobotanical assessments are provided under the relevant POSIs.

HISTORICAL CONTEXT

At the far end of the Kouphos Valley, the stream enters a gorge and runs between steep limestone hills to the open plain commanded by the modern village of Politiko. As one proceeds northward through this gorge, it is only 4 km from the gossan of Kokkinorotsos to the Archaic–Roman town of Tamassos (within Politiko). Tamassos is the major Archaic–Classical site in the region and the only possible administrative center that could have controlled any contemporary mines in the Kouphos Valley. Of considerable relevance to the archaeometallurgical activities in SIA 7 are finds of slag and other evidence of copper working in the Archaic period at the sanctuary of Chomazoudhia, just inside the city walls (Buchholz 1974:607; 1978:165–166, 171; 1985a:240–242; Buchholz and Unteidt 1996:53–57). Tamassos may well have had prehistoric forerunners, witnessed by the quantity and quality of material from such sites as Politiko *Lambertis* (SCY020, PreBA to ProBA tombs) or Politiko *Troulia* (SCY322, a PreBA settlement, with abundant evidence of walls, ground-stone material, and Red Polished pottery) (Catling 1962:153, 159, 168).

A moderate scale of copper production is indicated by the excavations at Phorades (SCY100). Most likely, this site was only one of several similar workshops spread around the mining areas in the foothills of the Troodos. Such sites would have been integrated readily into a broader economic and ideological system. Situated in agriculturally unproductive areas, they also would have needed subsistence support, perhaps provided by villages such as Aredhiou *Vouppes* (SCY010). In light of the site patterning evident in and around the SCSP area, we suggest that a Bronze Age smelting site like Phorades, along with its agricultural support village, would have been linked to a network of sites running from the mining zone in the southern stretches of the SCSP region, in a northerly and then northwesterly direction to a coastal site on Morphou Bay, perhaps associated in part with Morphou *Toumba tou Skourou*.

FIELD METHODOLOGY

The area of SIA 7 measures approximately 500 m east to west and 800 m north to south. In addition to transect survey, extensive block survey was carried out in 1995 and especially in 1996. In 1997, we conducted more block survey to investigate the Kouphos river terraces, as the geomorphologist had suggested they might reveal cultural remains. The primary aim of block survey in SIA 7 was to consider closely the relationships amongst the gossan at Kokkinorotsos, the Bronze Age smelting site (SCY100), the two "knolls" (SCY101, SCY123), and the surrounding arable land.

SCY100 was investigated in 1996 by both geomorphological and archaeometallurgical teams. We collected diagnostic samples of slag, furnaces, and tuyères from the surface and then from the stratified geomorphological section. The surrounding area was examined systematically through block survey during 1996. The 1997–1998 excavation methods used at SCY100 (Politiko *Phorades* 1) are presented in detail elsewhere (Knapp, Donnelly, and Kassianidou 1998; Knapp et al. 1998, 1999, 2001). SCY101 (Politiko *Phorades* 2) was investigated in 1995 by means of block survey (5 m spacing) but with very small units. SCY118 was first examined by a survey team in 1996, but not as part of regular transect. SCY123 (Politiko *Phorades* 3) was surveyed as one unit in 1995, and then gridded with 1 m squares in 1997, after more material had been brought to the surface.

SCY100: POLITIKO *PHORADES* 1:
PROTOHISTORIC BRONZE AGE
SMELTING WORKSHOP

SCY100 (Politiko *Phorades* 1) was first surveyed by ordinary transect (unit 3168) after its discovery by project geomorphologist Jay Noller, who was searching the dry creek beds in the southeastern sector of the SCSP region for exposed sections of stream sediments. Taking into consideration the singular nature of the material at SCY100 and the fact that the site was threatened by erosion, we decided to collect all refractories but only diagnostic samples of slag (based on shape, size, type, and inclusions). This initial collection was taken from the surface in the eroded area only, while the stratified deposits were left for later sampling.

Sampling was conducted within a grid system (1 m high by 2 m wide) established by Noller in his initial recording of this POSI. After a surface collection and with the permission of the Cypriot Department of Antiquities, the section was cleaned back in order to expose better the stratigraphy of the deposit. Samples were taken from nine identified strata that represented smelting and erosional events at the site (for details, see Knapp, Donnelly, and Kassianidou 1998:249–250, Fig. 2). During a systematic survey of the area around SCY100 (1996), Iron Age material was found in some quantity. The preliminary interpretation of this POSI as a smelting site with a unique type of slag, dated to the beginning of the Late Bronze Age, was subsequently demonstrated by excavation and radiocarbon dating.

Slag collected during the survey came from unique slag "cakes" of plano-concave shape, and the refractory material included rims, curved wall fragments, bottom/wall corner pieces, furnace bottoms, and tuyères. The single indicator of the possible date of smelting activity was a White Slip I sherd (seventeenth to sixteenth century BC; see table 4.15); this date has now been confirmed by further ^{14}C dates and by other pottery and archaeometallurgical material excavated during the 1997, 1998, and 2000 seasons. The technology involved has no precedents on Bronze Age Cyprus, and the material recovered thus assumes unique importance. Politiko *Phorades* 1 is the earliest known properly dated primary smelting site yet discovered on Cyprus. The archaeometal-lurgical and technological developments seen at Phorades are unprecedented and of unique importance for reconstructing the history of metallurgy on Cyprus. Excavations were conducted at the site in 1997 and 1998 and were completed in May-June 2000 (Knapp 1999a; Knapp, Donnelly, and Kassianidou 1998; Knapp et al. 1998; 1999, 2001; Given et al. 1999:29–32; Kassianidou 1999).

GEOBOTANY

Natural vegetation cover in the area of the excavations at SCY100 was characteristically sparse with low species diversity (11 species). *Thymus capitatus* dominated with 25 to 30% ground cover. *Cistus* was codominant with *Thymus*. The alluvial stream bed and terrace adjacent to the smelting site were densely covered with grasses and herbaceous plants. Fifteen 10 x 10 m quadrats were sampled on and adjoining

Table 4.15 SCY100: analyzed pottery

Chronotype	Period	Qty
White Slip I	PoB	1
Cypriot Glazed, Brown and Green	Ott	1
Contemporary Eastern Mediterranean	Mod	3
Cypriot W4	MM	1
Glazed ware	MM	1
Coarse ware	Unk	1

Phorades, as was vegetation on adjacent landforms of the same geomorphology to the north, south, east, and west.

Using all species variables, two distinct clusters of sampling units and a number of outliers were sorted by the clustering analysis. Cluster analysis (CA) and principal components analysis (PCA) (see chapter 3.5) make it possible to conclude that the vegetation on site at Phorades, at both the species and community level, was not significantly different from adjoining and surrounding vegetation to enable us to make a geobotanical indicator or predictive correlation. This lack of significantly different vegetation is noteworthy: all other slag or smelting sites examined were identifiable by the vegetation, and the level of smelting activity revealed by the excavations at SCY100 could reasonably have been expected to affect soil chemistry enough to cause change in the site vegetation. There is no explanation for this anomaly.

SCY101: POLITIKO *PHORADES* 2: ROMAN ESTATE

Some 500 m north of Phorades lies a small multi-terraced knoll, about 150 m in diameter, which rises steeply on its north face to a height of about 20 m and enjoys a commanding view of agricultural fields stretching 300 to 500 m farther north and west (figure 4.37). To the east is a narrow terraced field, and to the south the knoll slopes gently toward the copper smelting workshop at Phorades. SCY101 is ideally situated along a communication corridor that runs approximately 4 km north to Tamassos.

SCY101 was first discovered during the regular survey of transect 519.5. Because of the dense concentrations of cultural material, we designated the area a POSI and conducted more intensive botanical, geomorphological, and pottery studies. Because of the numerous small terraces on the knoll and in its immediate surroundings, the 1995 field team chose to survey these small, narrow areas as indi-

vidual units; the imposition of a grid or circles would not have produced uniform samples because of the narrowness of the terraces. In effect, this resulted in a block survey, but with much smaller units. Each unit was then surveyed by a field team—spaced at the usual 5 m—who collected a representative sample of the artifacts within each unit. The pottery recovered ranges in date from the Iron Age to the Late Roman period. Subsequent visits to SCY101 also uncovered fine wares from the Classical through Late Roman periods.

Dense concentrations of mainly Roman pottery and tile fragments were found on the northern and eastern slopes; few finds were seen on the southern slope and none on the western. From the top of the knoll down its steep northern slope there was a quantity of what seemed to be building rubble; the large size and quantity of these stones, some of which seem to have been worked, exceed what we would expect for use in terrace walls. These stones were most likely brought into the site, as there is no stone of similar type in the Kouphos drainage; the likely origin is the diabase dikes exposed in drainages to the south. Numerous large lichens on the exposed surfaces of these stones enabled geomorphologist Jay Noller to use a preliminary lichen dating curve (based on findings of lichens on dated surfaces elsewhere in the survey area), which suggested a period of about 1500 years for their exposure and use.

Although Early Roman material is never found in quantity in the SCSP survey area, the eastern side of the knoll (unit 1599) contained several Early Roman fine wares, dated AD 50 to 250, perhaps indicating some sort of affluence at this location (table 4.16). Late Roman pottery sherds predominate at SCY101, in both weight and number. This material was found all along the northern, eastern, and southern slopes. Despite the quantity of Late Roman material, and unlike the Early Roman period, there were relatively few sherds of fine ware (most came from imports such as African Red Slip and Phocaean Red Slip wares). This lack of fine wares also contrasts with most other Late Roman assemblages known from the survey area. The most common Late Roman sherds were amphora, basin, and pithos fragments, all arguably agricultural storage vessels, perhaps not surprising given the location in the midst of a large section of arable land. The surrounding agricultural fields show significant pottery densities only to the north and east,

Figure 4.37
SCY101: the
terraced knoll
from the north,
with the upper
Kouphos Valley
directly behind.

toward Tamassos, and these densities are much lower than the density of sherds on the slopes of the knoll.

Another interesting feature of SCY101 is the large quantity of tile fragments, again primarily distributed along the northern and eastern slopes of the knoll, with very little at the top of the knoll or on the western and southern slopes. For example, unit 1605, a narrow terrace approximately 80 m in length and situated halfway down the northern slope of SCY101, had 155 tile fragments, most quite large in size. Most of these fragments date from the fourth to sixth centuries AD. The near absence of slag, otherwise common throughout the SCSP universe, must also be considered. Despite its location not more than 400 m from the mines and ore bodies of SIA 7, SCY101 produced only thirteen slag fragments on and around the knoll.

Based on a broad array of evidence gathered by different specialists, we can suggest that SCY101 was inhabited from the Iron Age through the end of late antiquity. The rubble and numerous building tiles suggest the existence of a few small buildings on the northern and perhaps eastern slopes of the knoll during the fourth to sixth centuries AD. The function of these buildings is unclear. There were no Late Roman cooking wares (for example, "frying pans") typical of other large Late Roman assemblages in the SCSP region. Were these few small buildings used by individuals who farmed in the nearby plains? Although the site is located near several copper mines, there is no obvious connection between the two, and SCY101 seems to have been involved primarily in agriculture, as a large farmstead or estate, or perhaps as a support village for those who worked the mines. The physical landscape reveals that it was easy for the people who lived here to obtain supplies or to sell, exchange, or disperse their produce at Tamassos, only 4 km away, which we know had a basilica and bishopric during the fourth to fifth centuries AD (Buchholz and Untiedt 1996:60, 78).

GEOBOTANY

The floristics and structure of the native vegetation at SCY101 were recorded from two transects. The first comprised six adjoining 10 x 10 m quadrats on the north slope of the knoll. On the lower slopes of the knoll the batha community, dominants of *Thymus capitatus* and *Sarcopoterium spinosum* existed in roughly equal proportions, together making up 25% of ground cover. On the upper slopes, the vegetation cover was denser but the species diversity lower: *Thymus* declined and *Sarcopoterium* became dominant. The second transect of three adjacent 10 x 10 m quadrats on the eastern slope, perpendicular to the first transect, also showed a decline in the proportion of *Thymus* in the quadrats ascending the knoll.

Table 4.16 SCY101: analyzed pottery (units 1599–1615)

Chronotype	Period	Qty
Soft Red-Orange-Ar	Ar	2
Amphora-Cl	Cl	2
Plain White-Cl	Cl	7
Cooking ware-GAC	GAC	1
Amphora-AC	AC	2
Amphora, Torpedo	AC	2
Plain White-AC	AC	6
Plain ware-AC	AC	12
Soft Red-Orange-AC	AC	1
TOTAL Geometric to Classical		35
Black Glaze-He	He	1
Casserole, Cypriot Flanged	ER	12
Cooking ware-ER	ER	4
Cooking ware, ER Cooking Pot	ER	2
Cooking ware, Offset Rim Pot	ER	1
Cooking ware, Offset Rim Pot B	ER	1
Cypriot Sigillata	ER	1
Eastern Sigillata A	ER	1
Amphora, Pseudo-Koan	HER	1
TOTAL Hellenistic to Early Roman		24
African Red Slip	LR	2
African Red Slip 50	LR	1
Amphora-LR	LR	13
Amphora, LR 1	LR	11
Basin-LR	LR	23
Basin, Piecrust Rim	LR	3
Coarse ware-LR	LR	6
Coarse ware, LR Wheel-Ridged	LR	5
Cooking ware-LR	LR	2
Cypriot Red Slip	LR	1
Cypriot Red Slip 1	LR	1
Cypriot Red Slip 2	LR	3
Cypriot Red Slip 9	LR	1
Flat-Grooved	LR	40
Frying Pan	LR	2
Phocaean ware (LR C)	LR	1
Phocaean ware 3	LR	4
Pithos-LR	LR	1
Tile-LR	LR	2
TOTAL Late Roman		122
Amphora-Hi	Hi	1
Pithos-PC	PC	4
Tile, Corinthian Pan	PC	1
Tile, Cover	PC	1
Tile, Ridged and Rounded	PC	4
Coarse ware-Unk	Unk	37
Cooking ware-Unk	Unk	6
TOTAL		235

At the summit, *Sarcopoterium* was the sole dominant at 50% ground cover. In all, nine 10 x 10 m quadrats were sampled across the north and eastern slopes of the knoll and adjacent to the site.

Using all species variables in the quadrats, the cluster analysis grouped the quadrat sampling units into three clusters without any obviously meaningful groups. More significantly, sampling units from the control transect were not sorted into a separate cluster but grouped within clusters containing sampling units from on-site quadrats. A second CA returned a grouping of three clusters with a clear separation of the off-site sampling units from the on-site (see figure 4.38). On the knoll, the sampling units were sorted into two clusters, one comprised of units in the midslope areas of the north and eastern sides of the knoll and the other of units from the footslopes and summit.

Generalizing from these data, it appears that the midslope was characterized by higher densities of roof tile pieces and building blocks, while the footslopes and summit cluster areas were characterized by higher densities of pottery sherds. Since these areas corresponded to the locations of the clusters, we concluded tentatively that the vegetation array was commensurate with these different aspects of the site. We also concluded that the clusters themselves should be considered the vegetation "indicator areas" for the remote sensing investigation. Accordingly, the three clusters were carried forward into the satellite imagery interpretation as separate training areas and light signatures. The classification of the alluvial subregion using these signatures and background signatures for grain fields, grasslands, pine, and other batha heath lands, showed that the vegetation on SCY101 was a distinct thematic grouping of pixels seldom repeated in the surrounding area (plate XXX).

SCY116: POLITIKO *KOKKINOROTSOS* 1: ARCHAIC ORE ROASTING AND SMELTING SITE

SCY116 was first surveyed by ordinary transect. The field team noted that one of the bulldozed terraces in this area cut through stratified layers of furnace conglomerate and tap slags, roasting conglomerate, and crushed iron and copper ores—remains similar to those recorded at Agrokipia *Kriadhis* (SCY022). This area was thus designated a POSI, and the archaeometallurgical team recorded and sampled the remains systematically. This was fortunate timing, as a revisit by team members in 2000 revealed that the site had been entirely destroyed by bulldozing for the creation of new fields.

SCY116 is located just beyond the eastern side of the Kokkinorotsos gossan within sight of a dense slag scatter (SCY121). A collapsed adit, covered by trees and pine needles, lies about 10 to 12 m to the south on the same terrace. In front of the adit were compacted layers of silica and crushed gossan (with some large pieces of gossan). These do not appear to be roasting remains but rather mining waste. No datable material is available in relation to this adit.

Given this diversity of material, SCY116 may be regarded as a possible ore roasting and smelting site, substantially disturbed by bulldozers creating terraces for reforestation. A large part of the remains was removed in the cutting of this terrace, and the top surface was covered by extraneous material that washed down the slope (presumably when the road which runs along the top was constructed). An additional complication is that pine trees have grown on the slope, obscuring this top surface. SCY116 consists of a 4-m section as well as a bowl-shaped depression that cuts into the side of the hill along that section (figure 4.39). Because this is an active landscape, we cannot ascertain whether this depression is artificial or natural (perhaps created by water erosion in a part of the section which consists almost exclusively of finely crushed iron oxides).

To expose the stratigraphy better, the section was cleaned back with trowels and small picks. Material in danger of being lost during this process was collected even if its exact location was not clear. After cleaning, the section was recorded in a detailed drawing, which shows a total of 35 layers in the main section (figure 4.40), and 12 others in the rear wall of the eroded bowl-depression (figure 4.41).

The layers consisted of furnace and tap slag (most of which was badly corroded), crushed and in some cases finely ground ore and charcoal. The furnace conglomerate and tap slags were observed in layers 11 and 26 and layers 7 and 14. Roasting conglomerate was observed in layers 13 and 14 but in fact it was not as abundant as at Agrokipia *Kriadhis* (SCY022; see chapter 4.1). Roasted and/or crushed iron or copper, however, was plentiful and in section A–B was observed in layers 3, 5, 8, 11 to 14, 16, 18, 21 to 23, 25 to 30, and 32 to 34, and in section C–D in layers 2 to 5 and 7 to 12. In an effort to understand

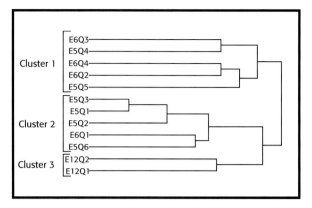

Figure 4.38 SCY101: dendrogram showing cluster analysis of geobotanical data

the formation of these deposits of finely crushed material, we took a sediment column sample of these layers within the bowl depression for micromorphological analysis; the results are discussed below.

Apart from a piece of furnace floor and a tuyère fragment found before cleaning the section and which may in fact have washed down the slope, no refractory material was recovered from any of these strata. Nor was any pottery observed in the section, although some Cypro-Archaic sherds were collected in the immediate vicinity (units 3103–3104); more Cypro-Archaic and other Iron Age pottery (about 50 sherds) was collected on and around the main slag deposit 100 m to the west (SCY121; unit 3096). Given the eroded and disturbed nature of these surface finds, they cannot be linked directly with metallurgical activities at SCY116.

Charcoal, on the other hand, was abundant in most layers of SCY116, while layer 20 consisted almost entirely of this material. Three samples were chosen for ^{14}C dating (appendix B); the results fall within the Iron Age, from the eighth to fifth centuries BC, which is in close accord with the pottery evidence. The Archaic period has always been regarded as one of intense metallurgical activity, and here we may see one of its earlier phases.

ARCHAEOMETALLURGICAL ACTIVITIES

In the attempt to understand the processes taking place in this POSI, a combination of analytical techniques was used on seven samples of various types of slag from the stratified deposits (see chapter 5.4). Bulk chemical analysis revealed slags very rich in iron (the iron oxide content ranged from 59.4 to 70.7%) and very low in manganese. This is not surprising,

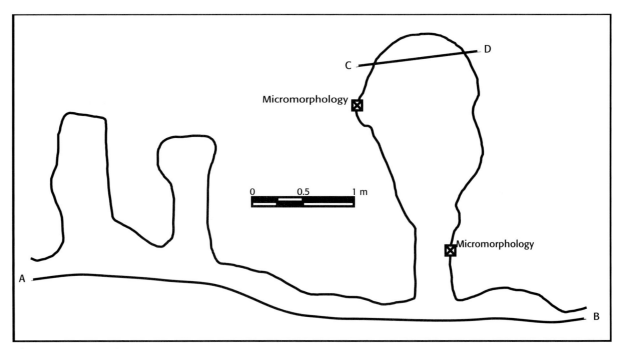

Figure 4.39 SCY116: plan

but it is generally assumed that the use of manganese as a fluxing agent dates to the Roman period. Microscopic analysis showed the iron to be in the form of fayalite crystals, as well as wüstite (the iron oxide). The copper content is variable and ranges from 0.7% to 7.6%. The highest percentage comes from one of the so-called furnace conglomerate pieces (Sample SCY116–30). Optical microscopy and microanalysis with a SEM detected matte inclusions in all of the analyzed samples. These samples, therefore, clearly resulted from a primary smelt of sulfide ores. Samples SCY116-30 and SCY116-32, however, contained copper prills with iron-rich globules. These perhaps indicate that secondary smelting of matte to black copper was also taking place in the same workshop.

With respect to the layers of finely crushed material that characterize this POSI, Dr. Peter Grave conducted micromorphological analysis. Within the sediment column were detected numerous fine rounded pores, which suggest steam bubbles along with carbonized plant remains. These indicate that at least some of the layers, of the very fine-grained sediment horizontal strata, were formed while the material was still hot. In other words, these layers are very likely related to ore roasting processes. The fact that chemical analysis of this material has not detected any significant amount of copper or sulfur should not surprise us. These are spoil heaps and waste dumps: it is natural that they should consist chiefly of detritus, because of the low content of copper metal. The copper rich part of the ore would have been processed further to produce copper metal and was only an intermediate product of the overall process.

In this relatively small section of a metallurgical waste heap we found crushed iron oxides, furnace conglomerate, and smelting slags deriving from both a primary and a secondary smelt, representing multiple aspects of producing black copper from sulfide ores. The fact that the site is located in direct proximity to ore deposits, as well as to fuel sources, makes a sharp contrast with other sites such as Phorades (SCY100) which is earlier, or Mitsero *Koulouphakis* (SCY021) and *Sykamies* (SCY024) which are much later. It is, however, similar to contemporary sites within the survey region, for example Agrokipia *Kriadhis* and Mitsero *Kokkinoyia*, as well as Ayia Varvara *Almyras*, where again the full sequence is well recorded (Fasnacht 1999; Fasnacht and Kassianidou 1992).

SCY123: POLITIKO *PHORADES* 3: ARCHAIC SETTLEMENT

SCY123 was first surveyed by ordinary transect. From the large scatter of pottery (and a few tiles and lithics) on the summit of this knoll, twenty-six sherds were collected in 1995. The concentration of material was limited to the top of the knoll, perhaps because the

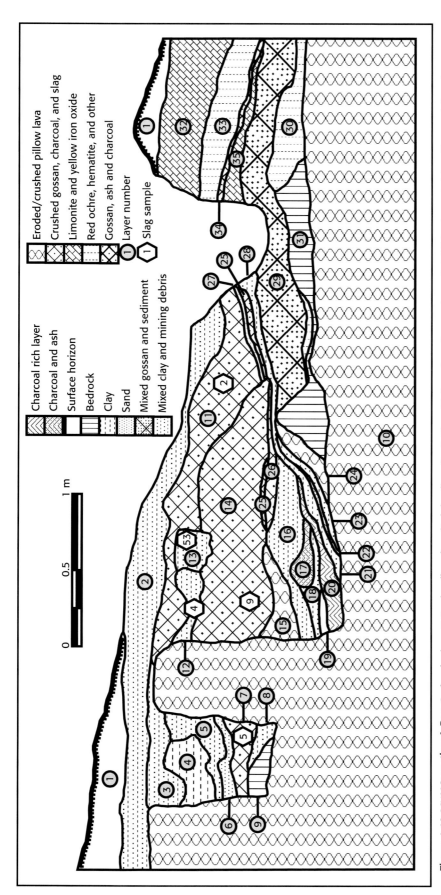

Figure 4.40 SCY116: section A-B: **1**, Surface horizon; **2**, Erosionally redeposited clay, limonite; **3**, Clay with limonite and some charcoal; **4**, White clay material; **5**, Clay, marl, limonite, some charcoal; **6**, Sand, marl, some charcoal; **7**, Slag with charcoal and limonite, crushed pillow lava; **8**, Limonite, some charcoal, some crushed pillow lava; **9**,Bedrock? (looks like 15); **10**, Crushed eroded pillow lava, marled clay; **11**, Crushed roasted haematite, slag, limonite, charcoal; **12**, Clay, marl, limonite, some charcoal; **13**, Ash, charcoal, limonite, refractory material; **14**, Slag, charcoal, crushed pillow lava, refractory, limonite; **15**, Crushed pillow lava; **16**, Clay, marl, limonite, some charcoal; **17**, Ash, charcoal, crushed pillow lavas; **18**, Clay, marl, limonite, some charcoal; **19**, Marl; **20**, Charcoal, some marl; **21**, Clay, marl, limonite, some charcoal; **22**, Dark brown soft fine earth, charcoal; **23**, Clay, marl, limonite, some charcoal; **24**, Clay, marl, some crushed pillow lava; **25**, Fine yellow clay and marl, limonite charcoal; **26**, Crushed slag, some charcoal, some limonite; **27**, Fine red iron oxides; **28**, Fine red iron oxides; **29**, Pieces of marly gossan; **30**, Ochre-coloured fine material; **31** Gray pillow lava bedrock; **32**, Finely crushed yellow ochre, a little charcoal; **33**, Yellow/red iron oxides, crushed limestone, charcoal; **34**, Fine red and purple iron oxides, charcoal; **35**, Yellow limonite, crushed pillow lava

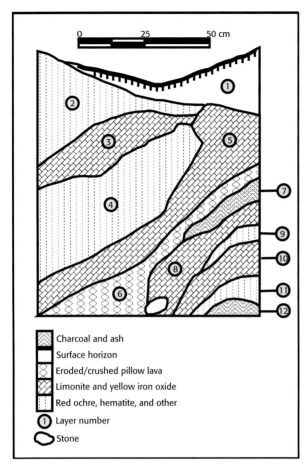

0 25 50 cm

Charcoal and ash
Surface horizon
Eroded/crushed pillow lava
Limonite and yellow iron oxide
Red ochre, hematite, and other
① **Layer number**
◯ **Stone**

Figure 4.41 SCY116: section C–D: **1**, Surface horizon; **2**, Reddish limonite, red iron oxides; **3**, Limonite, marl; **4**, Iron oxides, limonite, marl, charcoal; **5**, Marl/clay, some limonite; **6**, Crushed pillow lava; **7**, Ash, limonite, iron oxides, charcoal; **8**, Limonite, sand; **9**, Red iron oxides, charcoal, sand; **10**, Limonite, marl; **11**, Red iron oxide, some charcoal; **12**, Ash, iron oxide, limonite, charcoal

south and west sides have collapsed or eroded away. Traces of walls were visible on the top of knoll, though much of the stonework seems to have tumbled down the southern slope, perhaps originally robbed or destroyed by human agency (figure 4.42). The unexpectedly large boulders on SCY123 are imported diabase, the nearest source for which is the Pedhiaios River Valley.

An intensive 1 m gridded collection of material from SCY123 was carried out in 1997 (figure 4.42). An initial grid was laid out covering 8 x 8 m on a north/south axis, with a 2 m extension on the eastern edge. During three different phases of collection, 335 sherds were collected. The pottery from this POSI is predominantly Cypro-Archaic to Cypro-Classical with a small amount of possibly late Cypro-Geometric material (table 4.17). SCY123 is the source of most

of SIA 7's decorated wares, for example White Painted (cat. 1596.1.1, 3096.2.1), Bichrome (cat. 1629.2.1), Red Slip and Black-on-Red, as well as for most imports, for example Red Slip and Greek Black Glaze (cat. 1595.3.1). This contrasts with SCY101, where the majority of Plain White wares were found. In addition to the domestic wares at SCY123, three roof tile fragments, two lamps (cat. 1625.3.1) and a single loomweight (cat. S-0061) were found, while two basin fragments suggest washing or cooking activities. It may be noted, then, that SCY123 contains not only the greatest amount of Iron Age material within SIA 7 but also represents the widest range of activities: storage—cat. 1596.1.1, 3097.3.1; cooking—cat. S-0067; industrial; possibly serving—cat. 1625.5C.1, 1629.2.1 and S-0066; and weaving. It is also where we find elite imported materials such as Greek pottery.

SCY125: POLITIKO *KANNOURIS*: ANCIENT CHECK DAM

This POSI is a small check dam constructed of large stones preserved on a ridge about 100 m upstream (southwest) from Politiko *Phorades* (SCY100). Large (0.3 to 0.6 m diameter), subangular to subrounded stone boulders of basalt, diabase, and gossan are arranged in nested, stacked courses, approximately 3 m high and 8 m wide (including what are likely collapsed blocks at its perimeter); its preserved length is about 20 m. The uppermost course is two boulders wide. The lower courses are permeated with a fine-grained (sand to silt) matrix.

This structure is clearly of human manufacture. Many of the boulders are exotic to the Kouphos River drainage. Most of the stones reveal little sign of water wear, which is interpreted to indicate that they were not carried by and collected from the Kouphos. Large, subangular blocks of gossan came from quarries located several hundred meters to the northwest on or around Politiko *Kokkinorotsos*. Other sources of these types of stones derive from an even greater distance.

The Kouphos displays a distinct change in geomorphological character at this structure. Overall the Kouphos River has parallel sets of terraces along straight reaches marked by angular bends largely governed by the nature of the underlying basalt bedrock. The floodplain is distinctly wider and higher behind the dam. Immediately upstream from the Kouphos is a set of nested, curvilinear terraces along

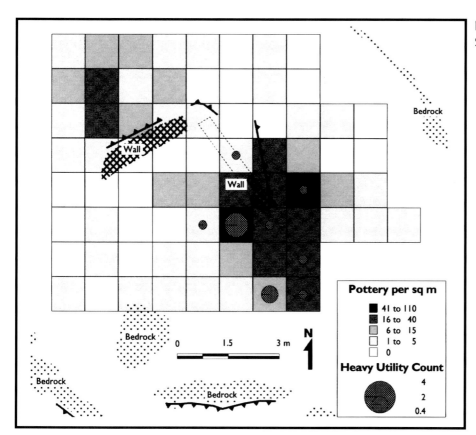

Figure 4.42
SCY123: walls and grid

the cut bank of the channel. Such terraces in this position are unusual; they are present elsewhere only on the inside or slip-off slope of channel bends. SCY125 is on the inside of a slip-off slope of the meandering Kouphos River.

The purpose of the structure is to impede the flow of water in the Kouphos. It is less clear if the intention was to store water (dam) or to trap sediments (check dam). The dam was constructed across the bottom of what was likely to have been the active channel of the Kouphos River at the time. It is oriented at right angles to the fall line of the Kouphos. Exposed on the upstream side of the dam are fine-grained deposits that may represent sediment trapped behind the structure. The fine-grained material within the structure represents constructed infilling or trapped sediments.

The spatial and stratigraphic relationships of the structure with nearby features provides some insight into its purpose. The base elevation of the structure is about 2 to 2.5 m above the bed of the modern channel, which coincides with the channel elevation at the time the smelting site at SCY100 (Phorades) was in operation. Hence, one possible purpose would have been to store water for the smelting site. How-

ever, other evidence and reasoning lead us to conclude that it was a check dam. The use of check dams on this landscape was common in all periods, and SCY125 could be the earliest of its type. Although less likely, a dam construction date of earlier than or contemporary with the smelting at SCY100 cannot be ruled out. Whether or not it was originally designed for water storage, its purpose is essentially that of check dam, as it effectively trapped at least 2 m of sediment. Incision migrating up the Kouphos led to the attack on the pillow basalt at the northern end of the dam, where it is relatively easier to erode compared to the massive boulder structure. As the channel migrated to the north it has undercut the ridge topped by SCY123. Pottery and construction stones from this ridge-top site ran down the eroded cut-bank. Thus, the dam cannot be significantly older than the Iron Age structure at SCY123. The prism of alluvial fill behind the dam allows for formation and preservation of the unique terraces of the Kouphos that are present here. The dam itself is now being undercut and eroded away by a downstream migrating meander of the Kouphos River that is attacking the underlying basalt bedrock.

Figure 4.43 SCY119: mining adit (twentieth century?)

Table 4.17 SCY123: analyzed pottery

Chronotype	Period	Qty
Amphora-Ar	Ar	2
Cooking ware-Ar [S-0067]	Ar	23
Green ware-Ar	Ar	20
Pithos-Ar	Ar	1
Plain ware-Ar [S-0066]	Ar	10
Red Slip-Ar	Ar	1
Soft Red-Orange-Ar	Ar	1
Black Glaze-Cl	Cl	1
Cooking ware-Cl	Cl	26
Greek Red Slip	Cl	2
Plain ware-Cl	Cl	10
Plain White-Cl	Cl	15
Green ware-Cl	GAC	6
Amphora-AC	AC	14
Black Slip-AC	AC	2
Cooking ware-AC	AC	61
Loomweight-AC [S-0061]	AC	1
Plain ware-AC	AC	36
Plain White-AC	AC	4
White Painted-AC	AC	2
Coarse ware-Unk	Unk	1
Cooking ware-Unk	Unk	3
Fine ware-Unk	Unk	1
Unknown	Unk	1
TOTAL		244

Note: Figures in brackets refer to cataloged items (see chapter 5.1 for pottery, chapter 5.3 for loomweight).

SLAG HEAPS AND ADITS ON THE GOSSAN RIDGE

On the top and flanks of the long gossan ridge which runs along the western edge of SIA 7 are a series of slag heaps, slag scatters, and adits. These were discovered partly by block survey, partly by purposive exploration; each was recorded individually (table 4.18; figure 4.43).

SCY121: POLITIKO *KOKKINOROTSOS* 6: SLAG HEAP AND GEOBOTANY

The slag heap at SCY121 lies over a spur in an elevated position on the ridge line south of the gossan. Much of it was exposed in a road cut, hence the discovery of 22 sherds and five tuyère fragments, dating mainly to the Archaic and Classical periods. The geobotanist examined seven 10 x 10 m quadrats in two transects crossing the slag heap. One transect, over the larger and more northerly part of the slag heap, has a tree canopy of *Pinus brutia* with an average density of 25% site coverage. Beneath this the vegetation is dominated by *Cistus villosus* and *Pinus* scrub.

At the other part of the slag heap, three quadrats, one over the slag deposits and one on the adjoining nonslag substrate, revealed similar vegetation: a *Pinus* tree canopy (15% density) over a shrub community of *Cistus villosus/Fumana procumbens* with *Thymus capitatus* as a subdominant. In both cases the sampled vegetation on the nonslag substrate was upslope from the slag. An initial cluster analysis, using both the indicator species and the indicator community levels, merely sorted the sampling units into clusters corresponding to the original transects (figure 4.44). However, with PCA, ordination within the clusters separated the sampling units on slag from those off-slag in both groups, when species variables with > 2% cover were used (figure 4.45).

BLOCK SURVEY

Geometric to Classical. The only pre-Iron Age material apart from SCY100 (Phorades) was a possible Bronze Age body sherd from SCY123, but more than 600 sherds from Cypro-Geometric to Classical date were identified. Densities are nowhere very great, but the eroded nature of the landscape must be taken into account (plate XXXI). The principal concentrations come from the less eroded part of the valley in

Table 4.18 SIA 7: POSIs on gossan ridge

ID	Locality	Unit	Grid Ref.	Description
SCY117	Kokkinorotsos 2	3089	519090/3874880	Heap of tap slag; 3-m diameter
SCY118	Kokkinorotsos 3	–	519125/3874960	Small heap of tap slag; bulldozed
SCY119	Kokkinorotsos 4	3071	519110/3874900	Adit, 15+ m., figure 4. 45
SCY120	Kokkinorotsos 5	3072	519165/3874885	Adit, 3+ m. Descends at 45°
SCY121	Kokkinorotsos 6	3096	518975/3874550	Slag heap with Ar–Cl pottery
SCY347	Kokkinorotsos 8	–	518975/3874765	Mining gallery in gossan
SCY348	Kokkinorotsos 9	–	518915/3874620	Modern drill/prospecting hole
SCY349	Kokkinorotsos 10	–	518840/3874510	Shallow mining hollows
SCY350	Kokkinorotsos 11	–	519110/3874820	Mining gallery or tunnel
SCY351	Kokkinorotsos 12	–	519120/3874905	Open cast pit? Very eroded
SCY352	Kokkinorotsos 13	–	519120/3874850	Shallow pit in gossan
SCY353	Kokkinorotsos 14	–	518955/3874820	Mining pit
SCY354	Kokkinorotsos 15	–	518965/3874835	Collapsed adit, 4+ m long
SCY355	Kokkinorotsos 16	–	519120/3874945	Mining hollow with gossan pile
SCY356	Kokkinorotsos 17	–	519025/3874915	Mining hollows? Eroded

the north, at SCY101 and in a series of plowed fields 200 m to its west. In both areas the pottery index is never more than 5000—considerably less than at SIA 6. Further into the valley, the main concentration is unsurprisingly at SCY123 (although the pie chart in plate XXXI shows only pottery from transect survey, not from the gridding of the site). Two other minor peaks in density coincide interestingly with archaeometallurgical activities: SCY118 and SCY121, both slag heaps with tap slag. A light scatter across the entire SIA, in spite of the considerable erosion, demonstrates the generally high level of activity in the valley during the Archaic and Classical periods.

Although no Cypro-Geometric (CG) I or II sherds were found in SIA 7, a few pieces dating either to CG III or Cypro Archaic (CA) I have been identified (table 4.19). Included are the following Geometric/Archaic examples: one White Painted rim fragment, one Black-on-Red sherd, and a Bichrome jug fragment (cat. 1629.2.1). Of 142 sherds that may be classified as Cypro-Archaic, few belong to CA I (for example, cat. 1596.1.1 and S-0066). More plain ware shallow bowl rims may be dated to the CA II period; also of CA II date are the carinated body sherds of a Bichrome jug and a White Painted vessel (cat. 3096.2.1). A kitchen ware jug from SCY123 (cat. S-0067) is similar in profile to CA II vessels from Kourion. Among 136 sherds datable to the Classical period, we note an amphora rim of Cypro-Classical I (cat. 3097.3.1) and a bowl of Cypro-Classical II date (cat. 1625.5C.1). Sherds from imported material, such as a Greek Red Slip bowl with inturned rim, also suggest that SIA 7 was inhabited during the Classical era,

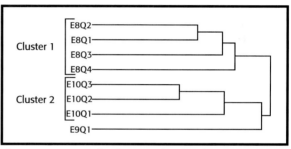

Figure 4.44 SCY121: dendrogram showing cluster analysis

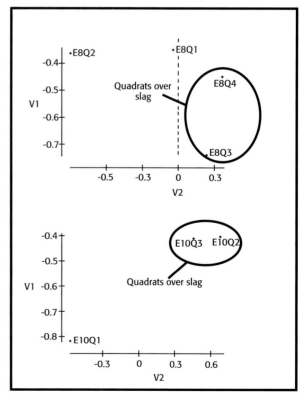

Figure 4.45 SCY121: PCA scatterplots showing separation of on-slag and off-slag samples

Table 4.19 SIA 7: analyzed pottery from block survey (excluding units 1599–1615)

Chronotype	Period	Qty	Chronotype	Period	Qty
Red Slip-PeB	PeB	1	Coarse ware-ER	ER	3
Base Ring 1	PoB	1	Cooking ware-ER	ER	1
			Cooking ware, ER Cook Pot	ER	3
TOTAL Prehistoric		2	Cooking ware, Offset Rim Pot A	ER	1
			Cooking ware, Square Rim Pot	ER	1
White Painted-Geo	Geo	1	Cypriot Sigillata	ER	3
Amphora-Ar	Ar	13	Eastern Sigillata A	ER	2
Basin-Ar	Ar	1	Lamp-ER	ER	1
Bichrome-Ar	Ar	2	African Red Slip	LR	3
Black-on-Red-Ar	Ar	1	Amphora-LR	LR	4
Cooking ware-Ar	Ar	22	Amphora, LR 1	LR	2
Green ware-Ar	Ar	2	Basin, Piecrust Rim	LR	1
Pithos-Ar	Ar	1	Coarse ware-LR	LR	3
Plain ware-Ar	Ar	24	Coarse ware, LR Wheel-Ridged	LR	6
Red Slip-Ar	Ar	6	Cypriot Red Slip	LR	1
Soft Red-Orange-Ar	Ar	10	Flat-Grooved	LR	1
White Painted-Ar [1596.1.1, 3096.2.1]	Ar	4	Frying Pan	LR	2
Wide Shallow Bowl-Ar	Ar	1			
Black-on-Red-GA	GA	1	TOTAL Hellenistic to Late Roman		44
Amphora-Cl [3097.3.1]	Cl	6	Cypriot W6	Ott	7
Black Glaze-Cl	Cl	1	Pithos-Ott	Ott	1
Cooking ware-Cl	Cl	14	Coarse ware-Mod	Mod	1
Greek Red Slip	Cl	3	Contemporary Imported Asian	Mod	2
Lamp-Cl	Cl	1	Cypriot W7	Mod	2
Plain ware-Cl	Cl	15	Water Pipe-Mod	Mod	2
Plain White-Cl	Cl	28	Cypriot W1	MM	1
Red Slip-Cl	Cl	1	Cypriot W4	MM	15
Coarse ware-GAC	GAC	1	Glazed ware	MM	1
Green ware-GAC	GAC	8			
White Painted-GAC	GAC	2	TOTAL Medieval to Modern		32
Amphora-AC	AC	30	Plain White-HA	HA	6
Amphora, Pithoid	AC	1	Pithos-PC	PC	25
Amphora, Torpedo	AC	4	Tile-PC	PC	11
Basin-AC	AC	1	Tile, Corinthian	PC	1
Bichrome-AC	AC	1	Tile, Corinthian Pan	PC	7
Black Glaze-AC	AC	1	Coarse ware-Unk	Unk	158
Coarse ware-AC	AC	11	Cooking ware-Unk	Unk	8
Cooking ware-AC	AC	35	Fine ware-Unk	Unk	1
Green ware-AC	AC	2	Unknown	Unk	1
Lamp-AC	AC	1			
Pithos-AC	AC	3	TOTAL		652
Plain ware-AC	AC	75			
Plain White-AC	AC	13			
Red Slip-AC	AC	2			
White Painted-AC	AC	7			
TOTAL Geometric to Classical		356			
Black Glaze-He	He	3			
Fine ware-He	He	3			

Note: Figures in brackets refer to cataloged items (see chapter 5.1).

and some pieces date later to the Hellenistic period (for example, cat. 1595.3.1, 1625.3.1).

Decorated pottery of the Iron Age is present only in limited numbers; most sherds consist of plain wares, large coarse wares, and kitchen wares. Storage, kitchen, and table wares are found throughout SIA 7 but are concentrated in SCY123, SCY101, and SCY121. Most decorated wares and imports were found at SCY123, along with a variety of items suggesting domestic activities (see above). Only 5% of the Geometric to Classical pottery collected consisted of Cypriot decorated wares; most were plain utilitarian wares that probably served food preparation or storage functions. Viewed from the perspective of its pottery, SIA 7 contains mainly domestic elements, including five large pithos fragments as well as transport and other amphorae indicative of permanent storage. No figurines or statuary have been found in this area, nor have any funerary deposits. Such a pattern contrasts with much of the rest of Cyprus during this period (Reyes 1994:104–121).

The inhabitants of the SIA 7 region were most likely linked economically to a polity centered on Tamassos. They lived (SCY123, SCY101) and worked (SCY116) in agricultural, metallurgical and domestic capacities in the hinterland of Tamassos and may have provided some food, ores, or other goods and services to that center, in return for the few luxury items they received, such as imported Greek pottery. There are no indicators of pottery production in the SIA 7 area, and such goods may have been obtained from, for example, Ayios Mnason (SIA 6), a center of pottery production on the outskirts of Tamassos. Finally, the lack of evidence for ceremonial activities in SIA 7 suggests that they would have taken place elsewhere, perhaps in SIA 6 or in Tamassos itself. Many of the known sites from Iron Age Cyprus are funerary or ceremonial in nature (tombs and "sanctuaries"), and the habitational character of POSIs such as SCY123 and SCY101 thus deserves emphasis. Similarly, industrial activities have often been found in connection with sanctuaries (Smith 1997:90–91) but rarely in isolation (compare Fasnacht and Kassianidou 1992) or associated with domestic habitation (cf. Idalion–Gaber and Dever 1996:92–99).

Hellenistic to Roman. There is almost no Hellenistic to Roman material in the southern part of the Kouphos Valley (plate XXXI). Because of the surviving Archaic and Classical material, this cannot be entirely due to erosion. Unlike the Mitsero area, we have no Roman material from the slag heaps, so it seems likely that the copper mines of Kokkinorotsos were not being exploited during this period. The peak of material at SCY101 is abundantly clear, with the densest unit almost reaching a pottery index of 10,000. Both this and the smaller numbers in the fields 200 m to the west show an interesting continuity with the Classical period, unlike the area to the south. The fields to the north and west of SCY101 have a general, very light scatter of pottery. This could conceivably be due to manuring, but considering the bulldozing this area has undergone, the pottery is more likely to have drifted from the main activity areas.

Only seven fine wares sherds from SIA 7 can be dated to the Hellenistic period, all apparently Cypriot made. Survey throughout SIA 7 revealed 40 sherds from the Early Roman period. Only six belonged to fine wares; the remainder were either coarse wares or, primarily, cooking pots. At the same time, there was almost a complete lack of amphorae sherds. The Early Roman fine wares included, primarily, Cypriot Sigillata (locally produced), plus three Eastern Sigillata A pieces from Syria (first to second centuries AD). There were 151 Late Roman sherds, most of them from SCY101 (see above). Of the 31 that came from elsewhere, only three were fine wares—two African Red Slip and one Cypriot Red Slip. The rest were coarse wares with but few cooking pots.

Medieval to Modern. Throughout the area of Kokkinorotsos, there are a few sherds of Medieval to Modern material (Chronotypes W4 and W5), and a total absence of any Byzantine material. There is only one possible Ottoman item, a fragment of curved tile found in an isolated setting (unit 5006) and thus of little significance. Elsewhere in the SCSP area, wherever we find Late Roman material in any quantity, we also find Medieval and Ottoman. This absence of later material is therefore unusual for the survey area and suggests the absence of mining and agriculture in the Kouphos Valley during those periods, despite the Medieval and Ottoman period settlement at Politiko itself.

SLAG DENSITIES

The slag density map for SIA 7 (plate XXXII) reveals unsurprisingly high concentrations around all the slag heaps (SCY117, SCY118, SCY121), and at Politik *Phorades* (SCY100). There are also peaks around two adits

(SCY119, SCY120) and at the presumed roasting and beneficiation area (SCY116). More surprisingly, there are large quantities in several fields west of SCY101 (units 3050–55) that contain noticeable amounts of Iron Age (Archaic) and Late Roman material.

CONCLUSION

With the exception of the copper smelting workshop at Phorades (SCY100), the most notable concentration of archaeometallurgical activity is found on the slopes of Kokkinorotsos or close to its edge. The evidence consists primarily of tap slag, which is probably much later in date than the material from Phorades. SCY116 (Politiko *Kokkinorotsos* 1), situated along the eastern side of the gossan, has a large slag scatter nearby (SCY121) and is defined by an exposed section with stratified layers of roasting conglomerate, furnace lining, and furnace floor. The evidence indicates that SCY116 was a place where black copper was being produced from sulfide ores during the Iron Age. Combined with the extensive evidence for Iron Age, copper-producing workshops at nearby Tamassos, the long-term, industrial significance of the SIA 7 landscape becomes apparent.

It is likely, furthermore, that notable changes occurred not only in the nature of production but also in the spatial organization of production sites, from the Late Bronze Age through the Iron Age to the Roman period. During the Bronze Age, proximity to secondary resources such as water, clay, and fuel seems to have been critical, while the different scale of Iron Age and Roman smelting activity perhaps made it possible for smelting to take place closer to the ores. The Iron Age pattern, at least, is repeated in the SCSP area at Agrokipia *Kriadhis* (SIA 1).

The check dam or revetment wall some 100 m southwest of SCY100 (Politiko *Kannouris*—SCY125) verifies an earlier and different course for the Kouphos River. Geomorphological analyses of this drainage system indicates a pre-Roman date for the dam; if it were contemporary with Phorades, then we have good evidence for the association between water resource management and smelting during the Bronze Age. On the other hand, this check dam could be related to agricultural activities carried out from the Iron Age to Late Roman periods, or even more recent periods. It is important to recognize and emphasize the agricultural and habitational aspects of the SIA 7 landscape.

People have exploited and modified the landscape in and around Politiko *Kokkinorotsos* (SIA 7) for at least four millennia. Much of that activity has focused on extracting the area's copper ore resources, which also will have impacted the environment in other ways, not least through collecting and burning fuel, smelting, building transport and communication routes, and subsistence activities. The dramatic landscape changes that took place during that time, revealed primarily by geomorphological fieldwork, obscure much of our evidence and therefore must be understood and factored into any attempt to interpret the social landscape. At the same time these changes demonstrate the complex interaction between people and their surroundings.

4.8 SIA 8: Mitsero Basin

Compiled by Caroline Whitehill
Fieldwork: Caroline Whitehill, Lisa Wells, and Jay Noller
Soil chemistry: Caroline Whitehill with Jay Noller
Contributions for SIAs and POSIs: Lita Diacopoulos,
Michael Given, Vasiliki Kassianidou, Jay Noller, Kylie Seretis,
Sven Van Lokeren, Lisa Wells

Grid reference: NW corner: 509000/3878500.
                    SE corner: 514000/3873500
Cadastral plan: XXIX/53
Aerial photographs: 1993, run 177, nos. 40–46;
                    run 176, Nos 7–12; run 175,
                    nos. 222–226; run 174, nos.
                    194–196
Survey units: 76–81, 123–239, 503–672,
                    1000–1018, 1253–1267, 1311–
                    1321, 2500–2610, 4000–4051,
                    4088

Mitsero Basin is a 20 km^2 catchment located in the northern foothills of the Troodos Mountains; it is the westernmost drainage basin in the SCSP survey area (plate XXXIII). Intensive geomorphological studies in the Mitsero Basin began in the winter of 1996 and continued during the 1997 and 1998 field seasons. One of SCSP's main goals was to characterize the complex relationship among human landuse, landscape evolution, and the surface distribution of cultural artifacts. Mitsero Basin was chosen for intensive geomorphological study because three SIAs and 22 POSIs lie within it, and because the modern culture and land use of the Mitsero area has been examined in detail.

Table 4.20 Mitsero Basin channel dynamics

Phase	Interpreted Fluvial Process	Channel Dimensions	C14 Age Constraints	Archaeological Age Constraints
1	Deposition-Hat$_1$	Min. dimension = Mitsero Basin	8448–7486 BC	Early Neolithic
2	Incision-Hat$_1$/Bedrock	170 m wide x 5 m deep	Pre-1050 BC	Early Iron Age
3	Deposition-Hat$_2$	160 m wide x 1.5–2 m thick	Pre-AD 1500	Late Medieval
4	Incision-Hat$_2$	≤ 20 m wide x 2–3 m deep	Pre-AD 1550	Late Medieval-Pre-Early Ottoman
5	Deposition-Hat$_3$	≤ 20 m wide x 1–2 m deep	Pre-AD 1889	Early Ottoman
6	Incision-Hat$_3$	5 m wide x 1–2 m deep	Pre-AD 1889–Post AD 1550	Post-Early Ottoman
7	Deposition-Hat$_4$	Point bar	No C14	Modern

Note: Reconstructions based on interpretations of Kryon Neron channel profiles. Age constraints taken from radiocarbon data (appendix B).

The main research goals of the work carried out in the Mitsero Basin were to characterize the alluvial stratigraphy and basin geomorphology and to interpret the relationship among artifact distribution, landscape evolution, and land use throughout the time that humans have occupied the area. A further goal dealt with elsewhere (Whitehill 1999) was to describe, quantify, and compare soil development of the alluvial terraces and hillslopes through soil chrono-sequence (time series), and topo-sequence (hillslope position series) studies.

METHODOLOGY

Field mapping, soil chemistry, and computer analyses all contributed to the integration of field and laboratory data. Field mapping of the basin was carried out using the 1993 1:8000 scale aerial photographs and included the alluvial, hillslope, and anthropogenic features of the entire basin. The Kryon Neron River, the central drainage of the five that constitute the Mitsero Basin, was the subject of more detailed studies. The integration of field-identified geomorphic features, physical and chemical properties of soils, and surface archaeological data provides a means for spatial characterization of the extent of land use impact on landscape evolution and on artifact distribution.

FLUVIAL GEOMORPHOLOGY

Mitsero Basin is drained by five fifth-order channels and has a maximum relief of 320 m. The basin divide has an average elevation of 540 m. The surface area in the alluvial plain region is dominated by the Hat$_1$ terrace, the oldest of four Late Pleistocene-Early Holocene alluvial terraces. The upper basin is underlain by ophiolites and the northernmost areas by the uplifted and tilted contact between the Creta-

ceous pillow basalts and the Miocene limestones, chalks, and marbles of the Dhali and upper Lapithos Groups. *Pinus brutia*, the dominant vegetation of the basin, was planted in a reforestation initiative by the British colonial Forestry Department. This initiative commenced in the late nineteenth century in an effort to restabilize the barren Cypriot landscape. Incipient soil development on the summits and steep hillslope shoulders and the distinct absence of late Holocene alluvial sedimentation suggest a very recent shift to landscape stabilization. Remnants of previous destabilization phases resulting in colluvial activity are preserved in the toeslope sediments that drape the foothill base and are interfingered with the alluvial stratigraphy.

Alluvial stratigraphy of the Kryon Neron records a minimum of seven depositional and erosional phases (table 4.20; figure 4.46). Age constraints for each phase were provided by radiocarbon dating of buried A and B horizons of the three oldest terraces, olive tree dating, and archaeological stratigraphy. Maximum channel dimensions were derived from topographic profiles measured at several channel locations.

Conventional dating of a bulk soil sample from the upper buried horizon (3Abk) of Hat$_1$ profile A060998 suggests that carbon accumulation in this horizon began at least 10,000 years ago, and therefore provides a minimum age for Hat$_1$. Thick deposits (over 2 m in some places) of well-rounded cobble layers of Hat$_1$ cover a broad erosional surface, which can be interpreted as an ancient braided floodplain now stranded more than 6 m above the modern channel. These observations suggest a Late Pleistocene climate wetter than the present day, one that would have supported a river discharge greater than today and represented a period of significant channel widening.

The deep incision of Hat$_1$ and the underlying bedrock (phase 2) represents a shift to a narrowly

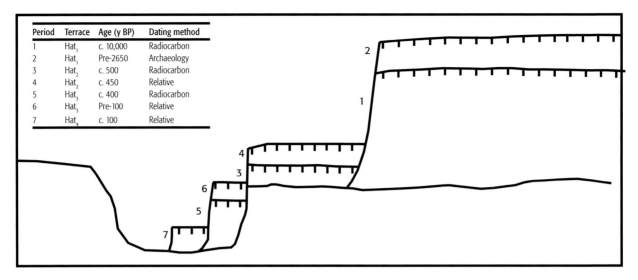

Period	Terrace	Age (y BP)	Dating method
1	Hat₁	c. 10,000	Radiocarbon
2	Hat₁	Pre-2650	Archaeology
3	Hat₂	c. 500	Radiocarbon
4	Hat₂	c. 450	Relative
5	Hat₃	c. 400	Radiocarbon
6	Hat₃	Pre-100	Relative
7	Hat₄	c. 100	Relative

Figure 4.46 Radiocarbon-dated terrace stratigraphy

incising river. The predominant channel activity of the past 9500 years has been deep incision with net sediment loss. The end of this incision phase predates AD 1430 to 1535 (the maximum age of Hat₂). This means that for over 8000 years the channels of the Mitsero Basin incised vertically more than 5 m in depth while cutting laterally a maximum of 170 m to create a new channel cross section and profile.

The deposition of Hat₂ (phase 3) occurred sometime in the Medieval period. Hat₂ was created by a 1 m deep infilling of the scoured channel, which had been created during phase 2. Not long after the deposition of the Hat₂ sediments (< 100 year period), river dynamics shifted to incision (phase 4) of the 2 to 3 m deep channel at the end of phase 3.

Phase 4 is similar to phase 2 in that the river channel width and depth were dramatically reduced, bedrock incision occurred, and the result was a new bedrock channel 2 m wide and 3 m deep. Sediments of Hat₃ filled the bedrock channel during phase 5 (Early Ottoman period), and were then incised to bedrock depth (phase 6). Terrace sediments of Hat₃ and Hat₄ are slip-off slope deposits formed during the early Modern to Modern Phase 7.

The channel dimensions of Mitsero Basin have decreased through time with two distinct and dramatic changes in base level (phases 2 and 4). The amount of sediment transported decreased from the late Pleistocene-early Holocene deposition to mid-late Holocene deposition, the result of a change to a semi-arid climate and decreased tectonic activity (Poole et al. 1991). The change in erosional mechanisms from climate-dominated to anthropogenic-moderated pro-

duced a change in the nature of the sediments transported. The youngest sediments of Hat₁ are characterized by coarse, rounded, cobble-rich channel fills, 1 to 3 m thick, which crosscut the modern channel system. Sediments of Hat₂, Hat₃, and Hat₄ contain gravel-sized, subrounded to subangular clasts in a predominantly sandy matrix. Fining-upwards sequences associated with flood deposition are common.

As defined here, phases 1 through 7 are the simplest possible chain of phases that can explain this stratigraphy. However, more than 8000 years of stratigraphy are missing between the deposition of Hat₁ and Hat₂. Accordingly, it is difficult to say whether or not this represents a continuous period of incision or whether sedimentological and archaeological data have been lost. The absence of any remnants of intervening stratigraphy indicates that the early Holocene was characterized by erosion in this basin. An explanation for this erosion may be tied to a change in land use and population density or it may be negative evidence for an abrupt and short change to a wetter climate about 5000 years ago.

Overall, the history of alluvial sedimentation in Mitsero Basin is similar to that seen in previous studies of Mediterranean rivers (Vita Finzi 1969; van Andel and Zangger 1990; van Andel et al. 1990; Inbar 1992; various papers in Lewin et al. 1995). There are two distinct periods of alluviation, late Pleistocene-early Holocene sedimentation, and mid-late Holocene sedimentation. Sediments of the late Pleistocene-early Holocene were lain as a result of both intense climate change marking the end of Pleistocene glaciation and of increased

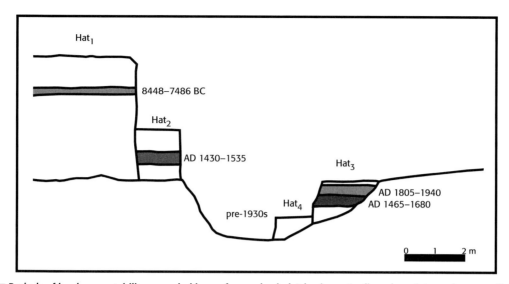

Figure 4.47 Periods of landscape stability recorded by surface or buried A horizons (radiocarbon dates as in appendix B)

tectonic activity in the Mediterranean region (Vita Finzi 1969; van Andel and Zangger 1990; Bull 1988; Poole et al. 1991). Pleistocene sediments are characterized by thick, cobble-rich channel fills typical of a broad, braided river system. Sedimentation of the mid-late Holocene period may be attributed to an increase in population and land use, especially deforestation, agriculture, and pastoralism. Van Andel and others have challenged Vita Finzi's model of climatically driven "Younger" and "Older" alluvial fills. From their research, they conclude that middle to late Holocene alluvial sedimentation in Mediterranean valleys coincided with an increase in clear-cutting for mining, wartime and domestic timber needs, as well as an increased need to farm marginal lands. Later studies have also attributed middle- to late-Holocene Valley fill to an increase in land use intensity. The Holocene stratigraphy of the Mitsero Basin is much younger than that observed in other Mediterranean valleys and the record of land use is therefore far less complete in Mitsero Basin.

HOLOCENE SOIL DEVELOPMENT

Soils and Landscape Stability. Previous studies have noted the significance of using soil development as a proxy for interpreting the duration of landscape stability (McFadden 1988; Holliday 1992; Ferring 1992; Noller 1993; Mandel 1988). Soil formation begins only once a surface has stabilized and all alluvial or colluvial deposition has ceased. The presence of buried A horizons represent past landscape

stability that was disturbed by an alluvial or colluvial depositional event (figure 4.47; Holliday 1992; McFadden 1988).

The alluvial soils of Mitsero Basin record a minimum of seven periods of landscape stability, represented as surface or buried A horizons (figure 4.47). Numeric and relative dating constraints place these periods of landscape stability of Mitsero Basin at about 10,000 years BP, pre-2650 BP, circa 500 BP, circa 450 BP, circa 400 BP, pre-100/post-400 BP, and circa 100 BP. The surface of Hat_1 has been stable since at least the Iron Age (pre-2650 BP). The landscape during the Medieval and Ottoman periods was characterized by brief periods of stability ($\leq$ 50 years), marked by sedimentation during short-lived events such as floods.

Soils and Human Land Use. A major aim of this investigation is to integrate pedological, archaeological, and geological data into a comprehensive history of surface processes and land-use impact. The intimate relationship between these three components cannot be overestimated. To understand one of them fully, the dynamic interface of the three must first be explained (Butzer 1982; Birkeland 1984; Van Andel and Runnels 1987; Holliday 1992). Since the Neolithic period, human occupation of the landscape has been motivated, sustained, and terminated by the availability of arable soils. This intimate relationship between soil conservation, settlement patterns, and cultural viability has been the topic of several recent papers (Holliday 1992; Sandor 1992; Noller and Wells N.D.; Wells 2001).

Cultural land use in Mitsero Basin has had a definitive impact on the rate and degree of soil development. Evidence of these effects exists in the form of soil conservation through terracing, manuring, or plowing and in the form of a severely denuded landscape. The alluvial soil stratigraphy attests to anthropogenic landscape instability. The soils of Hat_2 and Hat_3 terraces have qualities of advanced soil development (structure and clay films) that did not form in such young soils. These features have been recycled from hillslope soils that were abruptly stripped from the landscape due to deforestation and soil mismanagement. The hillslope soils were incorporated into the alluvial system and deposited with much of their genetic features intact. Again, this soil recycling accounts for the relatively slower rate of soil development observed in comparing the Mitsero Soil Development Index (SDI) with that of the Sacramento and Merced study areas in California (soils considered comparable to those of the Mediterranean area).

A complementary study of the phosphate trace of human land use and settlement has determined that soils of settlement and of agricultural employment are enriched in phosphates (Sandor 1992). Results of phosphorus analyses of the Mitsero Basin show an increase in total extractable phosphorus of surface A horizons with increasing terrace age. The thick anthropic epipedon (organically enriched plowed surface) of Hat_1 is high in phosphorus levels as a result of agriculture and manuring. Other than this occurrence, the anthropogenic phosphate signature in the Mitsero Basin is subtle.

GEOARCHAEOLOGY

The geoarchaeological component of the field study of SIA 8 is twofold. First, it aims to provide a geomorphological interpretation of the modern landscape, landscape evolution, and land-use impact that addresses SCSP concerns regarding artifact distribution and land use impact. The absence, presence, or distribution of cultural artifacts can be understood fully only when surficial processes are taken into consideration (Butzer 1982; Holliday 1992; Beach 1998; Noller and Wells N.D.). Second, this study aims to provide an archaeological context for basin geomorphology. Can the archaeological data help geologists interpret the sedimentary and soil stratigraphic histories and the causes of changes observed?

The pottery distribution maps show that cultural material in the Mitsero Basin is concentrated on the slopes or at the base of Kriadhis (SIA 3) and Lambadhousa (SIA 4) but is nearly nonexistent in the broad alluvial valley south of modern-day Mitsero (plate XXXIII). There is a small increase in Medieval through Modern pottery on interfluve sections of Hat_1. The Mitsero landscape is a highly impacted and eroded basin that has only begun to restabilize in the past century. It is not surprising, then, that there is an impressive absence of cultural data on the southern hillslopes (headwaters) and in the alluvial valley south of the modern village. Although we can account for cultural occupation of the basin since the Chalcolithic period, and the upper terrace is as old as late Pleistocene, very few cultural artifacts are preserved.

There are clear geomorphological reasons for the relatively high densities of Classical to Ottoman pottery found at SIA 4 (Mitsero *Mavrovounos*) and SIA 3 (Mitsero *Kouloupakhis*). At Mavrovounos most of the surface artifacts derive from an incised series of sediments that originally accumulated behind a check dam, or else are preserved more or less in situ because of the greater stability of the slag heaps and structures (chapter 4.4). Most of the pottery at Kouloupakhis is located on early Holocene alluvial terraces (Hat_1 and a lower terrace Hat_2) and appears to be in situ. This implies that the alluvial stratigraphy preserved around SIA 3 is considerably older than the alluvial stratigraphy mapped and dated in the broader fourth order valley, and was probably in place by at least the Early Iron Age.

As the transects progress south of Mitsero village, pottery densities drop off significantly. Protohistoric Bronze Age (Late Bronze) to Iron Age material is not represented at all in the archaeological record of the fourth-order basin, while the Archaic to Byzantine periods are only sparsely observed in two field units on isolated interfluves of Hat_1. The Medieval to Modern periods are better represented, though Ottoman pottery dominates the alluvial landscape and is concentrated on the interfluves of Hat_1.

Both archaeological and geological concern has been raised by the implication of the lack of surface data, especially when such a strong cultural presence is preserved in the northern end of the basin. The absence of surface material is difficult to interpret, but most likely occurs for one of three reasons:

- Cultural material never existed on the landscape;
- Cultural materials have been lost because of surficial processes (for example, they have been buried, redistributed, or flushed from the system);
- Cultural materials were simply not observed by the survey teams.

In the upper parts of Mitsero Basin there is ample evidence for significant late Holocene erosion. Geological survey gave no indication that archaeological survey misrepresented the artifact distribution (or lack of such) in the upper basin. It follows that either the cultural material has been removed from the landscape through erosion or the broad southern end of the valley was not heavily occupied. Check dams and agricultural terraces whose trapped sediments have been partially or entirely deflated are testimony to a lost battle to conserve soil, and to the loss of soil, sedimentary and archaeological material. The modern landscape of the fourth-order basin (except for Hat_1) is only as old as the increase in occupation in the early Medieval period (ca. AD 1200) and was largely shaped by the land use impact of the Medieval and Ottoman increases in population.

In comparison with the thorough cultural representation in the northern end of the basin, the lack of Prehistoric to Byzantine, and especially Iron Age to Late Roman pottery on the Hat_1 terrace is puzzling. Historical and archaeological information about the northern region of the basin attests to a large and productive human presence, both industrially and agriculturally, from the Archaic to the Late Roman periods, with a peak in regional and local population and productivity during the Roman period. The best interpretation is that the archaeological record has always been sparsely distributed across the hillslopes and on the surface of Hat_1 and that settlement in the southern part of the basin has been limited throughout the history of occupation.

Some cultural materials were possibly incorporated into the fluvial system and either deposited in the alluvial plains of the Lykithia or flushed entirely from the system. The shallower gradient of the Lykithia, together with the broader alluvial valley and the deeper basin created at the southern base of Kriadhis and Lambadhousa, effectively serve as a reservoir for the heavier cultural artifacts (primarily pottery). This stratigraphy has since been incised and

exists now as Holocene alluvial terraces (Wells 2001). This scenario agrees with the geomorphology and stability maps of Kouloupakhis, and suggests a major erosional episode that occurred sometime during or just after the Byzantine period (circa AD 750–1191). This erosional phase resulted in the deposition of the sediments of the Hyal terrace mapped at Kouloupakhis. It seems likely, then, that before the Byzantine period Kouloupakhis and Mavrovounos were primarily industrial sites and that settlement and agriculture were concentrated on the more fertile and accessible plains of the Peristerona River northwest of the Mitsero Basin divide. Following the end of the Roman occupation and a decrease in population, industry, and agriculture, soil conservation efforts were either abandoned or limited to only choice agricultural lands. Hillslope terraces and check dams were abandoned, and unstable hillslope sediments were shed from the hillslides.

Deposition of the sediments of the Hat_2 (Middle to Medieval), Hat_3 (early Ottoman) and Hat_4 (modern, < 100 BP) terraces may be interpreted as a renewed stabilization of the basin in the form of check dams on fourth- and fifth-order drainages, in an attempt to rejuvenate a devastated landscape. Alternatively they may have resulted from further episodes of basin sedimentation following landscape destabilization. Given the effects of a massive Byzantine landscape denudation, it is most likely that the sediments of Hat_2 were deposited in the channel as a result the damming of the Lykithia at the constriction between Kriadhis and Lambadhousa to conserve the soil. Historical and archaeological data support a rise in population in the area and particularly in the Mitsero Basin. A population increase would demand soil conservation and reintegration of marginal lands into the local economy. Damming of the Lykithia would also explain the broad meander just south of the Kriadhis-Lambadhousa pass. A meander of this size could have formed only through a dramatic decrease on the channel gradient. Following this model, channel incision (formation of Hat_2) would imply a dam break and free flow of the sediments of the Kryon Neron and other fourth order channels into the Lykithia, through the mountains and into the Peristerona River.

Conversely, profile development indices suggest that sediments of Hat_3 are predominantly reworked hillslope soils, and probably represent a destabilization of the Troodos foothills (catchment headlands).

The sixteenth century saw yet another rise in population and increased demand on marginal lands for agriculture and forest resources. The Venetian and Ottoman periods were mostly characterized by intense taxation, which would have forced the exploitation of marginal lands to meet taxation demands. The increase in pastoralism during the Ottoman period would have further impeded reforestation and landscape restabilization.

Sediments and juvenile soils of Hat_4 are the result of another, modern basin restabilization. The Hat_4 sediments are very different from those of Hat_3 to Hat_1: they are predominantly medium- to coarse-grained, subangular to subrounded clast-supported deposits with only a thin juvenile A horizon. These are sediments that were shed in intense periodic storm phases following the modern reforestation effort and preceding the Troodos-wide damming of second- to fourth-order channels. Present-day channel abrasion is a result of this damming, which effectively traps sediments upstream.

Current land-use practices of Mitsero Basin are seemingly benign; they consist mostly of modest grain and cucumber production. In an attempt to stabilize the postmodern industrial landscape created by intensive mining in the early to mid-twentieth century, the Forestry Department is actively maintaining the reforestation effort. However, despite recent droughts and an island-wide shortage of groundwater, some farmers are bulldozing 1:1 terraces on soil-depleted hillslopes and planting almond or olive orchards. This is producing a very dangerous relationship between land use and hillslope stability. Within the basin and surrounding area, the population density is rising steadily as the national economy grows and real-estate prices rise in Nicosia. Urban sprawl accompanied by novice landowners is likely to impede the landscape rejuvenation process.

CONCLUSION

This integration of fluvial geomorphology, pedology, and geoarchaeology has demonstrated the impact of human land use on the landscape evolution of the Mitsero Basin. Absolute and relative dating methods have determined that the alluvial terraces of the Mitsero Basin are Late Pleistocene to latest Holocene in age and that the colluvial soils (where present)

are predominantly less than one hundred years old. The three youngest terraces (Hat_4, Hat_3, and Hat_2) were formed through a series of intense deposition/incision cycles that began in the early-mid Medieval period and continued through the Ottoman occupation of the basin. Soil chrono-sequence and topo-sequence analyses suggest that while the alluvial soils of Hat_4 and Hat_3 terraces have developed as unique in situ terrace soils, they exhibit characteristics such as increased rubification (reddening of soil when iron within the sand, silt, or clay particles is oxidized) and clay accumulation, which are typical of older, more mature soils. This implies that their dominant parent material was soil that was stripped from the surrounding hillslopes through abusive land-use practices such as deforestation, pastoralism, and abandonment. Coarse Hat_4 sediments and modern incision are a result of a modern shift to an emphasis on conservation including reforestation, damming, and a prohibition of pastoralism in the basin foothills.

A comparison of the archaeological and historical record of the basin to the stratigraphy of the soils and sediments appears to show that the modern landscape was formed primarily through the exploitation of marginal lands to sustain growing populations and increased taxation demands during the Medieval and Ottoman periods. From the Iron Age to the Modern period, survey results consistently show high concentrations of pottery at Mitsero *Kouloupakhis* (SIA 3) and Mitsero *Mavrovounos* (SIA 4). These locations, of course, have prominent, multilayered slag heaps, evidence of diachronic industrial occupation of the northern region of the basin. Transects in the southern part of the basin, however, revealed a notable dearth of cultural data. As the oldest terrace, Hat_1, has been stable throughout the human occupation of the basin, the survey data do, in fact, reflect the genuine distribution (or lack) of the artifacts. It is likely that the basin resources principally have supported mineral and forest exploitation and pastoralism since the Iron Age, while the principal agricultural produce was extracted from the more fertile plains north of the basin divide. As is the case today, people did not settle in the foothills but congregated at the main river confluence and north of the basin divide.

Figure 4.48 SIA 9: the church of Ayios Mamas from the northeast. SCY134 is in the middle ground on the right with check dams behind.

4.9 SIA 9: Klirou *Ayios Mamas*

Compiled by Timothy E. Gregory and Michael Given
Team leader: Bradley Creevey Geomorphology: Caroline
Whitehill, Jay Noller GIS analysis: Nathan Meyer
Pottery: Timothy E. Gregory, R. Scott Moore

Grid reference: 518200/3874100
Cadastral map: XXXVIII/8
Aerial photograph: 1993, run 174, no. 196
Survey units: 4500–26
POSIs: SCY134: Klirou *Ayios Mamas*
                    (possible Medieval to Otto-
                    man settlement); SCY206:
                    Klirou *Ayia Irini* (rubble piles)

The recently reconstructed church of Ayios Mamas lies 2.5 km southeast of Klirou in a gently sloping landscape, with broad east-west terraces crossing the upper part of a small valley (plate XXXIV). The area was selected for examination in response to local informants who told us about mining activity, ancient tombs, and the remains of two abandoned villages in the area. The church was rebuilt in 1994 on the remains of an earlier church, which can be made out on the 1963 aerial photograph, and whose position was marked on the cadastral map of the area. SCSP's main aims in this area were to carry out block survey and an intensive examination of the two reported settlements; to compare the oral traditions with the surviving material evidence and to investigate the creation of arable land in the valley by means of check dams.

PHYSICAL LANDSCAPE

The area round the church has been bulldozed radically, undoubtedly in connection with the church's reconstruction, and a gossan hill lies immediately to the north (figure 4.48). The bedrock is a mixture of weathered upper pillow lavas, very fine-grained diabase dykes and mottled gossan material. This latter contains a few areas of mineral exploration, particularly on the hill to the north of the church. The valley itself is about 200 m wide, and appears to have undergone intensive human modification for a long period of time. Along the main north-south drainage is a series of six plowed fluvial terraces. Because they have been plowed and exploited intensively through the use of check dams over some centuries, the differences between remnant fluvial terraces, risers, and agricultural terraces are very subtle.

A large number of stone-built check dams have been constructed along the valley to contain the north-south flow of water and to trap sediment for the planting of crops and the cultivation of olives on the stable surfaces—rich in fluvial silt—thus created. The result has been a gentle broadening of the contours of the valley and a series of agricultural fields straddling the original water course. The general trend of this water course can still be seen in the treads and risers of its terraces. This anthropogenic landscape contrasts sharply with the steep and eroded terrain in the next valley to the east as well as further north in the same valley, both of which are deeply incised and quite useless in terms of arable

Table 4.21 SCY134 and SCY206: analyzed pottery

Chronotype	Period	Qty
Cypriot Glazed	Med	2
Cypriot Glazed VII	Med	1
Cypriot Glazed VIIIB Late	Ott	1
Cypriot Glazed IX Late	Ott	1
Cypriot Glazed, Brown and Green	Ott	1
Cypriot W3	Ott	4
Cypriot W5	Ott	9
Cypriot W6	Ott	2
Contemporary Imported Asian	Mod	1
Cypriot W7 [S-0054]	Mod	26
Brown Glaze	MM	1
Cypriot W1	MM	4
Cypriot W4 [S-0043]	MM	159
Glazed ware	MM	1
Pithos-MM	MM	3
Tile-MM	MM	13
Pithos-PC	PC	1
Tile-PC	PC	11
Coarse ware-Unk	Unk	11
Cooking ware-Unk	Unk	2
TOTAL for SCY134		254
Cypriot W6	Ott	1
Cypriot W4	MM	20
Tile, Corinthian Pan	PC	1
TOTAL for SCY206		22

Note: Figures in brackets refer to cataloged items (see chapter 5.1).

agriculture. This is clear evidence of deliberate long-term alteration of the landscape to provide food production in an otherwise barren area.

The olive trees on top of these surfaces provide a rough date at least for their final phases. Several olives appear to be at least five hundred years old, and most of the larger trees are 200 to 350 years old. The rows of olive trees that run roughly northeast-southwest in the northern part of the SIA (plate XXXIV) are, for the most part, on the youngest fluvial terrace, which stands only 10 to 20 cm above the present base level of the drainage. The olive trees farther south stand on terraces that in some stretches stand over 1 m above the current base level. It appears that check dams have been constructed and maintained in this valley since at least the sixteenth century, a time when the entire SCSP area witnessed a major growth in population. This means of maximizing arable land and protecting it against erosion is common throughout the region (for example, SCY114; see chapter 4.16; Noller and Wells N.D.).

HISTORICAL CONTEXT AND ORAL TRADITION

To our knowledge, no historical documents refer to this area. Local informants regard the vicinity as important because of the isolated rural chapel of Ayios Mamas and its association with a sixteenth-century icon of the saint, now kept in the late nineteenth-century church of the Panayia in Klirou. The rediscovery of this icon gave rise to an annual procession from Klirou to the chapel of Ayios Mamas on 1 September, the eve of the Saint's festival. In 1997 a SCSP team was working in the area during this festival and was warmly welcomed by the participants; the event also proved to be a rich source of information.

According to local tradition there were once two villages in the area: Ayios Mamas, immediately around and west of the church and Ayia Irini (also referred to as Ayia Marina) 300 m to the southwest, toward the head of the valley. The village of Ayios Mamas depended primarily on grain; Ayia Irini, on pastoralism and olive cultivation. Both were reputedly wealthy, partly from agriculture but mostly from local gold mines, and they competed with each other in their display of wealth. On one occasion, when the headmen of the two villages happened to be brothers, they decided to have a contest to determine which of the two was wealthier. In turn they piled up gold on one of the threshing floors, and the oxen pulled the threshing sledge round and round it as if threshing grain. The heap of gold where the sledge kept going the longest before its blades struck the paving stones would be the winner. Such was the wealth of the winning village that the sledge managed to go round the floor three times before its blades cut down through the gold and reached the paving stones.

FIELD METHODOLOGY

We carried out block survey in three main areas: (1) the fields to the west of the church, most of them created artificially by means of check dams; (2) a series of terraces to the north of the church; and (3) a higher area to the south near the reported settlement of Ayia Irini. The rubble piles where the settlement of Ayios Mamas had been pointed out to us (SCY134) were collected as a series of irregular subunits conforming to the piles. We examined the area around these rubble piles by means of fifty-two circles, 2 m in diameter and radiating out from the rubble piles into the surrounding fields. The remains at Ayia Irini (SCY206) consisted mainly of one long rubble pile, which was divided into five subunits for collection. The check dams were examined and a geomorphological map of the area was produced.

SCY134: KLIROU *AYIOS MAMAS*:
POSSIBLE MEDIEVAL TO OTTOMAN SETTLEMENT

Fifty meters west of the church, an elongated north-south outcrop of bedrock rises above the arable land created by the check dams. Too rocky to be cultivated, its surface consists of bare bedrock, thin vegetation, and a series of substantial, if amorphous, rubble piles. Some of this rubble is clearly due to recent field clearance, but most of it is heavily patinated with lichens, including the very slow-growing *Rizocarpin tinei*. Combined with the amount of pottery and tile mixed up with the rubble, these piles suggest that there some sort of habitation existed here, though possibly not of the size described by local tradition.

The pottery from the rubble piles and from the lines of circles radiating out from them contained nothing that was definitely pre-Medieval (table 4.21). With only 3 sherds of Medieval and 18 of Ottoman, it is hard to pin down the precise date and nature of the activities carried out here. In this respect Ayios Mamas is very different from the much more substantial and well-documented Medieval settlement of Mitsero *Mavrovounos* (see chapter 4.4). What is striking about the pottery from Ayios Mamas is the large number of sherds of the coarse red-brown ware (Cypriot W4), with 159 pieces or 63% or the total (for example, cat. S-0043). Whether these rubble piles and the scatter of material round them represent an actual village, or a much smaller farmstead or seasonal settlement, the material appears to be distinctly utilitarian in function with a comparatively low proportion of fine wares. Tile fragments numbered 43; given that most rural houses had brushwood and mud roofs until the 1930s, these fragments may actually derive from the church's predecessor.

SCY206: KLIROU *AYIA IRINI*:
RUBBLE PILES AND VINEYARD SHELTER

The area indicated by local informants as the site of the village of Ayia Irini (or Ayia Marina) lies only 300 m southwest of Ayios Mamas, in the upper part of the valley above the check dams. The only indica-

tions of any sort of structure were a long rubble pile and a vineyard shelter. The rubble pile was about 50 m long and 1 to 3 m wide, heaped up against a bank some 2 m in height. It was collected in five subunits, but because small potsherds tend to fall through, only twenty-two sherds were collected, twenty of which were the same Cypriot W4 ware that dominated the rubble piles at Ayios Mamas (table 4.21). The 35 tile fragments from the rubble suggest some sort of roofed structure.

On the slope immediately above an abandoned vineyard on the northern edge of the rubble heap was a vineyard shelter, half built from basalt river cobbles and half dug into the weathered and friable basalt bedrock. The walls had been plastered on the interior with mud plaster containing large proportions of chaff, and it had been reroofed relatively recently with machine-cut wooden beams, corrugated iron, and sections of flattened oil drum. Its construction and interior dimensions of 1.30 x 0.95 m were characteristic of such vineyard shelters from the late Ottoman and early Colonial periods (chapter 7.4; Given 2000:223–225). As they were used for shelter while dressing the vines and plowing at a distance from the village, it is most unlikely that there was a settlement in its vicinity during this period. If the rubble at Ayia Irini does represent some sort of small habitation, which seems possible but by no means certain, it was presumably in the Medieval or earlier Ottoman periods.

BLOCK SURVEY

The survey of 27 units across the valley indicated a general concentration of material around SCY134 and one dense field adjacent to SCY206 (plate XXXV). This clearly relates to the Medieval to Modern pottery distribution (plate XXXVI). There also seemed to be some chronological stratification. The prehistoric and Archaic to Classical material made up only a light scatter, but it was clearly limited to the area north of the church. The six Early Roman and seven Late Roman sherds, by contrast, were scattered without concentration across the entire area, with a characteristic pottery index of 500 to 1000. Elsewhere we take such an even carpet of pottery at this low level to represent manuring (chapter 7.4), although judging from the check dams it seems unlikely that these fields existed in the Roman period. The three Early Roman fine wares were all locally

Table 4.22 SIA 9: analyzed pottery from block survey (units 4500–4526)

Chronotype	Period	Qty
Pithos-PoB	PoB	3
Black-on-Red-Ar	Ar	5
Red Slip-Ar	Ar	17
Fine ware-AC	AC	1
Plain White-AC	AC	2
TOTAL PoB-Classical		28
Cypriot Sigillata	ER	1
Lamp-ER	ER	3
Red Slip-ER	ER	2
Amphora, LR 1	LR	1
Basin-LR	LR	1
Coarse ware-LR	LR	1
Coarse ware, LR Wheel-Ridged	LR	1
Cooking ware, Dhiorios Pot	LR	1
Cypriot Red Slip	LR	1
Cypriot Red Slip 1	LR	1
TOTAL Early to Late Roman		13
Byzantine Glazed, Local	Med	1
Cypriot Glazed	Med	3
Cypriot Glazed IVC	Med	1
Cypriot Glazed VIIIB	Med	8
Cypriot Glazed IX	Med	6
Cypriot Glazed XI	Med	3
Cypriot W1 Early	Med	4
Maiolica ware	Med	1
Cypriot Glazed VIIIB Late	Ott	4
Cypriot Glazed IX Late [4514.1.1]	Ott	5
Cypriot Glazed, Brown and Green	Ott	7
Cypriot W3	Ott	4
Cypriot W5	Ott	7
Cypriot W6	Ott	43
Ottoman Glazed	Ott	2
Tile-Ott	Ott	1
Brick	Mod	8
Coarse ware-Mod	Mod	1
Contemporary Eastern Mediterranean	Mod	2
Contemporary Yogurt ware	Mod	1
Cypriot W7	Mod	75
Brown Glaze	MM	3
Cypriot W1	MM	8
Cypriot W4	MM	447
Glazed ware	MM	2
Tile-MM	MM	13
TOTALMedieval to Modern		660
Plain White-HA	HA	13
Tile-PC	PC	18
Tile, Corinthian Pan	PC	4
Coarse ware-Unk	Unk	62
Cooking ware-Unk	Unk	12
TOTAL		810

Note: Figures in brackets refer to cataloged items (see chapter 5.1).

produced and dated to the first to third centuries AD; two fragments of Roman Red Slip may come from the same bowl (table 4.22). The Late Roman material is mostly fourth to seventh century AD and while small in numbers has a broad range of storage, cooking, and fine wares, all manufactured on Cyprus.

Medieval to Ottoman pottery tended to concentrate in the central and southern part of the area, particularly round the rubble piles at Ayios Mamas (SCY134), where the pottery index for Medieval to Modern reached an impressive 11,000 in unit 4524 (plate XXXVI). This helps to confirm that these rubble piles represent more than field clearance. As for Ayia Irini (SCY206), an adjacent unit with reasonable visibility (unit 4514) had a Medieval to Modern pottery index of 5500, which is substantial, but in isolation not very meaningful. The 27 Medieval pieces from SIA 9 include the standard wares, with a definite concentration in the sixteenth century, rather than in earlier years. Notable is the single piece of sixteenth-century Italian Maiolica, probably a Venetian import to Cyprus. Nearly all 68 sherds assigned to the Ottoman period came from coarse, relatively undiagnostic vessels (Cypriot W3, W5, W6), although 13 glazed pieces could be identified.

The discovery of 152 tile fragments during block survey and POSI investigation within SIA 9 suggests some sort of settlement in this region (plate XXXV). Of these tile fragments, 50 came from the immediate vicinity of SCY134, while another 43 came from the rubble piles. Of the remainder, 35 stem from the rubble at SCY206.

CONCLUSION

The two main cultural issues raised by the material from SIA 9 are the existence and nature of any settlement, and the creation of arable land by means of check dams. There is certainly abundant evidence of activity in the area, with rubble piles, the church and check dams, and occasionally considerable densities of pottery. It seems probable that the rubble piles, when taken with the tile fragments and higher densities of pottery, do mark the positions of structures of some sort, presumably deriving from the foundations of mud-brick structures. The outcrop at SCY134 is roughly 100 x 20 m. This seems hardly large enough for anything we might term a village, though it might once have extended out into what are now fields.

On balance, there were probably one or a few structures at both SCY134 and SCY206 in the Medieval and Ottoman periods. At SCY134 this would have included the predecessor of the current church of

Ayios Mamas. If any actual houses existed, they are more likely to have been farmsteads or else the equivalent of the small groups of seasonal field houses in use elsewhere in the northern Troodos until the mid-twentieth century (Given 2000:223–224). Thus, there is no surface archaeological evidence for the two villages rich in gold that local tradition describes.

The impressive series of broad check dams extending down the valley points to wealth and success of a different kind. Though not very large, this part of the valley is fertile, stable, and easy to cultivate and now supports intensive production of barley and olives—in striking contrast to the rocky, eroded valleys to the east and north. These fields were deliberately created by building check dams to trap the sediment that the stream carried down, thus harnessing the landscape's own power not just to protect against erosion but to create arable land where previously there was none. Judging by the age of the olive trees and most of the pottery on these surfaces, the check dams were first constructed in the Medieval period, about the same time as the structures at Ayios Mamas and Ayia Irini. Perhaps the gold from the earth recalled by oral tradition should be seen as a metaphor for the fertile soil that human endeavor succeeded in winning from the landscape.

4.10 SIA 10:
Malounda *Panayia Khrysopandanassa*

Compiled by Michael Given

Team leaders: Bradley Creevey, Michael Given

Geomorphology: Jay Noller GIS analysis: Nathan Meyer,

Michael Given Lithics: Dina Coleman

Pottery: Timothy E. Gregory, R. Scott Moore, Joanna S. Smith

Grid reference: 516700/3877400
Cadastral maps: XXIX/55, XXIX/63
Aerial photograph: 1993, run 177, no. 51
Survey units: 1268–83, 4527–53
POSIs: SCY112: Malounda *Panayia*
                      Khrysopandanassa; SCY303:
                      Malounda *Tria Yephyria*
                      (bridge); SCY313: Malounda
                      Village

The eighteenth-century church of Panayia Khrysopandanassa (Our Lady, the Golden Ruler of All) lies among olive groves just beyond the northern outskirts of the village of Malounda (plate XXXVII). It overlooks an agricultural plain that stretches from Aredhiou in the north to Klirou in the south, and ends abruptly on each side at the gorge of the Koutis River on the east and the Akaki River on the west. This plain is a remnant of an alluvial terrace from an earlier and much larger river.

The SIA 10 area was first investigated during the 1995 season, initiating our new strategy of targeting potential areas of significance and making use of information generated by the GIS, and of team members' experience within Cyprus and in the survey area. In this case, the targeting bore fruit immediately: The first unit surveyed contained 1855 sherds. Even though the block survey was carried out at two different times of year, only 25 units were sufficiently free of crops or vegetation to merit survey. Most striking among the material recovered was the abundant presence of Late Roman, Medieval, and Ottoman components. This combination characterizes the majority of pottery scatters on alluvial plains within the survey area; at five such scatters, old or ruined churches are also found.

These findings raised questions about the definition of a settlement and the relationship between the artifact scatter, the church, and the modern village. Intriguing variations, particularly in the distributions of pottery and tiles and of Late Roman and Medieval pottery, were apparent in the material, even at the coarse resolution of a block survey. Such variability could have resulted from original deposition or subsequent geomorphological processes, or both. Because of this degree of variation, as well as the sheer density of surface material, we defined the two survey units immediately to the north of the church as a POSI (SCY112) and decided to conduct a spatial analysis at a finer resolution in an attempt to consider the broader questions. Because the relevant fields had been plowed between the 1995 and 1996 field seasons, a completely new set of material could be expected on the surface (Ammerman 1995). This resurvey would also provide opportunity to test the accuracy of SCSP's transect/block survey methodology (see chapter 3.7).

PHYSICAL LANDSCAPE

Malounda *Panayia Khrysopandanassa* is located on a riser between two alluvial terraces or pediments, probably Middle Pleistocene, along the eastern side of the Akaki River (plate XXXVII). The upper and lower pediments both have red, clayey A and B horizons and

Figure 4.49
SIA 10: church
of Panayia
Khrysopandanassa
from the
southeast

calcic subsoils. The soil of the riser is different from its contemporary landform, the lower pediment, and is less advantageous for growing grain. Relative to the adjoining pediment soils, the lower water-holding capacity, greater stoniness, and greater base saturation of the riser soil is better suited for groves, orchards, and other crops requiring such conditions. This is reflected in current farming practices, particularly in the northern part of the SIA, where the olive trees are mainly distributed along the riser.

Around the church, the riser has been reformed by human labor into artificial terraces, with stone walls separating the terrace treads. The ages of these terraces are not clear, although lichens on the stones suggest construction or reconstruction during the twentieth century. It is probable that the terrace level on which the church is located predates the actual structure (1763 or earlier) and its wall. The location of artifacts in the immediate vicinity of the church is primarily due to human activity: They lie where they fell or were dumped, or they were moved as farmers graded the riser to its present form.

In the SIA as a whole, the geomorphological processes associated with the risers and pediments are important for understanding artifact distribution. Units 1268 and 1281 both lie on the riser, which is the most active part of the landscape. Erosion can therefore be expected to be the dominant process, moving downslope from east to west. From a geomorphological point of view, then, units 1268 and 1281 can be expected to contain less cultural material than fields on the treads of the terraces on each side. Unit 1280, immediately to the west of unit 1281 and just on the far side of the riser had, as expected, a much greater density of artifacts, as shown by fig-

ures from the 1995 block survey. Bearing geomorphological factors in mind, then, variations in the distribution of artifacts in units 1268 and 1281 may not be indicative of the original spatial pattern of their deposition, although any variations from north to south along the riser are liable to be more meaningful than those from east to west across the riser.

HISTORICAL BACKGROUND

Ancient tombs have been reported from the vicinity of Malounda, both in the area of the village and on the hill to the north (Goodwin 1984:1053). Otherwise nothing is known from the historical or archaeological literature until the Medieval period. Malounda appears in four village lists from the Venetian period (1489–1570) as Malonda, Malonta, and Malounda. In the first three lists it is categorized as a *casal*, or full village; according to the fourth list, in 1565 it had eighteen adult male *francomati*, or fully emancipated Cypriots (Grivaud 1998:462). The village appears on Ortelius's map of 1573 as Milondo (Stylianou and Stylianou 1980:257) and figures repeatedly in seventeenth- and eighteenth-century maps (Stylianou and Stylianou 1980:291, 304, 305, 337, 372, 397).

Mälünda is included in the list of villages belonging to the *kaza* (subdistrict) of Dağ (Orini) in 1821 (Theocharides and Andreev 1996:27). In the first census taken under British rule in 1881, Malounda had a population of 90; this increased steadily to 164 in 1931 and 285 in 1982 (*MKE* 9:283–284).

The church of Panayia Khrysopandanassa (figure 4.49), some 200 m north of the village, was constructed in 1763, according to the date over its south door. Architectural fragments incorporated into its walls and a scatter of mason's castoffs and limestone wall-packers in the fields immediately round it clearly indicate that it was rebuilt on the site of an earlier church. An icon of the Virgin Orans, which includes a richly dressed donor in one corner, was almost certainly made for the earlier church and then transferred to the new one. The icons earlier layer dates to the fourteenth century and the later to the sixteenth (Papanikola-Bakirtzis and Iacovou 1998:122–123). Other icons in the church date to 1708 and 1723, and the iconostasis was made in 1853, using woodwork from its predecessor (Gunnis 1936:336).

FIELD METHODOLOGY

Rather than being discovered as part of a transect, this area was first investigated in 1995 because experience elsewhere in the survey area (for example, SCY105) had shown that pre-Modern churches were often associated with major pottery scatters. We carried out a certain amount of block survey on all sides of the church, finding considerable amounts of pottery, particularly in units 1268 and 1281. Thick stubble meant that many fields could not be surveyed. In 1996 we reinvestigated the two units with the densest material, using a grid of 2 m diameter circles (SCY112). This also served as a means of testing our survey methodology. Geomorphological mapping in the same season helped our interpretation of the artifact distribution.

Because the 1997 season took place in September, fewer fields were obscured by stubble. We could therefore fill some of the gaps in the original block survey and extend it toward the edge of the Akaki gorge. In the same season we examined the area around the bridge over the River Akaki, immediately below the SIA (SCY303: Malounda *Tria Yephyria*) and at the same time conducted a block survey of a dense scatter of Roman pottery on the opposite river terrace, originally discovered during transect survey in 1993 (SCY002: Malounda *Kharjis* 1).

SCY112: MALOUNDA *PANAYIA KHRYSOPANDANASSA*: GRIDDED CIRCLES

To investigate the variations in dates and types of material across the two densest units in the SIA (1268, 1281), we set out a grid of 42 circles, 2 m in diameter and 10 m apart, divided by the road that passes between the two units (plate XXXVIII). The church, with its enclosure wall, lies at the southern end of unit 1268.

Both fields had been plowed since the initial block survey; by placing the grid between the olive trees we ensured that all circles had full visibility.

The gridded circles illustrate dramatically the variations in density across the two fields, as well as the phenomenal amount of pottery they contained. Nearest the church in unit 1268 there were characteristically eight or nine artifacts per m^2; moving northward this number increased to a maximum of 22.3 sherds and 1.0 tiles per m^2 in the northeastern circle, just 60 m away. Across the road in unit 1281, the number of artifacts dropped immediately to a maximum of 9.6 per m^2 and decreased slowly going northward over the rest of the field to two or three artifacts per m^2. Clearly there has been a certain amount of spreading of material within each field because of plowing, but not between the fields. The tile fragments were clearly more numerous to the south; the average density in unit 1268 to the south was 0.7 per m^2, as opposed to 0.1 in unit 1281. Within unit 1268, however, there was only a slight increase toward the south.

In absolute terms, sherd counts for this more intensive strategy are considerably greater than those obtained by the standard unit survey method used in 1995. From these earlier results, the average density in unit 1268 would be 0.82 pottery and tile fragments per m^2 and in unit 1281 just 0.27, as opposed to averages from the circles of 8.8 and 3.7, respectively. Such a large disparity is most likely due to the greater concentration with which a fieldwalker examines a 2 m circle, as opposed to a strip 5 m wide and some 60 to 100 m long. This in turn suggests that the figures from the transect and block survey, although consistent within themselves, cannot be compared in absolute terms with the figures deriving from much more closely scrutinized POSIs.

One major benefit of the gridded circles, as opposed to unit survey, is their much greater spatial resolution, most evident in the distribution of Late Roman pottery. The survey of the units merely recorded the Late Roman pottery index for each unit as a whole. The gridded circles demonstrate a distinct rise in the presence of Late Roman material toward the north of the POSI. The distribution of Medieval pottery is less clear because of the difficulty of distinguishing Medieval, Ottoman, and Modern coarse wares, but there is certainly a gradual increase in material across both units going southward toward the church, and concentrations of up to 8.3 sherds

Table 4.23 SCY112: analyzed pottery

Chronotype	Period	Qty
White Painted-Ar	Ar	1
Fine ware-Cl	Cl	1
Coarse ware-GAC	GAC	3
Plain White-AC	AC	15
White Painted-AC	AC	2
TOTAL Geometric to Classical		22
Fine ware-He	He	1
Eastern Sigillata A	ER	2
Amphora-LR	LR	2
Basin, Piecrust Rim	LR	3
Coarse ware-LR	LR	25
Coarse ware, LR Wheel-Ridged	LR	3
Cypriot Red Slip	LR	3
Phocaean ware (LR C)	LR	1
Tile-LR	LR	2
TOTAL Hellenistic to Late Roman		42
Cypriot Glazed	Med	9
Cypriot Glazed IV	Med	5
Cypriot Glazed VI	Med	1
Cypriot Glazed VIIIB	Med	3
Cypriot Glazed IX Late	Ott	3
Cypriot W3	Ott	4
Cypriot W6	Ott	5
Ottoman Glazed	Ott	4
Coarse ware-Mod	Mod	2
Fine ware-Mod	Mod	2
Tile-Mod	Mod	1
Coarse ware-MM	MM	188
Cypriot W1	MM	5
Cypriot W4	MM	1
Glazed ware	MM	31
Pithos-MM	MM	3
TOTAL Medieval to Modern		267
Pithos-PC	PC	27
Tile-PC	PC	1
Coarse ware-Unk	Unk	445
Fine ware-Unk	Unk	2
TOTAL		806

rims give some evidence of an Early Roman component, but despite the ubiquity of this type throughout the survey area it is notoriously difficult to date. The standard fine wares of late antiquity are all represented, with imported wares from Africa, Asia Minor (Phocaean ware), and Egypt (Egyptian Red Slip) as well as the standard, locally produced red slip ware (Cypriot Red Slip). Chronologically, these examples span the period from the mid-third century AD to at least the mid-seventh, although it may be more than chance that no pottery can be dated certainly between AD 250 and 550. Indeed, the bulk of the identifiable ancient pottery from this unit can be assigned to the last century before the Arab invasions in the mid-seventh century AD.

No examples of purely Byzantine wares were noted in this unit, but many pieces could be assigned to the Frankish period, after circa AD 1200. Interestingly, there are relatively large amounts of early Medieval material but a comparatively small number of late Medieval sherds, which reverses the norm in the survey area. Among the wares identified were Lemba ware (thirteenth to fourteenth centuries AD) and large amounts of Cypriot Glazed Ware Groups IV (thirteenth to fourteenth centuries AD), VIIB, and IX (sixteenth century AD). There are numerous pieces from the Ottoman period, including a fragment of a Turkish pipe bowl (1268.67.1) but virtually no pieces that can be identified as modern (apart from plastics and the like left in the field), even though the church of Panayia Khrysopandanassa is still in use. Of the 23.3% Medieval/Modern pottery from the POSI, much may in fact be modern.

SCY303: MALOUNDA *TRIA YEPHYRIA*: EARLY COLONIAL BRIDGE

The depth and steep sides of the gorge incised by the River Akaki make crossing places few and highly significant in the regional communications system. In 1887 the commissioner of Nicosia underlined the importance of the bridge at Malounda *Tria Yephyria* in linking Nicosia with the vine and fruit villages of the Dağ (that is, Orini), Morphou, and Limassol districts; in winter it was the only line of communication with this mountain region (SA1/1156/1887). Another report in 1889 described it as being "On the Palaeokhorio-Nicosia Road, the direct line of communication between wine villages and the capital" (SA1/481/1889:3). The route was probably equally

per m² within 40 m of the church. The low level of overlap between Late Roman and Medieval material is particularly striking. Given that erosional differences are minimized going north to south along the riser, there seems to be a general increase in Late Roman material toward the north and Medieval toward the south.

Apart from a picrolite pendant (cat. S-0020; almost certainly Chalcolithic in date) in unit 1268, most of the material from SCY112 was Archaic, Classical, Roman, and Medieval (table 4.23). Two cooking pot important in the Medieval and Ottoman periods: the Akaki River valley is the easiest route from Nicosia to the eastern section of the Troodos range, where from the sixteenth century at least there were a considerable number of villages (Grivaud 1998:466–70).

One of the best places to cross the Akaki lies immediately below SIA 10, where large gullies on each side give the opportunity for a road to traverse down into the gorge and up the other side. The three arches of the current bridge presumably give the locality its name of Tria Yephyria, or Three Bridges. Its late Medieval or Ottoman predecessor was replaced by the current bridge probably in the 1890s by the Public Works Department of the British colonial government (SA1/481/1889; compare Gunnis 1936:336).

What survives now is clearly a late nineteenth or early twentieth century rebuilding, in the usual colonial "brownstone" style. The width, measured underneath, is 3.01 m. The central arch of the north side has a plaque with the word *rebuilt* over the keystone, painted red inside the incised lettering. Whatever might have been written above that, such as the date, has been obscured by later concrete. The east and west arches of the north side have similar but noninscribed plaques. In the spandrel between the east and central arches on the north side, 80 cm below the parapet, is a circular plaque about 25 cm in diameter, clearly taken from the bridge's predecessor. It shows a cross on a stepped base with rosettes above the two arms. A circle of small bosses frames most of the composition, apart from where the stepped base meets the edge. Gunnis, somewhat inventively, describes this as "a defaced shield with a Lusignan coat of arms" (1936:336). At a later stage, the bridge was widened by 1.24 m on the south by reinforced concrete, which was also poured on top (Goodwin 1984:1052–1053). This extension obscured any plaques above the keystones on the south side.

BLOCK SURVEY

Because of bad visibility in the many stubble fields, our block survey was not as extensive or continuous as we might have wished. Nonetheless, it provided a reasonably complete picture of the variation in material on a broad strip running from the edge of the Akaki gorge to the northwest, running past the church toward the current village of Malounda in the southeast. The density map for pottery of all periods shows seven units with densities among the forty highest in the survey area (plate XXXIX). These figures are not as high as SIA 6 (Politiko *Ayios Mnason*) on the eastern edge of Tamassos, but they are still considerable. The highest density clearly focuses on the area immediately north and northwest of the church. The tile density similarly shows a very clear peak immediately north of the church, with a light scatter around it forming a halo about 350 m in diameter. The unit with the most tile fragments, 1286, is equivalent in density to the units on the edge of Tamassos (see plate XXV), but much more restricted in area.

Apart from the picrolite pendant from SCY112 and one sherd of Protohistoric Bronze Age coarse ware, there was no evidence of prehistoric or early Iron Age activity at SIA 10. The Archaic to Classical periods (plate XL) showed a light scatter across the whole area, with a pottery index of less than 800. Given the alluvial topography, and comparing these figures to those of other, similar areas, this is evidently the result of general agriculture and manuring. Most of this material consisted of plain utilitarian wares.

Immediately northwest of the church lies an area about 250 m across with rather higher densities (units 1268, 1280–81, SCY112). With a pottery index of 2000 to 3000, this was not as high as Tamassos or the discrete Late Roman peaks in the Tamassos plain. The material from this concentration had a more specific function profile than those found in other units (table 4.24). In addition to several plain utilitarian wares, there was at least one imported ware (one Greek Black Glaze and possibly a fine ware fragment) as well as White Painted fragments, one piece of certainly identified Red Slip, three pithos fragments (for example, cat. 1268.39A.1), a loomweight (cat. 1281.29.1) and two pieces identified as amphorae. Thus this area might have been a community or elite storage or production center in the Archaic and Classical periods.

The Hellenistic to Late Roman periods (plate XL) show a broadly similar pattern to the Archaic and Classical, though it is dominated by Late Roman material. The whole area has a general background scatter, probably owing to agricultural practices, and there is a distinct concentration north and northwest of the church, rather broader in extent than in the Archaic to Classical periods. This coincides exactly with the scatter of tile (plate

Table 4.24 SIA 10: analyzed pottery from block survey

Chronotype	Period	Qty
Coarse ware-PoB	PoB	1
Amphora-Ar	Ar	1
Plain ware-Ar	Ar	5
Red Slip-Ar	Ar	9
Soft Red-Orange-Ar	Ar	4
White Painted-Ar	Ar	1
Black Glaze-Cl	Cl	1
Loomweight-Cl [1281.29.1]	Cl	1
Plain ware-Cl	Cl	2
Plain White-Cl	Cl	5
Coarse ware-GAC	GAC	1
Fine ware-GAC	GAC	1
Green ware-GAC	GAC	4
Pithos-GAC [1268.39A.1]	GAC	1
Amphora-AC	AC	9
Amphora, Pithoid	AC	1
Basin-AC	AC	6
Coarse ware-AC	AC	1
Fine ware-AC	AC	1
Pithos-AC	AC	2
Plain ware-AC	AC	35
Plain White-AC	AC	83
Rolled Lug Handle-AC	AC	1
White Painted-AC	AC	1
TOTAL PoB to Classical		177
Black Glaze-He	He	2
Fine ware-He	He	1
Casserole, Cypriot Flanged	ER	2
Cooking ware-ER	ER	16
Cooking ware, Square Rim Pot	ER	9
Cypriot Sigillata	ER	4
African Red Slip	LR	4
Amphora-LR	LR	15
Amphora, LR 1	LR	29
Basin-LR	LR	21
Basin, Piecrust Rim	LR	1
Coarse ware-LR	LR	10
Coarse ware, LR Wheel-Ridged	LR	9
Cooking ware-LR	LR	4
Cooking ware, Dhiorios Pot	LR	1
Cypriot Red Slip	LR	5
Cypriot Red Slip 1	LR	1
Cypriot Red Slip 2	LR	4
Cypriot Red Slip 9	LR	9
Egyptian Red Slip	LR	4
Flat-Grooved	LR	14
Frying Pan	LR	6
Phocaean ware (LR C)	LR	4
Phocaean ware 3	LR	1
Phocaean ware 10	LR	1
Amphora-REL	REL	1
TOTAL Hellenistic to Late Roman		178

Chronotype	Period	Qty
Coarse ware-Med	Med	34
Cypriot Glazed [1269.23.1]	Med	33
Cypriot Glazed IV	Med	14
Cypriot Glazed IVC	Med	5
Cypriot Glazed V [1268.53.1]	Med	6
Cypriot Glazed VI [1269.22.1]	Med	5
Cypriot Glazed VIIIB	Med	4
Cypriot Glazed IX	Med	6
Cypriot Glazed XI	Med	7
Cypriot W1 Early	Med	1
Glazed ware, Italian	Med	1
Imported Sgrafitto [1268.60.2, 1269.21.1-2]	Med	3
Lemba ware [1268.62.1]	Med	8
Zeuxippos ware	Med	3
Cypriot Glazed IX Late	Ott	4
Cypriot Glazed, Brown and Green	Ott	62
Cypriot W3	Ott	35
Cypriot W5	Ott	45
Cypriot W6	Ott	13
Ottoman Glazed	Ott	35
Purple Painted ware	Ott	5
Turkish Pipe [1268.67.1]	Ott	1
Brick	Mod	3
Coarse ware-Mod	Mod	24
Contemporary Eastern Mediterranean	Mod	4
Contemporary Imported Asian	Mod	17
Contemporary Local wares	Mod	18
Contemporary Yogurt ware	Mod	25
Cypriot W7	Mod	21
Lapithos ware	Mod	1
Lapithos ware, Green	Mod	7
Lapithos ware, Yellow	Mod	28
Tile-Mod	Mod	4
Brown Glaze	MM	12
Cypriot W1	MM	8
Cypriot W4	MM	616
Glazed ware	MM	56
Pithos-MM	MM	2
Water Pipe-MM	MM	1
TOTAL Medieval to Modern		1213
Plain White-HA	HA	8
Red Slip-HA	HA	1
Amphora-Historical	Hi	7
Pithos-PC	PC	40
Tile-PC	PC	43
Tile, Corinthian Pan	PC	2
Tile, Flat Pan	PC	7
Coarse ware-Unk	Unk	574
Cooking ware-Unk	Unk	85
Fine ware-Unk	Unk	2
Table ware-Unk	Unk	8
Unknown	Unk	1
TOTAL		2346

Note: Figures in brackets refer to cataloged items (see chapter 5.1 for pottery, chapter 5.3 for loomweight and Turkish pipe).

XXXIX). The rimmed tile that predominates here is unfortunately hard to date, but it is most likely to be Late Roman or Byzantine.

The only Hellenistic pottery in SIA 10 consists of two sherds of Black Glazed fine ware, dated 300 to 100 BC. The Early Roman pottery, mainly concentrated in the northwestern part of the SIA, is more numerous, with 30 sherds, of which 27 are locally produced light utility wares, probably used for cooking or general kitchen purposes. The Early Roman fine wares are all locally produced Cypriot Sigillata, dating to the first century AD.

There was a total of 143 Late Roman sherds from SIA 10. Although all types of wares are represented, the light utility wares are unusually low in number. In contrast, both storage/transport wares (52 sherds, or 36%) and fine wares (33 sherds, or 23%) were relatively high. The storage/transport wares were predominantly Late Roman I amphorae, manufactured during this period at Amathus, Kourion, and Nea Paphos and probably used for the transport and storage of olive oil. All four major Late Roman fine wares are represented in SIA 10, accounting for 33 (23%) of the 143 Late Roman sherds: African Red Slip, Cypriot Red Slip, Egyptian Red Slip, and Phocaean ware. Of these, 14 are imported, suggesting a certain degree of affluence in the area. From a diachronic perspective, the fine wares show a decided increase in the period AD 550 to 650, including both local and imported pieces. This is a general feature of the Late Roman pottery in the survey area and may indicate a further increase in affluence, or even an increase in population (see chapter 6.3).

The Medieval to Modern pottery shows a distinctly different distribution (plate XLI). There is one clear peak immediately round the church, which extends farther east and south than the Archaic/Classical and Late Roman concentrations but not as far north. This same pattern can be seen at a larger scale and higher resolution in the gridded circles (plate XXXVIII). Presumably this scatter is somehow related to the church, whose predecessor probably dated to the Medieval period. Farther north and west there is another general concentration, particularly of Ottoman material. This is clearly greater than agricultural background but does not coincide with the tile distribution, and the typical pottery index of 4000 is not high enough from this period to be indicative of intensive human activity such as settlement.

This material may be owing to prolonged dumping of household trash outside the confines of the village. The relatively high quantities of modern material in particular are almost certainly because of this dumping.

The unusually high number of early Medieval sherds from SIA 10 is of particular interest, with 36 dated to the thirteenth to fourteenth centuries AD. These include three fragments of Zeuxippos ware, presumably from the Aegean, and eight Lemba ware pieces from the Paphos district (for example, cat. 1268.62.1). The findspots of this early Medieval material suggest a marked concentration immediately around the present church. Although visibility was poor to the south of the church, limiting our block survey, this concentration seems too restricted to be a settlement, and the high quality of the pottery suggests some sort of elite activity, perhaps a manor house or some activity associated with a predecessor of the church. Material from the sixteenth century, in contrast, primarily Cypriot Glazed XI, was not found close to the church but rather was much more widespread in the distant fields.

CONCLUSION

There has been a significant level of human activity in the area of Malounda *Panayia Khrysopandanassa* since the Archaic and Classical periods, although until the Medieval period it is rather hard to tie down in spatial terms. A slight density peak northwest of the church in the Archaic and Classical periods stands out because of its greater proportions of fine wares and storage pottery. A slightly larger peak in the Late Roman period in the same area coincides with the tile distribution, and the pottery includes notable amounts of imported fine wares as well as storage and transport vessels. The concentration of high-quality early Medieval pottery around the church is most unusual in the survey area, and clearly marks some focus of elite activity.

The church in the center of the village is modern, and there is no known predecessor on the site; Panayia Khrysopandanassa on the outskirts is the oldest known building by several centuries. Although the village of Milondo is known in the sixteenth century, it may have been closer to Panayia Khrysopandanassa than to its current situation. This could be fully determined only by

Figure 4.50
Kokkinoyia
mine from the
south, with
spoil heaps,
open-cast pit,
and modern
mine structures

further block survey, and much of the evidence is lost beneath the developing outskirts of the modern village. In the 1920s, a new church was built in the center of the current village to act as the focus of the settlement (Given N.D.). Whatever its earlier role, the old church of Panayia Khrysopandanassa now lies well outside the village and functions as a rural church with private dedications and festivals on the saint's day.

The significance of the area to its population at different periods results not just from the series of broad river terraces and their good alluvial soil but also from its proximity to a major crossing of the Akaki River and gorge. Historical documentation demonstrates the importance of this route in the Late Medieval to Modern periods, and the bridge at Tria Yephyria (SCY303) confirms it. Even before then, this seems to have been an important communications node. Both the Archaic/Classical and the Roman components of Panayia Khrysopandanassa are matched by similar concentrations of pottery above the gorge on its western side, immediately beside the route up from the bridge (SCY002: Malounda-Kharjis 1). There were also major Roman settlements at Klirou village and Klirou *Manastirka* (SIA 2) and smaller estates or farmsteads all over the Akaki River Valley, such as Malounda *Panayia Khrysopandanassa*. The Tria Yephyria route supplied the best access from these settlements to the mining territory of Agrokipia and Mitsero and thus linked the city of Tamassos to some of its principal mines.

4.11 SIA 11: Mitsero *Kokkinoyia*

Compiled by Sven Van Lokeren
Team leaders: Sven Van Lokeren, Susan Bain, Bradley Creevey
Archaeometallurgy: Sven Van Lokeren
Geomorphology: Jay Noller Historical Archaeology: Kylie Seretis
Pottery: Joanna S. Smith

Grid reference: 509850/3877950
Cadastral maps: XXIX/52, XXIX/53
Aerial photograph: 1993, run 177, no. 40
POSI: SCY219 (subunits SCY219-1 to
                     SCY219-10)

The large abandoned mining complex of Mitsero *Kokkinoyia* is situated in the northwestern sector of the SCSP area, about 900 m northwest of the Kokkinopezoula mine and 1.6 km west of Mitsero village. It lies near the base of the southern slopes of Mount Lambadhousa and is visible from a distance of 2 to 3 km because of its spectacularly colored gossan (figure 4.50).

After their discovery in 1997, the ancient mining and smelting remains were designated as a POSI (SCY219), with component subunits. Subsequently, the whole area was upgraded to SIA 11 because of its unusual extent of preservation and the wide range of production facilities found there. Although known from Bear's (1963) description of the modern mining industry, this mine and its surroundings had received no systematic archaeological attention before SCSP began work here. With the exception of a small entry in the MKE mentioning ancient mining remains (Panayiotou 1989a), and some analyses of unsystematically collected surface samples of slag (Koucky and Steinberg 1982a; Tylecote 1977; Wallace 1982:243), this study provides the first comprehensive archaeometallurgical examination of the site with contextualized data.

Both ancient and modern mining remains (plate XLII) as well as ancient slag heaps attest to the long-term and large-scale production of copper metal at Kokkinoyia, and to its unique place in Cypriot archaeometallurgy. In contrast to the more dispersed and only partially preserved remnants of metallurgical exploitation at SIAs 1 and 7, Kokkinoyia forms a self-contained complex consisting of mining, ore crushing, roasting, smelting, and administrative facilities from at least three and possibly four distinct periods within a single topographically and technologically enclosed location.

Thanks to the unusual range of archaeological and historical remains, SIA 11 offered a unique opportunity to evaluate the relationship between the spatial and technological organization of metal production, while the active interface between ancient and modern mining landscapes also resulted in the increased visibility and detection of some older workings. In most cases, the reopening of the Cypriot mines at the beginning of the twentieth century led to the systematic destruction of archaeometallurgical remains (Bear 1963; Davies 1928–1930). At Kokkinoyia, however, slag heaps have been sectioned, revealing a stratified deposit of technological developments, while mine shafts have been exposed, allowing us to study the selection of ore layers in ancient mining technology.

The importance of Tamassos, located about 12 km southeast of Kokkinoyia, as the administrative center controlling the Iron Age mines in the SCSP area, has already been noted (chapter 4.7). The fact that SIA 11 has only three main phases of exploitation in antiquity seems to fit well chronologically with the socioeconomic interpretation of the SCSP area serving as part of the industrial hinterland of Tamassos (Knapp 1999b:246–247). The highly localized ore layers at Kokkinoyia and the associated, well-dated slag heaps even suggest that this area may have been established directly as a consequence of Tamassos's economic expansion.

PHYSICAL LANDSCAPE

The distribution of the ore bodies indicates that the mine is located in the upper pillow lavas, which, judging from the remains of ancient sea floor volcanoes in the area, have been altered hydrothermally on the sea floor. One of the most spectacular and brilliantly colored gossans overlays the disseminated noncupreous ores at Kokkinoyia. This leached capping was formed on the portion of the ore body that lies in the oxidation zone. In this case, the gossan actually signaled an economic deposit and not merely the oxidized roots of eroded bodies, as geochemical prospecting had originally indicated in the early 1950s. The gossan contained abundant silica, jarosite, and hematite, indicating derivation from massive ore. The size and grade of the economic ore bodies, according to the Hellenic Mining Company, was 14,000 tons with some cupreous ore, 30% sulfur, and negligible amounts of zinc (Bear 1963:40–42, 71).

About 200 m to the southwest lie the slag heaps of Mitsero *Sykamies* with the Mavrovouniotis River running past them into the Mitsero Basin (chapter 4.4). To the south of Sykamies begins the Adelphi Forest, with its steep diabase slopes covered in *Pinus brutia*. No channels or extensive forests, however, are now visible in the highly eroded and culturally altered environment of Kokkinoyia. In fact, very little flora of any sort remains in this industrial landscape. Even so, the original pine forests on top of the gossan layers have recently started to regenerate.

FIELD METHODOLOGY

Based on previous publications and Davies' (1928–1930) description explaining how modern mining engineers followed ancient remains underground to prospect for new ore layers, we decided to visit this area. The concept of an archaeometallurgical landscape, explained in chapter 2.6, helped us to develop a predictive model with expected categories of material and types of production areas (see also chapter 3.6; Bachmann 1982a:1–7). We hoped that the complete production chain might still be preserved in its technologically distinct production units. Eventually, 10 subunits were identified during the course of two field seasons (1997 and 1998). Sections of the stratified slag heap and modern open-cast mine, showing the location of ancient adits, were drawn for further study.

The application of the theoretical model of a self-contained metallurgical area made up of specific site types, which in itself forms part of a microregional organization (Knapp, Donnelly, and Kassianidou 1998) and is to a lesser extent identifiable at SIAs 1 and 7, also helped in assessing the diachronic development of metallurgical technologies and landscapes. Moreover, we needed to consider the chronological and technological relationship with the nearby slag heaps at Mavrovounos (SIA 4). As a result, the idea of a wider production network integrated into the natural and sociotechnical landscape (Knapp 1999b:236–238; Pfaffenberger 1992), rather than a traditional review of isolated entities, stood at the forefront of our reconstruction.

SCY219: MITSERO KOKKINOYIA: MINING, ROASTING AND SMELTING REMAINS
SCY219-1: SLAG SCATTER

Following the path that branches off the main road from Mitsero, a small slag scatter was discovered about 50 to 60 m from the southern end of the modern spoil heaps. The 10.5 x 2.6 m layer of compacted slag, about 0.50 m thick, was heavily eroded by a creek bed shifting laterally over its surface through time. The remaining slag, located at present between two channels at the bottom of a gully between two hills, is unlikely to be even partly in situ. No slag was found in the creek beds further uphill, only pieces eroded from this unit farther downstream. Several pieces of pottery collected from its surface—undecorated utilitarian and storage vessel fragments—were consistent with an Archaic to Classical date. More such eroded remains are likely present in the immediate environment, washed down from the spoil heaps above or extant as residues from smaller slag scatters.

SCY219-2: SLAG SCATTER

Farther uphill toward the modern mining tower, we encountered a large scatter of crushed slag—about 41 m wide and 7 m high from top to bottom—on an artificial hillside (plate XLII). In addition there was a heavily packed, thin slag layer ranging from 3 to 10 cm thick on a modern track above the crushed slag and leading to the top of the spoil heaps. Located at the southeastern end of the modern spoil heaps, this obviously contained the remains of a secondary deposit, where slag was used as road metal to stabilize the topsoil. Bruce (1937:642) had already mentioned this practice. The metal was probably quarried from the ancient slag heaps near the modern open cast.

SCY219-3: MINE DUMPS AND ANCIENT MINING TIMBERS

Immediately to the north of SCY219-2 in the eastern part of the site, the first modern dump of crushed pyrites was found in front of the modern mining tower and the ore crushing and loading facility. Several mining props, all broken, were found in these dumps. These props were most likely mined along with the pyrites when the ancient mining remains were cut by the modern operations and crushed along with the ores. The loading facility for trucks, adjacent to the modern ore-processing plant and powerhouse, contained a mechanism for filtering out the coarser pieces of ore and debris.

This subunit resembled some of the modern mine dumps visible in open casts, where open flat areas are littered with small cone-shaped piles of mining waste, often misinterpreted as ore enrichment remains (Conrad and Rothenberg 1980: 69, 72–73). Immediately behind the large mining tower, an excellently preserved rail track about 150 m long led into a modern, semicircular mining tunnel 2.5 m high and 4 m wide at its base. This tunnel extended about 80 m into Mount Lambadhousa but was boarded up at that point. The interior of the gallery was constructed from iron sets with wooden planks behind them for lagging to hold back rubble (Ritchie and Hooker 1997:13). To the southwest of the rail track stand many of the original and, now rusty, mining carts.

SCY219-4: MINE DUMPS, CRUSHED SLAG, AND ANCIENT MINING TIMBERS

Farther up the dirt road to the west, toward the large modern open-cast pit, we found more slag scatters for road metalling, timber supports from galleries, and dumps of crushed pyrites in the modern spoil heaps. The props in these dumps were all at least partially replaced by leached secondary oxides and sulfates, while some showed evidence of crudely shaped ends for fitting cross beams. They thereby seem to resemble earlier finds from the northern Troodos (Bruce 1937:653). Consequently, the slightly

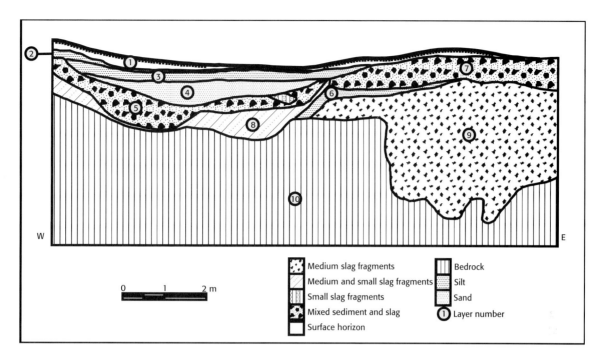

better preserved pieces may be interpreted as being later in date. The size of the galleries, which can be derived from the reconstructed timbers, does not resemble any of the larger tunnels dug by modern companies. The galleries in question would have provided only a very limited workspace and no easy access or evacuation of ore/debris.

SCY219-5: ROAD METALLING AND SLAG SCATTERS

SCY219-5 contained only secondary deposits of tap slag from dumped road metalling material and naturally redeposited wash. This subunit is situated immediately west of SCY219-4 and at the northern edge of the modern spoil heaps, in the center of the Kokkinoyia site. As such, it is safe to assume that this material was scattered during the quarrying of the slag heap for road metal; it would also have improved access to the modern open-cast mine.

SCY219-6: SLAG HEAP WITH STRATIFIED DEPOSITS

This subunit consists of an area wedged in between spoil heaps from the modern mine and the modern mine entrance. It contains the southernmost remains of a large slag heap with stratified layers, quarried for road metalling in the modern mine, including one section at its northernmost limit. This cut section is situated to the west of the modern mining pit and was drawn in detail (figure 4.51). Eighteen pieces

Figure 4.51 SCY219-6: section: **1**, Surface horizon and slag. Fine clay/silt with frequent fragments of tap slag (maximum 8 cm). Much root disturbance, 2.5 YR 4/4; **2**, Compact, very fine clay/silt thin lens. Moderate inclusions of broken tap slag. More clay content, more purple and more compact than 1, 2.5 YR 4/4; **3**, Moderately compact fine clay/silt. Occasional sub-angular, stone inclusions (maximum 4 cm) 7.5 YR 5/8; **4**, Pale orange, moderately compact fine sand (4D). Very occasional sub-angular stone inclusions (max, 4 cm); **5**, Loose mid-gray/brown sandy silt. Occasional small (2 cm) sub-angular pebble inclusions. Frequent fragments of broken tap slag (maximum 6 cm), 2.5 YR 5/4; **6**, Moderately compact sandy silt, 7.5 YR 5/6; **7**, Fine sandy silt (micaceous). Quite frequent loose fragments of tap slag (6–8 cm), 2.5 YR 5/4; **8**, Small slag heap of very compact broken tap slag. Heavily eroded.; **9**, Large slag heap of very compact broken tap slag. Heavily eroded. Large copper oxide inclusions (2 cm); **10**, Bedrock

of pottery were counted and 13 diagnostics collected on the surface of this subunit, mostly in front of the southern end of the slag heap. Unfortunately, none was found in the section itself. Of all subunits, this was the only one with a significant modern component. Several pieces of modern coarse ware and tile were found among the pottery sherds farther away from the section, while two pieces were unidentifiable. The remaining four pieces, including one round handle, appear to be of Archaic to Classical date. Some of these undecorated utilitarian wares may once have been used for cooking.

Figure 4.52 SCY219-7a: cutting through ancient slag heap. Section SCY219-7a/7c is on the left side of the cutting.

SCY219-7: SLAG HEAP WITH STRATIFIED DEPOSITS, ANCIENT GALLERY, AND POTTERY SCATTER

Immediately east of subunit 6, on the western and eastern side of the modern mine entrance, two large, stratified slag sections were found; these belonged to the same slag heap, originally about 27.5 m long and 7.8 to 10.0 m high (figure 4.52). Its base was still preserved in full and visible enough to be measured. The original large slag heap had been cut by modern miners to allow easy access to the big modern open-cast pit, thereby resulting in two well-preserved sections, the western one of which was measured and drawn (Section SCY219-7a). The tap slag was broken up into small and medium-sized pieces and was characterized by considerable secondary copper oxide staining. No complete slag cakes were found. The slag heap was formed by consecutive layers of crushed slag, forming a clear stratigraphy of production and dumping phases. It also contained pottery, possible furnace lining, and several hard-packed working floors with some charcoal inclusions.

Previous analyses of slag samples from the Kokkinoyia mine all came from undated surface collections, and consequently the data can serve only as a guideline for comparative interpretations. Samples previously taken from this slag heap (Kokkinoyia B [Mitsero]-CY6) were described as a lighter, yellow ochreous slag. The slags were non-magnetic and of the dendritic wüstite type with some

golden sulfide stringers but no copper globules (Tylecote 1977:319, 323–324).

The earliest publication of the American Expedition to Idalion included an appendix with the first large-scale analytical program of Cypriot slags and ores. From the seven samples ascribed to Kokkinoyia (nos. 72–77, 81), only one can be associated with the site under investigation (no. 81). All the others seem to belong to Mitsero *Mavrovounos* farther down the hillslope to the south. The single sample in question had a copper content of 0.75%, no detectable sulfur and a manganese content of 5.45% (Koucky and Steinberg 1974:156–162).

The Akhera survey of 1979 noted four distinct slag heaps near the Kokkinoyia mine (including the two at Mavrovounos), as well as evidence of ancient mining. Samples taken from the slag heap in our subunit 7 were classified as high-iron blocky type slags (so-called Type B) with a homogeneous black interior and thin brown-black alteration on the exterior. They clustered near the fayalite-wüstite eutectic and had a low viscosity indicated by the flattened surfaces. Such high density slags retained sulfides, but copper prills were rare. Some Cypro-Classical sherds were found in the same pile (Koucky and Steinberg 1982a; Wallace 1982:243).

SCSP's analysis of nine samples taken from the stratified slag heap at the modern mine entrance (figure 4.53) demonstrate the use of a different production technology than the one reconstructed for Mavrovounos. No manganese oxide was detected, which points to a different fluxing and slagging technology for these earlier remains. The zinc content was often considerable and ranged between 0.6 and 2.5% zinc oxide, most likely reflecting the exploitation of specific sphalerite-rich ore layers. The copper content of 0.8 to 3.1% copper oxide clearly indicated the production of copper metal, and in one specific case several distinct copper prills were visible. Both matte and remaining pyrite inclusions were found (see chapter 5.4).

In the center of the section, remains of an installation 1.50 m long and 0.85 m high were still visible (figure 4.54). Badly damaged furnace lining remains were next to a big block of limestone and several stratified layers of redeposited soil and slag. One meter to the right was an area with seven consecutive layers of working floors containing charcoal, fine silt, and packed soil. Both features were situated about 2 m above the present ground level. Similarly at Skouriotissa and Mitsero *Kouloupakhis* (SIA 3), structures were embedded in such slag heaps (Knapp 1999b:239; Tylecote 1977:324).

Three plain utilitarian sherds of Archaic to Classical date, characterized by some yellowing from the prolonged exposure to a sulfur- and iron-rich environment, were found in the section (table 4.25 summarizes the pottery from all ten subunits of SCY219). One piece was clearly part of a rim from a juglet and one from a thin walled cup. Another eight pieces were collected from the collapsed section debris, lying in front of the section itself. Again, all these plain sherds were Archaic to Classical in date. Three of them, including a flat, turned-out rim (cat. S-0057) and a strap handle, were definitely or possibly from storage amphorae and one possibly from a torpedo transport amphora. Another piece may come from a deep bowl. The remaining three sherds came from indeterminate utilitarian wares. One possible ground stone or mining hammer was also noted.

Pottery was also collected from the more eroded eastern section (7b), which was 29.8 m long and averaged 4.2 m high. The slag heap, therefore, originally sloped down toward this side. Four Archaic to Classical sherds were discovered in the section. All were plain utilitarian and storage wares, including one amphora fragment and one possible torpedo transport amphora fragment alongside two pieces of utilitarian and possibly cooking wares. One sherd was found in the debris beneath the slag heap, together with a piece of extremely weathered furnace lining.

Table 4.25 SCY219: analyzed pottery

Chronotype	Period	Qty
Cooking ware-Ar	Ar	3
Green ware-Ar	Ar	1
Plain ware-Ar	Ar	1
White Painted-Ar [S-0058]	Ar	1
Amphora-Cl [S-0057]	Cl	2
Plain White-Cl	Cl	2
White Painted-Cl	Cl	1
Plain ware-Cl	Cl	2
Amphora-AC	AC	5
Cooking ware-AC	AC	1
Plain ware-AC	AC	10
Plain White-AC	AC	1
Coarse ware-Mod	Mod	8
Amphora-Hi	Hi	1
Tile-PC	PC	3
Coarse ware-Unk	Unk	1
Unknown	Unk	1
TOTAL for SCY219		44

Note: Figures in brackets refer to cataloged items (see chapter 5.1)

At the northern end of this subunit, where the entrance to the modern open-cast mine cuts down into bedrock, the remains of a gallery (SCY219-7c) were found just above the bottom of the modern pit, about 4 to 6 m from the northern edge of slag section 7a. Although heavily eroded at its entrance, this gallery still contained some pottery and malachite-azurite nuggets within, buried beneath some mining debris. The friable rock contained no tool marks and seemed to follow a distinct vein with remaining carbonate staining underground. The preserved height was 1.30 m and the measured width 1.80 m at its widest point. Of all the subunits, this one can be most closely dated. Two White Painted pieces from the rim of a hydria or amphora were joined, probably dating to the Cypro-Archaic I or II period (cat. S-0058; for possible parallels see Gjerstad 1948: Figs. XXX.4, LI.7 and material from Tamassos in Buchholz and Untiedt 1996:Fig. 26.b). The remaining piece—a plain utilitarian sherd—is Classical in date.

Atop the slag heap (SCY219-7d), above the western face of Section 7a, six sherds were collected for identification, although about two dozen were scattered across this surface. Not all could be collected because of the danger of the section collapsing. Except for one sherd, which was a possible Roman amphora handle, all pieces were Archaic to Classical in date. They included two amphora fragments and three utilitarian, possibly cooking ware, fragments.

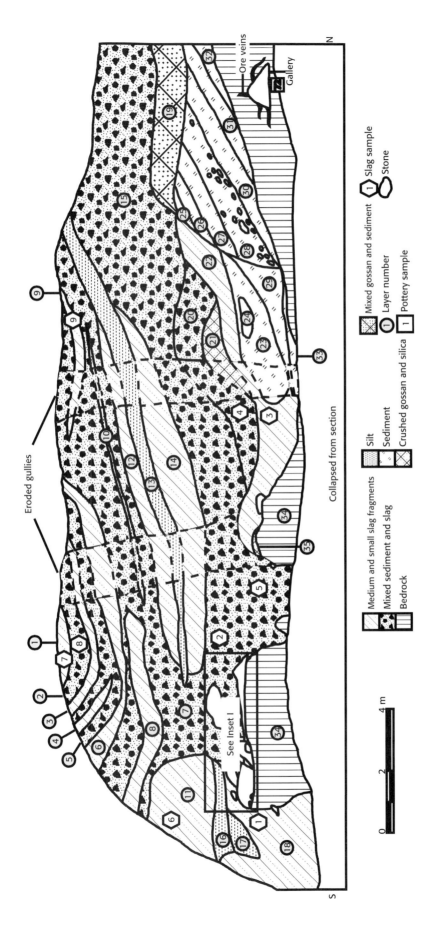

Figure 4.53 SCY219-7a: section 7a: **1**, Medium to small crushed slag; **2**, Mixed sediment and slag fill; **3**, Medium to small crushed slag; **4**, Mixed sediment, slag fill; **5**, Medium to small crushed slag; **6**, Medium to small crushed slag; **7**, Mixed sediment, slag fill; **8**, Medium to small crushed slag; **9**, Medium to small crushed slag; **10**, Fine silt layer; **11**, Medium to small crushed slag; **12**, Medium to small crushed slag; **13**, Fine silt layer; **14**, Medium to small crushed slag; **15**, Mixed sediment, slag fill; **16**, Fine silt layer; **17**, Fine silt layer; **18**, Medium to small crushed slag; **19**, Mixed gossan, gray sediment; **20**, Mixed reddish sediment, slag; **21**, Crushed gossan, silica; **22**, Medium to small crushed slag; **23**, Red orange sediment; **24**, Red orange sediment; **25**, White sediment; **26**, Mixed gray and white sediment; **27**, White sediment; **28**, Mixed gray and white sediment; **29**, Mixed gray and white sediment; **30**, White sediment; **31**, Mixed gray and white sediment; **32**, White sediment; **33**, White sediment; **34**, Bedrock: pillow lava; **35**, Crumbled gossan, silica

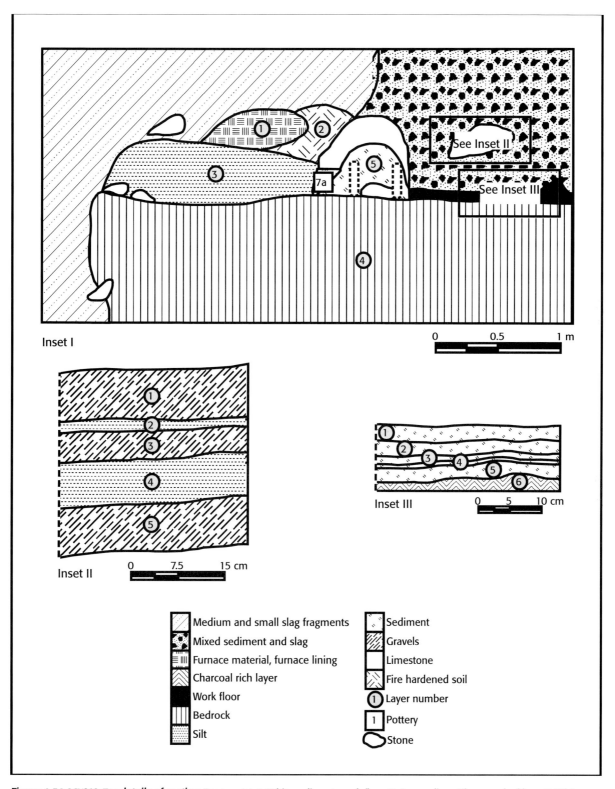

Inset I

Inset II

Inset III

Medium and small slag fragments
Mixed sediment and slag
Furnace material, furnace lining
Charcoal rich layer
Work floor
Bedrock
Silt

Sediment
Gravels
Limestone
Fire hardened soil
Layer number
Pottery
Stone

Figure 4.54 SCY219-7a: details of section 7a: *Inset I*: **1**, White sediment, work-floor; **2**, Gray sediment from crushed lava; **3**, White sediment, work-floor; **4**, Red sediment, work-floor; **5**, White sediment, work-floor; **6**, Charcoal rich layer; *Inset II:* **1**, Fine gravel, reddish sediment; **2**, Fine silt, reddish sediment; **3**, Gravel, gray sediment; **4**, Silt, reddish sediment; **5**, Gravel, gray sediment; *Inset III:* **1**, Collapsed cavity from installation; **2**, Fire-hardened soil by installation; **3**, Stratified fine silt layers; **4**, Furnace lining from installation; **5**, Impacted gray sediment with linear impressions next to furnace lining and large limestone

SCY219-8: OPEN-CAST MINE WITH ANCIENT GALLERIES AND MINING TIMBERS

In the large open-cast pit to the north of SCY219-7, we found abundant evidence of ancient mining remains. The western side contained at least 10 ends of partially preserved, rock-cut galleries located just below the gossans, in the contact zone between the gossan layer and upper pillow lavas and the main low-grade ore layer (Panayiotou 1989a:86; see figure 4.55). On both sides of the pit, large numbers of irregular vertical adits penetrate the gossan—starting quite near what must have been the original surface—and provide further evidence of ancient prospecting and planning in this area. All over the mining pit were unusual amounts of (secondary) malachite and azurite nodules, as well as some minor pyrite veins stuck inside the pillow lavas. Minute traces of possible chalcopyrite were also visible in several places.

Several mining timbers (SCY219-8a; see figures 4.56, 4.57) were still in situ about 5 to 6 m above the bottom of the open-cast mine. Two upright posts with crossbeam and remains of wooden roofing had an internal stratigraphy of redeposited clay-like and finely crushed gossan layers. They provide proof of the use of "sets," pre-cut timber frames used for propping the sides and roofs of drives (Ritchie and Hooker 1997:14). Two joining rim sherds, of cooking ware fabric and possibly of Iron Age to Hellenistic date, were found about 10 m to the south of Section 8a, mixed in with the eroded and collapsed material from the western section of the open cast.

On the eastern side, opposite 8a, more collapsed and partially permeated props were found (SCY219-8b; see figure 4.56) about 4 to 5 m above the bottom of the open-cast pit. No real ends of galleries (for example, cavities cut into the rock) were apparent here because of the heavily eroded lower sections of the pit on that side. However, negative imprints of galleries were preserved in the top half of the modern open-cast face. Having been filled in with leached mud and clay as well as chunks of gossan from above, the interior of these galleries became heavily compacted through time. These galleries did not need extra support from mining props when they were quarried, so when they were cut by modern mining activities, only the filled-in clay-like layers were left, forming distinctive rectangular and square orange-

brown patches on the rock face. Similar fills had been noted before at Mavrovouni and Skouriotissa (Bruce 1937:648). None of these was accessible for further study. Their estimated width and height ranged from 0.5 to 1.5 m.

In Section 8c, a rock-cut gallery was still partially preserved over a length of 2.5 m directly into the rock face. It measured about 2.5 to 3.0 m across and had a roughly concave shape. Distinctively irregular, rounded traces of hammering were still visible as evidence of the use of stone hammers rather than metal picks (Craddock 1995:38–39).

The northernmost end of the modern pit is formed by a large convex cavity cut into the basalt. Few in situ signs of ancient activity remained here. Section 8d contained some remains of upright timber props, heavily replaced by mineralization and cut down to about 15 cm above the present floor level. They extended for 3 to 4 m and were originally part of a horizontal gallery. At the northernmost end of SCY219-8, a rock-cut gallery of roughly rectangular shape was still visible some 75 to 80 m above the bottom of the modern pit. The bottom of the open cast was encrusted with secondary copper sulfates forming malachite-green crystals and a large mining lake during the wetter winter months.

SCY219-9: SLAG SCATTERS, SECTION, AND ORE-ROASTING SITE

To the west of SCY219-8, modern spoil heaps contain bulldozed slag scatters as well as secondary copper oxides and the remains of a stratified slag section (SCY219-9a), 3 m high and 5 m wide with crushed tap slag. The slag section was situated on the easternmost side of this subunit, immediately above the western edge of the mine pit; it formed part of the main slag heap. This subunit furthermore contained the only possible remains of a stratified section of an ancient ore processing and roasting area, 4 m long and 0.60 m high (SCY219-9b). The identification of these remains was based on their similarity with those in SCY022 (chapter 4.1; Koucky and Steinberg 1982b:149), and on the field identification of small samples (see chapter 3.6).

The earliest expedition to this area in 1973 took the first samples from the Kokkinoyia site, from the area above the modern open-cast pit. Interestingly enough, the first group (Kokkinoyia A [Mitsero]—

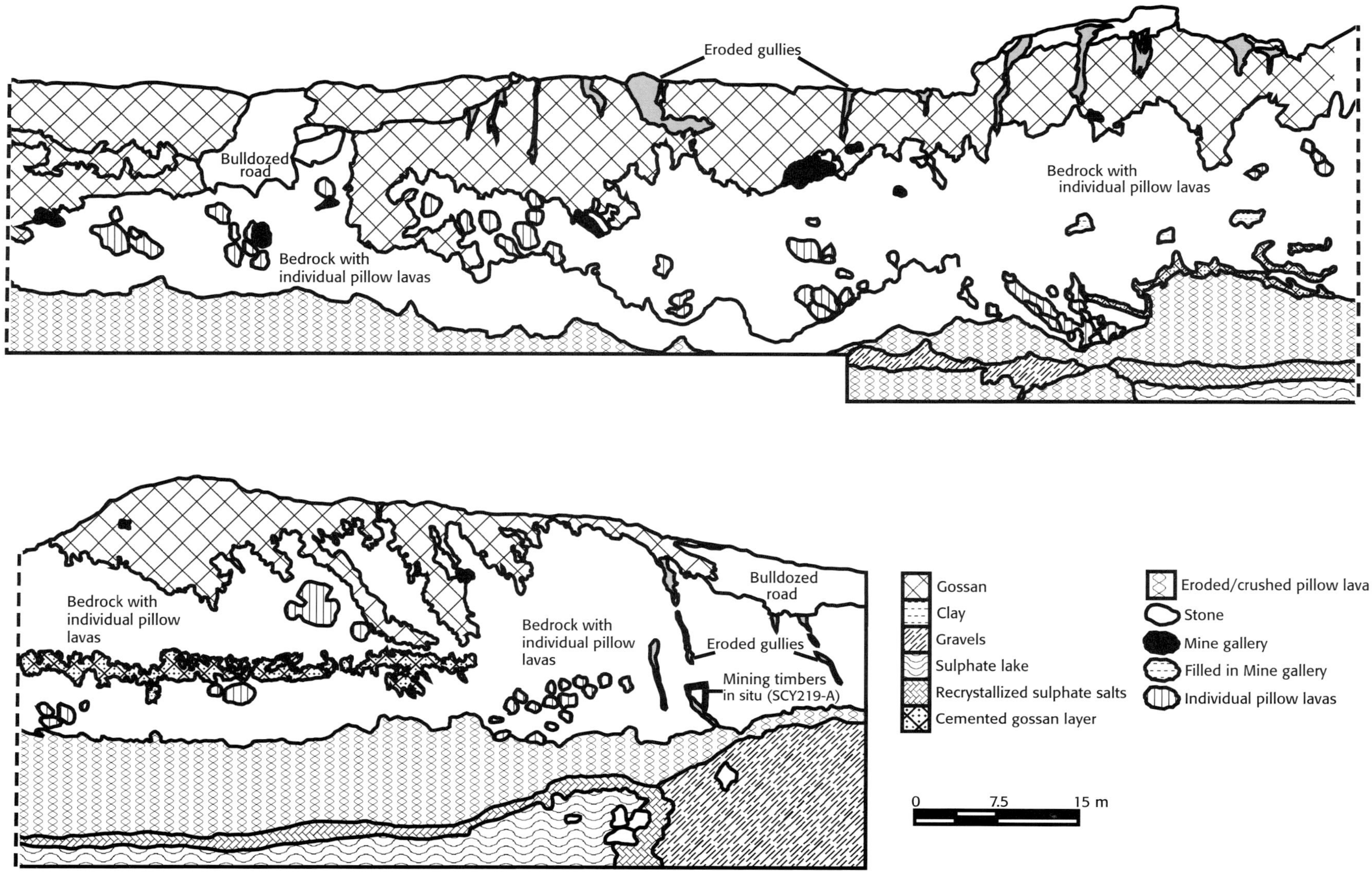

Eroded gullies
Bulldozed road
Bedrock with individual pillow lavas
Bedrock with individual pillow lavas
Bedrock with individual pillow lavas
Bedrock with individual pillow lavas
Bulldozed road
Eroded gullies
Mining timbers in situ (SCY219-A)
Gossan
Clay
Gravels
Sulphate lake
Recrystallized sulphate salts
Cemented gossan layer
Eroded/crushed pillow lava
Stone
Mine gallery
Filled in Mine gallery
Individual pillow lavas
0
7.5
15 m

Figure 4.55 SCY219-8: section

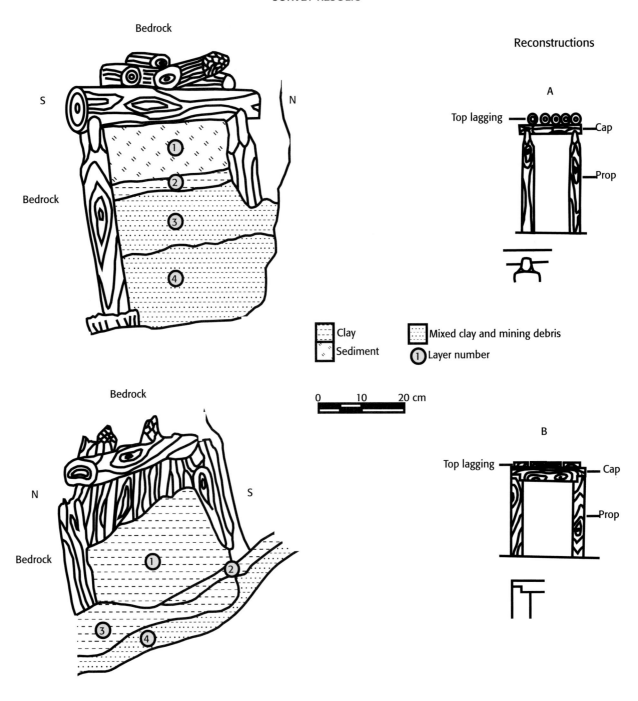

Figure 4.56 SCY219-8a/8b: ancient mining timbers: SCY219-8a: **1**, Compact gray/white washed-in sediment with secondary malachite staining; **2**, Heavy and compact yellow clay; **3**, Yellow clay, crushed pillow lava; **4**, Crushed gossan, pillow lava and hematite in heavy gray yellow clay; SCY219-8b: **1**, Red clay fill; **2**, Yellow clay; **3**, Red-beige clay; **4**, Beige clay with hematite and secondary malachite nodules

CY5) was described as "a conglomerate of charcoal, gossan (perhaps as flux), small slag etc., all cemented together with precipitated iron from the surface waters" (Tylecote 1977:323–324). The same area also seems to have contained a considerable amount of malachite traces, which seems to point at least partially to the roasting location described under SCY219-9b. Analysis revealed that the reddish, porous, and highly magnetic slag contained no golden sulfide stringers or copper globules. Its microstructure consisted of a fayalite and a dendritic wüstite phase. The high magnetism was explained as a result of the fairly unweathered interior and high Fe_3O_4 content (Tylecote 1977:323–324). This location was also revisited by Koucky and Steinberg and in turn interpreted as highly oxidized, red Type P (Phoenician) slag, without any associated sherds (Koucky and Steinberg 1982a; Wallace 1982:243). Because the minute charcoal inclusions disintegrated at our every sampling attempt, no dates are available.

SCY219-10: SLAG SCATTERS AND MODERN ADITS

SCY219-10 consisted of impressively colored gossan remains, which must have originally continued across the modern mine pit. Once again, this area contained large quantities of secondary malachite and copper sulfates. Near the northwestern edge of the unit, we encountered a well-preserved adit descending about 6 m on a 40 to 45° slope, with a second gallery starting at the bottom (now collapsed but once leading into the bedrock at a 45° angle from the adit). This inclined shaft, or underlay (Ritchie and Hooker 1997:13) obviously served as a principal entrance to a mine to follow the dip of an ore body. It was quite distinct from the tunnel remains located in SCY219-8. All the rock-cut remains in the latter had rounded side walls and roofs and distinctly uneven surfaces compatible with the use of stone hammers or hand-held metal tools (Craddock 1995:38–40). The underlay in SCY219-10, on the other hand, had a very regular rectangular shape with quite even surfaces, most likely part of the twentieth century AD underground explorations.

About 4 to 5 m to the northwest of SCY219-10a, we located another adit (10b) beneath a large pine tree. It sloped down at a 50 to 60° angle for 2 m, after which it turned upward at roughly the same angle. It was again very well cut and filled in with collapsed material from the roof.

Figure 4.57 SCY219-8a: ancient mining timbers

DATING

Although the relative dates derived from our pottery are not so accurate as those obtained from radiocarbon dating (see Panayiotou 1989a:85), there seems to be general agreement about the range of periods. It is at times difficult to distinguish between Cypro-Archaic and Cypro-Classical coarse wares in the SCSP area. The consecutive periods that fall within the eighth to fourth centuries BC could therefore be present without being necessarily distinguishable. Two joining White Painted sherds (cat. S-0058), interestingly found inside an ancient gallery, were definitely Cypro-Archaic, while another amphora handle was possibly Roman. Two sherds of unknown date in SCY219-8 could also belong to the Hellenistic period.

The pottery from Kokkinoyia thus suggests significant Archaic to Classical (and to a much lesser extent possible Hellenistic and Roman) presence in association with archaeometallurgical activity. All these vessel types would have been used by those involved in the mining and smelting activities, for storage, transport, or subsistence. This situation and chronology are roughly paralleled at the other Archaic to Classical metallurgical type site of Ayia Varvara-Almyras (Fasnacht 1999). It seems likely that the amphorae were used as water vessels, especially in the hot and dry environment of a mining/roasting/smelting site, rather than as containers for the collection of percolating copper sulfate as has been suggested previously (Bruce 1937:640; Koucky and Steinberg 1989).

MINING TECHNOLOGY AND ORES AT KOKKINOYIA

Mining Timbers. The timbers found in situ, as well as in the modern mining debris at Kokkinoyia, form one of the most unusual finds from any mine in Cyprus. They represent some of our best evidence for the deliberate targeting of specific ore layers by ancient miners, since they show the exact location of galleries and adits within the geological stratigraphy. Of several such in situ finds noted in the past, all have since been obliterated by recent exploitation (Bruce 1937:651–658). Most mining timbers unfortunately were discovered in piles of crushed pyrites and gangue, but nevertheless can offer useful information on the size and planning of underground workings.

SCY219-3 contained several caps, heavy timbers placed horizontally on top of two vertical timbers to support the roof of a drive or tunnel. Some pieces of props, wooden posts used as supports for the caps, were also discovered (Ritchie and Hooker 1997:12–14; Weisgerber 1982:Pls I.1 and II.1–3). Most pieces found at Kokkinoyia were broken up in the modern crushing and loading facility immediately to the north of this concentration. Based on a pattern of systematic processing and dumping of crushed pyrites and the high concentrations found in the western part of the subunit, one could suggest that they originated from one specific area in the open-cast mine. The props with a circular section were cut with an adze instead of sawn and were often encrusted with secondary metals. This is regarded as the best indicator of ancient mining timber in the absence of radiocarbon dates (Bruce 1937: 650). The differences in appearance between the sawn and unaltered timbers, most likely from the underground explorations in the 1950s (Bear 1963:72), were clear.

Another concentration of 18 caps and props was noted in SCY219-4. The timbers here were often preserved over their full length (up to 170 cm) and were once again encrusted with secondary metals and roughly cut. The best example—a 90 x 15 cm cap with an 8 cm deep cut on either side—implies a narrow working space of less than 1 m in width. All sets were probably made from *Pinus brutia* or cypress (Bruce 1937:650; Knapp 1999b:237). The timbers were all found in the top layers of the modern mining dumps and, thus, may be assumed to derive from the bottom of the open cast, that is, the last exploitation phases before all activity ceased at this location. Such a conclusion fits well with the timbers found still in situ near the bottom of the open-cast pit in SCY219-8, in opposite sections of the modern open-cast mine.

The western remains in SCY219-8a consist of two wooden props with one cap on top, on which several remaining timbers from top-lagging are visible. Lagging consists of secondary timbers placed behind the main timber supports in a shaft or drive to hold back rubble or loose country rock (Ritchie and Hooker 1997:13). They were made of thinner trunks and big branches. SCY219-8b was heavily encrusted with secondary minerals. In fact, most of the original wood seems to be completely replaced by encrustation and the very rough manner of construction points to older remains. Two props and one cap are partially visible with pieces of collapsed side- or roof-lagging behind them; thus we may be dealing with a cut side-section instead of a front-section as in 8a. These remains are situated at roughly the same height above the bottom of the mining pit, and may therefore be interpreted as belonging to the same level of drives but possibly to different galleries.

One further preserved example from the Kokkinoyia mine is on display in the archaeometallurgical section of the Cyprus Museum in Nicosia. This completely preserved shaft collar, also known as cribbing, consists of composed timbers horizontally laid one upon another and used as the framework around the neck of a vertical shaft (Bruce 1937:670–671; Ritchie and Hooker 1997:14; Weisgerber 1982:Pl. I.2). It is said to come from this site, but no exact geological or topographical information was available. Interestingly, the set-up has been reconstructed as going down a gossan layer, a plausible explanation and possible clue to its original use. It was probably used as a reinforced timbered surface entry to an underground tunnel (Ritchie and Hooker 1997:14).

The wooden props from Kokkinoyia have already been discussed briefly by Panayiotou (1989a). Some in situ timbers discovered during modern exploitation were dated by radiocarbon to three different periods: ninth to seventh centuries BC, sixth to third centuries BC, and third to fifth centuries AD (roughly the Archaic, Classical, and Roman periods). The exact source of the original samples is not given. Every ore layer discovered in the modern mine, however, had already been exploited by ancient miners. Panayiotou comments that the underground workings were particularly impressive, especially for the period of the eighth to seventh century BC, and that the galleries reached as deep as 200 m below the surface in certain places. The ancient tunnels were located mostly between the upper pillow lava zone, which contained the gossan and secondary enrichment layers, and the compacted low-grade ore layers immediately above the stockwork zone (Panayiotou 1989a:85–86).

Reconstruction of Mining Technology. By assessing the location of ancient mining remains within the geological stratigraphy, and by comparing the ore types to the analytical results of the sampled slag, we are able to establish which specific ore types were mined by the ancient smelters at Kokkinoyia.

Evidence of mining activities has been encountered most frequently in the massive sulfides in the pillow lavas where the ore easily could have been excavated with the available tools (Craddock 1995:38–40). At Kokkinoyia, after open casts had been used for mining out the upper copper carbonate-rich layers, adits (or drives) were possibly run from the surface into the hillside for the purpose of intersecting the ore body in the first instance; no real traces remain because of all the later disturbances. Galleries or levels would then have branched out depending on the location of ore-bearing veins into underground mines. Some of the vertical shafts visible in the long section (figure 4.55) show prospecting trenches, excavated with a view to locating a reef. The fact that several do not continue farther down shows that miners were not always successful in locating ore-bearing veins or else stopped when high-grade ores ran out. The existence of stopes, underground excavations from which ore is extracted, seems to have been confined to the upper levels of the ore bodies in SCY219-8 and might

have been characteristic for the earlier phases of underground exploration. The rock-cut cavities are the partially preserved remains of this stoping process (Ritchie and Hooker 1997:14–15). The lower levels, where the in situ timbers were found, were clearly less stable than the stoping levels, but Panayiotou's (1989b) work indicates that the timber sets were used from the outset.

The change in specific ores mined, reflected in the differing zinc content of the earlier Kokkinoyia and later Mavrovounos slag, was thus probably the result of the gallery system being extended to lower levels and/or less accessible layers. Accordingly, we can attribute a refined knowledge of mining geology to the ancient miners of this region.

Modern Mining at Kokkinoyia. The large slag dump nearby was already noted during renewed prospecting activity this century as providing evidence of considerable mining activity by the ancients. Although the mine is mainly known for its copper ores and pyrite production (figure 4.58), several other minerals had been exploited there. Between 1937 and 1940, the gossan was worked for gold and silver, but prospecting was only started in 1953 on an actual disseminated cupreous pyrite deposit. A considerable amount of underground exploration was involved, as a result of which relatively small tonnages of ore (14,000 tons with an average of 28% sulfur and 0.5% copper) were recovered during 1954 and 1955. In 1956 work on the deposit ceased, but prospecting recommenced in 1960 to 1962 and resulted in the discovery of a major ore layer at 100 m (Bear 1963:71–72; Panayiotou 1989a:85). Compared to some of the nearby workings, such as the Agrokipia open-cast lease, where 157,888 tons of ore were mined and 39,818 tons of pyrites were produced in 1957 alone, Kokkinoyia represents a rather limited operation (Bear 1963:69, Table 24).

Between 1973 and 1979 the amounts of ore extracted came to 481,000 tons with an average copper content of 2%. The exploitation of the mine and of the ore-enrichment facilities indisputably contributed to the economic and social development of the villages in the area, particularly Mitsero. It altered the traditional agricultural character of the area and resulted in a mixed agricultural and industrial economy with an extensively modified natural and cultural landscape (chapter 4.5; Knapp 1999b:236; Panayiotou 1989a:86). The export of the crushed pyrites and the contemporary workings in the

Figure 4.58
Ore-loading
dock and spoil
heaps at
Kokkinoyia
mine, from the
northeast

nearby Kriadhis and Kokkinopezoula mines (Bear 1963:67–72) in fact mirrored the larger archaeometallurgical organization and landscape of the Archaic to Roman periods as well as its interaction with the outside world.

CONCLUSION

The Mitsero Kokkinoyia mine and slag heaps represent one of the most important SCSP areas for studying ancient mining and smelting technology, within the proposed model of a spatially and technologically organized *chaîne opératoire* (chapter 2.6). Together they constitute the micro-regional and localized subunits of the overall organization of the archaeometallurgical production system (Knapp, Donnelly, and Kassianidou 1998:263–266), with distinct, interacting production units spread across several locations. Both Kokkinoyia and Mavrovounos (SIA 4; see chapter 4.4) have provided ample evidence of ancient smelting procedures and industrial organization in the form of stratified slag heaps, with clear examples of waste management. They both belong to the same chaîne opératoire which, although characterized by technical changes in the smelting process and the spatial shifts of certain production units, probably remained essentially unchanged in its organizational system.

The slag at Kokkinoyia, compared to that from Mavrovounos, is characterized by higher zinc and copper contents, and a total lack of manganiferous slags. In light of the mainly Archaic to Classical dating of the Kokkinoyia remains there, it becomes clear that a shift in the location of the smelting sites occurred first in the Archaic to Classical periods to the eastern slag heap at Mavrovounos (SCY024E), and then gradually to the western slag heap (SCY024W) during the Roman period. Furthermore, there was a simultaneous change in technology, with the development of a more efficient copper-extracting and slagging technique. This led to a specific spatial organization of the technology involved, with what seems to be a high degree of deliberate planning based on the stratigraphy of the slag heaps with incorporated remains of installations (SCY024E-1, SCY024E-2).

Possible reasons for these changes in location could include the exhaustion of raw materials such as local fuel and timber such as *Pinus brutia* or *Platanus orientalis* for the furnaces and mining galleries (Bruce 1937:650; Knapp 1999b:237), or even the easier access to communication routes via the Mavrovouniotis Valley toward Tamassos. Indirectly, we can even assume it was a consequence of an increase in scale. After all, the slag heaps at Mavrovounos constitute a significant rise in production over those at Kokkinoyia, even judged by the rather limited evidence of the estimated size of the slag heaps involved.

PLACES OF SPECIAL INTEREST (POSIs)

4.12 SCY010: Aredhiou *Vouppes*: Protohistoric Bronze Age Agricultural Settlement

Compiled by A. Bernard Knapp   Team leaders: Steve O. Held,
Priscilla Keswani   Geomorphology: Jay Noller
Pottery: Priscilla Keswani, Joanna S. Smith

Grid reference: 519015/3878700
Cadastral map: XXIX/56
Aerial photograph: 1993, run 177, no. 54
Survey unit: 338

Aredhiou *Vouppes* was found during regular transect survey. Although none of the pottery was recognizable by type/date in the field, a Late Cypriot (LC) wall bracket and a Black Slip Wheelmade sherd were identified among the collected material once it had been washed. On a revisit to unit 338, several LC pithos sherds were collected. The predominance of utilitarian wares and the presence of the wall bracket fragment, along with the occurrence of ground-stone implements, indicate that SCY010 was a farmstead or small settlement. Tombs may have been situated adjacent to or nearby the settlement. In 1992 SCSP collected a few White Slip 2, Black Slip Wheelmade, and Red-on-Black sherds eroding from a hillock less than 1 km east of Vouppes, at Aredhiou *Koladhes* (SCY001, see Knapp et al. 1992:331). In addition, there are probable tombs at the south end of SCY010.

Aredhiou *Vouppes* may be described tentatively as an "agricultural support village" (Knapp 1997:59–60, 66). The pithos fragments found there come from storage vessels of diverse sizes, including some very large examples (Keswani's Groups II and III, see Keswani 1989). Such finds first led to the suggestion that Vouppes may have been an officially managed agricultural village involved in provisioning one or more mining or smelting sites in the Troodos foothills (for example, Politiko *Phorades* 1). Webb and Frankel (1994) suggest that a similar agricultural village and collection center was located at Analiondas *Palioklichia* some 10 km southeast of Vouppes. The recovery of a Mycenaean sherd from the surface of Vouppes in 1995 offers some evidence of trading contacts with other sites that had access to imported goods.

PHYSICAL LANDSCAPE

Aredhiou *Vouppes* is located on an alluvial terrace along the banks of the Aloupos River drainage where the sedimentary plains and the igneous foothills meet. Today, the land at and around Vouppes is given over to cultivated barley fields and a dairy farm. Overall, the landscape in the immediate area seems to have been relatively stable over the last few thousand years, except for minor episodes of soil removal or filling associated with terracing and construction of various sorts. At least part of this POSI, immediately north of the bend in the track (see figure 4.59), consists of in situ soils, a factor that was critical in choosing where to place our grid for intensive collection (see Field Methodology, below).

HISTORICAL CONTEXT

Among several changes that characterize the archaeological record of the Protohistoric Bronze Age (ProBA) or LC period, the most relevant in the present context is that a number of towns engaged in copper production and overseas trade arose throughout the coastal regions of Cyprus. While some of these towns were located in reasonable proximity to major ore deposits in the Troodos Mountains, others were much farther away; it is usually presumed that the more distant towns acquired their copper supplies through extensive trade networks (Keswani 1993; Webb and Frankel 1994; Knapp 1997). Within north-central and northwestern Cyprus, site locational factors and artifact assemblages suggest the existence of multiple networks of copper procurement and transport linking rural settlements to coastal centers in the Morphou Bay area, and/or in eastern Cyprus (Keswani and Knapp N.D.). The general character of these interactions between coastal and inland communities became increasingly hierarchical during the course of the Late Bronze Age.

From a topographic perspective, it might seem unlikely that Aredhiou *Vouppes* formed part of a link in a chain of sites leading toward Morphou Bay. Admittedly there are numerous ridges and streams that separate Vouppes from sites farther north/northwest (for example, Akhera and Akaki), but Vouppes is also accessible from Politiko and the modern transport route leading north/northeast. On the basis of

Figure 4.59 SCY010: topographical map

survey and funerary evidence alike, Keswani and Knapp (N.D.) note that prestige goods flowing into this part of the island appear to be less numerous and striking than those used by the highest status groups in the coastal centers and may not have been equivalent in value to the copper this region exported. In other words, we may be dealing here with unequal or hierarchical trading relationships with one or more centers located several kilometers distant.

FIELD METHODOLOGY

Aredhiou *Vouppes* was found in the course of standard transect survey in 1993 and surveyed as unit 338. During the 1996 season, when visibility of material on the ground had improved considerably over 1993, we carried out an intensive collection of surface finds at Vouppes (figure 4.59). The grids for intensive collection were established only where the geomorphologist had identified in situ soils. The densest scatter of archaeological data was recovered along the western side of the fields adjacent to the cliff, an area that fortunately is characterized by in situ soils.

Vouppes is similar to many POSIs, inasmuch as it requires a variety of approaches for gridded collection. Because only a small portion of the modern fields at SCY010 had an intact, Bronze Age surface,

we carried out a 10 m fixed-grid collection in those fields (subunits W3S0-S6S2). The collection included three squares along the bank where visibility was excellent. In addition, half of the squares in the stubble fields were collected according to a checkerboard pattern. Because the surface of the adjacent part of the stubble field had changed dramatically since antiquity (so that no material would be in context), we carried out an iron cross collection of 11 circles (subunits E0N0–W1N0), partly to test the geomorphological observation, and partly to obtain a representative collection of material from the four quadrats. In line with Keswani's goal of collecting a broad and representative sample of material, the team also obtained separate representative collections, walking at 5 m spacing, in a part of the 1993 unit 338, where visibility was excellent and a lot of material was present.

POTTERY

The densest scatter of material lay in the westernmost sector of the agricultural fields, immediately adjacent to the cliff, where the soils essentially are preserved from the Bronze Age. The pottery certainly indicates that the primary period of occupation was toward the end of the Bronze Age (LC IIC), and the few lithics collected do not contradict that placement.

The surface pottery from Aredhiou *Vouppes* included 22 pithos sherds, 10 plain ware sherds, one fragment of Black Slip Wheelmade ware, one sherd tentatively ascribed to White Painted Wheelmade 2/3 (pastoral style), and one terra-cotta (plain ware) wall bracket (338.2.1), all of which are Late Cypriot in date (table 4.26). A single sherd from a Red Polished bowl may attest to an earlier, PreBA 2 (Middle Bronze) component at the site.

The pithos sherds recovered from SCY010 by the SCSP teams reveal various types and sizes of storage vessels, ranging from the relatively small, short-necked variety (Group I, Keswani 1989) to the very large, usually long-necked vessels, which may have been used for supra-household level storage over long periods of time (Groups II and III). One pithos ware sherd also belonged to a large rectangular tub. Among the plain ware were two rim sherds representing medium to large utilitarian bowls and one flat strap handle fragment possibly deriving from a krater. The fabrics, rim profiles, and pithos body decoration (parallel raised lines, incised horizontal and wavy lines) observed in this material are closely paralleled by pithos ware from Kalavasos *Ayios Dhimitrios*, Kition *Chrysopolitissa*, Maa *Palaekastro*, Pyla *Kokkinokremnos*, Myrtou *Pighades* and Apliki *Karamallos* (see Keswani, in Knapp et al. 1994:337–338). Occupation of Aredhiou *Vouppes* must have been at least partly contemporaneous with these other Late Cypriot sites.

CONCLUSION

The Protohistoric Bronze Age in Cyprus was a time of increasing population when new urban centers were built, overseas contacts multiplied, and internal production (pottery, copper) and interregional contacts (Knapp 1986b) became more intensified and developed. Settlements like Aredhiou *Vouppes* would have been common elements of the habitational, locational, and trading systems that prevailed in the LC IIC/ProBA 3 period (Keswani 1993; Knapp 1997). The pottery recovered from Vouppes, in particular the abundance of large pithos sherds, supports the notion that this was an agricultural support village, functioning as one element in a microregional production system. At the same time, Vouppes would have formed part of a broader, hierarchical settlement system. In such villages, surplus agricultural produce (grains, olive oil) were

Table 4.26 SCY010: analyzed pottery (unit 338, grid, circles, and grabs)

Chronotype	Period	Qty
Fine ware-PoB	PoB	5
Pithoid Tub	PoB	1
Wall Bracket [338.2.1]	PoB	3
Mycenean	PoB	3
Pithos-PoB [S-0030, S-0032, S-0034]	PoB	52
TOTAL Protohistoric Bronze Age		64
Amphora-Ar	Ar	1
Basin-AC	AC	3
Black Glaze-He	He	1
Amphora-LR	LR	1
Flat-Grooved	LR	1
Cypriot Glazed	Med	1
Pithos-Mod	Mod	1
Brown Glaze	MM	1
Coarse ware-MM	MM	4
Glazed ware	MM	2
TOTAL Archaic to Modern		16
Plain White-HA	HA	9
Amphora-Hi	Hi	1
Pithos-PC	PC	6
Coarse ware-Unk	Unk	51
Fine ware-Unk	Unk	3
TOTAL		150

Note: Figures in brackets refer to cataloged items (see chapter 5.1 for pottery, chapter 5.3 for wall bracket).

collected, processed and redistributed, but whether to mining sites or "up the line" to secondary or primary centers we do not know.

SCY010 was and remains important for SCSP because it was the first and only definitive Late Cypriot settlement site found, and one of the very few known in this region. The striking quantity of pithos material strongly suggests the storage function of this POSI. Although we have suggested a model wherein villages like Vouppes provide agricultural support and habitation for miners and other copper-producing specialists, it must be noted that there are no industrial sites in the igneous zones covered by SCSP which are strictly contemporary with SCY010. Politiko *Phorades* 1 (SCY100) belongs to a phase of the Bronze Age that could be up to 400 years earlier than Vouppes. The rarity of sites like Vouppes and the ongoing disinterest in excavating the small rural sites of Cypriot prehistory (cf. Frankel and Webb 1996) make it all the more significant. It is but one of several "sites" recovered by SCSP that would likely repay archaeological excavation.

4.13 SCY019: Politiko *Kelaïdhoni*: Lithics Scatter

Compiled by Dina Coleman (with Carole McCartney).
Team leader: Susan Bain Chipped stone: Dina Coleman
Geomorphology: Caroline Whitehill
Pottery: Timothy E. Gregory, Joanna S. Smith

Grid reference: 520800/3876350
Cadastral plan: XXX/57
Aerial photograph: 1993, run 13, no. 52
Survey unit: 101

Located on a spur 750 m northeast of Politiko *Phournia* (SCY200), the site of Politiko *Kelaïdhoni* has an excellent northerly view over the Tamassos Plain. The bedrock surrounding the site consists of interbedded chalky limestone, chalk, and limestone. In contrast to Politiko *Ayios Mnason* (SIA 6) just 900 m to the east, these beds have been tilted to the west and the resistant and protective limestone cap has been eroded away, leaving the underlying chalks exposed to heavy weathering and erosion. A dense concentration of lithics and a lighter scatter of pottery lie on an isolated stable surface on top of one of these eroded ridges.

A 3 m grid was placed over the densest area of artifact concentration, with outlying squares to test the fall-off in material. Within each square the total number of lithics and potsherds was counted, and a sample of 306 chipped stones and 20 sherds was collected. This strategy provided quantity and distribution data within the site. While the field team worked on the grid, the geomorphologist mapped the area, so that artifact density could be measured against surface stability (plate XLIII).

The density peak in the center is very clear, with the bladelets even more closely clustered in the central southern area of the concentration. The eastern edge shows a clearly defined fall-off with the deterioration in surface stability; this side of the small ridge has the most abrupt break in slope (marked by the boundary between the unstable and eroding areas). The same phenomenon holds in the west, where the fall-off is particularly abrupt. There are some local exceptions, however, particularly in the north and south. The four squares along the north

of the main concentration have no lithics, in spite of being in the most stable part of the site. A similar situation applies in the south. In both cases there is a light scatter beyond the main concentration, but these are mostly on eroding or eroded areas, and some have probably been washed down from above. Geomorphological scrutiny, then, suggests that this was originally a small, dense location of activity rather than a remnant of a much wider activity area that happens to have survived erosion.

Analysis of the sample collection of lithics revealed that 70% of the chipped stone material consisted of stone implements and utilized flakes, while only 30% was manufacturing debris (table 4.27). Based on these data, the site does not appear to be a primary knapping location but some sort of task-specific workplace where stone implements may have been both used and rejuvenated. This would explain the very small percentage of cores and hammer stones that were found and the tertiary character of almost all the debitage. To gain a better understanding of the site's function, it is necessary to look more closely at the types of stone implements.

Notches, denticulates, scrapers, and borers comprised some of the least numerous categories of implements, and backed or truncated blades are rare. The majority of scrapers consisted of end and notched scrapers; there were fewer circular and angular scrapers. Blades typically exhibited some degree of sharpening and/or cutting fractures on one or other lateral margin. The utilized flakes made up the second most common implement type.

The most numerous implements at Kelaïdhoni consisted of small blade segments and bladelets, which comprised one-third of all tools and nearly one-quarter of the site's entire chipped stone sample (table 4.27). Bladelets are here defined by the following attributes: They are twice as long as wide; they have two parallel sides; and they range in length from 2.0 to 4.5 cm. It is worth noting that bladelets were rarely found in the project area, and no other site yielded a similar assemblage. Approximately 20% showed polish (or sickle sheen) along a single lateral use margin. This information suggests that one of the tasks conducted at or near the site was the reaping of crops. Since these blades are probably too small to be used individually, several bladelets may have been inserted into a larger sickle tool, such as a long bone or an antler. Examples of such sickles are well known from the prehistoric Levant.

Table 4.27 SCY019: summary of chipped stone

Type	Qty	%
Hammer stones	3	1
Cores	3	1
Borers	4	1
Indeterminable	8	3
Incomplete (scrapers)	11	4
Blades	18	6
Incomplete (blades)	19	6
Scrapers	26	9
Utilized flakes	54	18
Micro blades	69	23
(TOTAL tools)	(215)	(70)
Debitage	90	30
TOTAL	305	100

Table 4.28 SCY019: analyzed pottery

Chronotype	Period	Qty
Coarse ware-PoB	PoB	1
Cooking ware-Ar	Ar	7
Cooking ware-AC	AC	4
Plain ware-AC	AC	6
Amphora-LR	LR	1
Cypriot Glazed IV	Med	1
TOTAL		20

This heavily blade-based assemblage shows the use of an opposed platform naviform related core technology on the basis of the high-quality translucent chert used, frequent bidirectional dorsal scars, a few crested blades, a "ski spall" platform rejuvenation, and a single broken upsalon blade. The tools, while dominated by simply utilized blades, bladelets, and flakes, also show numerous pièces esquillées, burins, and glossed ("sickle") blades. The burins are dominated by burins-on-break but include a number of dihedral examples. The glossed tools frequently exhibit fine denticulation and include a number of oblique or straight truncations, a basal thinned example, and a limited number of curvilinear backed "crescent" segments. A few of the glossed tools exhibit gloss at an oblique angle to the tool edge. A bilaterally retouched blade segment and a bifacially retouched piece, with flat to abrupt covering retouches are suggestive of attempts to manufacture projectile points. These technical and typological traits suggest an early Pre-Pottery Neolithic date for the chipped stone assemblage (McCartney and Peltenburg 2000; Peltenburg et al. 2001).

Only 20 pottery sherds and 4 pieces of ground-stone fragments accompanied the chipped stone scatter (table 4.28). In spite of one Protohistoric Bronze Age, one Late Roman, and one Medieval sherd, the majority of the pottery dated to the Archaic to Classical periods (750–312 BC). The contrast in date between the Pre-Pottery Neolithic chipped stone assemblage and the pottery indicates distinct eras of occupation at the site. Chalcolithic Phournia is less than 1 km away, and the area of Tamassos saw settlement from as early as the Prehistoric Bronze Age (chapter 6.1). The plain to the north and east was well cultivated in the Archaic and Classical periods (chapter 6.2) and presumably also supported the prehistoric settlements of the Tamassos area. Thus, it is conceivable that the people who occupied Kelaïdhoni contributed, in some measure, to the early subsistence and economy of the area.

4.14 SCY102: Agrokipia *Palaeokamina*: Lithics Scatter

Compiled by Dina Coleman (with Carole McCartney)
Team leaders: Bradley Creevey, Ian Johnson
Archaeometallurgy: Sven Van Lokeren Chipped Stone: Dina Coleman, Alice Kingsnorth Geomorphology: Caroline Whitehill
Pottery: Timothy E. Gregory, Joanna S. Smith

Grid reference:	514500/3878500
Cadastral map:	XXIX/55
Aerial photograph:	1993, run 177, no. 48
Survey units:	1025–28

SCY102, or Agrokipia *Palaeokamina*, is one of the most intriguing chipped-stone POSIs found within the SCSP area. From the time it was first identified in 1993, SCY102 invited considerable attention because of its remarkable collection of chipped stone implements manufactured from good quality lithic materials. There are several notable examples of knife blades and scraper implements made from soapy-textured, translucent, cryptocrystaline chert. In addition to chipped stone, numerous ground-stone objects, pottery sherds, slag, and glass fragments were found scattered across the site. Several small pits, or depressions, were noted throughout this POSI, some of which may have been collapsed tombs.

PHYSICAL LANDSCAPE

SCY102 is situated within the northern foothills of the Troodos Mountains on the edge of the floodplain and 500 m northeast of the modern village of

Agrokipia. This POSI occupies the upper slopes of an eroding limestone knoll, and is bordered by a small river originating in the Troodos. The river appears to divide the low-lying range to the east and larger range to the west; directly across the river is a steep limestone scarp.

The knoll occupied by SCY102 is characterized by limestone bedrock covered with a thin layer of soil. The surface of the knoll likely once had a greater soil overlay. Erosional processes have transported small soil particles downslope, while larger rocks and artifacts remained at or near the top of the knoll. There are no rills or drainages on the knoll, but enough erosion has occurred to expose the limestone pavement. Thus, the surface of the knoll that existed during antiquity is almost certainly not the same surface that exists today.

An orchard now occupies the top of the knoll where the soil above the limestone is up to 0.5 m thick in places. The hillslopes of the knoll and those of the immediate foothills are accented by abandoned agricultural terraces, although a few well-preserved stone walls remain standing, including some around the plowed orchard. Vegetation on the knoll (excluding the orchard) is sparse and consists of pine, hawthorn, thyme, and rockrose. The rocks on the surface consist of intensely weathered and lichen-covered limestone cobbles, as well as many rounded to subrounded basalt cobbles from the nearby river.

In addition to natural erosional processes, SCY102 has undergone a significant degree of modern disturbance. Plastic shotgun shells and military refuse are scattered in several areas of the site. Agricultural activities (the orchard) have substantially affected the POSI's integrity. Dirt roads encircling the knoll lead to Agrokipia and to a large gravel mine located approximately 0.75 km east.

DESCRIPTION

SCY102's cultural features were found primarily along the upper north-, west-, and south-facing slopes of the knoll. The adjoining ridge and surrounding easterly hills were also surveyed, but revealed no cultural remains except agricultural terrace walls. The denser concentrations of chipped stones, pottery, and slag were recovered in pockets along the westernmost upper slope of the knoll, particularly in units 1026

and 1027. Several ground-stone objects were found along the northeastern face of the knoll (unit 1028).

Six depression features were identified along several faces of the knoll (figure 4.60). Two of these were situated on the southwest-facing slope, two on the northwest and two on the northeast. The depressions on the west side of the knoll were made by enhancing naturally occurring limestone cavities in the ground, whereas the eastern depressions were created by excavating the surface soil. The function, purpose, and age of these depressions is uncertain, but might be related to modern military or hunting activities (bunkers or shelters).

Three additional depressions—two on the north face of the knoll and one on the west—had very different characteristics to the others: They were smaller in size and appear heavily weathered, whereas the other six lacked lichens or other vegetative overgrowth. These depressions are similar to collapsed Roman tombs at Ayios Mnason (SIA 6), but they contained no diagnostic pottery or artifacts.

CHIPPED STONE

In total, the chipped stone sample collected from SCY102 includes 642 pieces (table 4.29). This collection consists primarily of manufacturing debris (59% of the total). Although cores, core fragments, core trimming elements, and four hammer stones were recovered, the low occurrence of these items suggests that the predominant activity here was tool manufacture rather than primary core reduction. Scrapers and "knife" blades are relatively common, as are utilized and marginally retouched flakes and blades. Other tools include trapezoids, a few boring implements, burins, hammer stones and blades exhibiting sheen. Despite the natural and human disturbances apparent at SCY102, many of the chipped-stone implements were found in well-preserved condition. Some pieces were actually pristine, whereas others were caked with calcium carbonate, at least on one side of the stones.

Technical attributes such as the use of high-quality translucent chert, bidirectional dorsal scars on the prismatic blades dominating the sample, and a number of well-prepared butts, including one punctiform example, all suggest a relatively early Aceramic Neolithic date for at least part of the assemblage. The bitruncated segments or "trapezoids," some of which are microlithic, pièces esquillées, and glossed

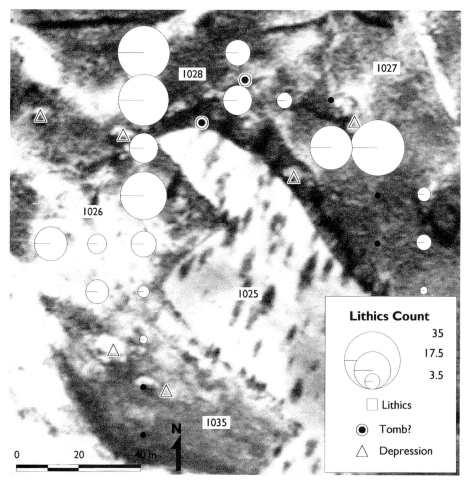

Figure 4.60 SCY102: topographical map and lithics distribution. *Based upon the aerials of the Department of Lands and Surveys with the sanction of the Government of the Republic of Cyprus. State copyright reserved*

blades with fine denticulation in the tool sample likewise argue for an early date. The presence of a significant proportion of more moderate raw materials (including basal Lefkara chert and jasper), the predominantly unidirectional blades exhibiting plain butts, as well as backed or truncated blades in the sample are elements which suggest a second, later phase in this Pre-Pottery assemblage dating to the latest stage of the early Pre-Pottery Neolithic, perhaps extending into the "classic" Khirokitia phase.

Beyond the chipped stone assemblage described above, over two-thirds of the pottery sherds collected here date to the Medieval and Modern periods. The slag and glass fragments also imply historic period occupation. Analysis of Palaeokamina's pottery (table 4.30) reveals that 67% of the sherds date to the Medieval and Modern periods. Only two percent of the sherds date to the Archaic period, 1% to Hellenistic, 3% to Early Roman, and 2% to Ottoman while 25% of the sherds could not be dated confidently. Thus a multiphase chronological scenario is

indicated with prehistoric, early historic as well as late historical components. Such conclusions can be substantiated only through excavation.

CONCLUSION

Artifactual evidence shows that this POSI was most likely occupied during two phases of the early Pre-Pottery Neolithic, followed by a considerable gap to the Archaic period, after which the site was occupied more frequently, right down to modern times. Although it was intensively surveyed and a representative sample of material collected, certain aspects concerning Palaeokamina remain enigmatic. Is it possible that it was somehow related to the archaeometallurgical site at Agrokipia *Kriadhis* (SIA 1), which is about 1 km to the west? The presence of slag at Palaeokamina, however, most likely means that it was deposited sometime after SCY102 was abandoned. Given the evidence of both agricultural and mining activities, the possibility of

Table 4.29 SCY102: summary of chipped stone

Type	Qty	%	Catalog #
Hammerstones	4	1	
Trapezoids	6	1	SCY102.1.8,
			SCY102.9.3,
			SCY102.16.1.8,
			SCY102.19.1.1
Borers	10	2	SCY102.9.2,
			SCY102.14.1.1
Cores	11	2	
Denticulates	14	2	
Indeterminable	41	6	
Utilized flakes	62	10	SCY102.16.1
Scrapers	64	10	SCY102.1.1,
			SCY102.1.2,
			SCY102.1.3,
			SCY102.1.6,
			SCY102.16.1.9,
			SCY102.1L.2.1
Blades	68	11	SCY102.1.4,
			SCY102.1.10,
			SCY102.5.31.98,
			SCY102.14.1.2,
			SCY102.1E.1.1,
			SCY102.1K.1.1
Debitage	359	56	
TOTAL	639	100	

Note: For catalog see chapter 5.2.

Table 4.30 SCY102: analyzed pottery

Chronotype	Period	Qty
Red Slip-Ar	Ar	3
Fine ware	He	1
African Red Slip	LR	1
Cooking ware, Offset Rim Pot	ER	1
Eastern Sigillata B II	ER	1
Amphora-LR	LR	1
Coarse ware, LR Wheel-Ridged	LR	1
Cypriot W5	Ott	1
Cypriot W6	Ott	1
Cypriot Glazed VIIIB	Med	1
Cypriot Glazed IX	Med	1
Cypriot Glazed XI	Med	2
Glass	Med	1
Cypriot W7	Mod	2
Cypriot W1	MM	1
Cypriot W4	MM	12
Coarse ware	Unk	16
TOTAL		47

tombs, and proximity to natural resources, Palaeokamina may have been a locus of industrial as well as domestic activity.

4.15 SCY110: Klirou *Mazerka*: Extensive Pottery Scatter

Compiled by Michael Given   Team leader: Bradley Creevey

Grid reference: 515400/3876200
Cadastral plan: XXIX/63
Aerial photograph: 1993, run 176, no. 15
Survey units: 1178–96

Five hundred meters southwest of Malounda village is a broad remnant terrace of the River Akaki, now bordered by the deeply incised river gorge. In May 1995, we examined this heavily cultivated area in the course of surveying transect 515.5. Only nine units had adequate visibility, and they showed substantial, though never large, densities of pottery: a sparse scatter of Archaic to Classical, with only one unit reaching a pottery index of 2000; a Hellenistic to Roman "carpet" with pottery index of less than 1000, plus one restricted density peak with pottery index of 4000; and a Medieval to Modern pattern similar to the Hellenistic to Roman but with a slightly larger density peak.

To test these apparent patterns at a greater level of intensity, and to circumvent the visibility problem, we returned in September 1997 and laid down three lines of 5 m diameter circles, each 20 m apart (plate XLIV). These seventy-four circles gave us a much higher spatial resolution in analyzing the history of human activity and post-depositional processes in this area.

The overall pottery count shows two apparent peaks, both of them roughly in the center of the crossing arms of circles. These counts rise smoothly from 0.5 to 8.0 sherds per m² over a distance of about 200 m (plate XLIV; table 4.31). There were also thirty-four slag fragments broadly spread across this POSI, but the gridded circles contained only one or two fragments each, apart from one with three.

The map (plate XLIV) shows very clearly the difference between the total pottery counted and the amount of pottery we were able to date accurately. This difference consists of pieces that were counted but not collected, collected pieces that could not be dated, and collected pieces that fall into very broad categories (for example, Post-classical). Both the Geometric to Classical and Hellenistic to Roman groups show a broad and even but very light scatter of pottery. This never rises above 0.5 sherds per m² (broadly equivalent to a pottery index of 1000 from the survey units). The Geometric to Roman material shows no correlation with the density peaks of total pottery. Given the small size of the field plots visible in the aerial photograph, it is unlikely that this broad distribution resulted from plowing, and earlier field boundaries were probably as small as or smaller than the current ones. The most likely explanation for this pattern is that these sherds were brought out from settlements with manure, and therefore spread evenly across the fields (see chapter 7.4). If this is the case, cultivation (or at least manuring) was slightly more intensive in the Hellenistic to Roman periods than in the Geometric to Classical.

The largest proportion of datable pottery falls into the Medieval to Modern group of periods, though it never rises above one sherd per m². In general terms, Medieval to Modern densities rise and fall along with the densities of total pottery, suggesting that much of the undated pottery could also belong to this period. If so, there are distinct peaks in density. Such peaks could result from differential manuring or plowing practices, or else from localized work undertaken by the people who lived in or utilized farmsteads, field shelters, or other sites of intensified agricultural activity.

4.16 SCY114: Mitsero *Lambadhiotissa*: Check Dams and Byzantine Church

Compiled by Michael Given

Architecture and survey: Michael Given

Check dams: Jay Noller and Lisa Wells

Geomorphology: Lisa Wells

Grid reference: 510720/3878600
Cadastral map: XXIX/53
Aerial photograph: 1993, run 177, no. 42
Survey units: 668–672

The modern church of Panayia *Lambadhiotissa* and its Byzantine predecessor lie immediately above a spring on the east-facing slopes of Lambadhousa (figure 4.61). The spring has long been regarded as sacred and emerges through a recently built tunnel-like shrine (Jeffery 1918: 302). Its waters—gathered by a concrete cistern constructed beside its masonry predecessor—are distributed among the orchards

Table 4.31 SCY110: analyzed pottery

Chronotype	Period	Qty
Black-on-Red-Ar	Ar	8
Red Slip-Ar	Ar	8
Black Glaze-Cl	Cl	1
Coarse ware-GAC	GAC	12
Green ware-GAC	GAC	9
Plain ware-GAC	GAC	3
Amphora-AC	AC	2
Cooking ware-AC	AC	6
Plain ware-AC	AC	23
Plain White-AC	AC	11
Red Slip-AC	AC	1
TOTAL Geometric to Classical		84
Cooking ware-ER	ER	13
Cooking ware, Square Rim Pot	ER	9
Cypriot Sigillata	ER	4
Amphora-LR	LR	11
Amphora, LR 1	LR	9
Basin-LR	LR	15
Basin, Piecrust Rim	LR	4
Coarse ware-LR	LR	8
Coarse ware, LR Wheel-Ridged	LR	15
Cooking ware-LR	LR	11
Cypriot Red Slip	LR	1
Cypriot Red Slip 9	LR	2
Fine ware-LR	LR	1
Flat-Grooved	LR	3
Frying Pan	LR	3
Spirally Grooved	LR	1
Coarse ware-Byz	Byz	1
TOTAL Early Roman to Byzantine		111
Byzantine Glazed, Local	Med	2
Cypriot Glazed	Med	8
Cypriot Glazed IVC	Med	2
Cypriot Glazed VIIIB	Med	4
Cypriot Glazed IX	Med	2
Cypriot Glazed XI	Med	2
Imported Sgrafitto ware	Med	1
Cypriot Glazed IX Late	Ott	8
Cypriot Glazed, Brown and Green	Ott	32
Cypriot W3	Ott	3
Cypriot W5	Ott	3
Cypriot W6	Ott	6
Ottoman Glazed	Ott	11
Purple Painted ware	Ott	1
Contemporary Eastern Mediterranean	Mod	7
Contemporary Yogurt ware	Mod	2
Cypriot W7	Mod	61
Lapithos ware, Green	Mod	5
Lapithos ware, Yellow	Mod	14
Brown Glaze	MM	1
Cypriot W1	MM	1
Cypriot W4	MM	242
Fine ware-MM	MM	1
Tile-MM	MM	7
TOTAL Medieval to Modern		426
Plain White-HA	HA	7
Amphora-Historical	Hi	12
Pithos-PC	PC	23
Tile-PC	PC	24
Tile, Corinthian Pan	PC	1
Coarse ware-Unk	Unk	329
Cooking ware-Unk	Unk	82
Table ware	Unk	2
TOTAL		1101

Figure 4.61
SCY114: modern
church of
Panayia
Lambadhiotissa
from the
northwest, with
Mitsero Village
below

Figure 4.62
SCY114: plan of
Byzantine church
of Panayia
Lambadhiotissa

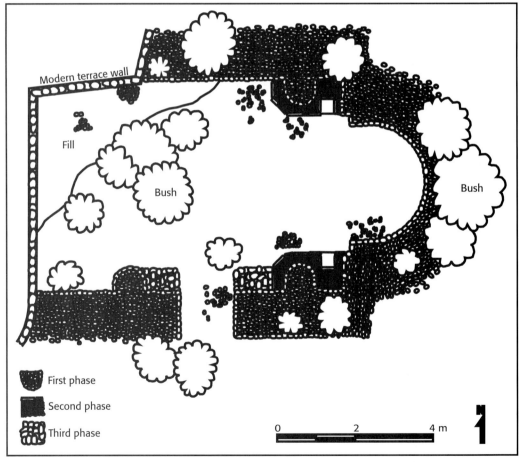

and small fields that lie below. Farther down, the stream is joined by four second-order streams, and becomes the third-order Argaki *Kokkinobamboula*. In the 800 m between the spring and the River Likythia in the valley below, there are at least five major check dams trapping the water-born sediment, as well as numerous smaller ones in the upper reaches. Regular rebuilding and raising of these check dams show that people have been using this method of creating arable land in the Lambadhiotissa area since circa AD 800.

SCSP teams in this area recorded the architectural remains of the Byzantine church, conducted block survey to the extent permitted by the generally poor visibility, and mapped the geomorphology. The geomorphologists carried out a detailed description and examination of the series of check dams, to be published separately (Noller and Wells N.D.).

PHYSICAL LANDSCAPE

The church and ruins at Mitsero *Lambadhiotissa* are located at the headwaters of the Argaki ("creek") Kokkinobamboula. The areas of gentle slope on which the structures and surrounding fields are constructed are small bowls in the mass of a large complex Pleistocene landslide. The southern slopes of this basin have multiple inset failure and shallow landslides. The spring has its source in the headscarp of one of these subsidiary landslides.

The area immediately surrounding the church consists of broken limestone that has been carried down the slope in the upper part of the highest landslide. The fields directly below the church lie in steep rubble with little flat tillable land, which accounts for their use as orchards instead of field crops. The small spring results from the exposure of an aquifer in the headscarp of a secondary landslide; it may have been in existence since the landslide occurred sometime during the Pleistocene. The Pleistocene date for this landslide is estimated by the erosion of the head scarp and the amount of fill that has accumulated in the hollows within the landslide mass.

BYZANTINE CHURCH

The walls of the church survive to a height of 1 to 2 m; both they and the interior are quite overgrown. Little survives of the outer faces of these walls, which in most cases had to be estimated. The west end of the church has been obliterated by a retaining wall supporting the modern church. Papageorgiou (*MKE* 8:194) dates the initial building to the early twelfth century, based on the style of the surviving frescoes and the construction of the *parastadhes* (engaged columns). Its condition has clearly deteriorated since it was inspected it by Papageorgiou, as only a few small patches of frescoes remain.

The church faces due east, and its surviving interior length is 10.2 m (figure 4.62). The apse has a diameter of 3.0 m, and widens out into the nave in two stages. Immediately west of the apse, the north and south walls have small niches about 0.8 m above the current ground level. The nave of the church, as originally built, is 5.7 m wide. The central dome was supported by four semicolumns, two of which preserve fragments of fresco. One of the stones in the southwest semicolumn has a fragment of fresco on an inner surface, and has clearly been reused. This implies that the semicolumns were built or repaired after the original construction of the church. Between the two semicolumns of the south wall is a door 1.4 m wide. Another small area of fresco is preserved in its original position on the west side of the door, and other fragments are scattered about in and near the church.

Some considerable time after the church's construction, the north and south walls were widened on the interior. This addition completely hid the two eastern semicolumns. The masonry consists of medium-sized angular stones set in thick mortar and faced with slabs; the transition to the nave was achieved by facing the new construction with slabs set diagonally. Parts of the frescoes on the original semicolumns can still be seen, with the later mortar adhering. The frescoes were damaged either during or before this construction, as the mortar has fresco fragments within it. At some later period the south wall was further strengthened, with a new wall 1.0 m wide running along the original south wall on either side of the door and abutting the earlier strengthening wall. The masonry is rough, and there are no facing stones. The north wall of the church shows no such addition, presumably because it did not have a door and was therefore stronger.

By the early twentieth century the church was in ruins. The modern church was built immediately above and to the west in about 1950, according to village memory, following a healing miracle granted by the Panayia Lambadhiotissa (Paraskevopoulou 1982:150).

Table 4.32 SCY114: analyzed pottery from block survey

Chronotype	Period	Qty
Cypriot Glazed	Med	3
Cypriot Glazed VIIIB	Med	1
Lapithos ware, Green	Mod	1
Cypriot W4	MM	3
Glazed ware	MM	7
Plain White-HA	HA	1
Coarse ware	Unk	7
TOTAL		23

BLOCK SURVEY

Today only half of the field system around the church and spring is still cultivated, and consists entirely of orchards, with olives, lemons, mandarins, apricots, figs, and almonds. All are irrigated from the spring. A wider expanse of now unused terraces and fields can be seen both on the ground and on the 1963 aerial photograph. Several of the olive trees are of substantial age, including one perhaps 350 years old.

Only five fields had sufficient visibility for survey, and one (unit 668) was a modern bulldozed terrace that contained only three undiagnostic sherds. The other four fields produced varying densities of sherds, never very great. Unit 669 immediately southeast of the old water tank contained 63 sherds, of which nine were datable, all Medieval or Medieval/ Modern, including one fine Cypriot Glazed VIIIB base (table 4.32). Unit 671, in the fields below the spring, had similar numbers and periods of material. With pottery indices of 2500 and 1100, respectively, neither of these units can be regarded as dense; only one sherd in the whole area was definitely ancient. There was a certain amount of tile, mostly pre-Modern, including 11 fragments found in survey units and many more used as packers in the masonry of the older water tank.

Without better visibility and more block survey, it is hard to draw any definite conclusions from these survey results. There was certainly no evidence for any sort of settlement that might have been one of the supposed predecessors of Mitsero (Goodwin 1984:1184). The pottery in unit 669 seems to indicate some level of activity in the Medieval to Modern periods, while the neighboring units suggest something rather less. The most likely explanations are traffic due to worship and annual festivals at the church, and agricultural exploitation of the area provided with water and sediment by the Argaki Kokkinobamboula. This latter explanation is confirmed by an examination of the check dams.

CHECK DAMS

There are at least five major check dams that cross the Argaki Kokkinobamboula and many smaller ones along its length. In the lowest part of the stream, just upstream of its confluence with the Likythia, check dam 1 was constructed of stone and may be of some antiquity, but this sequence was not studied in detail. At 180 m up the channel from the confluence, check dam 2 and its associated terraces were constructed with a bulldozer and are clearly of modern date. The agricultural land supported by this check dam covered an area of 0.4 ha. Another 70 m farther upstream, check dam 3 was a small, low feature that supported 0.3 ha of agricultural land. Check dam 4, a large multigenerational wall, lay 90 m beyond. It once supported about 0.3 ha of agricultural land, but extensive erosion has removed at least half of it. Another 90 m upstream, check dam 5 was located at the confluence of five second-order streams. Its stone walls being in good repair, no outcrops of trapped sediment were exposed. This check dam supported 0.7 ha of agricultural land, on which were grown market vegetables and grain irrigated by water piped in from upslope. Finally, in the upper 530 m of the channel, numerous smaller check dams supported one or a few olive trees, as well as small grain or vegetable fields. One of these olive trees is estimated to be 350 years old, thus giving an approximate terminus ante quem for the small terrace on which it stood.

The walls, sediments, and soils associated with check dams 3, 4, and 5 were described in detail. The sediments are angular, poorly sorted gravels, with sedimentary structures indicating that they were deposited either by rapidly flowing waters or else by siltation from slowly flowing or standing water. The upper portions of the sedimentary sequences are relatively fine-grained materials that make up the surface of the most recently active fields. Check dam 3 was the smallest feature, held in place by a few very large boulders (3 m in diameter), behind which the sediment was trapped. It is questionable whether this dam was deliberately constructed, but the low-lying sediment trapped behind it was being used as agricultural land. Associated with each generation of wall in check dam 4 was a thin A horizon, indicating a period of landscape stability and agriculture on the terrace surface. No pottery or lithics were found in any of the stratigraphic sequences. Because of the channel geometry in these narrow V-shaped canyons, building higher walls substantially increased the potential agricultural area. It may be that the increase in wall height was not driven by failure of the walls, but rather by market or population pressures to produce more crops. The sequence of soils and sediments behind check dam 4 indicated at least six construction events and six times in which agriculture was expanded in this part of the basin. Check dam 5 had four major generations of wall construction, each with associated sediments and soils.

The base and tops of check dams 4 and 5 were of similar form and position, suggesting that the chronology of these terraces is similar. The major difference between these terraces is that check dam 4 had been allowed to fail in the recent past, while check dam 5 has been maintained to the present day. Charcoal was collected from buried A horizons in the soils behind check dam 4. The oldest radiocarbon dates from the base of this sequence indicated that wall construction and associated sedimentation began about AD 800 (Noller and Wells N.D.). The lowest part of the sedimentary sequence, in soil that predated the first radiocarbon date, appears to have been trapped behind a large naturally occurring boulder rather than behind an intentionally constructed wall, and is similar in context to check dam 3. The youngest radiocarbon dates came from charcoal in soil at depths of about 2 m below the youngest wall in the third buried soil horizon. Two separate analyses yielded ages of 135 ± 40 BP and 140 ± 40 BP (Noller and Wells N.D.) for the third to the youngest soil. From this we may infer that the most recent construction of the uppermost wall occurred in the recent past. The wall failure and erosion of a narrow canyon through 6 m of fill occurred in less than one hundred years. The base of the modern channel is now flowing on and eroding into ophiolite or landslide mass along the length of the Argaki Kokkinobamboula.

As well as this sequence of check dams, hillslope terraces contour the hillsides on both sides of the Argaki. On the south side, the terraces were larger and supported 10.6 ha of agricultural fields on the lower slopes near the toe of the landslide. Such terraces were constructed to increase the surface area

of the swales in the landslide mass. On the north side, the slope is very steep, and limestone and marl are exposed in some places. Small hillslope terraces accounted for less than 0.3 ha of agricultural land north of the channel, and individual terraces frequently provided just enough flat land to support a single olive tree.

CONCLUSION

The church of Panayia Lambadhiotissa from the twelfth century is only one small aspect of human activity on the eastern slopes of Lambadhousa. Even the limited amount of block survey allowed by the visibility suggests that some sort of broader, probably agricultural, activity across arable land has taken place here since the early Medieval period. This was confirmed by stratigraphic investigation of the check dams, along with ^{14}C dating of their sediments.

The earliest possible date of check dam construction is AD 800 (Noller and Wells N.D.), which falls at the beginning of a little-known period in the SCSP area. During the preceding Late Roman period (AD 300–750), major copper smelting took place and some sort of settlement existed at Mitsero Kouloupakhis (SIA 3), just 500 m to the southeast. In general, this was a prosperous and well-populated period in the SCSP area, one which would have required intensive agriculture. The building of check dams may have been one means of expanding the available arable land, in which case we would expect it to be a common phenomenon during the Late Roman period. Alternatively, it may have been a means of coping with massive erosion that resulted from widespread abandonment of intensively cultivated land on the hillslopes, as may have happened at the end of the Late Roman period (circa AD 750).

In the early Medieval period (twelfth to thirteenth centuries AD), the population and economy of the area began to increase substantially. The church of Panayia Lambadhiotissa is one manifestation of this; a hoard of 145 twelfth-century coins discovered at the monastery of Ayios Panteleimon (2 km to the northeast) is another (Flourentzos and Nicolaou 1987). From this period onward people continued to use and repair the check dams along the Argaki Kokkinobamboula and to build them higher in order to reclaim more land. During the fifteenth to sixteenth centuries fields such as these were supporting considerable populations at the nearby villages of Mitsero, Mavrovounos, and Agrokipia. During another period of high population in the area, in the nineteenth century, the check dams were still being maintained and extended. This continuing technology demonstrates the inhabitants' close association with and understanding of their landscape. The Panayia Lambadhiotissa, whose successive churches stood just above the holy spring at the source of the Argaki Kokkinobamboula, provided not just the water to irrigate the crops but also the soil in which they grew.

4.17 SCY200: Politiko *Phournia*

Compiled by A. Bernard Knapp
Team leaders: Susan Bain Geomagnetic survey: Iain Banks
Geomorphology: Jay Noller, Lisa Wells, Caroline Whitehill
Geophysical Survey: Iain Banks, Michael Donnelly, Paul Duffy
GIS analysis: Nathan Meyer, A. Bernard Knapp
Lithics: Dina Coleman Pottery: Joanna S. Smith,
Diane Bolger, Jennifer Webb

Grid reference: 520150/3875950
Cadastral plan: XXX/57
Aerial photograph: 1993, run 176, no. 51

Chalcolithic sites are not that common in Cyprus, even though the Middle to Late Chalcolithic era extended from about 3500–2500 BC. The location of a Late Chalcolithic site in the north-central Troodos region, however, is not unprecedented. The three sites of Kato Moni *Kambia*, Kato Moni *Monarga*, and Orounda *Stavros tou Koundi* (Held 1990:14; Held in Knapp et al. 1992:332–333), situated about 15 to 20 km west of Phournia, form what Peltenburg (1985:1–2) terms a characteristic "settlement cluster" of the Chalcolithic period. The remnants of Phournia are located in an arable field (colluvium) in the Kouphos River Valley; initial visits revealed a scatter of what were first thought to be Prehistoric Bronze Age (PreBA), specifically Middle Cypriot wares, ground-stone implements and chipped stone tools. In fact, most cultural material from Politiko *Phournia* proved to be Late Chalcolithic in date, with a smaller component (Black Topped ware) possibly going back to the beginning of the Middle Chalcolithic period. There are, in addition, a few Philia transitional elements. Within the same month (August 1997), SCSP carried out a 5 m gridded collection of material at Phournia, and over the course of the following year several pottery specialists examined the material in our storeroom. In October of 1999,

topographic and geophysical survey (resistivity and magnetometer) was conducted at Phournia, across 20 m grids at 1 m intervals.

PHYSICAL LANDSCAPE

The arable field (colluvium) within the Kouphos River Valley that comprises SCY200 slopes gently to the southeast and is cut by a single agricultural terrace on the south. It is situated on a mid-Holocene river terrace whose minimum age is likely to be the Bronze Age. That is, for some period of time, prior to and probably ending in the Bronze Age, the Kouphos River flowed close to the elevation of Phournia, which would have been situated on the floodplain along the river. During the Late Chalcolithic and Bronze Age periods, the river appears to have had a more braided character with a broader channel and wider floodplain. Incision and confinement of the channel have occurred subsequently. Phournia is currently bounded on three sides by deep gullies and on the northwest by a shallower gully traversed by the modern dirt track.

In a (colluvial?) field (unit 5016) about 100 m northeast of Phournia, one sherd of Chalcolithic pottery was found. Across the dirt track to the northwest of Phournia lies another colluvial field (unit 5015) which contained five Chalcolithic sherds, concentrated in the southern half of the field. This suggests a possible alternative interpretation, namely that all the material from units 5016 and 5015 as well as Phournia may have eroded down from a point higher in the slopes to the northwest; we have not adopted that scenario here (see further under pottery section, and figure 4.63).

HISTORICAL CONTEXT:
PHOURNIA IN ITS CHALCOLITHIC TO
EARLY BRONZE AGE CONTEXT

To consider Phournia in its wider Late Chalcolithic context, we need to examine briefly some assumptions (for example, regionalism) and features (material, locational, social) typically associated with that period. Although the concept of regionalism, for example, has had a major influence on the way Cypriot archaeologists think about the early prehistory (Neolithic to Bronze Age) of the island, it refers primarily to divergent pottery styles within a cultural

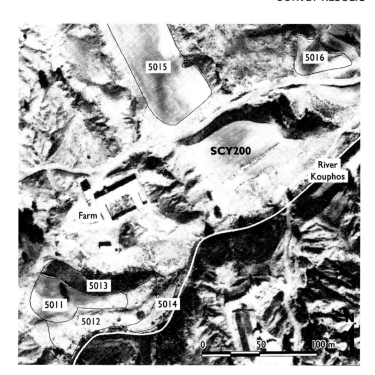

Figure 4.63 SCY200: topographical map. *Based upon the aerials of the Department of Lands and Surveys with the sanction of the Government of the Republic of Cyprus. State copyright reserved*

tradition that was otherwise quite uniform. Localized centers of pottery production existed at least from the Middle Chalcolithic period onward (Bolger 1991), and the study of the pottery fabrics from Phournia confirms this impression.

The main material characteristics of the Chalcolithic period that we can identify at Phournia are curvilinear architecture; Red-On-White, Red Monochrome, and Red Lustrous wares (and other diagnostic pottery); some distinctive ground-stone tools and utensils; and one picrolite bead. When we consider the transition from Chalcolithic to Bronze Age society on Cyprus, we find that PreBA culture and economy are for the most part direct successors to those of the agriculturally based Chalcolithic culture, and this is the case at Phournia as well.

Recent survey evidence (for example, Sørensen and Rupp 1993; Swiny 1989; Todd 1989) indicates an island-wide settlement expansion at the beginning of the Bronze Age, as well a continuing tendency toward site clustering in the north and northwest, and all around the metal-bearing areas of the Troodos Mountains. Because the earliest exploitation of copper resources had already begun (Knapp 1990:159–160) in the latter area, the location of sites like Phournia near the interface between the agricultural central plain and the mineral-rich foothills of the Troodos is entirely expected. Phournia, in

other words, is located in an area we might have predicted on the basis of available settlement data.

FIELD METHODOLOGY

Construction of the dirt road adjacent to SCY200 will have disturbed some archaeological finds, while agricultural activities disturbed or destroyed other material. At the same time, some of this plowing brought other materials to the surface.

When the field was gridded and collected (September 1997), the cereal crop had been harvested but the stubble remained. A 5-m grid was laid out roughly parallel to the northwest edge of the field (figure 4.64). However, the size of the field, approximately 3400 m², and the discrete nature of the scatter, precluded collecting from every subunit. Instead we decided to be selective in the collection strategy, to concentrate on the area of the scatter and to locate its edges. The entire north row (N5, within the field) of the grid—consisting of ten 5 x 5 m squares—was counted and collected: One person counted each square and collected a representative sample of the pottery using our normal field procedure. Culturally modified lithics were collected while ground stone (hammerstones, bowls, mortars, querns, pestles) was counted and sketched in the field notebook but not collected.

Figure 4.64 SCY200:
pottery density

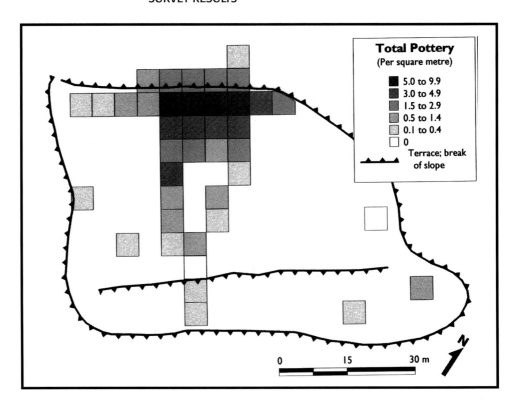

Figure 4.65 SCY200: geomagnetic plot

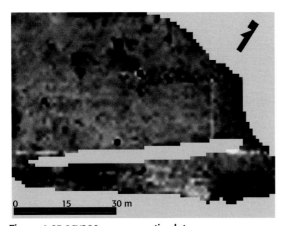

Figure 4.66 SCY200: geomagnetic plot, with structures as interpreted

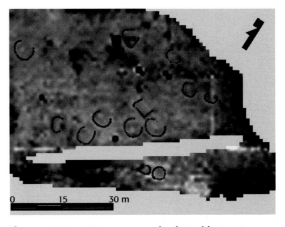

In examining the results of collecting the north-ernmost row, it became apparent that the densest area of cultural material was in the four subunits N5W3–N5E1. This information prompted the field team to collect some of the subunits running south from this area; these strips of subunits varied in width from 5 to 20 m. Four further subunits within the plowed area were collected and one other was simply counted. Six subunits were set up on the northern slope lead-ing down to the dirt track, immediately adjacent to the high density subunits in the plowed area; one fur-ther subunit was set up on the southeastern slope. The

material from these slope subunits was counted but not collected. With the exception of one subunit (S3W2) in the field and the six subunits on the north-ern slope, visibility was excellent (80 to 95) and background noise moderate.

Geophysical survey (resistivity) conducted at Phournia in October 1999 revealed several circular anomalies beneath the agricultural field (figures 4.65, 4.66). These anomalies range from 4 to 7 m in diam-eter, and all are consistent with archaeological features, such as walls. Several are situated close to-gether just above the ridge toward the bottom (southeast) of the field, nearest the river, with a few others on the northeastern edge of the field. The main area of overlap between these structural anomalies and the data available from SCSP's intensive collection of surface material—pottery, lithics, and ground stone—lies in the north and northeast sectors of the field.

ARTIFACTS

Pottery. Both the pottery and lithics from Phournia indicate Chalcolithic occupation. The wide variety of material recovered suggests a range of human activities on the site and likely occupation of the immediate area.

After the gridded collection and in the months prior to the 1998 SCSP study season, two pottery specialists (Jennifer Webb and Diane Bolger) visited the Mitsero storeroom to examine and classify the pottery from SCY200. Both confirmed a Late Chalcolithic date for the bulk of the material, with some Middle Chalcolithic and Late Chalcolithic-Philia transitional components (table 4.33). The largest part of the Phournia material is Late Chalcolithic (for example, Stroke Burnished and Coarse Painted wares), with a Middle Chalcolithic component (for example, Black Topped, Red-on-White, Red Monochrome Painted, and Spawled wares). Middle Chalcolithic Spawled ware is essentially the same as Late Chalcolithic Stroke Burnished ware except that it has limestone inclusions and is fired at a lower temperature: Stroke Burnished ware represents an improvement and refinement of Spawled ware technology. There are several sherds of Middle Chalcolithic Black Topped ware, which has a caramel-colored, polished surface and black interior polish (the black on the inside often extends over the rim of the vessel).

Some sherds with a very similar fabric and color actually belong to a transitional, Late Chalcolithic fabric but with highly polished red and black surfaces (Philia Red Lustrous ware, see Dikaios 1940). The fabric, shapes, and wall thickness of these pieces resemble the Chalcolithic assemblage, but the red and black polished surfaces are more similar to Philia wares. Red Lustrous ware is found at several other sites not too distant from Phournia (for example, Ambelikou *Ayios Georgios*, Kyra *Alonia*). Some other transitional sherds are apparent in the Phournia material, including one base and three spouts: These are hybrid pieces with fabric, shape, or technical

Table 4.33 SCY200: analyzed pottery

Chronotype	Period	Qty
Black Topped-Chalcolithic	EP	14
Coarse ware-Chalcolithic [S-0053]	EP	21
Coarse ware, Painted-Chalcolithic	EP	15
Philia Transitional [S-0055]	EP	2
Pithos-Chalcolithic [S-0046]	EP	7
Plain, with White Slip-Chalcolithic	EP	8
Red Lustrous-Philia Transit [S-0039]	EP	30
Red Monochrome Painted	EP	12
Red-on-White	EP	24
Spawled ware-Chalcolithic [S-0045]	EP	76
Stroke Burnished-Chalcolithic	EP	165
Plain White-PeB	PeB	1
TOTAL Prehistoric		**375**
Soft Red-Orange-AC	AC	3
Plain ware-AC	AC	3
Plain White-AC	AC	2
Brick	Mod	1
Tile-PC	PC	2
Unknown	Unk	3
TOTAL		**389**

Note: Figures in brackets refer to cataloged items (see chapter 5.1).

details reminiscent of Philia rather than Late Chalcolithic, but also including features that recall Late Chalcolithic material. Some pieces of Late Chalcolithic Stroke Burnished ware but with a black polished interior are probably a transitional ware between the usual Late Chalcolithic Stroke Burnished wares and the Red Lustrous. This could be significant in terms of "regional" pottery developments during this period.

Five additional sherds of Chalcolithic pottery were recovered from the lower slope of a field (unit 5015) no more than 50 m northwest of Phournia: one Middle Chalcolithic Red-on-White sherd; two Late Chalcolithic Stroke Burnished body sherds; one Stroke Burnished flat base/large vessel; and one Late Chalcolithic Coarse Painted sherd. Similarly, in unit 5016, about 100 m northeast of Phournia, one sherd of Middle Chalcolithic Spawled ware (burnished) was recovered. Regular SCSP transects to the east (units 1659–1682) and to the west (units 365–369) produced minimal amounts of cultural material, most of which ranged in date from Iron Age to Late Roman. There were also minuscule amounts of Archaic to Classical material amongst the Phournia collection.

A limited range of both open and closed shapes as well as spouts characterize this material. There is a clear majority of storage and table wares: trays, jugs,

Table 4.34 SCY200: frequency of tools, flakes, and cores

Type	Qty	Frequency (%)
Borers	8	4
Scrapers	28	15
Blades/Knives	4	2
Unknown/incomplete tools	18	10
(TOTAL Tools)	(58)	(31)
Utilized Flakes	29	16
Unutilized Flakes	43	23
Shatter	34	18
Cores	22	12
TOTAL	186	100

Table 4.35 SCY200: chipped-stone material types

Material	Qty	Frequency (%)
Lefkara Chert	11	6
Basal Lefkara	115	62
Chalcedony	15	8
Chert Silicates	20	11
Brown Jasper	12	6
Red Jasper	9	5
Green Jasper	4	2
TOTAL	186	100

pithoi (Late Chalcolithic), amphorae (smaller pithos-like pieces), bowls, a few jars, various spouted shapes, and coarse wares. The blackening of the spout ends and interiors probably resulted from the firing process. Along with the presence of a few bones and a picrolite bead, prima facie the material from Phournia does not seem very different in makeup from Lemba material (excepting the Philia transitional material).

Chipped Stone. The chipped-stone material from Politiko *Phournia* is of particular importance because of the site's Late Chalcolithic date (with Middle Chalcolithic components); this material helps to expand our limited knowledge of Cypriot Chalcolithic chipped stone data. Phournia also yielded an extensive study sample, including a significant percentage of stone tools. When compared with Cypriot Chalcolithic sites like Erimi *Pamboula*, Kissonerga *Mosphilia*, and Lemba *Lakkous*, or with the lithic findings from the Canadian Palaeopaphos Survey Project (Seton-Williams 1936; Betts 1985; 1986, D'Annibale 1992), the chipped-stone assemblage from Phournia reveals similarities in both manufacture and use-wear.

The lithic collection from Phournia was acquired by sampling in the highest artifact density area of the site: the north end of the harvested field (see Field Methodology above). Of the 58 recovered stone tools at Phournia, 28 were identified as scrapers (table 4.34). This is not surprising, as scrapers are commonly associated with Chalcolithic sites on the island (D'Annibale 1992:308; 1999:52). Four scrapers (200.1.1, 200.N4W1.1.16, 200.N5E3.2.5, 200.N2W3.1.1) have rounded shapes with edge modification evident along more than 50% of the margins. These pieces reveal an optimum use of durable edges. Of the larger scrapers found, there was some minimal homogeneity in shape; most appear to be of similar size with common use-wear that may be attributed to scraping (200.N5E2.1.1, 200.N5E2.1.3, 200.N3E1.2.1, 200.N4W1.1.2 and 200.N5E1.5.1).

Items 200.S1W3.2.1 and 200.N2E1.3.1 formed parts of a single triangular-shaped implement, which showed evidence of a corner-notched base and pointed distal tip. This implement exhibited retouch and use wear on the left lateral margin and on the distal tip. Although the two pieces fit together, the implement remains incomplete: it appears to have been broken recently in several places, perhaps the result of plowing. Despite its shape and base, it is unlikely to have been used as a projectile; rather, the wear scars and edge thickness suggest scraping activities.

Among the utilized flakes, several pieces were incomplete, which suggests that some may have been fragments of larger tools. When the complete appearance of a tool was uncertain, retouched fragments were grouped with the utilized flakes. Of 22 cores recovered, 13 were exhausted and 2 appear to be material testing cores. Five cores showed evidence of bipolar production technique.

Most materials for stone tool production were procured from local geological sources (table 4.35). More than half of Phournia's chipped-stone material came from basal Lefkara chert formations, characterized by a white to pinkish color with a texture varying from chalky to fine-grained silicates. The chalky materials appear to be too brittle for successful knapping. However, the exposure of the basal Lefkara materials to the elements may have weathered the material over time. No specific geological source was found for this material, but numerous small outcrops exist within the Kouphos River valley.

Ground Stone. Nineteen fragments of ground stone were recovered, all of basalt. They were measured and sketched in the field and a tentative function assigned based on a cursory examination: axe, hammerstone, bowl, rubber, and flat quern. One small butted polished basalt axe recovered from the top of the slope (southwest corner of the field) is stylistically similar to other Cypriot axe heads usually associated with the Neolithic; Bolger (1988:81–83), however, cites Chalcolithic parallels. Six possible bowl mortar fragments (three with rough interiors) were recorded. Six flat mortars, all comprised of one smooth surface, and three possible pestles were recovered. One of the pestles, triangular in section, may be a whetstone. The remaining three stones may have been used as hammerstones or pounding stones. One disc-shaped picrolite bead with a perforation near the edge was recovered (cat. S-0044; see chapter 5.3).

CONCLUSION

During the Chalcolithic period, Cyprus experienced a remarkable expansion of settlement and population (Held 1989:772, map D), best indicated in the archaeological record by excavated settlements such as Erimi *Pamboula*, Lemba *Lakkous*, and Kissonerga *Mosphilia* (Dikaios 1936; Heywood et al. 1981; Peltenburg 1985, 1991a, 1998). The characteristic Chalcolithic settlement cluster just to the west of the SCSP survey area shows two similarities with Phournia: (1) location on a fluvial terrace just beside or above a stream/river and (2) comparable surface material remains (for example, Red Monochrome and Red Lustrous wares, lithics, ground stone). The settlement cluster concept stipulates that when the diagnostic surface material of two or more neighboring sites of this period cannot be distinguished temporally, the sites would have served different functions within a single catchment area.

Having identified Phournia, should we expect to find other Late Chalcolithic sites (as part of a settlement cluster) in the near vicinity? Given the rarity of Late Chalcolithic sites island-wide, and particularly in the northern Troodos region, Phournia assumes a certain prominence among the overall survey results. Nonetheless, there are no other indicators of Chalcolithic occupation in transects covered by SCSP, nor in the river channels and many of the accompanying river terraces explored by SCSP's geomorphologists. Given the stray findings of Chalcolithic material in fields nearby SCY200, we wondered whether the original Chalcolithic site was actually situated at Phournia, or rather at some unknown locus farther up the hill and across the track from SCY200. Geophysical survey has resolved that question, and we now can confirm that Phournia, at least, appears to have architectural features beneath the surface.

Finally, the pottery and lithics from Phournia provide new information about the Chalcolithic period, not just in the north-central Troodos but over the whole of Cyprus. For example, it is now evident that Late Chalcolithic Stroke Burnished ware represents an improvement and refinement of Middle Chalcolithic Spawled ware. We can also see that certain fabrics, shapes, and wall thickness of various pieces resemble the Chalcolithic assemblage but have red and black polished surfaces more similar to Philia wares, for example, Philia Red Lustrous ware. In spatial terms, this pushes the extent of the Philia "facies" a bit further east on the island. Likewise, the chipped stone assemblage from Phournia, especially with half the stone tools identified as scrapers, shows close similarities in both manufacture and use wear with other Chalcolithic sites on the island.

With material dating from two transitional periods at either end of the Late Chalcolithic, Phournia has the potential, prima facie, to tell us as much about the Chalcolithic era and the transition to the Bronze Age as Kissonerga *Mosphilia*, perhaps the most important Chalcolithic site on the island. Its importance, thus, should not be underestimated, particularly now that geophysical prospection work has confirmed the coherence of the survey materials and the subsurface deposits.

4.18 SCY209: Episkopio *Kallinikos*: Extensive Pottery Scatter

Compiled by Michael Given Team leader: Susan Bain

Grid reference:	521500/3877600
Cadastral map:	XXX/49
Aerial photograph:	1993, run 177, no. 58
Survey units:	3654–3681

The broad and fertile plain west of Episkopio village is of great interest both for its agricultural potential and for its proximity to the Archaic to Byzantine city of Tamassos. Transects 520.5 and 521.5, surveyed in 1996, revealed considerable quantities of cultural material across this plain but with no immediately apparent focuses or density peaks. Preliminary GIS analysis in 1997 suggested one potential focus approximately 1 km north of Ayios Mnason. This area

Table 4.36 SCY209: analyzed pottery from circles

Chronotype	Period	Qty
Red-Burnished-Chalcolithic	EP	1
Coarse ware-PoB	PoB	4
Mycenean	PoB	1
TOTAL Prehistoric		6
Black-on-Red-Ar	Ar	1
Pithos-Ar	Ar	2
Red Slip-Ar	Ar	10
Black Glaze-Cl	Cl	2
Green ware-GAC	GAC	6
Amphora-AC	AC	5
Black Glaze-AC	AC	1
Coarse ware-AC	AC	1
Cooking ware-AC	AC	3
Plainware-AC	AC	62
Plain White-AC	AC	46
White Painted-AC	AC	2
TOTAL Geometric to Classical		141
Black Glaze-He	He	2
Çandarli ware	ER	1
Cooking ware-ER	ER	2
Cooking ware, ER Cooking Pot	ER	1
Cooking ware, Square Rim Pot	ER	1
Cypriot Sigillata	ER	1
Eastern Sigillata B II	ER	1
African Red Slip 50	LR	1
Amphora-LR	LR	2
Amphora, LR 1	LR	3
Basin-LR	LR	1
Coarse ware, LR Wheel-Ridged	LR	2
Cooking ware-LR	LR	1
Cooking ware, Dhiorios Pot	LR	3
Cypriot Red Slip	LR	1
Cypriot Red Slip 9	LR	1
Flat-Grooved	LR	1
Frying Pan	LR	1
TOTAL Hellenistic to Late Roman		26
Cypriot Glazed	Med	8
Cypriot Glazed V	Med	1
Cypriot Glazed VIIIB	Med	2
Cypriot Glazed IX	Med	2
Cypriot Glazed IX Late	Ott	1
Cypriot Glazed, Brown and Green	Ott	12
Cypriot W5	Ott	1
Ottoman Glazed	Ott	1
Contemporary Local wares	Mod	2
Contemporary Yogurt ware	Mod	1
Cypriot W4	MM	20
Glazed ware	MM	2
Pithos-MM	MM	1
Tile-MM	MM	1
TOTAL Medieval to Modern		55
Amphora-Historical	Hi	2
Pithos-PC	PC	12
Tile-PC	PC	33
Tile, Corinthian Pan	PC	1
Coarse ware-Unk	Unk	201
Cooking ware-Unk	Unk	24
Fine ware-Unk	Unk	1
Table ware-Unk	Unk	5
Unknown	Unk	1
TOTAL		508

showed a general background pottery index of 1000 to 2000 for all periods from Archaic to Modern, but with a notable peak of 10,000 in the Medieval to Modern periods, and a rather smaller one of 6000 in the same area (units 3568–69) during the Geometric to Archaic and Hellenistic to Roman periods (see chapter 7.4).

To investigate this area more intensively, we laid out an iron cross of 5 m diameter circles, 20 m apart, with a total of 37 circles (plate XLV), and another east-west line 600 m to the north, consisting of ten such circles.

The iron cross shows one relatively clear peak in the total density figures for pottery and tile, with figures just exceeding four sherds per m². The north-south arm appears to have a smaller peak, with the density reaching 2.2 sherds per m². This hardly suggests the large peak in units 3658–59 just 50 m north of the northern end of the line (plate LIII). Compared to Ayios Mnason, where the maximum density is 12.1, these figures are again relatively low. The very low number of tile fragments (17; maximum density 0.2 per m²) provides another contrast with Ayios Mnason and a further indication that this material most likely does not represent the remains of a settlement.

When broken down into specific groups of periods, the pottery is predominantly Geometric to Classical, though none of it is certainly Geometric (table 4.36). What is interesting about this distribution is its very even spread across the whole POSI, typically 0.1 to 0.3 sherds per m² (equivalent to a pottery index from the survey units of 1000 to 2000, a similar correspondence to that from SCY110). The Geometric to Classical material does not seem to be closely correlated with the undated pottery (compare SCY110; chapter 4.15), and so is probably fairly representative of the material from this period. Movement due to plow action is unlikely across the field boundaries, so this low but even spread of material would seem to be another good candidate for pottery spread as a result of manuring (chapter 7.4). It is unsurprising that there should have been intense agriculture 1 km from the rich Archaic to Classical city of Tamassos.

Material from the Hellenistic to Roman periods is much sparser and not so evenly spread. That from the Medieval to Modern periods is rather greater in density but characteristically more patchy in distribution, though the pattern might have been distorted by large numbers of Medieval to Modern sherds we were unable to identify.

4.19 SCY214: Klirou *Klirovourna*: Roman Estate/Farmstead

Compiled by R. Scott Moore Team leader: Bradley Creevey

Grid reference: 515500/3874000
Cadastral plan: XXXVII/7
Aerial photograph: 1993, run 174, no. 200
Survey units: 1143–1144

SCY214 is a raised river terrace surrounded on three sides by a water course. This POSI was first discovered during regular transect survey in 1995, in part because of its concentration of Roman tiles, including one round early Roman hypocaust tile, and large fragments. An examination of the 1963 aerial photographs revealed that the area had been extensively graded over the last 30 years. Located on the edge of the foothills of the Troodos Mountains, Klirovourna consists of two bulldozed terraces with a north/northeast aspect overlooking the agricultural area of Mazerka and the modern town of Klirou. It is situated close to a natural pass that leads south into the mountains and to the Medieval bridge over the Akaki river gorge (SCY302).

In 1963, SCY214 was a low, rocky hillside with several large trees. Distinct linear shadows on the aerial photograph seem to indicate the presence of a small to medium-sized building with at least two chambers, situated in the eastern part of subunits 2 and 14 or the western part of subunits 4 and 15, and an adjoining wall running east to west along a low bank, crossing subunit 4. This bank faces north with a good view of the Klirou/Mazerka area. The intensive plowing and grading of the hill has removed most traces of the buildings, but the features on the 1963 aerial photograph suggests that the building was in situ prior to the modern terracing of the hill.

SCSP collected and analyzed 126 pottery sherds collected from this POSI, and 25 tiles (table 4.37). A few of these dated to the Classical period, but there were none from the Hellenistic to Early Roman periods. The majority of identifiable sherds date to Late Roman times. All sherds derive from domestic wares such as basins and amphorae; no fine wares were discovered beyond a few from the Medieval to Ottoman periods. Several Late Roman 1 amphora fragments were present, from a type probably manufactured on the island.

Table 4.37 SCY214: analyzed pottery from subunits

Chronotype	Period	Qty
Pithos-Ar	Ar	2
Amphora, Knobbed Base	AC	1
Basin-AC	AC	1
Amphora, LR 1	R	17
Basin-LR	LR	9
Basin, Piecrust Rim	LR	2
Coarse ware-LR	LR	9
Pithos-LR	LR	2
Tile-LR	LR	2
Cypriot Glazed	Med	2
Cypriot Glazed IVC	Med	1
Ottoman Glazed	Ott	1
Cypriot W7	Mod	1
Cypriot W4	MM	25
Pithos-PC	PC	23
Tile-PC	PC	9
Tile, Corinthian Pan	PC	14
Coarse ware-Unk	Unk	29
Cooking ware-Unk	Unk	1
TOTAL		151

The large number of tile fragments (523) includes three main types (L-profiled angular. flat-rounded, low gable tiles), and one early Roman hypocaust tile. This pattern suggests the presence of a substantial building or a series of smaller buildings constructed on the site over several different periods. When the tile distribution is plotted against the pottery distribution (figure 4.67), the areas of highest pottery density are in the subunits with the highest tile density (subunits 3, 4, 5, and 15). These same subunits also have higher concentrations of Late Roman material, particularly Late Roman 1 amphorae and Late Roman basins. This distribution shows clearly that, during the Late Roman period, the building was located at the top of the knoll overlooking the agricultural areas, and that its rooms were probably used as storerooms for agricultural products. The nearby presence of dense scatters of stones suitable for the construction of mud-brick and tile buildings indicates that this building would have been very similar to traditional houses found throughout the survey area.

The lower terrace at SCY214 contained distinct distributions of tile and pithos fragments. These large amounts of settlement debris appear to have been deposited by normal processes, but more recently were bulldozed into a sickle-shaped terrace. This activity has resulted in very low pottery counts at the northwest end of the terrace and a dense concentration of tile and pithos sherds in its central area.

Figure 4.67 SCY214:
pottery and tile counts;
Late Roman 1 amphora

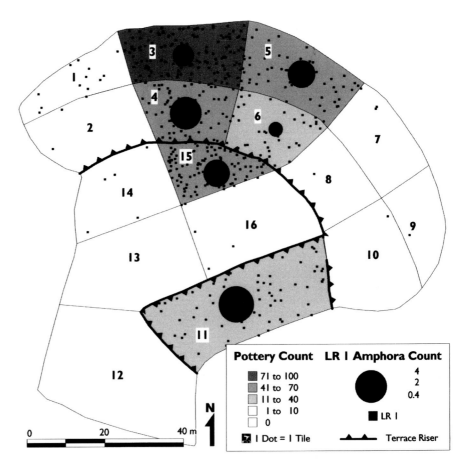

Pottery Count   LR I Amphora Count

▓ 71 to 100	4
▓ 41 to 70	2
░ 11 to 40	0.4
☐ 1 to 10	
☐ 0	■ LR I

▨ 1 Dot = 1 Tile   ▲▲ Terrace Riser

0   20   40 m

N

A significant number of tile and pottery fragments showed signs of burning, some at very high temperatures. Thus we might conclude that a structure on this POSI had been damaged or destroyed by fire. The mixture of burnt and unburnt material suggests that the building was damaged and then repaired, or else destroyed with another building constructed on the site at a later period.

Based on the material evidence and the location (in foothills with a marginal agricultural potential), SCY214 appears to have been a small farmstead devoted to the storage of produce; it may well have exploited other local resources to supplement the cereal production at the Roman village of Klirou *Limni* (SCY364). Other habitational elements situated to the south and southwest of Klirou (for example, SIA 2, SIA 9, SCY205) have large amounts of Roman material and are also involved with activities distinct from cereal production (for example, mining, smelting, and storage). It is also possible that the inhabitants of Klirou *Klirovourna* were involved in raising livestock, since the woods in these foot-

hills provide excellent fodder for grazing animals, such as pigs and goats. The locality now supports flourishing olive, almond, and fig groves with little modification. This POSI, together with Klirou *Manastirka* (SIA 2) and Klirou *Koutis* (SCY205) perhaps made up a series of radiating nodules of support for the Klirou area during the late Roman period, providing alternative resources and food produce to the cereal crops that would have been the focus of the settlement in and around Roman Klirou.

4.20 SCY215: Kalokhorio *Pontizos*: Extensive Pottery Scatter

Compiled by Michael Given   Team leader: Robert Schon

Grid reference: 514200/3875000
Cadastral map: XXXVIII/6
Aerial photograph: 1993, run 175, no. 229

During the 1995 and 1996 seasons it had become clear to SCSP teams that the alluvial plains of the Akaki and Pedhiaios Rivers contained broad spreads of

5.1 Pottery Catalog

Prehistoric: Priscilla Keswani, Sturt Manning, Elinor Ribeiro,
Joanna S. Smith Geometric to Hellenistic: Joanna S. Smith
Hellenistic to Roman: R. Scott Moore
Byzantine to Modern: Timothy E. Gregory

MODEL CATALOG ENTRY

(See appendix C for a list of chronotypes)

Cat. # **Period, Chronotype name, Form (chronotype abbreviation)**
Unit/POSI number, Grid reference/POSI name.
Plate number.
Description of shape, decoration, and any other relevant details. Exact date
if known. Function code (table 3.7). Fabric code (table 3.6).
Length/width/thickness in centimeters. Diameter if known. Surface
color (Munsell). Matrix color (Munsell).
Comparanda, if known (with references)

CATALOG

338.12.1 **Archaic to Classical Basin Rim and Handle (BAAC)**
Unit 338, SCY010 (Aredhiou *Vouppes*; see chapter 4.12).
Plate 1.
Rim of basin or tub with loop handle on side. Function HU. Fabric PI.
Length 17.5 cm. Width 16 cm. Thickness 2.6 cm.

550.4.1 **Medieval Cypriot Glazed IV Rim (CG4)**
Unit 550, Grid reference 510500/3877500.
Plate 14.
Fabric F. Function FW.
Length 1.8 cm. Width 2.6 cm. Thickness 0.4 cm.

551.2.1 **Ottoman Glazed Rim (OG)**
Unit 551, Grid reference 510500/3877500.
Plate 14.
Bowl with flaring broad rim. White slip and yellow glaze on interior and
over rim. Pendant half circles on interior of rim, with dots painted in green
glaze. Nineteenth century AD. Function FW. Fabric F.
Length 7.4 cm. Width 5.6 cm. Thickness 0.6 cm. Diameter 22 cm.
Surface 5YR 7/2. Matrix 5YR 7/2.

556.1.1 **Medieval Cypriot W6 Rim (W6)**
Unit 556, Grid reference 510500/3877750.
Plate 14.
Kouza (water jar) rim and strap handle. Function LU. Fabric C.
Length 5.4 cm. Width 3.1 cm. Thickness 0.7 cm. Diameter 9.0 cm.
Surface 5YR 5/6. Matrix 5YR 5/6.

1005.1.1 **Medieval Cypriot W1 Rim (W1)**
Unit 1005, SIA 3 (Mitsero *Kouloupakhis*; see chapter 4.3).
Plates 1, 14.
Galeftiri. Combing and molded decoration on exterior. Inturned
pointed rim. Function LU. Fabric C. Length 4.1 cm. Width 3.4 cm.
Thickness 1.6 cm. Surface 2.5YR 5/4. Matrix 2.5YR 6/3.

1009.1.1 **Late Roman Cypriot Red Slip 1 Rim (CRS1)**
Unit 1009, SIA 3 (Mitsero *Kouloupakhis*; see chapter 4.3).
Plate 1.
Cypriot Red Slip Form 1 rim. Function FW. Fabric F. Length 6.5 cm.
Width 3.0 cm. Thickness 0.5 cm. Diameter 27 cm. Surface 10R 5/
6. Matrix 10R 6/6.
Comparanda: Hayes Form 1, early-mid sixth century AD (Hayes 1972:374–
376, no. 14).

1012.2.1 **Archaic to Classical Double Rolled Strap Handle (DRSHAC)**
Unit 1012, Grid reference 511500/3878400.
Plate 1.
Double-rolled strap handle from plain ware jug. Function LU. Fabric
C. Surface 10YR 8/1. Matrix 10YR 8/1. Length 7.8 cm. Width
4.3 cm. Thickness 2.0 cm.

1015.1.1 **Archaic to Classical Greek Red Slip Handle (GRS)**
Unit 1015. Grid reference 511500/3878500.
Plate 1.
Greek red-slipped (glazed) rolled handle from skyphos or similar
shape. Function FW. Fabric F. Surface 5YR 6/4. Matrix 5YR 6/4.
Length 4.8 cm. Diameter 1.0–1.2 cm.

1034.2.1 **Geometric to Archaic Black-on-Red Body Sherd (BORGA)**
Unit 1034, Grid reference 514500/3878600.
Body sherd of Black-on-Red I (III) or II (IV) hemispherical bowl.
Red-slipped with black-painted horizontal bands on interior and
exterior. Cypro-Geometric III or Cypro-Archaic I. Function LU. Fabric
C. Length 2.9 cm. Width 3.0 cm. Thickness 0.5 cm.
Comparanda: Gjerstad 1948: Figs. XXIV.13, XXXVII.20.

1035.1.1 **Medieval Maiolica Ware Base (MW)**
Unit 1035, Grid reference 514500/3878450.
Plates 1, 14.
Blue maiolica low ring foot. Blue glazed interior and exterior, with
darker blue designs on interior. Sixteenth century AD. Function FW.
Fabric F. Length 2.5 cm. Width 2.0 cm. Thickness 0.4 cm. Surface
5YR 7/2. Matrix 5YR 7/2.

1035.2.1 **Medieval Cypriot Glazed IX Rim (CG9)**
Unit 1035, Grid reference 514500/3878450.
Plate 1, 14.
Bowl with plain vertical Group IX rim. White slip on interior and
over rim. Clear green glaze on tip of rim. Function FW. Fabric F.
Length 2.6 cm. Width 2.3 cm. Thickness 0.4 cm. Diameter 20 cm?
Surface 10YR 8/1. Matrix 10YR 8/1.

1054.13.1 **Medieval Lemba Ware Base (LW)**
Unit 1054, Grid reference 514500/3877450.
Plates 1, 14.
Glazed green ring foot from bowl of uncertain shape. White slip
and dark green glaze with circular sgraffito design at center.
Thirteenth century AD. Function FW. Fabric F. Length 6.6 cm. Width
3.3 cm. Thickness 0.7 cm. Surface 2.5YR 6/4. Matrix 2.5YR 6/4.

1057.2.1 **Late Roman Phocaean Ware 3 Rim (PHW3)**
Unit 1057, Grid reference 514450/3877450.
Very worn slip, grooves on outer edge. Function FW. Fabric F.
Length 6.0 cm. Width 2.8 cm. Thickness 0.4 cm. Diameter 18 cm.
Surface 7.5YR 6/6. Matrix 7.5YR 6/6.
Comparanda: Hayes Form 3f, second quarter sixth century AD (Hayes
1972:334–338, no. 25).

1081.2.1 **Ottoman Cypriot Glazed VIIIB Late Base (CG8BL)**
Unit 1081, Grid reference 514550/3874250.
Plate 1.
Bowl with low broad ring foot. Brown slip on exterior. Sgraffito
design on interior picked out in green glaze. Seventeenth century
AD. Function FW. Fabric F. Length 7.4 cm. Width 6.0 cm. Thickness
0.8 cm. Surface 2.5YR 6/4. Matrix 2.5YR 6/4.

1081.5.1 **Modern Lapithos Ware (Yellow) Rim (LPWY)**
Unit 1081, Grid reference 514550/3874250.
Plate 2.
Bowl with yellow plain folded rim, slip-painted design and yellow
glaze. Function FW. Fabric F. Length 3.0 cm. Width 2.8 cm. Thickness
0.5 cm. Diameter 22 cm. Surface 2.5YR 6/4. Matrix 2.5YR 6/4.

1144.9.1 **Late Roman 1 Amphora Body Sherd (AMRL)**
Unit 1144, Grid reference 515500/3874050.
Plate 2.
Amphora shoulder with dipinto. Function HU. Fabric C. Length
4.5 cm. Width 4.5 cm. Thickness 0.9 cm. Diameter 14 cm. Surface
10YR 8/1. Matrix 10YR 8/1.

1212.14.1 Modern Contemporary Yogurt Ware Rim (CYW)
Unit 1212, Grid reference 515550/3876900.
Plate 14.
Square vertical rim with groove on top. Thick yellow glaze on interior and over top of rim. Function LU. Fabric F. Length 2.8 cm. Width 2.2 cm. Thickness 0.6 cm.
Diameter 25 cm. Surface 5YR 6/4. Matrix 5YR 6/4.

1254.1.1 Geometric to Classical Pithos Rim (PIGAC)
Unit 1254, SIA 3 (Mitsero *Kouloupakhis*; see chapter 4.3).
Plate 2.
Rolled-out rim of pithos. Function PI. Fabric CR. Length 6.5 cm. Width 11.1 cm. Thickness 1.7 cm. Diameter 44 cm.

1257.12.1 Archaic Cypriot Red Slip III (V) Bowl Rim (RSAR)
Unit 1257, SIA 3 (Mitsero *Kouloupakhis*; see chapter 4.3).
Plate 2.
Down-sloping and concave surface rim of wide shallow bowl of Red Slip III (V) ware. Cypro-Archaic II. Function LU. Fabric TR. Length 2.4 cm. Width 7.5 cm. Thickness 0.6 cm.
Comparanda: Gjerstad 1948: Fig. LVI.6.

1257.13.1 Archaic Bowl or Cup Rim of Soft Red-Orange Fabric (SROAR)
Unit 1257, SIA 3 (Mitsero *Kouloupakhis*; see chapter 4.3).
Plate 14.
Rim of small bowl or cup. Possibly originally had red-slipped surface. Cypro-Archaic I. Function LU. Fabric TR. Length 3.0 cm. Width 1.7 cm. Thickness 0.3 cm. Diameter 16.5 cm. Surface 2.5YR 5/6. Matrix 2.5YR 5/8.
Comparanda: Gjerstad 1948: Fig. XLII.14.

1268.35.2 Late Roman Egyptian Red Slip Rim (ERS)
Unit 1268, SIA 10 (Malounda *Panayia Khrysopandanassa*; see chapter 4.10).
Plate 2.
One shallow narrow groove. Function FW. Fabric F. Length 4.1 cm. Width 2.4 cm. Thickness 0.8 cm. Diameter 42 cm. Surface 2.5YR 6/4. Matrix 2.5YR 6/4.

1268.39A.1 Geometric to Classical Pithos Rim (PIGAC)
Unit 1268, SIA 10 (Malounda *Panayia Khrysopandanassa*; see chapter 4.10).
Plate 14.
Rolled-out rim of small pithos. Function PI. Fabric CL. Length 10.7 cm. Width 3.7 cm. Thickness 1.5–1.9 cm. Diameter 22 cm. Surface 7.5YR 6/4. Matrix 5YR 6/4.

1268.53.1 Medieval Cypriot Glazed V Body Sherd (CG5)
Unit 1268, SIA 10 (Malounda *Panayia Khrysopandanassa*; see chapter 4.10).
Plate 2.
Rather thick-walled bowl. White slip and green glaze on interior. Sgraffito design. White slip on exterior. Possible Cypriot Glazed V (fourteenth century–AD). Function FW. Fabric F. Length 5.2 cm. Width 2.1 cm. Thickness 0.8 cm. Surface 2.5YR 6/4. Matrix 2.5YR 6/4.

1268.56.1 Ottoman Cypriot Glazed (Brown/Green) Base (CGBG)
Unit 1268, SIA 10 (Malounda *Panayia Khrysopandanassa*; see chapter 4.10).
Plate 2.
Brown slip and green glaze ring foot and base. Low, broad, almost nonexistent ring foot. Tripod mark. Eighteenth to nineteenth centuries AD. Function FW. Fabric F. Length 5.0 cm. Width 4.9 cm. Thickness 1.0 cm. Surface 5YR 6/4. Matrix 5YR 6/4.

1268.60.2 Medieval Imported Sgraffito Ware Rim (ISW)
Unit 1268, SIA 10 (Malounda *Panayia Khrysopandanassa*; see chapter 4.10).
Plate 3.
Bowl with plain rim. White slip and yellow glaze on interior and over rim. Import. Mend hole just under rim. Function FW. Fabric F. Length 2.6 cm. Width 2.0 cm. Thickness 0.4 cm. Diameter 28 cm? Surface 5YR 6/4. Matrix 5YR 6/4.

1268.62.1 Medieval Lemba Ware Body Sherd (LW)
Unit 1268, SIA 10 (Malounda *Panayia Khrysopandanassa*; see chapter 4.10).
Plates 3, 14.
Slip-painted body sherd. Glazed reddish and yellow inside. Function FW. Fabric F. Length 2.2 cm. Width 2.0 cm. Thickness 0.4 cm. Surface 2.5YR 6/4. Matrix 2.5YR 6/4.

1269.21.1 Medieval Imported Sgraffito Ware Base (ISW)
Unit 1269, SIA 10 (Malounda *Panayia Khrysopandanassa*; see chapter 4.10).
Plate 3.
Small low ring foot. Italian. White slip on interior and exterior. Yellow glaze on exterior. Interior medallion sgrafitto, yellow and green glaze. Sixteenth century AD. Function FW. Fabric F. Length 6.1 cm. Width 5.1 cm. Thickness 0.6 cm. Surface 5YR 6/4. Matrix 5YR 6/4.

1269.21.2 Medieval Imported Sgraffito Ware Base (ISW)
Unit 1269, SIA 10 (Malounda *Panayia Khrysopandanassa*; see chapter 4.10).
Plate 3.
Small, low ring foot. White slip on interior and exterior. Yellow glaze on exterior. Interior medallion sgraffito with yellow and green glaze. Sixteenth century AD. Function FW. Fabric F. Length 4.7 cm. Width 3.8 cm. Thickness 0.6 cm. Surface 5YR 7/2. Matrix 5YR 7/2.

1269.22.1 Medieval Cypriot Glazed VI Body Sherd (CG6)
Unit 1269, SIA 10 (Malounda *Panayia Khrysopandanassa*; see chapter 4.10).
Plates 3, 14.
Probable carinated shape. White crazed glaze on interior. Green and yellow glaze on exterior with sgraffito design. Fourteenth century AD. Function FW. Fabric F. Length 3.9 cm. Width 3.0 cm. Thickness 0.6 cm. Surface 10YR 7/4. Matrix 10YR 7/4.

1269.23.1 Medieval Cypriot Glazed Rim (CG)
Unit 1269, SIA 10 (Malounda *Panayia Khrysopandanassa*; see chapter 4.10).
Plate 3.
Blue and yellow glaze on rim with sgraffito design. Function FW. Fabric F. Length 2.5 cm. Width 1.6 cm. Thickness 0.4 cm. Diameter 34 cm. Surface 10YR 7/2. Matrix 10YR 7/2.

1280.5.1 Modern Lapithos Ware (Green) Rim (LPWG)
Unit 1280, SIA 10 (Malounda *Panayia Khrysopandanassa*; see chapter 4.10).
Plate 3.
Bowl with folded rim, slip-painted design and green glaze. Function FW. Fabric F. Length 6.5 cm. Width 2.8 cm. Thickness 0.5 cm. Diameter 26 cm. Surface 2.5YR 6/4. Matrix 2.5YR 6/4.

1285.12.1 Medieval Maiolica Ware Body Sherd (MW)
Unit 1285, Grid reference 516700/3878550.
Plates 3, 14.
Polychrome maiolica body sherd. Blue-white glaze on interior. Uncertain design in blue, white, yellow, and green on exterior. Sixteenth century AD. Function FW. Fabric F. Length 3.2 cm. Width 1.9 cm. Thickness 0.6 cm. Surface 10YR 8/2. Matrix 10YR 8/2.

1296.13.1 Early Roman Eastern Sigillata A Body Sherd (ESA)
Unit 1296, SCY105 (Aredhiou *Panayia Odhiyitria*).
Body sherd, with part of ring foot? Worn red slip interior and exterior. First century BC to first century AD. Function FW. Fabric F. Length 3.5 cm. Width 2.9 cm. Thickness 0.6 cm. Surface 5YR 7/2. Matrix 5YR 7/2.

1302.13.1 Archaic to Classical Plain White Bowl Rim (PWAC)
Unit 1302, SIA 1 (Agrokipia *Kriadhis*; see chapter 4.1).
Plates 3, 15.
Plain White IV, V, or VII flat, flanged rim of bowl with yellowish to white exterior. Function LU. Fabric C. Length 6.0 cm. Width 3.8 cm. Thickness 0.8 cm. Rim diameter 35 cm. Surface 10YR 7/3. Matrix 10YR 7/3.
Comparanda: Gjerstad 1948: Figs. XLIV.4, LVI.25, LXVII.17.

1307.1.1 Ottoman Cypriot Glazed (Brown/Green) Base (CGBG)
Unit 1307, SIA 1 (Agrokipia *Kriadhis*; see chapter 4.1).
Plate 4.
Very low almost disc base. Glazed green and beige on interior.
Eighteenth to nineteenth centuries AD. Function FW. Fabric F. Length
5.9 cm. Width 4.0 cm. Thickness 0.9 cm. Surface 5YR 6/4. Matrix
10YR 7/3.

1327.13.1 Early Roman Cypriot Sigillata Rim (CS)
Unit 1327, SCY105 (Aredhiou *Panayia Odhiyitria*).
Plate 15.
Hayes form 5. Function FW. Fabric F. Length 2.3 cm. Width 1.5 cm.
Thickness 0.4 cm. Diameter 16 cm. Surface 5YR 6/6. Slip 2.5YR
5/6. Matrix 5YR 5/6.
Comparanda: Hayes Form 5, Augustan and later (Hayes 1967:68–70).

1350.1.1 Early Roman Cooking Pot Rim (CKERP)
Unit 1350, Grid reference 516000/3876950.
Plate 4.
Rim with two grooves on upper surface. Function CU. Fabric CW.
Length 5.0 cm. Width 2.4 cm. Thickness 0.4 cm. Diameter 26 cm.
Surface 5YR 5/8. Matrix 5YR 5/8.

1595.3.1 Hellenistic Black Glaze Bowl Rim (BGHE)
Unit 1595, SIA 7 (Politiko *Kokkinorotsos*; see chapter 4.7).
Plate 4.
Rim of Greek Black Glaze bowl with two horizontal grooves below
rim on exterior. Worn, fragmentary. Gray core. Third century BC.
Function FW. Fabric F. Length 2.7 cm. Width 2.8 cm. Thickness
0.5 cm. Diameter 25 cm.
Comparanda: shape and size similar to the Bolster Cup, which is not a
common shape; see Rotroff 1997: 259, Fig. 13.166, Pl. 15.166, no. 166.

1596.1.1 Archaic White Painted IV Amphora Rim (WPAR)
Unit 1596, SIA 7 (Politiko *Kokkinorotsos*; see chapter 4.7).
Plates 4, 15.
Flat-flanged rim and part of neck of White Painted IV amphora.
Indent below rim and ridge at top of neck. Greenish fabric. Black
painted zigzag with vertical strokes on rim and wavy horizontal line
below rim. Cypro-Archaic I. Function LU. Fabric F. Length 9.5 cm.
Width 5.5 cm. Thickness 0.9 cm. Diameter 22.0 cm. Surface 10YR
7/2. Matrix 10YR 7/2.
Comparanda: for shape, see Gjerstad 1948: Fig. XXXV.14–15.

1599.1.1 Hellenistic/Early Roman Pseudo-Koan Amphora Rim (AMPK)
Unit 1599, SCY101 (Politiko *Phorades 2*; SIA 7; see chapter 4.7).
Plates 4, 15.
Pseudo-Koan amphora with angular rim and double handle.
Function HU. Fabric CL. Length 11.0 cm. Width 5.4 cm. Rim
thickness 1.0 cm. Diameter 18 cm. Surface 7.5YR 6/6. Matrix 5YR
6/6.

1599.12.1 Late Roman Cypriot Red Slip 2 Rim (CRS2)
Unit 1599, SCY101 (Politiko *Phorades 2*; SIA 7; see chapter 4.7).
Plates 4, 15.
Rim with two grooves on top, gouges, vertical on outside of rim.
Worn slip. Function FW. Fabric CR. Length 4.8 cm. Width 4.5 cm.
Thickness 1.4 cm. Surface 5YR 6/6. Matrix 5YR 6/6.
Comparanda: Hayes Form 2 (Hayes 1972:373–376).

1601.1.1 Late Roman Amphora Base (AMRL)
Unit 1601, SCY101 (Politiko *Phorades 2*; SIA 7; see chapter 4.7).
Plate 15.
Slipped amphora toe. Anemarium type A. Function HU. Fabric CL.
Length 9.2 cm. Width 6.7 cm. Base thickness 5 cm. Slip 10YR 7/4.
Matrix 5YR 6/4.

1603.3.1 Late Roman Pithos Base (PILR)
Unit 1603, SCY101 (Politiko *Phorades 2*; SIA 7; see chapter 4.7).
Plate 15.
Pithos toe. Inclusions 25 to 40%. Function PI. Fabric CR. Length
16.0 cm. Width 8.0 cm. Base thickness 3.8 cm. Body thickness
1.8 cm. Base diameter 16 cm. Surface 5YR 5/6. Matrix 5YR 5/6.

1604.4.1 Early Roman Offset Rim Cooking Pot Rim (CKOR)
Unit 1604, SCY101 (Politiko *Phorades 2*; SIA 7; see chapter 4.7).
Plate 16.
Rim, handle attachment, and strap handle. Handle slipped with
two grooves. Function CU. Fabric CR. Length 5.4 cm. Width 1.6 cm.
Rim thickness 0.9 cm. Handle thickness 0.7 cm. Diameter 17 cm.
Surface 2.5YR 5/6. Matrix 2.5YR 5/6.

1625.5C.1 Classical Plain Ware Bowl Rim and Body (PLCL)
Unit 1625, SCY123 (Politiko *Phorades 3*; SIA 7; see chapter 4.7).
Plate 16.
Rim and body of wide shallow bowl with carination below rim.
Cypro-Classical II. Function LU. Fabric CL. Length 7.0 cm. Width
6.1 cm. Rim thickness 1.8 cm. Body thickness 0.8 cm. Diameter
29.5 cm. Outer surface 5YR 6/6. Internal slip 7.5YR 7/4. Matrix
7.5YR 7/6.
Comparanda: Salles 1983:75, Fig. 29, no. 251.

1629.2.1 Geometric to Archaic Bichrome Jug Body Sherd (BIGA)
Unit 1629, SCY123 (Politiko *Phorades 3*; SIA 7; see chapter 4.7).
Plate 4.
Parallel black concentric lines on either side of a red circular band.
Overmarked by another set of black parallel lines. Cypro-Geometric
III to Cypro-Archaic II. Function LU. Fabric F. Length 4.5 cm. Width
3.6 cm. Thickness 0.5 cm. Surface 5YR 6/4. Matrix 5YR 6/4.
Comparanda: for decoration, see Gjerstad 1948: Figs. XXII.14, XXXIV.8,
XLIX.11.

1686.2.1 Medieval Cypriot Glazed VII Base (CG7)
Unit 1686, Grid reference 520450/3875000.
Plate 4.
High ring foot with white slip and clear glaze on interior and
exterior. Decadent sgraffito and green and yellow glaze on interior.
Function FW. Fabric F. Length 8.5 cm. Width 5.0 cm. Thickness
0.6 cm. Surface 5YR 6/4. Matrix 5YR 6/4.

1705.11.1 Modern Contemporary Local Ware Body Sherd (CLWM)
Unit 1705, SIA 6 (Politiko *Ayios Mnason*; see chapter 4.6).
Yellow-glazed body sherd. Hard yellow glaze on interior; poor
green glaze on exterior. Function FW. Fabric F. Length 4.1 cm.
Width 3.3 cm. Thickness 0.8 cm. Surface 10YR 8/2. Matrix 10YR
8/2.

1708.14.1 Early Roman Cooking Ware (Offset Rim Pot) Rim (CKOR)
Unit 1708, SIA 6 (Politiko *Ayios Mnason*; see chapter 4.6).
Plate 4.
Offset rim cooking pot. Function CU. Fabric CW. Length 3.2 cm.
Width 1.4 cm. Thickness 0.4 cm. Diameter 19 cm. Surface 5YR 5/
8. Matrix 5YR 5/8.

1709.27.1 Medieval Imported Sgraffito Ware Body Sherd (ISW)
Unit 1709, SIA 6 (Politiko *Ayios Mnason*; see chapter 4.6).
Plate 16.
Very sandy buff clay. White slip and pale yellow glaze inside and
out. Uncertain sgraffito design on interior. Import? Function FW.
Fabric F. Length 4.2 cm. Width 4.0 cm. Thickness 0.6 cm. Surface
10YR 6/4. Matrix 10YR 6/4.

1722.4.1 Late Roman Phocaean Ware 3 Rim (PHW3)
Unit 1722, SIA 6 (Politiko *Ayios Mnason*; see chapter 4.6).
Plate 16.
Imitation Phocaean Ware form 3 in Cypriot Red Slip. Function FW.
Fabric C. Length 4.0 cm. Width 3.3 cm. Rim thickness 1.6 cm.
Body thickness 0.7 cm. Diameter 30 cm. Slip 2.5YR 5/6. Matrix
2.5YR 6/6.

1727.16.1 Modern Lapithos Ware (Yellow) Rim (LPWY)
Unit 1727, SIA 6 (Politiko *Ayios Mnason*; see chapter 4.6).
Plate 4.
Plain folded rim with slip-painted design and yellow glaze. Function
FW. Fabric F. Length 4.6 cm. Width 4.0 cm. Thickness 0.5 cm.
Diameter 34 cm. Surface 2.5YR 6/4. Matrix 2.5YR 6/4.

1728.10.1 Late Roman African Red Slip 50 Rim (ARS50)
Unit 1728, SIA 6 (Politiko *Ayios Mnason*; see chapter 4.6).
Plate 16.
Hayes form 50b. Function FW. Fabric F. Length 2.1 cm. Width 1.3 cm. Thickness 0.4 cm. Diameter 35 cm. Surface 2.5YR 5/8. Matrix 2.5YR 5/8.
Comparanda: Hayes Form 50b, AD 350–400 (Hayes 1972:68–73, no. 60).

1733.2.1 Classical Knobbed Amphora Base (AMK)
Unit 1733, SIA 6 (Politiko *Ayios Mnason*; see chapter 4.6).
Plate 5.
Knobbed base of amphora. Cypro-Classical II. Function HU. Fabric CL. Length 4.7. Width 5.9 cm. Thickness 0.9 cm.
Comparanda: Gjerstad 1948: Fig. LXIX.11.

1733.3.1 Archaic to Classical Torpedo Amphora Handle (AMT)
Unit 1733, SIA 6 (Politiko *Ayios Mnason*; see chapter 4.6).
Plate 5.
Ear-shaped lug handle from torpedo amphora. Two joining fragments. Orange fabric that fragments parallel to surface of vessel. Function HU. Fabric CR. Length 7.6 cm. Width 2.6 cm. Thickness 1.3 cm.
Comparanda: Gjerstad 1960: Fig. 6.7–10.

1733.10.1 Archaic Bichrome V Bowl Rim (BIAR)
Unit 1733, SIA 6 (Politiko *Ayios Mnason*; see chapter 4.6).
Plate 5.
Flanged and slightly sloping rim of Bichrome V ware medium deep bowl. Slight ridge under end of rim. Black and red paint on rim as well as interior and exterior of body. Cypro-Archaic II. Function LU. Fabric TL. Length 2.9 cm. Width 6.7 cm. Thickness 0.3 cm.
Comparanda: for shape, see Gjerstad 1948: Fig. XLVII.12.

1740.1.1 Geometric to Classical Rolled Lug Handle (RLH)
Unit 1740, SIA 6 (Politiko *Ayios Mnason*; see chapter 4.6).
Plate 5.
Rolled lug handle of amphora, possibly pithoid, or other large closed shape such as a hydria. Very green fabric. Function HU. Fabric CL. Length 12.4 cm. Width 5.0 cm. Thickness 3.1 cm.

1741.1.1 Geometric to Classical Pithos Rim (PIGAC)
Unit 1741, SIA 6 (Politiko *Ayios Mnason*; see chapter 4.6).
Plate 5.
Rim of pithos with greenish exterior and many chaff impressions. Function PI. Fabric CL. Length 6.3 cm. Width 7.6 cm. Thickness 1.5 cm. Diameter 50+ cm.

1741.13.1 Archaic White Painted IV or V Amphora Rim (WPAR)
Unit 1741, SIA 6 (Politiko *Ayios Mnason*; see chapter 4.6).
Plate 5.
Concave rolled-out rim of White Painted IV or V amphora. Greenish fabric. Black paint on rim, inside rim, and around top of neck. Function HU. Fabric TL. Length 3.1 cm. Width 8.1 cm. Thickness 0.5 cm. Diameter 21 cm.
Comparanda: for shape of rim, see Gjerstad 1948: Figs. XXIX.12, L.9, LV.4.

1741.24B.1 Classical Plain Ware Jar Rim and Shoulder (PLCL)
Unit 1741, SIA 6 (Politiko *Ayios Mnason*; see chapter 4.6).
Plate 16.
Rounded rim and shoulder of jar. Fabric and surface same as terra-cotta sculpture hands from SIA 6 (5022.1.1; 5037.1.1; see chapter 5.3). Cypro-Classical I. Function LU. Fabric CR. Length 6.9 cm. Width 3.7 cm. Thickness 14.9 cm. Diameter 16 cm. Surface 10YR 7/3. Matrix 5YR 6/4.
Comparanda: Gjerstad 1948: Fig. LXII.2.

1742.1B.1 Archaic Pithoid Amphora Base (AMPI)
Unit 1742, SIA 6 (Politiko *Ayios Mnason*; see chapter 4.6).
Plate 16.
Flat pointed base of pithoid amphora. Exterior surface shaved. Cypro-Archaic II. Function HU. Fabric CL. Length 16.5 cm. Width 15.5 cm. Thickness 1.8–2.8 cm. Diameter 48 cm. Surface 2.5Y 7/4. Matrix 10YR 7/4.
Comparanda: Gjerstad 1948: Fig. LVII.23.

1742.4.1 Archaic to Classical Red Slip Jug Handle (RSAC)
Unit 1742, SIA 6 (Politiko *Ayios Mnason*; see chapter 4.6).
Plate 17.
Strap handle from straight rim of jug of Soft Red-Orange fabric with traces of red slip. Pot mark made after firing on upper part of handle: possibly /a/ in the Cypriot syllabary. Function LU. Fabric TR. Length 5.0 cm. Width 3.9 cm. Thickness 0.5 cm. Diameter 9 cm. Surface 2.5YR 5/6. Matrix 2.5YR 5/8.
Comparanda: similar pot marks appear in Masson 1996:179–180, nos. 2, 35.

1743.28.1 Late Roman Cypriot Red Slip 9 Rim (CRS9)
Unit 1743, SIA 6 (Politiko *Ayios Mnason*; see chapter 4.6).
Plate 17.
Slip worn on exterior. Function FW. Fabric F. Length 4.1 cm. Width 2.5 cm. Thickness 0.7 cm. Diameter 48 cm. Surface 5YR 5/8. Matrix 2.5YR 6/4.
Hayes Form 104b,–AD 570–580 (Hayes 1972:162–163, no. 15).

1745.1.1 Late Roman African Red Slip Rim (ARS45)
Unit 1745, SIA 6 (Politiko *Ayios Mnason*; see chapter 4.6).
Plate 17.
Large bowl, with broad flat rim. Hayes form 45c. Function FW. Fabric F. Length 5.2 cm. Width 4.4 cm. Thickness 0.7 cm. Diameter 32 cm. Slip 2.5YR 5/8. Matrix 2.5YR 6/8.
Hayes Form 45c, early to mid-fourth century AD (Hayes 1972:62–65, no. 10).

1746.2.1 Classical Plain ware Skyphos Handle and Rim (PLCL)
Unit 1746, SIA 6 (Politiko *Ayios Mnason*; see chapter 4.6).
Plate 17.
Loop handle and rim of skyphos. Function LU. Fabric TL. Length 5.0 cm. Width 2.3 cm. Body thickness 0.4 cm. Handle thickness 1.1 cm. Diameter 13 cm. Slip 7.5YR 8/4. Matrix 5YR 7/6.
Comparanda: for shape, see Gjerstad 1948: Figs. LXI.4, LXVI.12; Salles 1983:69, Fig. 27, no. 222; Buchholz 1985a:253–254, Fig. 13.a–c.

2102.12.1 Classical White Painted VI Jug Neck and Shoulder (WPCL)
Unit 2102, SIA 1 (Agrokipia *Kriadhis*; see chapter 4.1).
Plate 6.
Part of neck and shoulder of White Painted VI jug. Ridge around neckline. Black to purple-colored painted lines on either side of ridge, two vertical lines down shoulder, wavy line around lower part of neck. Cypro-Classical I. Function LU. Fabric TL.
Comparanda: Gjerstad 1948: fig. LVIII.9.

2105.5.1 Archaic Cooking Ware Wide Shallow Bowl Rim (WSBAR)
Unit 2105, SIA 1 (Agrokipia *Kriadhis*; see chapter 4.1).
Plate 6.
Flat rim and part of body of wide shallow bowl of cooking ware fabric. Function LU. Fabric TR. Length 3.6 cm. Width 2.5 cm. Thickness 0.4 cm.
Comparanda: for shape, see Gjerstad 1960: Fig. 1.6,11.

2105.8.1 Archaic to Classical Greek Amphora Rim (AMGR)
Unit 2105, SIA 1 (Agrokipia *Kriadhis*; see chapter 4.1).
Plate 6.
Rolled-out rim of amphora with handle scar below rim on neck. Micaceous dark red to brown fabric. Profile and fabric most similar to amphorae from Samos (though not examined through thin section). Compares with early sixth to early fifth centuries BC examples. Function HU. Fabric CL.
Comparanda: Grace 1971:73–74, Fig. 2.2, Pl. 15.1; Whitbread 1995:122, 124, 247.

2501.5.1 Medieval Cypriot Glazed IVC Ring Foot (CG4C)
Unit 2501, SIA 4 (Mitsero *Mavrovounos*; see chapter 4.4).
Plate 6.
Bowl with moderately high ring foot. Brown slip on exterior. White slip and clear glaze on interior, with sgrafitto design of squares. Function FW. Fabric F. Length 11.0 cm. Width 5.0 cm. Thickness 0.7 cm. Surface 5YR 6/4. Matrix 5YR 6/4.

2514.1.1 Classical Plain Ware Jar Rim and Shoulder (PLCL)
Unit 2514, SIA 4 (Mitsero *Mavrovounos*; see chapter 4.4).
Plates 6, 17.

Slightly bulbous rim and shoulder of plain ware jar. Cypro-Classical I. Function LU. Fabric C. Length 4.6 cm. Width 8.7 cm. Thickness 0.5 cm.
Comparanda: Gjerstad 1948: Fig. LXII.2.

2611.1.1   Archaic Black Glaze Ring Foot (BGAR)
Unit 2611, SIA 1 (Agrokipia *Kriadhis*; see chapter 4.1).
Plate 6.
Black-glazed ring foot. Possibly Hellenistic, but probably more similar to Archaic (sixth century BC) examples. Function FW. Fabric F. Length 3.4 cm. Width 2.5 cm. Thickness 0.4 cm. Diameter 5 cm. Surface 5YR 6/4. Matrix 5YR 6/4.
Comparanda: Sparkes and Talcott 1970:76–77, Fig. 3.240, Pl. 12.240–44; Rotroff 1997: Figs. 1.1, 39.530, Pl. 51.530.

2637.1.1   Contemporary Eastern Mediterranean Rim (CEM)
Unit 2637, Grid reference 513500/3878800.
Plate 6.
Bowl with flanged rim. Brown slip on exterior. Dark green glaze on interior. Function FW. Fabric F. Length 6.1 cm. Width 5.5 cm. Thickness 0.7 cm. Surface 10YR 7/3. Matrix 10YR 7/3.

2714.1.1   Medieval Cypriot Glazed VIIIB Base (CG8B)
Unit 2714, Grid reference 513500/3874250.
Plates 7, 17.
Heavy bowl with uncertain base. White slip and light yellow glaze on interior. Medallion sgraffito design carefully picked out in green glaze. Tripod mark. Sixteenth century AD. Function FW. Fabric F. Length 6.8 cm. Width 5.8 cm. Thickness 1.1 cm. Surface 5YR 6/4. Matrix 5YR 6/4.

3000.14B.1 Archaic Amphora Rim (AMAR)
Unit 3000, SIA 2 (Klirou *Manastirka*; see chapter 4.2).
Plate 17.
Straight, slightly flared and thickened amphora rim. Cypro-Archaic II. Function HU. Fabric CL. Length 4.9 cm. Width 3.9 cm. Thickness 1.2 cm. Diameter 17 cm. Surface 5YR 6/6. Matrix 5YR 6/6.
Comparanda: for shape, see Gjerstad 1948: Fig. LI.4.

3020.11.1   Archaic Plain Ware Bowl Rim (PLAR)
Unit 3020, SIA 2 (Klirou *Manastirka*; see chapter 4.2).
Plate 18.
Plain rim of medium deep bowl with slightly flared, rounded and tapered rim. Cypro-Archaic I. Function LU. Fabric TL. Length 2.4 cm. Width 2.6 cm. Thickness 0.5 cm.
Comparanda: for shape, see Gjerstad 1948: Fig. XXXVII.12.

3059.1.1   Late Roman Frying Pan Handle (LRF)
Unit 3059, SIA 7 (Politiko *Kokkinorotsos*; see chapter 4.7).
Plate 7.
Most of handle and part of rim of double-handle frying pan. Function LU. Fabric CR. Length 7.6 cm. Width 4.9 cm. Thickness 1.1 cm. Diameter 24 cm. Surface 5YR 5/8. Matrix 5YR 5/8.

3059.2.1   Late Roman Basin (Piecrust Rim) Rim (LRP)
Unit 3059, SIA 7 (Politiko *Kokkinorotsos*; see chapter 4.7).
Plate 7.
Basin rim with depressions on edge and two narrow grooves. Function LU. Fabric C. Length 10.5 cm. Width 6.4 cm. Thickness 1.0 cm. Surface 7.5YR 6/8. Matrix 7.5YR 6/8.

3096.2.1   Archaic White Painted V Body Sherd (WPAR)
Unit 3096, SCY121 (Politiko *Kokkinorotsos* 6; SIA 7; see chapter 4.7).
Plate 18.
Biconical (carinated) body sherd of White Painted V ware closed shape. Cypro-Archaic II. Function LU. Fabric CL. Length 4.2 cm. Width 3.2 cm. Thickness 0.7 cm. Surface 7.5YR 7/4. Matrix 7.5YR 7/6.
Comparanda: Gjerstad 1948: Fig. XLVII.1.

3097.3.1   Classical Amphora Rim (AMCL)
Unit 3097, SIA 7 (Politiko *Kokkinorotsos*; see chapter 4.7).
Plate 18.
Flat flanged rim of amphora. Cypro-Classical I. Function HU. Fabric

CL. Length 15.4 cm. Width 5.5 cm. Rim thickness 2.7 cm. Base thickness 8.5 cm. Diameter 28.5 cm. Surface 7.5YR 7/6. Matrix 7.5YR 6/6.
Comparanda: for shape, see Gjerstad 1948: Fig. LIX.2.

3194.13.1   Medieval to Modern Cypriot W3 Rim (W3)
Unit 3194, Grid reference 517000/3874400.
Plate 7.
Cooking pot or small pithos with triangular rim, flat on top. Similar to Phocaean Ware 3. Function LU. Fabric F. Length 3.5 cm. Width 3.2 cm. Thickness 0.4 cm. Diameter 50 cm. Surface 5YR 5/6. Matrix 5YR 5/6.

3224.13.1   Modern Glazed Body Sherd (GZ)
Unit 3224, Grid reference 516950/3874900.
Plate 18.
White porcelain body sherd with inscription. Made in Czechoslovakia. Function FW. Fabric F. Length 2.8 cm. Width 1.8 cm. Thickness 0.3 cm. Matrix 10YR 7/6.

3259.18.1   Late Roman Phocaean Ware Rim (PHW)
Unit 3259, Grid reference 517000/3875750.
Plate 18.
Pink clay. Phocaean Ware 3 imitation? Function FW. Fabric F. Length 3.5 cm. Width 2.2 cm. Rim thickness 0.8 cm. Body thickness 0.3 to 0.4 cm. Diameter 25 cm. Surface 2.5YR 6/6. Matrix 2.5YR 6/6.

3503.2.1   Classical Stroke Polished Flat Disc Base (SPCL)
Unit 3503, Grid reference 520500/3877750.
Plate 7.
Stroke-polished ware flat disc base of Soft Red-Orange (SRO) fabric. Open shape. Blackened striations on interior. Very worn, but traces of slip or paint remain. Function LU. Fabric C. Surface 2.5YR 5/6. Matrix 5YR 6/3. Length 5.8 cm. Width 4.5 cm. Thickness 0.4 cm.

3510.1.1   Prehistoric Bronze Age Fine Ware Spout (FWPEB)
Unit 3510, SCY106 (Ergates *Spileadhia*).
Plate 7.
Burnished spout. Function FW. Fabric F. Length 5.5 cm. Width 8.9 cm. Thickness 0.9 cm.

3510.3.1   Prehistoric Bronze Age Fine Ware Rim (FWPEB)
Unit 3510, SCY106 (Ergates *Spileadhia*).
Plate 7.
Straight tapered rim of Late Chalcolithic (?) open shape. Stroke burnished? Function FW. Fabric F. Length 5.2 cm. Width 4.0 cm. Thickness 0.7 cm. Diameter 50 cm. Surface 7.5YR 6/6. Matrix 5YR 5/3.

3533.3.1   Prehistoric Bronze Age Coarse Ware Spout (COPEB)
Unit 3533, Grid reference 519750/3877850.
Plate 8.
Basin spout. Red polished interior and exterior. Function UT. Fabric C. Length 4.4 cm. Width 4.0 cm. Thickness 0.7 cm. Surface 5YR 6/3. Matrix 5YR 6/3.

3653.27.1   Late Roman African Red Slip Rim (ARS)
Unit 3653, Grid reference 521500/3877300.
Plate 18.
Plain pointed rim. Mend hole at base. Function FW. Fabric F. Length 2.4 cm. Width 1.5 cm. Thickness 3.5 cm. Diameter 25 cm. Surface 10R 5/8. Matrix 10R 5/8.
Comparanda: Hayes ARS50b, AD 350–400 (Hayes 1972:68–73, no. 60).

3657.26.1   Early Roman Cypriot Sigillata Rim (CS)
Unit 3657, Grid reference 521500/3877450.
Plate 18.
Groove on top of rim. Function FW. Fabric F. Length 2.4 cm. Width 1.8 cm. Thickness 0.6 cm. Diameter 25 cm. Surface 5YR 7/6. Matrix 5YR 7/6.
Comparanda: Hayes Form 5 (Hayes 1967:70, no. 68).

3670.20.1 Medieval Cypriot W1 Early Rim (W1E)

Unit 3670, Grid reference 521450/3877900.
Plates 8, 18.
Beehive rim. Slipped. Function LU. Fabric CR. Length 5.0 cm.
Width 4.2 cm. Thickness 1.6 cm. Diameter 31 cm. Surface 7.5YR
5/4. Matrix 5YR 5/4.

4023.24.1 Modern Lapithos Ware Rim (LPW)

Unit 4023, SIA 3 (Mitsero *Kouloupakhis*; see chapter 4.3).
Plates 8, 18.
Ledge-lipped rim. Green glaze. Function FW. Fabric F. Length
3.7 cm. Width 3.2 cm. Thickness 0.5 cm. Diameter 18 cm. Surface
7.5YR 7/4. Matrix 7.5YR 7/4.

4023.25.1 Modern Lapithos Ware (Yellow) Rim (LPWY)

Unit 4023, SIA 3 (Mitsero *Kouloupakhis*; see chapter 4.3).
Plates 8, 19.
Worn Lapithos plain folded rim with slip-painted design and yellow
glaze. Function FW. Fabric F. Length 0.5 cm. Width 4.2 cm. Rim
thickness 0.9 cm. Body thickness 0.6 cm. Diameter 21 cm.
Surface 5YR 6/6. Matrix 5YR 6/6.

4041.4.1 Hellenistic Black Glazed Rim (BGHE)

Unit 4041, SIA 3 (Mitsero *Kouloupakhis*; see chapter 4.3).
Plates 8, 19.
Footed hemispherical bowl rim and ring foot, or late example of
echinus bowl. Black-dipped and painted interior decoration.
Second century BC. Function FW. Fabric F. Length 7.4 cm. Width
5.5 cm. Thickness 4.7 cm. Diameter 14 cm. Surface 10YR 6/3.
Matrix 10YR 7/1.
Comparanda: for shape, see Rotroff 1997:163–164, 343–344, Figs.
63.1025, 64.1044, nos. 1025, 1044.

4041.14.1 Geometric to Archaic Bichrome Jug Body Sherd (BIGA)

Unit 4041, SIA 3 (Mitsero *Kouloupakhis*; see chapter 4.3).
Plate 8.
Bichrome body sherd of jug. Friable overfired greenish fabric.
Reddish-purple and black-green paint. Group of lines flanked by
larger band. Cypro-Geometric III to Cypro-Archaic II. Function LU.
Fabric TL. Length 6.0 cm. Width 4.7 cm. Thickness 0.6 cm.
Comparanda: for decoration, see Gjerstad 1948: bichrome closed
shapes in Figs. XXII, XXXII, XLVIII.

4042.16.1 Medieval Glazed Rim (GZ)

Unit 4042, SIA 4 (Mitsero *Mavrovounos*; see chapter 4.4).
Plates 8, 19.
Yellow-glazed rim. Function FW. Fabric F. Length 5.3 cm. Width
2.6 cm. Thickness 0.7 cm. Diameter 25 cm. Surface 5YR 6/6.
Matrix 5YR 6/6.

4042.20.1 Medieval Cypriot Glazed XI Base (CG11)

Unit 4042, SIA 4 (Mitsero *Mavrovounos*; see chapter 4.4).
Plates 9, 19.
Bowl with low ring foot. White slip and clear glaze on interior,
marked with mottled gray splotches. Sixteenth century AD. Function
FW. Fabric F. Length 4.5 cm. Width 2.2 cm. Thickness 0.7 cm.
Surface 7.5YR 5/4. Matrix 7.5YR 5/4.

4052.6.1 Archaic Pithos Body Sherd of Soft Red-Orange Fabric (PIAR)

Unit 4052, SIA 2 (Klirou *Manastirka*; see chapter 4.2).
Plate 19.
Body sherd of pithos with two rows of impressed rope marks.
Probably from lower half of pithos where rope would have been
used for vessel stability during construction. Soft Red-Orange
fabric, like other Archaic pottery from Unit 4052. Function PI. Fabric
CR. Length 7.4 cm. Width 6.5 cm. Thickness 1.9 cm. Surface 5YR
5/6. Matrix 5YR 5/6.

4052.9.1 Archaic Skyphos Rim of Soft Red-Orange Fabric (SROAR)

Unit 4052, SIA 2 (Klirou *Manastirka*; see chapter 4.2).
Plate 19.
Rim and stub of handle of small cup or skyphos. Cypro-Archaic I.
Function LU. Fabric TR. Length 2.9 cm. Width 2.4 cm. Thickness

0.3 cm. Diameter 15 cm. Surface 5YR 4/6. Matrix 5YR 4/6.
Comparanda: for profile, see Gjerstad 1948: Fig. XXXVII.12; for handles
below the rim, see Gjerstad 1948: Fig. XXX.13.

4052.15.1,2,3 Archaic Medium Deep Bowl Rim (MDB)

Unit 4052, SIA 2 (Klirou *Manastirka*; see chapter 4.2).
Plate 19.
Three joining pieces of medium deep bowl with flat everted rim and
carinated lower body. Cooking ware fabric. Cypro-Archaic II. Function
LU. Fabric CD. Length 8.7 cm. Width 5.7 cm. Rim thickness 1.2 cm.
Body thickness 0.6 cm. Diameter 20 cm. Exterior surface 7.5YR 4/4.
Interior surface 7.5YR 5/4. Matrix 10YR 4/1.
Comparanda: for shape, see Gjerstad 1948: Fig. LIII.1.

4052.25.1 Hellenistic Black Glazed Rim (BGHE)

Unit 4052, SIA 2 (Klirou *Manastirka*; see chapter 4.2).
Plate 19.
Rolled-out rim and body of Hellenistic black slip bowl. Black slip on
interior and exterior. Function FW. Fabric F. Length 4.0 cm. Width
3.2 cm. Rim thickness 0.7 cm. Body thickness 0.35 cm. Diameter
18 cm. Surface 5YR 7/6. Matrix 5YR 6/4.

4068.11.1 Ottoman Cypriot Glazed IX Late Base (CG9L)

Unit 4068, SIA 2 (Klirou *Manastirka*; see chapter 4.2).
Plates 9, 20.
Large, very crudely made bowl, with low uneven ring foot and a
series of horizontal grooves above the base. Seventeenth to
eighteenth centuries AD. Function FW. Fabric F. Length 9.9 cm.
Width 6.2 cm. Thickness 1.2 cm. Base diameter 7.5 cm. Surface
7.5YR 6/6. Matrix 7.5YR 6/6.

4069.3.1 Early Roman Cypriot Sigillata Rim (CS)

Unit 4069, SIA 2 (Klirou *Manastirka*; see chapter 4.2).
Plate 20.
Slip completely worn. Function FW. Fabric F. Length 2.8 cm. Width
2.1 cm. Thickness 0.6 cm. Diameter 25 cm. Surface 2.5YR 6/8.
Matrix 2.5YR 6/8.
Comparanda: Hayes Form 11, circa AD 50–200 (Hayes 1967:71–72).

4505.5.1 Late Roman Cooking Ware (Dhiorios Pot) Rim (CKD)

Unit 4505, SIA 9 (Klirou-Ayios Mamas; see chapter 4.9).
Plates 9, 20.
Cooking pot with slightly flaring rim and thickened lip. Function CU.
Fabric TR. Length 4.1 cm. Width 3.1 cm. Thickness 0.7 cm. Surface
2.5YR 5/6. Matrix 2.5YR 4/3.

4514.1.1 Ottoman Cypriot Glazed IX Late Base (CG9L)

Unit 4514, SIA 9 (Klirou *Ayios Mamas*; see chapter 4.9).
Plates 9, 20.
Low, wide ring foot with brown slip, sgraffito decoration and green
glaze on interior. Function FW. Fabric F. Length 6.4 cm. Width
5.4 cm. Thickness 0.8 cm. Surface 7.5YR 6/6. Matrix 7.5YR 6/6.

4542.35.1 Late Roman Egyptian Red Slip Rim (ERS)

Unit 4542, SIA 10 (Malounda *Panayia Khrysopandanassa*; see
chapter 4.10).
Plate 20.
Function FW. Fabric F. Length 3.0 cm. Width 1.5 cm. Diameter
33 cm. Surface 5YR 7/6. Matrix 5YR 7/6.

5019.20.1 Classical Plain Ware Juglet Base and Body Sherd (PLCL)

Unit 5019, SIA 6 (Politiko *Ayios Mnason*; see chapter 4.6).
Plates 9, 20.
Flat disc base and lower half of body of small plain ware juglet.
Strap handle scar on body. Function SYM. Fabric CR. Length
4.6 cm. Width 4.5 cm. Thickness 0.9 cm. Diameter 4.0 cm.
Surface 5YR 6/6.
Comparanda: Salles 1983:82, Fig. 32, no. 276; Loulloupis 1989: Fig. 8;
Buitron-Oliver 1996:50, Fig. 51, no. H10.

5019.22.1 Medieval Cypriot Glazed VIIIB Base (CG8B)

Unit 5019, SIA 6 (Politiko *Ayios Mnason*; see chapter 4.6).
Plates 10, 20.

Base, part of base ring, some body walls. Function FW. Fabric F. Length 9.3 cm. Width 3.3 cm. Thickness 1.0 cm. Surface 5YR 7/6. Matrix 5YR 7/6.

5019.44A.1 Classical Green Ware Jar Rim and Shoulder (GWCL)
Unit 5019, SIA 6 (Politiko *Ayios Mnason*; see chapter 4.6). Plate 10.
Rim, neck, and shoulder of hole-mouth jar, cut prefiring just at junction to shoulder. Fired green, like a waster, with finger smudging of surface. Cypro-Classical I. Function LU. Fabric CL. Length 4.3 cm. Width 12.0 cm. Thickness 0.7 cm. Diameter 18 cm.
Comparanda: for shape, see Gjerstad 1948: Fig. LXII.2.

5021.51.1 Medieval Cypriot Glazed IX Late Base (CG9L)
Unit 5021, SIA 6 (Politiko *Ayios Mnason*; see chapter 4.6). Plates 10, 20.
Bowl with very low ring foot and graffito on base. Seventeenth to eighteenth century AD. Function FW. Fabric F. Length 7.0 cm. Width 4.5 cm. Thickness at side 1.3 cm. Thickness at middle 0.6 cm. Base diameter 7.0 cm. Surface 5YR 7/6. Matrix 5YR 7/6.

5026.8.1 Medieval Imported Sgraffito Ware Base (ISW)
Unit 5026, SIA 6 (Politiko *Ayios Mnason*; see chapter 4.6). Plate 20.
Imported sgraffito base. Function FW. Fabric F. Length 4.5 cm. Width 2.2 cm. Thickness 1.3 cm. Surface 5YR 6/6. Matrix 5YR 6/6.

5029.4.1 Early Roman Cooking Ware (Offset Rim Pot) Rim (CKOR)
Unit 5029, SIA 6 (Politiko *Ayios Mnason*; see chapter 4.6). Plates 10, 21.
Cooking pot with out-turned rim, rather thick, with horizontal handle. Wheel-ridged body and shoulder. Chocolate brown, fairly smooth clay. Function CU. Fabric CR. Length 8.2 cm. Width 5.3 cm. Rim thickness 1.5 cm. Body thickness 1.5 cm. Diameter 20 cm. Surface 2.5YR 4/4. Matrix 2.5YR 4/4.

5035.5.1 Contemporary Imported European Base (CIE)
Unit 5035, SIA 6 (Politiko *Ayios Mnason*; see chapter 4.6). Plate 10.
Glazed French plate. Function FW. Fabric F. Length 4.5 cm. Width 3.4 cm. Thickness 0.45 cm. Surface bright white. Matrix 2.5Y 8/2.

5035.29.1 Modern Contemporary Eastern Mediterranean Body Sherd (CEM)
Unit 5035, SIA 6 (Politiko *Ayios Mnason*; see chapter 4.6). Plates 10, 21.
Glazed blue-on-white body sherd. Function FW. Fabric F. Length 4.5 cm. Width 3.7 cm. Thickness 0.65 cm. Surface 10YR 7/4. Matrix 5YR 6/4.

5036.49.1 Medieval Imported Sgraffito Ware Base (ISW)
Unit 5036, SIA 6 (Politiko *Ayios Mnason*; see chapter 4.6). Plate 21.
Bowl with white slip and yellow glaze and uncertain sgraffito design on interior. Function FW. Fabric F. Length 6.2 cm. Width 2.6 cm. Base thickness 0.9 cm. Base diameter 7.6 cm. Surface 2.5YR 6/6. Matrix 2.5YR 6/2.

5037.4.1 Late Roman Phocaean Ware 3 Body Sherd (PHW3)
Unit 5037, SIA 6 (Politiko *Ayios Mnason*; see chapter 4.6). Plate 21.
Open shape. Thick slip, red and black on interior, and black partly over exterior. Three grooves on outside of rim. Function FW. Fabric F. Length 4.6 cm. Width 3.2 cm. Thickness 0.5–0.7 cm. Surface 7.5YR 6/2. Matrix 7.5YR 7/1.
Comparanda: Hayes Form 3e, circa AD 500 (Hayes 1972:337–338, no. 16).

5038.31.1 Hellenistic Fish Plate Base (FP)
Unit 5038, SIA 6 (Politiko *Ayios Mnason*; see chapter 4.6). Plates 10, 21.
Fish plate base. Second century BC. Function FW. Fabric F. Length 5.2 cm. Width 3.3 cm. Thickness 0.5 cm. Base diameter 55 cm. Surface 5YR 7/6. Matrix 5YR 7/6.

Comparanda: Hayes 1991:27, no. 4, Fig. 15.

5038.37.1 Late Roman Flat-Grooved Rim (LRG).
Unit 5038, SIA 6 (Politiko *Ayios Mnason*; see chapter 4.6). Plates 11, 21.
Flat horizontal rim with thickened rounded underside. Function LU. Fabric CR. Length 14.2 cm. Width 5.3 cm. Rim thickness 2.1 cm. Body thickness 1.1 cm. Diameter 46 cm. Surface 5YR 6/6. Matrix 5YR 6/6.

5039.13.1 Late Roman Phocaean Ware 10 Rim (PHW10)
Unit 5039, SIA 6 (Politiko *Ayios Mnason*; see chapter 4.6). Plates 11, 21.
Seventh century AD. Function FW. Fabric F. Length 6.7 cm. Width 3.4 cm. Rim thickness 1.6 cm. Body thickness 0.6 cm. Diameter 27 cm. Surface 2.5YR 6/8, 10R 5/8. Matrix 2.5YR 6/8.

5040.5.1 Early Roman Casserole (Cypriot Flanged) Rim (CFC)
Unit 5040, SIA 6 (Politiko *Ayios Mnason*; see chapter 4.6). Plates 11, 21.
Rim, neck, and shoulder. Function LU. Fabric TR. Length 8.9 cm. Width 4.3 cm. Neck thickness 0.6 cm. Shoulder thickness 0.4 cm. Diameter 17 cm. Surface 2.5YR 5/6. Matrix 2.5YR 5/6.

5040.34.1 Late Roman Cypriot Red Slip Rim (CRS10)
Unit 5040, SIA 6 (Politiko *Ayios Mnason*; see chapter 4.6). Plates 11, 21.
Seventh century AD. Function FW. Fabric F. Length 2.5 cm. Width 1.7 cm. Thickness 1.1 cm. Surface 10R 5/8. Matrix 10R 6/8.

5041.11.1 Hellenistic Coarse Rim and Handle (COH)
Unit 5041, SIA 6 (Politiko *Ayios Mnason*; see chapter 4.6). Plates 11, 21.
Rim, handle attachment, and part of handle of Brindisi amphora. Function UT. Fabric CR. Length 10.7 cm. Width 6.9 cm. Rim thickness 2.8 cm. Handle thickness 5.9 cm. Diameter 19 cm. Exterior surface 10YR 6/4. Interior surface 5YR 6/6. Matrix 2.5YR 6/6.

5041.32.1 Late Roman 1 Amphora Rim (LR1)
Unit 5041, SIA 6 (Politiko *Ayios Mnason*; see chapter 4.6). Plate 21.
Amphora with vertical round rim in rather fine light clay. Function HU. Fabric CL. Length 5.6 cm. Width 5.2 cm. Rim thickness 1.3 cm. Body 1.0 cm. Diameter 12.5 cm. Surface 2.5Y 7/3. Matrix 5YR 6/8.
Comparanda: van Alfen Type 1b (van Alfen 1996:193, Fig. 2).

5041.47.1 Early Roman African Red Slip Body Sherd (ARS)
Unit 5041, SIA 6 (Politiko *Ayios Mnason*; see chapter 4.6). Plate 22.
Small ARS body sherd. Function FW. Fabric F. Length 2.6 cm. Diameter 12 cm. Slip 2.5YR 5/8. Matrix 2.5YR 6/6.

5044.10.1 Late Roman Egyptian Red Slip A Rim (ERSA)
Unit 5044, SIA 6 (Politiko *Ayios Mnason*; see chapter 4.6). Plates 12, 22.
Function FW. Fabric F. Length 3.2 cm. Width 2.2 cm. Rim thickness 1.2 cm. Body thickness 0.6 cm. Diameter 20 cm. Surface 2.5YR 5/6, 10R5/6. Matrix 2.5YR 5/6.

5045.40.1 Ottoman Cypriot Glazed (Brown/Green) Base (CGBG)
Unit 5045, SIA 6 (Politiko *Ayios Mnason*; see chapter 4.6). Plates 12, 22.
CGBG (?) base. Function FW. Fabric F. Length 6.7 cm. Width 5.8 cm. Thickness 0.8 cm. Base diameter 6 cm. Surface 5YR 6/6. Matrix 5YR 6/6.

S-0029 (SCY204.1.27.1.1) Archaic to Classical Black-Glazed Body Sherd and Handle (BGAC)
SCY204 (Agrokipia *Kriadhis* 3; SIA 1; see chapter 4.1). Plates 12, 22.
Body fragment with part of handle of Black Glazed Attic skyphos. Possibly sixth century BC, but not enough preserved to be sure.

Arch-shaped handle. Function FW. Fabric F. Length 5.9 cm. Width 2.9 cm. Thickness 3.4 cm. Surface 5YR 6/6. Matrix 2.5YR 5/6. Comparanda: Sparkes and Talcott 1970:11, 109, Fig. 6.564, Pl. 25.564.

S-0030 (SCY010b.NE.3.1) Protohistoric Bronze Age Pithos Rim (PIPOB)
SCY010 (Aredhiou *Vouppes*; see chapter 4.12).
Plates 12, 22.
Pithos Group 2. Function PI. Fabric PI. Length 12.0 cm. Width 6.4 cm. Thickness 4.3 at rim, 2.1 at body. Surface 7.5YR 6/6. Matrix 7.5YR 6/6.

S-0032 (SCY010b.NE.2.1) Protohistoric Bronze Age Pithos Body Sherd (PIPOB)
SCY010 (Aredhiou *Vouppes*; see chapter 4.12).
Plate 12.
Applied wavy band on upper body. Function PI. Fabric PI. Length 8.7 cm. Width 5.8 cm. Body thickness 2.5 cm. Base thickness 2.3 cm. Base diameter 7.5 cm. Surface 10YR 7/3. Matrix 2.5YR 6/4.

S-0034 (SCY010b.NE.8.1) Protohistoric Bronze Age Pithos Body Sherd (PIPOB)
SCY010 (Aredhiou *Vouppes*; see chapter 4.12).
Plates 13, 22.
Two incised wavy lines on shoulder. Function PI. Fabric PI. Length 6.2 cm. Width 5.8 cm. Diameter 13–17 cm. Surface 10YR 7/4. Matrix 5YR 6/6.

S-0039 (SCY200.N4W3.9.1) Philia Transitional Red Lustrous Rim (RDL)
SCY200 (Politiko *Phournia*; see chapter 4.17).
Plate 22.
Thin tapered rim and part of body of Late Chalcolithic-Philia Culture red lustrous (black) bowl. Slip, polished surface; now all black, once red exterior? Function LU. Fabric TD. Length 4.5 cm. Width 3.5 cm. Rim thickness 0.4 cm. Body thickness 0.7 cm. Diameter 8.0 cm. Exterior surface 10YR 3/2. Interior surface 10YR 4/4. Matrix 10YR 4/1.

S-0043 (SCY134.57.8.1) Medieval to Modern Cypriot W4 Rim and Handle (W4)
SCY134 (Klirou-Ayios Mamas; SIA 9; see chapter 4.9).
Plates 13, 23.
Function LU. Fabric CR. Length 10.1 cm. Width 3.8 cm. Rim thickness 1.9 cm. Handle thickness 0.8 cm. Diameter 42 cm. Surface 2.5YR 4/6. Matrix 2.5YR 4/6.

S-0045 (SCY200.N4W1.4.1) Chalcolithic Spawled Ware Rim (SP)
SCY200 (Politiko *Phournia*; see chapter 4.17).
Plate 23.
Straight-sided rim of a spawled ware vessel. Fugitive red slip. Middle Chalcolithic. Function FW. Fabric CR. Length 7.2 cm. Width 7.1 cm. Thickness 1.2–1.4 cm. Diameter 35 cm. Surface 10YR 6/4.

S-0046 (SCY200.N5W4.3a.1) Chalcolithic Pithos Base (PICH)
SCY200 (Politiko *Phournia*; see chapter 4.17).
Plates 13, 23.
Flat disc base of Late Chalcolithic pithos. Red paint on interior, and possibly exterior. Unusual shape for Late Chalcolithic, but fabric and surface are normal. Function PI. Fabric CR. Length 9.7 cm. Width 8.4 cm. Body thickness 1.8 cm. Base thickness 2.1 cm. Base diameter 14 cm. Exterior surface 2.5YR 6/8. Interior surface 5YR 5/4. Matrix 5Y 4/1.

S-0047 (SCY110.59.5.1) Byzantine Coarse Handle (COB)
SCY110 (Klirou *Mazerka*; see chapter 4.15).
Plates 13, 23.
Function UT. Fabric CR. Length 6.9 cm. Width 4.8 cm. Thickness 1.5 cm. Surface 2.5YR 5/8. Matrix 10YR 5/3.

S-0053 (SCY200.N4W2.2.1) Chalcolithic Coarse Handle (COCH)
SCY200 (Politiko *Phournia*; see chapter 4.17).
Plate 23.
Handle in form of spout with indented end. Late Chalcolithic coarse ware. Function UT. Fabric CR. Length 5.3 cm. Width 3.8 cm. Thickness 2.4 cm. Surface 2.5YR 4/6. Matrix 7.5YR 4/3.

S-0054 (SCY134.56.5.1) Modern Cypriot W7 Pithos Body Sherd (W7)
SCY134 (Klirou *Ayios Mamas*; SIA 9; see chapter 4.9).
Plate 23.
Pithos body sherd with stamp. Function PI. Fabric CR. Length 9.6 cm. Width 6.6 cm. Thickness 3.8 cm. Surface 2.5YR 4/6. Matrix 2.5YR 4/8.

S-0055 (SCY200.S1W3.1.1) Philia Transitional Spout (PHTR)
SCY200 (Politiko *Phournia*; see chapter 4.17).
Plate 23.
Spout in Philia fabric, but Late Chalcolithic shape. Stroke burnished surface. Function LU. Fabric TL. Length 5.0 cm. Width 2.3 cm. Burnished surface 2.5YR 4/6. Interior 10YR 6/3. Matrix 10YR 5/1.

S-0057 (SCY219.7a.2.3.1) Classical Amphora Rim (AMCL)
SCY219 (Mitsero *Kokkinoyia*; SIA 11; see chapter 4.11).
Plate 24.
Flat out-turned rim of amphora. Cypro-Classical II. Function HU. Fabric CL. Length 2.6 cm. Width 2.2 cm. Thickness 1.2 cm. Diameter 35 cm. Surface 7.5YR 7/6. Matrix 7.5YR 7/6.
Comparanda: Gjerstad 1948: Fig. LXIX.2.

S-0058 (SCY219.7c.2.1–2) Archaic White Painted Jar Rim (WPAR)
SCY219 (Mitsero *Kokkinoyia*; SIA 11; see chapter 4.11).
Plate 24.
Two joining fragments of a concave flared-out rim of a White Painted IV or V amphora or hydria. Black paint faded to purple on rim and just below rim. Function LU. Fabric TL. Length 8.1 cm. Width 4.8 cm. Thickness 11.5 cm. Diameter 12.8 cm. Exterior surface 2.5Y 7/4. Interior surface 10YR 7/4. Matrix 5YR 6/6.
Comparanda: Gjerstad 1948: Figs. XXX.4, LI.7; Buchholz and Untiedt 1996: Fig. 26.b.

S-0066 (SCY123.N3E6.7.1) Archaic Plain Ware Rim (PLAR)
SCY123 (Politiko *Phorades 3*; SIA 7; see chapter 4.7).
Plate 24.
Rim and part of body of shallow bowl with hole, probably a repair hole. Cypro-Archaic I. Function LU. Fabric TL. Length 3.6 cm. Width 2.9 cm. Thickness 9.6 cm. Diameter 25 cm. Surface 7.5YR 7/6. Matrix 7.5YR 7/6.
Comparanda: for shape, see Gjerstad 1948: Fig. XXVIII.7, XXXVII.14; Buitron-Oliver 1996:44, Fig. 46, no. D7.

S-0067 (SCY123.N3E6.1.1) Archaic Cooking Ware Rim and Handle (CKAR)
SCY123 (Politiko *Phorades 3*; SIA 7; see chapter 4.7).
Plate 24.
Rim, strap handle, neck, and shoulder of cooking ware jug. Cypro-Archaic II. Function LU. Fabric TR. Length 8.4 cm. Width 3.6 cm. Base thickness 0.3 cm. Handle thickness 2.0 cm. Diameter 13 cm. Surface 5YR 6/6. Matrix 2.5YR 6/6.
Comparanda: Buitron-Oliver 1996:73, 75, Fig. 62, no. AA3.

SCY021.2.7.1 Classical Plain ware Rim with Rivet (PLCL)
SCY021 (Mitsero *Kouloupakhis*; SIA 3; see chapter 4.3).
Plate 33.
Rim, stub of strap handle and part of neck of plain ware jug. Applied clay rivet at top on side of handle. Function LU. Fabric CL. Length 4.2 cm. Width 4.3 cm. Thickness 0.4 cm. Diameter 5 cm.
Comparanda: for rivet next to strap handle, see Gjerstad 1948: Figs. LXII.18, LXVIII.9.

SCY204.3.3.1.1 Classical Plain Ware Rim (PLCL)
SCY204 (Agrokipia *Kriadhis 3*; SIA 1; see chapter 4.3).
Plate 33.
Rim and part of body of small thin-walled bowl of plain ware fabric. Cypro-Classical I. Function LU. Fabric TL. Length 4.5 cm. Width 3.0 cm. Thickness 0.3 cm.
Comparanda: Gjerstad 1948: Fig. LXI.30.

SCY204.3.5.1 Archaic White Painted Jar Rim (WPAR)
SCY204 (Agrokipia *Kriadhis 3*; SIA 1; see chapter 4.1).
Plate 33.

Rolled-out rim of White Painted IV or V hydria or amphora. Interior of rim concave. Two black painted lines around neck below rim on exterior. Function LU. Fabric CL. Length 4.9 cm. Width 3.5 cm. Thickness 0.6 cm.
Comparanda: Gjerstad 1948: Figs. LXXXV.13, L.13.

SCY204.4.12.1 Archaic Plain Ware Juglet Rim (PLAR)

SCY204 (Agrokipia *Kriadhis* 3; SIA 1; see chapter 4.1).
Plate 33.
Flat rim of mushroom-lipped juglet. Cypro-Archaic I. Function LU. Fabric CL. Length 3.3 cm. Width 1.2 cm. Thickness 0.4 cm.
Comparanda: for shape, see Gjerstad 1960: Fig. 8.2,5,8.

5.2 Chipped Stone Catalog

Dina Coleman

MODEL CATALOG ENTRY

Catalog No. Type—Period (if known)
Unit/POSI number, Grid reference/POSI name; SIA.
Plate number.
Description of material, type, retouch, use-wear and any other relevant details. Specific date if known. Length/width/thickness, in cm.

CATALOG

102-1-1 Scraper
SCY102 (Agrokipia *Palaeokamina*; see chapter 4.14).
Plate 25.
Light tan basal Lefkara chert. Two worked lateral margins; dorsal ridge; heavy use. Length 6.8 cm. Width 4.4 cm. Thickness 1.4 cm.

102-1-2 Ovate Scraper
SCY102 (Agrokipia *Palaeokamina*; see chapter 4.14).
Plate 25.
Light green cryptocrystalline. All of margin exhibits retouch. Length 5.7 cm. Width 4.4 cm. Thickness 0.8 cm.

102-1-3 Scraper
SCY102 (Agrokipia *Palaeokamina*; see chapter 4.14).
Plate 25.
Dark red jasper. Small round implement with fine retouch around 80% of margin. Length 1.5 cm. Width 1.5 cm. Thickness 0.5 cm.

102-1-4 Blade
SCY102 (Agrokipia *Palaeokamina*; see chapter 4.14).
Plate 25.
Light green cryptocrystalline. Thin delicate blade. Some wear evident on parallel lateral margins. Length 6.5 cm. Width 2.3 cm. Thickness 0.5 cm.

102-1-6 Small scraper
SCY102 (Agrokipia *Palaeokamina*; see chapter 4.14).
Plate 25.
Brown cryptocrystalline. Small ovate shape. 95% of margin exhibits retouch. Length 3.1 cm. Width 1.9 cm. Thickness 0.5 cm.

102-1-8 Trapezoid
SCY102 (Agrokipia *Palaeokamina*; see chapter 4.14).
Plate 26.
Olive green cryptocrystalline. Length 3.8 cm. Width 1.6 cm. Thickness 0.6 cm.

102-1-10 Blade
SCY102 (Agrokipia *Palaeokamina*; see chapter 4.14).
Plate 26.
Dark tan basal Lefkara chert. Both lateral margins and portion of proximal end exhibit fine retouch and some wear. Length 4.8 cm. Width 2.9 cm. Thickness 0.4 cm.

102-5-31-98 Blade
SCY102 (Agrokipia *Palaeokamina*; see chapter 4.14).
Plate 26.
Dark gray cryptocrystalline. Backed blade. Right lateral margin and distal end have been retouched. Cortex and lichens on backed left lateral margin. Length 7.8 cm. Width 3.5 cm. Thickness 1.0 cm.

102-9-2 Burin
SCY102 (Agrokipia *Palaeokamina*; see chapter 4.14).
Plate 26.
Brown cryptocrystalline. 90% of margin exhibits retouch. Distal end shows abrasive wear. Length 3.2 cm. Width 0.8 cm. Thickness 0.4 cm.

102-9-3 Trapezoid
SCY102 (Agrokipia *Palaeokamina*; see chapter 4.14).
Plate 26.
Light brown cryptocrystalline. Length 3.6 cm. Width 1.8 cm. Thickness 0.7 cm.

102-14-1-1 Burin
SCY102 (Agrokipia *Palaeokamina*; see chapter 4.14).
Plate 26.
Brown cryptocrystalline. Small burin pointed on two ends. Length 3.0 cm. Width 0.7 cm. Thickness 0.5 cm.

102-14-1-2 Sickle Blade
SCY102 (Agrokipia *Palaeokamina*; see chapter 4.14).
Plate 26.
Brown cryptocrystalline. Thin delicate blade with sickle polish along one lateral margin. Length 3.6 cm. Width 1.5 cm. Thickness 0.4 cm.

102-16-1-1 Utilized Flake
SCY102 (Agrokipia *Palaeokamina*; see chapter 4.14).
Plate 27.
Light tan jasper. Left lateral margin exhibits fine retouch. Length 4.6 cm. Width 3.7 cm. Thickness 1.5 cm.

102-16-1-8 Trapezoid
SCY102 (Agrokipia *Palaeokamina*; see chapter 4.14).
Plate 27.
Brown cryptocrystalline. Length 1.7 cm. Width 3.8 cm. Thickness 0.4 cm.

102-16-1-9 Small Scraper
SCY102 (Agrokipia *Palaeokamina*; see chapter 4.14).
Plate 27.
Olive green cryptocrystalline. Small roundish shape; retouch on 90% of margin. Length 1.6 cm. Width 1.5 cm. Thickness 0.6 cm.

102-19-1-1 Trapezoid
SCY102 (Agrokipia *Palaeokamina*; see chapter 4.14).
Plate 27.
Brown cryptocrystalline. Length 4.1 cm. Width 1.3 cm. Thickness 0.8 cm.

102-IE-1-1 Blade
SCY102 (Agrokipia *Palaeokamina*; see chapter 4.14).
Plate 27.
Coarse whitish tan chert. Both left and right lateral margins exhibit retouch. Length 5.0 cm. Width 2.0 cm. Thickness 0.9 cm.

102-IK-1-1 Blade
SCY102 (Agrokipia *Palaeokamina*; see chapter 4.14).
Plate 27.
Coarse white chert. Right lateral margin exhibits fine retouch on sharp edge. Length 5.8 cm. Width 2.7 cm. Thickness 0.9 cm. Specific date unknown (Archaic to Modern).

102-IL-2-1 Scraper
SCY102 (Agrokipia *Palaeokamina*; see chapter 4.14).
Plate 28.

Olive green cryptocrystalline. Distal end and right lateral margin exhibit retouch. Length 3.5 cm. Width 2.7 cm. Thickness 0.5 cm.

212-1-2   Scraper
SCY212 (Politiko *Gastres*).
Plate 28.
Tan basal Lefkara chert. 90% of margin exhibits retouch. Distal end shows signs of heavy wear. Length 6.0 cm. Width 4.1 cm. Thickness 1.2 cm. Specific date unknown (Archaic to Modern).

212-1-5   Burin
SCY212 (Politiko *Gastres*).
Plate 28.
White basal Lefkara chert. Length 2.8 cm. Width 1.3 cm. Thickness 0.4 cm. Specific date unknown.

212-S-1   Blade
SCY212 (Politiko *Gastres*).
Plate 28.
Blue-gray chalcedony. Backed right lateral margin. Abrupt retouch along left lateral margin. Length 8.3 cm. Width 3.5 cm. Thickness 1.5 cm. Specific date unknown.

212-S-2   Blade
SCY212 (Politiko *Gastres*).
Plate 28.
Dark brown cryptocrystalline. Serrated edges on lateral margins. Length 3.2 cm. Width 1.6 cm. Thickness 0.6 cm. Specific date unknown.

212-S-8   Blade
SCY212 (Politiko *Gastres*).
Plate 29.
Tan basal Lefkara chert. Length 4.1 cm. Width 2.0 cm. Thickness 0.5 cm. Specific date unknown.

212-S2E1-1 Side and End Scraper
SCY212 (Politiko *Gastres*).
Plate 29.
Tan basal Lefkara chert. Length 5.6 cm. Width 3.0 cm. Thickness 0.7 cm. Specific date unknown.

216-1-1   Burin
SCY216 (Agrokipia *Kottaphi*).
Plate 29.
Brown cryptocrystalline. Distal end comes to a point. Fine retouch along 95% of margin. Iron Age. Length 3.2 cm. Width 1.1 cm. Thickness 0.6 cm.

216-3-1   Blade
SCY216 (Agrokipia *Kottaphi*).
Plate 29.
Brown cryptocrystalline. Retouch along both lateral margins and distal end. Thin sharp edges. Iron Age. Length 7.6 cm. Width 3.5 cm. Thickness 0.8 cm.

1282-1-1   Dhoukani (Threshing Sledge) Blade
Unit 1282 (Threshing floor at Malounda; Grid reference 516780/3877040).
Plate 30.
Brown Lefkara chert. Modern. Length 4.6 cm. Width 2.5 cm. Thickness 1.2 cm.

5001-1-1   Projectile Point
Unit 5001, SIA 7 (Politiko *Kokkinorotsos*; chapter 4.7).
Plate 30.
White basal Lefkara. Distal tip broken. Heavily weathered material and much lichen growth on margins. Lateral margins are fine but not sharp. Length 8.9 cm. Width 3.3 cm. Thickness 0.9 cm. Specific date unknown.

Mit-Ex-1   Dhoukani (Threshing Sledge) Blade
From discarded threshing sledge found along transect 514.5.
Plate 30.

Tan Lefkara chert. Modern. Length 4.4 cm. Width 2.7 cm. Thickness 1.4 cm.

Mit-Ex-2   Dhoukani (Threshing Sledge) Blade
From discarded threshing sledge found along transect 514.5.
Plate 30.
Dark gray Lefkara chert. Modern. Length 5.1 cm. Width 1.6 cm. Thickness 0.5 cm.

5.3 Special Finds Catalog

Prehistoric: A. Bernard Knapp Geometric to Hellenistic: Joanna S. Smith Medieval to Modern: Timothy E. Gregory

MODEL CATALOG ENTRY

Cat. #   **Summary Description**
Unit/POSI number, Grid reference/POSI name.
Plate number.
Description of shape, decoration and any other relevant details. Period/date if known.
Length/width/thickness in cm. Diameter if relevant. Surface color (Munsell). Matrix color (Munsell).
Comparanda if known (with references and discussion)

CATALOG

338.2.1   Terra-cotta Wall Bracket
Unit 338, SCY010 (Aredhiou *Vouppes*; see chapter 4.12).
Plain Ware wall bracket fragment with large portion of flat handle or wall mount preserved. The pinkish-orange fabric contains dense black and red grit inclusions. A deeply incised vertical line down the center is bordered by one wavy line on each side.
Length 10.6 cm. Width 7.5 cm. Thickness 2.0 cm.
Comparanda: L. Åström 1972:518; Courtois 1984: Fig. 33, and Pl. XXIV; Karageorghis and Demas 1985: Pls. XLIV: 569/1, CC, CCVIII: 4186, CCXIII, Pl. CCXXXVIII: 928; Karageorghis and Demas 1988: CLXXX; Schaeffer 1949: Fig. 88; South et al. 1989: Fig. 27, and Pl. XI: 578; Du Plat Taylor 1952:162 and Pl. XXVI:e.
Publications: Knapp et al. 1994:337–338.

1007.2.1   Turkish Pipe Bowl
Unit 1007, western edge of SIA 3 (Mitsero *Kouloupakhis*; see chapter 4.3).
Plate 31.
Bowl fragment from Turkish pipe. Incised decoration. Black inclusions (3%). Ottoman.
Length 2.6 cm. Width 2.5 cm. Thickness 0.6 cm. Original diameter 3.0 cm. Surface 7.5YR 5/4. Matrix 10YR 6/1.

1010.1.1   Terra-cotta Human Figurine
Unit 1010, SIA 3 (Mitsero *Kouloupakhis*; see chapter 4.3).
Plate 31.
Terra-cotta, handmade, standing human figurine. No breasts, but not necessarily male (Knapp and Meskell 1997). Preserves part of solid body and parts of arms. From anthropomorphic figure with upraised arms. Cypro-Geometric III to Cypro-Archaic II.
Height 6.2 cm. Width 3.8 cm. Thickness 2.2 cm. Surface 5YR 6/4. Matrix 5YR 6/3.
Comparanda: Young and Young 1955:31, Pl. 8, no. 422; J. Karageorghis 1977:137–141; V. Karageorghis 1995:15, Pl. VII.6, no. 20.

1268.67.1 Turkish Pipe
Unit 1268, SCY112, SIA 10 (Malounda *Panayia Khrysopandanassa*; see chapter 4.10).
Plate 31.
Small part of bowl and hole. White glaze with design showing crossed swords drawn in black and covered in blue. Seventeenth to eighteenth century AD.
Length 3.0 cm. Width 2.8 cm. Wall thickness 1.1 cm. Surface 5YR 8/3. Matrix 5YR 8/3.

1281.29.1 Loomweight

Unit 1281, SCY112, SIA 10 (Malounda *Panayia Khrysopandanassa*; see chapter 4.10).
Plates 31, 34.
Complete flat discoid loomweight, pierced for string near one edge. Edges worn. Black, red, and yellow inclusions (25%). Classical or Hellenistic.
Diameter 7.7– 8.0 cm. Thickness 3.0 cm. Weight 200 gm. Surface 7.5YR 6/6. Matrix 7.5YR 6/4.
Comparanda: Smaller examples in Chavane 1975:84–85, Pl. 25–26, nos. 245, 247–251, 258.

1625.3.1 Hellenistic Lamp Rim and Body

Unit 1625, SIA 7 (Politiko *Kokkinorotsos*; see chapter 4.7).
Plate 34.
Rim and body of lamp. Wheelmade, biconical, undecorated, with inward sloping rim and ridge separating rim from body. Second half of third century BC.
Length 5.0 cm. Width 2.1 cm. Thickness 0.8 cm. Surface 10YR 6/4. Matrix 7.5YR 6/4.
Comparanda: Howland 1958:99, Pl. 15.41, no. 429; Bailey 1975:228, Pls. 96.Q499, 97.Q499, no. Q499; Oziol 1977:41, Pls. 6.74, 56.74, no. 74.

1728.11.1 Turkish Pipe Body Sherd

Unit 1728, SIA 6 (Politiko *Ayios Mnason*; see chapter 4.6).
Plate 31.
Central bowl of Turkish pipe, preserving bottom of fire box and top of bowl. Exterior of top of bowl decorated with vertical gouges. Burned partly black.
Length 3.5 cm. Width 3.4 cm. Thickness 0.5 cm. Surface 2.5YR 6/4. Matrix 5YR 7/1.

1741.8A.1 Terra-cotta Horse Figurine

Unit 1741, SIA 6 (Politiko *Ayios Mnason*; see chapter 4.6).
Plate 31.
Part of body, neck, and mane of terra-cotta horse figurine. Elongated body suggests date in the early sixth century BC, by comparison with Kourion examples.
Length 5.7 cm. Width 7.5 cm. Thickness 1.8 cm.
Comparanda: Young and Young 1955: Figs. 5–7; Buchholz 1991: Pl. 3a (horse figurines from Tamassos-Frangissa).

4052.2.1 Terra-cotta Horse Figurine

Unit 4052, SIA 2, SCY211 (Klirou *Mazovounos*; see chapter 4.2).
Plate 34.
Hind part of body, two rear legs, and tail of horse figurine. Tiny part of joining figurine on right hind leg shows this horse was once part of a chariot group. Soft Red-Orange fabric, like ceramics from same unit. Yellow, white, orange, and black inclusions (15%). Probably Archaic, by association with pottery of similar fabric.
Length 4.9. Width 3.3. Height 3.0. Surface 2.5YR 5/8. Matrix 5YR 4/4.

5017.37.1 Female Figurine Head

Unit 5017, SIA 6 (Politiko *Ayios Mnason*; see chapter 4.6).
Plate 31.
Mold-made female figurine head. Almond-shaped outlined eyes, bulbous nose, thick lips, left ear broken, headdress probably with flowers across top. Broken at neck. Back concave. Eyes and manufacture of figure similar to figures found near altar of Astarte-Aphrodite at Politiko-Choumazoudhia. Cypro-Archaic II.
Height 4.2 cm. Width 3.0 cm. Thickness 1.5 cm.
Comparanda: Buchholz 1978:220–221, Fig. 61.d–e; Buchholz and Untiedt 1996: Fig. 30.a,e. On date of altar, see Buchholz 1978:219, n. 124. See also Karageorghis 1987:21–22.

5017.39.1 Terra-cotta Mold-Made Foot

Unit 5017, SIA 6 (Politiko *Ayios Mnason*; see chapter 4.6).
Plate 32.
Mold-made foot, possibly wearing a shoe, or schematic pair of feet of terra-cotta statuette on a plaque. Hollow interior. Early Archaic figures with boots found nearby at Pera-Frangissa. Later example of rounded boots or shoes, painted with what may be lines to indicate sandals, from Cypro-Archaic II context at Polis-Peristeries. Archaic to Classical.

Length 6.3 cm. Width 7.5 cm. Thickness 3.7 cm.
Comparanda: For figure from Polis, see Serwint 1992:393, Pl. 19. On dating of that sanctuary, see Smith 1997. For Pera-Frangissa figures, see Karageorghis 1993:50–51, Pls. XXXIV.5, XXXV.1, nos. 152, 154.

5019.19.1 Terra-cotta Sculpture Fragment

Unit 5019, SIA 6 (Politiko *Ayios Mnason*; see chapter 4.6).
Plates 32, 34.
Terra-cotta sculpture fragment with two stamped chevron motifs. Probably from torso of statue, with decoration from part of clothing. Black and red-brown inclusions (25%). Archaic to Classical.
Length 6.6 cm. Width 5.7 cm. Thickness 0.9–1.6 cm. Surface 7.5YR 7/6. Matrix 7.5YR.

5022.1.1 Terra-cotta Hand

Unit 5022, SIA 6 (Politiko *Ayios Mnason*; see chapter 4.6).
Plates 32, 34.
Right hand of near life-size terra-cotta statue. Hand held palm up, fingers articulated from palm, underside undifferentiated. Archaic to Classical.
Length 11.9 cm. Width 8.4 cm. Thickness at thickest point 2.6 cm. Surface 10YR 7/3. Matrix 7.5YR 6/4.

5027.17.1 Terra-cotta Feet and Base

Unit 5027, SIA 6 (Politiko *Ayios Mnason*; see chapter 4.6).
Plates 32, 34.
Mold-made terra-cotta figurine feet and base of plaque around figure. Feet of figurine of type with head similar to 5017.37.1. Dark brown, black, white, and reddish-purple inclusions (40%). Cypro-Archaic II.
Length 4.7 cm. Width 4.4 cm. Thickness 2.2 cm. Surface 5YR 6/6. Matrix 5YR 6/6.
Comparanda: Buchholz 1978: Fig. 36.g; Buchholz and Untiedt 1996: Fig. 30a.

5037.1.1 Terra-cotta Hand

Unit 5037, SIA 6 (Politiko *Ayios Mnason*; see chapter 4.6).
Plates 32, 34.
Four fingers of life-size terra-cotta sculpture hand. Two dowel holes where hand was attached to rest of figure. Greenish color. Black, red, gray, and white inclusions (25%). Archaic to Classical.
Length: 9.1 cm. Width 4.4 cm. Thickness 2.4 cm. Surface 5Y 7/2. Matrix 2.5Y 7/3.
Comparanda: life-size and over life-size figures constructed from pieces attached with dowels also found at Pera-Frangissa (Buchholz 1991: Pls. 4b, 5a, 6a).

5040.1.1 Terra-cotta Standing Human Figurine

Unit 5040, SIA 6 (Politiko *Ayios Mnason*; see chapter 4.6).
Plates 32, 34.
Body and splayed base of standing handmade terra-cotta figurine. Solid body. No breasts, male? Arms broken off, but probably of upraised arms type. Black, brown, white, and reddish purple inclusions (40%). Cypro-Geometric III to Cypro-Archaic II. Height 8.0 cm. Width 2.8–3.4 cm. Surface 5YR 7/6. Matrix 5YR 7/6.
Comparanda: Young and Young 1955:31, Pl. 8. no. 422; J. Karageorghis 1977:137–141; V. Karageorghis 1995:15, Pl. VII.6, no. 20.

S-0020 (SCY112a.13.1) Picrolite Anthropomorphic Pendant

SCY112 (Malounda *Panayia Khrysopandanassa*; SIA 10; see chapter 4.10).
Plates 33, 35.
Highly schematized anthropomorphic picrolite pendant, with circular piercing. Resembles the "heads" on some very small cruciform pendants, with piercing in the same place. There are no exact parallels for this piece, although the attempt at double piercing is a common feature. Most likely Chalcolithic. We thank Marie Goodwin (Bryn Mawr College) for help in describing this piece.
Height 2.1 cm. Greatest width 1.75 cm. Thickness 0.4 cm.
Comparanda: Dikaios 1962:126, no. 27; Peltenburg 1998: Fig. 97, nos. 14, 25.

S-0044 (SCY200.N2W3.10.1) Picrolite Bead

SCY200 (Politiko *Phournia*; see chapter 4.17).
Plate 35.
Nearly round, flat picrolite bead. Drilled hole near one edge. Prehistoric.

Diameter 1.4 cm. Thickness 0.3 cm.
Comparanda: Niklasson 1991: Fig. 96 (bead); Dikaios 1961: Pls. 102.14, 17, 24.

S-0050 (SCY132.1.1.1) Loomweight with Stamped Impression

SCY132 (Klirou *Manastirka*; SIA 2; see chapter 4.2).
Plates 33, 35.
Discoid loomweight. Hole near one edge. Stamped impression on rounded rim, probably from a finger-ring, showing an unguentarium or possibly a figure holding an object. Black, shiny inclusions (25%). Classical or Hellenistic.
Diameter 5.3 cm. Thickness 2.9 cm. Diameter of hole 0.4 cm. Weight 100 gm. Surface 7.5YR 7/4. Matrix 7.5YR 7/4.
Comparanda: On shape and size of weight, see Chavane 1975:84–85, Pls. 25–26, nos. 245, 247–251, 258. Gems depicting vessels date to both the Classical (Boardman 1970: Pls. 470, 613, 770) and Hellenistic periods (Plantzos 1999: Pl. 81.655). Impression worn; probably a human figure, like those of a woman standing on a base-line holding something in her outstretched arm (for example, Plantzos 1999: Pls. 45.275-82, 47.294-305), in which case probably Hellenistic.

S-0061 (SCY123.N3E6.3.1) Loomweight Fragment

SCY123 (Politiko *Phorades* 3; SIA 7; see chapter 4.7).
Plate 35.
One quarter of a discoid lumpy loomweight. Central hole. Black, cream, and pink inclusions (5%). Archaic.
Length 5.5 cm. Width 2.6 cm. Thickness 2.2 cm. Surface 5YR 5/6. Matrix 5YR 4/6.
Comparanda: Chavane 1975:80, Pl. 24.224–225.

S-0070   Basalt Hand Axe

SCY200 (Politiko *Phournia*; see chapter 4.17).
Plates 33, 35.
Small-butted, basalt, highly polished hand axe. Small and ovoid proximal end; distal end is a 4.1-cm wide sharpened axe-edge. Axe-edge shows minimal evidence of fracturing from use. Permanent carbonate coating on one lateral side. Stylistically similar to Neolithic and Chalcolithic Cypriot axe-heads.
Length 11.0 cm. Width at broadest point 4.1 cm. Thickness 2.85 cm.
Comparanda: Bolger 1988:81–83, and Figs 24–25; Pls. 4:518, 5:27, 160; Dikaios 1961: Pl. 93 (various examples); Frankel and Webb 1996: Fig. 6.10 (axes); Le Brun 1981: Figs. 42.3, 43.4; Peltenburg 1991a: Fig. 26, Pl. 13 (KM1465); Swiny 1986: Fig. 45a.

SCY204.1.1   Terra-cotta "Astarte" Plaque Figurine

SCY204 (Agrokipia *Kriadhis* 3; SIA 1; see chapter 4.1).
Plate 35.
Body, arms and legs of mold-made plaque "Astarte" figurine holding her breasts and wearing a necklace. Head and feet missing. Rough and pitted exterior from corrosion by copper salts. CA I to early CA II.
Length 8.3 cm. Width 5.9 cm. Thickness 1.5 cm.
Comparanda: Although a well known type of Astarte figurine, this example has no exact parallels and seems to be earlier than published examples. Such figurines have been found both in tombs and in sanctuaries. Two examples were found in tombs at the""mining" site of Philani-Petaloudia, also located in the area of Tamassos (J. Karageorghis 1999:35, 42, 45; Buchholz 1978:186–189, Fig. 36:a–i). For a complete catalog of this type of Astarte figurine from Cyprus, see J. Karageorghis 1999:1–67. Parallels from sanctuaries include one from Tamassos: Buchholz and Unteidt 1996: Figure 30; J. Karageorghis 1999:37, catalog no. 98; close parallels from tombs include one from Amathus: J. Karageorghis 1999:8, 24, catalog numbers 13, 69; Karageorghis 1987:7, no. 64.

5.4 Archaeometallurgy: Data, Analyses, and Discussion

Vasiliki Kassianidou

Having recorded a number of archaeometallurgical sites in the survey area that date from the Late Bronze Age to the Late Roman period, we are in a good position to assess diachronic developments in Cypriot copper smelting technology. The following discussion is based on finds collected from various archaeometallurgical POSIs and on the analysis of slag samples. The slags, furnace material, stone tools, and so on presented below are archaeological finds and will be presented as such. The description is necessary as it will enable other archaeologists in the field to identify similar finds in their area of study. A number of other publications pay so much attention to analytical data that one often forgets that these are human artifacts. In what follows, analytical and archaeological data are combined.

Although a great deal of information has been collected, it is impossible here to discuss every item in detail or to present anything beyond a generalized discussion for each period. The analytical data (chemical analysis by XRF and microanalysis) are presented in tables 5.2 and 5.3, while figure 5.1 lists results for the six main elements (silica, iron, manganese, copper, sulfur, and zinc) in the form of a chart, in an effort to provide a quick and easy way to compare the composition of all samples. Table 5.4 presents the composition of metallic phases of some of the slag samples illustrated by the micrographs.

LATE BRONZE AGE

Politiko *Phorades* (SCY100) is the first primary smelting workshop of the Protohistoric Bronze Age (Late Cypriot) to be discovered and systematically excavated in Cyprus. After three seasons of excavations, we know more about the smelting technology of this period than that of any later periods represented by SCSP's archaeometallurgical POSIs. Because the excavations at Phorades have produced large numbers of furnace fragments and tuyères, our understanding of the smelting process is not based solely on the analysis and interpretation of slags, as is the case in all other POSIs or SIAs. Two preliminary excavation reports have already been

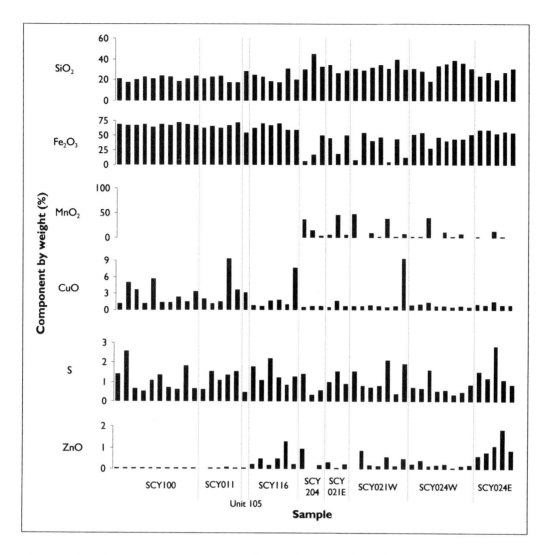

Figure 5.1. Concentrations of SiO_2, Fe_2O_3, MnO_2, CuO, S, and ZnO in the analyzed samples. Based on XRF analysis in table 5.1

published (Knapp, Donnelly, and Kassianidou 1998; Knapp et al. 1999), and the final excavation results and analyses will appear as a separate monograph. Here we provide some preliminary comments.

The finds themselves demonstrate that smelting took place in cylindrical furnaces with thick, flat bases built entirely of refractory clay rich in organic material (figure 5.2). The furnaces had an estimated diameter of 42 to 44 cm, but their full height is unknown. Ceramic tuyères formed an integral part of the smelting installation (figure 5.3), but the number used in each furnace and their position within the structure is also unknown. We have argued, however, that they must have been introduced from the top (Knapp et al. 1999:140). The products of the smelt were slag and matte, both of

which would have been in liquid form at the high temperatures of the process.

The slags from Phorades belong to a type previously unknown on Cyprus. All fragments derive from plano-concave cakes that had an estimated diameter of 40 cm at the top and a well-defined concavity at the bottom (figures 5.4, 5.5). It is evident that the concavity was left behind when the solid layer of matte had been removed. We believe the slags took this shape because the total contents of the furnace were tapped into a pit that was sometimes lined with river gravels. There they were left to cool, giving the two liquid phases (slag and matte/copper) ample time to separate. Experimental work by Bamberger and Wincierz (1990:133), following a technique described by Agricola, has demonstrated the feasibility of this procedure.

2 cm

Figure 5.2. SCY100: furnace lining, showing clearly the furnace bottom and part of the furnace wall ascending from it

2 cm

Figure 5.3. SCY100: side view of large tuyère fragment. This type with fine fabric generally has a 2.5 to 3 cm wide hole.

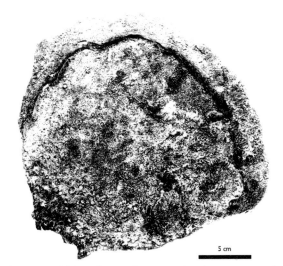

5 cm

Figure 5.4. SCY100: largest fragment of a plano-concave slag cake from Phorades. View shows bottom side with concavity. Some of the small gas vesicles are visible in the lower left corner of object.

What is striking about the slags from Phorades is that, in comparison with samples from other POSIs, they form a fairly homogeneous group in terms of shape, size, and also chemical composition. Chemical analyses of ten samples (tables 5.2; 5.3, nos. 1–10) reveal that the slags have a high iron content (average 67.8 %) and a relatively high copper content (average 2.64%; two examples have over 5%). As expected, manganese is present only as a trace element. The zinc content is also extremely low, unlike in the slags of later sites. Microscopic analysis has shown that the main phases are fayalite crystals and wüstite dendrites, with very little glass. According to Tylecote (1987:293), this is a common phenomenon in fayalitic slags. As fayalite is formed and the slag begins to cool down, excess iron is rejected as wüstite, while the remaining elements combine to form a glass. The slags are full of matte prills as well as angular sulfide inclusions, the composition of which is very close to chalcopyrite. The fact that these are angular rather than rounded may indicate that they represent crushed ore that did not have time to react.

Slags of the same type were collected in two other units in the SCSP area (Figures 5.6, 5.7). One is from unit 1746 (SCY011) and the other from unit 105. Neither of these units is located in an area where the slags could have been transported naturally (for example, by water) from Phorades, and so the three different locations have to be considered as independent. Although this type of slag was previously unknown on Cyprus, it is now well represented and closely dated by the Phorades excavations to the beginning of the Protohistoric Bronze Age. Thus, we might suggest that the examples of this type of slag from units 1746 and 105 should also be dated to the Protohistoric Bronze Age, but the pottery from those units is later in date. Unfortunately, no charcoal was found in the slags in those units; this might have provided another perspective. Nonetheless it should be pointed out that, at least in SCY011, the soil had eroded away almost entirely and most material collected lay directly on bedrock.

Analysis of six samples from these units (tables 5.2, 5.3, nos. 11–16) shows that they are very similar in composition to the Phorades samples and quite different from samples found in other POSIs, later in date. Generally speaking, the Phorades-type samples have much higher iron and copper contents, contain no manganese and, unlike the later samples,

Table 5.2 XRF analysis of slag samples: major and minor elements by weight (%)

#	Sample	POSI	Al$_2$O$_3$	SiO$_2$	S	K$_2$O	CaO	TiO$_2$	MnO$_2$	Fe$_2$O$_3$	CuO	ZnO	BaO
1	100-1	SCY100	5.0 ± 0.4	21.1 ± 1.1	1.39 ± 0.08	0.37 ± 0.02	1.48 ± 0.08	0.25 ± 0.02	0.070 ± 0.004	69.0 ± 1.7	1.23 ± 0.06	0.028 ± 0.002	
2	100-2	SCY100	5.7 ± 0.5	17.5 ± 0.9	2.6 ± 0.1	0.13 ± 0.01	1.40 ± 0.07	0.19 ± 0.01	0.070 ± 0.004	67.3 ± 1.7	5.01 ± 0.25	0.044 ± 0.002	
3	100-3	SCY100	6.0 ± 0.5	20.5 ± 1.0	0.64 ± 0.03	0.21 ± 0.01	1.38 ± 0.07	0.23 ± 0.01	0.066 ± 0.004	67.3 ± 1.7	3.70 ± 0.19	0.048 ± 0.002	
4	100-4	SCY100	4.7 ± 0.4	23.3 ± 1.2	0.53 ± 0.03	0.35 ± 0.02	1.66 ± 0.08	0.27 ± 0.01	0.080 ± 0.005	68.0 ± 1.7	1.12 ± 0.06	0.032 ± 0.002	
5	100-5	SCY100	6.0 ± 0.5	21.1 ± 1.1	1.10 ± 0.06	0.21 ± 0.01	1.07 ± 0.05	0.25 ± 0.01	0.065 ± 0.003	64.4 ± 1.6	5.6 ± 0.3	0.058 ± 0.003	
6	100-6	SCY100	3.5 ± 0.4	23.5 ± 1.2	1.34 ± 0.07	0.26 ± 0.01	1.22 ± 0.06	0.18 ± 0.01	0.057 ± 0.003	68.5 ± 1.7	1.28 ± 0.06	0.023 ± 0.001	
7	100-7	SCY100	5.9 ± 0.5	22.9 ± 1.1	0.70 ± 0.04	0.30 ± 0.02	1.80 ± 0.09	0.27 ± 0.01	0.090 ± 0.005	66.6 ± 1.6	1.32 ± 0.07	0.033 ± 0.002	
8	100-8	SCY100	5.0 ± 0.5	18.8 ± 0.9	0.63 ± 0.03	0.20 ± 0.01	0.73 ± 0.04	0.18 ± 0.01	0.055 ± 0.004	72.0 ± 1.8	2.40 ± 0.12	0.043 ± 0.002	
9	100-9	SCY100	4.4 ± 0.4	21.0 ± 1.0	1.85 ± 0.09	0.46 ± 0.02	2.2 ± 0.1	0.24 ± 0.01	0.080 ± 0.004	68.2 ± 1.7	1.45 ± 0.07	0.034 ± 0.002	
10	100-10	SCY100	4.0 ± 0.4	23.4 ± 1.2	0.67 ± 0.03	0.23 ± 0.01	1.26 ± 0.06	0.27 ± 0.01	0.080 ± 0.004	66.7 ± 1.6	3.3 ± 0.2	0.036 ± 0.002	
11	011-1	SCY011	4.6 ± 0.4	23.0 ± 1.1	1.55 ± 0.08	0.76 ± 0.04	3.2 ± 0.2	0.25 ± 0.01	0.12 ± 0.01	65.4 ± 1.6	1.10 ± 0.06	0.022 ± 0.001	
12	011-5a	SCY011	5.3 ± 0.4	24.2 ± 1.1	1.10 ± 0.06	0.83 ± 0.04	4.4 ± 0.2	0.23 ± 0.01	0.10 ± 0.01	62.3 ± 1.5	1.45 ± 0.07	0.024 ± 0.001	
13	011-5b	SCY011	2.3 ± 0.4	17.4 ± 0.9	1.34 ± 0.07	0.32 ± 0.08	1.64 ± 0.08	0.16 ± 0.01	0.090 ± 0.005	66.6 ± 1.6	9.32 ± 0.47	0.070 ± 0.004	
14	U1746-1	SCY011	9.1 ± 0.6	20.8 ± 1.0	0.63 ± 0.03	0.42 ± 0.02	3.7 ± 0.2	0.47 ± 0.02	0.12 ± 0.01	62.7 ± 1.5	2.05 ± 0.10	0.015 ± 0.001	
15	U1746-2	SCY011	3.6 ± 0.4	17.4 ± 0.9	1.53 ± 0.08	0.42 ± 0.02	2.3 ± 0.1	0.17 ± 0.01	0.073 ± 0.004	71.1 ± 1.8	3.65 ± 0.18	0.037 ± 0.002	
16	U105-1	Unit 105	9.2 ± 0.6	28.3 ± 1.4	0.49 ± 0.02	0.31 ± 0.02	3.3 ± 0.2	0.39 ± 0.02	0.13 ± 0.01	54.6 ± 1.4	3.17 ± 0.16	0.035 ± 0.002	
17	116-2	SCY116	7.1 ± 0.5	24.8 ± 1.2	1.77 ± 0.09	0.40 ± 0.02	1.81 ± 0.09	0.18 ± 0.01	0.090 ± 0.004	62.8 ± 1.5	0.81 ± 0.04	0.22 ± 0.01	
18	116-4	SCY116	2.8 ± 0.3	23.2 ± 1.2	1.07 ± 0.05	0.29 ± 0.01	1.44 ± 0.07	0.11 ± 0.01	0.11 ± 0.01	69.8 ± 1.7	0.70 ± 0.04	0.46 ± 0.02	
19	116-5	SCY116	7.0 ± 0.4	18.3 ± 0.9	2.2 ± 0.1	0.51 ± 0.03	2.2 ± 0.1	0.12 ± 0.01	0.090 ± 0.004	67.7 ± 1.7	1.73 ± 0.09	0.16 ± 0.01	
20	116-9	SCY116	4.1 ± 0.5	18.0 ± 0.9	1.22 ± 0.06	0.45 ± 0.02	2.8 ± 0.1	0.16 ± 0.01	0.12 ± 0.01	70.7 ± 1.8	1.78 ± 0.09	0.48 ± 0.02	
21	116-8	SCY116	4.3 ± 0.4	30.7 ± 1.5	0.86 ± 0.04	0.32 ± 0.02	1.49 ± 0.07	0.13 ± 0.01	0.066 ± 0.003	59.9 ± 1.5	1.05 ± 0.05	1.29 ± 0.06	
22	116-30	SCY116	6.9 ± 0.5	20.0 ± 1.0	1.28 ± 0.06	0.51 ± 0.03	3.8 ± 0.2	0.22 ± 0.01	0.12 ± 0.01	59.4 ± 1.5	7.6 ± 0.4	0.21 ± 0.01	
23	204-1	SCY204	9.2 ± 0.5	29.6 ± 1.5	1.39 ± 0.07	1.52 ± 0.08	11.6 ± 0.6	1.07 ± 0.05	37.8 ± 0.9	6.4 ± 0.3	0.58 ± 0.03	0.95 ± 0.05	
24	204-2	SCY204	12.0 ± 0.6	45.0 ± 2.2	0.34 ± 0.02	0.84 ± 0.04	7.6 ± 0.4	0.99 ± 0.05	14.8 ± 0.7	17.6 ± 0.9	0.66 ± 0.03	0.021 ± 0.01	0.12 ± 0.01
25	204-3	SCY204	7.8 ± 0.4	32.9 ± 1.7	0.56 ± 0.03	0.71 ± 0.04	3.1 ± 0.2	0.42 ± 0.02	2.9 ± 0.2	50.7 ± 1.3	0.68 ± 0.03	0.18 ± 0.01	
26	021-23	SCY021E	18.0 ± 0.5	34.5 ± 1.7	1.00 ± 0.05	0.54 ± 0.03	4.3 ± 0.2	0.51 ± 0.03	4.94 ± 0.3	45.4 ± 1.2	0.56 ± 0.03	0.29 ± 0.01	
27	021-22	SCY021E	12.3 ± 0.2	26.2 ± 1.3	1.54 ± 0.08	0.95 ± 0.02	1.8 ± 0.09	0.36 ± 0.02	45.4 ± 1.1	18.9 ± 1.0	1.62 ± 0.08	0.049 ± 0.002	0.85 ± 0.04
28	021-24	SCY021E	17.2 ± 0.5	29.1 ± 1.5	0.89 ± 0.04	0.44 ± 0.02	6.0 ± 0.3	0.68 ± 0.03	5.3 ± 0.3	49.5 ± 1.3	0.70 ± 0.03	0.22 ± 0.03	
29	021-10	SCY021W	13.7 ± 0.2	31.3 ± 1.5	1.53 ± 0.07	1.61 ± 0.08	3.2 ± 0.2	0.53 ± 0.03	48.9 ± 1.2	7.9 ± 0.4	0.63 ± 0.03	0.008 ± 0.001	0.79 ± 0.04
30	021-13	SCY021W	17.9 ± 0.5	29.4 ± 1.5	.78 ± 0.04	0.60 ± 0.03	4.1 ± 0.2	0.54 ± 0.03	0.68 ± 0.03	54.4 ± 1.3	0.69 ± 0.03	0.85 ± 0.03	
31	021-14	SCY021W	110.7 ± 0.5	31.9 ± 1.6	0.68 ± 0.03	0.56 ± 0.02	4.6 ± 0.2	0.49 ± 0.02	8.7 ± 0.4	41.3 ± 1.0	0.80 ± 0.04	0.17 ± 0.01	
32	021-15	SCY021W	19.1 ± 0.5	34.2 ± 1.7	0.78 ± 0.04	0.53 ± 0.03	5.5 ± 0.3	0.61 ± 0.03	1.26 ± 0.06	47.5 ± 1.2	0.72 ± 0.04	0.11 ± 0.01	
33	021-16	SCY021W	19.7 ± 0.5	30.5 ± 1.5	2.1 ± 0.1	1.21 ± 0.06	11.2 ± 0.6	0.70 ± 0.03	39.5 ± 1.0	4.0 ± 0.2	0.53 ± 0.03	0.54 ± 0.03	
34	021-19	SCY02W	19.6 ± 0.5	39.9 ± 2.0	0.38 ± 0.02	0.57 ± 0.03	3.5 ± 0.2	0.49 ± 0.02	1.55 ± 0.08	43.1 ± 1.2	0.69 ± 0.03	0.13 ± 0.01	
35	021-17	SCY021W	26.7 ± 0.5	29.6 ± 1.5	. 90 ± 0.09	0.44 ± 0.02	1.76 ± 0.09	0.57 ± 0.03	7.2 ± 0.4	42.1 ± 1.1	9.26 ± 0.46	0.48 ± 0.02	
36	024W-2	SCY024W	17.4 ± 0.5	31.1 ± 1.6	0.70 ± 0.04	0.48 ± 0.02	5.0 ± 0.2	0.56 ± 0.03	2.55 ± 0.13	51.1 ± 1.3	0.81 ± 0.04	0.22 ± 0.01	
37	024W-4	SCY024W	18.2 ± 0.5	28.0 ± 1.4	0.65 ± 0.03	0.36 ± 0.02	3.6 ± 0.2	0.50 ± 0.03	2.7 ± 0.1	54.8 ± 1.4	0.98 ± 0.05	0.39 ± 0.02	
38	024W-5	SCY024W	12.7 ± 0.2	18.2 ± 0.9	1.60 ± 0.08	0.75 ± 0.04	4.8 ± 0.2	0.23 ± 0.01	41.5 ± 2.1	28.4 ± 1.4	1.39 ± 0.07	0.11 ± 0.01	0.34 ± 0.02
39	024W-6	SCY024W	111.3 ± 0.6	33.3 ± 1.7	0.53 ± 0.03	0.36 ± 0.02	4.7 ± 0.2	0.60 ± 0.03	0.58 ± 0.03	47.6 ± 1.2	0.64 ± 0.03	0.19 ± 0.01	
40	024W-7	SCY024W	17.7 ± 0.5	35.6 ± 1.8	0.55 ± 0.03	0.48 ± 0.02	3.2 ± 0.2	0.34 ± 0.02	11.1 ± 0.6	40.0 ± 2.0	0.63 ± 0.03	0.23 ± 0.01	0.05 ± 0.01
41	024W-8	SCY024W	110.3 ± 0.5	38.4 ± 1.9	0.33 ± 0.02	0.33 ± 0.02	2.4 ± 0.1	0.76 ± 0.04	2.66 ± 0.13	44.2 ± 1.1	0.57 ± 0.03	0.040 ± 0.002	
42	024W-9	SCY024W	19.5 ± 0.5	36.2 ± 1.8	0.46 ± 0.02	0.44 ± 0.02	2.5 ± 0.1	0.44 ± 0.02	6.5 ± 0.3	43.2 ± 1.1	0.66 ± 0.03	0.14 ± 0.01	
43	024W-10	SCY024W	19.1 ± 0.6	30.5 ± 1.5	0.85 ± 0.04	0.40 ± 0.02	6.2 ± 0.3	0.44 ± 0.02	0.65 ± 0.03	51.1 ± 1.3	0.55 ± 0.03	0.16 ± 0.01	
44	024E-1	SCY024E	37.0 ± 0.5	23.9 ± 1.2	1.48 ± 0.08	0.46 ± 0.02	3.2 ± 0.2	0.49 ± 0.02	2.10 ± 0.11	59.8 ± 1.5	0.97 ± 0.05	0.58 ± 0.03	
45	024E-2	SCY024E	36.0 ± 0.5	27.1 ± 1.4	1.19 ± 0.06	0.51 ± 0.02	3.7 ± 0.2	0.56 ± 0.03	0.34 ± 0.02	59.0 ± 1.5	0.87 ± 0.04	0.75 ± 0.04	
46	024E-3	SCY024E	34.6 ± 0.4	20.4 ± 1.0	2.8 ± 0.2	0.43 ± 0.02	3.2 ± 0.2	0.36 ± 0.02	13.0 ± 0.7	52.5 ± 1.3	1.55 ± 0.08	1.08 ± 0.05	
47	024E-4	SCY024E	35.6 ± 0.4	27.2 ± 1.4	1.08 ± 0.05	0.59 ± 0.03	3.4 ± 0.2	0.44 ± 0.02	2.10 ± 0.11	56.9 ± 1.4	0.87 ± 0.04	1.84 ± 0.09	
48	024E-5	SCY024E	36.6 ± 0.4	30.9 ± 1.5	0.86 ± 0.04	0.62 ± 0.03	4.2 ± 0.2	0.54 ± 0.03	0.59 ± 0.03	54.0 ± 1.3	0.78 ± 0.04	0.87 ± 0.04	

Note: Cl value for No. 13 is 0.91 ± 0.05

Table 5.3 XRF analysis of slag samples: trace elements in parts per million (ppm)

A/#	Sample	POSI	V	Cr	Ni	Ga	Ge	As	Se	Br	Pb
1	100-1	SCY100	–	39 ± 8	–	–	–	4.1 ± 1.4	69 ± 3	3 .2 ± 1.0	–
2	100-2	SCY100	126 ± 24	130 ± 10	–	–	–	100 ± 5	81 ± 4	–	–
3	100-3	SCY100	–	54 ± 10	–	–	–	21 ± 2	39 ± 2	2.8 ± 1.0	–
4	100-4	SCY100	386 ± 26	85 ± 7	–	–	–	8.1 ± 1.6	31 ± 2	3.6 ± 0.9	–
5	100-5	SCY100	471 ± 26	58 ± 5	–	7.4 ± 3.3	–	42 ± 2	35 ± 2	1.9 ± 1.1	–
6	100-6	SCY100	170 ± 24	39 ± 8	–	–	–	2.9 ± 1.4	64 ± 3	3.2 ± 0.9	–
7	100-7	SCY100	150 ± 25	87 ± 7	–	6.7 ± 2.5	–	12 ± 2	32 ± 2	3.6 ± 0.9	–
8	100-8	SCY100	–	55 ± 9	–	19 ± 3	7.8 ± 2.0	44 ± 2	39 ± 2	–	–
9	100-9	SCY100	81 ± 25	60 ± 7	–	–	–	4.6 ± 1.5	66 ± 3	–	–
10	100-10	SCY100	178 ± 25	95 ± 8	–	–	–	30 ± 2	32 ± 2	1.9 ± 1.0	–
11	U1746-1	SCY011	141 ± 28	91 ± 8	–	7.7 ± 2.7	7.3 ± 1.9	–	114 ± 6	–	–
12	011-1	SCY011	68 ± 25	208 ± 14	–	–	–	–	61 ± 3	–	–
13	011-5a	SCY011	80 ± 25	210 ± 14	–	9 ± 3	–	3.1 ± 1.3	43 ± 2	–	–
14	011-5b	SCY011	130 ± 24	183 ± 12	–	7.5 ± 3.9	–	88 ± 4	39 ± 2	–	–
15	U1746-2	SCY011	44 ± 23	159 ± 11	–	9.1 ± 3.1	6.4 ± 2.1	36 ± 2	53 ± 3	–	–
16	U105-1	Unit 105	259 ± 27	321 ± 18	–	19 ± 3	2.5 ± 1.4	–	48 ± 2	4.2 ± 0.8	–
17	116-2	SCY116	123 ± 24	86 ± 7	–	16 ± 3	6.4 ± 1.8	41 ± 2	14 ± 1	–	–
18	116-4	SCY116	–	126 ± 9	–	10 ± 3	–	16 ± 2	18 ± 1	–	–
19	116-5	SCY116	148 ± 24	146 ± 10	–	10 ± 3	–	23 ± 2	25 ± 1	2.0 ± 1.0	–
20	116-9	SCY116	128 ± 19	65 ± 5	–	–	–	28 ± 2	26 ± 1	–	–
21	116-8	SCY116	105 ± 23	85 ± 7	–	70 ± 4	5.3 ± 2.1	46 ± 2	21 ± 1	–	–
22	116-30	SCY116	120 ± 25	37 ± 4	–	9.6 ± 3.2	–	389 ± 19	14 ± 1	–	–
23	204-1	SCY204	–	150 ± 42	44 ± 6	38 ± 3	–	33 ± 2	3.8 ± 0.8	–	–
24	204-2	SCY204	380 ± 25	177 ± 12	–	7.5 ± 1.1	–	16 ± 1	13 ± 1	–	–
25	204-3	SCY204	298 ± 29	184 ± 13	–	23 ± 3	3.0 ± 1.6	24 ± 2	38 ± 2	–	–
26	021-23	SCY021E1	580 ± 100	233 ± 16	–	6.5 ± 2.4	–	3.4 ± 1.0	17 ± 1	–	–
27	021-22	SCY021E1	406 ± 51	97 ± 21	–	–	–	–	74 ± 4	3.0 ± 1.0	–
28	021-24	SCY021E1	382 ± 31	126 ± 11	–	–	–	–	21 ± 1	–	–
29	021-10	SCY021W1	–	106 ± 33	–	–	–	12 ± 1	38 ± 2	3.4 ± 0.8	–
30	021-13	SCY021W1	280 ± 29	153 ± 12	–	40 ± 3	3.7 ± 1.9	9.0 ± 1.4	7.7 ± 1.1	–	–
31	021-14	SCY021W1	620 ± 80	276 ± 19	–	21 ± 2	–	2.4 ± 1.1	25 ± 1	–	–
32	021-15	SCY021W1	213 ± 32	178 ± 15	–	26 ± 2	–	5.9 ± 1.2	14 ± 1	–	–
33	021-16	SCY021W1	1200 ± 100	299 ± 41	–	12 ± 2	–	35 ± 2	2.5 ± 0.7	–	–
34	021-19	SCY021W1	292 ± 28	242 ± 16	–	20 ± 2	1.7 ± 1	20 ± 1	17 ± 1	–	–
35	021-17	SCY021W2	330 ± 29	–	–	58 ± 4	–	103 ± 5	105 ± 5	–	92 ± 10
36	024W-2	SCY024W1	481 ± 32	202 ± 15	–	19 ± 3	2.9 ± 1.5	–	22 ± 1	2.0 ± 0.8	–
37	024W-4	SCY024W1	159 ± 29	–	–	14 ± 3	–	8.5 ± 1.3	21 ± 1	–	–
38	024W-5	SCY024W1	500 ± 100	–	–	–	–	6.5 ± 1.5	89 ± 4	–	–
39	024W-6	SCY024W1	600 ± 150	165 ± 13	–	23 ± 2	3.5 ± 1.3	–	17 ± 1	4.5 ± 0.7	–
40	024W-7	SCY024W1	580 ± 80	142 ± 11	–	22 ± 2	3.3 ± 1.3	–	19 ± 1	1.8 ± 0.8	–
41	024W-8	SCY024W1	510 ± 95	52 ± 5	–	35 ± 2	–	15 ± 1	11 ± 1	–	–
42	024W-9	SCY024W1	282 ± 27	229 ± 16	–	24 ± 2	2.7 ± 1.3	2.1 ± 1.0	12 ± 1	–	–
43	024W-10	SCY024W1	334 ± 29	151 ± 12	–	44 ± 3	4.3 ± 1.6	–	13 ± 1	43 ± 2	271 ± 14
44	024E-1	SCY024E3	297 ± 28	119 ± 10	–	12 ± 3	–	–	23 ± 1	–	138 ± 7
45	024E-2	SCY024E3	220 ± 29	75 ± 7	–	38 ± 3	5.2 ± 1.9	13 ± 2	17 ± 1	–	–
46	024E-3	SCY024E3	123 ± 38	270 ± 17	–	64 ± 4	–	6.1 ± 1.6	18 ± 1	–	–
47	024E-4	SCY024E3	266 ± 27	131 ± 10	–	86 ± 4	–	–	10 ± 1	–	94 ± 5
48	024E-5	SCY024E3	79 ± 28	17 ± 2	–	44 ± 3	–	14 ± 3	7.3 ± 1.0	–	15 ± 3

Note: Fields marked with a dash signify no trace element detected.

have a very low zinc content. The similarity in the chemical composition indicates that the slags from the other two units were not only produced by the same technology but from a similar type of ore, low in zinc.

Microscopic analysis also revealed a similar microstructure in these Phorades-type slags, as they consist almost entirely of fayalite crystals, and wüstite with very little glassy matrix (figure 5.8). The copper is present mainly in the form of matte prills, but one sample contained large prills of copper in which small globules of copper-iron sulfide were found (figure 5.9; table 5.4). This may be an example of slag produced in a secondary smelting process where the roasted matte is converted into black copper. Alternatively, since it does not differ significantly from the other examples, it could very well represent an instance in which some copper was produced during the primary smelt. Whether this is possible will be better understood once a significant number of slag samples from Phorades have been analyzed.

GEOMETRIC TO CLASSICAL PERIODS

Two archaeometallurgical POSIs (SCY022, SCY116) dated by radiocarbon to the Geometric and Archaic periods are quite similar in nature. SCY022 (Agrokipia *Kriadhis* 1) consists of waste material produced during ore beneficiation (crushing, grinding, and roasting). The various stages of the ore beneficiation are represented by the waste material left behind: fragments of rocks that contain no metal; finely ground material that bears no trace of copper; and furnace conglomerate most likely related to the roasting process. The furnace conglomerate consists of small fragments of ore and charcoal loosely bound together and bearing the effects of heat, but not of intense temperatures (figure 5.10). As roasting is an intermediate step in the production of copper, one does not expect to encounter the material produced as this would have undergone further treatment. The only reason we find this material is that it was rejected as having too low a copper content.

A few pieces of slag were found in these sections, as well as fragments of tuyères (figure 5.11). These are quite small and derive from the back end of the tuyère where they terminate in a well-defined rim. All the examples are partly slagged (at the broken end). They are made of clay with a high proportion

Figure 5.5. SCY100: large fragment of a typical plano-concave slag cake from Phorades. View shows bottom side where concavity is clearly differentiated from the edge of the cake.

Figure 5.6 Unit 1746: plano-concave slag cakes

Figure 5.7 Unit 105: plano-concave slag cake

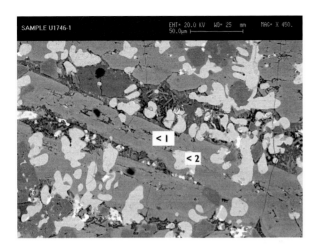

Figure 5.8 Micrograph of sample U1746-1. The slag consists of fayalite crystals (one of which is indicated by arrow 1), wüstite globules (arrow 2), and a small amount of glass.

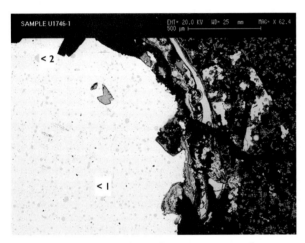

Figure 5.9 Micrograph of sample U1746. Arrow 1 shows an area which consists mainly of copper, while arrow 2 shows a copper-iron sulfide globule.

Table 5.4 Microanalysis of metallic prills in slag samples

Sample	Fig. #	Spot	Cu	Fe	S	Mn
U1746-1	5.4.9	1	99.09	0.9	–	–
U1746-1	5.4.9	2	76.27	4.72	19.00	–
116-8	5.4.12	–	68.22	12.24	19.54	–
116-30	5.4.13	–	97.02	2.98	–	–
116-9	5.4.14	1	98.80	1.20	–	–
116-9	5.4.14	–	78.77	2.09	19.14	–
024W-6	5.4.22	–	66.64	16.20	17.16	–
021-14	5.4.23	–	66.20	11.2	22.8	–

Note: Fields marked with a dash signify no element detected.

of inorganic temper and very little, if any, organic material. Although we cannot reconstruct their shape, the tuyères were clearly short (as the slagging ends 1 to 2 cm from the well-defined rim) and were perhaps introduced from the sides of the furnace wall. They are therefore quite different in size, shape, and material from those found at Phorades.

At SCY116 (Politiko *Kokkinorotsos* 1), in addition to the debris from ore beneficiation and roasting we also found slag that analysis has shown to derive from both primary and secondary smelting. Chemical analysis of six samples from this POSI (table 5.2, nos. 17–22) reveals that they are closer in composition to the samples from the Protohistoric Bronze Age than those which date to the Late Roman period. In general the iron content is relatively high, and manganese is present only as a trace element. Copper content is below 2% in all but one analyzed sample (which can be identified as furnace slag), while zinc is relatively high when compared to the earlier examples. We have suggested that the ore smelted at Phorades would have been mined at Kokkinorotsos, where SCY116 is also located. This difference in composition of the slags, however, indicates that the two sites exploited different deposits, not an unexpected development. It is entirely possible that rich copper-sulfide ores located close to the surface had been exhausted by the Protohistoric Bronze Age miners and that the ore for SCY116 had to be extracted from deeper deposits where sphalerite (the zinc-sulfide ore) was also present.

Microscopic analysis of the samples from SCY116 identified two types of slag. One is composed of fayalite crystals, wüstite dendrites, and matte prills embedded in a glassy matrix (figure 5.12); the second is composed of fayalite crystals, an even greater amount of wüstite dendrites, and copper prills (figure 5.13). Figure 5.14 shows a detail of a copper prill in which globules of copper iron sulfides can be detected. As argued above, the presence of the copper prills demonstrates that these slags derive from secondary smelting, which in turn shows that in this small, surviving part of SCY116 we have uncovered waste material from all the stages of copper production: crushing and grinding, roasting, primary and secondary smelting. In this, SCY116 is unique.

Apart from the waste material we also found three fragments of tuyère, unfortunately too small

Figure 5.10 SCY022: Furnace conglomerate

Figure 5.11 SCY022: Tuyère fragments

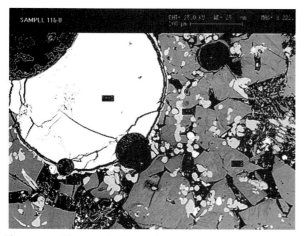

Figure 5.12 Micrograph of sample 116-8

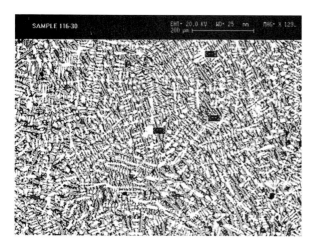

Figure 5.13 Micrograph of sample 116-30

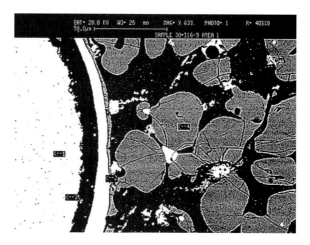

Figure 5.14 Micrograph of sample 116-9

to offer any information on their shape. Their material, however, is very similar to that of the tuyères collected in SCY022. There were no other finds related to the smelting installations, and so we have no way of knowing what these looked like or how they worked.

SCY219—MITSERO *KOKKINOYIA* (SVEN VAN LOKEREN)

The Archaic to Classical period is well represented by SCY 219-7, the slag heap located in direct proximity to the Kokkinoyia mine (SIA 11). There, Archaic to Classical period pottery was found in association with archaeometallurgical debris. Nine samples (nos. SCY219-7a-S1 to S9) collected from different layers of the section have been analyzed (table 5.5; see figure 4.53).

The samples, often heavily corroded on the outside, all belong to the so-called blocky, tapped slag (Koucky and Steinberg 1982a:118–119). Both the P (highly oxidized) and B (slightly oxidized) subtypes, however, were detected, a factor that underlines the limitations of their typology. In any case, at Kokkinoyia we have a whole range of other slag types that will help us to avoid an overly simplified chronological *cum* technological typology as adopted by Koucky and Steinberg (1982a, 1982b; 1989).

The surface texture of the Kokkinoyia samples shows some subdued flow structures, although the slag still seems to have a relatively high viscosity when tapped. Occasionally, long gas vesicles formed parallel to the surface, which disrupted the top surface. With one exception, the slag was not

Table 5.5 SEM-EDX data for spot analyses of main phases and inclusions of slag samples from Mitsero-Kokkinoyia (SCY219)

Sample #	Na_2O	MgO	Al_2O_3	SiO_2	P_2O_5	S	K_2O	CaO	TiO_2	V_2O_5	FeO	Fe	CuO	Cu	ZnO	Zn	Total	Phase Id.
SCY219-7A-S1-1	–	0.1	0.5	0.4	–	–	–	0.2	0.5	–	84.5	–	–	–	0.6	–	86.8	Wiistite dendrite
SCY219-7A-S1-2	–	6.5	–	30.9	–	–	–	1.1	–	–	59.9	–	–	–	1.1	–	99.5	Fayalite crystal
SCY219-7A-S1-3	–	0.5	–	0.6	–	–	–	–	0.3	0.2	94.4	–	–	–	0.5	–	96.5	Magnetite dendrite
SCY219-7A-S2-1	–	–	–	–	–	22.3	–	–	–	–	–	7.3	–	69.7	–	–	99.3	Matte prill
SCY219-7A-S2-2	–	–	–	–	–	20.3	–	–	–	–	–	0.6	–	78.6	–	–	99.5	Matte prill
SCY219-7A-S2-3	1.3	2.4	11.6	44	–	–	1.3	10.7	0.9	–	27.1	–	–	–	1.1	–	100.4	Glass matrix
SCY219-7A-S3-1	–	3.2	0.9	29.5	–	0.6	0.9	4.3	–	–	59.1	–	–	–	0.9	–	99.4	Fayalite needle
SCY219-7A-S3-2	–	0.6	0.9	0.4	–	–	–	–	–	0.2	93.7	–	–	–	–	–	95.8	Magnetite dendrite
SCY219-7A-S3-3	–	–	0.9	0.4	–	–	–	–	–	–	94.2	–	–	–	0.8	–	96.3	Magnetite dendrite
SCY219-7A-S4-1	–	3.3	0.7	30.4	–	–	–	2.5	–	–	59.3	–	–	–	4.1	–	99.6	Fayalite crystal
SCY219-7A-S4-2	–	0.1	0.6	–	–	–	–	–	0.3	–	87.1	–	–	–	0.6	–	88.7	Wiistite crystal
SCY219-7A-S4-3	–	–	–	1.3	–	33.3	–	–	–	–	–	32.3	–	28.6	–	3.9	99.4	Chalcopyrite ore
SCY219-7A-S5-1	–	2.1	1.6	30.6	–	0.2	–	1.7	–	–	62.4	–	–	–	0.6	–	99.2	Fayalite needle
SCY219-7A-S5-2	–	2.6	1.1	31.2	–	–	–	1.5	–	–	63.4	–	–	–	0.4	–	100.2	Fayalite needle
SCY219-7A-S5-3	–	–	0.8	–	–	–	–	–	0.3	–	90.8	–	–	–	0.5	–	92.4	Wiistite dendrite
SCY219-7A-S6-1	–	2.1	–	28.8	–	–	–	0.8	–	–	67.3	–	–	–	0.9	–	99.9	Fayalite crystal
SCY219-7A-S6-2	–	–	–	–	–	34.4	–	–	–	–	–	62.6	–	2.1	–	–	99.1	Pyrite ore
SCY219-7A-S6-3	–	–	–	–	–	34.9	–	–	–	–	–	63.1	–	1.8	–	–	99.8	Pyrite ore
SCY219-7A-S7-1	–	3.8	–	28.5	–	–	–	1.3	–	–	65.4	–	–	–	1.2	–	100.2	Fayalite crystal
SCY219-7A-S7-2	–	–	–	0.4	–	27.2	–	–	–	–	–	41.7	–	29.8	–	–	99.1	Chalcopyrite ore
SCY219-7A-S7-3	–	–	1.2	–	–	–	–	–	0.3	–	88.5	–	–	–	0.5	–	90.5	Wiistite dendrite
SCY219-7A-S8-1	–	1.7	3.7	28.4	–	0.2	–	1.2	–	–	64.4	–	–	–	1.3	–	100.9	Fayalite needle
SCY219-7A-S8-2	–	0.4	1.1	–	–	–	–	–	0.3	–	90.1	–	–	–	1	–	92.9	Wiistite dendrite
SCY219-7A-S8-3	0.8	–	9.8	39.6	–	0.6	–	–	–	–	47.4	–	–	–	0.9	–	99.1	Reacting gangue
SCY219-7A-S9-1	–	4.4	–	29.8	–	–	–	1.1	–	–	63.8	–	–	–	–	–	99.1	Fayalite crystal
SCY219-7A-S9-2	–	–	–	0.5	–	–	–	–	0.9	–	88.7	–	–	–	–	–	90.1	Wiistite dendrite
SCY219-7A-S9-3	–	–	–	–	–	–	–	–	–	–	–	3.6	–	96.6	–	–	100.2	Copper prill

Note: Figures in wt%.

ferromagnetic. Analysis of SCY219-7a-S3 showed a higher magnetite content than the other samples. No charcoal or large metallic inclusions were found. Some copper-oxide staining due to corrosion offered evidence of the remaining copper content. Subsequent polarizing microscopy and XRD phase identification analysis gave a coherent picture of a fayalite type slag, containing embedded iron oxide dendrites and globules (wüstite and magnetite) in a glassy matrix.

Further semiquantitative SEM-EDX analysis confirmed this interpretation (table 5.5). The main components are iron, ranging from 56.5 to 73.9% and generally averaging around 60 to 65 wt%, and silica ranging from 13.8 to 29.8%. Al_2O_3 contents are considerable. TiO_2, K_2O, Na_2O, MgO, and P_2O_5 are present as minor elements (although they are often below the detection limit). No manganese oxide (MnO_2) was detected. The overall copper content was relatively low. Moreover, embedded copper-iron-sulfur, that is, matte (SCY219-7a-S2 and -S9) and

metallic copper prills (SCY219-7a-S9), were discovered (figure 5.15). Sample SCY219-7a-S2 was characterized by a large number of spherical matte inclusions within an almost purely glass matrix. These prills often showed a notable iron content, most likely indicative of a matte-smelting process.

Samples SCY219-7a-S4 and S7 had remaining granular inclusions of reacting chalcopyrite ore, while SCY219-7a-S4 and S6 contained remnants of pyrite ore (figure 5.16). The latter FeS content, however, could also represent traces of the intermediary matting stage (Bachmann 1982a:22). Two samples, SCY219-7a-S1 and -S2, contained reacting gangue inclusions, possibly left from the added silica flux. Silica, rather than manganese fluxing, was therefore practiced at Kokkinoyia.

Zinc is present at relatively high levels (between 0.8 and 2.4 wt% ZnO), particularly in the case of SCY219-7a-S4, where it reached 8.1% because of a remaining sphalerite (ZnS) inclusion. The fact that the general ore type prevailing in the Cypriot

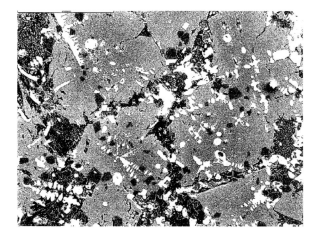

Figure 5.15 Digital micrograph of sample SCY219-7a-S9

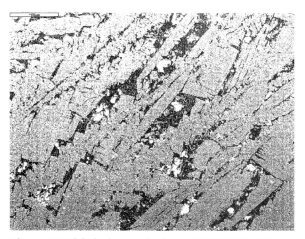

Figure 5.16 Digital micrograph of sample SCY219-7a-S6

ophiolites contains significant amounts of sphalerite in combination with all the other sulfides explains these results. During smelting the zinc content enters mainly into the slag, acting also as a flux and contributing to the glass phase, or else it remains in the matte, depending on the sulfur activity.

Although some fragments of furnaces have been found in the section, these are badly preserved and offer no information regarding their form and shape. Furthermore, no tuyère fragments have been collected. Thus our knowledge of the smelting technology of this period in the SCSP area relies heavily on slag analyses. The slags from the SCSP area, nonetheless, are very similar to those from the contemporary smelting workshop of Ayia Varvara *Almyras* (Fasnacht et al. 1989:63; Fasnacht et al. 1992:69–71) and those found in association with a double furnace at South Mathiati mine that also dates to the Archaic period (Fasnacht et al. 1996:108–109). It is possible, therefore, that the furnaces from Kokkinoyia would have been similar to those at Almyras: that is, they would have been free-standing, with an approximate height of 80 cm and a diameter of 40 to 60 cm. The Almyras furnaces also had a stone-built lower structure lined with clay and an upper structure constructed out of clay (Fasnacht et al. 1992:61).

LATE ROMAN PERIOD

We recorded two very large slags heaps that date to the Late Roman period, SCY021 (Mitsero *Kouloupakhis*) and SCY024 (Mitsero *Sykamies*). Unlike Phorades, where virtually all the slag belongs to the same type, the slag heaps of the Roman period consist of slag fragments that vary widely in shape,

size, and color. These differences are reflected in their chemical compositions, discussed below.

The most distinctive finds from these heaps are large slag cakes that weigh approximately 40 to 55 kg each (figure 5.17). Multiple layers in the slag cakes indicate that the contents of the furnace were tapped several times in the same pit. As pointed out in the discussion of these POSIs, however, most layers in the slag heap are not made up of the large cakes but instead consist mainly of medium (5 to 10 cm) and small (below 5 cm) sized slag fragments. Clearly much effort was devoted to crushing and even sorting them.

Crushing slag was a necessary step in early metallurgical processing, especially before the use of bellows and fluxes, as the metal was often trapped in the viscous slag (Tylecote 1987:300). This is not what one would expect of metallurgical workshops dating to Late Antiquity, and indeed the analyses show that the slag contains very little copper (apart from the fragments of furnace slag). Clearly the separation of metal from the slag does not seem to be the motive. Perhaps the reason behind the crushing was to achieve a more efficient disposal of the waste by creating a more stable heap that might also serve as a working floor. As we walked or climbed on these heaps, we immediately became aware that the layers containing the large slag cakes were unstable and prone to collapse. Presumably the slag was crushed on stone mortars (figure 5.18), examples of which have been found in the heaps, along with stone grinders (figure 5.19).

The blue/black colored slag in these heaps easily stands out from the rest and has been found on analysis to contain a large amount of manganese (for example,

Figure 5.17 Slag cakes from SCY021E-1 and SCY021W-2

are the "furnace" slags (figure 5.20). These are usually amorphous masses, sometimes covered in copper incrustations and often with small pieces of charcoal and clay furnace lining attached (for example, sample 021-17). Almost certainly this is the material that remained in the furnace once the bulk of the slag (and presumably the metal) had been tapped out.

We do not know what the furnaces looked like because no well-preserved examples were found. There is clear evidence, however, that some surfaces within these slag heaps were used as working floors, and we have recorded lenses of furnace material among the other layers which consist almost entirely of slag (for example, SCY021W-2; see chapter 4.3). Unfortunately, unlike the case of SCY100 (Phorades), none of the furnace material fragments is preserved in such a way as to indicate the furnaces' shape or dimensions.

At least we know what sort of materials were used to construct the furnaces. In these large slag heaps, and only there, we found rounded igneous rocks (mainly gabbro) coming from river channels that bear the traces of intense heat and slagging (figure 5.21). Some of these stones are quite large (figure 5.22) and clearly once formed part of a furnace installation. It is unclear whether they were lined with clay, as the examples collected have begun to melt, are slagged, and bear no traces of the clay lining. However, the clay may have been completely melted and incorporated into the slag layer. Apart from the slagged stones we also found fragments of slagged clay (figure 5.23). It is unclear whether these are fragments of the clay upper structure of a stone-built furnace (as is the case with the furnaces from Almyras; Fasnacht et al. 1992:63) or whether it derives from a metallurgical installation made entirely of clay and used in a different step of the process (like the much earlier furnaces of Phorades).

Although no tuyère fragments were found in the slag heaps, this does not mean they were not used (see Koucky and Steinberg 1974:169). Given the small amount of furnace material found, and even though thousands of installations must have existed to produce this phenomenal amount of slag, we need not expect any tuyère fragments to turn up.

SLAG ANALYSES

Let us turn now to the chemical and microscopic analyses of some slags from the POSIs under discussion (tables 5.2, 5.3, nos. 29–48). The basic

table 5.2, no. 024W-5). But the heaps also contain slags ranging in color from blue/black to red/black. In the past archaeologists, geologists, and mining engineers incorrectly dated slags according to their color. Reddish brown slags were believed to be Phoenician in date, while black slags were considered to be Roman (Bruce 1937:642; Muhly et al. 1980:86).

One striking difference between the slags from the Late Roman heaps and those from workshops dating to earlier periods (for example, SCY116) is that they are relatively free of copper carbonate incrustations. Looking at the chemical composition, it is clear why this is so: the copper content in these samples is normally below 1%. The only exceptions

Figure 5.20 SCY021-1E: fragments of furnace slag

Figure 5.21 SCY024E-2: slagged stone

Figure 5.18 Mortar stones from SCY021E-1(top) and SCY021W-1(bottom)

Figure 5.22 SCY021E-1: slagged stone

Figure 5.19 SCY021: Grinding stone

Figure 5.23 SCY024W-1: slagged furnace lining

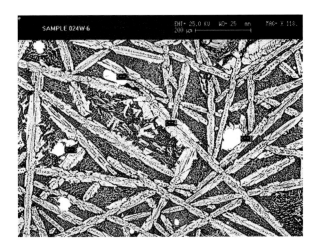

Figure 5.24 Micrograph of sample 024W-6

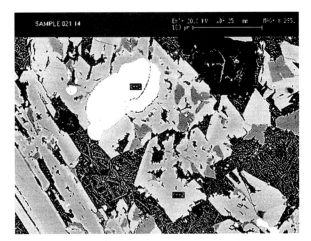

Figure 5.25 Micrograph of sample 021-14

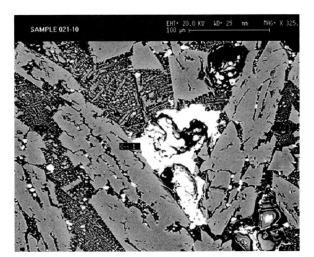

Figure 5.26 Micrograph of sample 021-10

difference in the chemical composition between those slags dated to the Late Roman period and those dated to earlier periods is the presence of manganese. However, as shown clearly in figure 5.2, the concentration of manganese varies greatly even between the samples within the same POSI: In some examples, it is below 2% and in others it is above 40%. In the examples with high manganese concentration, the iron content is lower than in the ones with low manganese concentration. In fact, the iron content of these slags is, in general, lower than in the examples from earlier sites. This is also reflected in their mineral composition, as shown by the microscopic analysis discussed below. The copper ores do not contain manganese and its presence in the slags indicates the deliberate use of manganiferous material as a flux in the charge. The material used was most likely umber, outcrops of which we have recorded in the vicinity of the mines. As we have not detected any manganese in the slags of earlier periods, the presence of manganese can act as an indicator of the date of a slag sample.

As a result of this observation, it might be suggested that the three samples collected from SCY204 (Agrokipia *Kriadhis* 3) date to the Late Roman period, not to the Archaic period (as suggested by the pottery; see chapter 4.1). The area is extremely disturbed and we cannot be certain that the slag is directly associated with the pottery. The rest of the chemical profile of these samples (particularly the low copper content) also agrees with the later date.

The other important difference between these later slags and their earlier counterparts is a low copper content, usually below 1% (apart from examples of furnace slag). This clearly results from the proper use of fluxes, which enable the formation of more fluid slags that allow the metal to separate more easily. Furthermore, in comparison to the earlier slags, the zinc content is relatively high, particularly in the samples from SCY024E-3. The presence of zinc in the slag shows that the ore used consisted of sphalerite as well as chalcopyrite and may indicate the exploitation of deeper deposits.

Microscopic analysis showed that most slags are composed of well-formed olivine crystals embedded in a glass phase. In samples where the manganese content is very low (for example, figure 5.24) the crystals are fayalites. In samples where there is a significant amount of manganese (for example, figure 5.25), some of the iron is replaced by manganese and the crystals are closer to the composition of knebélite. Finally, in samples with very high manganese content (for example, figure 5.26), almost all the iron is replaced and the olivine crystals are tephroite. The crystals are embedded in a glassy matrix. Unlike the slags from earlier periods, there are no iron oxides present, something that is reflected in their chemical composition. The only other phase present is represented by the few small prills of matte that are the brighter phases in the three micrographs. There are very few metallic prills, something which is again reflected in the bulk chemical composition. Everything points to a very efficient smelting technology that utilized fluxes and produced a fluid slag that separated well from the metal, leading to a reduction in the loss of copper in the slag.

Matte prills were detected in all the analyzed slag samples (every slag sample was studied under the optical microscope but only a selection was studied under the scanning electron microscope). In contrast, no copper prills—such as those detected in sample U1746-1 (Late Cypriot) or sample 116-9 (Geometric to Archaic)—were found in any of the samples dating to the Late Roman period. This may be coincidental, since we have analyzed only a small proportion of material from the bulk of the slag; on the other hand, it may indicate that even in the Late Roman period the final stages of smelting and refining were done elsewhere. As pointed out above, although we are in the historical period we know even less about the organization of the copper industry at this time than we do for the Late Cypriot period.

CONCLUSION

With the discovery of a primary smelting site dating to the Protohistoric Bronze Age, we have clear evidence that at least from the Late Cypriot period, if not earlier, production of copper on Cyprus was based on the exploitation of copper sulfide ores. The process followed was that of matte production; the matte then had to be roasted and smelted again to produce black copper. This process became the standard throughout the periods recorded in the SCSP area. From the evidence collected it is clear that although the technique is the same over the centuries, the installations are different (both in term of design and of material used for the furnaces and the tuyères), and so is the composition of the ore. This is not unexpected, as in later periods miners would have had to search for new deposits, some of which were quite deep underground. The amount of copper lost in the slag is gradually but significantly reduced, an advancement made possible by the better use of fluxes and probably also by the improved design of the smelting installations.

One of SCSP's important contributions has been to demonstrate that the theory proposed in various publications by Koucky and Steinberg (1974:169–176; 1989:294–304)—namely that copper was produced by a hydrometallurgical method—should finally be put to rest. We can show that most of their arguments are invalid; for example. that no tuyères have ever been found in or near the slag heaps, that no areas of crushing and grinding have ever been discovered, or that no copper matte has ever been found.

Another important thing that we have been able to demonstrate is the great variation in chemical compositions among the different sections of what can be considered to be the same slag heap (for example, SCY024W-1 and SCY024E-3), as well as between the slags from different strata of the same section. A single fragment of slag collected from a heap comprising a few hundred thousand tons of slag can no longer be regarded as a representative sample. Much more attention to detail is required if we are to record properly the history of the copper technology on the island that gave the metal its name.

Plate 1 *See Catalog for dimensions*

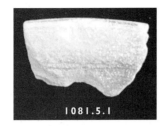

1081.5.1

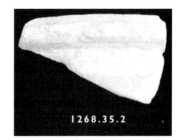

1268.35.2

1144.9.1

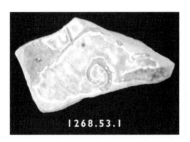

1268.53.1

1254.1.1

1257.12.1

1268.56.1

Plate 2 *See Catalog for dimensions*

1268.60.2

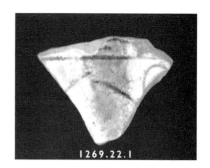

1269.22.1

1268.62.1

1269.23.1

1269.21.1

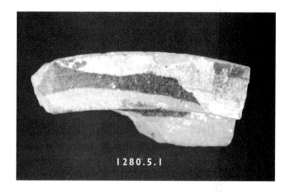

1280.5.1

1285.12.1

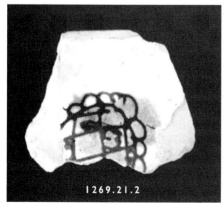

1269.21.2

1302.13.1

Plate 3 *See Catalog for dimensions*

POTTERY

1307.1.1

1599.12.1

1350.1.1

1629.2.1

1595.3.1

1596.1.1

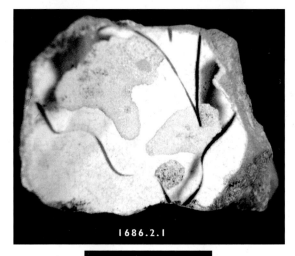

1686.2.1

1708.14.1

1599.1.1

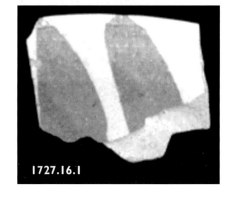

1727.16.1

Plate 4 *See Catalog for dimensions*

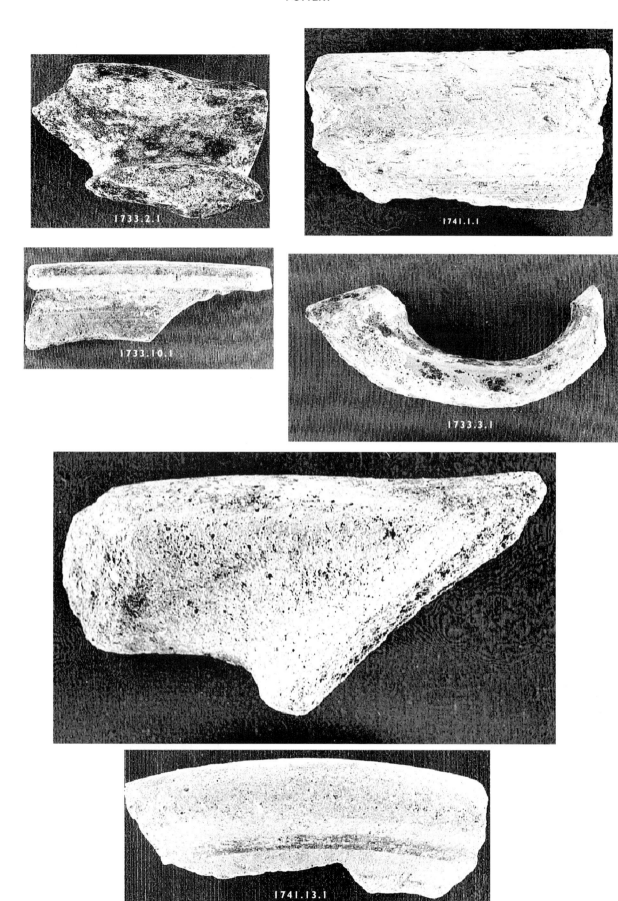

Plate 5 *See Catalog for dimensions*

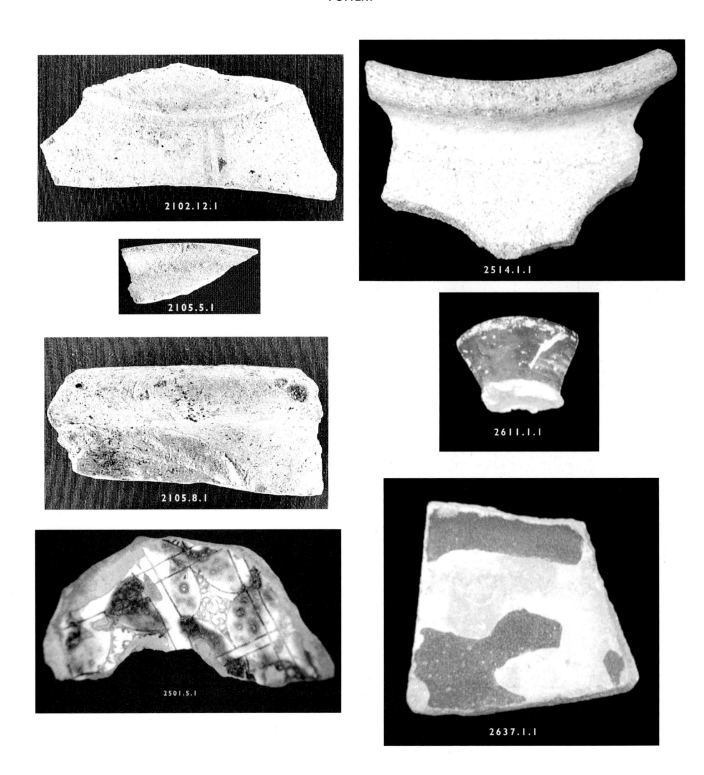

2102.12.1

2105.5.1

2105.8.1

2501.5.1

2514.1.1

2611.1.1

2637.1.1

Plate 6 *See Catalog for dimensions*

Plate 7 *See Catalog for dimensions*

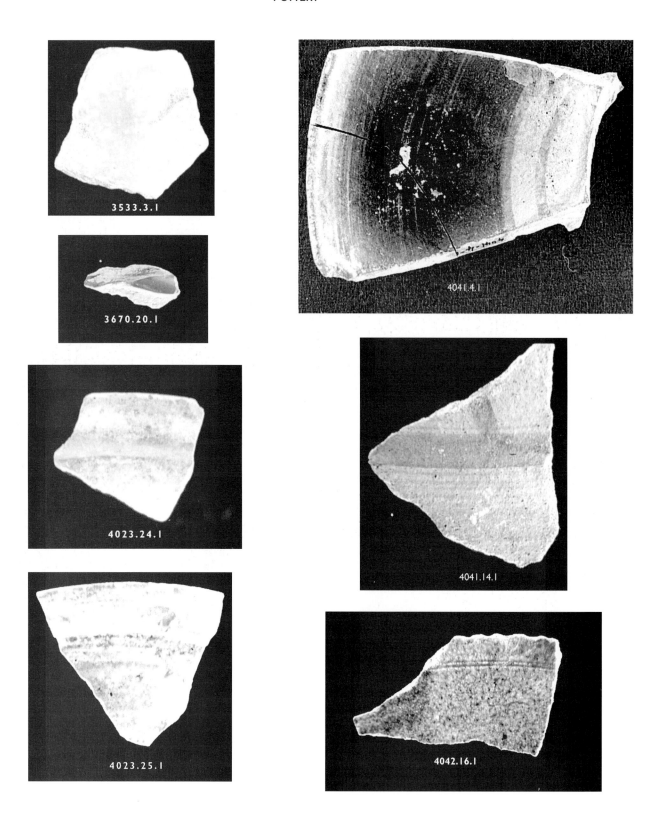

3533.3.1

3670.20.1

4041.4.1

4023.24.1

4041.14.1

4023.25.1

4042.16.1

Plate 8 *See Catalog for dimensions*

4042.20.1

4514.1.1

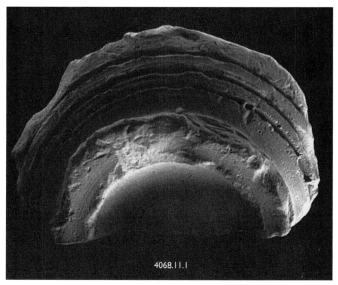

4068.11.1

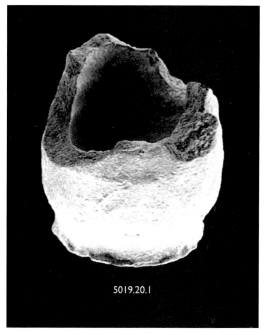

5019.20.1

4505.5.1

Plate 9 *See Catalog for dimensions*

POTTERY

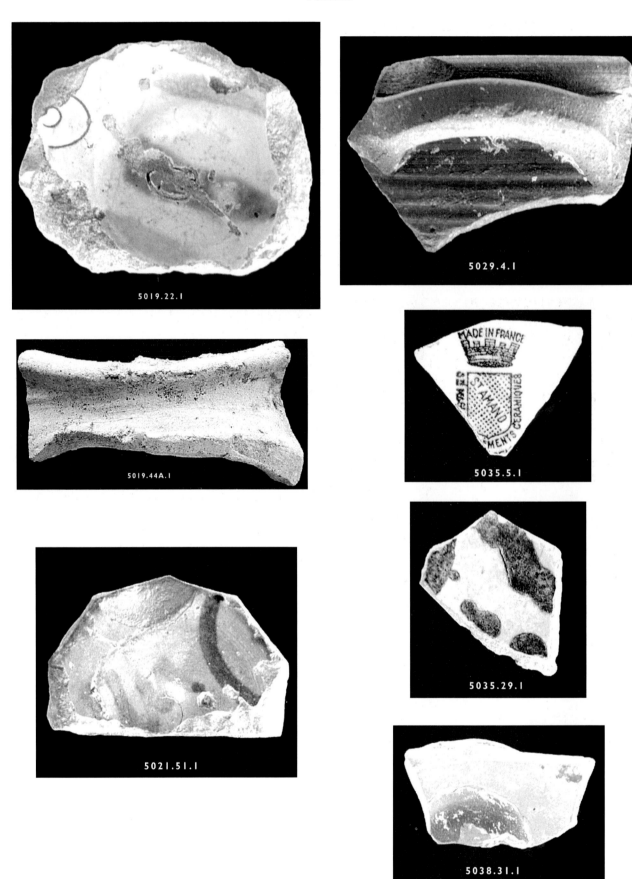

5019.22.1

5029.4.1

5019.44A.1

5035.5.1

5035.29.1

5021.51.1

5038.31.1

Plate 10 *See Catalog for dimensions*

238

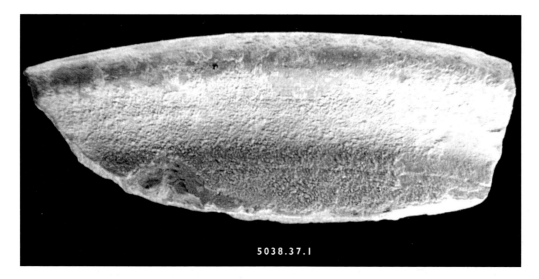

5038.37.1

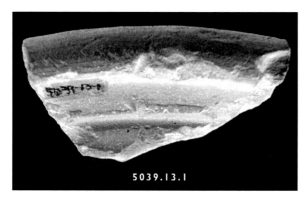

5039.13.1

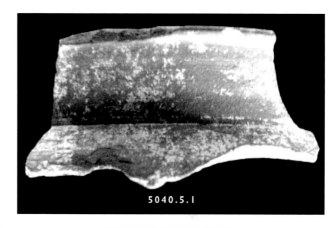

5040.5.1

5040.34.1

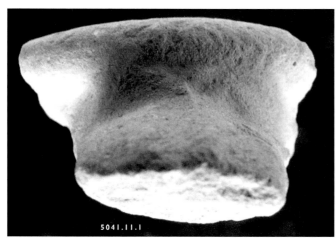

5041.11.1

Plate 11 *See Catalog for dimensions*

S-0030

5044.10.1

S-0029

5045.40.1

S-0032

Plate 12 *See Catalog for dimensions*

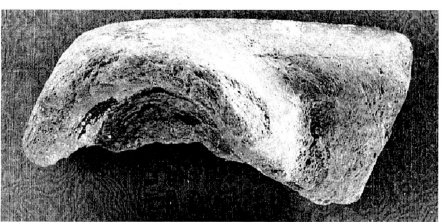

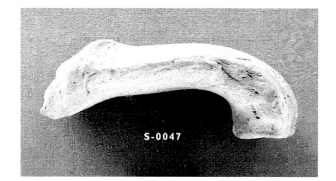

Plate 13 *See Catalog for dimensions*

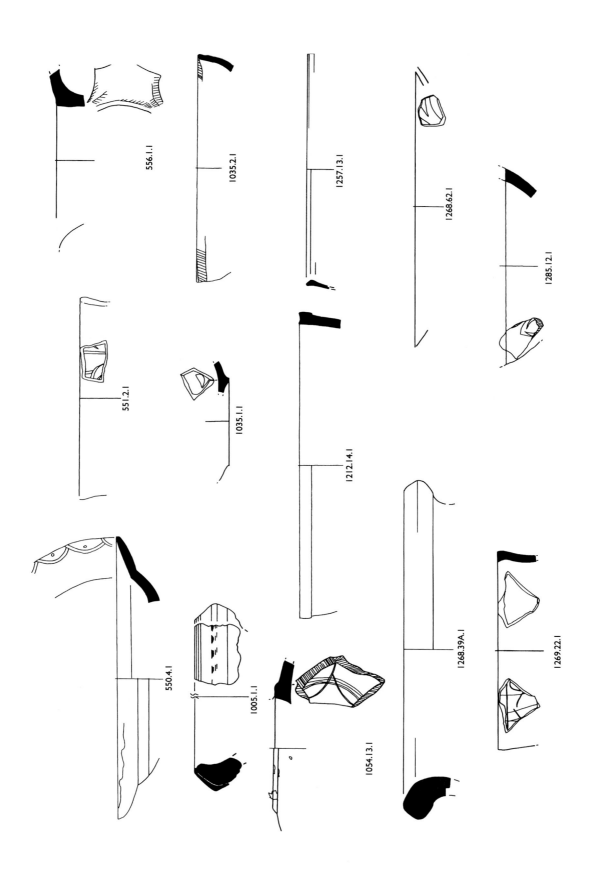

Plate 14 *See Catalog for dimensions*

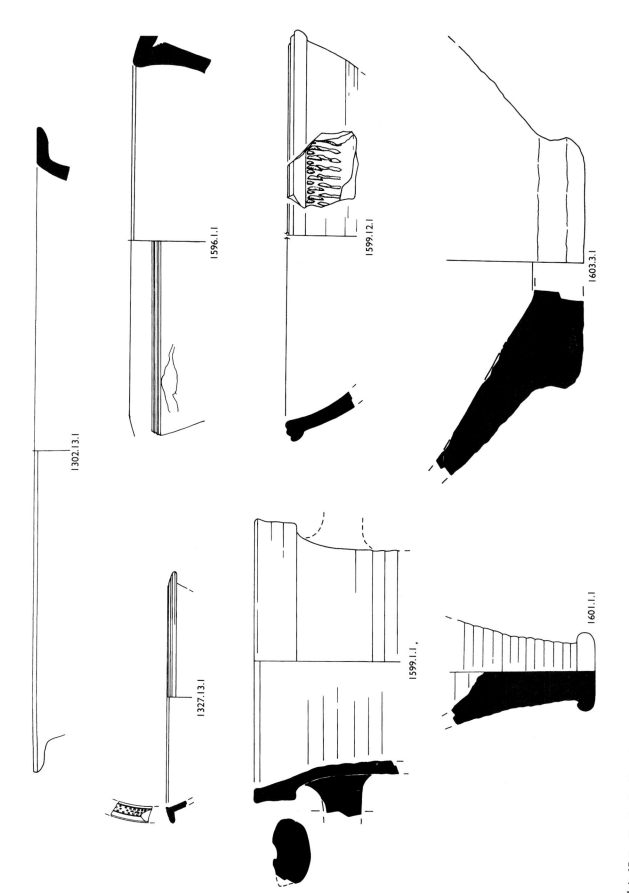

1302.13.1

1596.1.1

1599.12.1

1603.3.1

1327.13.1

1599.1.1.

1601.1.1

Plate 15 *See Catalog for dimensions*

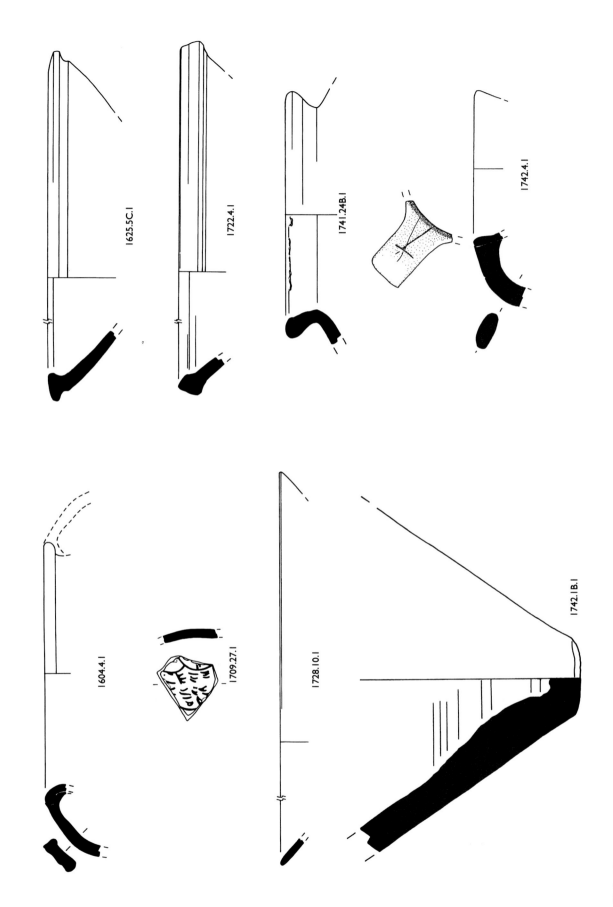

Plate 16 *See Catalog for dimensions*

1625.5C.1

1722.4.1

1741.24B.1

1742.4.1

1604.4.1

1709.27.1

1728.10.1

1742.1B.1

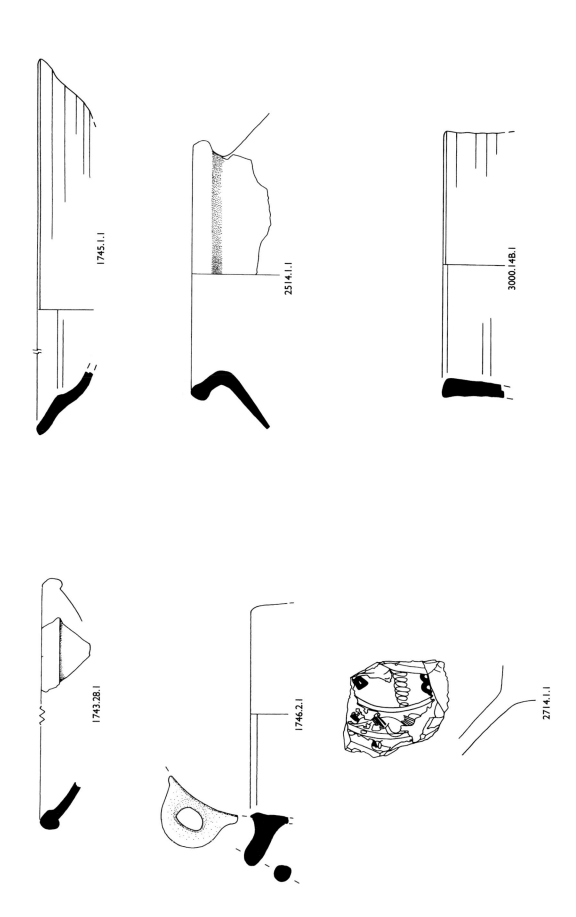

1745.1.1

2514.1.1

3000.14B.1

1743.28.1

1746.2.1

2714.1.1

Plate 17 *See Catalog for dimensions*

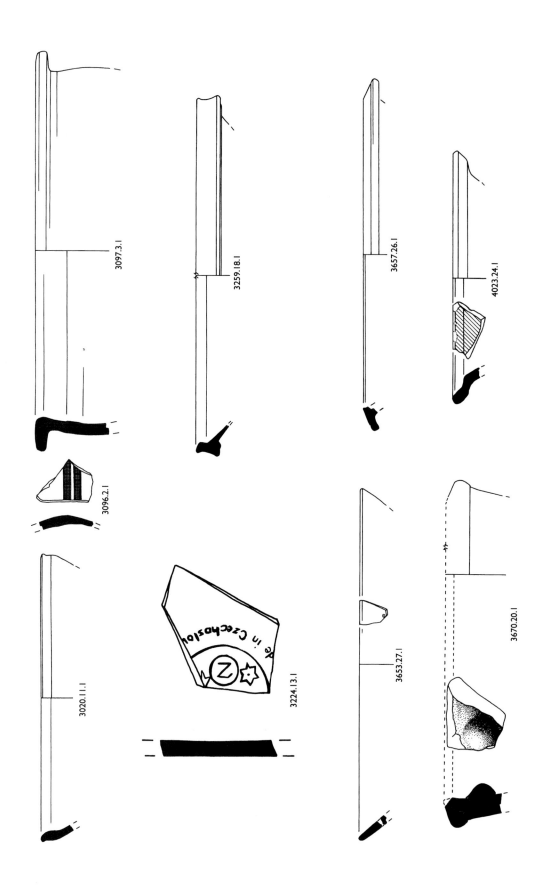

3097.3.1

3259.18.1

3657.26.1

4023.24.1

3096.2.1

3020.11.1

3224.13.1

de in Czechoslov

3653.27.1

3670.20.1

Plate 18 *See Catalog for dimensions*

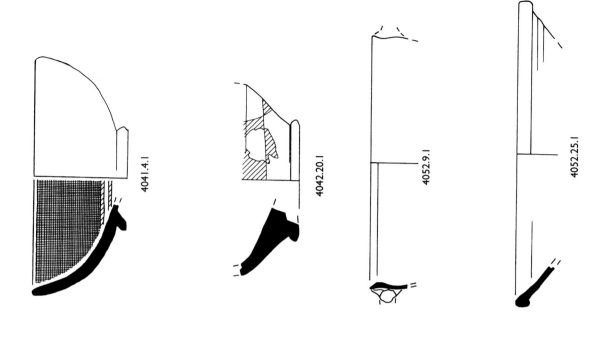

4041.4.1

4042.20.1

4052.9.1

4052.25.1

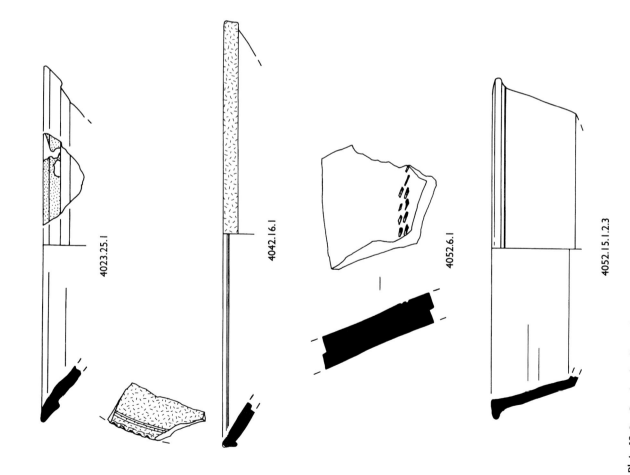

4023.25.1

4042.16.1

4052.6.1

4052.15.1.2.3

Plate 19 *See Catalog for dimensions*

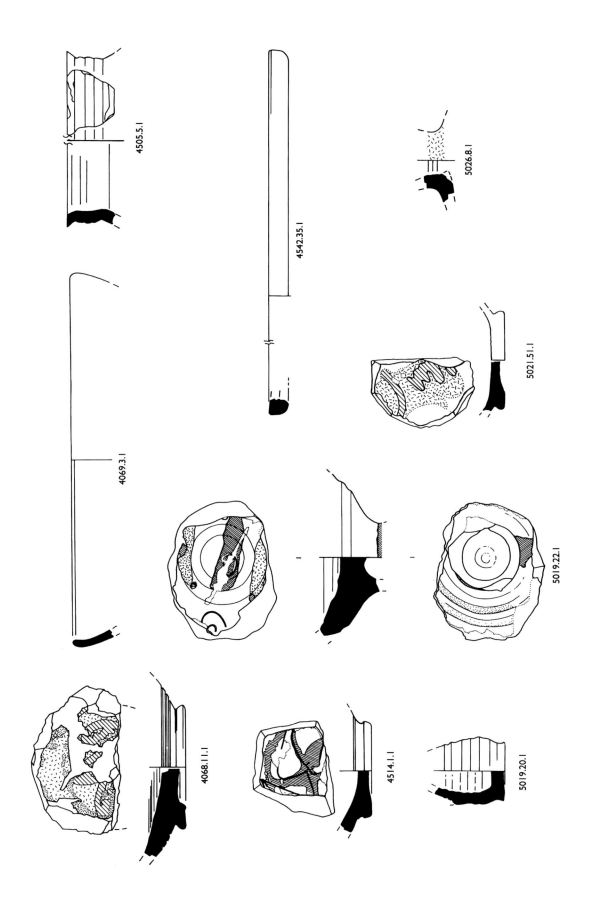

Plate 20 *See Catalog for dimensions*

4505.5.1

4542.35.1

5026.8.1

4069.3.1

5021.51.1

5019.22.1

4068.11.1

4514.1.1

5019.20.1

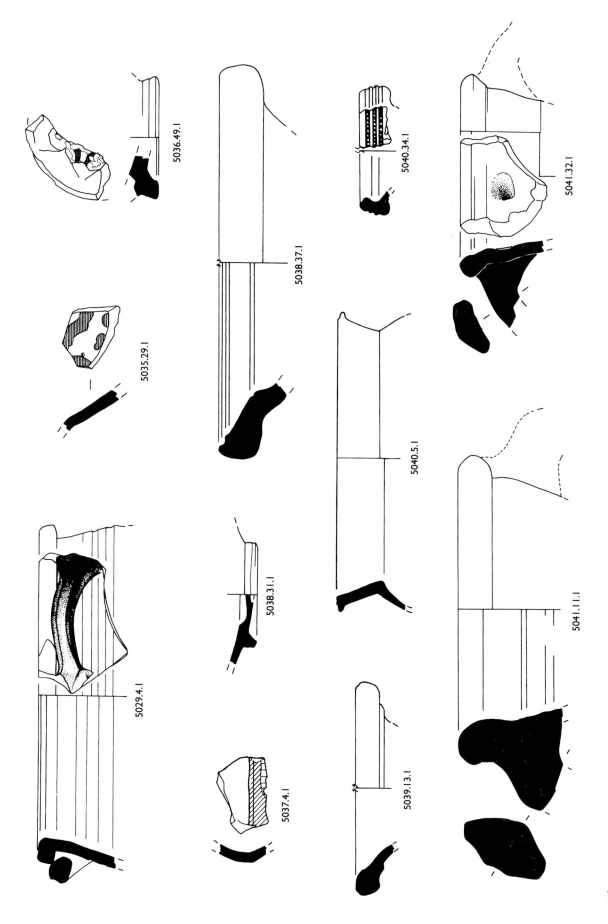

Plate 21 *See Catalog for dimensions*

5036.49.1

5038.37.1

5040.34.1

5041.32.1

5035.29.1

5040.5.1

5029.4.1

5038.31.1

5037.4.1

5039.13.1

5041.11.1

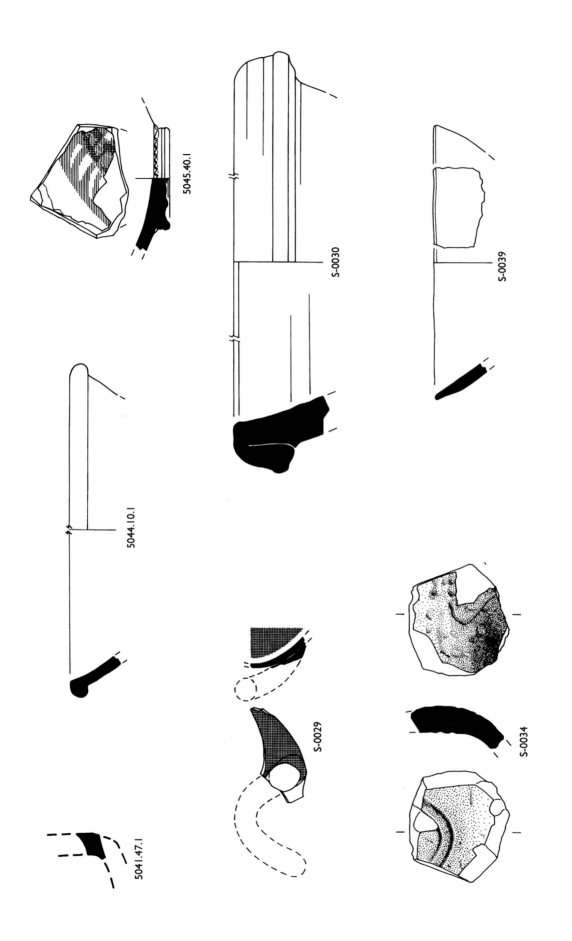

5045.40.1

S-0030

S-0039

5044.10.1

5041.47.1

S-0029

S-0034

Plate 22 *See Catalog for dimensions*

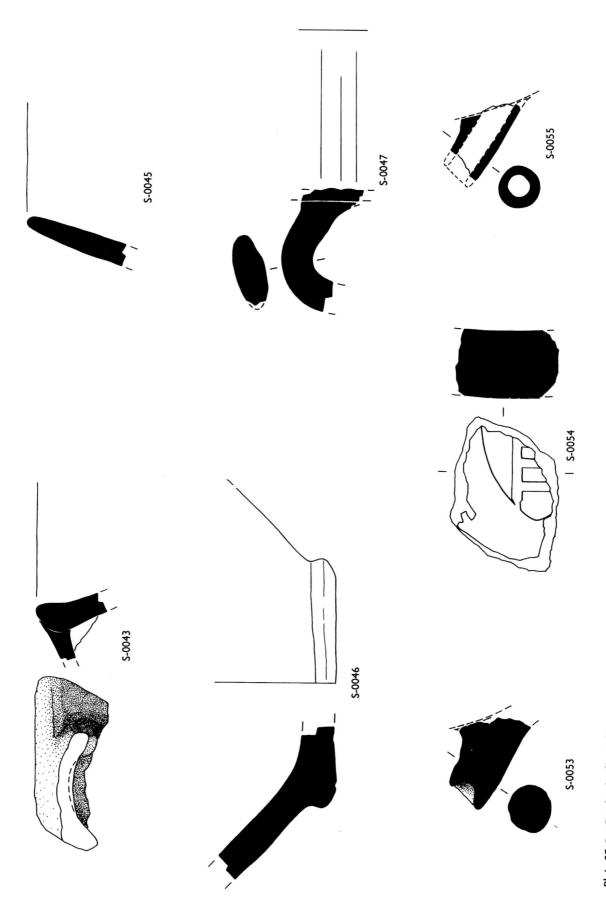

S-0045

S-0047

S-0055

S-0054

S-0043

S-0046

S-0053

Plate 23 *See Catalog for dimensions*

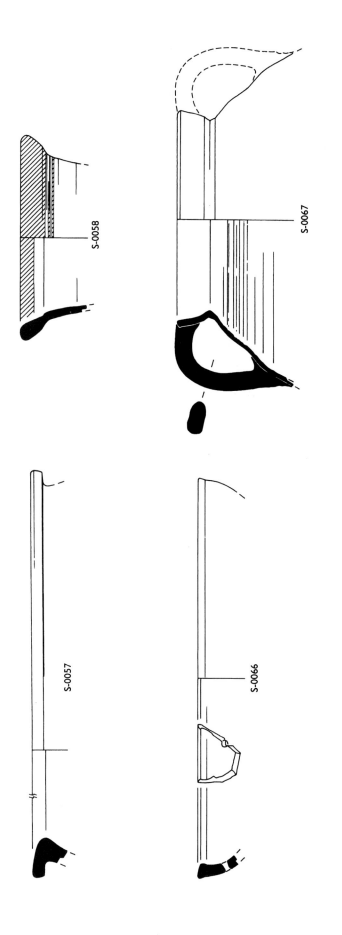

S-0058

S-0067

S-0057

S-0066

Plate 24 *See Catalog for dimensions*

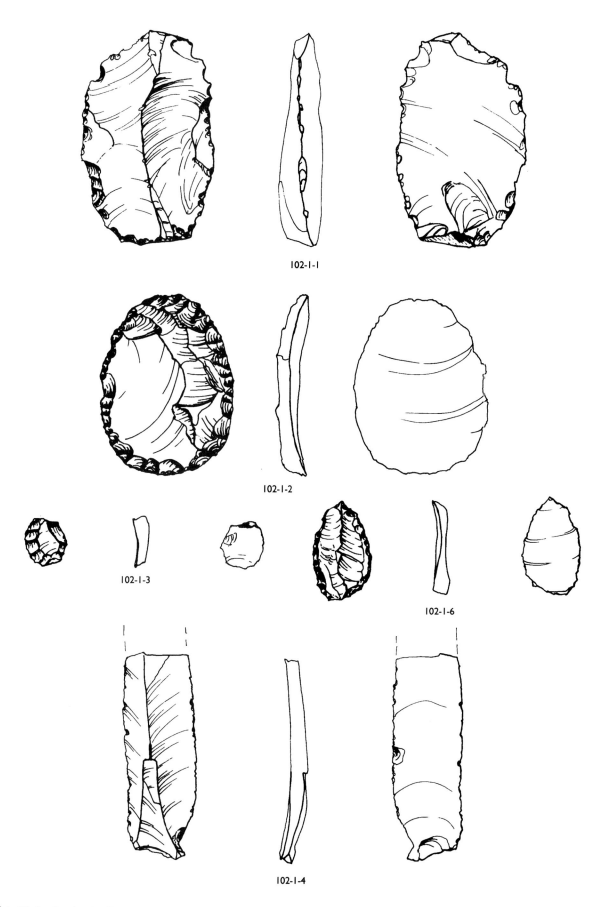

102-1-1

102-1-2

102-1-3

102-1-6

102-1-4

Plate 25 *See Catalog for dimensions*

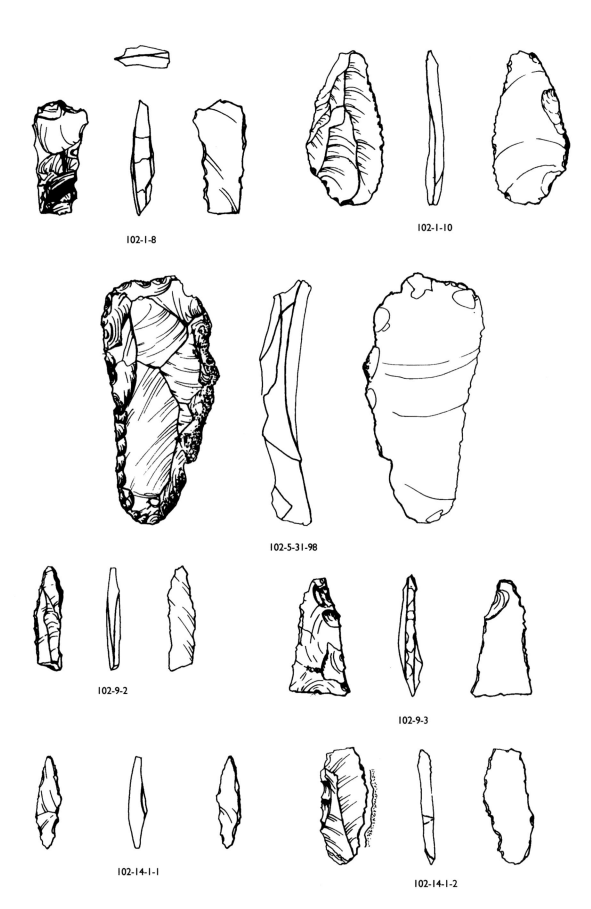

102-1-8

102-1-10

102-5-31-98

102-9-2

102-9-3

102-14-1-1

102-14-1-2

Plate 26 *See Catalog for dimensions*

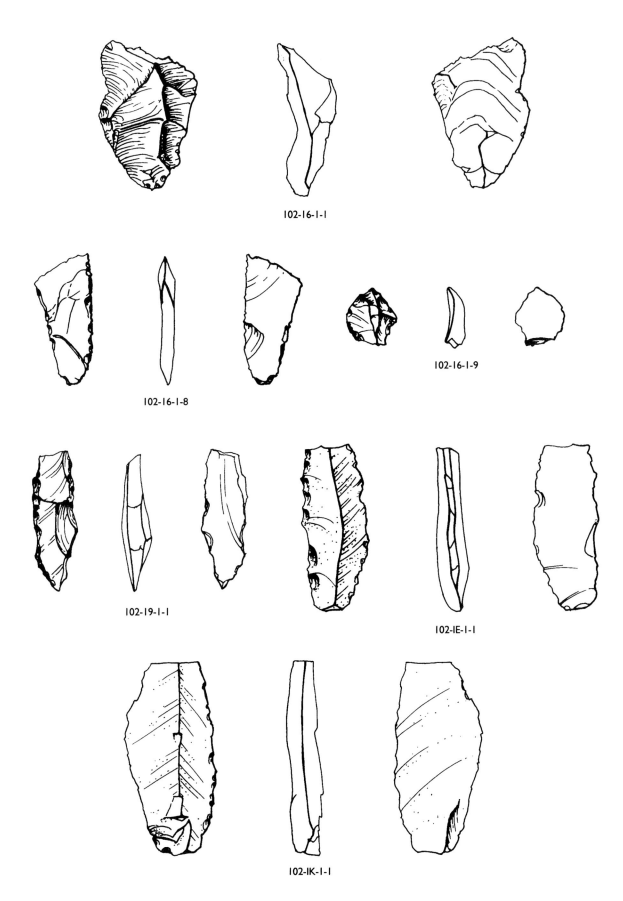

102-16-1-1

102-16-1-8

102-16-1-9

102-19-1-1

102-IE-1-1

102-IK-1-1

Plate 27 *See Catalog for dimensions*

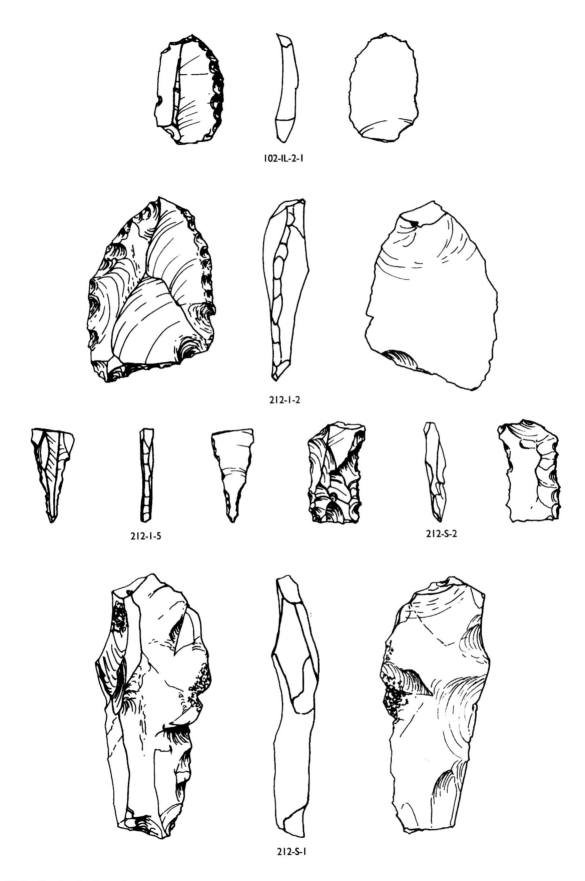

102-IL-2-1

212-1-2

212-1-5

212-S-2

212-S-1

Plate 28 *See Catalog for dimensions*

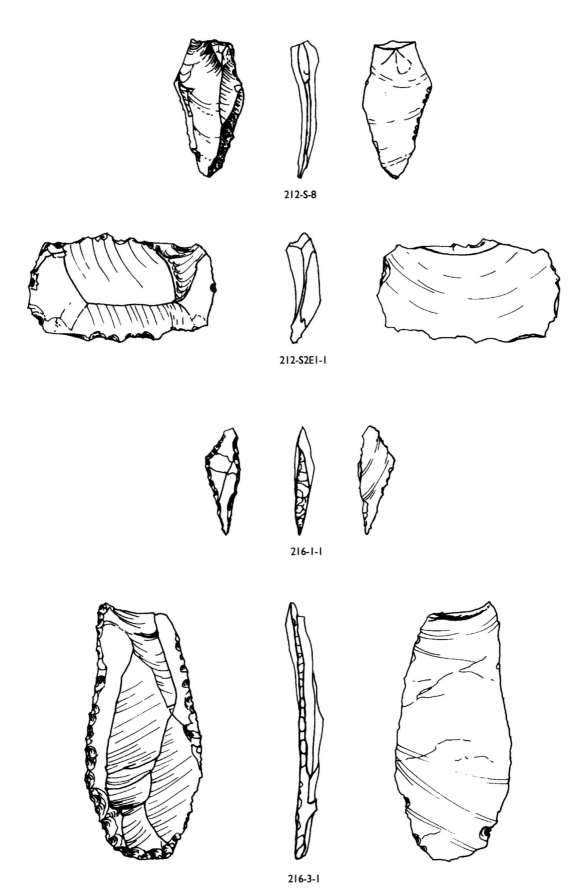

212-S-8

212-S2E1-1

216-1-1

216-3-1

Plate 29 *See Catalog for dimensions*

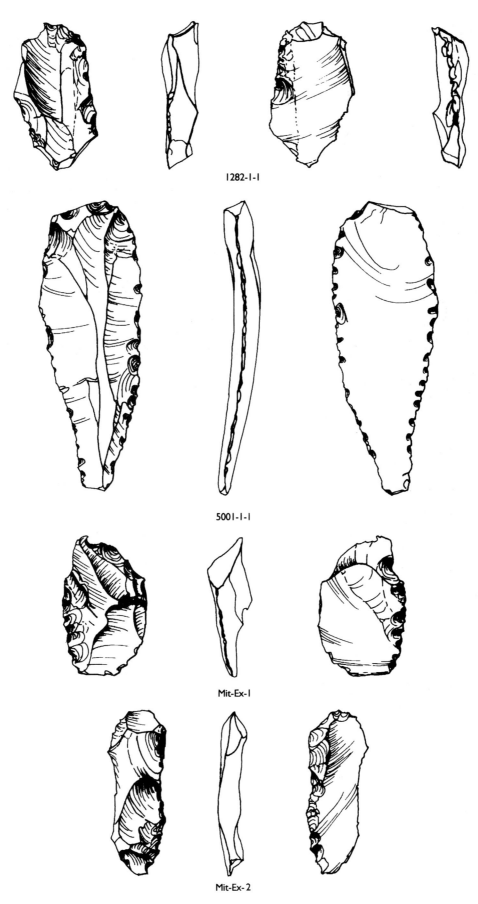

1282-1-1

5001-1-1

Mit-Ex-1

Mit-Ex-2

Plate 30 *See Catalog for dimensions*

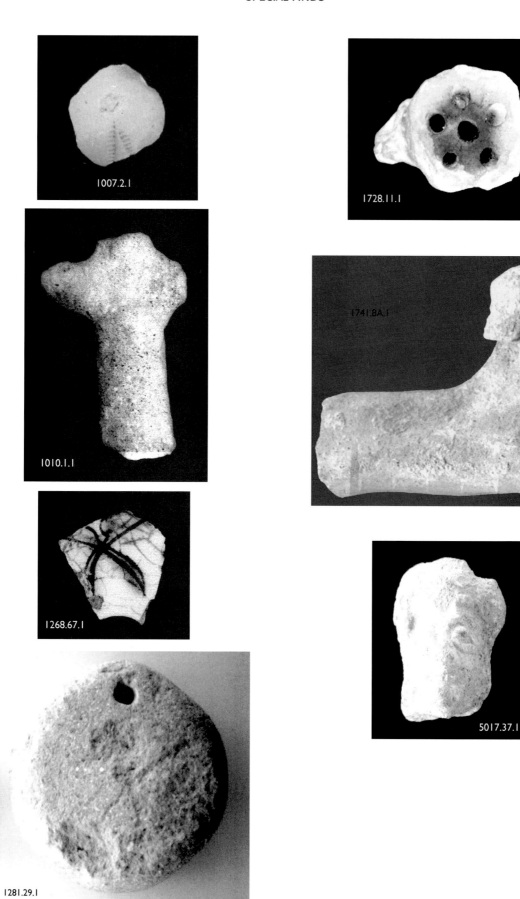

Plate 31 *See Catalog for dimensions*

5017.39.1

5019.19.1

5027.17.1

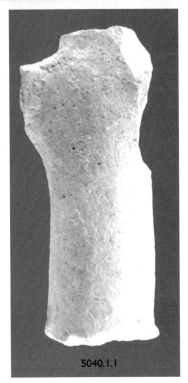

5040.1.1

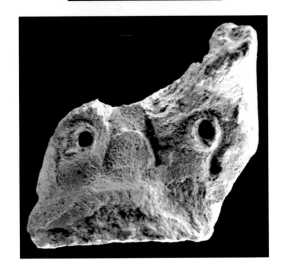

Plate 32 *See Catalog for dimensions*

S-0020

S-0050

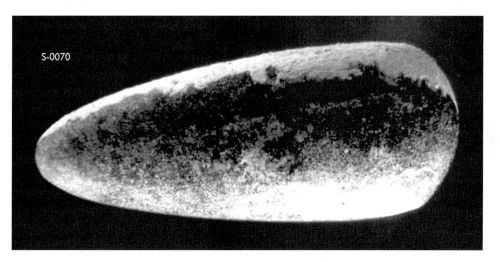

S-0070

SCY021.2.7.1

SCY204.3.5.1

SCY204.3.3.1.1

SCY204.4.12.1

Plate 33 *See Catalog for dimensions*

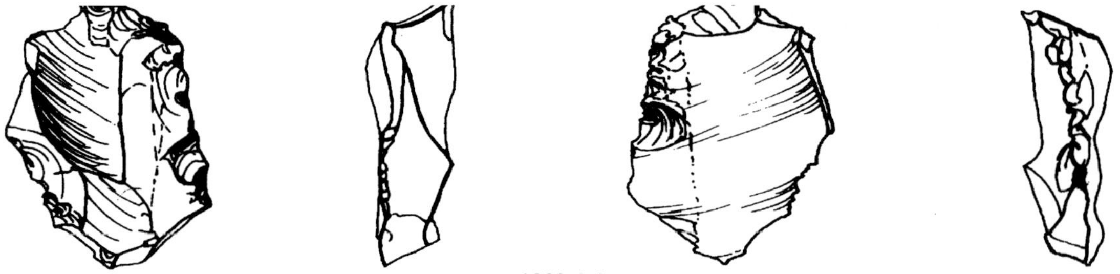

1282-1-1

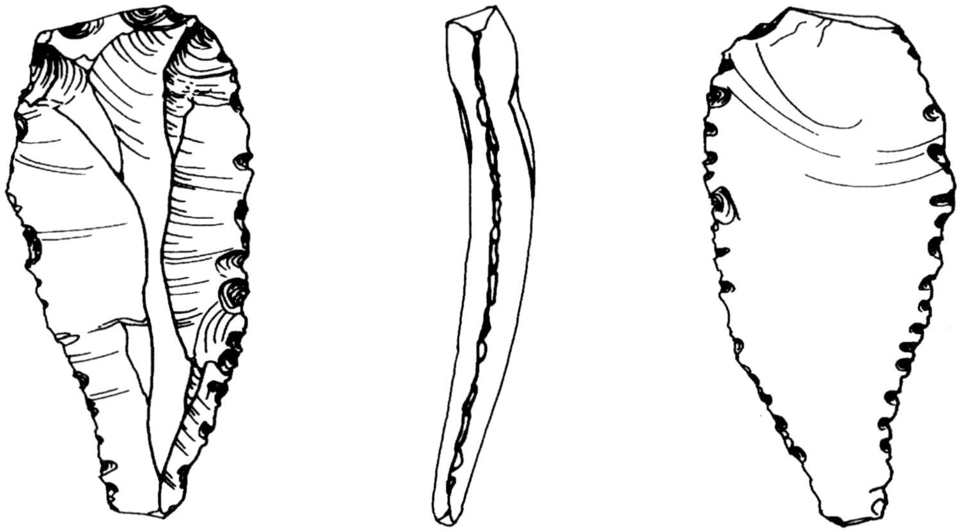

5001-1-1

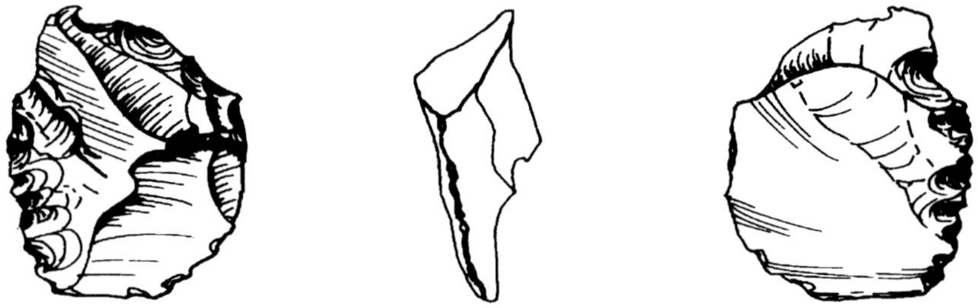

Mit-Ex-1

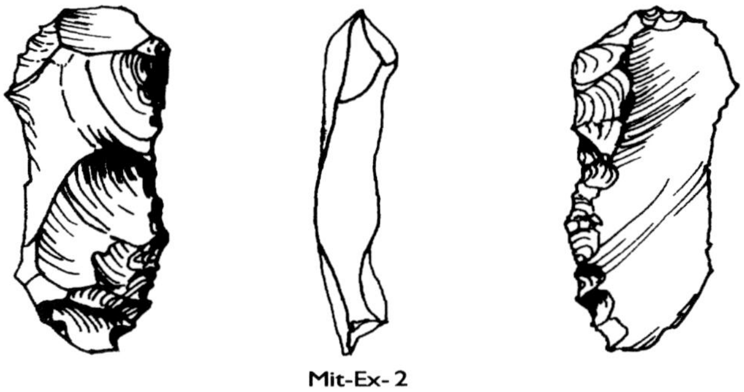

Mit-Ex-2

Plate 34 *See Catalog for dimensions*

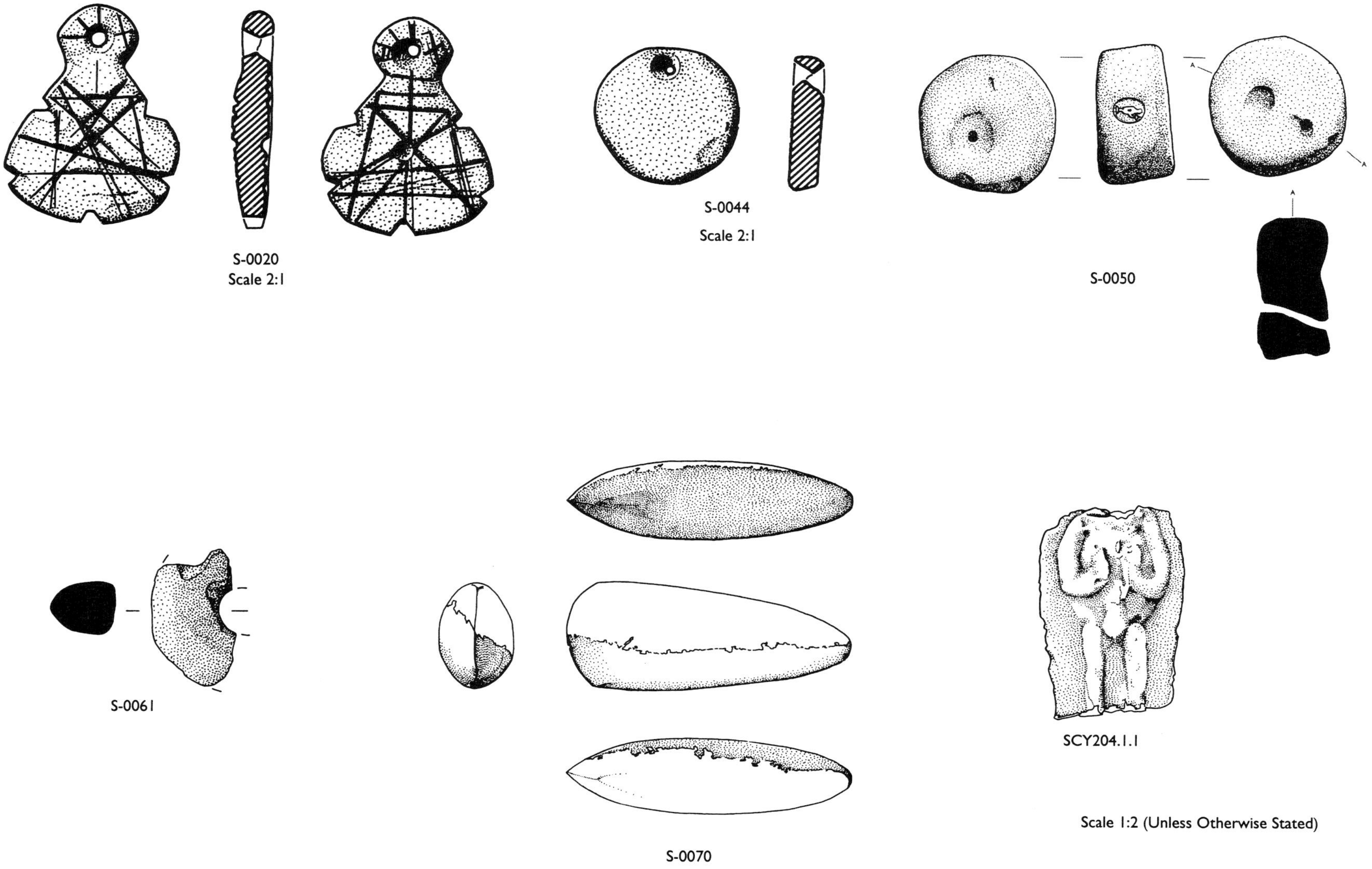

S-0050

SCY204.1.1

Scale 1:2 (Unless Otherwise Stated)

S-0044
Scale 2:1

S-0070

S-0020
Scale 2:1

S-0061

Plate 35 *See Catalog for dimensions*

6

DIACHRONIC LANDSCAPE HISTORY

In this chapter, we attempt to situate SCSP's work within the long-term geopolitical and cultural history of Cyprus and the Eastern Mediterranean. The emphasis on a diachronic study necessarily leads us into chronological periods when the course of Cypriot fortunes in the wider world may have influenced directly the settlement patterns and exploitation of resources in the survey area. These discussions use literary (where relevant) and archaeological sources to illustrate the geopolitical and communications background of Cyprus, and so help to map the SCSP region more effectively in each major time period. Wherever possible, we provide a complementary discussion of survey results pertaining to each chronological grouping, with direct reference to period maps showing the distribution of cultural material and POSIs over the survey area and their relation to known topographical features—for example, arable land, mineral resources, and communication foci.

6.1 Prehistoric Landscapes

(plate XLVII)

A. Bernard Knapp

PRE-POTTERY NEOLITHIC

Two predominantly lithics POSIs—Politiko *Kelaïdhoni* (SCY109) and Agrokipia *Palaeokamina* (SCY102)—provide the only indicators of a Pre-Pottery Neolithic presence in the SCSP area (McCartney and Peltenburg 2000). Both have notable amounts of diagnostic chipped stone material. Situated on chalky limestone outcrops, they are likely to have been task-specific workplaces rather than permanent settlement foci. The naviform related core technology and tool types found at these POSIs—including finely denticulated glossed blades, obliquely glossed crescents, *pièces esquillés*, bi-truncated "trapezoids," backed blades, and truncated blades—show similarities with materials from sites such as Kissonerga *Mylouthkia*, Parekklisha *Shillourokambos*, and Kalavassos *Tenta* (Peltenburg et al. 2000, 2001). The suggested time range would therefore be from the early Pre-Pottery Neolithic to the beginning of the "classic" Khirokitia phase (Guilaine et al. 2000; Peltenburg et al. 2001).

POTTERY NEOLITHIC

The earliest and only Pottery Neolithic POSI in the SCSP area is Mitsero *Kriadhis* (SCY012), a light scatter of Late Neolithic Red-on-White Broadline and Red Lustrous sherds, chipped-stone, and ground-stone material found near the top of a prominent, isolated hill that forms a dramatic backdrop to the village of Mitsero. At an altitude of over 600 m, Kriadhis occupies an unusual location for an Early Prehistoric site, and today is covered by uncultivated scrub (see also Knapp et al. 1992:333). Although we might have expected Neolithic settlement to occur in an area with a major river valley (the Akaki) and several smaller streams, along with sedimentary, alluvial bottomlands (good for agriculture), and igneous pine forests (good for lithic resources, hunting, and fuel), the density of Early Prehistoric sites in the Nicosia District ranges between one per 100 km^2 and one per 900 km^2, depending on the specific period and type of site (Held 1989:481–483). Thus, it seems unremarkable that SCSP found no other indisputable evidence of Neolithic presence.

CHALCOLITHIC

The concept of regionalism and regional groupings on prehistoric Cyprus has long conditioned the ways archaeologists think about prehistoric communications, movements of people, and cultural development and change (for example, Stewart 1962:296; Merrillees 1965, 1971; Åström and Åström 1972; Peltenburg 1978; Herscher 1981). Even if regional factions existed on prehistoric Cyprus, the emphasis on regionalism has obscured our understanding of the more dynamic aspects of producing, distributing, and consuming various goods and commodities, pottery and stone tools in particular.

Bolger (1991) has proposed the existence of "stylistic production" centers already during the Middle Chalcolithic. This phenomenon of local production also seems to typify the pottery and fabrics collected at Politiko *Phournia* (SCY200). Most Phournia pottery is Late Chalcolithic but with a Middle Chalcolithic component. Some of these wares are very similar in fabric and design: for example, the Late Chalcolithic Stroke Burnished ware represents a simple modification in the technology of Middle Chalcolithic Spawled ware. Moreover, some Late

Chalcolithic fabrics with highly polished red and black surfaces (for example, Philia Red Lustrous ware) are very similar to Middle Chalcolithic Black Topped wares, with their caramel-colored and black polished surfaces. Finally, we note that the Philia Red Lustrous ware found at Phournia is also found at several other sites in the surrounding regions (for example, Ambelikou *Ayios Georgios*, Kyra *Alonia*). Other examples exist, and are discussed more fully in chapter 4.17.

During the Middle Chalcolithic, there was steady population growth along the north coast and in the center of the island, in and around the SCSP study area, and very rapid growth in the southwest; in the southeast, population decline set in (Held 1990:203–204, 1992:138). In terms of Chalcolithic society, there is some evidence of social ranking at Kissonerga *Mosphilia* (Held 1993:28–29; compare Peltenburg 1991a, 1991b, 1993) and in the cemetery complex at Souskiou *Vathyrkakas* (Christou 1989; Vagnetti 1980; Baxivani 1997:61–65). Even if incipient social hierarchies existed in the Chalcolithic (Knapp 1993), they are unlikely to represent regionally empowered elites or social stratification as much as the side effects of ecological and subsistence strategies that helped to perpetuate a successful social and economic system. A rural, essentially self-sufficient way of life would have inhibited the emergence of central places (Held 1993:28). Thus, it seems likely that environmental and social constraints maintained both the population and the social system of the Chalcolithic at the level of egalitarian, autonomous agricultural villages.

How does settlement within the north-central Troodos, that is, in the SCSP area, fit into this situation? The only other known Late Chalcolithic sites in the north-central Troodos region, situated some 15 to 20 km west of Phournia, are Kato Moni *Kambia*, Kato Moni *Monarga* and Orounda *Stavros tou Koundi* (Held 1990:14; Held in Knapp et al. 1992:332–333). These sites fit the apparent pattern quite well, both in locational and functional terms. Peltenburg (1985:1–2) argues that the Kato Moni sites form one of the characteristic settlement "clusters" of the Chalcolithic period. Thus far, Phournia appears to be an isolated settlement, but its existence may signal the possibility of a site cluster in the SCSP region as well. The situation of Phournia, in close proximity to arable land and a perennial source of water, conforms very well to the typical agricultural village of the Late Chalcolithic period. Whether one or two of the lithic sites nearby (for example, SCY019—Politiko *Kelaïdhoni,*) might have had a Chalcolithic component is difficult to determine at this stage.

Geophysical survey (resistivity) conducted at Phournia (see chapter 4.17) has revealed several circular anomalies, 4 to 7 m in diameter, all of which are consistent with archaeological features such as walls, and none of which contradict in any way the pottery concentrations noted in the gridded collection of Phournia. We may conclude that Phournia is a bona fide Chalcolithic site.

TRANSITIONAL CHALCOLITHIC TO PREHISTORIC BRONZE AGE (PreBA)

The transition from Chalcolithic to Bronze Age society on Cyprus is still poorly documented, although recent excavations at Sotira *Kaminoudhia,* Marki *Alonia,* and elsewhere have begun to alter that situation (Frankel and Webb 1996, 1998; Swiny 1985, 1989). Whereas the economy and culture of the PreBA are in several respects direct successors to those of the agriculturally based Chalcolithic culture, the material evidence for the transition is ambiguous. The publication of a suite of radiocarbon dates from the PreBA site of Sotira *Kaminoudhia* (Manning and Swiny 1994) has demonstrated that the traditional pottery and technological phases—Late Chalcolithic, Philia, Early Cypriot (EC)—are sequential (thus corroborating Dikaios 1962) and actually overlapping within the suggested sequence.

At Marki *Alonia,* a large amount of Philia pottery has been recovered from primary, undisturbed stratigraphic contexts (Frankel and Webb 1994:60–62; Webb and Frankel 1999). At Phournia, the pottery contains several elements transitional to the PreBA (for example, between Late Chalcolithic Stroke Burnished wares and the Red Lustrous ware of the Philia "facies"). Most other Philia Culture sites are clustered in the north and northwest, with a few distributed loosely around the Troodos (Knapp 1990:154, Fig. 1) or in the south and southwest. Within the SCSP area, there are two Early Cypriot (PreBA 1) POSIs: Ergates *Spileadhia* (SCY106) and Episkopio *Vrysia* (SCY107). Spileadhia is located on a fanglomerate ridge top with a limited (30 x 6 m) flat, stable surface; several Red Polished pottery sherds and a small number of lithics were found on this ridge top and eroding down both its eastern and western slopes. Vrysia, in contrast, is situated on a small knoll that enjoys commanding views of the valley and plain surrounding the Iron Age to Byzantine site of Tamassos. Much of the area surrounding the knoll has eroded away, but several visits by SCSP personnel produced a small scatter of Red Polished sherds and some lithics. The top of the knoll (41 x 43 m) is currently a plowed, fallow field.

Given that PreBA settlement location overall was bound up with proximity to arable land and perennial watercourses (Swiny 1981:80–81), Episkopio *Vrysia* and Politiko *Phournia* repeat this pattern, while the ridge top at Ergates *Spileadhia* presents an enigma, one difficult to interpret without knowing more about that POSI. Elsewhere on the island, survey work (for example, Rupp 1987; Sørensen and Rupp 1993:3–6; Swiny 1989; Todd 1989) has shown that people were on the move at this time, as settlement expanded everywhere. The earlier Chalcolithic tendency toward site clustering in the northwest, along the north coast, and around the Troodos intensified (Swiny 1989). Incipient exploitation of copper resources had begun (Knapp 1990:159–160), but PreBA society still relied on a mixed agro-pastoral economy. In such a situation, site location near the interface between the agricultural central plain and the mineral-rich foothills of the Troodos is predictable; this helps to explain, at least in part, the location of every prehistoric site within the SCSP survey area.

PROTOHISTORIC BRONZE AGE
Priscilla Keswani and A. Bernard Knapp

During the Protohistoric Bronze Age (ProBA), a number of towns engaged in copper production, and overseas trade emerged along the coasts of Cyprus. While some of these towns were located within a few kilometers of major ore deposits in the Troodos Mountains, others were situated much farther away and presumably acquired copper through inter-island communications or trade. How were such systems structured in northwestern and north central Cyprus, within and adjacent to the SCSP area? Locational factors combined with a study of artifact assemblages suggest that multiple networks of copper procurement and transport linked rural, inland settlements involved in production to coastal centers involved in refinement, manufacture, consumption, and trade.

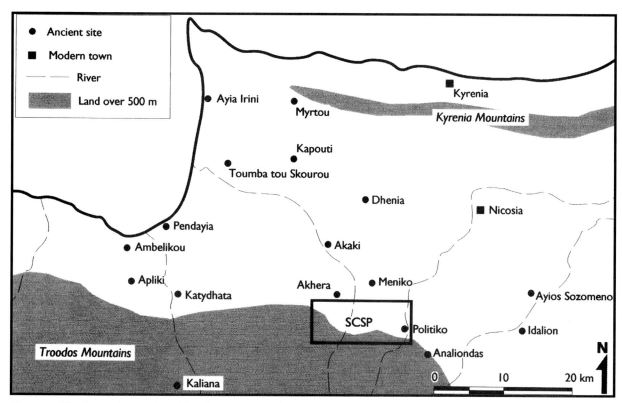

Figure 6.1 Northwest Cyprus: Protohistoric Bronze Age sites

The larger region under consideration encompasses the northern Troodos foothills and the Mesaoria plain, from Politiko in the east to Morphou Bay in the west. Several ProBA settlement and cemetery sites are known from excavation or survey in this region (figure 6.1). These include the important town at Morphou *Toumba tou Skourou*, the rural sanctuary at Myrtou *Pigadhes*, the mining village at Apliki *Karamallos*, the cemeteries of Katydhata and Pendayia *Mandres*, the cemetery and probable settlement sites at Akhera Chiflik *Paradisi*, Akaki *Trounalli*, Dhenia *Mali* and Dhenia *Kafkalla*, a possible agricultural village and rural collection center at Aredhiou *Vouppes* (SCY010), the smelting site at Politiko *Phorades* (SCY100), and a number of cemetery sites in the Politiko area—among others Politiko *Lambertis* (SCY020) and Politiko *Ayios Iraklidhios* (SCY322) (Masson 1964:202–204; Karageorghis 1965a). With the possible exception of Toumba tou Skourou, none of these could be regarded as a regional center.

Southwest of Toumba tou Skourou lie the rich ore bodies of the Mavrovouni and Skouriotissa mining districts, most likely exploited during the PreBA by the inhabitants of Ambelikou *Aletri* (Merrillees 1984), Katydhata, and Linou (Åström 1989). Even if Toumba tou Skourou exerted some sort of regional

influence, some system of local communications and contacts would have existed, perhaps mediated through a community such as Pendayia *Mandres*, strategically positioned along the main route between the Skouriotissa and Morphou areas. By the second phase of the ProBA (ca. 1400 to 1200 BC), however, Toumba tou Skourou may have acquired copper through a more formally administered transport and supply system encompassing mining villages such as Apliki *Karamallos* (Du Plat Taylor 1952).

Another chain in Toumba tou Skourou's transport links may have existed at the ProBA settlement and cemetery at Akhera (Karageorghis 1965b), only thirty minutes' walk from the mines of Agrokipia and Mitsero, and intermediary for sites such as Meniko *Mana tou Pedhon* and Akaki *Trounalli*, located along the plain between Akhera and Toumba tou Skourou. Surface finds collected by Wallace's 1979 survey in this area included typical Late Cypriot fine and utilitarian wares and numerous pithos fragments (Wallace 1982; finds examined by Keswani during the 1996 SCSP season). Material recovered from the unpublished, partially looted tombs at Akaki *Trounalli* indicates some form of contacts between Akaki, the Troodos mining district, and sites along the northwest coast of the island. Among the more unexpected finds (examined by Keswani in the Cyprus Museum and labeled "sherds") was a 9-cm-long piece of roasting conglomerate containing bits of copper, charcoal, and three smaller conglomerate fragments, perhaps indicating that some form of metallurgical activity occurred within the Akaki area.

Southeast of Akaki and Akhera, SCSP has identified two ProBA POSIs involved in the production of copper. The first, Politiko *Phorades* (SCY100), is a Bronze Age smelting site that seems to have produced more copper than required in the immediate area; it may thus have been linked into a broader, inter-island system. The second POSI, where we found Bronze Age pottery, pithoi, and a wall bracket fragment, is Aredhiou *Vouppes* (SCY010), situated on the banks of the Aloupis River drainage, where the agricultural plain interfaces with the igneous foothills. A third POSI, Aredhiou *Koladhes* (SCY001), produced a sparse scatter of Late Cypriot to Archaic sherds (perhaps the remains of a severely eroded tomb group, or else a farmstead); it is located just over 0.5 km southeast of Vouppes. The finds at Vouppes were scattered over about 2 ha, although this is by no means the definitive size of whatever type of habitation once existed there. The pithos fragments found at Vouppes came from storage vessels of diverse sizes, including some very large examples, raising the possibility that this may have been an officially managed agricultural support village that provisioned one or more mining encampments in the Troodos foothills. Webb and Frankel (1994) believe that a similar agricultural village and collection center was located at Analiondas *Palioklichia*, approximately 10 km southeast of Vouppes; such settlements may have been common elements in the transport and trading system of the ProBA. In villages like Vouppes or Palioklichia, surplus agricultural produce (grains, olive oil) would have been collected, processed, and redistributed, whether to mining sites or up the line to secondary or primary (coastal) centers (Knapp 1997).

In terms of transport and communication, we still do not know whether the sites near Politiko and Aredhiou fell within the domain of a coastal center such as Toumba tou Skourou to the west, Enkomi to the east, or some as yet unidentified local inland polity. From a topographic perspective, it is difficult to determine whether Aredhiou *Vouppes* or Politiko *Phorades* might have formed the terminal link in a chain of sites leading toward Morphou Bay. Several

ridges and small streams separate the SCSP environs from Akhera and Akaki and might have necessitated a circuitous transport route. However, both sites are easily accessible from Politiko and the modern transport route leading northeast toward Nicosia. Were these sites, then, part of a local polity centered in the Politiko area, perhaps a precursor of the Iron Age kingdom of Tamassos? While we cannot dismiss this possibility, neither SCSP nor any previous archaeological investigations in this region have encountered evidence for a Bronze Age urban center in the Politiko area. And yet a glance at the eastern part of plate XLVII reveals a veneer of ProBA pottery spread across the broad plains just northwest of Tamassos; could this indicate the manuring of fields surrounding a still undiscovered site in this area? If we are, in fact, dealing with a process of manuring, it is one that continues in this region throughout time (chapter 7.4). Although notably rich tombs of Middle Cypriot date are known at Politiko *Lambertis* (SCY020) and *Chomazoudhia* (Masson 1964:202–204), the Late Cypriot material from Politiko *Ayios Iraklidhios* Tomb 6, the only well-documented ProBA tomb in this region (Karageorghis 1965a), indicates a dearth of higher order valuables in this intensively investigated region. In other words, the Politiko-Aredhiou area seems to have participated in unequal exchange relationships with one or more centers located many kilometers distant.

Wallace (1982) suggested that the Politiko region may have been oriented to the southeast, that is, toward sites such as Idalion, Klavdhia, or Kition. This too would have entailed the negotiation of rugged terrain, although the general trend of the landscape, and of the Yialias and Alykos river valleys, lies toward the southeast, from the easternmost end of the SCSP area (see also Leonard 2000). Alternatively, or in addition, the Politiko area may have been linked to Enkomi via Nicosia *Ayia Paraskevi* and Sinda, a lengthy but perhaps less arduous journey over the Mesaoria plain. Peltenburg (1996) recently suggested that Enkomi exerted considerable influence throughout northwestern and north-central Cyprus at least as early as 1700 BC and established a security system of fortified sites along the northeastern flanks of the Troodos (ostensibly to procure copper) and along the southern flanks of the Kyrenia Range (ostensibly to prevent north coast sites from obtaining copper). However, none of the fortresses along the southern Kyrenia range have ever been excavated, and there is as yet no real evidence to link them with Enkomi. From the perspective of distance, it might be more plausible to postulate a link between the Kyrenia fortresses and Toumba tou Skourou. There is, of course, also the possibility that the entire region under discussion may have fallen within two or more overlapping transport and communications systems, one focused on Toumba tou Skourou or some other center of the northwest, and another focused on Enkomi or some other center in the southeast (that is, Kition or Hala Sultan Tekke).

OVERVIEW

One critical question that emerges from detailed consideration of the diachronic landscape is: why do we find so little prehistoric material in the SCSP survey universe? Several recent surveys in southern (lowland) Greece also indicate that prehistoric sites appear far less frequently than those of later period, especially Greco-Roman and Medieval date (Bintliff et al. 1999). Moreover, prehistoric surface artifact densities are much lower than those of later dates. Cherry et al. (1991:222–223, Fig. 9.7) concurred that prehistoric surface materials may be overlooked in a landscape dominated by the dense, off-site spread of sherds from later historical periods. The inevitable demographic conclusion has been that prehistoric populations must have been much lower than those inferred—on the basis of much larger amounts of surface material—for historic times. While there is little doubt that the pre-Neolithic through Chalcolithic (Early Prehistoric) population of Cyprus was smaller by comparison with that of later eras, the large town centers of the ProBA equalled or occasionally surpassed in size many towns of the Greco-Roman period. Thus, it is difficult to accept the demographic implications of Bintliff et al. (1999) for the Cypriot Bronze Age.

Bintliff et al. (1999) conclude (1) that the landscape (of southern Greece) holds an unidentified multitude of smaller, infrequently occupied, prehistoric sites; (2) that *vestigial* surface traces are all we can expect from small prehistoric settlements; and (3) that we should regard the often quite limited number of prehistoric sherds from later, higher density sites as another signpost to a prehistoric settlement. In at least three situations that Bintliff et al. cite, the use of more intensive methods

than they routinely practiced resulted in the discovery of discrete concentrations of prehistoric surface remains or, conversely and of equal importance, in the ability to determine where prehistoric surface remains did not survive.

In SCSP's case, and with respect to the first point, it seems unlikely that the landscape as it exists today—given erosional and other, taphonomic processes—has any undetected multitude of prehistoric sites. We have nine "prehistoric" POSIs in the SCSP region and several other POSIs that contain prehistoric sherds; if we had more reliable lithic data, this number would certainly increase throughout the survey area. Regarding their second point, in at least three different POSIs (SCY010—Aredhiou *Vouppes*; SCY100—Politiko *Phorades*; and SCY200—Politiko *Phournia*), the amount of surface material is anything but vestigial, even though two of these are nothing more than farmsteads or at the most small settlements, while the third is a limited-scale smelting site. Indeed we might not expect to find more Chalcolithic or Bronze Age sites in our 65 km² survey area (as noted earlier, Early Prehistoric site densities in the Nicosia district, as discovered by extensive survey, range from 1 to 9 per 100 km²). Concerning their third point, in three different SIAs (3, 6, 9) and one POSI (SCY209), we find a thin but perceptible spread of prehistoric sherds. In SIA 6 and SCY209, we suspect that the great density of sherds from most later periods is related to manuring or similar activity in the landscape rather than habitation (note, however, that the southeast edge of SIA 6 is also the edge of the site of Tamassos). SIA 9 contains only one ProBA sherd and this in a context with very heavy densities of Medieval to Modern sherds. SIA 3 is best characterized as an industrial landscape, with dense concentrations of Late Roman (to which the slag heap at Kouloupakhis has been dated by 14C analyses) and Medieval to Modern sherds. Here it is possible that we are dealing with some sort of prehistoric habitation, although we would not hazard a guess regarding the type.

Even with our most intensive efforts, surface survey projects are nothing more than sampling exercises; thus we regard the accumulated surface record of the SCSP survey universe as a reasonably accurate reflection of what is there, given our methodology and the ways in which we conducted our fieldwork. Our inability to recognize or define by period plain or undecorated wares is an issue that we acknowledge and one that must be addressed by other means, for example detailed fabric studies including petrographic analysis, in the attempt to establish and refine chronological markers (SCSP's chronotypes).

Therefore, although we would maintain that the accumulated surface record of the SCSP area, as we have defined it, is reasonably accurate, there remain many questions the record cannot address. On the positive side, and with respect to prehistoric material (Neolithic to Geometric), we believe we can present a much more accurate picture of habitation and land use in this area than ever existed prior to the inception of SCSP.

The map of prehistoric POSIs and pottery densities (plate XLVII) reveals that Early Prehistoric material is restricted primarily to the easternmost sectors of the SCSP survey area. With respect to the Protohistoric Bronze Age (Late Cypriot), this situation appears to coincide with the location of other Late Bronze Age sites and material found mainly to the north and northwest of the SCSP region and may be associated with a primary communications route through this region. In this light, it may be noted that the area around Mitsero (and approximately 1 km to the west) has been, until recent times, a veritable terminus of traffic from Nicosia. According to residents of the nearest villages to the west (for example Ayia Marina), only a few kilometers distant, they had no contacts with Mitsero and instead traveled to and from Nicosia by a different, more northerly route across another plain (but see the map in Gunnis 1936, which shows a track leading westward from Mitsero). Moreover, the southwestern quarter of the survey area is heavily dominated by pine forest, where it has always proven difficult to identify sites of any period.

With respect to Early Prehistoric materials, settlement location and land use patterns appear to conform to our expectations of Late Chalcolithic, Philia, and Early Cypriot sites over the rest of the island. With the exception of Pottery Neolithic Mitsero *Kriadhis* (SCY012) and Prehistoric Bronze Age Ergates *Spileadhia* (SCY106), all prehistoric sites are located immediately on or within 100 m of a water source, and, with the exception of the smelter at Politiko *Phorades* (SCY100), all other prehistoric POSIs are situated in the sedimentary zone and were most likely farmsteads or small agricultural villages.

For these small, prehistoric agricultural sites, the geological significance of the igneous-sedimentary zone transecting the SCSP area in a northwest-southeast direction is threefold:

1) The agricultural prominence of POSIs lying in the sedimentary zone on or near annual watercourses (perhaps perennial in the cases of the Akaki and Kouphos Rivers) is clear and establishes a pattern that unfolds on a much larger scale in later periods;

2) The industrial prominence of POSIs lying in or near the lower pillow lavas of the igneous zone is best exemplified by Politiko *Phorades* (SCY100) and is repeated on a larger scale during subsequent eras;

3) The existence of POSIs related to the production or consumption of chipped stone is based on easy access to the prevalent types of lithic raw materials, whether in the form of river-transported igneous rocks, or as chert embedded in the Lefkara Chalk Formation that fringes the upper pillow lavas throughout the SCSP area (Held, in Knapp et al. 1992:328).

Both the lithic and metallurgical resources of the igneous zone were exploited throughout the long history of production and settlement in the SCSP region. Within the SCSP area, there are three POSIs that have major lithic components (SCY019—Politiko *Kelaïdhoni*; SCY102—Agrokipia *Palaeokamina*; SCY212—Politiko *Gastres*); up to twenty further POSIs have notable amounts of lithics. Although SCSP has been more successful in dating archaeometallurgical POSIs than those comprised exclusively or primarily of chipped-stone material, this may simply reflect the broad archaeometallurgical expertise and interests of SCSP team members. Although we always maintained constant input from our lithic specialists, the complexity of Cypriot lithic studies precludes more definitive interpretations at this stage.

6.2 Geometric to Classical Landscapes
(plate XLVIII)
Michael Given and Joanna S. Smith

INTRODUCTION: CITY-KINGDOMS

The study of the Geometric to Classical landscapes of Cyprus has revolved almost entirely around the study of its city-kingdoms. Work has focused on the urban sites: the extensive necropoleis, the sanctuaries, the elite structures, and city walls. Rural sanctuaries are the only extra-urban areas that have attracted the attention of excavators. Ever since early excavations in the 1860s, the stone and terra-cotta sculptures found at these sanctuaries have been their primary attraction. Tamassos, just beyond the eastern edge of the survey area, is a typical example. During the 1970s, the Deutsche Tamassos-Expedition of the Deutschen Archäologischen Institut in Berlin examined the Cypro-Archaic elite tombs at Politiko *Chomazoudhia*, on the northern edge of the city, and excavated the adjacent sanctuary and various other tombs in the area (Buchholz and Untiedt 1996). Apart from some sporadic investigation of already known rural sanctuaries and traces of copper mining, the kingdom of Tamassos was treated as an all but unoccupied desert surrounding its urban oasis.

A further problem with the study of Geometric to Classical landscapes in Cyprus is that even the cities are known only through their tombs, sanctuaries, and walls. Little is known of urban domestic architecture, let alone settlements in the countryside (Reyes 1994:25–26, 45–46). SCSP's approach aimed to address both of these shortcomings by focusing on landscape activities such as industry, agriculture, settlement, religion, and ideology, as well as anything else that the analysis of intensive survey data might reveal. The wealth of material recorded by SCSP allowed us to examine not only the city and its kingdom but also the social and economic relations that incorporated them into a single human landscape.

POTTERY ANALYSIS

Our understanding of diachronic change during the Geometric to Classical periods within the SCSP area is reliant upon analyzing the material culture found in the landscape. This understanding is limited because of the difficulties involved in assigning precise dates to much of the surface material, that is, pottery. Often the sherds are quite worn and the majority are undecorated plain and coarse wares, usually in the form of (nondiagnostic) body sherds.

The current typology of Cypro-Geometric through Cypro-Classical pottery (Gjerstad 1948:48–91, 186–206, 240–318; Gjerstad 1960) is a masterful effort, based on the finds of the Swedish Cyprus Expedition (SCE) at a time when there was no overall

typology for Iron Age pottery. Though it remains a standard, it was not meant by the excavator to be the last word on material from those periods. In creating his typology, Gjerstad made it clear that much work remained to be done to determine the precise nature and sequence of the forms, fabrics, and decorations of pottery from each of the city-kingdoms on the island. Also he was aware that there were, as he called them, "local pottery schools" (1960:106); however, at the time of the SCE Iron Age publications, he stated explicitly that those regional differences did not form part of the basis for the typology he created.

Although there have been emendations to the typology laid out by Gjerstad (for example, Adelman 1976; Birmingham 1963; Demetriou 1978), its fundamental format and source material remain as they were when published in 1948. The difficulty of using the current typology to identify survey pottery is well known (for example, Sørenson 1993:37) and extends also to excavated finds on the island. The typological sequence relies more heavily on surface treatment and decoration than on shape (more helpful when studying sherd material). Plain ware is designated as Plain White, not allowing for the difference between vessels with a plain surface (called Plain ware by SCSP) versus those with a slipped or otherwise whitened surface (called Plain White by SCSP). Coarse wares are not included in the chronological sequence, making the narrow chronological classification of cooking wares and large storage vessels such as pithoi particularly challenging.

However, based on work with stratified Iron Age pottery found in the sanctuary of Polis *Peristeries* (Smith 1997:93, n. 3), reanalysis of the SCE typology (Smith 2000), with reference to recently excavated and published stratified material (especially finds from Kourion [Buitron-Oliver 1996; Oliver 1996] and Kition [Salles 1983]), it is clear that the general sequence of shapes and decorations currently used to identify Iron Age Cypriot pottery is useful in defining the more diagnostic sherds found by SCSP. Rims in particular could be defined within a narrow chronological range, as could some decorated pieces, partial profiles, and unusually distinctive handles and bases. Most material—body sherds, handles, and bases—could not be identified narrowly but appeared to be most similar to sherds that could be categorized as Archaic or Classical. The negligible amount of identifiable Geometric pottery made it impossible to ascertain how much of the remaining material might derive from that period. Imported material from Greece (mainly of Black Glazed pottery) could be identified quite narrowly, given the precise typologies of black and plain pottery, particularly from the Agora in Athens (Sparkes and Talcott 1970; Rotroff 1997). Nothing definitely of Phoenician origin was identified, which is interesting in view of the Phoenician hold over Tamassos from Kition in the fourth century BC. In contrast, there is ample evidence of Phoenician material at Idalion during the period of Phoenician control there (Hadjicosti 1997).

Regional differences, however, are crucial to understanding the pottery, and it remains to outline some details of all pottery types from Iron Age Cyprus, from site specific shapes, decorations, and fabrics, to regional styles, to island-wide groupings. Once these groupings are better defined, material from the SCSP area will probably prove to be most similar to stratified finds from Tamassos, which have appeared only very generally in publications (for example, Buchholz 1978, 1985a; Buchholz and Untiedt 1996). Finds from tombs in the area (for example, Hadjisavvas 1978), unpublished finds from the Akhera survey (Wallace 1982) and the sanctuary at Meniko (V. Karageorghis 1977) also form a basis for comparison.

SCSP chronotypes were created based on the most diagnostic surface treatments (wares) (for example, White Painted, Red Slip, Plain ware, and Plain White), fabrics (for example, Soft Red-Orange, Cooking Ware, and Coarse), shapes (for example, Amphora, Greek Amphora, Medium Deep Bowl, and Wide Shallow Bowl), and body parts (for example, Double Rolled Strap Handle and Rolled Lug Handle). We intended that all chronotypes should reflect the narrowest chronological date for any given piece. For example, if a sherd were clearly cooking ware but had a shape identifiable as a wide shallow bowl of Archaic date, the piece was identified as WSBAR (Wide Shallow Bowl [WSB] of Archaic shape [AR]) rather than a type of cooking ware (for example, no. 2105.5.1). Unlike later pottery found by SCSP, the great variability among Iron Age wares, as well as the already noted formative stages of the typology overall, made it difficult to assign chronotypes and achieve the most precise dating unless several period categories overlapped with different wares and shapes in various different combinations. Some-

times this led to a narrow date for one piece, such as a Bichrome V ware bowl rim (no. 1733.10.1) assigned the chronotype BIAR—Bichrome (BI) and Archaic (AR). Other Bichrome bowls could be identified only as Iron Age, in which case they were assigned the chronotype BIGAC—Bichrome (BI) and Geometric, Archaic, or Classical (GAC).

The study of the SCSP material has revealed very little definitively Geometric pottery. The earliest finds date to the Cypro-Geometric III period, although some pieces may ultimately be assigned to earlier Cypro-Geometric I or II periods. Pieces of Cypro-Geometric III date include possibly one piece of fine ware (FWG) from unit 3270 (1 km northeast of Klirou), one CG III (or conceivably CA I) White Painted skyphos rim from unit 3576 (the gossan in SIA 7), and no. 1034.2.1, a CG III Black-on-Red fragment of a hemispherical bowl (or possibly CA I). More common are pieces that could range in date from Cypro-Geometric III to Cypro-Archaic II (for example, no. 4041.14.1 from SIA 3; no. 1629.2.1 from SIA 7). This pattern fits in general terms with published material from Tamassos, where the earliest material, though sparse, dates to CG III. Perhaps two tombs have material that may be CG III rather than CA I, and only one published tomb has a secure CG III burial period (Hadjisavvas 1978:127–131). Two radiocarbon dates from Agrokipia *Kriadhis* (SIA 1) give a ninth-century BC date for the ore roasting, which would be contemporary roughly with the beginnings of Cypro-Geometric III.

Most of the pottery dates to the Archaic and/or Classical periods. As with the possibly Geometric material, many sherds were not diagnostic of a narrow chronological period and were categorized as Geometric, Archaic, or Classical (GAC, which accounts for 194 sherds) or Archaic or Classical (AC, which accounts for 2851 sherds). More narrowly defined are 632 Archaic sherds and 509 Classical sherds. A further 265 could be anything from Archaic to Late Roman and are classified as Historical Antiquity (HA). In addition there are 9010 completely unidentified sherds, some of which may one day be definable as Iron Age. Clearly this situation can improve only with further analyses of forms and fabrics and by the full publication of stratified material from controlled excavations elsewhere. Lumping together several of these period groupings, most usefully Archaic, Classical, GAC, and AC, using the SCSP GIS we can examine general trends in the distribution of material across the landscape for the Geometric to Classical periods as a whole (see plate XLVIII).

INDUSTRY

Of the six surviving ancient copper processing locations in the SCSP survey area, we know from stratified pottery and radiocarbon dating that at least three operated during the ninth to fifth centuries BC. The early date of much of this activity is noteworthy. The ore roasting and beneficiation site at Agrokipia *Kriadhis* (SCY022; see chapter 4.1) has two dates securely in the ninth century BC and another in the eighth to fifth centuries BC. The modern open-cast mine has cut through several mining galleries; presumably some of these will have dated to the Geometric and Archaic periods, as roasting was generally carried out immediately adjacent to the mines.

An ore-processing site just below the mining adits at Politiko *Kokkinorotsos* (SIA 7) was in use at some point during the eighth to fifth centuries BC; smelting as well as roasting was carried out (SCY116; see chapter 4.7). If the extensive slag piles stretching to the north and west of the dated section belong to the same period, this area was engaged in copper production on a notable scale, a mere 4 km from Tamassos. Mitsero *Kokkinoyia* (SIA 11), judging by the size of the slag heaps, produced copper at a similar scale, although it is dated less precisely by stratified pottery to the Archaic to Classical periods (chapter 4.11).

Our knowledge of the ownership or control of these resources is constrained by the lack of relevant sources. It is generally believed that the contemporary city-state kings were absolute monarchs, being both heads of state and leaders of the army; in the case of Paphos they were also the high priests (Hill 1940:114; Maier 1989:377–380; Stylianou 1992:402). Most likely they also owned the mineral resources and forests within their kingdoms, both of which would have provided substantial revenues (Spyridakis 1972:119). Their control over the forests is reflected in a passage by Theophrastus:

> For instance in Cyprus the kings used not to cut the trees, both because they took great care of them and husbanded them, and also because the transport of the timber was difficult. The timbers cut for Demetrius' ship of eleven banks of oars were thirteen fathoms long, and the timbers themselves were without knots and smooth, as well as of marvellous length.... (Theophrastus, *Enquiry into Plants*, 5.8.1)

Whether the kings of Cyprus were indeed so environmentally aware is hard to judge, but there is no question that the forests were important sources of charcoal for the copper industry. There are no direct references to royal control over mineral resources.

Another important industry taking place in the SCSP landscape during the Archaic and Classical periods was the manufacture of pottery. At Politiko *Ayios Mnason* (SIA 6), apparently in the same area as the Archaic/Classical sanctuary, iron-rich clay was used to produce a high-fired, reduced fabric with a light, sometimes buff color (chapter 4.6). This gave rise to a series of wasters, warped and vitrified pieces, and possibly vitrified kiln material. Other over-fired fragments had clearly been cut or sliced before firing and may have been parts of failed vessels that were cut up to support other vessels in the kiln. The location of this pottery workshop just beyond the city wall of Tamassos is worthy of note, as it may have been associated with the sanctuary.

A second pottery workshop in Klirou *Manastirka* (SIA 2) was very different in character. The clay used was also rich in iron, but it was low-fired to produce a soft and very friable fabric (Soft Red-Orange, or SRO). Many of the table, cooking, and storage wares found in SIA 2 were made of this fabric, even though it was so soft that in some cases it might have been impractical for use. Once again, this pottery manufacture was taking place near a sanctuary, where many of the vessels and one of the figurines were made from the same fabric. Was the pottery workshop mainly supplying nonfunctional products for symbolic use and dedication in the sanctuary? The SRO fabric is found elsewhere in the survey area but in much smaller quantities than in SIA 2.

Other industries in the SCSP landscape can only be presumed. The sanctuary architecture at Chomazoudhia, the city walls of Tamassos and, above all, the elite CA II tombs obviously required skilled stone masons and sculptors as well as quarry workers and builders, although SCSP found no traces of quarrying. The discovery of three loomweights from Klirou *Manastirka* (no. S-0050), Malounda *Panayia Khrysopandanassa* (no. 1281.29.1), and the settlement at Politiko *Phorades 3* (no. S-0061) make it clear that people were weaving in these areas. Two of these weights were found on plowed land, which means there could be fifteen times as many within the plow zone, quite apart from those lying undisturbed by the plow (Ammerman 1985:37). The loomweight from SIA 2 has a stamped impression, perhaps for personal identification or possibly as a marker for the weaver to insert a special weave (chapter 4.2).

AGRICULTURE

Little is known about agricultural practice and organization in the Geometric to Classical periods in Cyprus, largely because of the focus on tombs, elite urban buildings, and the artwork found within them. Sculpted figures found in sanctuaries frequently carry fruit, model oxen, or goats and occasionally ears of wheat, presumably as offerings (for example, di Cesnola 1885: nos. 112, 126, 806). The pyres from the fourth-century BC cemetery at Salamis *Cellarka* have remains of fruits such as grapes, olives, and almonds as well as pulses, wheat, and barley (Karageorghis 1970:170–202, 295–298, 318–335). Closer to the SCSP survey area, the sanctuary at Chomazoudhia on the edge of Tamassos contained extensive remains of animal bones around the altar, mostly sheep, goat, and oxen (Buchholz 1973:343–344; 1978:171) and bowls containing the remains of olives and grain (Buchholz 1978:169–70, 219). Such indicators of ceremonial activity within the Archaic and Classical kingdoms suggest that people both dedicated and sacrificed the agropastoral products of the region.

Of the various patterns discernible in the distribution of Archaic to Classical pottery across the SCSP area (plate XLVIII), some probably represent agricultural activity. The heavy concentration in the east is due partly to the rural sanctuary at Ayios Mnason (SCY365) and partly to location at the edge of Tamassos (SIA 6; see chapter 4.6). The scatters in SIA 7 are most likely associated with copper production. A pattern more likely to derive from agricultural activity is the broad but light scatter across the alluvial plains northwest of Politiko (the northeast corner of the survey area), east and southeast of Klirou, and perhaps west and southwest of Malounda. These units typically have a pottery index of 500 to 1000. In geomorphological terms most of this area is relatively stable Holocene alluvium (plate I), so the data are more meaningful than those from the heavily eroded southeast of the survey area. It is also good arable land, currently extensively used for barley, and to a lesser extent for olives.

If, as seems likely, these low-density but broad scatters of material represent manuring (chapter 7.4), then agricultural production must have been intensive in the plains nearest Tamassos and in some of the alluvial plain of the Akaki river. Transect 517.0 running just east of Klirou into SIA 2 is particularly clear: Apart from two major density peaks, the whole of this fertile plain has a light, even "carpet" of material. It is interesting that production in the Akaki valley is centered along the eastern parts of the plain. The two transects southwest of Klirou are only partly eroded, and block survey northwest of Kalokhorio (on stable alluvium) indicates that this area was intensively exploited in the Medieval to Modern periods. Neither of these areas revealed any notable amount of pottery from the Archaic to Classical periods. The same situation applies on the western side of the Akaki, where apart from a couple of scatters within easy reach of the Malounda river crossing, there is very little evidence of any activity.

Another pattern of pottery distribution is visible in the plain northwest of Politiko, where two clear density peaks enhance the main concentration around Tamassos and the adjacent sanctuary. These stand out very clearly from the low-density background (probably the result of manuring); the larger of the two almost reaches an impressive pottery index of 10,000. The same phenomenon is clear in the fertile alluvium east and southeast of Klirou where two very clear density peaks, both with a pottery index of about 5000, stand out from a similar level of background material. One of these is Klirou *Manastirka* (SIA 2; see chapter 4.2).

In the absence of any structural remains, it is hard to interpret these density peaks with any certainty; indeed, most were discovered only by means of GIS analysis of the pottery density rather than by observing anything particularly noteworthy in the field. Recalling the pattern of dispersed farmsteads spread across much of southern Greece during this same period (Alcock 1993:48), we might suggest that the alluvial plains in the SCSP area were exploited by people living on dispersed farmsteads, represented by our sudden and limited density peaks, with intensive production and manuring in the land between them. The clear eastern focus of this activity is no doubt based on the quality of the land and its proximity to Tamassos.

SETTLEMENT

Because of the relative rarity of diagnostic tile from this period, it is hard to distinguish settlement from other forms of intensive activity in the landscape. The eastern part of Politiko Ayios Mnason (SIA 6) was of considerable use here as a control, because we knew that the city of Tamassos extended more or less up to this area (chapter 4.6). One unit at the eastern edge of Ayios Mnason has revealed a level of pottery (pottery index of 11,000) which, combined with other data, indicates the presence of a settlement. This impression is confirmed by the Roman period in the same area, where similar levels of pottery are combined with large amounts of tile. The other density peak in SIA 6, however, which has even larger figures, is actually a sanctuary, not a settlement.

In identifying settlements the density figures must be viewed in conjunction with the nature of the pottery discovered. The pottery indices for the Archaic to Classical units at Politiko *Kokkinorotsos* (SIA 7; see chapter 4.7) are never more than 5000, but it seems clear that the pottery derives not from sanctuaries or tombs but from settlement, domestic, or even industrial activities. This applies particularly to Politiko *Phorades* 3 (SCY123), which has tiles, walls, a loomweight, and lamp fragments. Along with a wide range of wares for storing, cooking, eating, and drinking, these items represent use of this area from the Archaic to Hellenistic periods. Settlement areas identified in this way also include materials from Agrokipia *Kriadhis* (SIA 1; see chapter 4.1). If the finds there stem from a settlement located near the mining area, it would have been of a different type from that found in Politiko *Phorades* 3. The high percentage of imported Greek pottery outweighs the number of Geometric to Classical period imports in all other parts of the SCSP landscape, suggesting that Agrokipia *Kriadhis* was the locus of some kind of elite activity in the Archaic to Classical periods.

SACRED LANDSCAPES

Rural sanctuaries in Archaic and Classical Cyprus have been examined since the days of di Cesnola and Ohnefalsch-Richter (for example, Ohnefalsch-Richter 1893:1–28; Gjerstad et al. 1935:642–824). Any attempt at analyzing their distribution, however, has been limited by the accidents of discovery and by the lack of landscape context (for example, Given 1991:48–55; Wright 1992). SCSP's intensive survey led to the discovery of two rural sanctuaries; when combined with the four already known in the area we can propose a more systematic and contextual analysis of sacred landscapes for Archaic and Classical Cyprus.

Klirou *Mazovounos* (SCY211; see chapter 4.2) consists of a scatter of friable pottery and two figurine fragments on a small hill looking down a valley that was clearly exploited agriculturally in the Archaic to Classical periods. The other sanctuary in the survey area, Politiko *Ayios Mnason* 3 (SCY365; see chapter 4.6), is considerably larger, with a broad scatter of terra-cotta figurine and statue fragments, perhaps with an associated pottery workshop. It lies about 500 m west of Tamassos, on top of a rise overlooking the rich and intensively exploited Tamassos plain.

Other rural sanctuaries have been excavated or noted in the region surrounding the SCSP survey area (figure 6.2). Kalokhorio *Zithkionas* is a scatter of terra-cottas, including chariots and riders, on a high saddle overlooking the Klirou *Malounda* alluvial plain to the north (compare Gunnis 1936:244). Two "Ashtart" figurines in the Cyprus Museum come from Philani *Petalloudhes*, which may be a sanctuary (Buchholz 1978:168; Buchholz and Untiedt 1996:52). Statues and figurines made of bronze, limestone, and terra-cotta were discovered at Politiko *Mialathi*, in the current bed of the River Pedhiaios (Ohnefalsch-Richter 1893:10–11; Buchholz 1978:210–215; Buchholz and Untiedt 1996:46–47). The well-known sanctuary of Reshef/Apollo at Pera *Frangissa*, excavated by Ohnefalsch-Richter in 1885, lies on a terrace above a stream bed in the upper part of a small valley (Ohnefalsch-Richter 1893:7–10, 330–332; Buchholz 1991; Given 2001). Meniko *Litharkes* lies on a flat river terrace in open alluvial land, close to the banks of the River Akaki (Karageorghis 1977:17, Pl. I).

Two topographic patterns characterize the location of these sanctuaries. Mazovounos, Ayios Mnason, and Zithkionas lie on a hill or knoll with a view over agricultural land, rather than being in the agricultural land itself or on a high mountain top (compare Wright 1992:275–276). They overlook agricultural land that we know was exploited in the Archaic and Classical period. Frangissa, Mialathi, and Litharkes lie in valley bottoms close to rivers or streams, though still adjacent to good agricultural land. Dedications of agricultural produce were made in some sanctu-

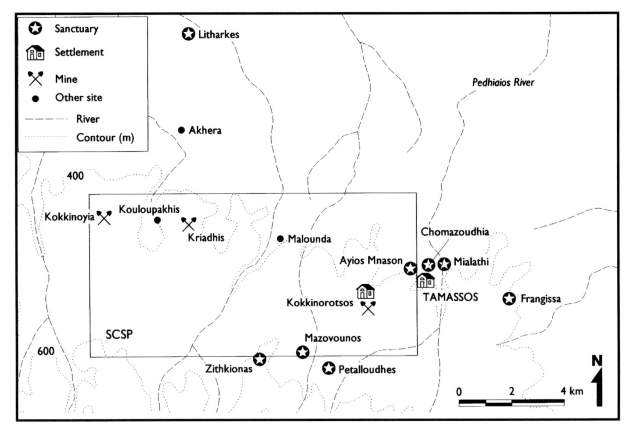

Figure 6.2 SCSP and surrounding area: Geometric to Classical sites

aries, especially those dedicated to the Cypriot goddess such as at Chomazoudhia. Other sanctuaries show evidence for storage of agricultural products (Smith 1997:91). Such functions perhaps help to explain this common feature of a sanctuary's location.

Mialathi and Ayios Mnason are within 500 m of the city, a pattern that is much more evident at Idalion, where eight sanctuaries ring the city, many of them on local high points overlooking agricultural land (Ohnefalsch-Richter 1893:5–6, 15–18; Given 1991:48–49). One pattern that clearly does not apply is any association between rural sanctuaries and copper production: of the seven sanctuaries in figure 6.2, only Petalloudhes lies in or adjacent to the pillow lavas, and there are none in the known Archaic to Classical copper production areas. The apparent association between figurines and copper production at Mathiati *Mavrovouni* is clearly not a general pattern, as it seems to be in the Bronze Age (Knapp 1986b; 1996a). Even there the association is uncertain, as the figurines merely underlie the slag, and so could be much earlier, even deriving from tombs in the area (Karageorghis 1984:964–965).

CONCLUSION: CITIES AND KINGDOMS

The SCSP landscape during the Archaic and Classical periods was heavily used and exploited, with the mining, roasting, smelting, and transportation of copper ore, intensive agricultural production in the alluvial plains within 6 km of Tamassos, rural sanctuaries with their associated activities such as dedications and processions, and people living in farmsteads or small settlements. Much of this activity clearly revolved around the urban center at Tamassos, which controlled the region politically. With their ostentatious tombs the local elite clearly benefited from the agricultural and mining activities that took place in the landscape. The city-kingdoms of the Archaic and Classical periods consisted of kingdoms as well as cities, in spite of the site-based perspective of much archaeological research.

The relationship between agricultural and industrial activities is very evident in the sanctuary of Politiko *Chomazoudhia*, just inside the city walls of

Tamassos. Not only were agropastoral products such as wheat, olives, and goats dedicated to the goddess here but also the products of hunting in the countryside—the animal bones included game such as hares, birds, and fallow deer (Buchholz 1973:343–344; 1978:171). The jugs and amphorae were presumably not dedicated as vessels but instead held wine and olive oil. The sanctuary lamps (Buchholz 1974:565) certainly needed oil. Even copper from the more remote countryside was dedicated to the goddess: There were workshops immediately adjacent to the sanctuary, and slag was found around the altar in the main courtyard of the sanctuary (Buchholz 1978:165–166; 1985a:242; Tatton-Brown 1985:71). Judging from its size, wealth, and position, this sanctuary was the principal one of Tamassos, but its religious significance clearly derived from the surrounding landscape.

6.3 Hellenistic to Roman Landscapes

(plate XLIX)

R. Scott Moore

HELLENISTIC PERIOD (323–100 BC)

When the Ptolemies regained control of Cyprus from the Antigonids following the death of Alexander the Great in 323 BC, they made the city of Nea Paphos their new administrative center (Fejfer 1995:22). Continuing the trend begun in the Classical period and seen throughout the eastern Mediterranean at this time (Lund 1993:141), the island continued to prosper. Some coastal areas, like the Akamas, underwent their first extensive land use during the Hellenistic period (Fejfer 1995:22) while others, like the Palaepaphos region, saw the continuation of growth that had begun in the Classical period (Sørensen 1993:185–197). Such growth and prosperity, however, is not apparent in the SCSP area; instead there seems to be a substantial drop-off from Classical times.

Within the SCSP area, the field teams discovered only a small amount of Hellenistic pottery, about 1% of the total sherds discovered during the survey. Two-thirds of the material found consisted of fine wares, and the vast majority of these were Hellenistic Black Glaze sherds (table 6.1). Very few cooking ware or coarse ware sherds were identified. The Hellenistic sherds were spread fairly evenly throughout the SCSP area, with the exception of concentrations in SIA 3 (Mitsero *Kouloupakhis*), SIA 6 (Politiko *Ayios Mnason*), and SCY101 (Politiko *Phorades 2*) (plate XLIX). Since SIA 3 and SIA 6

Table 6.1 Hellenistic, Early Roman, and Late Roman periods: fine wares and total sherds

Hellenistic		Early Roman		Late Roman	
Fish plates	2	Cypriot Sigillata	68	African Red Slip	71
Black Glaze	108	Eastern Sigillata A	26	Çandarli	6
		Eastern Sigillata B	14	Cypriot Red Slip	227
				Egyptian Red Slip	5
		(Red Slips, Hl-ER)	30	Phocaean ware	62
				Red Slips, unknown	15
TOTAL fine wares	110	TOTAL fine wares	108	TOTAL fine wares	386
TOTAL Hellenistic	204	TOTAL Early Roman	478	TOTAL Late Roman	2111

were close to well-established settlements near Mitsero and Politiko, elevated sherd counts are not surprising. The most interesting point about the Hellenistic sherds is their relationship to the preceding Classical and following Early and Late Roman periods. The number of Hellenistic sherds in any given area is almost always significantly smaller than that of both the Classical and Roman periods. Since sites containing Hellenistic pottery also revealed both Classical and Roman pottery, it seems likely that there was some continuity in settlement within the SCSP area from the Classical period to the end of the Roman era, at least at the larger sites. Many smaller Classical sites, however, seem to have been abandoned during the Hellenistic period.

One possible explanation is that small farms were phased out in favor of larger ones that would have been better able to meet outside demand for foodstuffs. Cyprus supplied grain and wine to the rest of the Mediterranean, particularly Rome, during the Hellenistic and Roman periods (Michaelides 1996:146–147). The lack of coarse, cooking, and transport wares would seem to indicate that this was not the case for the SCSP area; rather the region seems to have experienced a general decline in all aspects of work and habitation.

EARLY ROMAN PERIOD (100 BC–AD 300)

In the Early Roman period, Cyprus became an area of interest to Rome on several occasions, as the senate, and eventually the emperor, tried to fit it into the empire. In 58 BC the tribune, P. Clodius Pulcher, was able through legislation to reduce Cyprus to a province and confiscate the wealth of its king, Ptolemy (Cicero *De Domo Sua* 8.2, *Pro Sestio* 26.57). In 22 BC, Augustus ceded the island to the Senate as a senatorial province, but a minor one governed only by a praetor (Cassius Dio 54.4.1; Strabo 17.3.25:840).

Throughout the rest of the Early Roman period, the island was fairly quiet, with some clear exceptions. In AD 116, the Jewish insurrection of Artemion devastated part of the island, including the cities of Paphos and Salamis (Cassius Dio 68.32.1–3). In AD 164, a plague-like illness ravished the island. Later, in AD 269, the Goths invaded Cyprus (Trebellius Pollio *Vita Claudii* 12.1).

While there were numerous changes in political policy toward governing Cyprus, the prosperity of the Classical and Hellenistic periods continued for parts of the island, usually the coastal regions (Michaelides 1996:142–143; Sørensen 1993:193). During the period from 50 BC to AD 250, an economic downturn began to affect many parts of the eastern Mediterranean (Lund 1993:141). This situation may be seen on Cyprus in several regions, including the Akamas (Fejfer 1995:22–24). Within the SCSP area, there is actually a steady growth from the Hellenistic into the Early Roman period (table 6.1). Of the Early Roman sherds discovered in the SCSP area, approximately 1.5% of the total, the majority consisted of cooking wares. Most of these sherds belonged to a type of locally made Early Roman cooking pot characterized by a flat rim with narrow grooves. This type of cooking pot is similar to a series found at Aradhippou in the 1991 excavations at Panayia Ematousa (Sørensen and Grønne 1992:197–198, Fig. 9.45–9.47; Sørensen 1996:142–143, Fig. 2.20–2.23). It is also a common find at Paphos and Soli where it has been dated to the second century AD (Hayes 1991:82; Vessberg and Westholm 1956:15).

Another category of Early Roman pottery isolated for study was the transport class (amphorae, micaceous water jars). Although amphorae were manufactured to be sturdy and to resist breakage during transport or storage, some did break. If they had been shipped into the Mitsero-Politiko area, we would have expected to find multiple amphora sherds, but fieldwalking produced only six diagnostic pieces dated to the Early Roman period. Based upon finds made elsewhere of amphora with secondary ownership stamps, it has been suggested that amphorae were reused (Callender 1965:23; van Doorninck, Jr 1989:247–257). One possible explanation might be that wine was shipped to Mitsero in amphorae and then transferred to other containers while the amphorae themselves were refilled with olive oil and transported elsewhere. Even so, we would expect more broken or discarded sherds than we have found. The most parsimonious explanation is that few bulk goods (olive oil, wine, grain) were shipped into or out of the Mitsero-Politiko area during this period.

Of the Early Roman amphora sherds, the only distinctly identifiable one was a Pseudo-Koan handle. Pseudo-Koan is easily recognized because of its heavy bifid (double rounded) handles and sandy fabric, both of which strive to emulate the style of the Koan amphora, one of the most important wine transport vessels in the Mediterranean (Empereur and Hesnard 1987:22–23; Empereur and Picon 1989:225–229; Lund 1993:123–124; Zeest 1960:104–106). The site of origin is uncertain, but Pseudo-Koan ware is a common find in the eastern Mediterranean and has also been discovered in Italy and North Africa, where it is dated to the first and second centuries AD. Because the Koan amphora style upon which Pseudo-Koan wares were modeled most frequently contained wine (Peacock and Williams 1986:107–108), we might also assume that the vessels found in the SCSP area served the same purpose.

The lack of amphora sherds, both domestic and imported, suggests that there was little movement of bulk goods, such as wine and olive oil, in large quantities. Because both these products were important staples in the ancient diet, there are two possible ways to explain the lack of Early Roman amphora sherds in the Politiko-Mitsero region. First, the inhabitants of that region depended on local sources for wine and olive oil and had no need to import them. The communities would have engaged in a form of subsistence economy, producing adequate goods for local consumption, but with no surplus. Such a situation would have restricted contacts between the Mitsero-Politiko area and the surrounding regions. Nonetheless even this form of subsistence agriculture would have required storage containers, amphorae, or pithoi in which to store harvested goods throughout the winter; yet few examples of either were found during the course of the survey.

The second possibility is that very few people inhabited the Mitsero-Politiko area during the Early Roman period. However, the relationship between demographic growth and material remains, especially pottery, is fraught with difficulties (Bintliff 1997a; Hassan 1978:49–103; Cherry et al. 1991:403–454). The association between the amount of pottery recovered in the field and the amount of pottery actually used, not to mention the social aspects of its usage, is a very complex issue (Bintliff et al. 1999; Orton et al. 1993:23–35, 166–181; Rice 1987:286–304). For example, how many pottery vessels did a family use or destroy in a given span of time? How can one determine the number of original vessels from the number of sherds? Perhaps one way to assess the lack of Early Roman amphora sherds is to compare them to the Early Roman fine wares.

Fine wares constituted nearly one-third of the Early Roman material collected by SCSP. The largest class of Early Roman fine wares was Cypriot Sigillata, a locally produced "table ware" which accounted for nearly half of the total (see also Hayes 1967:65–77; 1972:10; Lund 1997:203). The only other Early Roman fine ware found in significant amounts was Eastern Sigillata A, from Syria. Other fine wares present in small numbers in the SCSP area included Eastern Sigillata B and B2 from the western half of Turkey, African Red Slip from North Africa, Çandarli from Pergamon, and one piece of Pompeiian Red Slip from Italy. While it is clear that the majority of the Early Roman fine wares discovered were locally manufactured on Cyprus, the complete absence of fine wares from the western Mediterranean (excepting one sherd of Pompeiian Red Slip), such as Italian Sigillata or Arretine Ware, indicates that such imports were not reaching the interior of island. In other words, the inhabitants of the Politiko-Mitsero area relied primarily on locally manufactured wares or on imports from eastern areas close to Cyprus (Syria or Anatolia). The presence of the Eastern Sigillatas A, B, and B2 indicates that some imports reached the island's interior, albeit in small numbers. While the lack of western wares perhaps results from the inconsistencies of the archaeological record, it is possible that the SCSP region's most direct trading links were with the easternmost Mediterranean.

As noted, Cypriot Sigillata made up the majority of Early Roman fine wares from our region. Recent work on this ware elsewhere on the island suggests that the main center of production was in the Nea Paphos region (Lund 1997:203), in the southwestern corner of Cyprus. Nea Paphos lies approximately 70 km and a rugged mountain range from the Mitsero region as the crow flies. Although the Cypriot Sigillata sherds may indicate contact between the two regions, they do not tell us whether the SCSP region was trading directly with the southwest or whether there were one or more intermediaries.

Analysis of the Early Roman fine wares thus reveals that there were more Early Roman than Hellenistic sherds, but far fewer (less than 50%) Early Roman than Classical sherds. As a result, we might suggest that, during the Early Roman period, the Mitsero-Politiko area relied primarily upon local production to meet most of its needs, with minimal import of bulk goods. When this area conducted commercial activities with other regions of Cyprus, it seems to have done so with areas that had strong eastern and weak western connections. This may be attributed to the network of roads constructed throughout the Early Roman period on the island by the Romans (Michaelides 1996:143). This emerging road system would have facilitated travel and exchange throughout the island, while the hinterland—including the SCSP region—would have benefited more than areas close to the large coastal cities. The territory between Politiko and Mitsero may have been considered marginal for agricultural production, at least on a commercial level, and thus would have been easier and more cost effective to exploit. This in turn would have promoted both commercial and population growth, unlike the situation in earlier periods.

If we compare the greater number of imported fine ware sherds to the amphora sherds, it is evident that the Early Roman trade in imported fine wares entering the SCSP region did not consist of "piggyback" trade (in which the major items of trade are shipped from a production center along with smaller items added to fill up any available space in the transport vehicle; Greene 1986:162–164, 1992:58–59). Piggyback trade is most often seen with cargoes of pottery, when the smaller fine wares fill in the free spaces around the large amphorae. Within the Mitsero-Politiko area, virtually no imported fine wares arrived with imported amphorae. Such a pattern suggests that nobody in this area was involved in direct long distance trade in bulk items, and that any trade in the Early Roman period was conducted through local Cypriot intermediaries or traveling merchants. Analysis of the Late Roman wares should help to illustrate whether a similar pattern existed in later periods.

LATE ROMAN PERIOD (AD 300–700)

Cyprus was considered to be a quiet backwater of a province during the Late Roman period, and intruded little on the larger geopolitical scene (Mitford 1980:1295). A series of plagues probably struck the island in 542, 558, 573, and 592 (Procopius *De Bello Persico*

Figure 6.3
Imported and local
Late Roman
fine wares

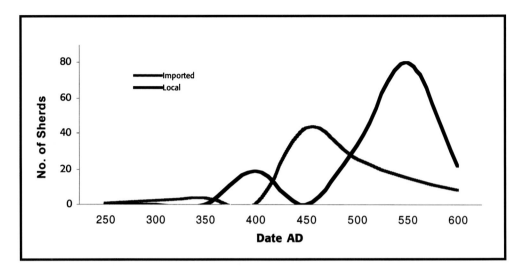

2.8; Chrysos 1993:8–9; Conrad 1986:143–163). Beyond such catastrophes, Cyprus remained relatively peaceful until the Arab Empire began to mobilize for an attack upon the Byzantine Empire, around AD 649 (Fejfer 1995:24–25).

From the survey, about 7% of the total sherds were positively identified as Late Roman/Early Byzantine in date. Among the sherds identified as Late Roman, the largest category both in weight and quantity was the coarse wares, followed by amphorae, and then fine wares; cooking ware formed the smallest component.

Of the Late Roman amphorae sherds discovered by SCSP, there was little variety in type. The largest category of identifiable amphorae sherds was Late Roman 1, dated from the fourth to seventh centuries AD. This type of amphora, manufactured on Cyprus at Amathus, Kourion, and Nea Paphos, as well as on the southern coast of Anatolia, typically carried olive oil (Lund 1993:130–131). The only clear imports were four North African amphora sherds and six Aegean amphora fragments. It is worth noting that Late Roman 2 amphorae sherds, found widely throughout the Mediterranean but typically concentrated in the Aegean and Black Sea regions, were not recovered in the SCSP area.

There are considerably more Late Roman amphora sherds than there were Early Roman, suggesting that bulk goods may well have moved into the Mitsero region from other areas during this later period. And yet there were still very few transport vessels from Italy, Africa, or the Aegean and Black Sea regions. The only possible non-Cypriot bulk goods reaching the SCSP area would have come from the east. None of the most commonly occurring amphorae in the eastern Mediterranean—such as the Gaza amphora (Peacock and Williams 1986:198–199; Riley 1979:223–224) and the Palestinian amphora (Peacock and Williams 1986:191–192; Riley 1979:223–224)—were found in the SCSP area. A comparison of these data with the analysis of the Late Roman fine wares should help complete the picture.

From the Late Roman fine wares identified by SCSP, the overwhelming majority fall into five specific wares: African Red Slip, Çandarli Ware, Cypriot Red Slip, Egyptian Red Slip, and Phocaean Red Slip ware, sometimes known as Late Roman C (table 6.1). As we might expect, the locally manufactured Cypriot Red Slip, probably from Nea Paphos (Lund 1997:203), was the most common Late Roman fine ware in the SCSP area. Among the imported fine wares, both Egyptian Red Slip and Çandarli Ware were discovered in very small amounts while Phocaean Ware and African Red Slip were far more common.

In considering carefully the specific forms of the fine wares, a clear chronological pattern emerges. Examining the wares by both quantity and weight over the time span from the first to seventh centuries AD, it is apparent that fine wares were scarce until about AD 350, became much more common until about 400 and then dropped off until AD 450 when they rose to a peak around 550, and fell off again toward AD 600. This pattern changes slightly when imported fine wares are compared with local ones (figure 6.3). The imports are relatively uncommon until the fifth century AD when there is a sudden increase to their highest level, followed by a gradual decline toward the seventh century.

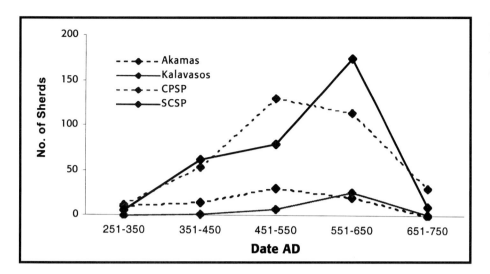

Figure 6.4
Late Roman
fine wares by
archaeological project

Local fine wares follow the same pattern but peak somewhat later, in the sixth century, and decline slowly toward the seventh century. It is interesting to note that a rise in imported fine wares offsets the decline in local fine wares, while a decline in imported fine wares corresponds with a rise in the local examples. This suggests that the pottery needs of people in the Politiko-Mitsero area were finite and could be met by either imported or local wares. Such a scenario also suggests that the imported wares were preferred whenever available, since the local fine wares were produced continuously without major interruption. Thus, the periods when imported wares were dominant (sixth to seventh centuries AD) were times of strong external contacts; at other times (third and fourth centuries AD) little foreign trade reached the SCSP area. Another possibility is that the periods when imported wares peaked were times of prosperity when the local inhabitants could afford the more exotic and expensive imports.

In general, then, this pattern suggests that the SCSP area was relatively isolated until the fifth century AD, when it developed strong trading and communication links with the outside world. These connections lasted for almost two centuries before they deteriorated, perhaps due to the Arab invasion of AD 648/49 and the area's subsequent involvement in the conflict between the Arab world and the Byzantine Empire. During this time, the imported wares, such as African Red Slip and Phocaean ware, slowly were replaced by the local fine ware, Cypriot Red Slip, which itself disappeared after AD 600.

In considering the Late Roman fine wares from three other projects—Akamas (Fejfer 1995), the Canadian Palaepaphos Survey Project (CPSP; Lund

1993), and Kalavasos *Kopetra* (Rautman and McClellan 1992)—with those recovered by SCSP, similar trends may be seen in each region (figure 6.4). Examining this material by quantity from the third to seventh centuries AD reveals that fine wares were scarce until about AD 350, then rose to a peak around 550 before falling off after AD 650. While this chronological trend is evident in all regions, SCSP and Kalavasos *Kopetra* peak slightly after CPSP and Akamas, about one century later (about AD 550–650).

In examining the types of imported fine wares found by each of the projects, several patterns emerge. First, all areas relied mainly on locally produced Cypriot Red Slip as the primary fine ware. Unusually, the SCSP region shows the highest percentage of African Red Slip, even though it lies farthest from the coast. Since Mitsero-Politiko is inland and more difficult to reach than Paphos, the high number of African Red Slip sherds becomes something of an anomaly.

One possible explanation is that the main trade connections of the SCSP area were with an area not associated with the other three regions but one that had a significant North African link. The Akamas, Paphos, and Kalavasos areas seem to have had stronger trade links with Anatolia than with North Africa. Yet the material itself makes it clear that the Politiko-Mitsero region received Cypriot Sigillata and Cypriot Red Slip most likely manufactured in the Nea Paphos region (about 5 km from the CPSP area). It seems unlikely that the SCSP region would have traded exclusively with one particular region over a span of several centuries and not with other regions in the immediate vicinity. Two other, perhaps more likely scenarios may help us to understand the better trade and communications during these periods.

First, the Mitsero-Politiko region may have traded with an intermediary who had connections both with the manufacturers of Cypriot Sigillata and Cypriot Red Slip, and with a distributor of African Red Slip. If so, we must still consider why more African Red Slip did not reach the CPSP area. Second, the Mitsero-Politiko region may have had several different trading partners. One in the Nea Paphos area or an intermediary would have provided a source for locally produced fine wares, while another would have offered a source for imported wares.

Based on the comparison of SCSP data with archaeological evidence from other sites in Cyprus, we might suggest the following. The Paphos, Akamas, and Kalavasos areas are located, respectively, in the southwestern, western, and southern sectors of the island, and much of the trade and communications in these areas is thought to have passed through Paphos. The Troodos Mountains, in turn, formed a natural and formidable barrier between Paphos and the SCSP area, which may have conducted much of its trade through the port of Soli. Soli was connected by road to Tamassos, in the eastern sector of the SCSP area. Suggested as a possibility during the Bronze Age, the natural topography of this region may have funneled traffic from the SCSP region north and northwest through the Morphou plain toward Soli. This would also have allowed the copper mined in the Tamassos region to be sent north to Soli for further refinement and export.

Tamassos was one of the few cities not located along the Cypriot coast to continue in existence from the Classical through the Roman period. The site of Tamassos, partially covered by the modern city of Politiko, controlled the Pedhiaios River Valley, a rich agricultural area; the city also derived considerable mineral wealth from its copper mines (Strabo 4.6), which according to a passage in the *Odyssey* were known in Homeric times (*Odyssey* 1.184). While the city is only infrequently mentioned in the ancient literature during the Roman period (Pliny *NH* 5.130; Ptolemy 5.13.6), it is included on the Peutinger Table, which shows a direct connection between Tamassos and the port city of Soli (Miller 1916:827–829; Mitford 1980:1331–1337). Soli was an important and wealthy city in northwest Cyprus. Located on the Morphou plain, it amassed its wealth from flax crops raised on the plain and from the copper mines near Skouriotissa, supposedly the richest on the island (Galen *De Temp. Fac. Simp. Med.* 9). The city seems to

have flourished during the Antonine and Severan periods, AD 96–235.

In turn, this situation raises questions about the social stature and economic position of the people who lived and worked in and around the SCSP area. It has been suggested that the SCSP area served as an organized, perhaps state-run agricultural support district for miners working in the ore deposits south of Tamassos (Politiko). Indeed, the increased pottery density as one approaches Tamassos would seem to indicate increased activity around that town (plate XLIX). As one of the few hinterland centers to survive into the Roman period, Tamassos would have relied on the surrounding areas to provide agricultural support for its inhabitants as well as the miners, unless all needed supplies were shipped in. But does the pottery distribution support such a scenario?

The paucity of storage vessels would seem to weigh against the theory of large-scale, organized support centers dedicated to cultivating crops for the inhabitants of Tamassos. What it does suggest is that several small villages or estates in the region may have traded with Tamassos on a purely local level. The pottery distribution on the Tamassos plain seems to indicate the presence of numerous small estates or villas that increased in number as they approached Tamassos. Individual farmers or estate owners in the SCSP area, in other words, would have traded with Tamassos whenever they had a surplus and in return gained access to imported, prestige goods from beyond the region, or even beyond Cyprus (for example, the African Red Slip ware). Tamassos' trade links with Soli would have provided the means, but these probably fluctuated along with the agricultural yields of the area.

During periods of prosperity, the inhabitants of the Mitsero-Politiko region would have traded their agricultural surplus at Tamassos to purchase prestige goods or other imports (for example, the Roman fine wares). Tamassos thus may have served a dual function in this region: while a source of copper for outside markets, it also may have functioned as an intermediary or local market for smaller villages and estates of the surrounding region. Copper mining in the region around Tamassos permitted the town to survive and thrive away from the coastal area and in turn provided a local market for the exchange of locally produced goods, primarily agricultural in nature.

6.4 The Byzantine Problem

Timothy E. Gregory

The problem underlying the absence of Byzantine material in the SCSP area is difficult to solve, especially given the lack of stratigraphic excavations there. Such excavations would at least provide information about the appearance of Byzantine pottery in the Mitsero-Politiko region. The problem we face—the invisibility of the Byzantine period—stands in marked contrast to the fascination among historians with the question of the so-called *condominium*: this involves the question of the legal and political status of Cyprus as it lay between the competing powers of Byzantium and the Arab caliphate (Dikogoropoulos 1940-1948; Kyrris 1984; Oikonomakis 1984). There is general agreement that Cyprus was left as a kind of buffer between the two great powers, each of which had the right to tax the island and use it as a naval base for operations against the other. Disagreement exists about the degree to which the Byzantines and Arabs exercised political authority on the island (compare Dikigoropoulos 1940–1948; Papageorghiou 1964; Megaw and Hawkins 1977:31, n. 130).

However this particular question is answered, the literary evidence makes it clear that Cyprus was inhabited during the period from 648 to 965 and that it was under full Byzantine suzerainty from 965 to 1192. As Papageorghiou (1966:25) wrote: "Despite the Arab invasions, however, life did not come to an end and the cities were not abandoned, as was formerly thought." Although the emperor Justinian II sought to remove the people of Cyprus and transplant them—along with their bishop—in 690-91 to Justinianopolis in the Hellespont, this experiment failed and the Cypriots returned to their homeland. After that, Cyprus became a place of refuge for Christians from Syria and Palestine and a religious center, as one can see from the writings of Theophanes or the Lives of St. Peter of Aosta and St. Constantine the Jew. During the course of the eighth and ninth centuries vaulted basilicas, and later domed churches, began to make their appearance on Cyprus, further testimony to the continuation of life on the island and some degree of economic prosperity. Papageorghiou (1966:26–27) assigns construction of the vaulted middle aisle of the *katholikon* of Ayios Iraklidhios and the first phase of the church at Peristerona to the 8th cen-

tury: both structures lie just beyond the SCSP area. Chrysos (1993:6–8), for his part, argues that the early Byzantine period in Cyprus was one of prosperity and peace. The general lack of noteworthy disasters accounts for the silence of the historical sources about Cyprus in the period. Of course, the restoration of Byzantine rule in 965 brought with it an efflorescence of building activity, and some of the churches in the survey area were probably constructed during that time.

All this, however, only serves to highlight the problem of the lack of Byzantine material in the SCSP area, since it is difficult to believe that this region was abandoned at that time. Chrysos (1993:9) points to the different pictures given by the literary and the archaeological sources, but argues that is due "...more to methodological differences between the two disciplines rather than to the evidence and its possible interpretations." An important aspect of this phenomenon is the remarkable contrast between the Late Roman and the Byzantine periods in terms of the quantity of survey data: Late Roman finds are among the most plentiful in the survey area (also the case in other parts of Cyprus and other areas of the eastern Mediterranean), while the Byzantine period is barely represented. All these factors, of course, relate to the broader question of the "fall of the Roman Empire," and it is tempting to suggest that the Arab invasions simply put an end to organized life in the area (see Foss 1977 on such a "catastrophic" military explanation in Asia Minor). Indeed, researchers elsewhere have noted a similar high-water mark in Late Antiquity, followed by marked collapse in the early Byzantine period. At the same time, recent scholarship has shown a certain diminution in material culture in the second half of the sixth century, a phenomenon which (if correct) would make the apparent collapse less sudden and perhaps less difficult to explain (Kennedy 1985; Russell 1986; Pentz 1992; Fejfer 1995). In particular, several recent studies (Megaw 1993; Rautman and McClellen 1992; Rautman et al. 1993) have provided a more nuanced understanding of the end of antiquity in Cyprus. These studies have shown how populations may have moved in the light of new and more dangerous situations, for example, and how pottery forms evolved at the end of antiquity.

Be that as it may, the most recent Late Roman material from SCSP most likely can be assigned to the middle of the seventh century AD, and there is no securely dated later pottery information until the thirteenth century, a remarkable gap of 600 years. Given the scenario implied by the written sources, it seems most peculiar that we would have found no Byzantine pottery. The most likely explanation is that we are unable to identify the pottery of this period and separate it from the pottery of the sixth and seventh centuries. It is well known that shapes and decorations of many earlier amphorae changed quite slowly in the eighth to tenth centuries, and it is possible that some of the sherds identified as Late Roman (sixth to seventh centuries) really belong to the Byzantine period. Cooking pots and Byzantine glazed wares are well known, however, and should certainly have been identifiable. Their absence does suggest reduced activity and a narrowing of contacts during this period, perhaps also a smaller population—all phenomena that would be in keeping with the historical sources. In addition, it is possible that the inhabitants of the Miterso-Politiko area during this time had an essentially aceramic culture and that instead of pottery they used utensils and containers made of more perishable materials—for example, wood, metal, leather, and plant-products such as gourds. Such a hypothesis cannot be proven or disproved at this time, and so we are left with this less than satisfactory solution. Finally, it is worth reiterating that systematic excavations in this region would go a long way in helping us sort out pottery chronologies that would shed light on this crucial historical question.

6.5 Medieval to Modern Landscapes

(plate L)
Michael Given and Timothy E. Gregory

The post-Roman periods in the Mediterranean are among the most rewarding for an intensive, interdisciplinary survey project to investigate, as recent work in Greece has demonstrated (for example, Sutton 1991; Bintliff 1997b; Bintliff et al. N.D.; Vroom 1998). Cyprus in the Medieval (1191 to 1571), Ottoman (1571 to 1878), and Modern (1878 to 2000) periods has the same potential (Baram 1995b; Given 2000). Relevant documentary sources include administrative records, travelers' reports, historical maps and accounts, and the records of individual estates and monasteries. There is also a series of studies on architecture, art, and coinage. To this

rather narrowly historical and stylistic perspective, archaeological survey brings an approach that examines the social and landscape context of human activity. This provides both the methodology for an interdisciplinary investigation of the landscape at specific periods and a large database of relevant information.

One of SCSP's most striking results has been the extent and intensity of activity across the landscape during these periods. Of the 8130 sherds that could be dated to precise periods, 9% were Medieval, 19% Ottoman, and 17% Modern. To these should be added another 7128 sherds dated to the Medieval/Modern period overall, as well as a wide range of buildings, roads, agricultural structures, and tools. These materials and our methods of analyzing them shed light on a wide range of human activities within the landscape: industries such as pottery production and copper mining; agriculture at various different levels of intensity; modes of habitation in villages and countryside; communications and trade; religion and ideology; and the impact on society of imperial rule by the Lusignans, Venetians, Ottomans, and British.

MEDIEVAL TO MODERN POTTERY

The Medieval to Modern pottery collected and studied by SCSP has a number of characteristics that at once differentiate it from and invite comparison with pottery found in excavations and surveys throughout Cyprus and beyond. The most striking similarity is the complete absence of early Byzantine pottery, from the seventh through at least the tenth centuries (discussed fully in the preceding section), and the very small number of pieces that can be assigned to the later Byzantine period, before the Frankish and later Venetian occupation in the late twelfth century. This situation is not uncommon elsewhere on Cyprus, where true Byzantine wares are remarkably scarce (Gregory 1987:202). Likewise, in broad terms, the number of pieces that can be assigned to specific centuries rises steadily from the thirteenth to the twentieth centuries, although there are localized rises and falls throughout this period. Again, this general phenomenon has been noted elsewhere, especially in southwestern Cyprus, in the CPSP survey area (Gregory 1993:157) (see table 6.2 and figure 6.5).

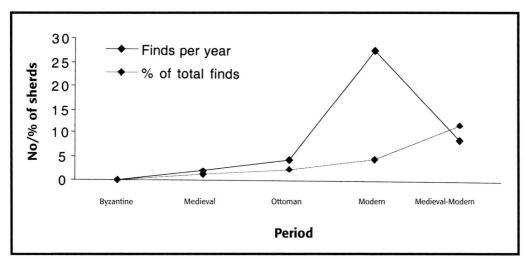

Figure 6.5
Byzantine to
Modern pottery:
percentages and
finds per year

Especially noteworthy is the increasing number of sherds identified as one gets closer to the present and, of course, the large number of sherds left in the catchall category Medieval to Modern. The Medieval to Modern category was created in large part to encompass the dark brownish/reddish coarse ware found so ubiquitously throughout Cyprus. Pottery of this same clay is still being made at centers such as Kornos and Phini, but it is clear that very similar fabrics were produced in earlier times, and pithoi with dates scratched in them can be found from the eighteenth century onward (London 1987; Papadimitriou 1972–1974; Pieridou 1960). The omnipresence of this type of pottery causes real problems in interpreting the archaeological data. In the end, we were able to distinguish six individual fabrics, termed Cypriot Coarse Ware W1, W3-W7 (see appendix C)—the differences between them were not always clear, and some doubt always exists about assigning individual pieces to one category or another.

Glazed Medieval Pottery. The classification and dating of Cypriot glazed pottery is based on a series of early studies (Dikigoropoulos and Megaw 1940–1948; Du Plat Taylor 1933, 1935; Du Plat Taylor and Megaw 1937–1939). Table 6.3 (p. 295) summarizes the basic classification system. Comparison with material from Polis on the northwest coast allows the clear differentiation of Groups I through III from the later groups:

1) The dominant characteristic is the upturned ring foot, not found after AD 1300.
2) The thirteenth-century pottery had a better quality fabric that is usually red, in contrast to the pinkish buff typical of later wares.

Table 6.2 Byzantine to Modern pottery: percentages of total finds and finds per year

Period	Finds	%	Years*	Finds/year
Byzantine	4	0.0	548	0.01
Medieval	744	1.3	373	1.99
Ottoman	1,514	2.6	325	4.66
Modern	2,764	4.7	100	27.64
Medieval-Modern	7,107	12.1	798	8.91
Total, all periods	58,500	100.0	–	5.85

* Years in period

3) The slip is thin.
4) There is no pink underslip, which is characteristic of fourteenth-century wares.

Most of the material studied by Dikigoropoulos, Du Plat Taylor, and Megaw came from tombs, many of them robbed, and most of which lacked sound archaeological context. Although the basic dimensions of this chronology are sound, further developments followed the discovery of evidence of production sites at Lemba (near Paphos), Lapithos, and Enkomi. Papanikola-Bakirtzis (1989, 1993, 1996) has studied all these data and provided new information and typologies, in some cases based on material brought to light in earlier years and now in the Cyprus Museum. She suggests that the Lemba workshop operated from the early thirteenth to the mid-fourteenth centuries AD and the Lapithos workshop from the fourteenth to the sixteenth centuries AD while the chronology of the Enkomi workshop is not known. The fabrics for the Lemba workshop comprise mainly the dark red ware, but there is some

Figure 6.6 Glazed
Medieval wares:
chronotypes and
numbers by period

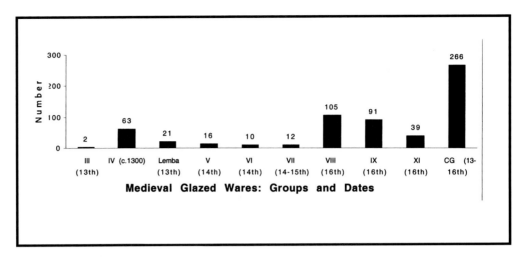

variation, and the upturned ring foot is an important characteristic. In general, Lemba ware is to be equated with SCSP's Groups III–IV (see figure 6.6 and table 6.3). The Lapithos fabric is buff-red, fine-grained, and dense; it is to be associated with Groups IVC and following. Megaw and Jones (1983) discuss the difference between these fabrics.

For the present study, Lemba ware was employed as a regular category whenever it could be identified, but otherwise the traditional groups were used since they are fairly standard. Note, however, that the distinction between Lemba and Lapithos wares is primarily chronological and, as mentioned, by far the largest quantities of datable Medieval pottery come from the sixteenth century, and apparently were made primarily at Lapithos. In addition, Lemba ware is generally recognizable, regardless of the condition of the sherd, because of its fabric. All the other groups may, we assume, be assigned to Lapithos, a region that would certainly have had close connections with the SCSP area in nearly all periods. The largest group of Medieval glazed pottery—here termed simply Cypriot Glazed/Lapithos—is also presumed to be from Lapithos. All these sherds may safely be assigned to the Medieval period. This distinction between places of manufacture is mainly chronological, with Lemba ware assigned to the thirteenth century and Lapithos production probably beginning in the fourteenth century and continuing unbroken up to the modern era. Figure 6.6 shows the relative numbers for all the glazed Medieval pottery recovered by SCSP. Assuming that none of the glazed pottery came from Enkomi, 13.8% of it derived from Lemba (that is, thirteenth century) while 86.2% derived from Lapithos (that is, fourteenth century and later).

The overwhelming amount of glazed Medieval ware recovered by SCSP was of Cypriot origin. The few imported glazed sherds encountered include four examples of sixteenth-century Italian sgraffito, five pieces of Zeuxippus Ware (Megaw 1968), and ten pieces of sgraffito wares from unknown sources (not Cyprus). No Proto-Maiolica (south-Italian product) wares were encountered in the survey area, but five examples of sixteenth-century Maiolica—presumably from northern Italy—were recovered, joining the Italian sgraffito to demonstrate close connections of the area with the Venetian rulers of the island.

Coarse Medieval Pottery. Surprisingly little coarse or cooking ware was assigned to the Medieval period, in large part because (as noted above) it was nearly impossible to separate the Medieval from the Modern versions of vessels made in the typical brownish red local fabric. Hesitantly, one class of this clay (W1E) was identified as Medieval: 22 sherds were found in the field. Furthermore, a brown-glazed coarse ware was regarded as Medieval, but only four examples of this ware were recovered. Strangely, none of the cooking pots found by Megaw at Saranda Kolones were identified in the SCSP survey area.

Glazed Ottoman Pottery. Unfortunately, the Ottoman period pottery of Cyprus is not well studied, and precise chronological assignments are difficult to make in the absence of new stratigraphic excavations. The best evidence remains the groups of pottery published by Megaw (1937–1939). In the SCSP area the high-quality Asia Minor and contemporary Italian (Maiolica) fabrics seem to be completely absent (on typical Ottoman wares, see Atsoy and Raby 1989; Hayes 1992:233–270), although Megaw (1937–1939) shows that they, and even Chinese products, could be found in contemporary Nicosia. Rather, the dominant wares,

Table 6.3 Cypriot glazed wares: traditional classification

Group	Name	Century/AD	Description
I	Sgraffito Wares, Monochrome		
IA	Fine Point	12th	
IB	Incised/Champlevé	12th–14th	Imported
IC	Cypriot Sgraffito		Local: either fine point or incised; usually only a simple design in center; sometimes glazed on exterior
II	Slip-Painted wares	12th	
III	Early Brown and Green Sgraffito		
IIIA		13th	Dashes of yellow-brown or green added to IC bowls; all have low ring feet with upturned base ring; variety of shapes: chalice, bowls with rounded sides and flaring rim, straight flaring rim, vertical but slightly externally concave rim; coarse red gritty clay, often fired gray
IIIB		end 13th	Transitional between IIIA and later forms; clay same as IIIA; introduces the common shape of later classes: bowl with vertical rim, but lacks the inward bevel of rims of later groups; same ring feet as IIIA
IV	Brown and Green Sgraffito with External Glaze	Late 13th–early 14th	Characterized by unslipped glazed exterior that produces a brown color; simple ring foot and bevel on interior of rim
IVA			Coarse red gritty clay covered with fine pinkish slip; often white slip on interior
IVB			Harder, better silted clay than IVA; dark red to crimson, often fired gray
IVC			Hard well-silted pinkish to light buff clay; slip as IVA; glaze very shiny; tendency to make a higher foot
V	Brown and Green Sgraffito with Plain Slipped Exterior	14th	Development of IVC; main difference is the use of a white slip over the whole of the body
VI	Brown and Green, Overall Sgraffito	14th	Continuation of previous group, fine pinkish-buff clay, but rather softer than V; thick white slip and sgraffito decoration inside and out
VII	Brown and Green Decadent Sgraffito	14th–15th	Characteristic form is bowl with tall foot; designs carelessly executed with considerable economy of line
VIII	Green Painted Sgraffito		
VIIIA		15th	Fine, soft reddish clay, micaceous; bowls with thin slightly everted rims and flat ring foot; yellow glaze and simple, normally non-figural sgraffito designs picked out in green; rare, perhaps inspired by Mamluke pottery
VIIIB		16th	Similar to Group VI, creamy slip and yellowish green glaze on interior and exterior to foot (related to VII; low foot and high variety of fabrics and surface treatments are common features)
IX	Green Painted	16th	Allied to VIIIB, white slip and yellow or yellowish-green, with meaningless lines in green
X	Green Glazed Sgraffito	13th	Coarse red clay; white slip and rich olive green glaze on interior of bowls and exterior of jugs
XI	Plain-Glazed wares		
XIA	Brown Glazed	Medieval	
XIB	Green Glazed		Perhaps related to Groups IV V, and X
XIC	Clear Glazed	16th	Found with Maiolica
XII	Imported wares		

Figure 6.7 Glazed Ottoman wares: chronotypes and numbers by period

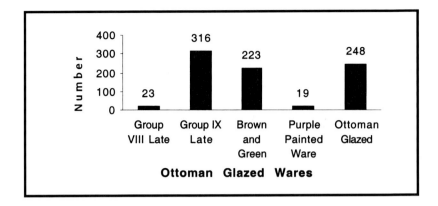

especially in the seventeenth to eighteenth centuries, are continuations of the traditions of Cypriot glazed manufacture begun in the thirteenth century (figure 6.7). Thus, two of the most common wares are clearly variations of Cypriot Glazed Groups VIII and IX. This continuity is seen elsewhere in the Greek world, for example, in Athens (Frantz 1942), where the local sgraffito tradition continued well into Ottoman times (compare Gourgiotis 1981).

Apparently, the most important early local glazed Cypriot wares of the Ottoman period are characterized by the application of poorly applied streaks of green on the glazed surface, called here Group IX Late. This phenomenon can be paralleled in Hayes (1992: Pl. 47c), a bowl in a subclass of his Ware B dated to the fifteenth to seventeenth centuries (Hayes 1992:272–273, 280). Similar to this is Group VIII Late, which has added sgraffito decoration, paralleled by Hayes's Ware D (1992: Pl. 47 h, j), assigned to the sixteenth century and later (Hayes 1992:272, 274, 280, 284). Another ware, here called Cypriot Glazed Brown and Green, was perhaps contemporary with the former classes, but was manufactured elsewhere. It is characterized by a brownish slip and clear glaze along with streaks of green similar to those in the two previous classes. All three of these wares are presumably to be assigned to the seventeenth to eighteenth centuries. Probably from the nineteenth century comes a better manufactured pottery with a creamy glaze and streaks of purple paint, here called Purple-Painted ware. A final category of probable Ottoman date is a nonhomogeneous collection of mainly plain-glazed wares, with the glaze usually applied directly to the fabric without a slip.

Arguably, glazed pottery may be taken as an indicator of wealth or social distinction and in traditional societies most families would not have pos-

sessed large quantities of these expensive goods. It seems reasonable, therefore, to measure the number of glazed sherds encountered in various periods, and to count the total number of sherds: Overall, 829 glazed sherds have been assigned to the Ottoman period and 649 to the Medieval period. This averages out as 1.98 glazed sherds per year in the Medieval period and 2.21 in the Ottoman, which is remarkably similar, although there would of course have been considerable social and cultural variation within each of these periods.

Coarse Ottoman Pottery. Coarse pottery of the Ottoman period was dominated by three versions of the typical brown or brownish red fabrics: Cypriot Coarse Ware W3 (120 sherds), W5 (289), and W6 (258). These fabrics were expressed in a number of vessels of different shapes. Typical of these shapes are small and large pithoi, *galeftiria* (milking pan), water jugs, and pitchers. Given our present state of knowledge about these wares, it is impossible to tell whether they represent different chronologies or different places of manufacture.

One final and especially interesting class of Ottoman vessels is the Turkish pipe (Hayes 1992:391–395; Baram 1995a). Four examples of tobacco pipes were found, all relatively simple and in the fine gray or light gray clay that Hayes (1992:393) dates to the seventeenth or early eighteenth century AD.

Glazed Modern Pottery. The primary work carried out on the modern pottery of Cyprus has been sociological or anthropological in nature—focusing on the methods of production and the workshops of the traditional ceramic industry—or otherwise aesthetic in focus (London 1987; Papadimitriou 1972–1974; Pieridou 1960). The fine Chinese and European ceramics of the nineteenth and twentieth centuries are well known, and the typologies that have been established are useful to archaeologists.

So far, however, no attempt has been made to relate this information to the archaeology of Cyprus (compare now Ionas 2001), or to study the local pottery produced in the Eastern Mediterranean, either in imitation of imported wares or, to a certain extent, maintaining some connection with traditional Cypriot production (on the study of modern pottery in Greece, see especially Hahn 1989 and Vroom 1996, 1997, 1998).

SCSP was not in a position to make a significant contribution to the study of this material, but we did attempt to collect and study the modern pottery in the same manner used for the pottery of all other periods. For these purposes several broad categories of pottery were defined. Among the glazed wares perhaps the most readily identifiable type was what we termed Lapithos ware, but which is elsewhere identified as Didimotycheion ware (Bakirtzis 1980; Hayes 1992:276–277). This is a slip-painted ware with decoration of crudely painted radiating lines and either a green or yellow glaze; by far the most common shape is a bowl with flaring sides and a hooked rim.

A total of 189 examples of this ware was collected in the SCSP area, including 52 with green glaze and 106 with yellow. Although the prototype for this ware may have been made in Didymoteichon, the large number of examples found throughout Cyprus strongly suggest a local center of production, perhaps Lapithos. Bakirtzis (1980) dates the ware to the nineteenth and twentieth centuries and, while Hayes (1992:276–277, Ware P) thinks production may have begun as early as the late seventeenth century, we have included it here as a phenomenon of the late nineteenth and twentieth centuries. Hayes (1992:442, n. 14) also points out that Frantz (1942:1–28, Figs. 22, 23, left, group 7, nos. 1–2) published several examples of this ware from Athens and dated them to the eighteenth century. Yet, these were probably local imitations of the Didymoteichon Ware, and one should imagine the same situation in Cyprus.

Most other modern glazed ceramics have been grouped into three broad categories: Contemporary, Eastern Mediterranean (125 sherds); Contemporary Imported, European (6); and Contemporary Imported, Asian (55). The broad category Fine Ware, Modern was set up to describe fragments so poorly preserved that they could not be distinguished further (89 sherds). The rest are largely characterized by their likely place of origin. Contemporary, Eastern Mediterranean wares represent the local glazed

traditions of Cyprus and the surrounding areas; they are most commonly plain glazed, either with or without an underlying slip, in continuation of styles of the Medieval and Ottoman periods, but with harder fired fabric. Contemporary Imported, European wares—surprisingly few in number—represent the well-known transfer print and other styles of European pottery imported into Cyprus. Contemporary Imported, Asian wares are not the high-quality Chinese and other oriental pottery of the past, but rather the relatively cheap mass-produced wares that have come to dominate the tableware market in recent years. Not surprisingly, the dominant pottery class of this period is the traditional eastern Mediterranean ware, a factor that indicates the relative isolation of the Mitsero area, even into the twentieth century. One imagines that the reasonably high number of Asian imports is the result of the region's opening up to the broader world, especially after 1960.

Coarse Modern Pottery. Coarse modern pottery would, of course, include the numerous brick (58) and tile (122) fragments found throughout the Cypriot landscape. In addition, the category includes hard-fired objects such as flower pots in a relatively well-levigated clay. These wares are designated simply as Coarse, Modern (122 sherds) and thus are distinguished from Cypriot Coarse Ware W7 (514 sherds), a softer fired chocolate brown fabric generally known as Kornos Ware. A special category of modern glazed pottery is the Contemporary Yogurt Pot (61 sherds), a vessel with nearly flat bottom, straight sides, and a grooved vertical rim, made in a stony red fabric and covered with a thick yellow glaze on the interior and at least part of the exterior.

INDUSTRY

There is no definitive evidence from the SCSP area for copper mining or smelting after the Late Roman period, although copper production from the Medieval period has been reported in the Polis region in the west of Cyprus (Raber 1987:306–307). From historical sources we know that there was a substantial net import of copper from Europe to the Levant during the later Medieval period, some of it sent via Cyprus (Ashtor 1983:81, 156–158). European travelers to Cyprus in the eighteenth century often mention the abandoned ancient copper mines, attributing their current lack of use either to the repressiveness of the Ottoman government or the idleness of the Greek inhabitants (Cobham 1908:243, 248, 266; Mariti 1909:10). The area of Tamassos was certainly well known for its history of copper, gold, and silver mining (Cobham 1908:165, 309; Mariti 1909:90).

A mineral product that was definitely exploited during the Medieval period was vitriol, a range of copper salts still found crystallizing out of the sulfurous pools in the open-cast mining pits. It was used for eye salve, tanning, and ink and, according to Heyman, writing in 1709, Cyprus in the Venetian period (1489–1571) exported "a great deal of very good vitriol" (Cobham 1908:248). It may well have been vitriol that was produced in the Polis region rather than metallic copper (Raber 1987:299). It was well known during the Ottoman period that the ancient mines of the Tamassos area were particularly rich in vitriol (Cobham 1908:206, 309), but SCSP found no traces of this activity, no doubt because modern open-cast mining has obliterated earlier traces. By the late eighteenth century vitriol was being imported to Cyprus from Venice (Cobham 1908:372).

The first recorded modern explorations of the copper deposits in the SCSP area were carried out in 1916 (Lavender 1962:108); some of the more regular adits at Politiko *Kokkinorotsos* appear to date to this phase (chapter 4.7). From the 1920s, there was more intense development of the Mitsero and Agrokipia mines, and the economy and social organization of these villages was radically altered. The result was a clear tension between the agricultural and mining landscapes of the area. Before the development of large-scale mining, the SCSP landscape was peopled with communities of peasant farmers and landholders living in stone and mud-brick houses in their family's village and working their own fields in the village territory. From the 1930s, this scenario was juxtaposed with a mining landscape of massive pits and spoil heaps, hierarchical labor structures, and artificial communities of wage laborers from all over the island and beyond, living in purpose-built housing. These tensions can be read in the structure and surrounding landscapes of villages such as Mitsero (chapter 4.5).

AGRICULTURE

Apart from the copper mining of the twentieth century, the mainstay of the survey area's economy from the Medieval to Modern periods was agriculture,

Table 6.4 Cereal production at Psimolophou Estate in 1317

Crop	Estate-Owned			Peasant-Owned		Total
	Sown	Harvested	Yield	Harvested	Tithed	
Wheat	405	1,173	1:2.9	5,011	1,671	6,184
Barley	310	1,230	1:4.0	9,108	3,036	10,338
Oats	67	41	1:0.6	0	0	41

Note. Figures in bushels (1 bushel = about 40 liters)
Source: Richard 1947:128, 140–143)

dominated by cereals, goats and sheep, vines, and, to a lesser extent, olives. During the Medieval period in Cyprus, there was usually a large surplus of wheat and barley that was exported to Venice; reports by European travelers indicate that in the Ottoman period there was a major drop in production (Christodoulou 1959:123–124).

A valuable source of information for the northern Troodos comes from a set of accounts for the estate of Psimolophou, immediately northeast of the survey area, carried out in 1318 because of the absent Frankish landlord's distrust of his bailiff, one Brother Bernard (Richard 1947). The estate itself consisted of a manor house and commercial farm, with a village around it large enough to support tanners and bakers. The accounts give precise figures for the 1317 cereal harvest (table 6.4).

These figures show surprisingly low yields; Christodoulou's estimate for wheat yield from circa 1540 until the mid-twentieth century is 1:7 (1959:123). The oats in particular clearly suffered a bad year, with less being harvested than was sown. The peasants as a whole were growing 4.3 times as much wheat as the estate, but 7.3 times as much barley. This difference presumably reflects their larger proportion of poor land that supported the hardier and normally better yielding barley. The peasants paid one-third of their produce to the estate as tithes, and they also had to provide labor working on estate-owned crops. During the 1317 harvest, for example, the estate employed 1332 men and 150 women and boys (Richard 1947:151).

The precise extent of the Psimolophou estate and the peasants it controlled is unknown, but most likely it extended into the northeastern part of our survey area. The same area, the flat alluvial plain north and northwest of ancient Tamassos and its successor Politiko, was also known in the Ottoman period as a fertile area. According to the historian Kyprianos, writing in 1788, "it has plentiful wheat, barley, olive oil, wine, silk, cotton, fruit, and other items useful for living" (Kyprianos 1788:42). In the eighteenth and nineteenth centuries this alluvial plain supported not just the villages of Episkopio and Politiko but the monasteries of Ayios Mnason (chapter 4.6) and Ayios Iraklidhios. The Ukrainian monk Basil Barsky visited the monastery of Ayios Iraklidhios in 1735, and admired its rich landholdings (Barsky 1996:79). The Archbishopric Property Codex for the same monastery in 1773 lists 1.7 ha of orchards, 7.3 ha of vines, 59.6 ha of fields, and 643 olive trees (Tsiknopoullou 1967:62). Even without the figures for peasant families in the villages, the intensity with which this area was cultivated is clear.

This documentary evidence compares well with the archaeological survey data. The pottery distribution for the Medieval to Modern periods as a whole in the northeastern corner of the survey area (plate L) shows one clear density peak at Politiko *Ayios Mnason* (SIA 6; chapter 4.6) and another smaller one to the north (SCY209—Episkopio *Kallinikos*; chapter 4.18). The first is due to the monastery of Ayios Mnason and perhaps dumping on the outskirts of the village of Politiko; the second may be some sort of farmstead. Of great interest is the spread of low-density pottery between and north of these peaks. With a characteristic pottery index of 500 to 1000, this is most likely the result of intensive manuring in the fields nearest the village (chapter 7.4). From documentary and oral evidence we know that the most valuable fields were the *sokhorafa*, the infields nearest the village which could be manured most easily (Christodoulou 1959:41; Panaretos 1967:71). The survey data suggest that this was indeed being done. Interestingly, this low-density "carpet" of pottery does not extend to the next transect 1 km to the west but is limited to a 1 to 1.5 km halo round the main villages. Such a pattern stands in striking contrast to the Roman period, when the low levels of pottery extended much more widely, interrupted by small rural estates (chapter 6.3); apparently the most intensive land use in the Medieval to Modern periods was restricted to the areas around the settlements.

There is no documentary evidence with the same level of detail for the other parts of the SCSP area, but the archaeological survey data shows a very similar pattern (plate L). In the fertile alluvial plain of the Akaki river, there are a series of substantial villages and settlements (Aredhiou, Malounda,

Klirou, Kalokhorio, Klirou *Manastirka*), which show substantial amounts of pottery on their edges, and a relatively broad but low-density halo of pottery in the surrounding fields. This halo generally seems to be about 1 km or a little more in radius. Much of the pottery could not be dated any more closely than Medieval/Modern, but there are clearly substantial Ottoman and Modern components in this central area. Farther west, there is a corridor of activity following the modern road from Malounda through Agrokipia and Mitsero to Mavrovounos (SIA 4). Other than Mavrovounos, where the settlement itself was surveyed, most of this material, which includes some Medieval and Ottoman pottery as well as Modern, probably represents manuring and dumping outside the settlements. In terms of arable agriculture, then, the central Akaki plain may have been even more important than the Tamassos plain in the east, in spite of the bias of the documentary sources toward the estates and monasteries of the eastern area. This is supported by the location of the Ottoman period water mills: There were six along the Akaki in this section, as opposed to only one in the equivalent stretch of the Pedhiaios (Given 2000:219).

Pastoralism has been of major economic importance throughout the period, particularly in the mountainous south of the survey area where there was little arable land but good grazing land. Apart from examining the location of structures such as goatfolds (chapter 7.4), it is hard to associate sherd distribution patterns with pastoralism, though passing goatherds certainly provide a likely explanation for the frequent stray finds of coarse wares in remote, uncultivable land. In spite of this, a comparison of population and grazing animal figures from different communities and periods is very relevant to an investigation of the landscape (table 6.5).

What is immediately clear is the large scale of agricultural production at the Medieval and Ottoman estates and monasteries (Given 2000:218–221). Both the Psimolophou estate and the monastery of Ayios Iraklidhios are producing dairy, meat, and hide products at a similar scale to a small modern village such as Malounda. When their arable production is taken into account, they match a more substantial village such as Mitsero and would have had a similar impact on the landscape and society of the region. The Psimolophou estate had a permanent staff of some

Table 6.5 Population and grazing animals

	Psimolophou Estate	Ayios Iraklidhios	Malounda	Mitsero	Politiko
Date	1318	1773	1982–1985	1982–1985	1982–1985
Population	(minimum staff) 40	(monks in 1825) 12	285	704	309
Goats	131	(just goats) 302	105	690	1743
Sheep	151	(sheep and goats) 190	47	206	139
Cattle	74	3	36	190	4
Total Animals	356	495	188	1086	1886

Sources: Richard 1947:130–131, 145; Tsiknopoullou 1967:62, 66; *MKE* 9:283–284; 10:83; 11:372.

forty to fifty people but employed almost 1500 people for the harvest and controlled a large number of peasant families. Similarly, the twelve monks of Ayios Iraklidhios would have had an equivalent number of servants and numerous tenants and temporary wage laborers. The agricultural landscapes of the Medieval and Ottoman periods were as intensively worked and socially complex as those of today.

SETTLEMENT

Although the settlement pattern during the Medieval to Modern periods clearly consists mainly of nucleated villages, intensive archaeological survey has demonstrated some of the complexities and changes within this system. Village lists from the sixteenth century, historical maps from the sixteenth and seventeenth centuries, and archaeological survey all indicate that during the Medieval period settlements were smaller but more numerous. Mavrovounos (SIA 4; chapter 4.4) is a good example, appearing in Venetian village lists and maps and, according to our pottery analysis, abandoned probably in the seventeenth century. Klirou *Ayios Mamas* was probably a similar example (SIA 9; chapter 4.9), and the oral tradition about the predecessors of Mitsero reflects the same phenomenon (chapter 4.5). In general the seventeenth century shows a population decline and a consolidation into fewer villages (Papadopoullos 1965:37–43; Grivaud 1998:280–292).

The complexities of seasonal agricultural labor mean that a model consisting of nucleated settlements and farmers commuting to their fields each day is inevitably simplistic. Vine-dressing and plowing in January required stone-built shelters, or temporary structures made of brushwood. Mountain villages with little arable land needed summer settlements down on the plains for the production of cereals. Some monasteries and estates owned outlying estates or farmsteads to work their remotest land.

More fundamentally, the inhabited landscape was divided between the nucleated villages of peasant families and the great estates and monasteries.

The locations of the Medieval to Modern villages in the SCSP area and its vicinity are of considerable interest (plate L). In areas of reasonable arable land they are characteristically 2 km apart (Mitsero, Agrokipia, Malounda, and Aredhiou; Malounda, Klirou, and Kalokhorio; Ergates, Episkopio, Politiko, and Pera); in rougher land they are typically 4 km apart (Aredhiou and Episkopio; Mitsero and Kato Moni). Each one of these villages, moreover, tends to lie in a bowl of hills with its arable land around it and a ridge dividing it from the next. None of the villages in the survey area are intervisible and, apart from mountaintops and ridgelines, there are very few spots where two villages are visible simultaneously. The abandoned settlements of Mavrovounos and Ayios Mamas fill the same conditions; this is a pattern clearly going back to the Medieval period. The landscape, then, is divided into territories comprising what can be seen from the village; these viewsheds, the areas which can be seen from each village, correspond closely with the very modern administrative boundaries of the villages, which derive from the colonial and Ottoman periods.

Each of these settlements is distinguished by another very visible feature: the church and its bell tower. There are no hilltop chapels in the survey area, and in Cyprus, in contrast to Greece, they are almost unknown. There are apparently rural chapels, but in almost every case archaeological investigation has shown that they mark the sites of abandoned settlements: the ruins of Ayios Yeoryios at Mavrovounos (SIA 4; chapter 4.4); Ayios Mamas (SIA 9; chapter 4.9); and Panayia Khrysopandanassa outside Malounda (SIA 10; chapter 4.10). No habitation remains were found around Panayia Lambadhiotissa (SCY114; chapter 4.16), but a strong local tradition indicates that there was once a settlement there. This oral tradition demonstrates that the association between church and settlement is a locally held belief, not just an academic observation. Exploration elsewhere in Cyprus has confirmed that this association is a common feature of the Cypriot landscape. Churches, then, define villages, and villages in turn are defined by churches. No mosques are known in the survey area, even in the once mixed village of Aredhiou, but elsewhere in the region mosques occur only in villages and seem to have a similar function of marking and defining a village.

COMMUNICATIONS

The principal routes of the Medieval and Ottoman periods can be discerned by investigating the lie of the land, the locations of settlements, and the presence of bridges. North-south movement is relatively easy, thanks to the river valleys leading into the mountains to the south. The gorge incised by the Akaki River, however, is a major barrier to east-west movement. Of its two bridges, the one at Malounda *Tria Yephyria* (SCY303; chapter 4.10) was rebuilt in the 1880s from a mid-Ottoman or earlier predecessor, while that at Kalokhorio *Mutoyephiron* (SCY302) has clearly been rebuilt on several occasions, but may originally have been Medieval.

The location of the villages and the broader agricultural activities indicated by the pottery distribution suggest that there was a principal axis of communication running down the eastern side of the Akaki River valley and another along the Pedhiaios River to the east, coming past Psimolophou and down to Politiko. A subsidiary route clearly crossed the Akaki at Malounda *Tria Yephyria* and headed westward to Agrokipia, Mitsero, and *Mavrovounos*. Some sections of the main routes must have been passable by oxcarts in the summer, as the Psimolophou estate accounts list various types of carts and carriages, together with their component parts, value, and draught animals (Richard 1947:148–149). The heavy taxation in kind extracted by all successive imperial powers also required efficient transportation to bring goods or products from remote villages to regional centers, while estates producing cash crops needed good access to seaports for exporting their wheat, cotton, or wine.

The British colonial rulers, soon after assuming administration of the island in 1878, were keen to improve the road system, both to give villagers access to markets and to allow the army fast access to

quell potential rebellions (Schaar et al. 1995:37–40). A road from Nicosia to Klirou is first shown on a 1903 map, with an extension to the southwest still in progress (Bellamy 1903:28). The Malounda bridge was rebuilt in the 1880s because, according to the commissioner of Nicosia, in the winter it was the only link between Nicosia and the wine and fruit villages of mountain regions to the south and southwest (SA1/1156/1887). With the advent of the commercial mining of the mid-twentieth century, the Hellenic Mining Company developed the access road to Agrokipia and Mitsero for their own benefit and, incidentally, that of the villagers (chapter 4.5).

CONCLUSION: IMPERIAL LANDSCAPES

Apart from the last forty years, for the whole of the Medieval, Ottoman, and Modern periods Cyprus was under the imperial rule of the Byzantines, Lusignans, Venetians, Ottomans, and the British. Even though the Lusignan dynasty actually resided in Cyprus, they clearly distinguished themselves from the Greek inhabitants and acted as a colonial power. This control had a very clear expression in the landscape. One major reason for a nucleated settlement pattern, for example, was the tax collectors' need to take tithes in kind (see Davis 1991). It was much easier to control crop processing and to collect tithes from the threshing floors if they were in one place immediately adjacent to the village, as at Mitsero *Kato Alonia* (chapter 4.5), rather than being scattered throughout the landscape.

Settlements also grew out of Medieval estates and the houses of the estate servants and laborers clustered around them. It is clear from the Psimolophou accounts that just such a community existed there and ultimately developed into what is now a thriving town close to the outskirts of Nicosia. Similarly, a late fifteenth-century Venetian manuscript records forty-one Cypriot villages that belonged to the Grand Commandery of the Knights of St. John. These included Achiera (Akhera, immediately north of the survey area), Agrochipia, Mavrovunos, and Micero (Mitsero) (de Mas Latrie 1852–1861 III:502–503). Their inhabitants were exploiting the surrounding landscape not just for themselves but for the Frankish knights.

Communications are also important for an imperial power, not just to bring in troops to quell rebellions but also to carry out the task that lay at the heart of imperial rule: tax collection. Basil Barsky, the Ukrainian monk who traveled round the monasteries of Cyprus in 1735, was sympathetic to the monks who gave him hospitality and was quick to see the impact of its location on the monastery of Ayios Iraklidhios:

> The monastery's name is famous, its architecture is beautiful and its buildings are well spread out. It owns vineyards, orchards, sheep, and fields, from which it derives an income to feed those who live in it and its visitors, and with which to pay the taxes and other forms of persecution by the Turks. No other monastery is so persecuted as this one, as it stands on the crossroads and is surrounded by many villages. It is also not far from the large town of Nicosia, and therefore many Saracens arrive seeking recreation and from them many indignities are suffered by the poor monks and the hegumen [abbot]. (Barsky 1996:79)

The apparent richness of the fertile alluvial plains and the broad scatters of pottery across them that indicate intensive agriculture are, clearly, only part of the story. The intensity of the agriculture, the large villages, and the good communications are a response to the need to produce a large surplus for taxation, with the help of an infrastructure provided by the colonial power for the purpose. The landscapes of the Medieval, Ottoman, and the earlier part of the Modern periods were undoubtedly busy with human activity, but this was as much a product of repression as it was of prosperity.

7

SOCIAL LANDSCAPES AND REGIONAL ARCHAEOLOGICAL SURVEY

After tracing the history of SCSP from the Pre-Pottery Neolithic to the present day, we now turn to a thematic study of that landscape. The integration of geomorphology and archaeology allows a close examination of the ongoing dynamic between people and the natural and anthropogenic landscapes in which they live. We report on our ability to detect sites remotely using satellite imagery and geobotanical indicators. The survey area at all periods is then analyzed in terms of our three main research goals, with a discussion of its industrial, agricultural, and ideational landscapes. The concluding section aims to synthesize this broad array of data and perspectives by integrating the concept of social landscapes with the goals and methodologies of regional archaeological survey.

7.1 Human and Physical Landscape Dynamics

Jay Noller and Lisa Wells

AT THE BREAK IN SLOPE

Located in the northern foothills of the Troodos Mountains, the SCSP region straddles an important geological and geomorphological divide. This divide is visible from distant satellites as the break (or break in slope) from the steep-sided hill slopes of the mountains to the stepped plains of the *Mesaoria*—literally between the mountains (an apt term as the imposing slopes of the Kyrenia Range bound it on the north). The SCSP area cuts across a series of tilted bedrock strata that represent the essential geological inheritance of Cyprus. This complete cross section also suggests how the varying geological formations may have influenced social developments on the island.

At human scales, such as the case of someone's field or other land-holding, the landscape becomes more complex, yet still holds the basic form and function inherited from its parent geological formations. To interpret this complex landscape requires only a simple framework of two major geological formations and two major agents of landscape change: running water and human beings. Water—as rainfall, stream-flow, and a weathering agent—has shaped the underlying bedrock into something close to its modern form. People have interacted with the flow of water and the results of its actions over the past five millennia to embellish and alter radically the "naturally" produced landforms.

295

BEDROCK GEOLOGY

The SCSP survey area is nested within a landscape that emerged from the depths of a Cretaceous sea-floor to its present epi-montane form. An ancient Tertiary coastline has been stripped back to its once-vibrant, now-fossil coral reef, revealing a landscape spread with pillow lavas and the intrusive bodies that fed their flow across the seafloor. On the seafloor, sparsely distributed hydrothermal systems heated by the magma below drew in sea water and filtered metals into dome-shaped life-encrusted mounds. These mounds sprang to life over and over again in the past few millennia as people quarried out ore bodies of copper and other precious metals.

Seaward of the ancient reef lie the deposits eroded from the emergent peaks of the early Troodos Mountains. The *Mesaoria* Plain is underlain by these sedimentary rocks, and they provide the basis for the relatively fertile soils that develop there. Intercalated in these gravel-filled, sandy deposits are beds of bentonite clay, which resulted from an alteration of volcanic ash that settled throughout the Mediterranean Sea. In addition to their modern industrial uses, outcroppings of these deposits and the soils they form along the edge of the *Mesaoria* appear to have been exploited in premodern times for pottery manufacture and brick or tile making.

In geological terms, the bedrock exposed in the SCSP area consists of upper and lower pillow basalts of the Upper Cretaceous Troodos Ophiolite. This is overlain by <30 m of marl, with interbeds of clays and cherts of the Palaeogene Lefkara Formation, and by 50+ m of marl and chalk of the Miocene Pakhna Formation. This sequence is capped by a 30 to 100 m thick biohermic (reef-like) limestone of the Upper Miocene Koronia Limestone.

The natural resources of the SCSP area have been made available through the convergence of geologic forces worked across the deep time of the earth's history. With this brief overview of how the earth beneath SCSP came to be, we now consider how this landscape has been shaped in the most recent geologic epoch, the Holocene, or the last ten thousand years, roughly coinciding with the period of human occupancy on Cyprus.

SURFACE PROCESSES

The gently north-sloping bedrock formations of the area have been eroded and reshaped primarily by river (fluvial) processes, and secondarily by hill slope (colluvial) and landslide (mass-wasting) processes. Wind (eolian) and tectonic transformations have been negligible during the recent past. Nearly all exposed surfaces have undergone weathering and/or soil-forming processes that have left them chemically, physically, and/or biologically altered.

Streams. Two types of streams drain the area, the mountain stream and the plains stream. The mountain stream is the most prevalent and is chiefly responsible for the lay of the land. Mountain streams originate in the wetter, steeper slopes of the Troodos and accordingly have higher annual discharges. These streams carry greater loads than their plains counterparts: more sediment, larger clasts (individual fragments of rock), and more resistant rocks. Episodically for the past million or so years, mountain streams altered their courses, leaving an intact deposit of river sediments. The new stream ran to either side of its predecessor, because it was easier there for the river to incise the pillow basalts and marls and thus to make its new valley course. With each successive change in course, the mountain streams became lower in elevation than they had been originally, and former courses are now the ridgelines and the terraced "steps" flanking the ridges. Their previous courses left behind clear traces, in the form of a 1 m or more thick deposit of water-lain silt, sand, and gravel. These deposits can be as much as 1 km wide and typically extend across the entire north to south extent of the SCSP area. These are the alluvial terraces or pediments on which much of the contemporary, local agriculture has been established.

In contrast, the plains streams have episodic and flashy discharge, which is considerably less frequent and lower in flow. The significantly lower flow required of these streams results from their low elevation at the edge of the Mesaoria. Compounding the lower flow is the lower amount of rain delivered to these drainage basins and the significantly higher rate of discharge lost to infiltration into the underlying sedimentary bedrock. The water that actually enters the stream tends to seep into the river channel rather than flow very far downstream. Many of the channels that begin in the SCSP area end a short distance to the north of it. The sediment load available for these streams is significantly smaller or more sparse in gravel content. All these factors combine to make plains streams narrow, steeply V-shaped in cross section, and highly inclined. Tributaries and headwaters of the plains streams have similar morphology and together form a badlands landscape. The badlands are considerably less well vegetated and until the last fifty years were seldom cultivated.

Hill Slopes. As the streams incise they develop in their wake hill slopes that are situated mainly at or near the angle of repose (the maximum slope without collapsing) of the underlying material. Generally, hill slopes in the Troodos are steepest because of their erosion-resistant bedrock, and slopes underlain by sedimentary rocks of the *Mesaoria* are steeper than those underlain by pillow basalts. Nonetheless, exceptions to this generality abound, particularly at the human scale. Where stream erosion is pronounced, such as in the badlands, hill slopes have a thin mantle of sandy to pebbly scree. Where stream incision rate is lower, there are slope deposits (colluvium). Soils are developed in most of these hill-slope colluvia and are conserved and augmented by the agricultural practice of terracing.

On the slopes of the large hills Lambadhousa and Kriadhis, massive landslides have cumulatively displaced up to 1 km² or more of sedimentary bedrock. The landslides have developed complex morphologies due to their recurring failure. A large landslide (over 0.3 km²) will spawn many smaller failures within its own mass as well as along its margins. Many of these landslides have increased in size through incremental failure of their upper margins. Arch-shaped head scarps, from 10 to 100 m or more high, mark the upper margin of the landslides. Such mass-wasting features have accentuated the imposing aspect of these hills.

Below the head scarps, topographic depressions formed in the pull-away zone, the depression in a hillslope vacated by a landslide. These depressions subsequently trapped sediment, and surface water flow was integrated with the drainage network. Small, closed depressions (< 0.25 ha) have persisted locally in the slide masses, and many of these have been used for seasonal water storage, shallow wells, or sunken gardens. Large limestone hummocks are present in the upper slopes of most landslides. Convex rock- and debris-strewn slopes along streams mark their down-slope terminus.

Landslide activity began during the Pleistocene as the mountain streams undercut their slopes along the gorges through the limestone ridge. Holocene landslide activity is limited to shallow slips in the landslide head scarps and rock falls along the landslide margins. Thus, the landslides are a static part of the geologic substrate for the period of human history presented here.

SHAPED LAND

Human activities have extensively reshaped much of the Cypriot landscape into what is largely a stepped topography. In other words, the landscape everywhere has been made into flat-lying surfaces, or treads. Steeply sloped surfaces, or risers, separate these treads. Agricultural fields, terraces, roads, and trails have a tread and one or more risers, which may be built into, or constructed of, earth or stone. As shaped lands tend to be areas of significant (or at least extant) human land use, it is useful to consider their vulnerability to erosion and hence their removal from the archaeological record. The fate of contextualized cultural materials rides on the erosional susceptibility of the substrate.

Fields. Agricultural fields are recognized by generally low-sloping ground with standing crops or orchards, furrowed soil, piles of field stones, and associations with farming structures and implements. The surface expression of these fields varies depending upon use (for example, orchard versus row crop), date of tilling, and type and density of vegetation. Fields vary in shape and area depending on the underlying slope, from small (40 m²) irregularly shaped fields on steep hill slopes to large (>1 ha) orthogonal field boundaries on flat alluvial plains. Fields behind check dams have margins that generally conform to the pre-check-dam contours of the gully.

Until recently, the badlands and bare rock slopes of the Troodos foothills escaped the onslaught of bulldozers. Major technological improvements in grading equipment have now overcome the difficulties of ripping up the bedrock. The shapes of newly formed fields conform to engineered boundaries rather than the long-held constraints of landform and substrate.

The potential for and character of erosion on agricultural fields varies widely depending on the slope, soil properties, crops, and maintenance of erosion control features. Fields with relatively steep slopes (>5°), especially if downslope from a high (>2 m) riser or the mouth of a gully, tend to have the highest incidence of erosional landforms. Rills (small stream channels) are most pronounced in fields underlain by alluvial or colluvial deposits that have not been contour plowed. They tend to follow the surface swales (slight depressions) that mark older infilled gullies. Gullies advance upslope by headward erosion through the sediments trapped in colluvial hollows or behind check dams.

Both rills and gullies contain channelized water and therefore present the most danger to the original context of the surface archaeological record. The mechanized plow and grader has created the profound ability to level the land, cutting off high areas and filling in low-lying areas. Without recognizing this, an artifact's context in such a disturbed field could be misinterpreted quite easily. To improve our understanding of the context of surface artifacts, it is useful to consider the types and characters of anthropogenically shaped lands.

Roads and Trails. The SCSP region is crossed by roads and trails, including asphalt-paved two-lane roads, quarry haul roads, various grades of field roads, and foot or donkey trails. Nearly all trails connect the fields to the villages. Permanent trails are commonly located along field boundaries, while temporary trails develop within fields during the harvest. Premodern trails and roads connecting villages are most visible in the disused badlands, typically distinguished as topographic lineaments and unusually aligned gullies and ridge-line depressions.

Most of the roads in the area have been constructed since World War II, when bulldozers moved in to develop mines, quarries, and mills for the large-scale extraction of mineral resources. Based on comparison of the 1963 and 1993 aerial photographs and our own observations (1995–1999), dirt roads are replacing many of the foot trails. Some of these are graded and leveled every one or two years. Culverts and other drainage controls are limited to the improved roads that are maintained by a local mining company. Gullying of road treads and collapse of road cuts have made some roads impassable. We have observed that this may occur in as little as one or two rainy seasons.

Hill-Slope Terraces. Hill-slope terraces are wedged-shaped deposits of colluvium and moved earth fill, typically supported on the downslope side by a vertical to near-vertical stone wall. The walls are comprised of a dry-stack wall and rock screen that traps sediment and surface soil. Typical walls are at least three courses (about 0.5 m) high, slope gently up-valley, and are only a single stack thick. Most variability in wall morphotypes is in the size, shape, and arrangement of stones.

Check Dams. Check dams are stone wall constructions purposefully built to block the flow in channels or gullies, apparently built as systems along the

length of small drainages and streams. Failure of these dams and gully erosion has often exposed thick sequences of fill behind stone edifices. Below Mitsero *Lambadhiotissa* (SCY114), a single 4.5 m thick deposit consists of at least six superposed check dams built over 1300 years (see chapter 4.16). At the base of this deposit is a soil Ap horizon (anthropogenically disturbed surface soil) with wood (burnt and unburnt), seeds, insect tests, charcoal, and snail shells with an irregular patchy distribution. Radiocarbon age estimates from three charcoal samples in the Ap soil horizons indicate agricultural use of this surface during the Late Roman Period (ca. AD 700 ± 200) (Noller and Wells N.D.). A sequence of largely conformable deposits and check dams of Medieval to early Modern date comprise the overlying stratigraphy. The sequence consists of repeating sedimentary units, each made up of a check dam, trapped sediment, and an agricultural soil formed in that order. The lower units are debris-flow deposits while the upper units are channelized flow deposits. Rarely do individual beds achieve thickness exceeding 20 cm.

This stratigraphic sequence indicates changes in the processes controlling deposition within the drainage during the period of human activity. Prior to human modifications, alternating processes of fluvial deposition and channel incision predominated. During the Byzantine period, modifications resulted in a shift to fluvial deposition, as local base levels were raised by the construction of the first check dams. During the Venetian to Late Ottoman periods, hill slope processes dominated and resulted in the deposition of debris flows and colluvium. This is suggestive of a decrease in hill slope stability probably resulting from land use change. Finally, during the colonial through modern periods there is a return to fluvial deposition as the hill slopes became stabilized. The maintenance of the check dams has recently been abandoned, and river erosion is rapidly removing the dams and the trapped sediments at this location. This rapid recent incision indicates that overtopping of the dams, or undermining by piping, quickly leads to erosion. Given that most of the sequence lacks unconformities, we can infer nearly continuous maintenance of these features over the last 1300 years.

Check dams appear to have a long history of use in the SCSP area. A check dam at SCY125 in the Kouphos River drainage in SIA 7 (see chapter 4.7) may have been constructed as early as 1600 BC and is the oldest recognized sediment and soil conservation structure in SCSP. As such it points out that human intervention in soil erosion, sediment yield, and transport has a long history in the region. The construction materials hint at an association with mining activities just 400-500 m up the hill, which makes this structure of particular interest. It may well represent an organized connection between mining, with its collateral erosive effects of earth moving and vegetation removal, and agriculture with its husbandry of soil and soil substrate. Such evidence of cause-effect-response is well worth further study and consideration.

CONCLUSION

From at least the Chalcolithic period onward, the SCSP landscape has undergone profound changes as a result of human activities and because of conservation, management, and use of sediment and soil on hill slopes and drainages. Centuries, if not millennia, of efforts to arrest and promote soil development in what were marginal lands have been abandoned in the past 50 to 75 years. Traditionally non-agricultural areas, in contrast, are now sprouting up fruit orchards. The natural processes of erosion and transport to the fluvial system, which the villagers of old once battled against, are now promoted and accelerated by the actions and inaction of their modern descendants.

7.2 Geobotany

Neil Urwin

GEOBOTANICAL INDICATORS

The objective of the multivariate analyses of seven vegetated archaeological sites using a hierarchical cluster analysis and species cover variables was to test the hypothesis that POSIs in the SCSP study area might be indicated by the natural vegetation that occurred on them. We also wanted to verify, if possible, that the indicator would be the result of chemical and possible physical effects in the soil environment. Multivariate clustering of the botanical data indicated a significantly different on-site vegetation for a number of the POSIs when compared with control (off-site) vegetation samples (table 7.1).

POSIs indicated at the species level (SCY017 and SCY021) are not necessarily characterized by the oc-

currence of individual indicator species. Clustering at the "all species" level means that the entire species array, including the presence or absence of very low frequency species which occur in one or more of the subunits being analyzed has determined the result. While the identification of some indicator species is achieved as a by-product of this analysis (for example, at SCY021 Mitsero *Kouloupakhis*), it is recognized that a different experimental design would be needed specifically to confirm the existence of indicator species.

The Mitsero *Kouloupakhis* slag heap was indicated by an array of individual indicator species, because they were all positively correlated with that POSI (that is, present on-site and absent off-site). On the other hand, we concluded that the species level indicator of Mitsero *Kokkinoyia 1* (SCY017) was not necessarily a case of individual species indicators, because the clustering strategy reacted not only to the presence of some low frequency species on site but also to the absence of some others which occurred elsewhere.

POSIs indicated at the community level clearly represent real community geobotanical indicators. The removal of occasional and low frequency species from the data reduced the species array of the total data set for all layers combined to an average of only six to seven different species of flowering plants, with 60% of them in the dominant shrub layer. Thus, with the occasional and low frequency species excluded from the analysis, the clustering identified the changes in the relative percentage cover of only dominant species in the sample units on- and off-site, which characterized the vegetation community.

Of the five POSIs that successfully showed geobotanical indicators (at either the species or community level), three were slag heaps where the vegetation was most likely responding to chemical effects in the soil environment. One of these, Mitsero *Kouloupakhis*, has been subject to extensive recent physical disturbance and may also be partly characterized by vegetation typical of waste ground colonizers. A fourth POSI, Mitsero *Kokkinoyia* 1, was associated with slag that probably did not originate on site and has not been in situ long enough for its effects on soil chemistry to be the predominant determinant of the vegetation type. Instead, it shares influence with the effects of geomorphological processes. The fifth POSI, Politiko *Phorades* 2, had no observable source of chemical effects in the archaeological record. Rather, the archaeological record suggested that it was a building site and therefore more likely to be a source of physical effects on the soil environment (soil moisture, aeration, compaction), which in turn influences the vegetation.

We therefore concluded that, for the limited number of POSIs tested, geobotanical indicators were detectable to some degree in the majority of cases and, further, that these indicators resulted from a range of determinants depending upon the type of site.

GEOBOTANICAL INDICATORS AND REMOTE SITE PREDICTION

The testing of a second hypothesis focused on the classification of satellite imagery in subscenes centered on the archaeological POSIs. The hypothesis proposed that the geobotanical indicators could be detected remotely and developed as a site-prediction tool. Five POSIs demonstrated positive geobotanical correlations with archaeological sites at the community level through multivariate analysis. These geobotanical correlations were used as light signatures to classify the satellite imagery, after which the performance of the thematic maps, in terms of usefulness in site prediction, was assessed on three levels:

1) *Primary Test of Differentiation.* This test posed the question: Does the classification correctly map the training area from which the site signature was derived (that is, the original POSI area)? The assessment focused on whether the light signature for the vegetation on the archaeological POSI is distinct from its surroundings. If it is, the classification will map the original site accurately. If it is not distinct, it means that the signature for site vegetation appreciably overlaps the signatures of the background land cover classes. Where this overlap is sufficient to preclude accurate mapping of the site vegetation, the image is unstable and the signature will be of no use for remote site detection.

2) *Primary Test of Predictive Ability.* This test posed the question: Does the classified map identify any other known areas of the same kind (for example, other slag heaps)? The assessment focused on whether the light signature for the vegetation on the archaeological POSI has any application or relevance for areas other than it-

self. Where this does not occur, it may be that the vegetation is still a valid indicator of the archaeological feature but is also responding to added edaphic or other conditions peculiar to that site. In this case, it will be of limited application elsewhere when these site conditions do not prevail. Alternatively, it might be the case that there are no known similar features nearby (within the same geomorphological area) to identify.

3) *Secondary Test of Predictive Ability.* This test posed the question: Does the classified map identify other unknown areas with the same light signature that, by virtue of their geomorphology, location, and configuration suggest the potential for the existence of similar archaeological features? This assessment tested the most attractive and useful facility of image classification and thematic mapping—the ability to extrapolate from the known to the unknown. The concept is simple, involving the identification of other pixels and pixel groups in the image that match the signature of the reference area—in this case, the site vegetation community. In practice, the ability of image classification strategies to do this can be a powerful predictive tool.

These tests were applied to the findings from the thematic maps derived from the reference signatures from the five POSIs (table 7.2).

Within the confines of the experimental design and the small number of cases studied, the findings show that the prediction of potential site areas by the use of vegetation community indicators and satellite imagery is achievable and has the potential to be developed as a survey tool. The degree of success of this methodology depends upon a number of conditions being met. The main ones are:

• An in-depth environmental profile of the study area is required to establish the appropriate experimental design, data sampling protocols, and analysis strategy. In particular, research on the autecology of community dominants is essential preparatory work.
• The degree to which the indicator community on a site is found to be differentiated from the surrounding vegetation. This needs to be determined by a multivariate clustering or grouping

Table 7.1 Geobotanical indication of POSIs

POSIs indicated by Geobotany		POSIs not indicated
Species level	Community level	
SCY017 Mitsero *Kokkinoyia* 1	SCY021 Mitsero *Kouloupakhis*	SCY100 Politiko *Phorades* 1
SCY021 Mitsero *Kouloupakhis*	SCY024 Mitsero *Sykamies*	SCY102 Agrokipia *Paleokamina*
	SCY101 Politiko *Phorades* 2	SCY107 Episkopio *Vrysia*
	SCY121 Politiko *Kokkinorotsos* 6	

Table 7.2 Remote site prediction using geobotanical indicators

Site of reference signature	1) Maps reference area?	2) Identifies other known areas?	3) Predicts other unknown areas?
SCY021 Mitsero *Kouloupakhis*	Yes	Yes (Kouloupakhis 2 and 3 identified)	Yes (other areas in the Kouloupakhis triangle and west of Mitsero UTM 511086/3878620 and 510990/3878530)
SCY024 Mitsero *Sykamies*	Yes	Yes (smaller slag heap at UTM 3877530-509500)	Yes (site at UTM 509490/3878080 with positive preliminary finds)
SCY101 Politiko *Phorades* 2	Yes	N/A (no similar features known in area)	Yes (at least four other areas on the alluvial plain at UTM 519300/3875650, 519200/3875250, 520650/3875000, 520800/3875700)
SCY121 Politiko *Kokkinorotsos* 6	No (unstable thematic map)	–	–

strategy as a first sieve of potential reference sites.

- The environmental conditions to which the indicator vegetation is responding. Chemical effects arising from the archaeological feature appear to be readily detectable in the vegetation of the SCSP area, although the glaring exception at SCY100 Politiko *Phorades* 1 requires further examination and explanation.

- The type of vegetation. The vegetation should be natural, in that present human cultural practices affecting plant growth are minimized, although the methodology also appeared capable of performing well with a data set that contained waste ground and disturbance pioneer species. The finding from this survey was that the vegetation should be a perennial woody shrubland or grassy heath without significant tree cover: that is, a batha or garrigue form such as occurs in the SCSP study area.

7.3 Industrial Landscapes

Vasiliki Kassianidou, Sven Van Lokeren,
and A. Bernard Knapp

UNESCO's newest categories of cultural or "natural" landscapes include the "organically evolved landscape" and a subcategory defined as "relict." Relict landscapes are, in fact, industrial landscapes and include sites involved in the mining, quarrying, and production of metals, glass, and textiles (Cleere 1995:66). Industrial landscapes are part of what the U.S. National Park Service terms historic vernacular landscapes, while in Great Britain the National Register provides specific criteria to help identify and preserve the integrity of these (usually) rural landscapes (Hardesty 1990).

The material culture of mining plays a major role in the configuration of industrial landscapes (Hardesty 1988; Knapp 1999b:236–237). Mining communities were located not just with respect to ore bodies but also with concern for access to water, timber, and agricultural land; people who lived in mining communities also needed to eat, have shelter, and establish some means to transport the product of their labors. Given the bulkiness and weight of unprocessed ores, the primary production of metals occurred most frequently in close proximity to the ores and the mines. Other factors also affected social production and economic demand, for example: ease of access to the ore, microenvironments for the beneficiation and smelting of ores, the degree to which the labor force was free or servile, and the presence of water for energy or drinking.

Industrial landscapes can be considered from two perspectives. On the one hand, we need to assess the extent to which the location of the different types of archaeometallurgical sites (for example, the mines, ore beneficiation sites, primary and secondary smelting sites, distribution centers) was determined by the physical landscape and to what extent by other parameters. On the other hand, we need to evaluate how these processes altered the "natural" landscape and gradually turned it into an industrial landscape. These two processes are obviously interconnected: As the physical landscape is exploited and natural resources become depleted (for example, as forests are destroyed), workshops and miners must move to an area better able to sustain the industry.

INDUSTRIAL LANDSCAPES AND THE *CHAÎNES OPÉRATOIRES*

In addition to considering the range of factors that may have dictated the location of an industrial site, we also need to take into account the operational parameters of Cypriot smiths, in particular the fact that they had to extract copper from sulfide ores with the aid of existing pyrotechnologies. Pfaffenberger's (1992, 1998) work on *chaînes opératoires* (Leroi-Gourhan 1943) and sociotechnical systems offers one means of conceptualizing these parameters. The notion of the *chaîne opératoire* is concerned with both the extant material remains and the industrial and social processes involved (Schlanger 1994:143). In such an approach, material remains stem from the social actions of past individuals. The dynamic among producer, locus of production, and product is both flexible and firm, leaving room to maneuver and interact with social constructs. From a practical perspective, an individual participating in a specific society learns a type of behavior that may be inscribed into a collective operation. The technical organization of production is largely determined by the social organization of its producers and, when individuals become members of a social group, they gradually acquire certain technical skills. Because tools (in this case a mining hammer, a furnace, a tuyère, or even a piece of slag) acquire meaning only through use that renders them technically efficient, the *chaînes opératoires* approach can serve as a means to unify our own approach to archaeometallurgical data, spatial analysis, and social organization.

In this dynamic, people choose a specific technological organization, and the resulting technical processes, to some extent, affect their social organization. "The use of even the most rudimentary tools, after all, requires some degree of socialization and knowledge and is thus a social as well as a material phenomenon" (Pfaffenberger 1998:294). Technology comprises both material things and human actions, which necessitate social organization and which interact through the application of knowledge. The purely technical part of these *chaînes opératoires*, as reconstructed from the data, can therefore be used to infer a type of social organization not immediately apparent in the archaeological remains. In other words, identifying technical characteristics or technological design will help to reconstruct the production process and its socioeconomic organization. Archaeometallurgical remains, which Bachmann (1982a:2–7) viewed as "process indicators," reflect a whole range of production operations from mining to metal casting, which in turn are affected by and influence the social organization of metal production.

The *chaîne opératoire* is not just a standardized, apprenticed production process reflecting the social division of technical tasks; it also illustrates the spatial organization of production units such as mining adits, roasting heaps, slag heaps, furnace installations, and the like (Pfaffenberger 1998:294–295). Perhaps equally important, this approach foregrounds the problem of spatial organization. How and where did the ancient miners and smelters organize production in the landscape? Did the intersecting sequences of the mining-smelting process affect the selection criteria for a suitable production location? Let us consider the interrelationship between the *chaînes opératoires* and an industrial landscape more closely.

LOCATIONAL FACTORS IN AN INDUSTRIAL LANDSCAPE

As an aspect of the physical landscape, the basal geology is a key determining factor in selecting an ore deposit and opening a mine. Other, equally natural features in the landscape—for example, a bright gossan outcrop or a certain type of vegetation associated with the existence of an ore body—would be obvious to anyone involved in the production of metals, whether prospector, miner, or farmer supporting a mining community (Constantinou 1992). Otherwise, industrial processes are neither delimited nor restricted. Several factors may influence the place where other aspects of ore preparation and production are carried out. For example, ore beneficiation is a process wherein the ore is ground and crushed and perhaps washed to remove the sterile gangue. Some or all of these steps can take place near the mine, thus reducing the volume of material that has to be carried to the smelters. If washing is part of the process, then ore beneficiation must take place near a water source or, as in the case of Laurion in Greece (Jones 1984:69), a system must be created where water is collected and stored for use in beneficiation. Thus the ore would be transported to a water source which may or may not lie in close proximity to a mine. Unlike the actual location of the mine, the producer's choice of location for ore beneficiation is contingent on various factors other than the ore body.

The same holds true for roasting and smelting operations. Primary smelting is most often located in the immediate vicinity of a mine in order to avoid transporting or carrying the ore too great a distance. Yet, when one considers the amount of fuel needed to smelt sulfide ores, the determining factor may become the availability of timber; in this scenario, ores are transported to the fuel source rather than the other way around. Another possibility is that the smiths may choose to establish a smelting workshop near a water source. Water is necessary both for constructing the smelting installations and for drinking. Apart from the water itself, a river provides a source of other essential raw materials (for example, clay and cobbles) used in the construction of smelting furnaces. In other cases it may be important to locate the smelting workshop in an area easily accessible and well connected to a transport system, which would facilitate the further refinement, manufacture, or distribution of copper ores. Roads and distribution routes also function to bring supplies to the workforce, which may have been a significant factor in times of intensive or large scale production, for example, in the Late Roman period or perhaps in the Protohistoric Bronze Age (Late Cypriot period).

Several other factors may have been instrumental in determining the location of copper smelting workshops and/or the administrative centers that directed them. Because copper is a precious commodity, smiths occasionally establish their workshops in a secure and easily defensible, or even remote, position, particularly during times when political unity or economic organization is lacking. Although never clearly stated in the relevant written sources, some of the conflicts that arose between city kingdoms during the Classical Period may have been sparked in an attempt to control the mining districts; such control would have provided substantial revenues. For example, historians explain the Phoenician expansion from Kition to Idalion and thence to Tamassos (Cross 1974:78) in just these terms. King Pnytagoras of Salamis asked that he be given Tamassos as a reward for helping Alexander in the siege of Tyre (Hill 1940:50). In both cases the mines in question are those around Tamassos, some of which SCSP has recorded during the course of fieldwork.

THE INDUSTRIAL LANDSCAPE OF SCSP

Bearing in mind the concept of the *chaînes opératoires* and the various factors that may affect the location of mines and smelters within the natural landscape, let us consider now the workshops SCSP has encountered and try to understand why they were chosen and how they changed through time. The distribution map of metallurgical POSIs (plate LI) reveals that all except one are located within the Upper Pillow Lavas—where the ore deposits are also situated—or in the Lower Pillow Lavas. The only exception is SCY011 where Phorades-type slag was found. Very few archaeometallurgical finds of any sort were collected from units in the alluvium.

Not all metallurgical POSIs were sited in direct proximity to the mines: The most notable example is SCY021 (Mitsero Kouloupakhis), the large Late Roman slag heap approximately 2 km from both the Kokkinoyia mine (SIA 11) and the Agrokipia mine (SIA 1). There are also concentrations of slag in areas that were not associated with a mine (for example, in units of Transect 517, east of Klirou village). The one thing that all metallurgical POSIs have in common is their location near river channels, clearly a key link in the archaeometallurgical *chaînes opératoires* represented in the SCSP area.

When we consider the distribution of the relevant POSIs through time, it appears that diverse factors dictated the choice of an industrial or mining site in different periods; no single variable can be cited as characteristic. SCY100 (Politiko *Phorades* 1), the primary smelting workshop of the Late Cypriot period, was sited 500–600 m from the closest ore deposit (Kokkinorotsos) and very close to an active river channel. From what has survived, Phorades seems to have been involved solely in smelting ores. No architectural remains have been identified and the closest known Late Cypriot sites lie 2 to 3 km away. It would seem that a primary factor in site location at that time was the presence of the river channel and perhaps also the natural spring nearby, which would have provided those operating the smelter with drinking water.

The two metallurgical POSIs of the Geometric and Archaic periods, SCY022 (Agrokipia *Kriadhis* 1) and SCY116 (Politiko *Kokkinorotsos* 1), are both located in the direct vicinity of a mine, and both have waste deriving from more than one stage of the copper production process. SCY116, in fact, reveals evidence of all stages (that is, ore beneficiation, primary and secondary smelting). The somewhat later (Archaic to Classical) SCY219-7, Mitsero *Kokkinoyia* 2, is a large slag heap also located in direct association with a mine (see SIA 11); the remains of an ore beneficiation procedure (SCY219-9) are not far away. If SCY219-7 and 219-9 are contemporary (neither was dated by radiocarbon and no pottery was found in 219-9), the *chaînes opératoires* would seem to have been organized in such a way that all stages took place in close proximity to a mine, albeit with each stage somewhat separate from the other.

The Late Roman slag heaps at Mitsero *Kouloupakhis* (SCY021) and Sykamies (SCY024) are both located at some distance from a mine: Sykamies about 500 m southwest of the Kokkinoyia mine and Kouloupakhis about 2 km from both Kokkinoyia and Kriadhis (SIA 1). This spatial arrangement seems to suggest another change in the social organization of production, since the smelting workshops are no longer found in direct association with a mine; in the case of Kouloupakhis it is actually at a notable distance. At Kouloupakhis we found walls constructed of mortared limestone with finely cut blocks, and we could see that substantial building activity had taken place prior to the beginnings of copper production (see chapter 4.3). Moreover, at least one building appears to have been abandoned prior to the start of smelting operations. Yet we also found slag covering and in direct contact with some of the existing walls, suggesting that these walls lay in ruins at some point

during the lifespan of copper production at this site. Roman tiles, pottery, and mortars recovered within the "workshop" walls suggest that they were refurbished while the copper industry still flourished. Another wall exposed on the lower terrace at Kouloupakhis had been constructed before copper production began, and then was used in some industrial process before being turned into a dump.

From this *chaîne opératoire* of mining and archaeometallurgy, it follows that, prior to the industrial activity we observe so clearly, substantial Classical or Hellenistic structures existed in and beyond the buildings at Kouloupakhis. Later they became integrated into a significant copper smelting enterprise, and underwent refurbishing during the Roman period. Thus, the Kouloupakhis slag heaps and the surrounding area reveal solid evidence for long-term human occupation as well as a considerable investment in the copper industry.

According to analytical work conducted on the slags, both Kouloupakhis and Sykamies were involved in the primary smelting of ores; there is no evidence of ore beneficiation in either case. The shift in location farther from a mine but closer to a river (in the case of Sykamies), or closer to a river and perhaps to a settlement or administrative center (in the case of Kouloupakhis) may be explained in different ways. It may have been necessary to move to an area where trees could provide fuel: The smelters of the Archaic to Classical period who produced the slag heap at Kokkinoyia (SCY219) would have used a substantial amount of charcoal, while the mines themselves required timber supports in the mining galleries. Perhaps the trees around Kokkinoyia had been reduced to the point that they could no longer regenerate: Sulfur dioxide fumes are quite toxic and have the capacity to eliminate most natural life around a smelting workshop. In such a scenario it would have been necessary to establish new workshops in timber-rich areas. Alternatively, perhaps the new locations nearer a river were chosen because it was easier to move the ore downhill than it was to move the fuel uphill and next to the mine. In the case of Kouloupakhis, it may have been the presence of an administrative center or settlement that decided the issue. Evidence for such a settlement exists in the notable presence of Roman pottery around SIA 3 (Mitsero *Kouloupakhis*—see plate XIII) and in the number of Roman tombs in this area, all excavated by the Cypriot Department of Antiquities.

Thus, a range of evidence collected by SCSP reveals the diverse *chaînes opératoires* involved in the emergence and development of an early industrial landscape in the north-central Troodos region of Cyprus. Because we have no idea if even earlier workshops lie below or within these enormous slag heaps, perhaps we should not place too much weight on these observations. Yet there appears to be a clear spatial differentiation in the workshops—vis-à-vis mines and ores, fuel, and water—during different time periods. Perhaps this results in part from the transformation of the natural landscape into an industrial landscape, and the need to expand to new areas unaffected by the copper industry.

INDUSTRIAL LANDSCAPES IN CONTEXT

The interrelationships—economic, social, ideological—among agricultural settlements, mining communities, industrial sites, and the landscape vary with respect to the scale and the organizational level of production (various papers in Knapp, Pigott, and Herbert 1998; Raber 1987: 301–302). Industrial sites like Politiko *Phorades*, or Mitsero *Kouloupakhis* and *Sykamies*, fulfilled the basic production needs of the economy, especially in terms of raw materials and refined goods. But when the production of copper exceeded local or regional capacity, mining communities rapidly became integrated into supraregional or national trading networks. In turn, this development brought outside goods into mining communities, along with migrant labor and other factors that led to sociostructural changes within the industrial landscape.

In the SCSP area, the large spoil heap of the modern, open cast Kokkinoyia mine, juxtaposed with the nearby ancient slag heap at Sykamies (in SIA 11), is a remarkable example of long-term human modification of a landscape (see Frontispiece). These two industrial remnants dominate the interspersed agricultural fields and actually emulate, unintentionally, the surrounding foothills. The major spoil heaps and slag heaps in the SCSP area reflect both the social organization and economic significance of an industrial landscape that affected the everyday life and work of people in this region.

The archaeometallurgical landscape was a profoundly influential factor in creating and maintaining social identities. In turn, people used this landscape and imbued it with personal, ideological, and economic significance (Given et al. 1999). SCSP's fieldwork and its research design have enabled us to view an industrial landscape as a space that serves as a medium for and the outcome of human activity (Tilley 1994:10). Although the manufacture of metals essentially characterizes such a landscape, it is the dynamic between metallurgical production and agricultural enterprise that typifies the SCSP region.

7.4 Agricultural Landscapes

Michael Given, Dina Coleman, R. Scott Moore, and Jay Noller

Even before industrialization, agriculture always required complex technologies, involving such operations as selective breeding, the designing of specialized tools and processes, and the movement of vast quantities of earth and water. This technology, along with the necessity of agricultural products for human survival, engenders a complex and highly organized set of economic and social activities across the landscape. During the annual cycle of food production, people interact with their environment, with the members of their families and communities, and with external structures such as corporations, factions, states, and empires. Tasks may be shared, or divided between specialists, or done in turn or in different parts of the landscape. Agriculturalists may support only themselves, or produce a surplus for industrial communities or exploitative elites, or for cash exchange. One task that SCSP set for itself was to attempt to detect such economic and social patterns across the landscape.

Landscape archaeology brings to this investigation a strong emphasis on spatial analysis and, ideally, the integration of several relevant disciplinary approaches. SCSP carried out the geomorphological mapping of soils and the human and natural processes that have affected them since the first occupation of the area. Many agricultural activities leave structural traces in the landscape, most notably in the check dams and hillside terraces investigated by the project's geomorphologists, but also in the form of field walls, wells, and cisterns, and in a variety of temporary shelters. The analysis of settlement patterns is also critical for a better understanding of agricultural production and the social organization that structured it.

Thanks to an intensive survey of the landscape, rather than individual sites, we can even detect some of these agricultural processes. Manuring leaves a diagnostic pattern of broad but low density scatters of sherds in arable land. Stone clearance is identifiable not just from the stone heaps at the edges of fields but more subtly from different average stone sizes in different fields. Threshing, when carried out by means of threshing sledges, can be identified by the discovery of paved or earthen threshing floors and by the characteristic chipped stone inserts that studded the underneath of the sledges. These various patterns need to be analyzed, taking into account survival biases and postdepositional processes. Once that has been done, we can compare the agricultural activities with environmental resources, local cultural factors, and social organization—all at a landscape level of analysis.

This section has been written by a survey archaeologist, a lithics specialist, a pottery specialist and a geomorphologist, all of whom worked together in the field. We examine the soils of the survey area and the structures used by farmers to manipulate them, and then give an overview of the sites, structures, and artifacts that relate to agricultural processes in the survey area. By combining this information with GIS analyses of SCSP survey data, we are able to assess the changing relationship among agricultural activities, social organization, and the landscape.

SOILS AND SOIL-HOLDING STRUCTURES

Agricultural soils have a plowed organic-rich surface horizon (Ap) underlain by a subsoil ranging from an immature, slightly weathered horizon (Cox) to an ancient, red clay-rich and deeply weathered horizon (Bt). These soils are best differentiated in the field on the basis of stoniness, texture, structure and color; a dark brown soil, for example, indicates a high level of organic matter. In hill-slope positions, such as on terraces and in check dams, at least one buried Ap horizon is present within the deposits. Ap horizons also include mollusks, seeds, charcoal, insect tests, and invertebrate fecal matter (especially in large pores or worm bores). Roots are many, fine to thick with a dominantly vertical orientation on active and fallow fields, but a more random to horizontal orientation beneath the surface crust in abandoned fields. Pores formed by penetrating roots and soil invertebrates are generally round, less than 3 mm in diameter and randomly oriented. These characteristics attest to the deeper infiltration of water in active soils.

Variations in soil properties and position (surface or buried) reflect a combination of land use, soil age, and soil improvements such as manuring, cultivation, and the clearing of field stones. Fields frequently have marginal deposits of cleared stones that may form berms, small hills, or field corner cairns. Some fields appear to have been deliberately spread with stones, as this can counteract soil erosion by wind and water, increase soil moisture, provide better drainage in the root zone, and reduce weeds.

Hill slope terraces have traditionally been used for planting grains, grape vines, and olive and fruit trees. Some olive trees on the terraces are 400 or more years in age. Soil development on these terraces suggests long use through plowing in field stubble and perhaps, but not necessarily, manure. Grain would add proportionally more organic matter to soils than other crops, and this might explain the quantity of organic matter accumulated in these soils.

Much of what we know about the fate of sediment and soils in the SCSP area comes from the study of sequences of trapped sediments and the soils which developed on them. Of particular interest are the systems of check dams and hill-slope terraces across much of the survey area (see chapters 4.9, 4.16, and 7.1). Deposits impounded behind the check dams are almost entirely fluvial in origin, and anthropogenic fill is used only as part of check dam construction. Perhaps the check dams represent "speculative" reclamation of waste or village lands for future agricultural use. In the shorter term, the check dams should have served to ameliorate the loss of soil from nearby terraces, presumably from stream undercutting of terrace walls. The use of these valley bottoms for agricultural use would not occur immediately after these structures were built. Eventually these reclaimed lands were used for growing grain and olives and thus represent a tradition in this region stretching back at least 600 years (based on olive trees still growing behind check dams).

AGRICULTURAL SHELTERS AND SETTLEMENTS

Patterns of residence and movement form an essential part of investigating the social organization of agriculture across the landscapes. The paucity of Bronze Age POSIs in the SCSP area, and their very poor state of surface preservation, reveal very little about prehistoric agricultural regimes. The Archaic to Roman landscape presents a very different picture of agricultural settlement from the nucleated villages of the Medieval to Modern periods. Large town centers such as Tamassos (SIA 6) and Klirou (SCY364) serve as spatial centers of communication, with elite displays and multiple functions. Lower down the settlement hierarchy there were numerous small agricultural settlements scattered throughout the survey area. These seem to have been rather smaller in the Archaic and Classical periods (chapter 6.2), and were perhaps farmsteads, while they were often rather bigger in the Roman periods, perhaps more like estates (chapter 6.3).

The pottery assemblages for farmsteads and small estates in the SCSP survey area show certain common features. In the Archaic to Classical periods, the relevant sites are characterized by substantial numbers of domestic wares and a few fine wares. In the Hellenistic to Late Roman periods, the sites still have cooking wares and coarse wares, such as the Late Roman frying pan, Late Roman basins, and Late Roman 1 amphorae, but they also have an increased amount of fine wares, such as Cypriot Red Slip, Phocaean ware, and African Red Slip. This pattern makes it easy to draw distinctions in the Hellenistic to Late Roman periods between estates or villas, with elements of elite consumption and display, and more basic agricultural sites restricted to intensive production. Sites such as SCY101, and the clear density peaks on the Tamassos (SCY108, SCY127, SCY209) and Klirou (units 3237, 3239) plains, have a mixture of fine wares and coarse wares, and are here interpreted as estates or villas. Sites such as SCY214, on the other hand, reveal large quantities of coarse wares and no fine wares; we interpret their function as limited to intensive agricultural production. This trend continues in the early Medieval period, but in the late Medieval to Modern periods the sites return to the Archaic to Classical pattern, with manifold coarse wares but few fine wares.

Most of the agricultural settlements were small in area and probably consisted of only one or two buildings with a few rooms, for example, SCY214. Larger centers, for example, SCY101, which are fewer in number in the SCSP area, consisted of several buildings grouped together in one central location. Usually situated in the foothills overlooking the flat agricultural plains surrounding the larger towns, these agricultural compounds are characterized by an extensive tile scatter (particularly in the Roman

period) and large numbers of coarse wares and cooking wares. Only the larger estates, such as SCY101, have fine or imported wares in any significant numbers. All the coarse wares and cooking wares, such as the Late Roman 1 amphorae, seem to have been manufactured on the island. While storage vessels such as amphorae and pithoi are present, they are not numerous enough to suggest a large-scale operation under the control of a nearby town. Rather they are consistent with what would we might expect from small, independently owned and worked farms or estates that communicated both socially and economically with the town centers. Chronologically, such sites seem to have flourished from the Archaic to Late Roman periods.

Even with a system of nucleated villages, such as that which prevailed during the Medieval to British colonial periods, farmers and laborers often need to spend one or more nights in their fields, to deal with labor-intensive tasks at specific times of year. This applies particularly to vine-dressing, which takes place in January and often at considerable altitudes. A characteristic series of stone-built vineyard shelters were clearly in use in the northern Troodos mountains during the early twentieth century, and very likely before then (Given 2000:229-231). Two examples from the SCSP survey area are typical. Episkopio *Peratis* (SCY341) is a stone-built structure measuring 3.2 x 2.8 m externally, with the collapsed remains of beams and cane roof, and an entrance in the northwest corner. Klirou *Ayia Marina* (SCY206) is half built and half excavated into the rocky slope, with an internal space of 2.3 x 1.0 m. Both are situated in abandoned vineyards, 2.5 km from the nearest village.

Apart from water mills, the other type of structure associated with agricultural activity and relatively common in the northern Troodos is the goat fold (*mandra*). In the Ottoman and early colonial periods, families tended to keep about ten goats or sheep in the courtyard of their village houses. Larger landowners and monasteries, however, often had flocks of eighty or more, which required a specially built goat fold, usually situated well away from arable land (Given 2000: 227–229). The two examples from the SCSP area are rather smaller and simpler than the elaborate versions surviving in the Makheras and Adelphi forests to the south, but they have the same essential elements. Mitsero *Klouvaes* (SCY325) sits on the edge of the current forest overlooking the

Figure 7.1 Plank from threshing sledge, with notches for inserting the blades

Mitsero Basin, and consists of a semicircular 9 x 12 m courtyard, with two low rooms along the straight (northern) side. These rooms are 4 x 3 m and 5 x 3 m, and by comparison with other goat folds we can suggest they were probably used for storage and for shelter by the shepherd, while the animals remained in the enclosure. Politiko *Mersinoudhi 1* (SCY341) is a very similar structure, with a single stone-built room measuring 6.0 x 3.7 m, and a roughly trapezoidal 19 x 12 m enclosure on its northeastern side.

The agricultural landscape of the Ottoman and colonial periods was very much based on nucleated villages with occasional temporary settlement in specialized vineyard shelters and goat folds. Judging by the distribution of off-site pottery, the Medieval period was much the same, apart from the large estates (for example, Richard 1947).

THRESHING

While the examination of sites and structures is important for examining patterns of residence and movement in agricultural practice, systematic and intensive collection of off-site data gives us information about specific agricultural processes. Two such processes are threshing and manuring.

Because the practice of manual threshing persisted in Cyprus into the 1950s, we anticipated that we would find evidence of this technology within the SCSP landscape, particularly because agriculture has always been a vital subsistence mode in the area. We used various methods to investigate the technology of premechanized threshing and its appearance throughout the landscape. Aerial photographs from 1948 (provided by the Hellenic Mining Company) proved helpful in identifying the location and number of threshing floors (*alonia*) throughout the project area. In 1997 and 1998 we conducted interviews with local residents in the village of Mitsero; they described the threshing process as well as the locations where the tasks were carried out and in which family members were involved. They also told of the visits of traveling *athkiakadjes* (flint knappers) from the north coast of Cyprus.

Historical documents provided additional information, particularly concerning the history of Cypriot threshing and how long threshing has occurred in Cyprus (see also Whittaker 1999). The earliest reference to threshing sledges in the region dates to 1318, when the accounts of the estate of Psimolophou record the purchase of "six boards with which the wheat is threshed on the threshing floors" (Richard 1947:150). Later travelers such as the Englishman Alexander Drummond, who traveled through Cyprus in 1745, describe the process in more detail (Cobham 1908:287). Finally, surface survey of the project's landscape generated data regarding the occurrence and distribution of threshing-related artifacts and structures throughout the landscape. One set of threshing floors was examined in more detail (chapter 4.5).

During the 1995 field season, an abandoned threshing sledge plank (*dhoukani*) was located near the village of Mitsero and collected for study purposes (figure 7.1). Although the sledge was weathered and in poor condition, it provided a typical example of a wooden plank, metal braces, and embedded stone blades. The fragment consisted of a single wooden plank measuring 210 cm long, 26 cm wide, and 3.7 cm thick; originally it would have been attached to a second similar plank. One hundred and fifty-two notches were carved into one side of the board in nineteen offset rows of eight notches, for inserting stone blades. Most of the blades were missing from the board, but twelve remained in heavily weathered notches, providing examples of size, shape, material type, and use-wear patterns. Each blade was analyzed to identify common attributes. This information was combined with threshing sledge blade attributes defined by Carole McCartney (1993). The set of known attributes was then used to identify sledge blades among the project's chipped stone sample.

Many of the blades from the chipped stone collection were fairly uniform in size, shape, and material type. Occasionally the size and shape of the pieces appeared anomalous, but the distinctive heavy abrasive fracturing seen on lateral use margins helped to identify them. Of roughly 3000 chipped stone examples collected during field survey, 120 were identified indisputably as threshing sledge blades. This seemed surprisingly low, and we considered several explanations. First, the established set of attributes was not guaranteed to identify all such blades. Moreover, 15% of the chipped stone collection consisted of incomplete stone implements, and threshing sledge blades may have made up a large part of this grouping. It is also likely that blades had a comparatively high economic value, and scattered blades have been collected for reuse. This might be a realistic explanation in times when skilled knappers were unavailable or raw material sources unknown.

Once the threshing sledge blades were sorted from the larger chipped stone collection, their location was plotted on a distribution map (plate LII). The clearest concentration is immediately east of Aredhiou, where most of the village's threshing floors were located; it is surprising that more were not found at the equivalent location immediately north of Mitsero. SCY101 (Politiko *Phorades* 2) also shows a major concentration, in an area where there is no Medieval to Modern pottery at all (chapter 4.7). This suggests that these threshing sledge blades may be contemporary with the Roman estate there. The fertile alluvial river terraces north of Politiko and around Malounda and Klirou are notable for a broad but very thin scatter of threshing sledge blades. As the next section suggests, these scatters are more likely to reflect manuring practices from the villages than the actual locations of threshing.

MANURING

In the Roman period and, to a lesser extent, in the Medieval to Modern periods, stable alluvial plains throughout the survey area show a relatively even carpet of sherds at a consistently low level of density, with a typical pottery index of less than 1000 (plates XLIX, L). This pattern is clearest in the broad alluvial plain northwest of Tamassos and SIA 6, apart from two clear density peaks (plate LIII). The same broad but low spread of Roman pottery can be seen in other areas of alluvial land in small pockets east of Aredhiou (SCY105) and at SIA 9 (chapter 4.9), and all the way across the broad alluvial valley of the River Akaki, from Aredhiou and Malounda to Klirou and Kalokhorio.

Similar phenomena have been noted in many intensive survey projects in Europe, the Mediterranean, and the Middle East—with many possible explanations:

- Erosion from major pottery concentrations can cause light scatters downhill (Alcock et al. 1994:164). This is clearly not the case here, as these scatters occur on stable and flat alluvium. The same applies to sedimentation derived from pottery-rich areas; these parts of our survey area do not show sedimentation (plate I).

- Plow action over a long period of time can drag pottery from distinct concentrations backward and forward until it becomes an even, light carpet, its density peaks obscured (Ammerman 1985; Yorston et al. 1990). This effect, however, is less on flat surfaces, and plowing cannot carry sherds across the field boundaries on which our survey units were based.

- General activity in the landscape, most notably travel and labor in the fields, brings a certain amount of material into the landscape because of breakage of water jars and other containers. It is highly unlikely that this would have produced so widespread and consistent a pattern.

- Dumping of household garbage outside major settlements can cause a halo of material for up to 1 km around that settlement.

- Night soil was often collected, along with household garbage, and spread on fields. This is well attested for Classical Greece (Alcock et al. 1994:148–149) and is supported by the identification of *koprones* or cesspits in fourth-century BC houses at Halieis in southern Greece (Ault 1999).

- Manuring of fields required the transport of manure from villages, farms, and estates out to the surrounding farmland, often containing household garbage and broken pottery. This is very well attested in the prehistoric Middle East

(Wilkinson 1989), during the Classical to Roman periods in the central Mediterranean (Alcock et al. 1994:149–153), and in Medieval and later Europe (Astill and Davies 1997:28–32; Gerrard 1997:69–70).

For the Roman to Modern periods in the survey area, some combination of dumping, night soil, and manuring seems the most likely explanation for these broad but low-density pottery scatters. This can to some extent be tested by the analysis of phosphate levels (Cavanagh et al. 1988:81–82; Wilkinson 1989:33; Alcock et al. 1994:163; Sarris and Jones 2000:41–48). Whitehill's analysis of successive river terraces in the Mitsero Basin (see chapter 4.8) shows that total phosphorus levels are higher than expected in old surface horizons; they even increase with the age of the surface horizon, suggesting that older surfaces have been exploited and manured for longer than younger ones.

For the Roman period in the survey area, it is perfectly possible that domestic garbage and night soil were dumped near the major settlements such as Tamassos and Klirou. This does not explain, however, the much broader expanse of pottery in alluvial areas, which is more likely to be deliberate fertilizing through manuring, whether animal or human in derivation. This situation would clearly allow greater productivity, as fallowing can be kept to a minimum. When combined with estates or large farms such as Politiko *Phorades* 2 (SCY101) and Klirou *Klirovourna* (SCY214), this evidence implies intensive and highly organized agriculture across the alluvial plains of the survey area, especially during the Late Roman period. Production was clearly aimed at a much higher level than that of subsistence alone and was capable of supporting a wide range of nonproducers, such as the elites who constructed the tombs, sanctuary buildings, and churches of Tamassos and the mining communities of Mitsero *Kouloupakhis* (SIA 3) or Mitsero *Mavrovounos* (SIA 4).

The Medieval to Modern periods show a rather different distribution pattern. There are widespread and significant scatters around the main known settlements, most clearly Politiko and Episkopio in the east of the survey area. Interestingly, these scatters coincide with the distribution of threshing sledge blades, apart from the major peaks of blades at threshing areas (plate LII). The pottery scatters are denser than their Roman equivalents, typically with a pottery in-

dex of about 2000 to 3000, but they are distinctly more limited in area. This fits in much better with the halo pattern of dumping around settlements and suggests that manuring was less significant.

The nucleated settlement pattern and extensive farming of the Medieval to Modern periods meant that the animals were kept at a distance from the fields, usually in the villages. This made manuring much more difficult. Before the use of artificial fertilizers, it was only the *sokhorafa* (the fields immediately adjacent to the village) which were manured (Christodoulou 1959:41). Instead, the bare fallow technique was used, where the field was plowed every second year to kill the weeds and then left fallow (Halstead 1987:78, 81–83). This technique has been widespread in Cyprus certainly for the last two centuries, and probably for all the Medieval to Modern periods (Christodoulou 1959:43, 126). The evidence for manuring practice is visible in the survey data through the heavier halos or concentrations of material around the villages, but with a less extensive carpet of material across alluvial land.

CONCLUSION

The relationship among agricultural production, metallurgical exploitation, and social organization across the SCSP landscape has at all periods been complex, dynamic, and constantly changing. From the localized subsistence and production strategies of Early Prehistoric sites to the intensive elite-sponsored production of the Bronze Age (copper) or Roman period (grain) to the more organic household-based organization of the Ottoman and Modern villages, people's relationship with each other and with their environment has changed dramatically. These different agricultural landscapes can still be read, thanks to the integration of geomorphology, historical records, the contextual examination of artifacts and structures, and intensive archaeological survey.

Even from the pottery-poor hillslopes, we can learn about the rich record of soil conservation through long-used agricultural technologies. Expansion of agriculture onto hillslopes of ever greater steepness was not always followed directly by increased loss of soil and rock, as earlier workers have concluded elsewhere in the Mediterranean or around the world. Rather, the first affirming steps of sediment collection in gullies led to the creation of substantial terraces of rich agricultural soils. The direct organization of the check dams and hillslope terraces points to a structured organization of the agricultural communities of the SCSP area, at the very least on a family or household level. Ethnohistorical data on threshing practices, for example, suggest that this level of activity could easily be carried out by the household with occasional extra support from extended family or other members of the community.

SCSP survey data from earlier periods, above all the Late Roman, show that agricultural organization often transcended the family or household level. Estates such as SCY101 (chapter 4.7) or SCY214 (chapter 4.19) required wealthy landowners, professional management, and a considerable labor force. The carpet of Roman pottery across the Tamassos plain and elsewhere from manuring similarly suggests intensive production, good communications and market facilities, and a well-organized system of land ownership. The height of agricultural production came in the Late Roman period, and judging by the Kouloupakhis and Mavrovounos slag heaps it coincided with the most intensive copper production. This was a landscape controlled by the state and organized for mass production of food and copper. The grain, oil, and other foodstuffs supported the urban elite and craft specialists such as miners and smelters; its production was therefore an integral part of the operation of a complex and exploitative state power.

7.5 Ideational Landscapes

A. Bernard Knapp

Mediterranean archaeologists have treated several distinctive types of landscapes—civic, sacred, rural, and urban among them (Knapp 1997:21–27). In previous attempts to reconstruct the sacred landscape of prehistoric Cyprus (Knapp 1996a), or to discuss the long-term ideational landscape of the island (Knapp 1999b), it was untimely to refer to SCSP data and analyses. The present section thus seeks to link SCSP to the current literature and at the same time to assess the notion of ideational landscapes by using SCSP data, by definition both prehistoric and historic.

Whereas Johnston maintains that the study of landscapes is a "multi-disciplinary project" (1998), all variations of perceived landscapes still fall under two basic rubrics: the cultural and the ideational (or cognitive). For Tilley, the landscape is an "unstable" concept swinging between these polar extremes

(1994:37). More recently, Bender suggested that landscapes are multiple, contested, embodied, and an integral part of everyday human activity (1998:8–9). Most contemporary archaeologists likely would agree that certain social and symbolic elements are ingrained in the concept of landscape, which in turn means that the landscape is a dynamic, fully integrated part of the human experience. But we still need to consider how we might identify such social and symbolic elements in the field, particularly during the course of pedestrian survey.

Cultural landscapes are shaped by peoples' everyday lives, routines, habits, morals, and beliefs. Yet the usual archaeological notion of a cultural landscape makes a uniformitarian assumption that past events and cycles create or influence the present through some predictable association. Such deterministic ideas neutralize the social factors that were involved in constructing the landscape or forming perceptions of it. Landscapes should not be characterized as passive backdrops for human dramas, nor as inculcating neutral, binary relationships between people and nature (Meinig 1979:2). There may be a dynamic tension between the natural world and the socially constructed images of landscape (Richards 1996:314). Yet only an intellectual distinction separates real and perceived landscapes; the two concepts are indivisible for anyone who dwells in that space (Tuan 1977). As Brück points out, activities typically labeled as functional, practical or ritual are based on a logic for action and a model of the world that is distinctively western, and modern (1999). Within individual or collective memories, everything from mythological or cosmological concepts to cemeteries and cathedrals provide a means of organizing and inhabiting the landscape (Basso 1996; Schama 1995). People perceive the physical landscape through their own social and cognitive filters, often in what contemporary archaeologists relate to the ritual or symbolic. The environment is manifested as landscape only when people order, transform, and experience space as a living place (Knapp and Ashmore 1999:20–21).

Archaeologists usually regard *ideational* as a term equivalent to the sacred or symbolic; some associate it with "landscapes of the mind" (Knapp and Ashmore 1999:12–13; Bintliff 1996:250). An ideational landscape might refer to a mental image of something (imaginative aspect) or else it might elicit some spiritual value or ideal (emotional aspect). Whereas ideational is meant to convey an insider's perspective, archaeologists impose such notions from the outside. Ideational is distinct from ideological, but at the same time conveys a broader meaning than either sacred or symbolic. Ideational landscapes may keep track of genealogies, elicit sacred emotions or moral messages, and recount or recall oral or mythic histories. Ideational is an alternative term to sacred or ideological, at once more encompassing and with fewer specific implications for how particular meanings were generated or perpetuated in the past. At the same time, is it intended to embrace sacred as well as other kinds of meanings attached to and embodied in landscapes.

Peoples' ideas about the world, their identities, and their cognitive understandings mediated every part of a prehistoric landscape (Bender et al. 1997:150). Although archaeologists often distinguish between the constructed (built) landscape and the conceptualized (natural) landscape, the concept of an ideational landscape is meant to encompass both analytic realms and the range of meaning archaeologists impose upon landscapes. As argued elsewhere (Knapp and Ashmore 1999:13), ideational landscape is a construct approaching Johnston's (1998) notion of the inherent, where landscape is not perceived separately but embedded within ways of living and being.

IDEATIONAL LANDSCAPES ON CYPRUS

A. Bernard Knapp and Michael Given

Cypriot archaeologists have argued, often implicitly, that power and authority reside in the construction or elaboration of monumental architecture in urban centers. This position ignores the strategic or symbolic value of special places in rural or hinterland settings or in any other aspect of the nonconstructed landscape. Natural features such as mountains, mineral deposits, streams, caves, trees, and forests may also be defined and interpreted through social practices and experience (see various chapters in Ashmore and Knapp 1999).

Notions of ideology and authority extending from the Late Chalcolithic to the Middle Cypriot period (Prehistoric Bronze Age) have been considered in the context of building models (Peltenburg 1994) and figurines (Knapp and Meskell 1997), both of which provide information relevant to the con-

cept of the ideational landscape. Knapp (1996a, 1999b) has suggested that the ideational landscape of prehistoric Cyprus was closely linked to industrial activities, and to Bronze Age elites who exploited supernatural knowledge in order to gain control over the appropriation, distribution, and consumption of mineral resources (especially copper), labor, and land. By the Late Cypriot period (Protohistoric Bronze Age), the spatial patterning of settlement, cemetery and sanctuary had changed (Merrillees 1973), and there is good evidence for ceremonial structures in both urban and rural centers, the latter characterized by their isolation and location on some topographic prominence.

Rural sanctuaries are widely regarded as crucial for assessing the symbolic aspects of ideational landscapes (among others, see Webb 1988, 1999; Wright 1992; Knapp 1999b). In general, rural sanctuaries have been characterized by the specific types of material culture they contain (Alcock 1993:172–214): figurines and bucrania, precious or unique artifacts, distinctive architecture and installations, and repositories for storing unusual (cultic) items. On Bronze Age Cyprus, certain symbols associated with the production of copper—seals, bronze stands, pottery, and miniature ingots (Knapp 1986b)—also formed part of the ideational landscape. The sanctuaries themselves may also have been involved in the production and transport of raw materials and in the limited storage of agricultural products, such as olive oil. Not infrequently, we find installations in rural sanctuaries—workshops or entire production units—clearly associated with metalworking.

Knapp (1997:53–61) argued that the rural sanctuary should be added as a fourth component to the widely used tripartite scheme devised to portray Cyprus's Bronze Age settlement and economy (Catling 1962; Keswani 1996): (1) coastal trading centers; (2) inland, rural, agriculturally based settlements; and (3) inland copper production sites. Although, during the Late Cypriot period, some sanctuaries were situated within the new town centers (for example, Enkomi, Kition, Kouklia *Palaepaphos*, and others), several more were located inland and are thought to have been special-purpose, sanctuary, or ritual, sites (Webb 1999): for example, Myrtou *Pigadhes*, Ayios Iakovos *Dhima*, and Athienou *Bamboulari tis Koukounninas.* Webb (1999) has identified twenty-nine possible Late Cypriot cult units in fourteen different sites, most of which she regards as public or ceremonial in nature (on funerary cult sites, see Webb 1992:92–96). Catling (1975:193), who first proposed the tripartite system (1962), suggested that these rustic sanctuaries might have been intermediary points in an internal trade that brought copper and prestige goods to the town centers; yet he failed to distinguish these sanctuaries from any other type of inland settlement.

Returning to the SCSP context, we also need to consider how—or if—survey data can shed light on past ideational or conceptual landscapes, on rural sanctuaries or similar sites. It must be observed straightaway that none of our prehistoric POSIs or SIAs can be identified plausibly as a rural sanctuary, much less as part of an ideational landscape. During excavation of the Bronze Age smelting site at Politiko *Phorades* (SCY100), we encountered caprid jaw bones and some long bones of ovicaprid type in context with a massive, intrusive boulder. The bones probably highlight no more than daily activities at Phorades (for example, remains of a worker's lunch), although they could be taken to indicate some sort of feasting. The pottery at Phorades also inspires questions about the type of activities associated with copper smelting as well as the status of copper workers within Cypriot Bronze Age society. The presence of what we have traditionally regarded as elite pottery styles such as White Slip, Base Ring, Red Lustrous, and a possible Aegean import might be taken to imply that somebody at Phorades had access to high-status goods. On the other hand, maybe we should ask whether and why Bronze Age Cypriots would have regarded these wares as elite. Finally, the excavations at Phorades uncovered a large conical boulder (0.66 m in height by 0.49 m wide at its widest point). The stone is diabase and thus not local to this area. Although this type of rock was used to make tools, such as anvils and pestles for crushing ores, the Phorades example bears no wear marks typical of such actions. Along with a small deposit of (calcined?) bone found at the base of this rock, its conical shape, size, and exotic character may suggest some nonfunctional use, for example as a *baetyl*, or sacred stone (Karageorghis 1992:212). Even if we allow for some association here between metallurgical production and ceremonial activity, without the excavation of Phorades none of this material would have entered into the discussion.

There are seven Iron Age rural sanctuaries in and immediately around the survey area, two of which were discovered by SCSP (chapter 6.2; figure 6.2). To these can be added the major urban sanctuary of Politiko *Chomazoudhia*, within the city of Tamassos. Copper workshops were found immediately adjacent to this sanctuary (Buchholz 1985a:240–242). In addition to copper slag, there is evidence of agricultural products—for example, bones of wild and domestic animals, olive pits, grain, and, judging from the vessels, oil and wine—in the town sanctuary at Tamassos. Can we assume that copper as well as products from the surrounding countryside were dedicated or processed in a sanctuary setting (Given 1991:54–55)?

Of the rural sanctuaries, only Pera *Frangissa* has been excavated, and that in the 1880s, so we know nothing about the dedication of agricultural or other rural products. The courtyards of these sanctuaries were full of statuary ranging from over life-size to a mere 10 cm; whether their walls were low enough to allow the statues to be visible from outside we have no idea. Mazovounos lies on a small hill in the middle of a valley, Zithkionas overlooks the fertile Akaki plain, and Ayios Mnason similarly overlooks the fertile plain northeast of Tamassos—which our intensive survey shows was certainly cultivated in the Archaic and Classical periods. Frangissa and Mialathi are more discreet, one in a small upland valley, the other in the Pedhiaios River bed. Whatever reasoning governed the initial choice of these sacred sites, their architecture and what became a centuries-long tradition of visiting and offering dedications, made them highly significant nodes within the ideational landscape of the Archaic to Classical periods.

No rural sanctuaries are known from the Roman period in or around the SCSP area, and indeed they are rare throughout Cyprus. Our survey data suggest a landscape given over to intensive production and exploitation of natural resources, especially in the Late Roman period. The alluvial plains were intensively cultivated; there were villas, estates, and farmsteads in the mountain valleys as well as in the plains, and marginal land was colonized for agriculture using check dams. Even the inhospitable pillow lavas saw intensive mining and processing of copper ore, with the settlements and workshops that such a technical process required. The natural hillocks and outcrops of the pillow lavas were rivaled by slag heaps rising to 10 m in height. This was a landscape tamed, dominated, and exploited by human activity. There seem to be no significant sacred places outside the city, and the view in every direction was one of extracting agricultural and mineral wealth at a nearly industrial level.

The contrast with the Byzantine, Medieval, and Ottoman periods is dramatic. It is unlikely that the landscape become fully depopulated under Byzantine rulers and the Byzantine/Arab *condominium*, but even so anyone still living in the SCSP area left almost no traces of their existence. Even when cultural materials again become evident in the thirteenth century, it is clear that a totally different dynamic existed between people and their landscape. Settlements from the Medieval period to the first half of the twentieth century were firmly nucleated. The inhabitants lived in a series of defined communities, such as Mavrovounos, Mitsero, and Agrokipia; unless specific agricultural tasks required otherwise, they returned to these communities from their fields each night. There were still estates, such as Psimolophou and Akhera, but these were on the same scale as a village, and most Medieval estates actually became villages.

Each village is marked by its church, which was the focus of the community's religious, social, and often economic life (Given N.D). Of the five apparently rural churches in the survey area, each one turned out to be associated with an abandoned settlement or monastery. The village's most valuable fields were the *sokhorafa* or infields closest to it, which could be visited most often and manured the most easily. This is well known from oral sources (for example, Panaretos 1967:71), and confirmed by our intensive survey (chapter 7.4). Beyond the area controlled by and visible from the village was the wilderness, inhabited by characters such as bandits and goatherds (Sant Cassia 1993:775–778), or the three-eyed giant Trimmatos who lived in a cave 1 km northwest of Mitsero.

A series of folk traditions express this tripartite view of the landscape, with the village and its protecting church, the infields, and the wilderness. On the feast day of Saint Tryphon, for example, villagers take holy water from the village church and scatter it on their fields and vines to protect them from disease (Panaretos 1967:226, 247). On Olive Sunday they take olive leaves from the church and scatter them in the fields to bless them (Panaretos 1967: 228). An epidemic among the animals or people of a village can be controlled by the *nimatoma*, circling the village church with a rope made of cloth (Panaretos 1967:240); the metaphor here is one of enclosing and therefore protecting the community, symbolized by the village church.

Even in the wilderness, there are islands of safety. Monasteries such as Ayios Mnason are enclosed by a wall, with the cells looking inward to the church. Goatfolds are similarly walled, as the examples from the SCSP area show (chapter 7.4), and there is a host of traditions to protect the animals inside. One such tradition from Xylophagou relates that when a shepherd finds some of his animals are missing, he puts the bread-shovel backward into the oven, with its handle in the middle; this will protect the sheep from foxes (Panaretos 1967: 240). Again, the metaphor is one of being inside (the *domus*), whether the oven, the goatfold, or the village and therefore being protected against the wilderness outside (the *agros*). The contrast with the dispersed settlement and nearly industrial-level activity all over the landscape during the Late Roman period could hardly be greater.

CONCLUSION

As Brück (1999:326) has recently argued, the post-Enlightenment rationalism that demands a sharp distinction between ritual and secular action, or between the symbolic and the practical, is not a concept that is universally shared. By rejecting the analytical value of this post-Enlightenment notion, we can view the landscape as a place where people engaged in a practical manner with all variety of material conditions. Activities usually regarded by ethnographers or archaeologists as ritual or symbolic in nature need not be seen as qualitatively different from other areas of practice. Rather, as Brück (1999:327) points out, all activities are shaped by a very different type of rationality and a different understanding of causation from those of contemporary western culture. In terms of human-environment relations specifically, this viewpoint is the equivalent of Pálsson's communalism, which rejects any separation between people and the natural world (Pálsson 1996:66–67).

A great variety of sites, features, installations, and settlements will have formed part of the ideational landscape. Within that landscape people negotiated differing interests and manipulated their social and spatial worlds. Such locations were not haphazard, but instead were linked closely to human settlement and social needs in the landscape. People collectively develop and maintain certain places, or entire towns and regions, in symbolic or ceremonial or otherwise unusual (to us) terms. Sanctuaries, shrines, monuments, and a whole range of natural features (caves, grottoes, gardens, high places) serve as social spaces where ceremonial activities are carried out and where local authority is generated and maintained. These places, in turn, help to form and express a people's social identity. Within the ideational landscape, people carry out sacred or symbolic or even mundane acts, which further serve to establish their social identity or authority, and to reinforce social, economic, or religious institutions. In the end, we need to consider just how such landscape elements affect human relations and how people and institutions are empowered in spatial and temporal terms.

Many of these issues can be addressed only by data from an intensive and interdisciplinary survey such as SCSP. When we discuss isolated sites such as settlements and rural sanctuaries, we exclude whole areas of human activity; by relying on the perceived function of those sites, we fall easily into the trap of artificially distinguishing ceremonial or ritual from mundane, everyday activities. By collecting and analyzing material from an entire survey area, with a careful eye to the geomorphological processes within the area, we have identified a wider, more fully contextualized range of human activities in the landscape. Undertakings such as copper production, extensive large-scale farming, or dedications in a rural sanctuary cannot be seen in isolation. To investigate past ideational landscapes, we also need to detect natural and anthropogenic changes to the terrain, investigate patterns of movement, map the arable land and mineral resources that were being exploited, and reconstruct the social hierarchies and dynamics played out in those landscapes.

7.6 Conclusion

A. Bernard Knapp and Michael Given

AGRICULTURE AND METALLURGY

At the outset of SCSP, we predicted we would find both industrial sites (for example, smelting areas, slag heaps, mines, and lithic production areas) and the agricultural villages that supported them. At the same time, we always operated within the framework of the total cultural and social landscape. This allowed us, for example, to consider not only the Classical to Roman slag heaps in and around the village of Mitsero but also the huge, modern spoil

heap and open cast mine (Kokkinopezoulas) that dominate the village and the surrounding agricultural countryside.

SCSP's attempt to gain a broader, diachronic, regional and social perspective has been underpinned by our focus on the landscape and our attempts to learn how people lived in it and used it. One of our primary goals was to learn more about the relationship among metallurgical resources, agricultural production, and trade, from earliest prehistory to the present day. Based on intensive survey work, excavation, and geomorphological study of the region around the Bronze Age smelting site at Phorades, we proposed a reconstruction of a prehistoric industrial landscape. The integration of geobotanical and geomorphological fieldwork demonstrated that earlier landscapes in the Mitsero-Politiko region were noticeably different from those we see today. Rivers channels flowed higher and on different courses, while the surrounding floodplains were more extensive, and much less eroded and chopped up; intensive mining and agriculture together have stripped the natural ground cover and altered the landscape beyond recognition. Within the igneous setting, ores for smelting came from mines along the gossan ridge (Kokkinorotsos) in the southeastern sector of the SCSP area or from mines and ore deposits in the pillow lavas stretching along the northwestern sector, and centered on the villages of Agrokipia and Mitsero. These Upper Pillow Lavas (see plate LI) contain the richest deposits of Cyprus's sulfide ores, and the array of unprecedented technological and archaeometallurgical finds from the SCSP area overall will prove immensely significant for reconstructing the long-term history of metallurgy on Cyprus.

The SCSP survey area was chosen, amongst other reasons, to include significant parts of the pillow lavas, where the ore resources are situated in immediate proximity to the sedimentary/alluvial zone that holds the most fertile soils. From the main era of intensive copper mining (Protohistoric Bronze Age to Late Roman), we discovered sixteen major POSIs—most directly involved in copper production—located within the pillow lavas close to exploited ores (this figure excludes the fifteen minor slag scatters, adits, and pits from SIA 7 recorded in table 4.18). From the same period, not including low-density spreads of pottery deriving from manuring, we have eighteen POSIs located on good arable land in the sedimentary zone probably involved in farming. Given that we were careful to sample these different zones at the same intensity, these numbers are roughly equivalent.

During times of extensive copper production, for example in the Late Roman period when the slag heaps of Mavrovounos and Kouloupakhis arose, there was a need for a corresponding system of intensive agricultural production to provide a surplus large enough to feed miners, metalworkers, and the elite who controlled the system. The estates and the widespread cultivation in the Tamassos region clearly filled this need. At periods of lower production, the symbiosis between agriculture and mining was more subtle, flexible, even unpredictable. This observation even applies during the mid-twentieth century, as oral sources testify. For example, in the village of Mitsero during the 1950s, Konstantinos Ttaouxis would walk in the evening with his donkey to his most distant fields (7 km away), sleep a little, and harvest all night on his own. Then, in the morning, he would walk back to the pyrites washing plant, where he would leave his donkey and spend all day breaking up pyrites by hand with a hammer, to return home only in the afternoon before walking back out to his fields in the evening (interviewed 16 June 1998). Such stories are expressed in the landscape through the system of copper mining and production sites, agricultural fields, and villages. This changing dynamic between agriculture and mining in the SCSP landscape can be investigated further by examining the settlement hierarchies of the survey area.

SETTLEMENT HIERARCHIES

Models of settlement hierarchy for Bronze Age Cyprus (Catling 1962; Keswani 1996; Knapp 1997) have always defined a system in which some coastal centers were larger, wealthier, more stratified socially, and more diverse in their forms of production than were inland towns. In turn, inland towns are distinguished in similar ways from the still smaller agricultural settlements or rural sanctuaries. Mining sites/communities and pottery manufacturing villages are not necessarily distinguished by size or extent but by their productive functions. Following some general statements on prehistoric settlement hierarchies, we consider whether such phenomena of any period are even apparent in the SCSP landscape. Iron Age city-kingdoms, and later city-states and villages have not been discussed in the terms

associated with prehistoric polities, so it is difficult to be inclusive in what follows. We can state at the outset, however, that data from previous survey projects on Cyprus do not contradict the concept of a settlement hierarchy; indeed, they indicate the significance of site size and location, especially in terms of proximity to either the coast or mineral resources (also Portugali and Knapp 1985). Figure 7.2 shows a working model that gives a diachronic overview of some of the suggested settlement hierarchies of the SCSP area.

Site or settlement hierarchies arise as a result of the ideology of elite landowners. socioeconomic costs and benefits (for example, resource location, sharecropping, or slavery), modes of transport, and mechanisms of trade. The upper tiers of a settlement hierarchy may be shaped by force (for example, resettlement; mercantile legislation) or by intention (colonization; relocating). Town dwellers often own, control, or otherwise dominate both land and people in the rural sector (Cherry et al. 1991:460–461). Wagstaff and Cherry (1982:250) suggest that the degree of settlement hierarchy, and the settlement nucleation or dispersal that produces it, vary directly with the political or economic relationships that exist between different regions. In attempting to assess settlement hierarchies by using survey data, we also need to bear in mind the idiosyncrasies of surface remains, their density, their fluctuation from year to year, their visibility, and the fact that surface finds often do not coordinate well with subsurface features (Ammerman 1993: 370–371; 1995; Barker 1991:5; Bintliff et al. 1999; see also Davis and Sutton 1995). Surface materials must also be studied within a geomorphological context (for example, local rates of erosion, alluviation, and colluviation).

The settlement system proposed for Bronze Age Cyprus is far from perfect. Primary centers not only have multiple functions overlapping with those of secondary and tertiary centers inland, some also have an inland location much closer to the mines than the coast. The existence of imported prestige goods not just at inland centers, as we might expect, but also at rural sanctuaries and agricultural villages suggests either that the latter sites were involved in wider networks of regional exchange or that we need to reassess whether what we envision as prestige goods were regarded that way in the past. Or, perhaps, these imports reached rural sites indirectly (Webb and Frankel 1994:17).

In the SCSP area, we need to determine whether access to Cyprus's minerals and arable lands or to other sources of wealth and prestige was controlled by one centralized political organization or by more local or regional elites. This situation certainly will have varied through time. Other issues may be more equivocal but must be noted. For example, the prominence of storage facilities at agricultural support villages and inland sites implies that agricultural products were produced and stored in the hinterland but redistributed to specialized producers or to elites upon demand. To take another example: If the status of Enkomi continues to be anomalous compared to other *early* Late Cypriot sites (that is, Protohistoric Bronze Age 1, or MC III–LC I), it must be noted that we do have prima facie evidence for the existence of a king, as documented in the Amarna letters of the fourteenth century BC. Moreover, a king of *Alashiya* (Cyprus) is now mentioned by name—Kushmeshusha—in a new cuneiform tablet found at Ugarit in Syria (Malbran-Labat 1999).

Turning now to SCSP evidence for the Prehistoric periods, nine POSIs have been defined as Prehistoric while several others had prehistoric sherds among the material collected. Early Prehistoric finds derive mainly from the eastern part of the SCSP area (plate XLVII). PreBA (Chalcolithic, Philia, and Early Cypriot) settlement location and land use patterns mirror those of contemporary sites elsewhere in Cyprus. With two exceptions (PreBA Ergates *Spileadhia*—SCY106; ProBA Politiko *Phorades*—SCY100), all prehistoric sites are situated in the sedimentary zone and within 100 m of a water course. All were either farmsteads or very small agricultural villages.

Of three ProBA POSIs (SCY001—Aredhiou *Koladhes*; SCY010—Aredhiou *Vouppes*; and SCY100—Politiko *Phorades*), the first two are either farmsteads or very small rural compounds while the third is a copper smelting site. Unlike the situation with Iron Age and later Tamassos, there is no known primary center in the SCSP area, and the three POSIs just mentioned belong to the third (rural agricultural settlements) and fourth (production sites) tiers of the proposed settlement hierarchy. We can speculate but we cannot demonstrate that sites like Vouppes, with pithoi fragments belonging to storage vessels of diverse sizes, were agricultural support villages provisioning mining sites or encampments

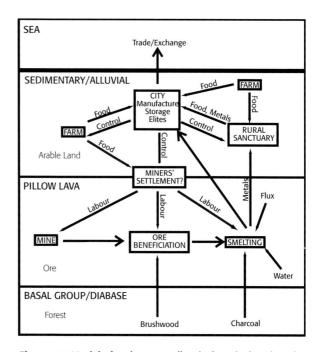

Figure 7.2 Model of archaeometallurgical, agricultural, and social processes in the landscape. The thick arrow follows the course of copper ore/metal/artifacts. 'Ore beneficiation' refers to both crushing and roasting. 'Farm' means an agricultural production centre such as a villa, estate, or agricultural support settlement.

like Phorades (these two sites are not necessarily contemporary). Such sites are also assumed to be key elements in ProBA transport and storage systems, where surplus grains and olive oil would have been collected, processed, and redistributed, either to mining sites or to the inland towns and coastal centers (Knapp 1997). As discussed above (chapter 6.1), the location of ProBA (Late Cypriot) sites and materials to the north and northwest of the SCSP area could be associated with some sort of communications route running into and through the region.

From the eighth century BC to the beginning of the Hellenistic period the least equivocal evidence for a settlement hierarchy comes from the ten or so independent or semi-independent city-kingdoms. The eastern end of the SCSP survey area includes just the edge of Tamassos, and the surface material there stands out from the rest of the survey area for its density, extent, variety, and quality. It is not difficult to determine that this is the edge of a major cosmopolitan center. The map of POSIs and, more helpfully, pottery density for this period (plate XLVIII) shows a relatively clear second order of site, mostly density peaks of limited area in the arable plains, in the midst of broader carpets of low-density pottery probably derived from manuring. These may be farming hamlets or farmsteads, on the Classical and early Hellenistic Greek model (Alcock 1993:37–49). In addition, there are four specifically mining and metallurgical sites, probably dependent on Tamassos, which according to literary sources controlled the copper resources of its territory (chapter 6.2). Other than the imported Greek pottery from SIA 1, presumably from tombs rather than metallurgical installations, there is little evidence for elite activity in the landscapes. Even the rural sanctuaries seem to be marked by large numbers of locally made terra-cotta figurines and statues rather than by ostentatious elite display on the level of the Chomazoudhia sanctuary or the royal tombs of Tamassos itself.

The picture in the Roman period, and especially the data-rich Late Roman period, seems to be similar to that of the Archaic and Classical periods but on a larger scale. The city of Tamassos extended slightly farther west with even more material than before, the manuring covered a greater proportion of the arable land, and the density peaks in these arable areas seemed larger, if fewer (plate XLIX). The large-scale copper production of the period required larger sites, possibly with related settlements as at Kouloupakhis, and a greater supply of agricultural surplus. There was, of course, a level in the hierarchy above that of the city, in that the province of Cyprus was controlled by and paid a proportion of its income to Rome. This may be reflected in the intensity and apparent organization of both agricultural and copper production.

During most of the Medieval to Modern periods, Nicosia, 22 km northeast of the center of the survey area, was the state and district capital. Thus, it became the ultimate destination of tithed produce and the source of political control, but until communications improved in the late nineteenth century it played a minor role in local exchange networks and the settlement hierarchy. Until that time, there was very much one level of settlement: the village. Even though some villages coalesced from estates with their settlement of waged estate workers (as is recorded for Psimolophou and Agrokipia), all were of equivalent size and function. Apart from the relatively independent monasteries, the only other sites in the landscape beyond the village were seasonal or temporary settlements for specific agricultural purposes. This single-level settlement pattern also was reflected administratively: successive governments divided the island into villages—each with their territories—and taxed and controlled the population accordingly.

SCIENCE AND ARCHAEOLOGY

SCSP employed an intensive survey methodology; invested a great deal of time and specialist expertise in developing a complex, relational database; carefully linked that database to a GIS and analyzed an immense amount of data statistically (which resulted in the thematic maps that display the data spatially and quantitatively); integrated the work of a geomorphological team to assess the context of the archaeological material and to reconstruct past landscapes; engaged geobotanical ground truthing with satellite imagery to develop a predictive model geared to locating sites; used various archaeometallurgical analyses to gain a fuller understanding of ancient smelting and production techniques; and provided as many radiocarbon analyses as possible to set the chronological parameters of past landscapes. We adopted and sought to follow an interdisciplinary ethic, not a multidisciplinary approach. Its usefulness must now be judged in terms of the results presented elsewhere in this volume. Here we emphasize only some of the highpoints.

Our most fully integrated scientific approach has been to collect and analyze data on material culture found throughout the landscape according to a system that takes an appropriately sized and chosen sample, is repeatable, and is based on experimentation and testing. Rather than giving an impressionistic account of the material's location in the landscape, we quantified this information using statistical methods to factor in effects that impact our data, such as poor visibility. Ultimately this produced a set of GIS maps showing variability and distribution of human activity in the landscape, which could then be interpreted within the frame of a social archaeology of landscape.

XRF and SEM analyses of slag samples from all main archaeometallurgical POSIs have shown significant changes in technology between the Protohistoric Bronze Age and the Late Roman period, including the use of different ore sources and fluxes and the improving efficiency of the process. When combined with the twelve radiocarbon dates from stratified archaeometallurgical deposits, this has contributed a new and much-needed chronological control in assessing the development of ancient copper production on Cyprus. Our geomorphological mapping and analysis of land forms and surface processes were essential for gauging the integrity of the SCSP surface material. With the help of a further seven radiocarbon dates and the analysis of exposed soil sections and stratified deposits behind check dams, SCSP's geomorphologists were able to shed new light on the evolving relationship between people and their landscape. Investigating the geobotanical indicators of archaeometallurgical and other sites has shown that it is indeed possible to detect such sites remotely by using ground-truthed satellite photographs.

Beyond this, we must ask if real interdisciplinary collaboration is possible in a project so decisively archaeological in its origins, goals, and outlook? A difficult question, perhaps, and one more readily answered by specialists from the other disciplines involved or by readers who will judge the success of our efforts. And yet we must bear in mind that archaeological knowledge is often intangible and certain to be modified as more evidence accumulates or as new and different interpretative approaches take hold. Some archaeologists are very skeptical about engaging with science; others are all too ready to accept that the results of scientific approaches and analyses outweigh those derived strictly from archaeological methods and theory. The truth hangs somewhere in the balance between social archaeology and archaeological science, between social and scientific. Science clearly has the potential to help us evaluate archaeological issues and problems but scientific analyses alone can never adjudicate between cultural possibilities or social potential. On the contrary, analytical data are open to multiple social interpretations and must always be assessed by collaborating specialists working together with archaeologists (Knapp 2000).

Metals, grains, dairy products, and oil were produced by miners, shepherds, and farmers who understood much more about the basic technologies involved than did the elites, merchants, and traders who exported both primary and secondary (luxury) commodities. All these goods, even standardized bulk commodities, have social meaning layered on top of economic value and technological expertise. Science can help us to understand the technologies involved or to evaluate certain quanti-

tative aspects of production, but archaeology alone holds the key to unpacking social meaning.

THE SOCIAL ARCHAEOLOGY OF LANDSCAPES

Our highest level research goal has been to understand the social and spatial aspects of human habitation on Cyprus as expressed by material in the landscape. To do this, we have attempted to make meaningful statements about the emergence, development, and transformation of social landscapes and complex communities in the northern Troodos foothills of Cyprus. Have we succeeded in these goals? Can "social archaeology" ever be any more than the attempt to put people back into past spaces and places and to look at individuals, communities, or regions through their material remnants? To comment on what they produced, how they organized production, where and when they carried it out? And to speculate on why they did what they did, in the ways they did?

Landscape archaeology traditionally has focused on changes in settlement patterns and the exploitation of natural resources within a defined region. SCSP has operated under the assumption that social and natural landscapes are equally important, and we have tried to look at the way people interact with the landscape in terms of their own individual or collective experiences. The notion of settlement systems as dynamic social constructions, bearing culture and material culture through space, time, and memory, is relatively new to archaeological thinking (see Roberts 1996). The relationship between the environment and the people who use it is conditioned by both human consciousness and material reality. Landscapes influence personal and social identity and leave their material imprint on the cultural heritage of any given land.

The SCSP area has undergone major transformations over geological time. In human terms, it is safe to say that the people who inhabited the SCSP region during the Chalcolithic period—some 5000 years ago—would simply not recognize the landscape today, even if we were able to remove all the towns, people, and modern conveniences. With the exception of the Troodos Mountain complex, human and natural processes alike have modified the forest and plains and river valleys beyond recognition. The exploitation of the area's natural resources commenced no later than the Chalcolithic, when people living at *Phournia* exploited the local basal Lefkara chert formations and created a habitational space along the banks of a river (Kouphos) that had a much broader channel and wider floodplain than those we see today. People began creating new tracts of agricultural land using hillslope terraces and check dams that transformed rocky gullies like the one at Ayios Mamas (SIA 9) into smooth and fertile valleys. We can only speculate on the exact ways in which social identities are defined by place, but the agricultural character of the SCSP region took its first form in the Chalcolithic and thereafter was maintained and reconfigured as dictated by social needs or economic demand.

Excavations at the copper smelting workshop at Phorades reveal another level of articulation between landscape and social identity by the beginning of the Late Bronze Age. Many sites similar to Phorades must have existed in the Troodos foothills, each supported by one or more agricultural villages. The smelting of copper seems to have taken place during down time in the agricultural calendar, and here we see, perhaps for the first time in the SCSP region, an example of how the rhythms of agricultural and metallurgical production became interlinked in the life cycles and memories of the people who inhabited this landscape. We know from evidence beyond the SCSP region that the exploitation of Cyprus's copper resources had a major transformative effect on Late Cypriot society, a pattern that still has its legacy in the contemporary Cypriot landscape, deeply scarred and massively restructured by twentitehth century AD mining companies and conglomerates.

Social identity as expressed in the landscape is not a momentary or purely synchronic phenomenon: It is contained in memory, history, and perceived continuities and changes. The continuity of settlements in the survey area between the Late Roman and Medieval periods is very striking, even when there is no intervening material from the Byzantine period. Village memory today always recalls the ruined churches, even when no remains are visible. In almost all cases where we inquired about antiquities in an area, we were told first of the churches. The people of Klirou knew where the long-gone church of Ayios Mamas had been (SIA 9) and so in the early 1990s decided to rebuild it: continuity with the past

was felt to be important. The monastery of Ayios Mnason (SCY346) is now in ruins, but it is still widely known that Saint Paul converted its patron nearly 2000 years ago. Interestingly, the monastery is very close to the site of an Archaic and Classical rural sanctuary, and one of its outer walls is possibly ancient; this may be a memory of a sacred landscape that goes back even further. Most people in Mitsero have memories of their recent mining past, but because of the monumental ancient slag heaps on the edge of the village—and the team of archaeologists working in the area since 1992—they make connections with the skills and suffering of an older population of mineworkers.

Despite the wealth of information available on mining, manuring, hydrological regimes, and intensive agricultural practices, and despite all the regional survey work that has been conducted in the Mediterranean throughout the past forty years, it remains a challenge to attempt to reconstruct landscapes or even to present a coherent landscape history of any given region. In this volume, we have sought to look at the landscape holistically, as natural, social, and cultural, and we have considered the dynamic between these aspects. But archaeologists are not the only ones who consider the long-term relationship between people and their landscapes: in diverse ways and to various degrees, the inhabitants of those very landscapes involve themselves in examining and nurturing or debasing that relationship. The articulation between social identity and landscape, whether on the individual or collective level, helps us to understand the active role of landscapes—how place is formed, maintained, and reconfigured. As people create or modify places in the landscape, their identity too is defined or redefined. Within the SCSP landscape, we have considered the social dynamics occurring over a period of seven thousand years and we have seen how people transformed the landscape even as their livelihoods were changing, their social relations adjusting to the new or reorienting to the traditional. And now, we take these newly found understandings with us to a new survey project in another, little explored area of the northwest Troodos Mountains of Cyprus, where we too must adjust and adapt to a different tempo and mode of village life, itself forever changing.

Appendix A

LIST OF POSIs

ID	Village/Locality	Grid reference	Periods	Basic description	Page
SCY001	Aredhiou *Koladhes*	519700/3878600	ProBA; Ar	Sparse scatter of sherds on eroded hillock; WS, LC III, Archaic Red Slip	177
SCY002	Malounda *Kharjis* 1	516080/3877650	GAC, Roman	Dense scatter of sherds in plowed field. Mostly Cl and LR	164
SCY003	Aredhiou *Vamvakis*	517700/3879300	?	Unknown	
SCY004	Klirou *Kokkinoyia*	513350/3876300	?	Spoil heap from modern mining exploration, with ancient slag fragments	
SCY006	Mitsero *Petramoutti* 1	511600/3878700	?	Unknown	
SCY007	Mitsero *Kambos tou Kriadhi* 1	512200/3878900	?	Unknown; terrace may have redeposited material	
SCY008	Politiko *Argaki ton Kastron* 1	522150/3874350	?	Sparse scatter of sherds, tapped slag fragments and lithics in valley bottom	
SCY009	Politiko *Argaki ton Kastron* 2	521700/3874300	?	Very sparse scatter of worn sherds and slag fragments	
SCY010	Aredhiou *Vouppes*	519015/3878700	ProBA	Dense scatter of LC pottery and pithos in fields; wall bracket fragment	179–181
SCY011	Politiko *Kafkalla*	521500/3875775	AC; some Med–Ott	Concentrated scatter of sherds from small vessels and slag fragments.	
SCY012	Mitsero *Kriadhis*	512800/3878500	EP	High hilltop with pottery, chipped and ground stone. Knapp et al. 1992: 333	265
SCY013	Eliophotes *Ova*	509400/3880200	EP	Extensive ground stone, some chipped stone, little pottery. Knapp et al. 1992: 332	
SCY014	Kato Moni *Monarga*	508190/3881800	EP	Fluvial terrace; light scatter of pottery and chipped stone. Knapp et al. 1992: 332–333	
SCY015	Kato Moni *Kambia*	507300/3880600	EP	Fluvial terrace with lithics and ceramics. Knapp et al. 1992: 332	
SCY016	Politiko *Mazovounos*	522100/3873400	?	Chipped and ground stone. Knapp and Given 1996: 345–346	
SCY017	Mitsero *Kokkinoyia* 1	510050/3878020	?	Slag scatter; exploratory mine workings; pre-modern foundation of large blocks	
SCY018	Aredhiou *Trakhonia*	518400/3878370	?	Plowed field with scatter of lithics; pottery from several historic periods	
SCY019	Politiko *Kelaïdhoni*	520800/3876350	Pre-Pottery Neolithic	Eroded hilltop with dense scatter of lithics; many bladelets	182–183
SCY020	Politiko *Lambertis*	522450/3875900	ProBA	Low hill with MC-LC pottery, apparently from tombs. Catling 1962: 153, 159, 168	133
SCY021	Mitsero *Kouloupakhis* 1	511680/3878220	GAC-LR	Slag heap with workshop floors and structure; probable settlement. SIA 3	84–93
SCY022	Agrokipia *Kriadhis* 1	513300/3878100	GAC-LR	Ore roasting heap in modern mine. SIA 1	64–69
SCY023	Mitsero *Mavrovounos*	509500/3877550	Med–Ott	Ruined settlement of "Maurochio". SIA 4	103–109
SCY024	Mitsero *Sykamies*	509600/3877550	Roman	Twin slag heaps. SIA 4	100–104
SCY025	Agrokipia *Kokkinous*	514500/3877400	Med	Plowed fields with scatter of pottery. Knapp and Given 1996: 324–325	
SCY026	Ayia Marina *Mavrovouni*	507200/3879900	Cl, Roman	Slag heap with extensive pottery and nearby rubble heaps	
SCY100	Politiko *Phorades* 1	519528/3874570	ProBA	Copper smelting workshop. SIA 7	133–134
SCY101	Politiko *Phorades* 2	519500/3875100	Roman	Knoll in valley with very dense sherds and tile fragments	134–137
SCY102	Agrokipia *Paleokamina*	514600/3878500	Pre-Pottery Neolithic	Ridge top with extensive chipped and ground stone	183–186
SCY103	Agrokipia *Autinina*	513550/3877860	Hl, LR, Med	Plowed field with scatter of lithics and sherds	60
SCY105	Aredhiou *Panayia Odhiyitria*	518400/3878300	Cl–LR; Med–Mod	15th century church; extensive sherd scatter	
SCY106	Ergates *Spileudhiu*	520500/3878700	PreBA	Eroded hillock with Red Polished pottery and lithics	266
SCY107	Episkopio *Vrysia*	520490/3878100	PreBA; Ott–Mod	Cultivated knoll with Red Polished sherd scatter	266
SCY108	Episkopio *Kokkinos*	520500/3877700	Cl, Hl, LR	Eroding gully with dense scatter of pottery and lithics	
SCY109	Kalokhorio *Kladhous*	514600/3874300	Med–Mod	Fields on river terrace with broad but sparse scatter of sherds and slag	
SCY110	Klirou *Mazerka*	515400/3876200	GAC-LR; Med–Ott	Fields on river terrace with very broad scatter of sherds	186–187

continued

ID	Village/Locality	Grid reference	Periods	Basic description	Page
SCY111	Politiko *Ayios Mnason 1*	521600/3876430	GAC–LR; Med–Mod	Archaic–Roman necropolis; ruined monastery; extensive sherd scatter. SIA 6	121
SCY112	Malounda *Panayia Khrysopandanassa*	516700/3877740	GAC–LR; Med–Mod	Church, with extensive and dense pottery scatter in fields. SIA 10	159
SCY113	Malounda *Pervolia*	516000/3877000	LR; Med–Ott	Fields on river terrace with broad scatter of sherds	109
SCY114	Mitsero *Lambadhiotissa*	510720/3878560	Byz–Mod	12th-century church, with modern successor; spring; check dams	187–192
SCY115	Mitsero *Kalorka*	509500/3876800	Med–Ott	Walled enclosure on mountain ridge. Goat fold?	137–140
SCY116	Politiko *Kokkinorotsos 1*	519120/3874525	Geo–Ar	Extensive slag heap, and roasting site. SIA 7	146
SCY117	Politiko *Kokkinorotsos 2*	519090/3874880	GAC?	Gossan and scatter of tap slag fragments. SIA 7	146
SCY118	Politiko *Kokkinorotsos 3*	519125/3874960	?	Gossan and slag heap. SIA 7	146
SCY119	Politiko *Kokkinorotsos 4*	519110/3874900	?	Mining adit. SIA 7	146
SCY120	Politiko *Kokkinorotsos 5*	519165/3874885	?	Mining adit. SIA 7	146
SCY121	Politiko *Kokkinorotsos 6*	518975/3874550	GAC?	Slag heap cut by road. SIA 7	142–143
SCY123	Politiko *Phorades 3*	519410/3874570	GAC–Hl	Eroded knoll with dense sherd scatter and foundation walls. SIA 7	140
SCY124	Agrokipia *Moutti ton Spitoudhion*	513470/3877140	Mod?	Small clusters of lithic reduction debris	
SCY125	Politiko *Kannouris*	519440/3874520	?	Substantial stone check dam. SIA 7	140–142
SCY126	Politiko *Phorades 4*	519515/3874660	?	Lithics scatter. SIA 7	130
SCY127	Politiko *Parthenou*	520500/3877030	Hl, LR, Mod	Terracing with sparse pottery scatter	
SCY128	Agrokipia *Mavroyia*	513400/3877200	Mod?	Small clusters of lithic reduction debris	
SCY129	Politiko *Mali*	522200/3875700	GAC, Cl, Roman	Scatter of pottery and slag	
SCY130	Kalokhorio *Alonia*	513390/3874300	Ott–Mod	Settlement of 5 ruined buildings, including one cut stone house	
SCY131	Agrokipia *Panayia Khrysopandanassa*	514200/3878300	Roman? Ott–Mod	Church, cemetery, and slag heap	
SCY132	Klirou *Manastirka*	517370/3873500	GAC–LR; Ott–Mod	Monastery on knoll, with dense pottery and slag scatter. SIA 2	74–81
SCY133	Klirou *Kokkinous ton Pitidhion*	517000/3875790	Med–Mod?	Mud brick fragments	
SCY134	Klirou *Ayios Mamas*	518360/3874230	Med–Mod	Ottoman settlement, with rubble piles and pottery; modern church. SIA 9	155
SCY135	Politiko *Kokkinorotsos 7*	520150/3876050	LR; some Ar	Slope with pottery and unusual slag-like but natural concretions	143
SCY200	Politiko *Phournia*	520150/3875950	Chalcolithic	Field and slope with dense pottery scatter and lithics (mid–late Chalcolithic)	192–197
SCY201	Klirou *Lithinon*	516800/3873500	Roman?	Cemetery on steep hillslope. SIA 2	78
SCY202	Mitsero *Kato Alonia*	511350/3878250	Modern	Threshing floors. SIA 5	109
SCY203	Agrokipia *Kriadhis 2*	513120/3878030	?	Tapped slag and grid of square cobbled floors. SIA 1	69–70
SCY204	Agrokipia *Kriadhis 3*	513280/3878060	Ar–?Roman	Crushed slag layer; workshop floors; pottery. SIA 1	70–71
SCY205	Klirou *Koutis*	517700/3874400	Ar–Cl	Dense slag scatter, with Ar–Cl pottery; adit	81
SCY206	Klirou *Kouloupaedhes*	518180/3874000	Med–Mod	Rubble piles and tile fragments; later vineyard shelter. SIA 9	155
SCY207	Mitsero *Kambos tou Kriadhi 2*	512280/3878400	?	70-m long fortification wall, 1–2 m thick, with room or tower	
SCY208	Mitsero *Loukkos tou Ellina*	509510/3878110	Ar–Cl	Steep gully with sherds and slag fragments; detected by geobotany	99
SCY209	Episkopio *Kallinikos*	521500/3877600	GAC, ER, LR, Med, Ott	Plowed fields with extensive scatter of pottery	197–198
SCY210	Klirou *Mavridhes*	518260/3874530	Mod	20th-century garbage dump: domestic and building materials, including pottery	
SCY211	Klirou *Mazovounos*	517240/3873245	Cl, Hl, LR	Sherd scatter on knoll; from tombs? SIA 2	78
SCY212	Politiko *Gastres*	522000/3874520	Ar, Cl, ER	Valley with lithic clusters, pottery, water pipe and aqueduct	
SCY213	Mitsero *Spilios*	511500/3878200	?	Terracing; source for Basal Lefkara chert	
SCY214	Klirou *Klirovourna*	515500/3874100	LR; some Ar–Cl	Settlement debris, with many storage vessels	198–200
SCY215	Kalokhorio *Pontizos*	514200/3875000	ER, LR, Med–Ott	River terraces with extensive pottery scatter	200–201
SCY216	Agrokipia *Kottaphi*	514050/3878750	?	High hilltop with chipped stone	
SCY217	Kalokhorio *Kounnas*	514050/3875570	?	Chipped stone and ground stone	
SCY218	Agrokipia *Ayios Kournoutas*	514400/3879700	Ott–Mod?	Saddle in ridge with ruined church	
SCY219	Mitsero *Kokkinoyia 2*	509850/3877950	Ar, Cl, Mod	Sections through slag heaps and workshops; galleries; modern mine. SIA 11	166–175
SCY220	Agrokipia *Kriadhis 4*	513240/3878100	?	Slag scatters. SIA 1	71–72
SCY221	Agrokipia *Kriadhis 5*	513280/3877980	?	Mining galleries with timbers cut by modern mine. SIA 1	72
SCY222	Agrokipia *Kriadhis 6*	513330/3878000	?	Slag scatters on spoil heaps of modern mine. SIA 1	72
SCY223	Mitsero *Petromoutti 2*	511650/3878400	Ar	Tunnel-like hole; perhaps tomb	
SCY300	Mitsero *Rodhanos*	511600/3878700	Mod	Gold works; mining gallery 140 m long	116
SCY301	Mitsero *Kokkinopezoulas*	510500/3877300	Mod	Open cast mine, with some structures remaining. Scattered ancient slag	116
SCY302	Kalokhorio *Mutoyephiron*	514150/3874550	Med–Mod	Bridge with pointed arches, much restored and repaired	
SCY303	Malounda *Tria Yephyria 1*	516200/3877450	Ott–Mod	Bridge with round arches, rebuilt ca. 1890, with older plaque	160
SCY304	Malounda *Asproyi*	516420/3878260	Ott	Water mill with hopper; surviving wheel chamber	
SCY305	Malounda *Kharjis 2*	516180/3878030	Ott	Water mill with shaft; surviving channel and wheel chamber	
SCY306	Malounda *Tria Yephyria 2*	516200/3877450	Ott	Water mill (marked on cadastral map)	
SCY307	Kalokhorio *Potamous*	515900/3877150	Ott	Water mill with shaft; surviving channel and adjacent rooms	

continued

ID	Village/Locality	Grid reference	Periods	Basic description	Page
SCY308	Kalokhorio *Satas*	515280/3876470	Ott (1757)	Water mill with hopper; Greek inscription (1757)	114
SCY309	Klirou *Kavala*	516250/3875800	Roman	Cemetery, under school and modern cemetery	
SCY310	Mitsero Village	511300/3878000	Med–Mod	Village. SIA 5	109
SCY311	Agrokipia Village	514200/3878200	Med–Mod	Village	64
SCY312	Klirou Village	516300/3875400	Med–Mod	Village	164
SCY313	Malounda Village	516800/3877100	Med–Mod	Village	157
SCY314	Aredhiou Village	517800/3878500	Med–Mod	Village	
SCY315	Kalokhorio Village	514800/3873900	Ott–Mod	Village	
SCY316	Ergates Village	522300/3879300	Ott–Mod	Village	
SCY317	Episkopio Village	522500/3877900	Byz–Mod	Village	
SCY318	Politiko Village	522200/3876300	Ar–Mod	Village	
SCY319	Mitsero *Ayios Panteleimon*	512800/3879300	Byz; Ott–Mod	12th-century coin hoard; 18th-century monastery	
SCY320	Agrokipia *Ayia Varvara*	513000/3877700	Mod	1950s mining settlement for foremen. SIA 5	116
SCY321	Mitsero *Kolasis*	512450/3877700	Mod	1950s miners' housing. SIA 5	116
SCY322	Politiko *Troulia*	522200/3875900	PreBA	Settlement, with walls eroding out of gully. Ground stone; RP pottery	
SCY323	Malounda *Asprolakxia*	516270/3878260	Ott	Water mill with shaft; little survives	
SCY324	Mitsero *Moutti tou Trimithou*	509500/3878500	?	Group of small structures and rubble piles on ridge line	109
SCY325	Mitsero *Klouvaes*	510490/3876680	Ott–Mod	Ruined goat fold with two rooms and semi-circular enclosure	109
SCY326	Politiko *Ayios Iraklidhios*	522250/3887000	LR–Mod	18th-century monastery with remains of LR church, tombs, mortuary chapel	126
SCY327	Eliophotes *Petrokholetra*	509750/3879400	Ott–Mod	Lime kiln built in tiers, 5 m high	
SCY328	Mitsero *Ayios Yeoryios*	509300/3877400	Med–Ott	Ruined church, with extensive tile scatter. SIA 4	107
SCY329	Mitsero *Spilios 2*	511000/3878400	Ott–Mod	Goatfold (marked on cadastral map)	
SCY330	Mitsero *Kambos tou Kriadhi 3*	512260/3878830	Ott–Mod	Lime kiln	
SCY331	Mitsero *Rotsos Stidhos*	512700/3878200	Ott–Mod	Lime kiln	
SCY332	Mitsero *Papaphingos*	511850/3875750	Ott–Mod	Lime kiln (marked on cadastral map)	
SCY333	Politiko *Kato Kilistraes*	519700/3877650	Ott–Mod	Lime kiln (marked on cadastral map)	
SCY334	Politiko *Petrovounaro*	520450/3876350	Ott–Mod	Lime kiln (marked on cadastral map)	
SCY335	Politiko *Kokkinoyia*	521100/3876700	Ott–Mod	Lime kiln (marked on cadastral map)	
SCY336	Mitsero *Kapsalis*	510520/3878950	Mod	Gypsum quarry and two built stone kilns (2–2.5 m diameter); ash deposits	
SCY337	Mitsero *Petromoutti 3*	512040/3878730	Ott–Mod	Collapsed lime kiln	
SCY338	Klirou *Kouloupadhis*	518800/3876100	Ott–Mod	Isolated farmstead; chain of wells, water tanks, enclosure	
SCY339	Politiko *Mersinoudhia 1*	520470/3874330	Med–Mod?	Isolated stone built structure, at least 3 x 10 m	
SCY340	Politiko *Mersinoudhia 2*	520480/3874270	Ott–Mod?	Isolated structure with enclosure; goatfold?	
SCY341	Episkopio *Perati*	519520/3876860	Ott–Mod	Vineyard shelter; stone built with cane roof	
SCY342	Mitsero *Kouloupakhis 2*	511800/3878400	?	Adit and soil heap. SIA 3	93
SCY343	Kalokhorio *Kokkinorotsos*	514200/3874400	?	Exposed gossan face with several mining galleries	
SCY344	Agrokipia *Volidhiaridhes*	514200/3877200	Ott–Mod	Alakati (wheel-well)	
SCY345	Agrokipia *Vathia*	514150/3877400	Ott–Mod	Stone-built open water tank	
SCY346	Politiko *Ayios Mnason 2*	521600/3876430	Ott–Mod	Monastery and church. SIA 6	123–126
SCY347	Politiko *Kokkinorotsos 8*	518975/3874765	?	Mining gallery in gossan	143
SCY348	Politiko *Kokkinorotsos 9*	518915/3874620	Mod	Modern drill/prospecting hole	143
SCY349	Politiko *Kokkinorotsos 10*	518840/3874510	?	Shallow mining hollows	143
SCY350	Politiko *Kokkinorotsos 11*	519110/3874820	?	Mining gallery or tunnel	143
SCY351	Politiko *Kokkinorotsos 12*	519120/3874905	?	Open cast pit? Very eroded	143
SCY352	Politiko *Kokkinorotsos 13*	519120/3874850	?	Shallow pit in gossan	143
SCY353	Politiko *Kokkinorotsos 14*	518955/3874820	?	Mining pit	143
SCY354	Politiko *Kokkinorotsos 15*	518965/3874835	?	Collapsed adit, 4+ m long	143
SCY355	Politiko *Kokkinorotsos 16*	519120/3874945	?	Mining hollow with gossan pile	143
SCY356	Politiko *Kokkinorotsos 17*	519025/3874915	?	Mining hollows? Eroded	143
SCY357	Mitsero *Arkhangelos Mikhail*	511410/3878010	Ott–Mod	Village Church	111
SCY358	Mitsero Village 2	511355/3878370	Mod	Village cemetery	113
SCY359	Mitsero Village 3	511365/3878005	Mod	"House of Symbols"	113
SCY360	Mitsero Village 4	511420/3877995	Mod	Old school	113
SCY361	Mitsero Village 5	511430/3878015	Mod	Old olive press	113
SCY362	Mitsero *Kokkinoyia 3*	509000/3877955	Mod	Modern mine pithead buildings. SIA 11	113
SCY363	Mitsero *Yeropalloura*	510275/3877835	Mod	Kokkinopezoulas Mine office complex	116
SCY364	Klirou *Limni*	516200/3875700	Hl–Roman	Slag, pottery, tiles in construction trenches in Klirou village	
SCY365	Politiko *Ayios Mnason 3*	521620/3876220	Ar–Cl	Rural sanctuary with terra-cotta statuettes and statue fragments	122–123

Appendix B

RADIOCARBON DATES

Comments on Age Estimates

Treatment of materials for dating, including sampling, handling, preparation, and analysis, has been performed in accordance with the standards of good practice (Noller et al. 2000). Reporting of radiocarbon age estimates is based on the suggested format of Stuiver et al. (1998). Calibrations of radiocarbon laboratory results were performed using CALIB rev. 4.2 (Stuiver and Reimer 1993; Stuiver et al. 1998). Atomic Mass Spectrophotometry (AMS) determined radiocarbon age estimates were corrected for isotope fractionation using lab-determined values of ^{13}C ($\pm$ 2.5‰) through the normalization on a $^{13}C_{PDB}$ value of -25‰. Conventional radiocarbon results, for which we have one (GX25438), do not need such corrections.

We report the Method A curve intercepts at 1σ (68.3% confidence interval) as well as the Method B probability distribution at 2σ (95.4% confidence interval). Whereas the former is more familiar to workers in the region, the latter result is the most robust estimate of the calendrical age of the dated material and provides a means of objectively distinguishing which of the age ranges are most likely accurate. The relative areas under the probability curve for the 2σ interval are listed in table A2.2 as percentage of total area and only those age ranges with areas equal to or greater than 10% are reported. An age range with 100% of the relative area should incorporate the actual age of the sample at the 95.4% confidence level.

APPENDIX B: RADIOCARBON DATES

Table A2.1 Radiocarbon dates from archaeometallurgical samples

SCSP No.	Lab No.[a]	Unit	Layer	Material	Δ^{13}C (%)	^{14}C Date BP[b]	Calibrated ± 1σ[c]	Calibrated ± 2σ[c]
SCY021-26	GU-8330	SCY021W-2	14	Charcoal	-22.50	1660 ± 60	AD 245–425	AD 210–475 (89%)
SCY021-27	GU-8332	SCY021W-2	19	Charcoal	-23.40	1660 ± 60	AD 255–305, 315–425	AD 210–540 (98%)
SCY021-29	AA-34133	SCY021W-1	–	Charcoal	-25.4	1535 ± 45	AD 435–605	AD 420–640 (100%)
SCY021-32	GU-8333	SCY021W-5	5	Charcoal	-22.8	1860 ± 70	AD 25–45, 50–235	BC 55–AD 265 (94%)
SCY022-52	AA-34134 (GU-8341)	SCY022-1A	26	Charcoal	-26.85	2555 ± 50	BC 795–55, 720–540, 530–25	BC 800–480 (93%)
SCY022-53	GU-8337	SCY022-1A	42	Charcoal	-22.4	2690 ± 50	BC 970–60, 925–815	BC 1010–780 (100%)
SCY022-54	GU-8338	SCY022-1B	16	Charcoal	-23.1	2660 ± 50	BC 900–800	BC 985–785 (99%)
SCY022-139	AA-34131 (GU-8335)	SCY022-1B	19	Charcoal	-21.0	2505 ± 65	BC 805–760, 680–65, 635–590, 580–55	BC 835–480 (93%)
SCY024-13	AA-34130 (GU-8334)	SCY024E-1	–	Charcoal	-23.1	1590 ± 45	AD 385–534	AD 320–565 (94%)
SCY116-37	GU-8331		7	Charcoal	-24.9	2490 ± 50	BC 790–480, 470–50, 445–10	BC 790–480 (88%)
SCY116-56	GU-8336		14	Charcoal	-23.7	2540 ± 70	BC 805–760, 685–660, 645–545	BC 830–480 (92%)
SCY116.48 (GU-8339)	AA-34132		20	Charcoal	-23.4	2450 ± 45	BC 780–410	BC 775–475 (85%) BC 475–410 (15%)

a. Analyses were carried out at the Scottish Universities Research Reactor Centre (SURRC). Samples with an AA coding were measured at the University of Arizona AMS Facility.

b. ^{14}C ages are quoted in conventional years BP (before AD 1950). The errors are expressed at the one sigma level of confidence. Values rounded to nearest 5 years.

c. The calibrated age ranges were determined using CALIB rev. 4.2 2000, Radiocarbon Dating Program, by the University of Washington, Quaternary Isotope Laboratory, according to Stuiver et al. (1998). Parentheses show the relative percent area under probability distribution for 2-σ age estimates. Values rounded to nearest 5 years.

Table A2.2 Radiocarbon dates from geomorphological samples (Mitsero Basin)

SCSP No.	Lab No.[a]	Position	Soil hori.	Material	Δ^{13}C (%)	^{14}C Date BP[b]	Calibrated ± 1σ[c]	Calibrated ± 2σ[c]
CYSS0025	AA25273	Hat$_3$	Bw	Charcoal	-25.0	285 + 60	AD 1490–1665, 1785–1790	AD 1465–1680 (84%) AD 1755–1805 (10%)
CYSS0055	AA31326	Hat$_3$	2Ab	Charcoal	-25.1	80 + 60	AD 1673–1955, with 12 identified intercept ranges	AD 1800–1930 (59%) AD 1680–1740 (26%)
CYSS0067	GX25438	Hat$_1$	3Abk	Charcoal	-25.5	8930 + 235	BC 8450–7490	
CYSS0093 (86)	AA31330	Toeb	2Cox	Partially burned wood	-23.7	275 + 60	AD 1485–1660	AD 1440–1680 (88%) AD 1735–1805 (10%)
CYSS0117	AA29389	Hat$_2$	2Ab	Charcoal	-23.3	390 + 140	AD 1400–1645	AD 1285–1695 (90%)
CYSS0117	AA31327	Hat$_2$	2Ab	Charcoal	-24.0	145 + 60	AD 1655–1892, 1905–1955	AD 1635–1955 (99%)
CYSS0118	AA31328	Hat$_2$	2Cox	Charcoal	-22.0	215 + 60	AD 1520–1590, 1625–1670, 1780–1800	AD 1450–1695 (72%) AD 1725–1815 (20%)

a. Analyses were carried out at the University of Arizona AMS Facility (AA) and the Geochron Lab, Krueger Enterprises, Inc. (GX). From Whitehill (1999). Analyses were funded by U.S. National Science Foundation (NSF Award SBR9728841 to L. Wells and J. Noller).

b. ^{14}C ages are quoted in conventional years BP (before AD 1950). The errors are expressed at the one sigma level of confidence. Values rounded to nearest 5 years.

c. The calibrated age ranges were determined using CALIB rev. 4.2 2000, Radiocarbon Dating Program, by the University of Washington, Quaternary Isotope Laboratory, according to Stuiver et al. (1998). Parentheses show the relative percent area under probability distribution for 2-σ age estimates. Values rounded to nearest 5 years.

Appendix C

CHRONOTYPES

Explanation of chronotypes: chapter 2.3. List of functions: table 3.6. List of periods: table 3.1. Pottery catalog: chapter 5.1

Summary of Chronotypes by Period

Chronotypes codes are given in the same order they appear in the List of Chronotypes

Period	Period Name	Chronotype Codes
EP	Early Prehistoric	BLT, BBP, COCH, COP, PHTR, PICH, PWCH, RB, RDL, RMP, RM, ROB, ROW, SP, SB
PEB	Prehistoric Bronze Age	COPEB, FWPEB, RPW, RSPEB, RPW, RSPEB
POB	Protohistoric Bronze Age	BR1, COPOB, FWPOB, MEA, MYC, PTPOB, PIPOB, PWH, PLPOB, RMPOB, WS1, WS2
PH	Prehistoric (EP–Geometric)	COPH
Geo	Geometric	FWG, WPGEO
Ar	Archaic	AMAR, BAAR, BIAR, BGAR, BORAR, CKAR, DRSHAR, FWAR, GWAR, MDB, PIAR, PLAR, RSAR, SROAR, TIAR, WPAR, WSBAR
GA	Geometric to Archaic	BIGA, BORGA
Cl	Classical	AMCL, BICL, BGCL, BORCL, DRSHCL, FWCL, GRS, GWCL, LPCL, PWCL, PLCL, RSCL, SROCL, SPCL, TICL, WPCL, WSBCL
GAC	Geometric to Classical	AMGAC, BS, BORGAC, COGAC, CKGAC, DRSHGAC, FWGAC, GWGAC, PIGAC, PLGAC, RLH, SROGAC, WPGAC, WP3
AC	Archaic to Classical	AMAC, AMGR, AMKB, AMPI, AMT, BAAC, BIAC, BGAC, BORAC, COAC, DRSHAC, FWAC, GWAC, LPAC, PIAC, PWAC, PLAC, RSAC, SROAC, TIAC, WPAC, WSBAC
ClHe	Classical to Hellenistic	BACH
He	Hellenistic	AMHE, BGHE, BSHE, COH, FWHE, FP, PWHE, RSHE
ER	Early Roman	AMER, CW, CAO, CFC, COER, CKER, CKERP, CKOR, CKORA, CKORB, CKSR, CS, CS5, ESA, ESB, ESB1, ESB2, FWER, LPER, RSER
LR	Late Roman	ARS, ARS45, ARS50, AMLR, AMLR1, AMRED, LRB, LRP, COLR, COWR, CKLR, CKD, CRS, CRS1-CRS12, CRSI1-CRSI10, ERS, ERSA-ERSC, FWLR, LRG, LRF, LRFD, LPLR, PHW, PHW1-PHW10, PILR, PILR12, RSLR, LRSG, TILR
REL	Early to Late Roman	AMREL, COREL, FWREL, LPREL, RSREL, WWR
Byz	Byzantine	AMB, COB, FWB
Med	Medieval	BGL, COMED, CG, CG1C, CG3B, CG4, CG4A-CG4C, CG5-CG8, CG8A, CG8B, CG9, CG11, W1E, FWMED, GZI, ISW, LW, MW, PMW, ZW
Ott	Ottoman	COOT, CG8BL, CG9L, CGBG, W3, W5, W6, OG, PIOT, PPW, TIOT
Mod	Modern	AMMOD, BRK, COMOD, CEM, CIA, CIE, CLWM, CYW, W7, FWMOD, LPW, LPWG, LPWY, PIMOD, TIMOD
MM	Medieval to Modern	BGW, COMM, W1, W4, FWMM, GZ, PIMM, TIMM, WA
HA	Historical Antiquity (Ar-LR)	PW, RS
Hi	Historical (Ar-Mod)	AM
PC	Post Classical (He-Mod)	PI, TI, TICR, TICP, TICO, TIFP, TILA, TIRR
Unk	Unknown	CO, CK, FW, TW, UNK

continued

List of Chronotypes

Chronotype	Code	Function	Period	Cat. Examples
African Red Slip	ARS	FW	LR	1728.10.1, 3653.27.1, 5041.47.1
African Red Slip 45	ARS45	FW	LR	1745.1.1
African Red Slip 50	ARS50	FW	LR	
Amphora, Archaic	AMAR	HU	Ar	3000.14B.1
Amphora, Classical	AMCL	HU	Cl	1733.2.1, 3097.3.1, S-0057
Amphora, Geo/Ar/Cl	AMGAC	HU	GAC	
Amphora, Archaic/Classical	AMAC	HU	AC	
Amphora, Greek	AMGR	HU	AC	2105.8.1
Amphora, Knobbed Base	AMKB	HU	AC	1733.2.1
Amphora, Pithoid	AMPI	HU	AC	1742.1B.1
Amphora, Torpedo	AMT	HU	AC	1733.3.1
Amphora, Hellenistic	AMHE	HU	He	
Amphora, Early Roman	AMER	HU	ER	
Amphora, Pseudo-Koan	AMPK	HU	HER	1599.1.1
Amphora, Late Roman	AMLR	HU	LR	1144.9.1, 1601.1.1
Amphora, Late Roman 1	AMLR1	HU	LR	5041.32.1
Amphora, Aegean Red	AMRED	HU	LR	
Amphora, Roman	AMREL	HU	REL	
Amphora, Byzantine	AMB	HU	Byz	
Amphora, Historical	AM	HU	Hi	
Amphora, Modern	AMMOD	HU	Mod	
Base Ring 1	BR1	LU	PoB	
Basin, Coarse ware, Archaic	BAAR	LU	Ar	
Basin, Coarse ware, Archaic/Classical	BAAC	LU	AC	338.12.1
Basin, Coarse ware, Cl/He	BACH	LU	ClHe	
Basin, Coarse ware, Late Roman	LRB	LU	LR	
Basin, Coarse ware, Piecrust Rim	LRP	LU	LR	3059.2.1
Bichrome, Archaic	BIAR	LU	Ar	1733.10.1
Bichrome, Geometric/Archaic	BIGA	LU	GA	1629.2.1, 4041.14.1
Bichrome, Classical	BICL	LU	Cl	
Bichrome, Archaic/Classical	BIAC	LU	AC	
Black Glaze, Archaic	BGAR	FW	Ar	2611.1.1
Black Glaze, Classical	BGCL	FW	Cl	
Black Glaze, Archaic/Classical	BGAC	FW	AC	S-0029
Black Glaze, Hellenistic	BGHE	FW	He	1595.3.1, 4041.4.1, 4052.25.1, 5038.30.1
Black Slip, Geometric/Archaic/Classical	BS	FW	GAC	
Black Slip, Hellenistic	BSHE	FW	He	
Black Topped, Chalcolithic	BLT	LU	EP	
Black-on-Red, Archaic	BORAR	LU	Ar	
Black-on-Red, Geometric/Archaic	BORGA	LU	GA	
Black-on-Red, Classical	BORCL	LU	Cl	
Black-on-Red, Geo/Ar/Cl	BORGAC	LU	GAC	
Black-on-Red, Archaic/Classical	BORAC	LU	AC	
Brick	BRK	AR	Mod	
Brown Burnished/Polished	BBP	LU	EP	
Brown Glazed ware	BGW	LU	MM	
Byzantine Glazed, local	BGL	FW	Med	
Çandarli ware	CW	FW	ER	
Casserole, Angular Offset	CAO	LU	ER	
Casserole, Cypriot Flanged	CFC	LU	ER	5040.5.1
Coarse ware	CO	UT	Unk	
Coarse ware, Chalcolithic	COCH	UT	EP	S-0053
Coarse ware, Painted, Chalcolithic	COP	UT	EP	
Coarse ware, Prehistoric Bronze Age	COPEB	UT	PeB	1034.2.1, 3533.3.1
Coarse ware, Protohistoric Bronze Age	COPOB	UT	PoB	
Coarse ware, Prehistoric	COPH	UT	PH	

continued

Chronotype	Code	Function	Period	Cat. examples
Coarse ware, Geo/Ar/Cl	COGAC	UT	GAC	
Coarse ware, Archaic/Classical	COAC	UT	AC	
Coarse ware, Hellenistic	COH	UT	He	5041.11.1
Coarse ware, Early Roman	COER	UT	ER	
Coarse ware, Late Roman	COLR	UT	LR	
Coarse ware, LR Wheel-Ridged	COWR	UT	LR	
Coarse ware, Roman	COREL	UT	REL	
Coarse ware, Byzantine	COB	UT	Byz	S-0047
Coarse ware, Medieval	COMED	UT	Med	
Coarse ware, Ottoman	COOT	UT	Ott	
Coarse ware, Modern	COMOD	UT	Mod	
Coarse ware, Medieval/Modern	COMM	UT	MM	
Contemporary, Eastern Mediterranean	CEM	FW	Mod	2637.1.1, 5035.29.1
Contemporary imported, Asian	CIA	FW	Mod	
Contemporary imported, European	CIE	FW	Mod	5035.5.1
Contemporary local wares	CLWM	FW	Mod	1705.11.1
Contemporary yogurt ware	CYW	LU	Mod	1212.14.1
Cooking ware	CK	CU	Unk	
Cooking ware, Archaic	CKAR	CU	Ar	S-0067
Cooking ware, Classical	CKCL	CU	Cl	
Cooking ware, Geo/Ar/Cl	CKGAC	CU	GAC	
Cooking ware, Early Roman	CKER	CU	ER	
Cooking ware, ER Cooking Pot	CKERP	CU	ER	1350.1.1, 3052.2.1
Cooking ware, Offset Rim Pot	CKOR	CU	ER	1604.4.1, 1708.14.1, 5029.4.1
Cooking ware, Offset Rim Pot A	CKORA	CU	ER	
Cooking ware, Offset Rim Pot B	CKORB	CU	ER	
Cooking ware, Square Rim Pot	CKSR	CU	ER	
Cooking ware, Late Roman	CKLR	CU	LR	
Cooking ware, Dhiorios Pot	CKD	CU	LR	4505.5.1
Cypriot Coarse ware 1	W1	LU	MM	1005.1.1
Cypriot Coarse ware 1 Early	W1E	LU	Med	3670.20.1
Cypriot Coarse ware 3	W3	LU	Ott	3194.13.1
Cypriot Coarse ware 4	W4	LU	MM	S-0043
Cypriot Coarse ware 5	W5	LU	Ott	
Cypriot Coarse ware 6	W6	LU	Ott	556.1.1
Cypriot Coarse ware 7	W7	LU	Mod	S-0054
Cypriot Glazed	CG	FW	Med	1269.23.1
Cypriot Glazed IC	CG1C	FW	Med	
Cypriot Glazed IIIB	CG3B	FW	Med	
Cypriot Glazed IV	CG4	FW	Med	550.4.1
Cypriot Glazed IVA	CG4A	FW	Med	
Cypriot Glazed IVB	CG4B	FW	Med	
Cypriot Glazed IVC	CG4C	FW	Med	2501.5.1
Cypriot Glazed V	CG5	FW	Med	1268.53.1
Cypriot Glazed VI	CG6	FW	Med	1269.22.1
Cypriot Glazed VII	CG7	FW	Med	1686.2.1
Cypriot Glazed VIII	CG8	FW	Med	
Cypriot Glazed VIIIA	CG8A	FW	Med	
Cypriot Glazed VIIIB	CG8B	FW	Med	2714.1.1, 5019.22.1
Cypriot Glazed VIIIB Late	CG8BL	FW	Ott	1081.2.1
Cypriot Glazed IX	CG9	FW	Med	1035.2.1, 1081.2.2
Cypriot Glazed IX Late	CG9L	FW	Ott	4068.11.1, 4514.1.1, 5021.51.1
Cypriot Glazed XI	CG11	FW	Med	4042.20.1
Cypriot Glazed, Brown and Green	CGBG	FW	Ott	1268.56.1, 1307.1.1, 4030.2.1, 5045.40.1
Cypriot Red Slip	CRS	FW	LR	
Cypriot Red Slip 1	CRS1	FW	LR	1009.1.1
Cypriot Red Slip 2	CRS2	FW	LR	1599.12.1
Cypriot Red Slip 3	CRS3	FW	LR	
Cypriot Red Slip 4	CRS4	FW	LR	
Cypriot Red Slip 5	CRS5	FW	LR	

continued

Chronotype	Code	Function	Period	Cat. examples
Cypriot Red Slip 6	CRS6	FW	LR	
Cypriot Red Slip 7	CRS7	FW	LR	
Cypriot Red Slip 8	CRS8	FW	LR	
Cypriot Red Slip 9	CRS9	FW	LR	1743.28.1
Cypriot Red Slip 10	CRS10	FW	LR	5040.34.1
Cypriot Red Slip 11	CRS11	FW	LR	
Cypriot Red Slip 12	CRS12	FW	LR	
Cypriot Red Slip Imitation Form 1	CRSI1	FW	LR	
Cypriot Red Slip Imitation Form 2	CRSI2	FW	LR	
Cypriot Red Slip Imitation Form 3	CRSI3	FW	LR	
Cypriot Red Slip Imitation Form 4	CRSI4	FW	LR	
Cypriot Red Slip Imitation Form 5	CRSI5	FW	LR	
Cypriot Red Slip Imitation Form 6	CRSI6	FW	LR	
Cypriot Red Slip Imitation Form 7	CRSI7	FW	LR	
Cypriot Red Slip Imitation Form 8	CRSI8	FW	LR	
Cypriot Red Slip Imitation Form 9	CRSI9	FW	LR	
Cypriot Red Slip Imitation Form 10	CRSI10	FW	LR	
Cypriot Sigillata	CS	FW	ER	1327.13.1, 3657.26.1, 4069.3.1
Cypriot Sigillata 5	CS5	FW	ER	
Double Rolled Strap Handle, Archaic	DRSHAR	LU	Ar	
Double Rolled Strap Handle, AC	DRSHAC	LU	AC	1012.2.1
Eastern Sigillata A	ESA	FW	ER	1296.13.1
Eastern Sigillata B	ESB	FW	ER	
Eastern Sigillata B I	ESB1	FW	ER	
Eastern Sigillata B II	ESB2	FW	ER	
Egyptian Red Slip	ERS	FW	LR	1268.35.2, 4542.35.1
Egyptian Red Slip A	ERSA	FW	LR	5044.10.1
Egyptian Red Slip B	ERSB	FW	LR	
Egyptian Red Slip C	ERSC	FW	LR	
Fine ware	FW	FW	Unk	
Fine ware, Prehistoric Bronze Age	FWPEB	FW	PeB	3510.1.1, 3510.3.1
Fine ware, Protohistoric Bronze Age	FWPOB	FW	PoB	
Fine ware, Geometric	FWG	FW	Geo	
Fine ware, Archaic	FWAR	FW	Ar	
Fine ware, Classical	FWCL	FW	Cl	
Fine ware, Geo/Ar/Cl	FWGAC	FW	GAC	
Fine ware, Archaic/Classical	FWAC	FW	AC	
Fine ware, Hellenistic	FWHE	FW	He	
Fine ware, Early Roman	FWER	FW	ER	
Fine ware, Late Roman	FWLR	FW	LR	
Fine ware, Roman	FWREL	FW	REL	
Fine ware, Byzantine	FWB	FW	Byz	
Fine ware, Medieval	FWMED	FW	Med	
Fine ware, Modern	FWMOD	FW	Mod	
Fine ware, Medieval/Modern	FWMM	FW	MM	
Fish Plate	FP	FW	He	5038.31.1
Flat-Grooved	LRG	LU	LR	5038.37.1
Frying Pan	LRF	LU	LR	3059.1.1
Frying Pan, Double	LRFD	LU	LR	
Glazed ware	GZ	FW	MM	3224.13.1, 4042.16.1
Glazed ware, Italian	GZI	FW	Med	
Greek Red Slip	GRS	FW	Cl	1015.1.1
Chronotype	Code	Function	Period	Cat. Examples
Green ware, Archaic	GWAR	LU	Ar	
Green ware, Classical	GWCL	LU	Cl	5019.44A.1
Green ware, Geo/Ar/Cl	GWGAC	LU	GAC	
Green ware, Archaic/Classical	GWAC	LU	AC	
Imported Sgrafitto ware	ISW	FW	Med	1268.60.2, 1269.21.1, 1269.21.2, 1709.27.1, 1720.7.1, 5026.8.1, 5036.49.1
Lapithos ware	LPW	FW	Mod	4023.24.1
Lapithos ware, Green	LPWG	FW	Mod	1280.5.1

continued

Chronotype	Code	Function	Period	Cat. examples
Lapithos ware, Yellow	LPWY	FW	Mod	1081.5.1, 1727.16.1, 4023.25.1
Lemba ware	LW	FW	Med	1054.13.1, 1268.62.1
Maiolica ware	MW	FW	Med	1035.1.1, 1285.12.1
Medium Deep Bowl	MDB	LU	Ar	4052.15.1,2,3
Minoan, East Aegean	MEA	FW	PoB	
Mycenean wares	MYC	FW	PoB	
Ottoman Glazed	OG	FW	Ott	551.2.1
Philia Transition	PHTR	LU	EP	S-0055
Phocaean ware (Late Roman C)	PHW	FW	LR	3259.18.1
Phocaean ware 1	PHW1	FW	LR	
Phocaean ware 2	PHW2	FW	LR	
Phocaean ware 3	PHW3	FW	LR	1057.2.1, 1722.4.1, 5037.4.1
Phocaean ware 4	PHW4	FW	LR	
Phocaean ware 5	PHW5	FW	LR	
Phocaean ware 6	PHW6	FW	LR	
Phocaean ware 7	PHW7	FW	LR	
Phocaean ware 8	PHW8	FW	LR	
Phocaean ware 9	PHW9	FW	LR	
Phocaean ware 10	PHW10	FW	LR	5039.13.1
Pithoid Tub	PTPOB	HU	PoB	
Pithos	PI	PI	PC	
Pithos, Chalcolithic	PICH	PI	EP	S-0046
Pithos, Protohistoric Bronze Age	PIPOB	PI	PoB	S-0030, S-0032, S-0034
Pithos, Archaic	PIAR	PI	Ar	4052.6.1
Pithos, Geo/Ar/Cl	PIGAC	PI	GAC	1254.1.1, 1268.39A.1, 1741.1.1
Pithos, Archaic/Classical	PIAC	PI	AC	
Pithos, Late Roman	PILR	PI	LR	1603.3.1
Pithos, Late Roman 1/2	PILR12	PI	LR	
Pithos, Ottoman	PIOT	PI	Ott	
Pithos, Modern	PIMOD	PI	Mod	
Pithos, Medieval/Modern	PIMM	PI	MM	
Plain White	PW	LU	HA	
Plain White, Classical	PWCL	LU	Cl	
Plain White, Archaic/Classical	PWAC	LU	AC	1302.13.1
Plain White, Hellenistic	PWHE	LU	He	
Plain White, Handmade	PWH	LU	PoB	
Plain, White Slip, Chalcolithic	PWCH	LU	EP	
Plain ware, PoB	PLPOB	LU	PoB	
Plain ware, Archaic	PLAR	LU	Ar	3020.11.1, S-0066, SCY204.4.12.1
Plain ware, Classical	PLCL	LU	Cl	1625.5C.1, 1741.24B.1, 1746.2.1, 2514.1.1, 5019.20.1, SCY021.2.7.1, SCY204.3.3.1.1
Plain ware, Geo/Ar/Cl	PLGAC	LU	GAC	
Plain ware, Archaic/Classical	PLAC	LU	AC	1302.13.1
Proto-Maiolica ware	PMW	FW	Med	
Purple Painted ware	PPW	FW	Ott	
Red Burnished, Chalcolithic	RB	FW	EP	
Red Lustrous, Chalcolithic	RDL	FW	EP	S-0039
Red Monochrome, PoB	RMPOB	FW	PoB	
Red Monochrome, Painted, Chalco	RMP	LU	EP	
Chronotype	Code	Function	Period	Cat. Examples
Red Monochrome, Unpainted, Chalco	RM	FW	EP	
Red-on-Black	ROB	LU	EP	
Red-on-White	ROW	LU	EP	
Red Polished ware	RPW	LU	PeB	
Red Slip, Prehistoric Bronze Age	RSPEB	FW	PeB	
Red Slip, Archaic	RSAR	LU	Ar	1257.12.1, 1742.4.1
Red Slip, Classical	RSCL	FW	Cl	
Red Slip, Archaic/Classical	RSAC	FW	AC	
Red Slip, Hellenistic	RSHE	FW	He	
Red Slip, Early Roman	RSER	FW	ER	

continued

Chronotype	Code	Function	Period	Cat. examples
Red Slip, Late Roman	RSLR	FW	LR	
Red Slip, Roman	RSREL	FW	REL	
Red Slip, Historical Antiquity	RS	FW	HA	
Rolled Lug Handle, Geo/Ar/Cl	RLH	LU	GAC	1740.1.2
Soft Red-Orange, Archaic	SROAR	LU	Ar	1257.13.1, 4052.9.1
Soft Red-Orange, Classical	SROCL	LU	Cl	
Soft Red-Orange, Geo/Ar/Cl	SROGAC	LU	GAC	
Soft Red-Orange, Archaic/Classical	SROAC	LU	AC	
Spawled ware, Chalcolithic	SP	FW	EP	S-0045
Spirally Grooved, Late Roman	LRSG	HU	LR	
Stroke Burnished, Chalcolithic	SB	FW	EP	
Stroke Polished, Classical	SPCL	LU	Cl	3503.2.1
Table ware	TW	LU	Unk	
Tile	TI	AR	PC	
Tile, Archaic	TIAR	AR	Ar	
Tile, Classical	TICL	AR	Cl	
Tile, Archaic/Classical	TIAC	AR	AC	
Tile, Late Roman	TILR	AR	LR	
Tile, Ottoman	TIOT	AR	Ott	
Tile, Modern	TIMOD	AR	Mod	
Tile, Medieval/Modern	TIMM	AR	MM	
Tile, Corinthian	TICR	AR	PC	
Tile, Corinthian Pan	TICP	AR	PC	
Tile, Cover	TICO	AR	PC	
Tile, Flat Pan	TIFP	AR	PC	
Tile, Laconian	TILA	AR	PC	
Tile, Ridged and Rounded	TIRR	AR	PC	
Unknown	UNK	UNK	Unk	
Water Pipe	WA	PO	MM	
Water/Waste System, Roman	WWR	AR	REL	
White Painted III	WP3	LU	PeB	
White Painted, Geometric	WPGEO	LU	Geo	
White Painted, Archaic	WPAR	LU	Ar	1596.1.1, 1741.13.1, 3096.2.1, S-0058, SCY204.3.5.1
White Painted, Classical	WPCL	LU	Cl	2102.12.1
White Painted, Geo/Ar/Cl	WPGAC	LU	GAC	
White Painted, Archaic/Classical	WPAC	LU	AC	
White Slip 1	WS1	LU	PoB	
White Slip 2	WS2	LU	PoB	
Wide Shallow Bowl, Archaic	WSBAR	LU	Ar	2105.5.1
Wide Shallow Bowl, Classical	WSBCL	LU	Cl	
Wide Shallow Bowl, Archaic/Classical	WSBAC	LU	AC	
Zeuxippos ware	ZW	FW	Med	

Appendix D

HOW TO READ THE GIS MAPS

The maps reproduced in color were generated from SCSP's survey data using the Geographic Information System software MapInfo Professional. Our main objective in using them is to interpret changing human activity in the landscape. To do this we have plotted the density and distribution of surface artifacts, particularly pottery. These analyses are affected by natural factors such as erosion and deposition, by anthropogenic factors such as cultivation and dumping, and by our collection methods. Here we summarise briefly how we have accounted for these factors in our analysis. A fuller version can be read in chapter 3.7, and in the interpretation of the individual maps in the text.

Pottery Index

The "Pottery Index" is a relative scale of density, rather than an absolute number of sherds. It takes into account the following factors: (1) the surface area of the survey unit; (2) ground visibility; (3) background confusion; and (4) a projection from the sherds *collected* in the survey unit to the total number of sherds *counted* in the unit. This last factor calculates the probable number of sherds of a particular period, based on the sample of sherds from that period which we collected and analyzed. See chapter 3.7 for a full explanation of this calculation.

In general terms, we would suggest that a Pottery Index of 500 to 1,000 indicates a light scatter of pottery derived from practices such as ancient manuring (see chapter 7.4). A Pottery Index of 10,000 indicates the very high densities that might be found on major settlements such as Tamassos (see chapter 4.6).

Pie charts

Most of the pottery distribution maps use pie charts. While they tend to obscure the shape of the survey unit underneath them, they do show patterns of distribution when the scale is too small for shading within the units to be visible. Where they overlap, the smallest pie charts is always shown on top. The aim is to give a general idea of the patterning across the landscape, rather than to convey a precise value for each individual survey unit. Note that the diameter of each pie charts is proportional to the Pottery Index of its survey unit, rather than directly representing the unit's surface area.

Wherever possible we have kept to the same scale, whereby 2 cm indicates a Pottery Index of 5,000. For reasons of legibility and presentation, the maps of the entire survey area (plates XLVII, XLVIII, XLIX, and L) use a different scale, whereby 2 cm indicates a Pottery Index of 10,000.

Periods

A high proportion of surface pottery can only be dated to very broad bands of periods, as follows: Prehistoric (9000–1050 BC), Geometric-Classical (1050–312 BC), Hellenistic-Roman (312 BC–AD 750), and Medieval-Modern (AD 750–2000). Each set of pie charts refers to one of these period bands. Most of our material is from the last three, and given that there is almost no material from AD 750-1000, they are all more or less 1000 years long and therefore roughly comparable. Within each pie chart, we split up the main component periods, but leave in the general period that covers the entire band (for example, "Medieval-Modern"). See table 3.1 for a breakdown of the chronological periods.

BIBLIOGRAPHY

ABBREVIATIONS

PWD MBAR Public Works Department, Mines Branch Annual Report. Nicosia: Government of Cyprus.

ARIM Annual Report of the Inspector of Mines. Nicosia: Government of Cyprus.

MKE 1984–91 *Megali Kipriaki Enkiklopedhia* (*Great Cypriot Encyclopaedia*). 14 volumes. Nicosia: Filokipros.

SA1 Unpublished government correspondence preserved in the Cyprus State Archives, Nicosia. Copyright remains with the Government of Cyprus.

Åström, L., and P. Åström
1972 *The Swedish Cyprus Expedition* IV: 1D. *The late Cypriote Bronze Age. Other arts and crafts.* Lund: Swedish Cyprus Expedition.

Åström, P.
1989 *Katydhata. A Bronze Age site in Cyprus.* Studies in Mediterranean Archaeology 86. Gothenburg: P. Åström's Förlag.

Adams, R. E. W., W. E. Brown, Jr., and T. P. Culbert
1981 Radar mapping, archaeology and ancient Mayan land use. *Science* 213 (4515):1457–1463.

Adelman, C.
1976 *Cypro-Geometric pottery: Refinements in classification.* Studies in Mediterranean Archaeology 47. Gothenburg: P. Åström's Förlag.

Agricola, G.
1950 *De Re Metallica.* Translated by H. C. Hoover and L. H. Hoover. New York: Dover.

Alcock, S. E.
1993 *Graecia Capta: The landscapes of Roman Greece.* Cambridge: Cambridge University Press.

1994 Breaking up the Hellenistic world: Survey and society. In *Classical Greece: Ancient histories and modern archaeologies,* edited by I. Morris, 171–190. Cambridge: Cambridge University Press.

Alcock, S. E., J. F. Cherry, and J. L. Davis
1994 Intensive survey, agricultural practice and the classical landscape of Greece. In *Classical Greece: Ancient histories and modern archaeologies,* edited by I. Morris, 137–170. Cambridge: Cambridge University Press.

Aldenderfer, M. S., ed.
1987 *Quantitative research in archaeology.* Newbury Park: Sage Publications.

Ammerman, A. J.
1981 Surveys and archaeological research. *Annual Review of Anthropology* 10:63–88.

1985 *The Acconia Survey: Neolithic settlement and the obsidian trade.* Institute of Archaeology, University of London, Occasional Papers 10. London: University College London, Institute of Archaeology.

1992 Taking stock of quantitative archaeology. *Annual Review of Anthropology* 21:231–255.

1993 Review of J. F. Cherry, J. L. Davis, and E. Mantzourani, *Landscape archaeology as long-term history: Northern Keos in the Cycladic Islands. Journal of Field Archaeology* 20:367–372.

1995 The dynamics of modern landuse and the Acconia Survey. *Journal of Mediterranean Archaeology* 8:77–92.

Arnold, D. E.
1993 *Ecology and ceramic production in an Andean community.* Cambridge: Cambridge University Press.

Ashmore, W., and A. B. Knapp, eds.
1999 *Archaeologies of landscape: Contemporary perspectives.* Oxford: Blackwell.

Ashtor, E.
1983 *Levant trade in the later Middle Ages.* Princeton: Princeton University Press.

Astill, G., and W. Davies
1997 *A Breton landscape.* London: University College London Press.

Atasoy, N., and J. Raby

1989 *Iznik. The pottery of Ottoman Turkey*. London: Alexandria Press.

Ault, B. A.

1999 *Koprones* and oil presses at Halieis: Interactions of town and country and the integration of domestic and rural economies. *Hesperia* 68:549–573.

Bachmann, H.–G

1982a *The identification of ancient slags from archaeological sites*. Occasional Publication 6. London: Institute of Archaeology, University College London, .

1982b Copper smelting slags from Cyprus: Review and classification of analytical data. In *Early metallurgy in Cyprus, 4000–500 BC*, edited by J. D. Muhly, R. Maddin, and V. Karageorghis, 143–152. Nicosia: Pierides Foundation.

Bailey, D. M.

1975 *A catalogue of the lamps in the British Museum* I: *Greek, Hellenistic, and Early Roman pottery lamps*. London: British Museum.

Baird, D.

1985 Survey in Peyia Village territory, Paphos, 1983. *Report of the Department of Antiquities, Cyprus*: 340–349.

Bakirtzis, C.

1980 Didymoteichon: Un centre céramique post-Byzantine aux XIIIe et XIVe siècles. *Balkan Studies* 21:147–153.

Bamberger, M., and P. Wincierz

1990 Ancient smelting of oxide copper ore. In *The ancient metallurgy of copper*, edited by Benno Rothenberg, 123–57. London: Institute for Archaeometallurgical Studies, Institute of Archaeology.

Baram, U.

1995a Notes on the preliminary typologies of production and chronology for the clay tobacco pipes of Cyprus. *Report of the Department of Antiquities, Cyprus*: 299–309.

1995b Questions and answers for the material culture of Cyprus from the sixteenth through the nineteenth centuries. In *Visitors, immigrants and invaders in Cyprus*, edited by P. W. Wallace, 125–134. Albany: Insitute of Cyprus Studies.

Barker, G.

1991 Approaches to archaeological survey. In *Roman landscapes: Archaeological survey in the Mediterranean*, edited by G. Barker and J. Lloyd, 1–9. Archaeological Monograph 2. London: British Schoool at Rome.

Barker, G., ed.

1995a *The Biferno Valley survey: The archaeological and geomorphological record*. Leicester: Leicester University Press.

1995b *A Mediterranean valley: Landscape archaeology and Annales history in the Biferno Valley*. Leicester: Leicester University Press.

Barsky, B.

1996 *A pilgrim's account of Cyprus: Bars'kyj's travels in Cyprus. Essay, Translation, and Commentaries*. Translated by Alexander D. Grishin. Sources for the History of Cyprus 3. Altamont, NY: Greece and Cyprus Research Center.

Basso, K. H.

1996 *Wisdom sits in places*. Albuquerque: University of New Mexico Press.

Baxivani, E.

1997 From settlement to cemetery burial: The ideology of death in the Early Bronze Age societies of Cyprus and Crete. In *Cyprus and the Aegean in antiquity: From the prehistoric period to the 7th century ad*, edited by D. Christou, 57–69. Nicosia: Department of Antiquities.

Beach, T

1998 Soil constraints on northwestern Yucatán, Mexico: Pedoarchaeology and Maya subsistence at Chunchucmil. *Geoarchaeology* 13:759–791.

Bear, L. M.

1960 *The geology and mineral resources of the Akaki-Lythrodondha area*. Memoir 3. Nicosia: Geological Survey Department, Ministry of Science and Industry, Cyprus.

1963 *The mineral resources and mining industry of Cyprus*. Bulletin 1. Nicosia: Geological Survey Department, Ministry of Science and Industry, Cyprus.

Bell, R., M. L. Labovitz, and D. P. Sullivan

1985 Delay in leaf flush associated with heavy metal enriched soil. *Economic Geology and The Bulletin of the Society of Economic Geologists* 80:1407–1414.

Bellamy, C. V.

1903 *A monograph on the main roads of Cyprus*. Nicosia: Government Printing Office.

Bender, B.

1998 *Stonehenge: Making space*. Oxford: Berg.

Bender, B., S. Hamilton, and C. Tilley

1997 Leskernick: Stone worlds; alternative narrative; nested landscapes. *Proceedings of the Prehistoric Society* 63:147–178.

Betts, A.

1985 The chipped stone. In *Lemba Archaeological Project* I: *Excavations at Lemba-Lakkous 1976–1983*, by E. J. Peltenburg, 94–95, 196–197, 276–278. Studies in Mediterranean Archaeology 70(1). Gothenburg: P. Åström's Förlag.

1986 The chipped stone. In Excavations at Kissonerga-Mosphilia, by E. J. Peltenburg and project members. *Report of the Department of Antiquities, Cyprus*: 10–15.

Biersack, A.

1999 Introduction: From the "new ecology" to the new ecologies. *American Anthropologist* 101:5–18.

Binford, L. R.

1964 A consideration of archaeological research design. *American Antiquity* 29:425–441.

Bintliff, J. L.

1991 *The Annales school and archaeology*. Leicester: Leicester University Press.

1996 Interactions of theory, methodology and practice: Retrospect and commentary. *Archaeological Dialogues* 3:246–255.

1997a Regional survey, demography, and the rise of complex societies in the ancient Aegean: Core-periphery, neo-Malthusian, and other interpretive models. *Journal of Field Archaeology* 24:1–38.

1997b The archaeological investigation of deserted Medieval and post-Medieval villages in Greece. In *Rural settlements in Medieval Europe*, edited by G. De Boe and F. Verhaeghe, 21–34. Volume 6. Zellik: I. A. P. Rapporten.

1997c Catastrophe, chaos and complexity: The death, decay, and rebirth of towns from antiquity to today. *Journal of European Archaeology* 5 (2):67–90.

Bintliff, J. L., and A. Snodgrass

1988 Mediterranean survey and the city. *Antiquity* 62/234:57–71.

Bintliff, J., P. Howard, and A. Snodgrass

1999 The hidden landscape of prehistoric Greece. *Journal of Mediterranean Archaeology* 12:139 168.

Bintliff, J., E. Tsougarakis, and D. Tsougarakis, eds.

N.D. *New approaches to Medieval and post-Medieval Greece*. Athens: British School of Archaeology at Athens.

Birkeland, P. W.

1984 *Soils in geomorphology*. New York: Oxford University Press.

Birmingham, J.
1963   The chronology of some early and middle Iron Age Cypriote sites. *American Journal of Archaeology* 67:15–42.

Boardman, J.
1970   *Greek gems and finger rings: Early Bronze Age to late Classical.* London: Thames and Hudson.

Bolger, D.
1988   *Erimi-Pamboula: A Chalcolithic settlement in Cyprus.* BAR International Series S443. Oxford: British Archaeological Reports.
1991   The evolution of the Chalcolithic painted style. *Bulletin of the American Schools of Oriental Research* 282–283:81–93.

Braidwood, R. J., and B. Howe
1960   *Prehistoric investigations in Iraqi Kurdistan.* Studies in Ancient Oriental Civilization 31. Chicago: University of Chicago Press.

Braudel, F.
1980   History and the social sciences: The *longue durée.* In *On History*, 25–54. Chicago: University of Chicago Press.

Braun-Blanquet, J.
1932   *Plant sociology.* New York: McGraw Hill.

Brooks, R. R.
1983   *Biological methods of prospecting for minerals.* New York: John Wiley.

Brooks, R. R., and D. Johannes
1990   Geobotany and exploitation of ancient mines. In *Phytoarchaeology*, by R. R. Brooks and D. Johannes, 15–55. Historical, Ethno- and Economic Botany Series 3. Portland: Dioscorides Press.

Bruce, J. L.
1937   Antiquities in the mines of Cyprus. In *Swedish Cyprus Expedition: Finds and results of the excavations in Cyprus 1927–1931*, by E. Gjerstad, J. Lindros, E. Sjoqvist and A. Westholm, 639–671. Volume 3. Stockholm: Swedish Cyprus Expedition.
1949   Cyprus mines copper again. *Transactions of the American Institute of Mining and Metallurgical Engineers* 181:205–232.

Brück, J.
1999   Ritual and rationality: Some problems of interpretation in European archaeology. *European Journal of Archaeology* 2:313–344.

Buchholz, H.–G.
1973   Tamassos, Zypern, 1970–1972. 1 Bericht. *Archäologischer Anzeiger*:295–388.
1974   Tamassos, Zypern, 1973. 2 Bericht. *Archäologischer Anzeiger*:554–614.
1978   Tamassos, Zypern, 1974–1976. 3. Bericht. *Archäologischer Anzeiger*:155–230.
1985a   Der Beitrag der Ausgrabungen von Tamassos zur antiken Baugeschichte Zyperns. In *Archaeology in Cyprus 1960–1985*, edited by V. Karageorghis, 238–255. Nicosia: A. G. Leventis Foundation.
1985b   Die Deutschen Ausgrabungen in Tamassos von 1970 bis heute. In *Praktika tou Dhefterou Dhiethnous Kiproloyikou Sinedhriou* (Lefkosia, 10–25 Apriliou 1982) I: *Arkheon T'mima*, edited by T. Papadopoullou and S. A. Hadjistilli, 229–271. Nicosia: A. G. Leventis Foundation.
1991   Tamassos-Frangissa (1885). *Centre d'études Chypriotes, Cahier* 16:3–15.
1994   Sakralschaufeln im antiken Zypern. *Report of the Department of Antiquities, Cyprus*: 129–154.

Buchholz, H.-G., and K. Unteidt
1996   *Tamassos. Ein Antikes Königreich auf Zypern.* Studies in Mediterranean Archaeology and Literature, Pocket-book 136. Jonsered: P. Åström's Förlag.

Buitron-Oliver, D.
1996   Pottery from the Archaic precinct. In *The sanctuary of Apollo Hylates at Kourion: Excavations in the Archaic precinct*, edited by D. Buitron-Oliver, 41–71. Studies in Mediterranean Archaeology 109. Jonsered: P. Åström's Förlag.

Bull, W. B.
1988   *Geomorphic response to climate change.* New York: Oxford University Press.

Butzer, K.
1982   *Archaeology as human ecology.* Cambridge: Cambridge University Press.

Callender, M. H.
1965   *Roman amphorae.* London: Oxford University Press.

Canuto, M. A., and J. Yaeger, eds.
2000   *The archaeology of communities: A New World perspective.* London: Routledge.

Casey, E. C.
1987   *Traditional methods Cyprus 1935.* Ludlow, England: n.p.

Catling, H. W.
1962   Patterns of settlement in Bronze Age Cyprus. *Opuscula Atheniensia* 4:129–69.
1975   Cyprus in the late Bronze Age. In *Cambridge ancient history*, edited by I. E. S. Edwards, C. J. Gadd, N. G. L. Hammond and E. Sollberger, 188–216. Volume 2: Part 2. Cambridge: Cambridge University Press.

Cavanagh, W. G., S. Hirst, and C. D. Litton
1988   Soil phosphate, site boundaries, and change point analysis. *Journal of Field Archaeology* 15:67–83.

Chavane, M.-J.
1975   *Salamine de Chypre 6: Les petits objets.* Paris: de Boccard.

Cherry, J. F.
1983   Frogs round the pond: Perspective on current archaeological survey projects in the Mediterranean regions. In *Archaeological survey in the Mediterranean area*, edited by D. R. Keller and D. W. Rupp, 375–416. BAR International Series 155. Oxford: British Archaeological Reports.

Cherry, J. F., J. L. Davis, and E. Mantzourani
1991   *Landscape archaeology as long-term history: Northern Keos in the Cycladic Islands from earliest settlement until modern times.* Monumenta Archaeologica 16. Los Angeles: UCLA Institute of Archaeology.

Cherry, J.F., C. Gamble , and S. Shennan
1978   *Sampling in contemporary British archaeology.* BAR British Series 50. Oxford: British Archaeological Reports.

Christodoulou, D.
1959   *The evolution of the rural land use pattern in Cyprus.* World Land Use Survey, Monograph 2. Cornwall: Geographical Publications.

Christou, D
1989   The Chalcolithic cemetery at Souskiou-Vathyrkakas. In *Early society in Cyprus*, edited by E. J. Peltenburg, 82–94. Edinburgh: Edinburgh University Press.
1996   Politiko (Mission australienne). In Chronique des fouilles et découvertes archéologiques à Chypre en 1995. *Bulletin de Correspondance Héllenique* 120:1096.

Chrysos, E.
1993   Cyprus in early Byzantine times. In *The sweet land of Cyprus*, edited by A. A. M. Bryer and G. S. Georghallides, 3–14. Nicosia: Cyprus Research Centre.

Cleere, H.

1995 Cultural landscapes as world heritage. *Conservation and Management of Archaeological Sites* 1:63–68.

Clough, R.

1996 SCSP95: Archaeometallurgical remains in the SCSP area. In A report on the Sydney Cyprus Survey Project (SCSP), third season (1995), by A.B. Knapp and M Given. *Report of the Department of Antiquities, Cyprus:* 308–316.

Cobham, C. D., ed.

1908 *Excerpta Cypria: Materials for a history of Cyprus.* Cambridge: Cambridge University Press.

Coleman, J. E., J. A. Barlow, M. Mogelonsky, and K. W. Scharr

1996 *Alambra: A middle Bronze Age site in Cyprus. Investigations by Cornell University, 1975–1978.* Studies in Mediterranean Archaeology 118. Gothenburg: P. Åström's Förlag.

Conrad, H. G., and B. Rothenberg, eds.

1980 *Antikes Kupfer im Timna-Tal. 4000 Jahre Bergbau und Verhuettung in der Arabah (Israel).* Der Anschnitt, Beiheft 1. Bochum: Deutsches Bergbau-Museum.

Conrad, L. I.

1986 The plague in Bil al Shâm in pre-Islamic times. In *Proceedings of the Symposium on Bilâl al Shâm during the Byzantine Period* 2:143–163. Amman: al-Jami'ah al-Urduniyah.

Constantinou, G.

1972 The geology and genesis of sulphide ores of Cyprus. Ph.D. dissertation, Imperial College, University of London.

1982 Geological features and ancient exploitation of the cupriferous sulphide orebodies of Cyprus. In *Early metallurgy in Cyprus, 4000–500 bc,* edited by J. D. Muhly, R. Maddin and V. Karageorghis, 13–24. Nicosia: Pierides Foundation

1992 The mining industry of Cyprus in modern times. In *Cyprus copper and the sea,* edited by A. Marangou and K. Psillides, 328–367. Nicosia: Government of Cyprus.

Courtois, J.-C.

1984 *Les objects des Niveaux Stratifiés d'Enkomi. Fouilles C. F. A. Schaeffer 1947–1970.* Alasia III. Editions Recherches sur les Civilisations, Memoire 32. Paris: EDPF.

Cowgill, G.

1990 Toward refining concepts of full-coverage survey. In *The archaeology of regions: A case for full coverage survey,* edited by S. K. Fish and S. A. Kowaleski, 249–259. Washington, DC : Smithsonian Institution Press.

Cox, C.

1992 Satellite imagery, aerial photography and wetland archaeology: An interim report on an application of remote sensing to wetland archaeology—the pilot study in Cumbria, England. *World Archaeology* 24:249–267.

Crabtree, D. E.

1972 *An introduction to flintworking.* Idaho State University Museum, Occasional Paper 28. Pocatello: Idaho State University Museum.

Craddock, P. T.

1989 The scientific investigation of early mining and smelting. In *Scientific analysis in archaeology and its interpretation,* edited by J. Henderson, 178–212. Oxford University Committee for Archaeology, Monograph 19. Oxford: Oxbow.

1995 *Early metal mining and production.* Edinburgh: Edinburgh University Press.

Cross, F. M.

1974 Inscriptions from Idalion in Greek, Cypriot syllabic and Phoenician scripts. In *American expedition to Idalion, Cyprus. First preliminary report: Seasons of 1971 and 1972,* by L. E. Stager,

A. Walker and G. E. Wright, 77–81. Bulletin of the American Schools of Oriental Research, Supplement 18. Cambridge, MA: American Schools of Oriental Research.

D'Annibale, C.

1992 Lithic analysis. In D. W. Rupp, J.T. Clarke, C. D'Annibale, and S. Stewart, Canadian Palaipaphos survey project: 1991 field season. *Report of the Department of Antiquities, Cyprus:* 300–312.

1999 The chipped stone industry. In Prastio Agios Savvas tis Karonis monastery (Paphos district, Cyprus): 1994–1995 field season and 1992–1995 artifact analyses, by D. W. Rupp, J.T. Clarke, S.C. Fox, C. D'Annibale, E. Herscher, T.E. Gregory, M.C. McClellan, and J. Critchley. *Bulletin of the American Schools of Oriental Research* 316:52–55.

Davies, O.

1928–1930 The copper mines of Cyprus. *Annual of the British School at Athens* 30:74–85.

Davis, J. L.

1991 Contributions to a Mediterranean rural archaeology: Historical case studies from the Ottoman Cyclades. *Journal of Mediterranean Archaeology* 4:131–215.

Davis, J. L., and S. B. Sutton

1995 Response to A. J. Ammerman, The dynamics of modern landuse and the Acconia Survey. *Journal of Mediterranean Archaeology* 8:113–123.

de Mas Latrie, M. L.

1852–1861 *Histoire de l'Ile de Chypre sous le Règne des Princes de la Maison de Lusignan.* (3 volumes). Paris: Imprimerie Impériale.

Demetriou, A.

1978 Die Datierung der Periode Cypro-Archaic I nach Fundzusammenhangen mit grieschischer Keramik. *Archäologischer Anzeiger* 1978:12–25.

Denevan, W. M.

1992 The pristine myth: The landscape of the Americas in 1492. *Annals of the Association of American Geographers* 82:369–385.

Dewar, R. E.

1991 Incorporating variation in occupation span into settlement-pattern analysis. *American Antiquity* 56:604–620.

1994 Contending with contemporaneity: A reply to Kintigh. *American Antiquity* 59:149–152.

di Cesnola, L. P.

1885 *A descriptive atlas of the Cesnola Collection of Cypriote antiquities in the Metropolitan Museum of Art, New York* 1: *Sculpture.* Boston: James R. Osgood.

Dikaios, P.

1936 The excavations at Erimi, 1933–1935. Final report. *Report of the Department of Antiquities, Cyprus:* 1–81.

1940 *The excavations at Vounous-Bellapais in Cyprus, 1931–1932.* Archaeologia 88. London: Society of Antiquaries, Oxford.

1961 *Sotira.* University Museum Monograph, University of Pennsylvania. Philadelphia: The University Museum.

1962 The Stone Age. In *Swedish Cyprus Expedition* IV.1A, by P. Dikaios and J. R. Stewart, 1–204. Lund: Swedish Cyprus Expedition.

1969/71 *Enkomi, Excavations 1948–1958,* 3 vols. Mainz: Verlag Philipp von Zabern.

Dikigoropoulos, A. I.

1940/48 The political status of Cyprus A.D. 648–965. *Report of the Department of Antiquities, Cyprus:* 94–114.

Dikigoropoulos, A. I., and A. H. S. Megaw

1940/48 Early glazed pottery from Polis. *Report of the Department of Antiquities, Cyprus:* 77–93.

Dothan, T., and A. Ben-Tor

1983 *Excavations at Athienou, Cyprus, 1971–1972.* QEDEM 16. Jerusalem: Institute of Archaeology, Hebrew University.

Downs, R. M., and D. Stea

1977 *Maps in minds: Reflections on cognitive mapping.* New York: Harper and Row.

Dunnell, R. C., and W. S. Dancey.

1983 The siteless survey: A regional scale data collection strategy. In *Advances in archaeological method and theory*, edited by M. B. Schiffer, 267–287. Volume 6. New York: Academic Press.

Du Plat Taylor, J.

1933 Some notes on Byzantine glazed ware in Cyprus. *Report of the Department of Antiquities, Cyprus:* 24–25.

1935 Byzantine bowls acquired by the Cyprus Museum. *Report of the Department of Antiquities, Cyprus:* 34.

1952 A late Bronze Age settlement at Apliki, Cyprus. *Antiquaries Journal* 32:133–167.

Du Plat Taylor, J., and A. H. S. Megaw

1937/39 Cypriot medieval glazed pottery—notes for a preliminary classification. *Report of the Department of Antiquities, Cyprus:* 1–13.

Ebert, J. I.

1992 *Distributional archaeology.* Albuquerque: University of New Mexico Press.

Empereur, J.-Y., and A. Hesnard

1987 Les amphores hellénistiques. In *Céramiques hellénistiques et romaines*, edited by P. Lévêque and J.-P. Morel, 9–71. Volume 2. Paris: Les Belles Lettres.

Empereur, J.-Y., and M. Picon

1989 Les régions de production d'amphores impériales en Méditerranée orientale. In *Amphores romaines et histoire économique: dix ans de recherché*, 223-248. Collection de l'École Française de Rome 114. Rome: École Française de Rome.

Everitt, B.

1974 *Cluster analysis.* New York: John Wiley.

Fasnacht, W.

1999 Excavations at Ayia Varvara *Almyras:* A review of twelve years of research. *Report of the Department of Antiquities, Cyprus:* 179–184.

Fasnacht, W., R.S. Morris, K. Zubler, and M. Schenk

1989 Excavations at Ayia Varvara *Almyras. Report of the Department of Antiquities, Cyprus:* 59–76.

Fasnacht, W., and V. Kassianidou

1992 Copper at Almyras. A mining and smelting site in Cyprus. In *Cyprus, copper and the sea*, edited by A. Marangou and K. Psillides, 78–90. Nicosia: Government of Cyprus.

Fasnacht, W., J. Kunz, C. Deslex, K. Zubler, P. Boll, V. Kassianidou, A. Connolly an,d T. Maradi

1996 Excavations at Ayia Varvara *Almyras.* Fifth Preliminary Report. *Report of the Department of Antiquities, Cyprus:* 95–126.

Fasnacht, W., S. Schwarzländer, and P. Boll

1997 The Sia-Mathiatis-Ayia Varvara Survey Project (SMASP): second preliminary report. *Report of the Department of Antiquities, Cyprus:* 219–224.

Fasnacht, W., K. Zubler, R. S. Morris, D. Gerbothé, V. Kassianidou, A. Connolly, and T. Rehren

1992 Excavations at Ayia Varvara *Almyras:* Fourth preliminary report. *Report of the Department of Antiquities, Cyprus:* 59–74.

Feinman, G. M.

1994 Toward an archaeology without polarization: Comments on contemporary theory. In *Caciques and their people: A volume in honor of Ronald Spores*, edited by J. Marcus and J. F. Zeitlin, 13–43. Anthropological Paper 89. Ann Arbor: University of Michigan Museum of Anthropology.

Fejfer, J., ed.

1995 *Ancient Akamas: Settlement and environment.* Aarhus: Aarhus University Press.

Ferring, R. C.

1992 Alluvial pedology and geoarchaeological research. In *Soils in archaeology: Landscape evolution and human occupation*, edited by V. T. Holliday, 1–40. Washington, DC: Smithsonian Institution Press.

Fish, S. K., and S. A. Kowaleski, eds.

1990 *The archaeology of regions: A case for full coverage survey.* Washington, DC: Smithsonian Institution Press.

Flannery, K. V., ed.

1976 *The early Mesoamerican village.* New York: Academic Press.

Flourentzos, P.

1994 A workshop of Cypro-Classical terracottas from Marion. *Report of the Department of Antiquities, Cyprus:* 161–165.

Flourentzos, P., and I. Nicolaou

1987 The Ayios Panteleimon of Akhera hoard of Byzantine electrum scyphate coins. *Report of the Department of Antiquities, Cyprus:* 279–318.

Forbes, R. J.

1966 *Studies in ancient technology.* Volume 7. Leiden: Brill.

Fotiadis, M.

1992 Units of data as deployment of disciplinary code. In *Representations in archaeology*, edited by J.-C. Gardin and C. S. Peebles, 130–148. Bloomington: Indiana University Press.

1997 Cultural identity and regional archaeological perspectives. *Archaeological Dialogues* 4:102–113.

Foss, C.

1977 Archaeology and the "twenty cities" of Byzantine Asia. *American Journal of Archaeology* 81:469–486.

Fox, W. A., S. Zacharias, and U. M. Franklin

1987 Investigations of ancient metallurgical sites in the Paphos district, Cyprus. In *Western Cyprus: Connections*, edited by D. W. Rupp, 169–184. Studies in Mediterranean Archaeology 77. Gothenburg: P. Åström's Förlag.

Frankel, D., and Webb, J. M.

1994 Excavations at Marki *Alonia*, 1993–94. *Report of the Department of Antiquities, Cyprus:* 51–72.

1996 *Marki* Alonia: *An Early and Middle Bronze Age town in Cyprus. Excavations 1990–1994.* Studies in Mediterranean Archaeology 123.1. Jonsered: P. Åström's Förlag.

1998 Excavations at Marki *Alonia*, 1996–97. *Report of the Department of Antiquities, Cyprus:* 85–110.

Frantz, A.

1942 Turkish pottery in the Agora. *Hesperia* 10:1–28.

Frye, J. C., and H. B. Willman

1962 Note 27; Morphostratigraphic units in Pleistocene stratigraphy. *Bulletin of the American Association of Petroleum Geologists* 46:112–113.

Gaber, P., and W. G. Dever

1996 Idalion, Cyprus: Conquest and continuity. *Annual of the American Schools of Oriental Research* 53:85–113.

Gaffney, V. L., and M. Tingle

1988 *The middle farm project: An integrated survey of prehistoric and Roman landscapes on the Berkshire Downs.* BAR International Series S200. Oxford: British Archaeological Reports.

Gale, N. H.

1991 Copper ox–hide ingots: Their origin and their place in the Bronze Age metals trade. In *Bronze Age trade in the Mediterranean*, edited by N. H. Gale, 197–239. Studies in Mediterranean Archaeology 90. Jonsered: P. Åström's Förlag.

Gerrard, C.
1997   Misplaced faith? Medieval pottery and fieldwalking. *Medieval Ceramics* 21:61–72.

Gerth, R. A.
1998   Quantifying Anthropogenic Hillslope Erosion on Mount Kreatos, Cyprus. Senior honor's thesis. Department of Geology, Vanderbilt University, Nashville.

Giddens, A.
1979   *Central problems in social theory: Action, structure and contradictions in social analysis.* London: Macmillan.

Given, M.
1991   Symbols, power, and the construction of identity in the city kingdoms of ancient Cyprus, c.750–312 B.C. Ph.D. dissertation, Department of Classics, Cambridge University.
2000   Agriculture, settlement and landscape in Ottoman Cyprus. *Levant* 32:215–236.
2001   The fight for the past: Watkins vs. Warren (1885–6) and the control of excavation. In *Cyprus in the 19th century AD: Fact, fancy and fiction,* edited by Veronica Tatton-Brown, 255–260. Oxford: Oxbow Books.
N.D.   Wandering villages, stationary churches: Local definitions of sites and settlements in Ottoman Cyprus. In *New approaches to Medieval and post-Medieval Greece,* edited by J. Bintliff, E. Tsougarakis and D. Tsougarakis. Athens: British School of Archaeology at Athens.

Given, M., A. B. Knapp, and N. Meyer (with T. E. Gregory, V. Kassianidou, J. Noller, N. Urwin, L. Wells, and H. Wright)
1999   The Sydney Cyprus Survey Project: An interdisciplinary investigation of long-term change in the north central Troodos, Cyprus. *Journal of Field Archaeology* 26:19–39.

Gjerstad, E.
1948   *The Swedish Cyprus Expedition: The Cypro-Geometric, Cypro-Archaic and Cypro-Classical periods.* Volume 4.2. Stockholm: Swedish Cyprus Expedition.
1960   Pottery types: Cypro-Geometric to Cypro-Classical. *Opuscula Atheniensia* 3:105–122.
1980   The origin and chronology of the early Bronze Age in Cyprus. *Report of the Department of Antiquities, Cyprus:* 1–16.

Gjerstad, E., J. Lindros, E. Sjöqvist, and A. Westholm
1935   *The Swedish Cyprus Expedition: Finds and results of the excavations in Cyprus, 1927–1931.* Volume 2. Stockholm: Swedish Cyprus Expedition.

Goodall, D. W.
1954   Objective methods for the classification of vegetation III. An essay in the use of factor analysis. *Australian Journal of Botany* 2:304–324.

Goodwin, J. C.
1984   *An historical toponymy of Cyprus.* 4th edition. Nicosia: n.p.

Gould, P., and R. White.
1986   *Mental maps.* Boston: Allen and White.

Gourgiotis, G.
1981   Proima metavyzantina kerameika. *Archaiologia* 1:74–76.

Grace, V. R.
1971   Samian amphoras. *Hesperia* 40:52–95.

Greene, K.
1986   *The archaeology of the Roman Empire.* Berkeley: University of California Press.
1992   *Roman pottery.* Berkeley: University of California Press.

Gregory, T. E.
1987   Circulation of Byzantine and Medieval pottery in southwestern Cyprus. In *Western Cyprus: Connections,* edited by D. W. Rupp, 199–213. Studies in Mediterranean Archaeology 77. Gothenburg: P. Åström's Förlag.

1993   Byzantine and Medieval pottery. In *The land of the Paphian Aphrodite* 2. *The Canadian Palaipaphos Survey Project: Artifact and ecofactual studies,* edited by L. W. Sørensen and D. W. Rupp, 157–176. Studies in Mediterranean Archaeology 104(2). Gothenburg: P. Åström's Förlag.

Greig-Smith, P.
1964   Quantitative plant ecology. 2nd edition. London: Butterworths.

Grivaud, Gilles
1998   *Villages désertés à Chypre (fin XIIe–fin XIXe siècle).* Meletai kai Ipomnimata 3. Nicosia: Archbishop Makarios III Foundation.

Guilaine, J., F. Briois, J–D. Vinge, and I. Carrère
2000   Découverte d'un néolithique précéramique ancien chypriote (fin 9e, début 8e millénaires cal BC), apparenté au PPNB ancien/moyen du Levant nord. *Earth and Planetary Sciences* 300:75–82.

Gummerman, G. J., and T. R. Lyons
1971   Archaeological methodology and remote sensing. *Science* 172:126–132.

Gunnis, R.
1936   *Historic Cyprus: A guide to its towns and villages, monasteries and castles.* London: Methuen.

Hadjicosti, M.
1997   The kingdom of Idalion in the light of new evidence. *Bulletin of the American Schools of Oriental Research* 308:49–64.

Hadjisavvas, S.
1978   Politiko "Kouphos": An archaic cemetery. *Report of the Department of Antiquities, Cyprus:* 124–131.
1992   *Olive oil processing in Cyprus from the Bronze Age to the Byzantine period.* Studies in Mediterranean Archaeology 99. Nicosia: P. Åström's Förlag.

Hahn, M.
1989   Byzantine and post-Byzantine pottery from the Greek-Swedish excavations at Khania, Crete. In *Recherches sur la céramique Byzantine,* edited by V. Déroche and J.–M. Speiser, 227–232. Bulletin de Correspondance Hellénique, Supplement 18. Athens: École française d'Athènes.

Halstead, P.
1987   Traditional or ancient rural economy in Mediterranean Europe: Plus ça change? *Journal of Hellenic Studies* 107:77–87.

Hardesty, D. L.
1988   *The archaeology of mining and miners: A view from the silver state.* Special Publication 6. Pleasant Hill, CA: Society for Historical Archaeology.
1990   Mining property types: Inventory and significance evaluation. In *Death Valley to Deathwood: Kennecott to Cripple Creek,* edited by L. R. Barker and A. E. Houston, 39–43. San Francisco: National Registers Program.

Hartigan, J. A.
1975   *Clustering algorithms.* New York: John Wiley.

Hassan, F. A.
1978   Demographic archaeology. In *Advances in archaeological method and theory* 1, edited by M. B. Schiffer, 49–103. New York: Academic Press.

Hayes, J. W.
1967   Cypriot sigillata. *Report of the Department of Antiquities, Cyprus:* 65–77.
1972   *Late Roman pottery.* London: British School at Rome.
1991   *Paphos* III: *The Hellenistic and Roman pottery.* Nicosia: Department of Antiquities.

1992 *Excavations at Saraçhane in Istanbul* 2. Princeton: Princeton University Press.

Held, S. O.

1989 Early prehistoric island archaeology in Cyprus: Configurations of formative culture growth from the Pleistocene/Holocene boundary to the mid-3rd millennium B.C. Ph.D. dissertation, Institute of Archaeology, University of London.

1990 Back to what future? New directions for Cypriot Early Prehistoric research in the 1990s. *Report of the Department of Antiquities, Cyprus*: 1–43.

1992 Colonization and extinction on Early Prehistoric Cyprus. In *Acta Cypria: Acts of an international congress on Cypriote Archaeology*. Part 2, edited by P. Åström, 104–164. Studies in Mediterranean Archaeology and Literature, Pocket-book 117. Jonsered: P. Åström's Förlag.

1993 Insularity as a modifier of cultural change: The case of prehistoric Cyprus. *Bulletin of the American Schools of Oriental Research* 292:25–33.

Herbert, E. W.

1984 *Red gold of Africa. Copper in precolonial history and culture*. Madison: University of Wisconsin Press.

Herscher, E.

1981 Southern Cyprus, the disappearing early Bronze Age, and the evidence from Phaneromeni. In *Studies in Cypriote Archaeology*, edited by J. C. Biers and D. Soren, 79–85. Monograph 18. Los Angeles: UCLA Institute of Archaeology.

Heywood, H., S. Swiny, D. Whittingham, D. Croft, and P. Croft

1981 Erimi revisited. *Report of the Department of Antiquities, Cyprus*: 24–42.

Hidiroglou, P.

1971/1972 Kataloghos ton en to arkhio tou Kentrou Epistimonikon Erevnon Enapokimenon Othomanikon khiroghraphon. *Epetiris tou Kentrou Epistimonikon Erevnon* 5:257–385.

Hill, G.

1940 *A history of Cyprus* 1: *To the conquest by Richard the Lionheart*. Cambridge: Cambridge University Press.

Hocking, N.

1999 A modern potter's examination of Cypriot Iron Age white painted and bichrome wares. *American Schools of Oriental Research 1999 Annual Meeting Abstracts*: 40.

Hodcraft, A. J. T., and J. M. Moore

1988 Remote sensing of vegetation—a promising exploratory tool. *The Mining Magazine* (October 1988):274–279.

Hodder, I.

1982 Theoretical archaeology: A reactionary view. In *Symbolic and structural archaeology*, edited by I. Hodder, 1–16. Cambridge: Cambridge University Press.

Holliday, V. T.,

1992 Soil formation, time, and archaeology. In *Soils in archaeology: Landscape evolution and human occupation*, edited by V. T. Holliday, 101–107. Washington, DC: Smithsonian Institution Press.

Horler, D. N., J. Barber, and A. R. Barrington

1980 New concepts for the determination of chemical stress in plants. In *Remote sensing in geological and terrain studies*, edited by J. A. Allen and M. Bradshaw, 113–123. London: Remote Sensing Society.

Hosler, D.

1994 *The sounds and colors of power*. Cambridge, MA: MIT Press.

Howland, R. H.

1958 *Greek lamps and their survivals. The Athenian Agora*, Volume

IV. Princeton: The American School of Classical Studies at Athens.

Inbar, M.

1992 Rates of fluvial erosion in basins with a Mediterranean type climate. *Catena* 19:393–409.

Ionas, I.

1988 *La maison rurale de Chypre (XVIIIe–XXe siècle): Aspects et techniques de construction*. Nicosia: Cyprus Research Centre.

1998 *Pottery in the Cyprus tradition*. Publications of the Cyprus Research Centre 23. Nicosia: Cyprus Research Centre.

2001 *Traditional pottery and potters on Cyprus: The disappearance of an ancient craft industry in the 19th and 20th centuries*. Birmingham Byzantine and Ottoman Monographs 6. Aldershot, England: Ashgate.

Ireland, T., and N. Urwin

1993 Satellite imagery and landscape archaeology. *Mediterranean Archaeology* 5/6:121–146.

Jameson, M. H., C. N. Runnels, and T. H. Van Andel

1994 *A Greek countryside: The southern Argolid from Prehistory to the present day*. Stanford: Stanford University Press.

Jeffery, G.

1918 *A description of the historic monuments of Cyprus: Studies in the archaeology and architecture of the island*. Nicosia. Reprint. London: Zeno, 1983.

Jensen, S.

1979 Classification of lakes in southern Sweden on the basis of their macrophyte composition by means of multivariate methods. *Vegetatio* 39:129–146.

Johnston, R.

1998 Approaches to the perception of landscape: Philosophy, theory, methodology. *Archaeological Dialogues* 5:54–68.

Jones, J. E.

1984 Ancient Athenian silver mines, dressing floors and smelting sites. *Journal of the Historical Metallurgical Society* 18(2):65–81.

Karageorghis, J.

1977 *La grande déesse de Chypre et son culte*. Paris: E. de Boccard.

1999 *The coroplastic art of ancient Cyprus 5. The Cypro-Archaic period: Small female figurines*. Nicosia: A. G. Leventis Foundation.

Karageorghis, V.

1965a A late Cypriote tomb at Tamassos. *Report of the Department of Antiquities, Cyprus*: 11–29.

1965b Fouilles des tombes du Chypriote Récent à Akhera. In *Nouveaux Documents pour l'Étude du Bronze Récent à Chypre*. Études Chypriotes 3:71–156. Paris: E. de Boccard.

1970 *Excavations in the necropolis of Salamis* 2. Nicosia: Department of Antiquities.

1973 Chronique des fouilles et découvertes archéologiques à Chypre en 1972. *Bulletin de Correspondance Hellénique* 97:601–689.

1977 *Two Cypriote sanctuaries of the end of the Cypro-Archaic period*. Rome: Consiglio Nazionale delle Ricerche.

1984 Chronique des fouilles et découvertes archéologiques à Chypre en 1983. *Bulletin de Correspondance Hellénique* 108:893–966.

1987 The terracottas. In *La Nécropole d'Amathonte Tombes 113–367*, edited by V. Karageorghis, O. Picard, and C. Tytgat, 1–50. Études Chypriotes 9. Nicosia: École française d'Athènes et Fondation A. G. Leventis.

1992 Miscellanea from late Bronze Age Cyprus. 1. On "baetyls" in Cyprus. *Levant* 24:212.

1993 *The coroplastic art of ancient Cyprus 3. The Cypro-Archaic period:*

Large and medium size sculpture. Nicosia: A. G. Leventis Foundation.

1995 *The coroplastic art of ancient Cyprus* 4. *The Cypro-Archaic period: Small male figurines.* Nicosia: A. G. Leventis Foundation.

Karageorghis, V., and M. Demas

1985 *Excavations at Kition* 5. *The Pre-Phoenician levels.* Nicosia: Department of Antiquities.

1988 *Excavations at Maa-Palaeokastro 1979–1986.* Nicosia: Department of Antiquities.

Kardulias, P. N., and R. W. Yerkes

1996 Microwear and metric analysis of threshing sledge flints from Greece and Cyprus. *Journal of Archaeological Science* 23:657–666.

Karydas, A. G. and T. Paradellis

1993 Proton induced monochromatic x-ray beams. *X-Ray Spectrometry* 22:252–259.

1998 Proton induced monochromatic x-rays: A technique for solving interference problems in x-ray fluorescence analysis. In *American Institute of Physics, Conference Proceedings* 475, edited by J. L Duggan and I. L. Morgan, 460–463. Denton, TX: American Institute of Physics.

Kassianidou, V.

1999 Bronze Age copper smelting technology in Cyprus—the evidence from Politiko *Phorades.* In *Metals in antiquity,* edited by S. M. M. Young, A. M. Pollard, P. Budd and R. A. Ixer, 91–97. BAR International Series 792. Oxford: Archaeopress.

2000 Hellenistic and Roman mining in Cyprus. In *Acts of the Third International Congress of Cypriot Studies* (Nicosia, 16–20 April 1996), Volume A: Ancient Section, edited by G. K. Ioannides and S.A. Hadjistyllis, 745–756. Nicosia: Society of Cypriot Studies.

2001 New developments in the archaeometallurgy of Cyprus. In *Archaeometry issues in Greek prehistory and antiquity,* edited by Y. Bassiakos, E. Aloupi, and Y. Facorellis, 609–616. Athens: Hellenic Society for Archaeometry and Society for Archaeological Messenian Studies.

Kassianidou, V., and D. Michaelides

1996 Is there Cypriot gold? Geological facts versus the written sources. Paper presented at the International Conference The Fortune of Greek Gold in the Classical and Hellenistic Period, organized by The Aristoteleion University of Thessaloniki and PACT, Thessaloniki, 27 to 30 March, 1996.

Kassianidou, V., and H. Wright

1996 SCSP 1995: Agrokipia *Kriadis* mine (Unit 2013) and Mitsero *Sykamies* slag heap (Unit 2009). In A report on the Sydney Cyprus Survey Project (SCSP), third season (1995), by A. B. Knapp and M. Given. *Report of the Department of Antiquities, Cyprus*: 316–323.

Kealhofer, L.

1999 Creating social identity in the landscape: Tidewater, Virginia, 1600–1750. In *Archaeologies of landscape: Contemporary perspectives,* edited by W. Ashmore and A. B. Knapp, 58–82. Oxford: Blackwell.

Kennedy, H.

1985 From polis to madina: Urban change in late antique and early Islamic Syria. *Past and Present* 106:3–27.

Keswani, P. S.

1989 The pithoi and other plain ware vessels. In *Vasilikos Valley Project* 3: *Kalavasos-Ayios Dhimitrios* 2, by A. K. South, P. Russell, and P. S. Keswani, 12–21. Studies in Mediterranean Archaeology 71(3). Gothenburg: P. Åström's Förlag.

1993 Models of local exchange in late Bronze Age Cyprus. *Bulletin of the American Schools of Oriental Research* 292:73–83.

1996 Hierarchies, heterarchies, and urbanization processes: The view from Bronze Age Cyprus. *Journal of Mediterranean Archaeology* 9:211–249.

Keswani, P. S., and A. B. Knapp

N.D. Bronze Age boundaries and social exchange in northwest Cyprus. Unpublished manuscript.

Kiel, M.

1997 The rise and decline of Turkish Boeotia, 15th–19th century. In *Recent developments in the history and archaeology of central Greece,* edited by J. Bintliff, 315–358. BAR International Series S666. Oxford: British Archaeological Reports.

Kintigh, K. W.

1990 Comments on the case for full-coverage surveys. In *The archaeology of regions: A case for full coverage survey,* edited by S. K. Fish and S. A. Kowaleski, 237–242. Washington, DC: Smithsonian Institution Press.

1994 Contending with contemporaneity in settlement-pattern studies. *American Antiquity* 59:143–148.

Kliridhis, N.

1961 *Khoria ke Polities tis Kiprou.* Nicosia: N.p.

Knapp, A. B.

1986a Production, exchange and socio-political complexity on Bronze Age Cyprus. *Oxford Journal of Archaeology* 5:35–60.

1986b *Copper production and divine protection: Archaeology, ideology and social complexity on Bronze Age Cyprus.* Studies in Mediterranean Archaeology, Pocket-book 42. Gothenburg: P. Åström's Förlag.

1990 Production, location and integration in Bronze Age Cyprus. *Current Anthropology* 31:147–76.

1993 Social complexity: Incipience, emergence and development on prehistoric Cyprus. *Bulletin of the American Schools of Oriental Research* 292:85–106.

1996a The Bronze Age economy of Cyprus: Ritual, ideology, and the sacred landscape. In *The development of the Cypriot economy: From the prehistoric period to the present day,* edited by V. Karageorghis and D. Michaelides, 71–106. Nicosia: A. G. Leventis Foundation and the Bank of Cyprus.

1996b Power and ideology on prehistoric Cyprus. In *Religion and power in the ancient Greek world,* edited by P. Hellström and B. Alroth, 9–25. Acta Universitatis Upsaliensis, Boreas 24. Stockholm: Almqvist and Wiksell.

1997 *The archaeology of late Bronze Age Cypriot society: The study of settlement, survey and landscape.* Occasional Paper 4. Glasgow: University of Glasgow, Department of Archaeology.

1999a The archaeology of mining: Fieldwork perspectives from the Sydney Cyprus Survey Project (SCSP). In *Metals in antiquity,* edited by S. M. M. Young, A. M. Pollard, P. Budd and R. A. Ixer, 98–109. BAR International Series S792. Oxford: Archaeopress.

1999b Ideational and industrial landscape on prehistoric Cyprus. In *Archaeologies of landscape: Contemporary perspectives,* edited by W. Ashmore and A. B. Knapp, 229–252. Oxford: Blackwell.

2000 Archaeology, science-based archaeology and the Mediterranean Bronze Age metals trade. *European Journal of Archaeology* 3:31–56.

Knapp, A.B., ed.

1992 *Archaeology, Annales and ethnohistory.* Cambridge: Cambridge University Press.

Knapp, A. B., and W. Ashmore

1999 Archaeological landscapes: Constructed, conceptualised, ideational. In *Archaeologies of landscape: Contemporary perspectives*, edited by W. Ashmore and A. B. Knapp, 1–30. Oxford: Blackwell.

Knapp, A. B., M. Donnelly, and V. Kassianidou

1998 Excavations at Politiko *Phorades*—1997. *Report of the Department of Antiquities, Cyprus*: 247–268.

Knapp, A. B., and M. Given

1996 A report on the Sydney Cyprus Survey Project (SCSP), third season (1995). *Report of the Department of Antiquities, Cyprus*: 295–366.

Knapp, A. B., S. O. Held, I. R. Johnson, and E. Zangger

1992 The Sydney Cyprus Survey Project, first preliminary season (1992). *Report of the Department of Antiquities, Cyprus*: 319–336.

Knapp, A. B., S. O. Held, I. Johnson, and P. S. Keswani

1994 The Sydney Cyprus Survey Project, second preliminary season (1993). *Report of the Department of Antiquities, Cyprus*: 329–343.

Knapp, A. B., and I. Johnson

1994 Quantifying survey data from Cyprus: Using aerial photos for field recording and GIS input. In *Methods in the mountains: Proceedings of the UISPP Committee IV meeting*, edited by I. Johnson, 157–164. Archaeological Method Series 2. Sydney: Archaeological Computing Laboratory, Sydney University.

Knapp, A.B., V. Kassianidou, and M. Donnelly

1998 The 1997 excavations at Politiko *Phorades*, Cyprus. *Old World Archaeology Newsletter* 21(1):15–23.

1999 Excavations at Politiko *Phorades*—1998. *Report of the Department of Antiquities, Cyprus*: 125–46.

2001 The excavations at Politiko *Phorades* and the archaeology of ancient Cypriot copper mining. *Near Eastern Archaeology* 64:202–208.

Knapp, A. B., and L.M. Meskell

1997 Bodies of evidence on prehistoric Cyprus. *Cambridge Archaeological Journal* 7:183–204.

Knapp, A. B., V.C. Pigott, and E. Herbert, eds.

1998 *Social approaches to an industrial past: The archaeology and anthropology of mining*. London: Routledge.

Knapp, A. B., and K. Seretis

1996 The Sydney Cyprus Survey Project (SCSP), fourth season (1996): Brief preliminary report. *Old World Archaeology Newsletter* 20:10–19.

Kolb, M. J., and J. E. Snead

1997 It's a small world after all: Comparative analyses of community organization in archaeology. *American Antiquity* 62:609–628.

Kottak, C. P.

1999 The new ecological anthropology. *American Anthropologist* 101:23–35.

Koucky, F.

1982 Appendix. Note on the slags near Mitsero and Agrokipia. *Report of the Department of Antiquities, Cyprus*: 243.

Koucky, F. L., and A. R. Steinberg

1974 Preliminary metallurgical research on the ancient Cypriot copper industry. In *The American Expedition to Idalion, Cyprus*, edited by L.E. Stager, A. Walker and G.E.Wright, 149–178. BASOR Supplementary Volume 18. Cambridge MA: American Schools of Oriental Research.

1982a The ancient slags of Cyprus. In *Early Metallurgy in Cyprus, 4000–500 BC*, edited by J. D. Muhly, R. Maddin, and V. Karageorghis, 117-142. Nicosia: Pierides Foundation.

1982b Ancient mining and mineral dressing on Cyprus. In *Early pyrotechnology: The evolution of the first fire-using industries*, edited by T.A. and S.F. Wertime, 149–180. Washington, DC: Smithsonian Institution Press.

1989 Ancient mining and mineral dressing on Cyprus. In *The American Expedition to Idalion, Cyprus, 1973–1980*, edited by L.E. Stager and A. Walker, 275–327. Oriental Institute Communications 24. Chicago: Oriental Institute, University of Chicago.

Kowaleski, S. A.

1997 A spatial method for integrating data of different types. *Journal of Archaeological Method and Theory* 4:287–306.

Kus, S.

1982 Social representation of space: Dimensioning the cosmological and the quotidian. In *Archaeological hammers and theories*, edited by J. A. Moore and A. S. Keene, 277–298. New York: Academic Press.

1987 The "Blue Height" and the "Village of a Thousand." In *Mirror and metaphor: Material and social constructions of reality*, edited by D. W. Ingersoll and G. Bronitsky, 351–364. Lanham, MD: University Press of America.

Kyprianos, Archimandrite

1788 *Istoria Khronoloyiki tis Nisou Kiprou*. Venice: N.p.

Kyrris, C. P.

1984 The nature of Arab-Byzantine relations in Cyprus from the middle of the 7th to the middle of the 10th century A.D. *Graeco-Arabica* 1:149–175.

1987 *The Kanakaria documents 1666–1850: Sale and donation deeds*. Texts and Studies in the History of Cyprus 14. Nicosia: Cyprus Research Centre.

Lance, G. N., and W. T. Williams

1968 A general theory for classificatory sorting strategies 2: Clustering systems. *Computer Journal* 10:271–276.

Larsson, L., J. Callmer, and B. Stjernquist, eds.

1992 *The archaeology of the cultural landscape: Field work and research in a south Swedish rural region*. Stockholm: Almqvist and Wiksell.

Lavender, D.

1962 *The story of the Cyprus Mines Corporation*. San Marino, CA: Huntington Library.

Le Brun, A.

1981 *Un site néolithique précéramique en Chypre: Cap Andreas Kastros*. Recherches sur les Grandes Civilisations. Memoire 5 (Études Néolithiques). Paris: Edition ADPF.

Lee, W. E.

2001 The Pylos Regional Archaeological Project, part IV: Change and the human landscape in a modern Greek village in Messenia. *Hesperia* 70:49–98.

Lemmonier, P., ed.

1993 *Technological choices. Transformations in material cultures since the Neolithic*. London: Routledge.

Leonard, A., Jr.

2000 The Larnaka Hinterland Project: A preliminary report on the 1997 and 1998 seasons. *Report of the Department of Antiquities, Cyprus*: 117–146.

Leroi-Gourhan, A.

1943 *Evolution et techniques: l'homme et la matière*. Paris: Albin Michel.

Lewin, J., J. M. Macklin, and J. C. Woodward, eds.

1995 *Mediterranean Quaternary river environments*. Brookfield, Vermont: Balkema.

Lloyd, J.

1991   Conclusion: Archaeological survey and the Roman land-scape. In *Roman landscapes: Archaeological survey in the Mediterranean*, edited by G. Barker and J. Lloyd, 233–240. Archaeological Monograph 2. London: British Schoool at Rome.

London, G. A.

1987   Cypriote potters: Past and present. *Report of the Department of Antiquities, Cyprus*: 319–322.

Loulloupis, M. C.

1989   A rural cult place in the Soloi area. In *Cyprus and the East Mediterranean in the Iron Age*, edited by V. Tatton-Brown, 68–83. Proceedings of the Seventh British Museum Colloquium, April, 1988. London: British Museum.

Ludwig, J. A., and J. Reynolds

1988   *Statistical ecology: A primer on methods and computers*. New York: John Wiley.

Lund, J.

1993   Pottery of the Classical, Hellenistic, and Roman periods. In *The land of the Paphian Aphrodite 2. The Canadian Palaipaphos Survey Project: Artifact and ecofactual studies*, edited by L. W. Sørensen and D. Rupp, 79–156. Studies in Mediterranean Archaeology 104(2). Gothenburg: P. Åström's Förlag.

1997   The distribution of Cypriot sigillata. In *Res maritimae: Cyprus and the Eastern Mediterranean from prehistory to late antiquity*, edited by S. Swiny, R. L. Hohlfelder and H. W. Swiny, 201–216. Cyprus American Archaeological Research Institute, Monograph 1. Atlanta: Scholar's Press.

Lyon, R. J. P.

1975   Correlation between ground metal analysis, vegetation reflectance, and ERTS brightness over a molybdenum skarn deposit, Pine Nut Mountains, Western Nevada. *Proceedings of the 10th international symposium on remote sensing and environment*, 1031–1037. Ann Arbor: Environmental Research Institute of Michigan.

McCartney, C.

1993   An attribute analysis of Cypriot *dhoukani* "teeth": Implications for the study of Cypriot chipped stone assemblages. *Report of the Department of Antiquities, Cyprus*: 365–379.

McCartney, C., and E. Peltenburg

2000   The colonization of Cyprus: Questions of origins and isolation. *Neo-Lithics* 1:8–11.

McFadden, L. D.

1988   Climatic influences on rates and processes of soil development in Quaternary deposits of southern California. In *Paleosols and weathering through geologic time: Principles and applications*, edited by J. Reinhardt and W. R. Sigleo, 153–177. Special Paper 216. Boulder: Geological Society of America.

McGlade, J.

1995   Archaeology and the ecodynamics of human-modified land-scapes. *Antiquity* 69:113–132.

McManamon, F. P.

1982   Probability sampling and archaeological survey in the northeast. In *Foundations in Northeast archaeology*, edited by D. R. Snow, 195–227. New York: Academic Press.

Madry, S. L. H.

1987   A multiscalar approach to remote sensing in a temperate regional archaeological survey. In *Regional dynamics: Burgundian landscapes in historical perspective*, edited by C. L. Crumley and W. H. Marquardt, 173–236. San Diego: Academic Press.

Maier, F. G.

1989   Priest kings in Cyprus. In *Early society in Cyprus*, edited by E. J. Peltenburg, 376–391. Edinburgh: Edinburgh University Press.

Malaisse, F., and R. R. Brooks

1982   Colonisation of modified metalliferous environments in Zaire by the copper plant *Haumaniastum katangense*. *Plant and Soil* 64:298–293.

Malbran-Labat, F.

1999   Nouvelles donnes épigraphiques sur Chypre et Ougarit. *Report of the Department of Antiquities, Cyprus*: 121–123.

Mandel, R. D.

1988   Geomorphology of the Pawnee River Valley, southwest Kansas. In *Phase II archaeological and geomorphological survey of the proposed Pawnee River watershed covering sub-watersheds 3 through 7, Ness, Ford, Lane, Hodgeman and Finney counties, southwest Kansas*, edited by R. D. Timberlake, 79–134. Salina: Kansas State Historical Society.

Manning, S. W., and S. Swiny

1994   Sotira *Kaminoudhia* and the chronology of the Early Bronze Age in Cyprus. *Oxford Journal of Archaeology* 13:149–172.

Manning, S. W., and D. H. Conwell

1992   Maroni Valley Archaeological Survey Project: Preliminary report on the 1990–1991 field seasons. *Report of the Department of Antiquities, Cyprus*: 271–283.

Mariti, G.

1909   *Travels on the island of Cyprus*. Translated by C. D. Cobham. Cambridge: Cambridge University Press.

Masson, O.

1964   Kypriaka I. Recherches sur les antiquités de Tamassos. *Bulletin de Correspondance Hellénique* 88:199–238.

1996   Inscriptions syllabiques et incisions diverses. In *The sanctuary of Apollo Hylates at Kourion: Excavations in the Archaic precinct*, edited by D. Buitron-Oliver, 179–180. Studies in Mediterranean Archaeology 109. Jonsered: P. Åström's Förlag.

Megaw, A. H. S.

1937/39 Three medieval pit-groups from Nicosia. *Report of the Department of Antiquities, Cyprus*: 45–68.

1968   Zeuxippus ware. *Annual of the British School at Athens* 63:67–88.

1993   The episcopal precinct at Kourion and the evidence for relocation. In *The sweet land of Cyprus*, edited by A. A. M. Bryer and G. S. Georghallides, 53–67. Nicosia: National Research Centre.

Megaw, A. H. S., and E. J. W. Hawkins

1977   *The church of the Panagia Kankariá at Lythrankomi in Cyprus. Its mosaics and frescoes*. Dumbarton Oaks Studies 14. Washington, DC: Dumbarton Oaks.

Megaw, A. H. S., and R. E. Jones

1983   Byzantine and allied pottery: A contribution by chemical analysis to problems of origin and distribution. *Annual of the British School at Athens* 78:235–263.

Meikle, R. D.

1977   *Flora of Cyprus*. Kew: Royal Botanic Gardens.

Meinig, D. W.

1979   Introduction. In *The interpretation of ordinary landscapes*, edited by D. W. Meinig, 1–7. Oxford: Oxford University Press.

Merkel J. F., I. Shimada, C. P. Swann, and R. Doonan

1994   Pre-Hispanic copper alloy production at Batan Grande, Peru: Interpretation of the analytical data for ore samples. In *Archaeometry of pre-Columbian sites and artefacts*, edited by D. A. Scott and P. Meyers, 199–229. Santa Monica: Getty Trust Publications.

Merrillees, R. S.

1965   Reflections on the late Bronze Age in Cyprus. *Opuscula Atheniensia* 6:139–148.

1971   The early history of late Cypriote I. *Levant* 3:56–79.

1973   Settlement, sanctuary and cemetery in Bronze Age Cyprus. *Australian Studies in Archaeology* 1:44–57.

1984   Ambelikou-Aletri: A preliminary report. *Report of the Department of Antiquities, Cyprus*: 1–13.

Michaelides, D.

1996   The economy of Cyprus during the Hellenistic and Roman periods. In *The development of the Cypriot economy: From the prehistoric period to the present day*, edited by V. Karageorghis and D. Michaelides, 139–152. Nicosia: A. G. Leventis Foundation and the Bank of Cyprus.

Miller, K.

1916   *Die Peutingersche Tafel.* Stuttgart: F. A. Brockhaus.

Mitford, T. B.

1980   Roman Cyprus. In *Aufstieg und Niedergang der Römischen Welt* II.7.2:1285–1384.

Morris, R. S.

1984   The Stylianides Mill—Evrykhou. *Kipriakes Spoudhes* 57:161–172.

Muhly, J. D.

1982   The nature of trade in the late Bronze Age Eastern Mediterranean: The organization of the metals trade and the role of Cyprus. In *Early metallurgy in Cyprus, 4000–500 BC*, edited by J. D Muhly, R. Maddin, and V. Karageorghis, 251–269. Nicosia: Pierides Foundation.

1986   The role of Cyprus in the economy of the eastern Mediterranean during the second millennium B.C. In *Acts of the international archaeological symposium: Cyprus between the Orient and the Occident*, edited by V. Karageorghis, 45–60. Nicosia: Department of Antiquities.

1989   The organisation of the copper industry in late Bronze Age Cyprus. In *Early society in Cyprus*, edited by E. Peltenburg, 298–314. Edinburgh: Edinburgh University Press.

Muhly, J. D., R. Maddin, and T. S. Wheeler

1980   The oxhide ingots from Enkomi and Mathiatis and late Bronze Age copper smelting in Cyprus. *Report of the Department of Antiquities, Cyprus*: 84–99.

Muir, R.

1999   *Approaches to landscape.* Macmillan: London.

Nance, J. D.

1983   Regional sampling in archaeological survey: The statistical perspective. In *Advances in archaeological method and theory*. volume 6, edited by M. B. Schiffer, 289–357. New York: Academic Press.

Niklasson, K.

1991   *Early prehistoric burials in Cyprus.* Studies in Mediterranean Archaeology 96. Jonsered: P. Åström's Förlag.

Noller, J. S.,

1993   Late Cenozoic stratigraphy and soil geomorphology of the Peruvian desert, 3°–18° S: A long-term record of hyperaridity and El Niño. Ph.D. dissertation, Department of Geological Sciences, University of Colorado, Boulder.

Noller, J. S., J. M. Sowers, and W. R. Lettis

2000   *Quaternary geochronology: Methods and applications.* Washington, D.C.: American Geophysical Union.

Noller, J.S., and Wells, L.E.,

N.D.   Bimilenary persistence of traditional systems of hill slope soil conservation in the Mediterranean. *Geoarchaeology. In press.*

O'Brien, W. ed.

1994   *Mount Gabriel. Bronze Age mining in Ireland.* Belfast: Galway University Press.

Ohnefalsch-Richter, M. H.

1893   *Kypros, the Bible and Homer: Oriental civilization, art and religion in ancient times.* London: Asher.

Oikonomakis, N. E.

1984   I Kipros ke i Araves (622–965 AD). *Melete ke Ipomnimata* 1:344–350.

Oliver, A., Jr.

1996   Pottery from the votive deposit. In *The sanctuary of Apollo Hylates at Kourion: Excavations in the Archaic precinct*, edited by D. Buitron-Oliver, 73–86. Studies in Mediterranean Archaeology 109. Jonsered: P. Åström's Förlag.

Orton, C., P. Tyers, and A. Vince

1993   *Pottery in archaeology.* Cambridge: Cambridge University Press.

Oziol, T.

1977   *Les lampes du Musée de Chypre.* Salamine de Chypre VII. Paris: de Boccard.

Pálsson, G.

1996   Human-environmental relations: Orientalism, paternalism and communalism. In *Nature and society: Anthropological perspectives*, edited by P. Descola and G. Pálsson, 63–81. London: Routledge.

Panaretos, A.

1967   *Kipriaki Yeoryiki Laografia.* Nicosia: Sinergatiki Kendriki Trapeza.

Panayiotou A.

1989a   Mitserou metallia. *Megali Kipriaki Enkiklopedhia* 10:85–86. Nicosia: Philokypros.

1989b   Metallia — Metallevma. *Megali Kipriaki Enkiklopedhia* 10:31–43. Nicosia: Philokypros.

Papadimitriou, E. K.

1972–1974 The modern pottery of Lapithos. *Laphithos Chronicle* 2–3:11–55.

1992   *Ethnographika Karpasias.* Nicosia: Society for Cypriot Studies.

Papadopoullos, T.

1965   *Social and historical data on population (1570–1881).* Nicosia: Cyprus Research Centre.

Papageorghiou, A.

1964   Les premières incursions arabes à Chypre et leurs consequences. In *Afieroma is ton Konstantinon Spiridhakin*, 152–158. Nicosia.

1966   Ereuna eis to naon tou Ayiou Spuridonos en Tremetousia (first preliminary report). *Kypriakai Spoudhai* 30: 17-33.

Papanikola-Bakirtzis, D.

1989   *Medieval Cypriot pottery in the Pierides Foundation Museum.* Larnaca: Pierides Foundation.

1993   Cypriot medieval glazed pottery: Answers and questions. In *The sweet land of Cyprus*, edited by A. A. M. Bryer and G. S. Georgallides, 115–125. Nicosia: Cyprus Research Centre.

1996   *Meseoniki Efialomeni Keramiki tis Kiprou: Ta ergastiria Paphou ke Lapithou.* Thessaloniki: A. G. Leventis Foundation.

Papanikola-Bakirtzis, D. and M. Iacovou, eds.

1998   *Byzantine Medieval Cyprus.* Nicosia: Bank of Cyprus Cultural Foundation.

Paraskevopoulou, M.

1982   *Researches into the traditions of the popular religious feasts of Cyprus.* Translated by P. Bosustow. Nicosia: Private publication.

Peacock, D. P. S., and D. F. Williams

1986   *Amphorae and the Roman economy: An introductory guide.* New York: Longman.

Peltenburg, E. J.

1978   The Sotira Culture: Regional diversity and cultural unity in late Neolithic Cyprus. *Levant* 10:55–74.

1985 *Lemba Archaeological Project* I: *Excavations 1976–1983.* Studies in Mediterranean Archaeology 70(1). Gothenburg: P. Åström's Förlag.

1991a *Lemba Archaeological Project* 2. 2. *A ceremonial area at Kissonerga.* Studies in Mediterranean Archaeology 70(3). Gothenburg: P. Åström's Förlag.

1991b Kissonerga-Mosphilia: A major Chalcolithic site in Cyprus. *Bulletin of the American Schools of Oriental Research* 282–83:17–35.

1993 Settlement discontinuity and resistance to complexity in Cyprus, ca. 4500–2500 B.C. *Bulletin of the American Schools of Oriental Research* 292:9–23.

1994 Constructing authority: The Vounous enclosure model. *Opuscula Atheniensia* 20:157–162.

1996 From isolation to state formation in Cyprus, c. 3500–1500 B.C. In *The development of the Cypriot economy: From the prehistoric period to the present day*, edited by V. Karageorghis and D. Michaelides, 17–44. Nicosia: A. G. Leventis Foundation and Bank of Cyprus.

1998 *Lemba Archaeological Reports.* Volume 2: 1A. *Excavations at Kissonerga-Mosphilia.* Studies in Mediterranean Archaeology 70(2). Jonsered: P. Åström's Förlag.

Peltenburg, E., S. Colledge, P. Croft, A. Jackson, C. McCartney, and M.A. Murray

2000 Agro-pastoralist colonization of Cyprus in the 10th millennium BP: Initial assessments. *Antiquity* 74/286:884–853.

Peltenburg, E., P. Croft, A. Jackson, C. McCartney, and M.A. Murray

2001 Well-established colonists: Mylouthkia I and the Cypro-Pre-Pottery Neolithic B. In *The Earliest Prehistory of Cyprus: From Colonization to Exploitation*, edited by S. Swiny, 61–93. Cyprus American Archaeological Research Institute, Monograph 2. Boston: American Schools of Oriental Research.

Pentz, P.

1992 *The invisible conquest: The ontogenesis of sixth and seventh century Syria.* Copenhagen: National Museum of Denmark.

Pfaffenberger, B.

1992 Social anthropology of technology. *Annual Review of Anthropology* 21:491–516.

1998 Mining communities, chaînes opératoires and sociotechnical systems. In *Social approaches to an industrial past. The archaeology and anthropology of mining*, edited by A. B. Knapp, V. C. Pigott, and E. W. Herbert, 291–300. Routledge: London and New York.

Phillips, P., ed.

1989 *Archaeology and landscape studies in North Lincolnshire.* BAR British Series 208. Oxford: British Archaeological Reports.

Pieridou, A. G.

1960 Kipriaki laiki tekhni. Kipriaki laiki angioplastiki. *Kipriakes Spoudhes* 24:153–165.

Plantzos, D.

1999 *Hellenistic engraved gems.* Oxford: Clarendon Press.

Plog, F.

1990 Some thoughts on full-coverage survey. In *The archaeology of regions: A case for full coverage survey*, edited by S. K. Fish and S. A. Kowaleski, 243–248. Washington, DC: Smithsonian Institution Press.

Plog, F., and J. A. Hill

1971 Explaining variability in the distribution of sites. In *The distribution of prehistoric population aggregates*, edited by G. J. Gummerman, 7–36. Prescott: Prescott College Press.

Plog, S., F. Plog, and W. Wait

1978 Decision making in modern surveys. In *Advances in archaeo-logical method and theory* 1, edited by M. B. Schiffer, 383–421. New York: Academic Press.

Poole, A. J., G. B. Shimmield, and A. H. F. Robertson

1991 Late Quaternary uplift of the Troodos Ophiolite, Cyprus: Uranium-series dating of Pleistocene coral. *Geology* 18:894–897.

Pope, K. O., and B. H. Dahlin

1989 Ancient Maya wetland agriculture: New insights from ecological and remote sensing research. *Journal of Field Archaeology* 16:87–106.

Portugali, J.

1992 Geography, environment and cognition: An introduction. *Geoforum* 23:107–109.

Portugali, J., and A. B. Knapp

1985 Cyprus and the Aegean: A spatial analysis of interaction in the 17th–14th centuries B.C. In *Prehistoric production and exchange: The Aegean and the eastern Mediterranean*, edited by A. B. Knapp and T. Stech, 44–78. Monograph 25. Los Angeles: UCLA Institute of Archaeology.

Preuschen, E.

1964 Kupfererzbergbau und vegetationsstörungen. *Archaeologia Austriaca* 35:87–88.

1965 Das urseitliche Kupfer-Verhuttungsgebiet von Lavarone (Trentino). *Der Anschnitt* 17:8–13.

Raber, P. A.

1984 The organization and development of early copper metallurgy in the Polis region, western Cyprus. Ph.D. dissertation, Pennsylvania State University, College Park.

1987 Early copper production in the Polis region, western Cyprus. *Journal of Field Archaeology* 14:297–312.

Raptou, E.

1996 Note sur les coutumes funeraires de Marion à l'époque classique. *Report of the Department of Antiquities, Cyprus*: 225–237.

Rautman, M. L., and M. C. McClellan

1992 Excavations at late Roman Kopetra, Cyprus. *Journal of Roman Archaeology* 5:265–271.

Rautman, M. L., B. Gomez, H. Neff, and M. D. Glascock

1993 Neutron activation analysis of late Roman ceramics from Kalavasos-Kopetra and the environs of the Vasilikos Valley. *Report of the Department of Antiquities, Cyprus*: 232–264.

Renfrew, A. C.

1984 *Approaches to social archaeology.* Edinburgh: Edinburgh University Press.

Renfrew, C., and S. J. Shennan, eds.

1982 *Ranking, resource and exchange: Aspects of the archaeology of early European society.* Cambridge: Cambridge University Press.

Renfrew, A. C., and M. Wagstaff, eds.

1982 *An island polity: The archaeology of exploitation on Melos.* Cambridge: Cambridge University Press.

Reyes, A. T.

1994 *Archaic Cyprus. A study of the textual and archaeological evidence.* Oxford Monographs on Classical Archaeology. Oxford: Clarendon Press.

Rice, P,

1987 *Pottery analysis: A sourcebook.* Chicago: University of Chicago Press.

Richard, J.

1947 Casal de Psimolofo et la vie rurale en Chypre au XIVe siècle. *Mélanges d'archéologie et d'histoire publiés par l'Ecole Française de Rome* 59:121–153.

Richards, C.

1996 Henges and water: Towards an elemental understanding of monumentality and landscape in late Neolithic Britain. *Journal of Material Culture* 1:313–336.

Rickard, T. A.

1930   Copper mining in Cyprus. *Transactions of the Institution of Mining and Metallurgy* 39:285–301.

Riley, J. A.

1979   The coarse pottery from Bernice. In *Excavations at Sidi Khrebish Benghazi (Berenice)*, volume 2, edited by J. A. Lloyd, 91–467. Tripoli: Department of Antiquities.

Ritchie, N., and R. Hooker

1997   An archaeologist's guide to mining terminology. *Australasian Historical Archaeology* 15:3–29.

Roberts, B. K.

1996   *Landscapes of settlement: Prehistory to the present.* London: Routledge.

Rosen, S. A

1997   *Lithics after the Stone Age: A handbook of stone tools from the Levant.* Thousand Oaks, CA: Altamira Press.

Rothenberg, Benno

1990a   *The ancient metallurgy of copper.* London: Institute for Archaeometallurgical Studies, University College London.

1990b   Copper smelting furnaces, tuyères, slags, ingot-moulds and ingots in the Arabah: The archaeological data. In *The ancient metallurgy of copper,* edited by B. Rothenberg, 1–74. London: Institute for Archaeometallurgical Studies, University College London.

Rothenberg, B., and A. Blanco Freijeiro

1981   *Studies in ancient mining and metallurgy in south-west Spain.* London: Institute for Archaeometallurgical Studies, University College London.

Rotroff, S. I.

1997   *Hellenistic pottery: Athenian and imported wheelmade table ware and related material. The Athenian Agora,* Volume XXIX. Princeton: The American School of Classical Studies at Athens.

Ruiz, M., R. Risch, P. G. Marcen, P. Castro, V. Lull, and R. Chapman

1992   Environmental exploitation and social structure in prehistoric southeast Spain. *Journal of Mediterranean Archaeology* 5:3–38.

Rupp, D. W.

1986   The Canadian Palaipaphos (Cyprus) Survey Project: Third preliminary report, 1983–1985. *Acta Archaeologica* 57:27–45.

1987   The Canadian Palaipaphos Survey Project: An overview of the 1986 season. *Echos du Monde Classique* n.s. 6:217–224.

Russell, J.

1986   Excavations at Anemurium (Eksi Anamur), 1985. *Echos du Monde Classique* n.s. 5:173–183.

Sakellariou, A. A.

1890   *Ta Kipriaka.* Volume A'. Centennial Publication 1991. Nicosia: Cultural Foundation of Makarios III.

Salkield, L. U.

1982   Appendix A. Reply to Koucky and Steinberg. In *Early pyrotechnology: The evolution of fire-using industries,* edited by T. A. Wertime and S. F. Wertime, 245–246. Washington, DC: Smithsonian Institution Press.

Salles, J.–F.

1983   *Kition-Bamboula 2: Les égouts de la ville classique.* Paris: Éditions recherche sur les civilisations.

Sanders, W. T., J. R. Parsons, and R. S. Santley

1979   *The basin of Mexico: Ecological processes in the evolution of civilization.* New York: Academic Press.

Sandor, J. A.

1992   Long-term effects of prehistoric agriculture on soils: Examples from New Mexico and Peru. In *Soils in archaeology: Landscape evolution and human occupation,* edited by T. Holliday, 217–246. Washington, DC: Smithsonian Institution Press.

Sant Cassia, P.

1993   Banditry, myth and terror. *Comparative Studies in Society and History* 35:773–795.

Sarris, A., and R. E. Jones

2000   Geophysical and related techniques applied to archaeological survey in the Mediterranean: A review. *Journal of Mediterranean Archaeology* 13:3–75.

Schaar, K. W., M. Given, and G. Theocharous

1995   *Under the clock: Colonial architecture and history in Cyprus, 1878–1960.* Nicosia: Bank of Cyprus.

Schaeffer, C. F. A.

1949   *Ugaritica* II. *Mission de Ras Shamra* 5. Bibliotheque Archeologique et Historique 47. Paris: Geuthner.

Schama, S.

1995   *Landscape and memory.* London: Harper Collins.

Schiffer, M. B., A. P. Sullivan, and T. C. Klinger

1978   The design of archaeological surveys. *World Archaeology* 10:1–27.

Schlanger, N.

1994   Mindful technology: Unleashing the chaîne opératoire for an archaeology of mind. In *The ancient mind. Elements of cognitive archaeology,* edited by C. Renfrew and E. B. W. Zubrow, 143–151. Cambridge: Cambridge University Press.

Schubert, R.

1953/54a Die Schwermetallpflanzengesellschaften des östlichen Harzvorlandes. *Wissenschaftliche Zeitschrift der Martin-Luther-Universität Halle-Wittenberg Mathematisch-naturwissenschaftliche Reihe* 3:51–70.

1953/54b Die Pflanzengesellschaften der Bottendorfer Hohen. *Wissenschaftliche Zeitschrift der Martin-Luther-Universität Halle-Wittenberg Mathematisch-naturwissenschaftliche Reihe* 3: 99-128.

Scott D. A.

1991   *Metallography and microstructure of ancient and historic metals.* Singapore: The Getty Conservation Institute and Archetype Books.

Serwint, N.

1992   The terracotta sculpture from ancient Marion: Recent discoveries. In *Acta Cypria: Acts of an International Congress on Cypriote Archaeology held in Gothenburg on 22–24 August 1991.* Part 3, edited by P. Åström, 38–426. Studies in Mediterranean Archaeology and Literature, Pocket-book 120. Jonsered: Paul Åström's Förlag.

Seton-Williams, V.

1936   The implements of flint and chert. In The Excavations at Erimi, by P. Dikaios. *Report of the Department of Antiquities, Cyprus:* 51–54.

Shanks, M., and C. Tilley

1987   *Social theory and archaeology.* Cambridge: Polity Press.

Shennan, S.

1995   *Bronze Age copper producers of the eastern Alps: Excavations at St. Veit-Klinglberg.* Universitätsforschungen zur Prähistorischen Archäologie 27. Bonn: R. Habelt.

1997   *Quantifying archaeology.* 2nd edition. Edinburgh: Edinburgh University Press.

Smith, J. S.

1997   Preliminary comments on a rural Cypro-Archaic sanctuary in Polis-Peristeries. *Bulletin of the American Schools of Oriental Research* 308:77–98.

1999 Changes in warp-weighted loom technology in late Bronze Age Cyprus. *American Schools of Oriental Research 1999 Annual Meeting Abstracts*:40.

2000 Iron Age Eastern Mediterranean ceramics from production to consumption. *American Schools of Oriental Research 2000 Annual Meeting Abstracts*.

2002 Changes in the workplace: Women and textile production on late Bronze Age Cyprus. In *Engendering Aphrodite: Women and society in ancient Cyprus*, edited by D. Bolger and N. Serwint, 281–312. ASOR Archaeological Reports 7. CAARI Monographs 3. Boston, MA: American Schools of Oriental Research.

Solomidou-Ieronymidou, Marina

2001 The discovery of six unique Cypro-Archaic statues at Tamassos. *Report of the Department of Antiquities, Cyprus*, 165–186.

Sørensen, L. W.

1993 In *The land of the Paphian Aphrodite 2: The Canadian Palaipaphos Survey Project, artifactual and ecofactual studies*, edited by L. W. Sørensen and D. W. Rupp, 185-197. Studies in Mediterranean Archaeology 104(2). Göteborg: P. Åström's Förlag.

1996 Preliminary report of the Danish archaeological excavations to *Panayia Ematousa*, Aradhippou 1993 and 1994. *Report of the Department of Antiquities, Cyprus:* 135–155.

Sørenson, L. W., and C. Grønne.

1992 Report of archaeological soundings at *Panayia Ematousa*, Aradhippou, Cyprus 1991. *Report of the Department of Antiquities, Cyprus*: 185–203.

Sørensen, L. W., and D. W. Rupp, eds.

1993 *The land of the Paphian Aphrodite* 2. Studies in Mediterranean Archaeology 104(2). Gothenburg: P. Åström's Förlag.

South, A. K., P. Russell, and P. S. Keswani

1989 *Vasilikos Valley Project* 3: *Kalavasos-Ayios Dhimitrios* 2: *Ceramics, objects, tombs, specialist studies*. Studies in Mediterranean Archaeology 71(3). Gothenburg: P. Åström's Förlag.

Sparkes, B. A., and L. Talcott

1970 *Black and plain pottery of the 6th, 5th and 4th centuries B.C. The Athenian Agora*, Volume XII. Princeton: The American School of Classical Studies at Athens.

Spyridakis, C.

1972 I ikonomiki politiki ton vasileon tis Kiprou. *Melete, Dhialexis, Loyi, Arthra. Tomos A. Istorikofiloloyike Melete ke Dhialexis*. Vol. 1:112–22. Nicosia: Tmima Dhimosiefseon Ellinikis Kinotikis Sinelefseos.

Steward, J.

1937 Ecological aspects of southwestern society. *Anthropos* 32:87–104.

Stewart, J. R

1962 The Early Cypriote Bronze Age. In *Swedish Cyprus Expedition* IV.1A, by P. Dikaios and J. R. Stewart, 205–401. Lund: Swedish Cyprus Expedition.

Stos-Gale, S., G. Maliotis, and N. Gale

1998 A preliminary survey of the Cypriot slag heaps and their contribution to the reconstruction of copper production on Cyprus. In *Metallurgica antiqua. In honour of Hans-Gert Bachmann and R. Maddin*, edited by T. Rehren, A. Hauptmann and J. D. Muhly, 235–262. Der Anschnitt, Beiheft 8. Bochum: Deutschen Bergbau Museum.

Strabo

1917/32 *The geography of Strabo*. Translated by Leonard Jones. Loeb Classical Library. London: Heinemann.

Stringer, W. J., and J. P. Cook

1974 *Feasibility study for locating archaeological village sites by satellite remote sensing*. Technical Report Series. Fairbanks: University of Alaska.

Stuiver, M., and P. J. Reimer

1993 Extended 14C database and revised CALIB radiocarbon calibration program. *Radiocarbon* 35:215–230.

Stuiver, M., P. J. Reimer, E. Bard, J. W. Beck, G. S. Burr, K. A. Hughen, B. Kromer, G. McCormac, J. van der Plicht, and M. Spurk

1998 INTCAL98 Radiocarbon Age Calibration, 24,000-0 cal BP. *Radiocarbon* 40:1041–1084.

Stylianou, A., and J. A. Stylianou

1980 *The history of the cartography of Cyprus*. Nicosia: Cyprus Research Centre.

1985 *The painted churches of Cyprus*. London: Trigraph.

Stylianou, P. J.

1992 The age of the kingdoms. A political history of Cyprus in the Archaic and Classical Periods. In *Travaux et Memoirs* II (*Melete ke Ipomnimata*), edited by T. Papadopoullos, 375–530. Nicosia: Archbishop Makarios III Foundation.

Sutton, S. B.

1991 Population, economy, and settlement in post-revolutionary Keos: A cultural anthropological study. In *Landscape archaeology as long-term history: Northern Keos in the Cycladic Islands from earliest settlement until modern times*, by J. F. Cherry, J. L. Davis, and E. Mantzourani, 383–402. Los Angeles: UCLA Institute of Archaeology.

1994 Settlement patterns, settlement perceptions: Rethinking the Greek village. In *Beyond the site: Regional studies in the Aegean Area*, edited by P. N. Kardulias, 313–335. Lanham, MD: University Press of America.

Swiny, S.

1981 Bronze Age settlement patterns in southwest Cyprus. *Levant* 13:51–87.

1985 Sotira *Kaminoudhia* and the Chalcolithic/Early Bronze Age transition in Cyprus. In *Archaeology in Cyprus, 1960–1985*, edited by V. Karageorghis, 115–124. Nicosia: Zavallis Press.

1986 *The Kent State University Expedition to Episkopi-Phaneromeni*. Studies in Mediterranean Archaeology. 74(2). Gothenburg: P. Åström's Förlag.

1989 From round house to duplex: A reassessment of prehistoric Bronze Age Cypriot society. In *Early society in Cyprus*, edited by E. J. Peltenburg, 14–31. Edinburgh: Edinburgh University Press.

Taçon, P. S. C.

1999 Identifying ancient sacred landscapes in Australia: From physical to social. In *Archaeologies of landscape: Contemporary perspectives*, edited by W. Ashmore and A. B. Knapp, 33–57. Oxford: Blackwell.

Tatton-Brown, V.

1985 Archaeology in Cyprus: 1960–1985. Classical to Roman periods. In *Archaeology in Cyprus 1960–1985*, edited by V. Karageorghis, 60–72. Nicosia: Pierides Foundation.

Terrenato, N., and A. J. Ammerman

1996 Visibility and site recovery in the Cecina Valley Survey, Italy. *Journal of Field Archaeology* 23:91–109.

Theocharides, I. P., and S. Andreev

1996 *Traghodhias 1821 Sinekhia Othomaniki Piyi yia tin Kipro*. Nicosia: Kykko Monastery Research Centre.

Theophrastus

1916 *Enquiry into plants*. Loeb Classical Library 70. Translated by Arthur Hort. Cambridge MA: Harvard University Press.

Thomas, D. H.

1975 Nonsite sampling in archaeology: Up the creek without a site? In *Sampling in archaeology*, edited by J. W. Mueller, 61–81. Tucson: University of Arizona Press.

Tilley, C.

1994 *A phenomenology of landscape*. Oxford: Berg.

Tixier, J.

1974 Glossary for the description of stone tools: with special reference to the Epipaleolithic of the Maghreb. Translated by M. H. Newcomer. *Newsletter of Lithic Technology, Washington State University* 36. Pullman, Washington.

Todd, I. A.

1989 The 1988 field survey in the Vasilikos Valley. *Report of Department of Antiquities, Cyprus*: 41–50.

Toumazou, M. K., R. W. Yerkes, and P. N. Kardulias

1998 Athienou Archaeological Project: Investigations in the Malloura Valley, Cyprus, 1990–1995. *Journal of Field Archaeology* 25:163–182.

Trigger, B. G.

1967 Settlement archaeology—its goals and promise. *American Antiquity* 32:149–159.

1968 The determinants of settlement patterns. In *Settlement Archaeology*, edited by K. C. Chang, 53–78. Palo Alto: National Press Books.

1989 *A history of archaeological thought*. Cambridge: Cambridge University Press.

Trumbore, S. E.

2000 Radiocarbon geochronology. In *Quaternary geochronology: Methods and applications*, edited by J. S. Noller, J. M. Sowers, and W. Lettis, 41–60. Reference Shelf 4. Washington, DC: American Geophysical Union.

Tsiknopoullou, I. P.

1967 *O Ayios Iraklidhios, I Iera Aftou Moni ke i Akolouthia*. Nicosia: Archbishopric.

Tuan, Y.

1977 *Space and place: The perspective of experience*. Minneapolis: University of Minnesota Press.

Tylecote, R. F.

1971 Observations on Cypriot copper smelting. *Report of the Department of Antiquities, Cyprus*: 53–58.

1976 *A history of metallurgy*. London: Institute of Metals.

1977 A report on metallurgical work carried out on material collected in Cyprus in 1973. *Reports of the Department of Antiquities, Cyprus*: 317–327.

1982 The late Bronze Age: Copper and bronze metallurgy at Enkomi and Kition. In *Early metallurgy in Cyprus, 4000–500 bc*, edited by J. D. Muhly, R. Maddin, and V. Karageorghis, 81–100. Nicosia: Pierides Foundation.

1987 *The early history of metallurgy in Europe*. London and New York: Longman.

Vagnetti, L.

1980 Figurines and minor objects from a Chalcolithic cemetery at Souskiou-Vathyrkakas. *Studi Micenei ed Egeo-Anatolici* 21:17–72.

van Alfen, P. G.

1996 New light on the 7th-c. Yassi Ada shipwreck: Capacities and standard sizes of LRA1 amphoras. *Journal of Roman Archaeology* 9:189–213.

van Andel, T. H., and C. Runnels.

1987 *Beyond the Acropolis: A rural Greek past*. Stanford: Stanford University Press.

van Andel, T. H., and E. Zangger

1990 Landscape stability and destabilzation in the prehistory of Greece. In *Man's role in the shaping of the eastern Mediterranean landscape*, edited by S. Bottema, G. Entjes-Nieborg, and W. van Zeist, 139–157. Rotterdam: Balkema.

van Andel, T. H., E. Zangger, and A. Demitrack

1990 Land use and soil erosion in prehistoric and historical Greece, 3. *Journal of Field Archaeology* 17:379–396.

van Doorninck, F. H. Jr.

1989 The cargo amphoras on the 7th century Yassi Ada and 11th century Serçe Limani shipwrecks: Two examples of a reuse of Byzantine amphoras as transport jars. In *Recherches sur la céramique byzantine*, edited by V. Déroche and J.-M. Spisser, 247–257. BCH Supplement 18. Athens: L'École Française d'Athénes.

Vessberg, O., and A. Westholm

1956 *The Swedish Cyprus Expedition* IV: *The Hellenistic and Roman periods in Cyprus*. Stockholm: The Swedish Cyprus Expedition.

Vita-Finzi, C.

1969 *The Mediterranean valleys: Geological chances in historical times*. Cambridge: Cambridge University Press.

von Wartburg, M.–L.

1983 The Medieval cane sugar industry in Cyprus: Results of recent excavations. *The Antiquaries Journal* 63:298–314.

Vroom, J.

1996 Coffee and archaeology: A note on a Kütahya ware find in Boeotia, Greece. *Pharos* 4:5–19.

1997 Pots and pans: New perspectives on medieval ceramics in Greece. In *Material culture in Medieval Europe*, edited by G. De Boe and F. Verhaeghe, 203–213. Papers of the Medieval Europe Brugge 1997 Conference 7. Zellik: I. A. P. Rapporten.

1998 Early Modern archaeology in central Greece: The contrast of artefact-rich and sherdless sites. *Journal of Mediterranean Archaeology* 11:131–164.

Wagner, G. A., and G. Weisgerber, eds.

1988 *Antike Edel-und Buntmetallgewinnung auf Thasos*. Der Anschnitt, Beiheft 6. Bochum: Deutschen Bergbau-Museums.

Wagstaff, M., and J. F. Cherry

1982 Settlement and resources. In *An island polity: The archaeology of exploitation on Melos*, edited by C. Renfrew and M. Wagstaff, 245–263. Cambridge: Cambridge University Press.

Wallace, P. W.

1982 Survey of the Akhera area. *Report of the Department of Antiquities, Cyprus*: 237–243.

Wandsnider, L., and E. L. Camilli

1992 Character of surface archaeological deposits and its influence on survey accuracy. *Journal of Field Archaeology* 19:169–188.

Webb, J. M.

1988 The archaeological and iconographic evidence for the religion of late Bronze Age Cyprus. Ph.D. Dissertation. Department of Classics, University of Melbourne.

1992 Funerary ideology in Bronze Age Cyprus —towards the recognition and analysis of Cypriote ritual data. In *Studies in honour of Vassos Karageorghis*, edited by G.K. Ioannides, 87–99. Nicosia: Society of Cypriot Studies.

1999 *Ritual architecture, iconography and practice in the late Cypriot Bronze Age*. Studies in Mediterranean Archaeology and Literature, Pocket-book 75. Jonsered: P. Åström's Förlag.

Webb, J. M., and D. Frankel

1994 Making an impression: Storage and surplus finance in late Bronze Age Cyprus. *Journal of Mediterranean Archaeology* 7:5–26.

1999 Characterising the Philia facies. Material culture, chronology and the origin of the Bronze Age in Cyprus. *American Journal of Archaeology* 103:3–43.

Weisgerber, G.
1982 Towards a history of copper mining in Cyprus and the Near East: Possibilities of mining archaeology. In *Early Metallurgy in Cyprus, 4000–500 BC*, edited by J. D. Muhly, R. Maddin, and V. Karageorghis, 25–32. Nicosia: Pierides Foundation.

Wells, Lisa E.
2001 A geomorphological approach to reconstructing archaeological settlement patterns based on surficial artifact distribution. In *Earth sciences and archaeology*, edited by P. Goldberg, V. Holliday, and C. R. Ferring, 107–141. New York: Kluwer Academic/Plenum.

Whitbread, I. K.
1995 *Greek transport amphorae: A petrological and archaeological study.* Fitch Laboratory Occasional Papers 4. Exeter: British School at Athens.

Whitehill, C. S.
1999 Fluvial geomorphology, Holocene soil development and land use impact, Mitsero Basin, Cyprus. M.S. thesis, Department of Geology, Vanderbilt University, Nashville.

Whittaker, J. C.
1999 *Alonia*: Ethnoarchaeology of Cypriot threshing floors. *Journal of Mediterranean Archaeology* 12:7–25.

Wilkinson, T. J.
1989 Extensive sherd scatters and land-use intensity: Some recent results. *Journal of Field Archaeology* 16:31–46.

Willey, G. R.
1953 *Prehistoric settlement patterns in the Viru Valley, Peru.* Bulletin 155. Washington, DC: Bureau of American Ethnology.

Williams, C.
1989 *Anemurium: The Roman and Early Byzantine pottery.* Toronto: Pontifical Institute of Mediaeval Studies.

Wright, G. R. H.
1992 The Cypriot rural sanctuary: An illuminating document in comparative religion. In *Studies in Honour of Vassos Karageorghis*, edited by G. C. Ioannides, 269–283. Nicosia: Society of Cypriot Studies.

Wylie, A.
1993 A proliferation of new archaeologies: Beyond objectivism and relativism. In *Archaeological theory: Who sets the agenda?*, edited by N. Yoffee and A. Sherratt, 20–26. Cambridge: Cambridge University Press.

Yorston, R. M., V. L. Gaffney, and P. J. Reynolds
1990 Simulation of artefact movement due to cultivation. *Journal of Archaeological Science* 17:67–83.

Young, J. H., and S. H. Young
1955 *Terracotta figurines from Kourion in Cyprus.* Philadelphia: University of Pennsylvania Museum of Anthropology and Archaeology.

Zarkadas, C., A. G. Karydas, T. Paradellis, C. Nicolaou, A. J. Manouras, and N. S. Apostolidis
1998 Improved detection limits of trace elements in biological samples through an optimized secondary target X-ray fluorescence system. In *Proceedings of the International Conference of Trace Elements in Humans: New Perspectives*, edited by S. Ermeidou-Pollet, 117–126. Athens.

Zeest, I. B.
1960 *Keramicheskaia tara Bospora.* Materialy i issledovaniia po arkheologii SSSR no. 83. Moskow: Izd-vo Akademii nauk SSSR.

Zwicker, U.
1986 Ancient metallurgical methods for copper production in Cyprus, Part 2—sulphide ore and copper-arsenic-alloy production. *Bulletin of the Cyprus Association of Geologists and Mining Engineers* 3:92–111.

Zwicker, U., H. Rollig, and U. Schwarz
1972 Investigations on prehistoric and early historic copper-slag from Cyprus (preliminary report). *Report of the Department of Antiquities, Cyprus*: 34–45.

ILLUSTRATION CREDITS

ARTIFACT DRAWINGS

Finalized by Helen Saunders

Claire Etienne: *102-1-1, 102-1-2, 103-1-3, 102-1-4, 102-1-6, 102-1-8, 102-1-10, 102-5-31-98, 102-9-2, 102-9-3, 102-14-1-1, 1021-14-1-2, 102-16-1-1, 102-16-1-8, 102-16-1-9, 102-19-1-1, 102-1E-1-1, 102-1K-1-1, 102-1L-2-1*

Caitlin Evans: *212-S-2, 212-S-8, 1743.28.1, 2514.1.1, 2714.1.1, 5001-1-1, SCY204.1.1, S-0070*

Jean Humbert: *1257.13.1, 1268.39A.1, 1281.29.1, 1327.13.1, 1599.1.1, 1601.1.1, 1603.3.1, 1604.4.1, 1625.5C.1, 1722.4.1, 1728.10.1, 1741.1B.1, 1741.24B.1, 1745.1.1, 3000.14B.1, 3096.2.1, 3097.3.1, 3224.13.1, 3653.27.1, 3657.26.1, 4042.16.1, 4042.20.1, 4052.2.1, 4052.6.1, 4052.9.1, 4052.15.1,2,3, 4052.25.1, 4068.11.1, 4069.3.1, 4542.35.1, 5026.8.1, 5035.29.1, 5036.49.1, 5038.31.1, 5040.1.1, 5041.32.1, 5041.47.1, 5045.40.1, S-0020, S-0029, S-0030, S-0034, S-0039, S-0043, S-0044, S-0045, S-0046, S-0047, S-0053, S-0054, S-0055, S-0057, S-0058, S-0061, S-0066, S-0067*

Janie Ravenhurst: *550.4.1, 551.2.1, 556.1.1, 1010.1.1, 1035.1.1, 1035.2.1, 1054.13.1, 1212.14.1, 1268.62.1, 1269.22.1, 1285.12.1, 1302.13.1, 1596.1.1, 1726.4.1*

Dorella Romanou: *1599.12.1, 1709.27.1, 1742.4.1, 1746.2.1, 3020.11.1, 3259.18.1, 3670.20.1, 4514.1.1, 5019.19.1,*
5019.20.1, 5019.22.1, 5027.17.1, 5038.37.1, 5039.13.1, 5040.5.1, 5041.11.1, 5044.10.1, S-0050

Krista Ubbels: *1005.1.1, 4023.24.1, 4023.25.1, 4041.4.1, 4505.5.1, 5021.51.1, 5022.1.1, 5037.1.1, 5037.4.1, 5040.34.1, 212-1-2, 212-1-5, 212-S-1, 212-S2E1-1, 216-1-1, 216-3-1, 1282-1-1, Mit-Ex-1, Mit-Ex-2*

ARTIFACT PHOTOGRAPHS

Finalized by Helen Saunders

Michael Given: *338.12.1, 1254.1.1, 1599.1.1, 1599.12.1, 1733.2.1, 1733.3.1, 1733.10.1, 1740.1.2, 1741.1.1, 174.8A.1, 1741.13.1, 2102.12.1, 2105.8.1, 4041.4.1, 5017.37.1, 5019.44A.1, S-0030, S-0032, S-0034, S-0043, S-0046, S-0047. Figures 5.6, 5.7, 5.10, 5.17, 5.18 (left), 5.19, 5.20, 5.22, 5.23, 7.2*

Megan Mebberson: *Figures 5.11, 5.18 (right), 5.21*

Xenophon Michael: *Figures 5.2-5.5*

Chris Parks: *1257.12.1, 1595.3.1, 2105.5.1, 5017.39.1, SCY021.2.7.1, SCY204.3.3.1.1, SCY204.3.5.1, SCY204.4.12.1, S-0029, S-0050.*

Karen Ulrich: *1005.1.1, 1009.1.1, 1012.2.1, 1015.1.1, 1035.1.1, 1035.2.1, 1054.13.1, 1081.2.1, 1081.5.1, 1144.9.1, 1268.35.2, 1268.53.1, 1268.56.1, 1268.60.2, 1268.62.1, 1269.21.1, 1269.21.2, 1269.22.1, 1269.23.1, 1280.5.1, 1285.12.1, 1302.13.1, 1307.1.1, 1350.1.1, 1596.1.1,*
1629.2.1, 1686.2.1, 1708.14.1, 1727.16.1, 1743.28.1, 2501.5.1, 2514.1.1, 2611.1.1, 2637.1.1, 2714.1.1, 3052.2.1, 3059.1.1, 3059.2.1, 3194.13.1, 3503.2.1, 3510.1.1, 3510.3.1, 3533.3.1, 3670.20.1, 4023.24.1, 4023.25.1, 4041.14.1, 4024.16.1, 4042.20.1, 4068.11.1, 4505.5.1, 4514.1.1, 5019.20.1, 5019.22.1, 5021.51.1, 5026.8.1, 5035.29.1, 5035.5.1, 5038.31.1, 5038.37.1, 5039.13.1, 5040.34.1, 5040.5.1, 5041.11.1, 5044.10.1, 5045.40.1

MICROGRAPHS

Peter Grave: Plate IV
Vasiliki Kassianidou: 5.8, 5.9, 5.12-5.14, 5.24-5.26
Sven Van Lokeren: 5.15, 5.16

SECTION DRAWINGS, PLANS, AND LINE MAPS

Finalized by Helen Saunders

Zoanna Carrol: *4.39–4.41*
Bradley Creevey: 4.6, 4.54
Michael Given: 4.22, 6.2
Petros Lapithis: 4.9
Megan Mebberson: 4.2, 4.4, 4.10, 4.12, 4.14-4.16, 4.18
Helen Saunders: 1.1, 6.1
Sven Van Lokeren: 4.25, 4.55, 4.57
Michelle McLean, Lara Proctor and Sven Van Lokeren: 4.5
Shona Nicol and Sven Van Lokeren: 4.32
Michael Given and Ann Goldberg: 4.26
Lara Proctor, Jacqueline Smith, Robert Suttie and Natalie Swords: 4.35

Susan Bain and Robert Suttie: 4.51
Sven Van Lokeren, Shona Nicol and Bradley Creevey: 4.53
Michael Given and Christopher Papalas: 4.62

DIAGRAMS

Finalized by Helen Saunders

Iain Banks: 4.65, 4.66
Michael Given: 7.2
Neil Urwin: 4.8, 4.20, 4.21, 4.38, 4.44, 4.45, 4.65, 4.66, *Plates II, XVI, XXX*
Caroline Whitehill: 4.46, 4.47

GIS MAPS; MAPS BASED ON AERIAL PHOTOGRAPHS

Digitizing by SCSP team members in Sydney, Mitsero, and Glasgow; data analysis by Nathan Meyer; map design by Michael Given: *4.59, 4.60, 4.63, 4.64, 4.67, Plates I, III, V-XV, XVII-XXIX, XXXI-LIII*

LANDSCAPE/SECTION PHOTOGRAPHS

Michael Given: *Frontispiece, 4.19, 4.24, 4.32, 4.34, 4.37, 4.50, 4.52, 4.58*
Megan Mebberson: *1.2, 4.7, 4.11, 4.13, 4.17, Prologue*
Kylie Seretis: *4.27–4.31, 4.33*
Karen Ulrich: *4.7, 4.36, 4.48, 4.49, 4.61*
Sven Van Lokeren: *4.43*

TABLES AND GRAPHS

Finalized by Michael Given

INDEX